What Kind of God?

Siphrut
Literature and Theology of the Hebrew Scriptures

1. *A Severe Mercy: Sin and Its Remedy in the Old Testament*, by Mark J. Boda

2. *Chosen and Unchosen: Conceptions of Election in the Pentateuch and Jewish-Christian Interpretation*, by Joel N. Lohr

3. *Genesis and the Moses Story: Israel's Dual Origins in the Hebrew Bible*, by Konrad Schmid

4. *The Land of Canaan and the Destiny of Israel: Theologies of Territory in the Hebrew Bible*, by David Frankel

5. *Jacob and the Divine Trickster: A Theology of Deception and Yhwh's Fidelity to the Ancestral Promise in the Jacob Cycle*, by John E. Anderson

6. *Esther: The Outer Narrative and the Hidden Reading*, by Jonathan Grossman

7. *From Fratricide to Forgiveness: The Language and Ethics of Anger in Genesis*, by Matthew R. Schlimm

8. *The Rhetoric of Remembrance: An Investigation of the "Fathers" in Deuteronomy*, by Jerry Hwang

9. *In the Beginning: Essays on Creation Motifs in the Bible and the Ancient Near East*, by Bernard F. Batto

10. *Run, David, Run! An Investigation of the Theological Speech Acts of David's Departure and Return (2 Samuel 14–20)*, by Steven T. Mann

11. *From the Depths of Despair to the Promise of Presence: A Rhetorical Reading of the Book of Joel*, by Joel Barker

12. *Forming God: Divine Anthropomorphism in the Pentateuch*, by Anne Katherine Knafl

13. *Standing in the Breach: An Old Testament Theology and Spirituality of Intercessory Prayer*, by Michael Widmer

14. *What Kind of God? Collected Essays of Terence E. Fretheim*, edited by Michael J. Chan and Brent A. Strawn

15. *The "Image of God" in Eden: The Creation of Mankind in Genesis 2:5–3:24 in Light of the* mis pi pit pi *and* wpt-r *Rituals of Mesopotamia and Ancient Egypt*, by Catherine McDowell

What Kind of God?

Collected Essays of
Terence E. Fretheim

edited by
Michael J. Chan and Brent A. Strawn

Winona Lake, Indiana
EISENBRAUNS
2015

Library of Congress Cataloging-in-Publication Data

What kind of God? : collected essays of Terence E. Fretheim / edited by
Michael J. Chan and Brent A. Strawn.
      pages   cm.—(Siphrut : literature and theology of the Hebrew
Scriptures ; 14)
      Includes bibliographical references and index.
      ISBN 978-1-57506-343-0 (hardback : alk. paper)
      1. Fretheim, Terence E.—Philosophy.   2. God—Biblical teaching.
   3. Bible. Old Testament—Criticism, interpretation, etc.   4. God
(Judaism)   5. God (Christianity)   I. Fretheim, Terence E.   II. Chan,
Michael J., editor.   III. Strawn, Brent A., editor.
      BS1192.6.W48   2015
      231—dc23

                                              2014045407

Contents

Part 1
On Fretheim

Part 2
God and the World

Part 3
God and Suffering

v

Editorial Preface

A word about the origins of this collection seems appropriate. The project itself originated over a dinner conversation at the house of Brent and Holly Strawn. While discussing the work of Terence E. Fretheim—something we had done on many occasions before—one of us remarked that a collection of his essays was nonexistent and would be a useful resource for the field. Although we approach Fretheim's corpus from different perspectives—Chan as a former student of Fretheim's, and Strawn as a long-time admirer of Fretheim's work—we share a deep respect and profound appreciation for how Fretheim has shaped conversations in biblical studies, especially in the area of Old Testament theology. We decided to mount this collection and, as our first choice, approached the editors of Eisenbrauns' Siphrut series (Nathan McDonald, Stephen B. Chapman, and Tremper Longman III) with the idea. We were delighted when the editorial board of Siphrut and Jim Eisenbraun accepted the project for publication.

The goal of the collection is to present in curated form a selection of writings that highlight Fretheim's most significant and enduring insights. To this end, the 30 pieces included here are organized into thematic subsections that are meant to capture major themes in Fretheim's work. The volume begins with 2 essays situating Fretheim and his work—one by the editors and one by Fretheim himself (part 1). The essays in part 2, "God and the World," deal with Fretheim's understanding of God and God's relationship to the created order. Part 3, "God and Suffering," features pieces on the suffering of God and the world and includes an excerpt from Fretheim's groundbreaking book *The Suffering of God*. Part 4 is titled "God and Wrath." The essays gathered here deal with three overlapping themes: the wrath of God, divine violence, and God's frequent association with violence in the Old Testament. Part 5, "God and the Pentateuch," contains 6 essays that focus especially on Genesis 1–11, Exodus, and Deuteronomy. The essays in part 6 on "God and the Prophets" deal with various theological themes in the former, major, and minor prophets—all marked by Fretheim's unmistakable style and approach. The last part of the collection, part 7, "God and the Church's Book," addresses specific issues related to Christian theology, with an eye on denominational and congregational contexts. The volume concludes with a bibliography of Fretheim's works (1969–2015).

The essays (or book excerpts) were published in many different places (see the acknowledgments for places of first publication), which means that they followed many different formats and styles. In order to bring a measure of uniformity to the collection as well as to facilitate reader comprehension, all citations were converted into footnotes that conform to *The SBL Handbook of Style*. Despite our best intentions, some minor variations will no doubt be occasionally detected in the footnotes, but these should not keep the reader from ascertaining the pertinent information or the source cited.

Also in light of their previous publications—and to facilitate cross-referencing and citation—we decided to embed the original pagination in the text with the use of square brackets. So, for example,

> From another perspective, it is often thought that the chapter is incoherent. It moves from the repentance of God (vv. 10–11) to an affirmation [596] that God does not repent (vv. 28–29), and then it returns to repentance in v. 35.[1]

In the original document, the page break came after the word "affirmation"; hence, the placement of [ ] immediately after this word. Everything that follows "affirmation" appears on p. 596, until "[597]" appears, and so on.

The process of converting previously published works into a new format presented a number of serious challenges. The "original" electronic documents that were used for many of the publications were generally not available, even to Fretheim. This left us with .PDF scans of the published versions, but these did not permit the sort of editorial reworking that was necessary for the project. Thus, using Optical Character Recognition (OCR) technology, every document reprinted here was scanned and then converted into a manipulable Word document. Although OCR is a convenient and powerful tool that makes tasks such as ours somewhat easier, it was often imperfect. In order to reduce errors, each of the essays included in the present collection underwent a multistage editorial process subsequent to the OCR procedure to ensure accuracy. We are particularly indebted to Aubrey Buster, Deborah van der Lande, Peter Susag, Collin Cornell, and the house at Eisenbrauns for providing crucial editorial and administrative assistance throughout this project. Despite this help, we assume responsibility for any errors that may remain.

A number of other parties must be thanked. To begin, we express our gratitude to the publishers and journals that gave us permission to reprint: *Catholic Biblical Quarterly*, Eerdmans, *Ex Auditu*, Fortress, *Horizons in Biblical Theology*, *Interpretation*, *Journal of Biblical Literature*, Liturgical Press, *Lutheran Theological Journal*, *Theology Today*, Wipf and Stock, Westminster John Knox Press, *Word and World*, and *Zeitschrift für die alttestamentliche Wissenschaft*. Special thanks are also due to Michael J. Gorman, who graciously hosted a session at the 2013 Annual Meeting of the Society of Biblical Literature (Baltimore, Maryland) in honor of Fretheim and the forthcoming publication of this volume. The session was chaired by Brent A. Strawn, and

---

1. Selected from Terence E. Fretheim, "Divine Foreknowledge, Divine Constancy, and the Rejection of Saul's Kingship," *CBQ* 47 (1985): 595–602 (= chap. 21 below).

the respondents included Samuel E. Balentine, Walter Brueggemann, Michael J. Chan, Dennis T. Olson, and Carolyn J. Sharp—with a final response by Fretheim. Last but certainly not least, we thank Terry himself, whose work and ways inspired this volume, for writing the sketch of his scholarly development. We are only two representative types—as former student and long-time reader—of the many people who have been inspired and changed by Fretheim and his work. We hope the present collection continues this trend.

—MICHAEL J. CHAN, Luther Seminary
—BRENT A. STRAWN, Candler School of Theology, Emory University

Acknowledgments

Chapter 3   originally appeared as "Divine Dependence upon the Human: An Old Testament Perspective," *Ex Auditu* 13 (1997): 1–13.

Chapter 4   originally appeared as "The Repentance of God: A Key to Evaluating Old Testament God-Talk," *Horizons in Biblical Theology* 10 (1988): 47–70.

Chapter 5   originally appeared as "The God Who Acts: An Old Testament Perspective," *Theology Today* 54 (1997): 6–18.

Chapter 6   originally appeared as "Some Reflections on Brueggemann's God," in *God in the Fray: A Tribute to Walter Brueggemann* (ed. Tod Linafelt and Timothy K. Beal; Minneapolis: Fortress, 1998), 24–37.

Chapter 7   originally appeared as "Introduction," in *The Suffering of God: An Old Testament Perspective* (Overtures to Biblical Theology; Philadelphia: Fortress, 1984), 1–12.

Chapter 8   originally appeared as "To Say Something—About God, Evil, and Suffering," *Word and World* 19 (1999): 339–50.

Chapter 9   originally appeared as "Suffering God and Sovereign God in Exodus: A Collision of Images," *Horizons in Biblical Theology* 11 (1989): 31–56.

Chapter 10 originally appeared as "'Evil' after 9/11: A Consequence of Human Freedom," *Word and World* 24 (2004): 205–7.

Chapter 11 originally appeared as "God and Violence in the Old Testament," *Word and World* 24 (2004): 18–28.

Chapter 12 originally appeared as "Theological Reflections on the Wrath of God in the Old Testament," *Horizons in Biblical Theology* 24 (2002): 1–26.

Chapter 13 originally appeared as "The Self-Limiting God of the Old Testament and Issues of Violence," in *Raising up a Faithful Exegete: Essays in Honor of Richard D. Nelson* (ed. K. L. Noll and Brooks Schramm; Winona Lake, IN: Eisenbrauns, 2010), 179–91.

Chapter 14 originally appeared as "'I Was Only a Little Angry'; Divine Violence in the Prophets," *Interpretation* 58 (2004): 365–75.

Chapter 15 originally appeared as "Preaching Creation: Genesis 1–2," *Word and World* 29 (2009): 75–83.

Chapter 16 originally appeared as "Creator, Creature, and Co-Creation in Genesis 1–2," in *All Things New: Essays in Honor of Roy A. Harrisville* (ed. Arland J. Hultgren, Donald H. Juel, and Jack D. Kingsbury; Word and World Supplement Series 1; St. Paul, MN: Luther Northwestern Theological Seminary, 1992), 11–20.

Chapter 17 originally appeared as "'God Was with the Boy' (Genesis 21:20): Children in the Book of Genesis," in *The Child in the Bible* (ed. Marcia J. Bunge, Terence E. Fretheim, and Beverly Roberts Gaventa; Grand Rapids, MI: Eerdmans, 2008), 3–23.

Chapter 18 originally appeared as "The Plagues as Ecological Signs of Historical Disaster," *Journal of Biblical Literature* 110 (1991): 385–96.

Chapter 19 originally appeared as "The Reclamation of Creation: Redemption and Law in Exodus," *Interpretation* 45 (1991): 354–65.

Chapter 20 originally appeared as "Law in the Service of Life: A Dynamic Understanding of Law in Deuteronomy," in *A God So Near: Essays in Old Testament Theology in Honor of Patrick D. Miller* (ed. Brent A. Strawn and Nancy R. Bowen; Winona Lake, IN: Eisenbrauns, 2003), 183–200.

Chapter 21 originally appeared as "Divine Foreknowledge, Divine Constancy, and the Rejection of Saul's Kingship," *Catholic Biblical Quarterly* 47 (1985): 595–602.

Chapter 22 originally appeared as "The Prophets and Social Justice: A *Conservative* Agenda," *Word and World* 28 (2008): 159–68.

Chapter 23 originally appeared as "Caught in the Middle: Jeremiah's Vocational Crisis," *Word and World* 22 (2002): 351–60.

Chapter 24 originally appeared as "The Character of God in Jeremiah," in *Character and Scripture: Moral Formation, Community, and Biblical Interpretation* (ed. William P. Brown; Grand Rapids, MI: Eerdmans, 2002), 211–30.

Chapter 25 originally appeared as "Is Anything Too Hard for God? (Jer 32:27)," *Catholic Biblical Quarterly* 66 (2004): 231–36.

Chapter 26 originally appeared as "The Exaggerated God of Jonah," *Word and World* 27 (2007): 125–34.

Chapter 27 originally appeared as "Jonah and Theodicy," *Zeitschrift für die alttestamentliche Wissenschaft* 90 (1978): 227–37.

Chapter 28 originally appeared as "The Old Testament in Christian Proclamation," *Word and World* 3 (1983): 223–30.

Chapter 29 originally appeared as "Christology and the Old Testament," in *Who Do You Say That I Am? Essays on Christology* (ed. Mark Allan Powell and David R. Bauer; Louisville: Westminster John Knox, 1999), 201–15.

Chapter 30 originally appeared as "Salvation in the Bible vs. Salvation in the Church," *Word and World* 13 (1993): 363–72.

Chapter 31 originally appeared as "The Authority of the Bible and Churchly Debates Regarding Sexuality," *Word and World* 26 (2006): 365–74.

Chapter 32 originally appeared as "What Biblical Scholars Wish Pastors Would Start or Stop Doing about Ethical Issues in the Old Testament," *Word and World* 31 (2011): 297–306.

Abbreviations

General

JB	Jerusalem Bible
KJV	King James Version
NAB	New American Bible
NEB	New English Bible
NIV	New International Version
NJPS	*Tanakh: The Holy Scriptures—The New Jewish Publication Society Translation according to the Traditional Hebrew Text*
NRSV	New Revised Standard Version
NT	New Testament
OT	Old Testament
REB	Revised English Bible
RSV	Revised Standard Version
TEV	Today's English Version

Reference Works

AB	Anchor Bible
ABD	*Anchor Bible Dictionary.* Edited by D. N. Freedman et al. 6 vols. New York: Doubleday, 1992
AnBib	Analecta Biblica
Bib	*Biblica*
BibS(N)	Biblische Studien (Neukirchen, 1951–)
BTB	*Biblical Theology Bulletin*
BZAW	Beihefte zur Zeitschrift für die alttestamentliche Wissenschaft
CBQ	Catholic Biblical Quarterly
CBQMS	Catholic Biblical Quarterly Monograph Series
CD	Karl Barth. *Church Dogmatics.* Edinburgh: T. & T. Clark, 1932–
ChrCent	*Christian Century*
ConBOT	Coniectanea Biblica: Old Testament Series
CTM	*Concordia Theological Monthly*
EvT	*Evangelische Theologie*
ExAud	*Ex Auditu*
HBT	*Horizons in Biblical Theology*
HTR	*Harvard Theological Review*
HTS	Harvard Theological Studies
HUCA	*Hebrew Union College Annual*
IBT	Interpreting Biblical Texts
ICC	International Critical Commentary
IDB	*Interpreter's Dictionary of the Bible.* Edited by G. A. Buttrick. 4 vols. Nashville: Abingdon, 1962

IDBSup	*Interpreter's Dictionary of the Bible: Supplementary Volume.* Edited by K. Crim. Nashville: Abingdon, 1976
Int	*Interpretation*
IRT	Issues in Religion and Theology
JBL	*Journal of Biblical Literature*
JBQ	*Jewish Bible Quarterly*
JQR	*Jewish Quarterly Review*
JR	*Journal of Religion*
JSOT	*Journal for the Study of the Old Testament*
JSOTSup	Journal for the Study of the Old Testament: Supplement Series
JTS	*Journal of Theological Studies*
LQ	*Lutheran Quarterly*
NIB	*New Interpreter's Bible.* 13 vols. Nashville: Abingdon, 1994–2004
OBO	Orbis Biblicus et Orientalis
OBT	Overtures to Biblical Theology
OTL	Old Testament Library
OtSt	Oudtestamentische Studiën
RR	*Review of Religion*
RSR	*Recherches de science religieuse*
SBLDS	Society of Biblical Literature Dissertation Series
SBLMS	Society of Biblical Literature Monograph Series
SBLRBS	Society of Biblical Literature Resources for Biblical Study
SBT	Studies in Biblical Theology
SJT	*Scottish Journal of Theology*
TDOT	*Theological Dictionary of the Old Testament.* Edited by G. J. Botterweck et al. Translated by J. T. Willis et al. 15 vols. Grand Rapids, MI: Eerdmans, 1974–2012
THAT	*Theologisches Handwörterbuch zum Alten Testament.* Edited by E. Jenni, with assistance from C. Westermann. 2 vols. Munich: Chr. Kaiser / Zurich: Theologischer Verlag, 1971–76
ThTo	*Theology Today*
TWNT	*Theologische Wörterbuch zum Neuen Testament.* Edited by G. Kittel and G. Friedrich. 10 vols. Stuttgart: Kohlhammer, 1932–79
TZ	*Theologische Zeitschrift*
VT	*Vetus Testamentum*
WBC	Word Biblical Commentary
WW	*Word and World*
ZAW	*Zeitschrift für die alttestamentliche Wissenschaft*

Part 1

On Fretheim

Introducing Fretheim:
His Theology and His God

MICHAEL J. CHAN AND BRENT A. STRAWN

This present volume is not a catchall collection of previously published essays. Instead, the goal in the selection and arrangement of the various works contained here aims to underscore and explicate the most enduring and significant contributions of Terence E. Fretheim to the field of Old Testament theology. His contributions are numerous, to be sure, but above all others is Fretheim's *understanding of the God-world relationship*. Relationality is at the center of his theology, though this is most pronounced in his publications subsequent to the late 1970s. In these later works, Fretheim's understanding of the God-world relationship recurs almost invariably—whether as an explicit argument or as a governing assumption. Given the importance of this notion throughout Fretheim's corpus—indeed, its status as the proverbial *sine qua non*—it is worth tracing its development so as to better understand it and, correlatively, Fretheim, his theology, and (so it goes) his God.

Relationality: Its Centrality and Development

Rembrandt's *Return of the Prodigal Son* (ca. 1669) is a fitting visual entrée to Fretheim's view of the God-world relationship. In this well-known painting, the pathos of the father is clearly evident. With strong but tender hands, the father embraces his ragged son. The beggarly son is touched by the father, but the father is obviously also "touched" (that is, emotionally) by the son. It is a genuine exchange in which both parties give, take, and are changed. Fretheim has contributed many things to theological reflection, but chief among them is the insight that the God of Israel—like the father in Rembrandt's painting—*touches* the world and *is touched by* the world. God *bestows* and *receives*, *teaches* and *learns*, *hopes* and *regrets*, *moves* and is *moved*. Creator and creation are in a genuine relationship, and neither party is unaffected.

To date, Fretheim's fullest description of the God-world relationship is found in his 2005 publication, *God and World in the Old Testament*.[1] There he makes the following claims:

---

1. Terence E. Fretheim, *God and World in the Old Testament: A Relational Theology of Creation* (Nashville: Abingdon, 2005).

- Relationality is basic to the very nature of God.
- This relational God freely enters into relationships with creatures.
- This relational God has created a world in which all creatures are interrelated.
- God so enters into relationships that:
  - God is not the only one who has something important to say.
  - God is not the only one who has something important to do and the power to do it.
  - God is genuinely affected by what happens in (or to) that relationship.
  - Human will can stand over against the will of God.
  - The future is not all predetermined.[2]

For Fretheim, "genuine" relationship is marked by risk, sacrifice, commitment, limitation, change, power-sharing, and the ability of both parties to shape the future, even God's future. All of creation is interconnected—like the strands in a spider web, he argues—so that the actions of one creature can have a profound effect on the well-being of other creatures.[3] Of course, God remains the more powerful party in this relationship, but God's power does not shield God from the real risks that mark any true relationship. God suffers because of, with, and for creation, and especially for Israel.[4] The limitations that mark God's relationship to the world, however, are not things to which God is somehow ontologically bound. They are, rather, constraints into which God *freely* enters[5]—an assertion that sets Fretheim outside process theology and philosophy proper.[6] In his own words:

---

2. This list actually combines two separate lists that Fretheim provides in *God and World*, 16–22.

3. Fretheim often uses this image of a spider web to describe the complex interrelations among creatures. For example, in "Preaching Creation: Genesis 1–2," *WW* 29 (2009): 78–79 (= chap. 15 below), he writes,

> All creatures live in a spider web of a world within which creaturely words and deeds set the web a-shaking, either positively or negatively—especially those perpetrated by human beings. This important relational point has not originated in recent scholarship; it is a strong biblical claim. Indeed, such interrelatedness is so basic to biblical reality that it is understood to be true of God as well as the world of creatures. Both God and world are who they are because of relationships.

For a still earlier use of the image, see "Creator, Creature, and Co-Creation in Genesis 1–2," in *All Things New: Essays in Honor of Roy A. Harrisville* (ed. Arland J. Hultgren, Donald Juel, and Jack Dean Kingsbury; Word and World Supplement 1; St. Paul, MN: Luther Northwestern Theological Seminary, 1992), 12 (= chap. 21 below).

4. Note the names of chaps. 7–9 in idem, *The Suffering of God: An Old Testament Perspective* (OBT; Philadelphia: Fortress, 1984): "God Suffers *Because*," "God Suffers *With*," and "God Suffers *For*" (emphases added).

5. Idem, *God and World in the Old Testament*, 17: "This relational God *freely* enters into relationships with the creatures" (emphasis added).

6. Both critics and fans of Fretheim's work occasionally associate him with "process thought" without realizing that it is exactly his view of divine freedom that distances him

Israel's God is transcendent, but transcendent in relationship with the world, not in isolation from it. In the words of Heschel, "God remains transcendent in his immanence, and related in his transcendence." God has taken the initiative and *freely* entered into this relationship, both in creation and in covenant with Israel. Having done so, God—who is other than world—has decisively and irrevocably committed himself to be in relationship with the world. Hence, the God who has freely made this commitment is no longer free to back out of the relationship; God will be faithful. Divine freedom now has to do with freedom *within* relationship, with freedom *for* the world, not from the world.[7]

Fundamental to God's relationship with the world is the claim that God is not the only one who holds power. All of creation has genuine power, and humanity in particular has been given a special charge to exercise power in service of life (see Gen 1:28).[8] The future, then, will be shaped by both

---

from the same. For example, Robert Karl Gnuse, *No Other Gods: Emergent Monotheism in Israel* (JSOTSup 241; Sheffield: Sheffield Academic Press, 1997), 300–301, writes:

> Process thought complements the historical recital of the biblical narratives by speaking of God in such a way as to metaphysically describe a divine reality capable of interaction, change, and even growth in relationship to the human reality. Terence Fretheim, for example, can look at a biblical thought through a modern worldview and see the biblical portrayal of God's relationship to the world as "organismic." (Note that Gnuse cites Fretheim frequently in his *Old Testament and Process Theology* [St. Louis, MO: Chalice, 2000]).

See similarly Brevard S. Childs, *Biblical Theology of the Old and New Testaments* (Minneapolis: Fortress, 1992), 356–58. But in a helpful essay, Roger Olson has demonstrated that Fretheim is not a process theologian. See Olson's "Process Theology (with special reference to Terence Fretheim)," http://www.patheos.com/blogs/rogereolson/2011/08/process-theology-with-special-reference-to-terence-fretheim/ (accessed 6/7/2014). Although Process Theology and Open Theism have many things in common, one key difference concerns *how* God comes into a relationship with the world. In process theology, God and the world are, to use Olson's terms, "necessarily ontologically interdependent (panentheism)." By way of contrast, Open Theism (a far better category for Fretheim's work) assumes that God has *freely chosen* self-limitation and relationship. Omnipotence and unmediated action are *voluntarily* relinquished by God for the sake of relationship.

7. Fretheim, "Divine Dependence upon the Human: An Old Testament Perspective," *ExAud* 13 (1997): 1–2 (= chap. 3 below). For the citation, see Abraham Heschel, *The Prophets* (New York: Harper & Row, 1962), 486.

8. See Fretheim, *Creation Untamed: The Bible, God, and Natural Disasters* (Grand Rapids: Baker, 2010), 34:

> Human beings are also created to 'have dominion' (*radah*) over 'every living thing that moves upon the earth' (Gen 1:26, 28). The language of dominion apparently was drawn from the sphere of ideal conceptions of royal responsibility (see Ezek 34:1–4, where 'force' and 'harshness' are needed to qualify the verb; so also Lev 25:43, 46). The verb should thus be understood in terms of caregiving, even nurturing, not exploitation (killing animals is a post-sin reality; Gen 9:2–3).

See also chap. 20 below.

divine and creational power. In sum, for Fretheim, it is relationality all the way down.

Relationality and the Suffering of God

Embedded within Fretheim's concept of relationality is a strong critique of classical theism, which typically emphasizes divine atemporality, immutability, omniscience, omnipotence, and the like. This polemic is powerfully articulated early in Fretheim's classic book, *The Suffering of God*:

> As one surveys the landscape of OT scholarship on the understanding of God, the portrait of God which normally emerges bears a striking resemblance to the quite traditional Jewish or Christian understanding of God regnant in synagogue or church. Save for matters relating to historical development (e.g., from henotheism to monotheism) one can read back and forth between church dogmatics textbooks and most God-talk in OT studies without missing a beat. Thus, for example, God is understood in terms of traditional categories: freedom, immutability, omniscience, and omnipotence; if not explicitly stated, they are commonly assumed. I cannot ever recall a commentator on an OT text dealing with the future, suggesting that God's knowledge of the future is limited, and that consequently the text should be interpreted with that in mind.[9]

At least on the matter of God-talk, Fretheim is clearly troubled by the dominance of dogmatic categories in the work of biblical scholars. The problem is that the methodological marriage between Christian theology and biblical studies has been unequal, with dogmatic categories dominating. What Fretheim proposes, instead, is to flip this arrangement on its head and to write a Christian theology of God, with Scripture serving as the bedrock, not predetermined (even if widely accepted) dogmatic categories. The Protestant (and specifically Lutheran!) impulse in this move is, of course, unmistakable. Be that as it may, the strategy of *The Suffering of God* is quite simple: to demonstrate through thoughtful theological readings of the Old Testament how classical forms of theism are far removed from the texts on which they supposedly depend.

An important point in Fretheim's argument against classical theistic categories that are not sufficiently biblical is how he construes the relationship between God and metaphor—or, in his own terms, "between metaphor and essential definition."[10] Prior to *The Suffering of God*, Fretheim

---

9. Idem, *The Suffering of God*, 17.

10. See ibid., 7 (= chap. 7 below). Although it is not as prominent in his later work, Fretheim's understanding of theophany also plays an important role in his polemic against classical theism, because theophany, for Fretheim, represents God's willingness to change and to experience something that God has never before experienced.

> For God to assume such a form means that God freely undergoes change, experiencing that which God has not experienced heretofore. Even if one were to say that God foreknew that God would assume such a form, one would still have to reckon

showed very little interest in metaphor qua metaphor. In *The Suffering of God*, however, metaphor becomes a pivotal methodological and theoretical issue. He writes:

> It is not enough to say that one believes in God. What is important finally is the kind of God in whom one believes. Or, to use different language: metaphors matter. The images used to speak of God not only decisively determine the way one thinks about God, they have a powerful impact on the shape of the life of the believer.[11]

Like many other contemporary scholars writing on metaphor, Fretheim does not view its function in terms of rhetorical embellishment—"mere metaphor," to use a well-worn phrase. Metaphors are rather "reality depicting."[12] This is a crucial point. Fretheim is not interested in metaphor as an interesting philosophical or theoretical topic. What matters is how metaphors relate to theology. So when Fretheim claims that metaphors are reality depicting, his point is primarily *theological*—namely, that metaphors, even the most anthropocentric or anthropopathic examples, are not simply some sort of accommodating discourse, God's "baby talk" to immature humans, as it were. Rather, an *essential* connection exists between metaphor and God.

To be sure, Fretheim is the first to admit that God "outdistances all our images," but he also argues that metaphors "reveal an essential continuity with the reality which is God."[13] It belongs to the work of interpretation to determine the "yes" and the "no" (i.e., the continuity and discontinuity) that inheres in every metaphor.[14] Matthew R. Schlimm has recently shown in an insightful study of divine pathos in the work of Fretheim, Walter Brueggemann, and Abraham Joshua Heschel,[15] that making this determination is precisely the point at which these renowned interpreters go

---

> with the fact that the actual experience of being "clothed" in the form of the human is different from merely foreknowing such. It is different to know something as actuality rather than only as possibility. In other words, the most basic form in which God reveals himself to Israel, namely the theophany, provides the most fundamental basis for considering a God who in freedom changes for the sake of personal encounter with the creation. ("The Repentance of God: A Key to Evaluating Old Testament God-Talk," *Horizons* 10 [1988]: 59 [= chap. 4 below]).

11. Fretheim, *The Suffering of God*, 1 (= chap. 7 below).
12. Ibid., 7 (= chap. 7 below).
13. See ibid., 7–8 (= chap. 7 below).
14. See ibid., 7 (= chap. 7 below).
15. See Matthew R. Schlimm, "Different Perspectives on Divine Pathos: An Examination of Hermeneutics in Biblical Theology," *CBQ* 69 (2007): 673–94. Fretheim has written that,

> given the fact that God is the subject of thousands of verbs in the OT, it is not as commonly recognized as it ought to be that one's theistic perspective will often profoundly affect how those verbs and sentences will be interpreted. It is the interdisciplinary theological conversation more than anything else which will make

their separate ways and reveal their deepest theological commitments.[16] In Fretheim's case, a reality-depicting understanding of metaphor funds his relational view of God and the world in fundamental ways. For instance, texts in which God "repents," "regrets," or "changes" God's own mind,[17] are not "mere metaphors," but rather literary windows into the nature of God and the world God has created.

A Shift to the Final Form

The Suffering of God represents the crystallization of a thesis that is both theologically significant and controversial,[18] but it also marks a funda-mental methodological shift in Fretheim's work. Reflecting certain intel-

---

us aware of the interpretive options. ("The Repentance of God," 49–50 [= chap. 4 below]).

16. For example, Fretheim and Brueggemann go their separate ways on the matter of covenant, a metaphor for the God-Israel relationship. According to Fretheim,

> For Brueggemann a "common theology" of the Near East has taken root in Israel, evident in creational and covenantal understandings that issue in "structure le-gitimation" and "contractual theology." This "tight system of deeds and conse-quences" allows "no slippage, no graciousness, no room for failure." Such a per-spective is reality for both Israel and God. But because "it lacks a human face," it needs to be submitted to sharp critique. I believe that this "system" is much looser than he supposes; it does not function mechanically, even in Deuteronomic theology. . . . The language of "contractual theology" will simply not do for the God-Israel relationship in any Old Testament tradition, though it had its adherents in popular understanding, then as now (e.g., the friends of Job). We should not forget that "covenant" is used metaphorically, carrying both a yes and a no with respect to the sociopolitical analogue. ("Some Reflections on Brueggemann's God," in *God in the Fray: A Tribute to Walter Brueggemann* [ed. Tod Linafelt and Timothy K. Beal; Minneapolis: Fortress, 1998], 28 [= chap. 6 below]).

17. For further discussions of this topic in Fretheim's corpus, see, e.g., "The Repentance of God" (= chap. 4 below); "Divine Foreknowledge, Divine Constancy, and the Rejection of Saul's Kingship," *CBQ* 47 (1985): 595–602 (= chap. 21 below); and "Divine Dependence upon the Human" (= chap. 3 below).

18. Note that some of the conclusions Fretheim reaches in *The Suffering of God* are found in nascent form in two earlier publications: (1) In *The Message of Jonah: A Theological Commentary* (Minneapolis: Augsburg, 1977), he writes:

> The third and final question now needs to be asked: What is involved in God's be-ing moved to spare? The use of the verb '*moved* to spare' points us to the fact that God's action has its effect upon God himself. This verb has reference to suffering action, action executed with tears in the eyes. . . . And so 'to have pity' would mean action undertaken with 'tears flowing down the cheeks.' It is suffering action. Here God takes upon *himself* the evil of Nineveh. He bears the weight of its violence, the pain of a thousand plundered cities, including Israel's. God chooses to suffer in place of Nineveh. His tears flow instead of theirs. Someday he may even choose to die. (p. 130, his emphasis; see idem, "Jonah and Theodicy," *ZAW* 90 [1978]: 236–37 [= chap. 26 below])

(2) In *Deuteronomic History* (Nashville: Abingdon, 1983), published just one year before *The Suffering of God*, Frethim writes the following about Judges:

lectual trends at the time, *The Suffering of God* pays very little attention to composition-historical issues and chooses instead to interpret the Old Testament in its "final form." The influence of Brevard Childs is rightly detected at this point,[19] and a shift toward the final form proves decisive in Fretheim's subsequent work. Prior to *The Suffering of God*, his work was tradition historical, even if theologically and "kerygmatically" oriented.[20] Fretheim's dissertation, in fact, focused on isolating and interpreting Israel's monarchic ark traditions.[21] The "early" Fretheim's approach to biblical texts is aptly illustrated in a 1972 article entitled, "The Jacob Traditions:

God's people, again and again, exhibit patterns of life which threaten their existence. God's response is remarkable in its variety and flexibility, in order to accomplish salutary purposes. A highly personal divine response is revealed, which values mercy above retribution; we see a God who chooses to experience suffering rather than visit the people with the finality of death; we are surprised by a God who finds ways of working in, with, and under very compromising situations in which people have placed themselves in order to bring about good. (p. 98)

19. Fretheim's dependence on Childs is particularly obvious in his emphasis on Genesis as the canonical introduction to the Pentateuch and indeed to the whole of the Old Testament. For instance, in an article on redemption and law in Exodus, Fretheim begins with reflections on the importance of Genesis's location in the canon:

As one contributing factor to this renewed enterprise, it is imperative to begin reading Exodus, indeed the entire Old Testament, with Genesis as the point of departure. The implications of this canonical placement are more far-reaching than is commonly realized. This canonical ordering was theologically significant for Israel. Those who put the canon together in its present form were certainly reflecting existing community perspectives rather than promoting an innovative theological strategy. ("The Reclamation of Creation: Redemption and Law in Exodus," *Int* 45 [1991]: 355 [= chap. 19 below])

Fretheim is transparent about his reliance on "canonical criticism" at this point, explicitly citing Childs's *Introduction to the Old Testament as Scripture* (Philadelphia: Fortress, 1979), 155: "The canonical role of Gen. 1–11 testifies to the priority of creation. The divine relation to the world stems from God's initial creative purpose for the universe, not for Israel alone." But Fretheim is also critical of aspects of Childs's work. See his "Review of Brevard S. Childs, *Biblical Theology of the Old and New Testaments: Theological Reflection on the Christian Bible*," *CBQ* 56 (1994): 324–25. Fretheim's relationship to Childs's project is thus best described as critical appreciation. The same could be said of Childs's response to Fretheim's work, and especially *The Suffering of God* (see Childs, *Biblical Theology of the Old and New Testaments*, 356–59).

20. The influence of Hans Walter Wolff on Fretheim's early work is palpable. In the preface to his first commentary on Jonah, for instance, Fretheim notes that his "most basic perspective" on composition-historical matters is informed by Wolff, with whom Fretheim had personal contact while on sabbatical in Heidelberg in 1975–76 (see *Jonah: A Theological Commentary*, 12). In an article entitled, "Theology of the Major Traditions in Genesis–Numbers" (*Review and Expositor* 74 [1977]: 301–20), Fretheim cites Walter Brueggemann and Hans Walter Wolff, *The Vitality of Old Testament Traditions* (Atlanta: John Knox, 1975) no less than 11 times (see "Theology of the Major Traditions," nn. 4, 12, 13, 14, 15, 24, 26, 27, 28, 29, 33).

21. See Fretheim, "The Cultic Use of the Ark of the Covenant in the Monarchial Period" (Ph.D. diss., Princeton Theological Seminary, 1968).

Theology and Hermeneutic."[22] He writes: "Every layer of interpretation in the biblical materials must be sought out and recognized by the church as a basis for speaking to the contemporary world."[23] This statement is representative of his early work, concisely and clearly revealing his approach to biblical texts at that time: critical tools were used to uncover the history of biblical traditions and texts, all in service to theological interpretation for the contemporary world.

There was also a period when Fretheim urged readers of the Bible to pay close attention to *both* the reconstructed forms of the text *and* the final form, though this appears to be a sort of transitional period ("middle Fretheim"?). In 1983, he wrote:

> The historical approach has given more concentrated attention to sources of biblical books than to their final form. This atomization of the literature has tended to discourage preachers, because of the preparatory time it takes to track down this theory or that, and because it often takes too much explaining before one can get on with the sermon.
>
> Recent literary and "canonical" studies have given renewed importance to the present form of the text. There is now scholarly permission, if you will, to work with the interpretive possibilities of the text as it stands. . . .
>
> At the same time, one ought not lose sight of the traditioning process that has preceded the final form, not only for its insights into individual texts, but also for the possibilities it bespeaks regarding relationships between texts and Testament. The Old Testament is seen to be the end product of a long history of many traditions.[24]

Despite Fretheim's nod here to composition-historical approaches, he has clearly found a new sense of freedom ("scholarly permission") to engage the text as a literary whole. In subsequent work, he increasingly distances himself from the composition-historical enterprise.[25] Viewing such approaches as fundamentally speculative, Fretheim's interest in the study of the multilayered prehistory of the Old Testament largely gives way to a focus on that aspect of the Bible that is most readily available to readers today—the text's final form.

Relationality Meets Creation

The next major development in Fretheim's thinking comes when his conception of divine relationality—exhibited so lucidly in *The Suffering of*

---

22. Idem, "The Jacob Traditions: Theology and Hermeneutic," *Int* 26 (1972): 419–36.

23. Ibid., 419.

24. Idem, "The Old Testament in Christian Proclamation," *WW* 3 (1983): 226 (= chap. 28 below).

25. Fretheim does not entirely disregard composition-historical concerns, of course, though they clearly take a back seat to literary and theological questions. See, e.g., idem, *First and Second Kings* (Westminster Bible Companion; Louisville: Westminster John Knox, 1999), 6–8; idem, *Jeremiah* (Macon: Smyth and Helwys, 2012), 1–4, 22–29.

God—became intertwined with his views on creation. "This relational God has created a world in which all creatures are interrelated," he writes in his magnum opus, *God and World in the Old Testament*.[26] *The Suffering of God* (1984) is reflected in the first part of this sentence, with its talk of the "relational God," but it is Fretheim's work on Exodus, culminating in his 1991 commentary that provides the balance of the sentence, which speaks of creation and creaturely relationality.[27] As noted earlier, Fretheim now deems relationality to be characteristic of *all creation*. To be sure, Fretheim always had an interest in creation. His very first book was a theologically oriented, tradition-historical analysis of the Primeval History.[28] In the late 1980s and early 1990s, however, Fretheim began to reimagine creation according to the relational theology he first developed in *The Suffering of God*. The following quotation from a 1989 article makes the point:

> I have come away from my study of Exodus with two primary theological convictions: (I) A theology of creation shapes the book of Exodus in a fundamental way; (II) The God of Exodus is both sovereign and suffering.[29]

Fretheim elaborates on these ideas further in his Exodus commentary. He notes that "God's work in creation provides the basic categories and interpretive clues for what happens in redemption and related divine activity. It is the Creator God who redeems Israel from Egypt."[30] What's more, Pharaoh is not only Yhwh's royal opponent, he is himself an anticreational force who works against God's (pro-)creational purposes in growing Israel from a family into a nation. The people whom God rescues from Pharaoh has a calling that is thus cosmic in scope.[31] These creational motifs are intertwined with images of a God who suffers with and because of God's own people.[32] In one of the boldest and most creative modern commentaries on Exodus to date, Fretheim masterfully integrates his earlier work on divine suffering with his emerging creational insights.

The ideas Fretheim developed around creation and divine suffering and sovereignty set the tone for much of his subsequent work on creation

---

26. Idem, *God and World in the Old Testament*, 19. He makes a similar point in *Creation Untamed*: "Everyone and everything is in relationship; reality is relational. Indeed, as we will see, such interrelatedness is true not only of the world of creatures; it is also true of God. Both God and the world are constituted by relationships within which one can speak of both commonality and distinction" (p. 9).

27. See idem, *Exodus* (Interpretation; Louisville: John Knox, 1991). Emphasis is also placed on creation in a 1989 article entitled, "Suffering God and Sovereign God in Exodus: A Collision of Images," *HBT* 11 (1989): 31–56 (= chap. 9 below).

28. See idem, *Creation, Fall, and Flood: Studies in Genesis 1–11* (Minneapolis: Augsburg, 1969).

29. See idem, "Suffering God and Sovereign God in Exodus," 32 (= chap. 9 below).

30. See idem, *Exodus*, 13.

31. Ibid., 13–14.

32. Ibid., 17.

and ecotheology, Abraham, divine violence, natural disasters,[33] and so on and so forth. We may consider two examples from his work during the last 15 years to demonstrate how powerfully these emerging convictions have shaped Fretheim's thinking. The first concerns divine violence in the prophets and the second God's involvement in natural disasters.

Fretheim on Divine Violence in the Prophets

In 2004, Fretheim wrote an essay entitled "'I Was Only A Little Angry': Divine Violence in the Prophets" for the journal *Interpretation*.[34] The witty title comes from Zech 1:15: "And I am extremely angry with the nations that are at ease; for while I was only a little angry, they made the disaster worse" (NRSV). Fretheim's article capitalizes on the space this verse creates between divine anger ("I was only a little angry") and the disproportionately violent actions of the nations ("they made the disaster worse").

Not surprisingly, Fretheim begins with some basic relational claims about God's dealings with the world and especially with created agents:

> After some introductory comments, I consider these basic claims: God's relationship with Israel is genuine; God acts in Israel and in the world in and through agents; God's agents of judgment commonly exceed their mandate; God's response to the consequent disasters includes tears, lament, and regret.[35]

From this passage, one sees clearly how deeply Fretheim's thinking about divine violence has been informed by his intervening work on creation and divine suffering. God acts in the world only through created agents, but when these agents exceed their mandate and cause undue suffering to God's people, God is saddened—even regretful.

---

33. On *ecotheology*, see, e.g., idem, "Divine Judgment and the Warming of the World," in *God, Evil, and Suffering: Essays in Honor of Paul R. Sponheim* (ed. Terence E. Fretheim and Curtis L. Thompson; Word and World Supplement 4; St. Paul, MN: Luther Seminary, 2000), 21–32; idem, *God and World*, passim; idem, "Genesis and Ecology," in *The Book of Genesis: Composition, Reception, and Interpretation* (ed. Craig A. Evans, Joel N. Lohr, and David L. Petersen; VTSup 152; Leiden: Brill, 2012), 683–708.

On *Abraham*, see idem, *Abraham: Trials of Family and Faith* (Studies on Personalities of the Old Testament; Columbia: University of South Carolina Press, 2007), 1–13.

On *divine violence*, see, e.g., idem, "The Self-Limiting God of the Old Testament and Issues of Violence," in *Raising up a Faithful Exegete: Essays in Honor of Richard D. Nelson* (ed. K. L. Noll and Brooks Schramm; Winona Lake, IN: Eisenbrauns, 2010), 179–91 (= chap. 13 below); idem, "'I Was Only a Little Angry': Divine Violence in the Prophets," *Int* 58 (2004): 365–75 (= chap. 14 below).

On *natural disasters*, see idem, "The God of the Flood Story and Natural Disasters," *CTJ* 43 (2008): 21–34; idem, *Creation Untamed*; idem, "The Authority of the Bible, the Flood Story, and Problematic Images of God," in *Hermeneutics and the Authority of the Scripture* (ed. A. H. Cadwallader; Adelaide: ATF Theology, 2011), 29–47.

34. Idem, "I Was Only A Little Angry" (= chap. 14 below).

35. Ibid., 365 (= chap. 14 below).

Fretheim leads, then, with the claim that to understand divine violence in the prophets one must recognize how God exercises power in the
world. Creatures "have been given genuine power (e.g., Gen 1:28), and
God so honors this relationship—indeed is unchangeably faithful to it—
that God will be self-limiting in the exercise of divine power within such
relationships."[36] Much of this is familiar from Fretheim's earlier work, but
he adds another level of nuance: because God is committed to relationships of integrity,[37] God chooses not to violate the will of those through
whom God is acting, *even when* the agent's actions are harmful to God's
people or to creation!

God's decision to accomplish things in this way means that God becomes associated with human agents whose character and actions are
less than ideal. God's agents include the likes of the Assyrian Empire (Isa
10:5), Nebuchadnezzar (Jer 25:9; 27:6, 7; 43:10), and Cyrus the Persian
(Isa 45:1).[38] In choosing to work through emperors such as these, God not
only depends on their agency but also risks associating God's own name
with their oftentimes despicable actions. Focusing on Jeremiah, Fretheim
observes that many of the same verbs used to describe the violent actions
of the Babylonians are also used to describe God's actions:

> And so, God in judgment will not "pity, spare, or have compassion" (Jer
> 13:14), because that is what the Babylonians, the agents of divine judg-
> ment, will not do (Jer 21:7). God will dash in pieces, destroy, scatter, and
> strike down (Jer 13:14, 24; 21:6), precisely because that is what Babylon,
> the chosen divine agent will do (Jer 48:12; 36:29; 52:8; 21:7).[39]

The lexical correspondences between divine and agential actions in Jeremiah suggest to Fretheim a deeper theological relationship: "Such hard
words are used with God as subject because they depict the actions of those
in and through whom God mediates judgment. *The portrayal of God's violent action is conformed to the means that God uses.*"[40]

God's decision to work through agents and depend upon them is, of
course, risky, requiring God to accept "any 'guilt by association' that may
accrue to the divine reputation."[41] Said differently, Fretheim offers no theodicy. He has no interest in getting God off the hook for how God acts in
the world. What Fretheim provides is not an *apologia* but, rather, an *explanation* of divine action that takes seriously both the flawed nature of human
agents and the highly relational nature of their Creator. While this might
be a *controversial* point in Fretheim's work, it is nevertheless a *consistent*

---

36. Ibid., 368 (= chap. 14 below).
37. For the language of "integrity," see idem, *The Suffering of God*, 35.
38. Ibid., 368–69 (= chap. 14 below).
39. Ibid., 369 (= chap. 14 below).
40. Ibid. (his emphasis) (= chap. 14 below).
41. Ibid. (= chap. 14 below).

one—the logical culmination of his thinking about freedom (human and divine), relationality, and the integrity of Creator, creation, and creature.

Fretheim is not oblivious to the problem of agential mismanagement. When God's agents exceed their mandates—which they often do—they find themselves no longer the selected object of God's work but the object of God's wrath. This switch demonstrates that the nations are not mere puppets in the divine hands. Rather,

> [t]hey retained the power to make decisions and execute policies that flew in the face of the will of God; the God active in these events is not "irresistible." . . . God risks what the nations will do with the mandate they have been given. One element of that risk is that God's name will become associated with their excessive violence.[42]

This excessive violence, insofar as it is a going beyond the divine mandate, is not to be confused with God's will, even if it is now somehow associated with God, who initially authorized the agency. Because of God's commitment to genuine relationality, God cannot simply "intervene" and fix the problem—somehow preventing the excessive act before it happens. In Fretheim's words, "[N]o resolution will be simple, even for God." Instead, in this situation no less than others, both God and the world have to face the consequences of their true relationality; both will even have to *suffer* because of God's primordial decision to interact with the world in a relational manner. "[T]his way of relating to people reveals a divine vulnerability, for God opens the divine self up to hurt should things go wrong. And things do go violently wrong, despite God's best efforts."[43] When this happens, God is angry at the nations for exceeding their mandate, and God regrets—even apologizes!—for the fact that these agents went too far: "I am *sorry* about the disaster that I brought upon you" (Jer 42:10; emphasis added).

In sum, Fretheim's work on divine violence in the prophets showcases how his earlier work on divine suffering and freedom-for-relationship is connected to his later work on creation, and especially God's use of creaturely agents. God's decision to relate to the world is genuinely risky on God's part, because God and God's reputation become closely associated with the agents whom God chooses to use. If and when those agents exceed their mandate, both God and Israel suffer. What could be a more accurate reflection of authentic relationality than that all parties involved are vulnerable?

Fretheim on Natural Disasters

Something about natural disasters prompts humans to raise their eyes (if not their fists) to the heavens and say, "Why?" Such disasters raise theological questions: How, if at all, is God involved? But this is just one such

---

42. Ibid., 372 (= chap. 14 below).
43. Ibid., 373 (= chap. 14 below).

question; there are many others: What role (if any) do natural disasters play in the ongoing development of creation? What is the relationship among human sin of whatever sort and natural disasters? Is God responsible for these catastrophes or are humans? And if it is God, is the action random (the proverbial "act of God") or direct: a response to human culpability, in which case humans are ultimately responsible? To what degree is human environmental irresponsibility (for example, global warming) to blame for natural disasters?

These are large, even intractable questions, but Fretheim has not shied away from them. Over the past decade or so, he has addressed them directly, drawing deeply from his relational-theological model. In many ways, the problem of natural disasters is an ultimate one for Fretheim and his project. His thinking on these matters and the specific problem of natural disasters has culminated in his 2010 book, *Creation Untamed: The Bible, God, and Natural Disasters.* [44]

At the heart of *Creation Untamed* is the conviction that natural disasters—while often devastating to human communities—are part of God's ongoing development of the created order. In Fretheim's opinion, natural disasters are not simply post-sin realities but are, rather, an integral part of *creatio continua*: "*natural disasters are a key agent of God in the continuing creation of the world.*" [45] According to him,

> [i]n the development of such a universe [as ours], God chooses to involve that which is other than God, from human beings to earthquakes, tsunamis, periodic extinction of species (over 90 percent to our point in time), volcanic eruptions, and storms galore. All of these creatures of God participate with God in the continuing creation of the universe. [46]

Just as God used created agents in Genesis 1 to bring about creation's beginning ("Let *the earth* bring forth. . . . *The earth* brought forth," Gen 1:11–12), God continues to use agents to bring about further acts of creation. Already in 1999, Fretheim anticipated the arguments of *Creation Untamed*:

> God has created a dynamic world; earthquakes, volcanoes, glaciers, storms, bacteria, and viruses have their role to play in this becoming of the world. This is an orderly process in many ways, but randomness also plays a role; in the words of Eccles 9:11, "time and chance happen to them all." Because we are part of this interconnected world, we may get in the way of these processes and get hurt by them. One thinks of the randomness of the gene pool or tragic encounters with certain storms or viruses. [47]

---

44. Idem, *Creation Untamed*.
45. See ibid., 151 (his emphasis).
46. See ibid., 66.
47. See idem, "To Say Something—About God, Evil, and Suffering," *WW* 19 (1999): 349 (= chap. 8 below).

Creation, with its wild and sometimes random processes, can be a dangerous place for humans. But creation itself does not bear all the blame. God, Fretheim insists—consistent with his work on divine violence in the prophets—does not get off the hook: "human suffering may occur in God's world because of the way in which God has created the world."[48] Once again, this kind of formulation demonstrates that Fretheim is uninterested in justifying or defending God's actions. There is no divine apology here, no theodicy—only a *deeply relational and nonanthropocentric exploration* of the role played by natural disasters in the ongoing development of the created order.

Among other things, Fretheim's argument provides an important corrective to any theology that considers the problem of evil only from the perspective of *human* suffering. People often wonder—especially in the face of suffering—"Is God good?" What people tend to mean by that question is really, "Is God good *to humanity*?" or even more specifically, "Is God good *to me*?" Fretheim's work suggests that any discussion of evil falters, if it assumes that "good" must always or somehow only begin with humanity as its central point of reference or definition. For some people, Fretheim notes, "if God is in any way involved in such disasters, it must mean that God is not good or loving—since suffering is not consistent with a good or loving God." The problem, he goes on to say, is that "[w]e tend not to consider carefully that suffering is sometimes a good thing if it serves life."[49]

But there is more to say. Even though natural disasters may have a constructive role to play in *creatio continua*, Fretheim also realizes that they can result from and/or be intensified by human sin. One need not venture far into the Old Testament to see that natural disasters are often associated with human sin in the Bible: the Flood (Genesis 6–9), the destruction of Sodom and Gomorrah (Genesis 18–19), the plagues against Egypt (Exodus 7–11), and so forth. In his comments on the plagues, for example, he argues that, "the collective image presented [in Exodus 7–11] is that the entire created order is caught up in this struggle against Pharaoh's anticreational designs, either as cause or victim."[50] Natural disasters, in other words not only contribute to the ongoing creation of the world; they function as agents of judgment, mediating divine wrath to sinful human beings.

One might wonder, of course, if God's natural agents also go sometimes too far, on analogy with the human agents discussed in the prophets. Is this possible? If so, perhaps God, too, is sorry about the extent of natural disasters. One wonders, that is, whether there is intertextual resonance between a text such as Jer 42:10, where God is sorry about the disaster brought on Judah (cited above), and a text such as Gen 9:20–22, where

---

48. See idem, *Creation Untamed*, 65.
49. See ibid., 150.
50. See idem, *God and World*, 115; and, further, idem, "The Plagues as Ecological Signs of Historical Disaster," *JBL* 110 (1991): 385–96 (= chap. 18 below).

God—if not actually sorry—at least changes the divine mind about strategies involving worldwide floods. Or, still further in this analogical connection to Fretheim's work on the prophets, one wonders if God's hands get a bit dirty, as it were, in the course of natural disasters, even if only because this created universe with its relational ways of being and working—all the way down—is one of God's own design and choosing.

Conclusion

This essay has sought to capture and analyze—at least in preliminary fashion—what we deem Fretheim's most important contribution to Old Testament theology, and Christian theology and faith more broadly— namely, *that the God of the Old Testament is a fundamentally relational God and that any attempt to understand the Old Testament and the God to whom it witnesses demands serious attention to this claim.* Behind this deceptively simple insight are years of creative reflection on biblical texts, contemporary issues, and classical expressions of Christian theology.[51] Fretheim did not stumble upon this insight in a single day; it developed over decades of engagement with the academy and with the church. And it was facilitated by an important methodological move: Fretheim's shift away from his historical-critical roots toward an approach that is largely interested in Scripture's final form.

To be sure, Fretheim has made many more contributions to the guild and to the church than the primary insight that we deem so central to all the others. His corpus is wide and deep; we have only scratched the surface of the treasures the reader will find in the following collection. Another boon is the fact that, since he continues to publish at a steady pace, we are confident that he will bequeath still-more distinctly "Fretheimian" gifts to students of the Bible for years to come.

---

51. His work, in turn, stands to benefit, not only the study of Scripture or the analysis of various contemporary issues, but also works of Christian theology. Note, for instance, how Fretheim's understanding of law and exodus as creational realities (see chaps. 18 and 20 below) corrects Robert W. Jenson's misdivision of creation from exodus and the Sinaitic revelation (*Canon and Creed* [Louisville: Westminster John Knox, 2010], 28–29).

Fretheim on Fretheim: Some Personal Reflections on a Biblical-Theological Journey

TERENCE E. FRETHEIM

My parents are probably most responsible for the biblical focus and theological perspective I have today, though they could not have imagined my journey.

I was brought up in a parsonage. Both of my parents were reared in Norwegian Lutheran pietism. Reading the Bible and talking about the faith was a regular part of our daily lives. My parents were always more concerned about whether I *used* the Bible regularly, not what I thought *about* the Bible. They discerned that such a use of the Bible would lead me to see its texts as a genuine resource for faith and life and that its importance for me would become established over time.

I was educated in Lutheran institutions for both my B.A. and M.Div. degrees but received my Ph.D.—and some Presbyterian blood—from Princeton Theological Seminary. I also studied at Oxford and Durham Universities in England, at Heidelberg University in Germany, and at the University of Chicago. My study with James Barr at Princeton was probably one of the more formative educational experiences for me. Under his leadership, no question of the text was considered inappropriate; indeed, the more unusual the question, the better. Learning to ask questions of the text and to field challenges to it reinforced the upbringing I received from my family.

I have been engaged in teaching seminary students from the beginning of my career in 1961 (paired with some college teaching in the early years). So, helping to prepare students for Christian ministry has been integral to my vocation for over 50 years. During 3 years of my early teaching experience, I also served as a pastor of a Lutheran parish in rural Minnesota. Given this experience, the importance of relating biblical materials to issues of daily life became ingrained in me. My home base for teaching Old Testament has been at Luther Seminary, St. Paul, Minnesota, since 1968. I was Academic Dean at Luther for 10 of those years, which served to stretch my interests into nonbiblical disciplines.

I have taught for shorter periods of time in several other theological institutions both in the United States (Princeton Theological Seminary, The University of Chicago, McCormick Seminary, The Graduate Theological

18

Union, Philadelphia Lutheran Seminary, Trinity Lutheran Seminary) and abroad (Sabah, Malaysia; Hong Kong; and Cairo, Egypt). Conversations with students and faculty in these various theological institutions have certainly shaped my studies of the biblical traditions and given them a more global perspective.

I have learned from family, teachers, and colleagues through the years that the biblical text itself must be central in any biblical study of consequence. What the Bible "actually says" in specific texts is crucial for theologically-interested work. At the same time, I have learned that biblical study is more than historical or literary work. Theological reflection on biblical texts is important, not least because the texts themselves are often engaged in reflection of this sort. To be true to these texts and their authors, one must explore as thoroughly as possible what sorts of theological issues are being raised. What kind of God is revealed in this or that text?

I learned from my parents and several teachers that the most important questions you can ask of a biblical text are God questions: What is God up to here? What kind of God is active in this text? Most basically, the tutelage of these individuals enabled me to see that the God of the Bible was best understood in highly relational terms. Now, after years of working on the God questions—a journey that is still very much in progress—I believe that a deeply relational understanding of God is basic to the biblical perspective. This relational angle of vision has increasingly come to animate my work with biblical texts.

An innovative curricular move made in the late 1970s at Luther Seminary proved important for my biblical-theological reflection. Six required interdisciplinary, team-taught courses were put in place, with biblical studies playing an important role in several of them. I became involved in one of these courses ("God, Evil, and Suffering"), which I team-taught with systematic theology professors for nearly 30 years (Paul Sponheim has been especially helpful). This team-teaching assignment involved a great deal of cross-disciplinary reflection for me, with special interest in Old Testament topics related to issues of God, creation, and suffering. These issues provided one significant focus for my work and generated one of my more important books, *The Suffering of God: An Old Testament Perspective.*[1] The God questions raised in that course by many excellent students throughout the years continue to animate me and provoke my theological work with the biblical texts.

Another important area of biblical-theological work for me has been creation theology, an interest that has followed me throughout my career. My first book was a study of Genesis 1–11.[2] I later wrote a commentary on

---

1. See *The Suffering of God: An Old Testament Perspective* (OTL; Minneapolis: Fortress, 1984).
2. See *Creation, Fall and Flood: Studies in Genesis 1–11* (Minneapolis: Augsburg, 1969).

Genesis, a volume entitled, *God and World: A Relational Theology of Creation*, and shaped my Exodus commentary by using a creation lens.[3] This ongoing interest in creation theology has brought me to see its central importance throughout the biblical story and has no doubt driven me into such topics as environmental theology, human sexuality, and issues of social justice.

I have written for the church from my earliest years. The rhythm of writing for both academy and church has characterized my entire career. I published a two-volume introduction to the Old Testament for laypeople in 1970 and have written a number of books and articles for this audience along the way.[4] In terms of other churchly service, one important stretch of time was a four-year stint of serving on the Evangelical Lutheran Church in America's Task Force on Sexuality. This project sent me out and about in the church having conversations about human sexuality—a remarkable journey. The major production of our study group was a volume entitled *Journey Together Faithfully* (part II) in 2005.[5]

Eberhard Jüngel in his book, *God as the Mystery of the World*, makes a point that has obsessed me for many years: the deeper one probes into the mystery of God, the more mysterious and interesting God becomes.[6] In other words, the more you know about God, the more you know you don't know. If so, it would follow that the less you know about God, the less of a mystery God is. And the less interesting God is! I have learned over time the truth of these sorts of claims, and this has driven me to probe the biblical text more pervasively regarding the God questions it raises. And I have urged others to do so as well. In teaching students who will serve in one form of ministry or another, I have felt that it is important for me to urge them to think about the God of the text and to learn how best to generate these sorts of God-and/in-text questions in other people. And importantly, as they think through their teaching and conversing about God with communities of faith, also to raise this question: will others find the God of the biblical text *interesting*?

---

3. See, respectively, "Genesis: Introduction, Commentary, and Reflections," *NIB* 1:319–674; *God and World in the Old Testament: A Relational Theology of Creation* (Nashville: Abingdon, 2005); and *Exodus* (Interpretation; Louisville: John Knox, 1991).

4. See *Our Old Testament Heritage* (Minneapolis: Augsburg, 1970). This aspect of my writing is emphasized in the introductory essay by Michael J. Chan and Brent A. Strawn in the present volume ("Introducing Fretheim: His Theology and His God"). A selection of these types of essays are found in part 7 ("God and the Church's Book") of the book.

5. Task Force for ELCA Studies on Sexuality, "Journey Together Faithfully: ELCA Studies on Sexuality—Part Two," online at: http://download.elca.org/ELCA%20Resource%20 Repository/Journey_Together_Faithfully2.pdf (accessed July 7, 2014). Additionally, see my "Authority of the Bible and Churchly Debates regarding Sexuality," *WW* 26 (2006): 365–74 (= chap. 31 below).

6. Eberhard Jüngel, *God as the Mystery of the World: On the Foundation of the Theology of the Crucified One in the Dispute between Theism and Atheism* (trans. Darrell L. Guder; Grand Rapids, MI: Eerdmans, 1983).

The God of the Bible is not demystified by further knowledge; indeed, the greater the understanding, the more the divine inexhaustibility becomes apparent. God outdistances all of our language about God, and our images and metaphors cannot even begin to capture God. Even more, a gap between the textual God and the actual God will always exist. That is, the God as presented in the biblical text will never fully reflect who God actually is, however trusting we are that the Bible's most basic word about God corresponds to the divine reality. Said differently, God remains hidden in all of God's ways, whether in God's revealing or in God's acting. At the same time, for all that God has revealed to us (for Christians, most supremely in Jesus Christ), I think we have not fully plumbed the depths of Scripture regarding the revelation it provides. We can trust Jesus' promise that the Holy Spirit will continue to lead us into the truth about God and God's ways in the world. This means that we have not yet arrived; much theological work is yet to be done, and theological insights are yet to be gained. I welcome any and all conversations that could raise further questions about God and bring me further along in my understanding.

Part 2

God and the World

Divine Dependence upon the Human: An Old Testament Perspective

To speak of "divine dependence," whether dependence on the human or any other created reality, stands over against many theological claims on the part of biblical scholars, let alone other theologians. Perspectives would vary somewhat with respect to the meaning given to "dependence."[1] No specific biblical vocabulary for dependence, independence, and inter-dependence seems to be available. To speak clearly about the human, it is necessary to speak clearly about God and the relationship that God has established with human beings and the world. *All* biblical thought about the human presupposes a certain understanding of God. Look under the rock of any anthropology and a view of God will constitute a substantial part of the ground upon which it rests. We should be as clear as we can both about that fact and about the understanding of God that is at work in our thinking about the human. The issue to be considered is not simply *that* the Israelites believed in God, but the *kind of God* in whom they be-lieved. The response will affect one's understanding of the *kind of human being* of which the OT speaks. For example, to speak of human relationality means that relational language regarding God must be clear and forthright, if image of God language is to ring true. We may well have a high view of the human and human relatedness, but this talk is all too often subverted,

---

This essay was originally published in *Ex Auditu* 13 (1997): 1–13.

1. I think of three related definitions: dependence in the sense of being unable to do without ("a baby depends upon its mother"); in the sense of contingency ("it depends on whether you agree"); in the sense of reliance or trust ("I depend on you to do that"). I believe that all three senses can be supported from biblical texts, though I will not try to sort them out precisely in such terms in this article.

The language of dependence often has a bad name, as in the clinical term "co-dependence"; but it need not be so understood. For a helpful use of this language for Christ's relationship to his father, see Robert Bertram, "Putting the Nature of God into Language: Naming the Trinity," in *Our Naming of God: Problems and Prospect of God-Talk To-day* (ed. Carl Braaten; Minneapolis: Fortress, 1989), 91–110. His striking formulation: "The one God on whom everything depends is simultaneously as we are, one who depends—a child! But the Child is not for that reason any less God. . . . The one who is depended upon is of course God, but the one who does the depending is likewise God, the selfsame God" (p. 92). My colleague, Gary Simpson, informed me of this reference, as well as that of Ted Peters, whose *God as Trinity: Relationality and Temporality in Divine Life* (Louisville: Westminster John Knox, 1993), 135–142, characterizes the God of Wolfhart Pannenberg as "Dependent Deity." In Peters' language, "the identity of God is dependent upon God's relations to the history of the world" (p. 137). One might also note the dependence of Jesus upon his followers for such things as food and shelter (e.g., Luke 8:1–3).

indeed made incoherent, by an understanding of God that is relational only in a perfunctory sense.

Israel's Kind of God

A basic understanding of God in the Bible is that God is in genuine relationship with the world.[2] This relatedness is grounded in the very character of God, who is *by nature* a relational being (witness the divine council, e.g., Jer 23:18–22). Biblical metaphors for God, with few if any exceptions, have relation with humans at their very core: for example, king-subject; husband-wife; parent-child; shepherd-sheep; redeemer-redeemed. Even non-personal metaphors, such as rock, are understood in relational terms (e.g., Deut 32:18; Ps 31:2–3). Not every metaphor speaks of the relationship in the same way or lifts up the same concerns with equal prominence, but relatedness is basic to all biblical speech about God.

Israel's God is transcendent, but transcendent in relationship with the world, not in isolation from it. In the words of Heschel, "God remains transcendent in his immanence, and related in his transcendence."[3] God has taken the initiative [2] and *freely* entered into this relationship, both in creation and in covenant with Israel. Having done so, God—who is other than world—has decisively and irrevocably committed himself to be in relationship with the world. Hence, the God who has freely made this commitment is no longer free to back out of the relationship; God will be faithful. Divine freedom now has to do with freedom *within* relationship, with freedom *for* the world, not from the world.

Moreover, God's relationship with the world is comprehensive in scope. In the words of Jer 23:24, God "fills heaven and earth." The world is full of God, and God is relational to all that is not God. Absence is not a divine possibility, though this may appear to be the case from the human side, and varying intensifications of divine presence would need to be considered (from presence in creation to theophany). More specifically, in terms of Ps 33:5 (and parallels), the world is "full of the steadfast love of God." God is thus not only present to every creature and active in every occasion, but God is *lovingly* present and active. God is, therefore, purposively and graciously at work in all things, even in judgment. The incarnation is the supreme exemplification of divine relatedness and its irrevocability (see Rom 11:29).

Given this kind of God-world relationship, what does it mean for a faithful, always present God to be in such a relationship with human be-

---

2. For detail, see my *The Suffering of God: An Old Testament Perspective* (OTL; Philadelphia: Fortress, 1984). In this volume I have used the language of dependence for God (e.g., p. 35). See also my "The God Who Acts: An Old Testament Perspective," *ThTo* 54 (1997): 6–18.

3. Abraham Heschel, *The Prophets* (New York: Harper & Row, 1962), 486.

ings? God enters into relationships in such a way that both parties to the relationship have something important to say and both parties have something important to do (e.g., dominion).

With regard to both having something important to say, one example, only noted here, would be God's gift of prayer, which is given for the sake of communication within the relationship. God, being faithful, will take human prayer into account in, e.g., moving into the future (Exod 32:9–14; 2 Kgs 20:1–7). It may even be asked whether God *is dependent* upon human prayer. That is to say, do not prayers make available to God some new ingredients (human will, energy, insight) with which to work the divine will in a situation, and without which the shape of the future would be different?[4] In what follows we will explore more closely the fact that both parties to the relationship have something important to do.

Relatedness is not only fundamental to the Godhead and to God's interaction with the world, there is also an interrelatedness among all creatures within the totality of God's creation. What it means to be human for Israel must be understood from within this complex of intra-creaturely relationships. The world for Israel could be imaged as a giant spider web. Every created entity is in a symbiotic relationship with every other entity in such a way that any act reverberates out and affects the whole, shaking the web in varying degrees of intensity. Being the gifted creatures they are, human beings have the capacity to affect the web in ways more intense and pervasive than any other entity, both positively and negatively.

One common OT perspective on this point would be that moral order affects cosmic order, positively or negatively. Human sin, for example, has an adverse effect upon the entire cosmos (e.g., Hos 4:1–3). Importantly, this symbiosis is not mechanistically understood. To be sure, there are the great, consistent rhythms of the world, to which Gen 8:22 bears witness: seedtime and harvest, cold and heat, summer and winter, day and night. At the same time, a certain [3] openness in the created order is recognized. God's speeches in Job 38–41, for example, reveal unpredictability, ambiguity, and "play" within the creation. Several texts even speak of chance (e.g., Eccl 9:11).

That the world is so interrelated makes complex our consideration of God's faithful relationship to it. Generally, we might say that God honors the nature and dynamics of this creaturely interrelatedness in relating to the world. God will take into account both the order and the play in speaking and acting within this relationship.

---

4. For detail, see Samuel Balentine, *Prayer in the Hebrew Bible: The Drama of the Divine-Human Dialogue* (Minneapolis: Fortress, 1993); Patrick Miller, "Prayer as Persuasion," *WW* 13 (1993), especially pp. 361–62; Terence Fretheim, "Prayer in the Old Testament: Creating Space in the World for God," in *A Primer on Prayer* (ed. Paul Sponheim; Philadelphia: Fortress, 1988), 51–62.

Israel's High View of the Human
in the Divine Economy

Several texts point to the significant role that God gives to the human in the carrying out of the divine purposes in the world. The relationships of which I have spoken above will be illustrated in such a way that the language of dependence and interdependence is seen to be helpful in thinking through the place of the human in God's world.

1. The Kind of Human Being God Has Created

As with the beginning of any book, Genesis 1–11 is of key importance for the interpretation of the entire canon. These chapters catch the reader up into a universal frame of reference; the canon as a whole is to be read through the understandings provided by this opening lens.[5] In what follows, I lift up the role of the human in Genesis 1–2. In any thoroughgoing consideration of the role of the human in Genesis 1–11, more attention would have to be given to human sin. For our purposes in this paper, it is sufficient to note the continuing use of image of God language for the human in the chapters that follow the introduction of sin in Genesis 3 (Gen 5:3 and 9:6).

It has become commonplace to contrast the imaging of God in Gen 1:1–2:4a and Gen 2:4b–25.[6] For example, the God of Genesis 1 is "in sovereign control" while the God of Genesis 2 has less control. Oftentimes in the theological work on these texts, Genesis 2 has been deemed naïve or primitive, while Genesis 1 speaks Israel's more mature views on creation. Such a critical analysis reinforces a traditional churchly image of God as a radically transcendent Creator, operating in total independence from the world.

Theologically, this is inadequate from two perspectives: from the relationship between Genesis 1 and Genesis 2; and from consideration of details in these chapters, particularly as they relate to the co-creational role given to human beings.

Tradition-historical studies of Genesis 1–2 reveal an ongoing theological conversation in Israel about matters of creation. The theological tension between these accounts, even if less than commonly claimed, gives evidence of differing theological perspectives. I would claim that these chapters no longer have (canonical) theological standing in independence from each other. The differing theological voices of the tradition *woven together* have become a more sophisticated theological perspective and more closely approximate the *truth* that Israel, finally, [4] discerned about God and creation. Each of the theological voices in its singularity is too simplistic; only

---

5. On this rhetorical strategy, see Terence Fretheim, *The Pentateuch* (Nashville: Abingdon, 1996), 43–44.

6. For a recent perspective, see David Carr, *Reading the Fractures of Genesis: Historical and Literary Approaches* (Louisville: Westminster John Knox, 1996), 64, 317.

in their combination is a sufficiently complex theological perspective on this matter made available. In other words, not all recoverable theological voices in the history of the tradition have the same value, for Israel or for ongoing use of the tradition. Rather, such earlier theological stages as can be discerned have been deemed by Israel to be theologically inadequate to stand by themselves in the search for the truth about the creation; only the chapters together present the theological perspective on creation that the canon wishes to leave with its readers. From a source-critical perspective it might also be noted that, if P is the redactor of J and other materials,[7] then P's special contribution in Genesis 1 was never intended to stand alone. The P perspective on creation is to be found *only* in Genesis 1–2 as a single whole.

One effect of this analysis is that the understanding of God's sovereignty in Genesis 1 is more qualified than commonly suggested and the creative role of the creatures (especially the human) is given an enhanced standing. Certain details in these chapters help fill out this picture.[8]

(1) The interchangeable use in Genesis 1 of the everyday verb *'śh,* "make, do," and *br',* "create," indicates that God's creative activity is not understood to be without analogy in the human sphere. This is reinforced by the creating verbs ("form," "build," "plant," etc.) of chapter 2.

(2) God's speaking *(dbr)* the creation into being is not simply presented as a unilateral act. In the creative process, God also speaks *with* that which has *already* been created, with the earth, the waters, and human beings (1:11, 20, 24, 28). "Let the earth bring forth . . . and the earth brought forth." This is mediate rather than immediate creation; it is creation from within rather than creation from without. God's word to the human beings (1:28) is comparable in its import; compare also the creative character of the human speaking in 2:23 (see below).

(3) In 1:6, the firmament is to "separate" *(bdl)* waters from waters, a task given elsewhere in this account to God (1:4, 7). In 1:16, 18 the heavenly bodies are to "rule" *(mšl)* over day and night. God gives the task of ruling in this respect over to that which is not God.

(4) It has commonly been noted[9] that the absence of a "seventh day" formula in 2:1–3 leaves the future open-ended for further creative activity, a task assumed not only by God (Ps 104:30), but by human beings and others (begun in 2:18–25).

---

7. See Frank Moore Cross, *Canaanite Myth and Hebrew Epic* (Cambridge: Harvard University Press, 1973), 293–325.

8. On the following see my commentary on Genesis in *The New Interpreter's Bible* (Nashville: Abingdon, 1994). See also Michael Welker, "What Is Creation? Rereading Genesis 1 and 2," *ThTo* 48 (1991): 56–71. Welker shows that these chapters speak of God-creature interdependence in creation.

9. See Jon D. Levenson, *Creation and the Persistence of Evil* (New York: Harper & Row, 1988).

(5) God is imaged in 1:26 as a consultant with other divine beings with respect to the creation of humankind. This way of creating human beings is unique and, importantly, dialogical in character. God shares the creative process with that which is not God. This relationship of mutuality within the divine realm ("let us make") is implicitly extended by God to those who are created in the divine image.

(6) Initially, this sharing of power with the human takes the form of a command, "Be fruitful and multiply" (1:28). It is remarkable that God's first word to the newly created human beings constitutes a sharing of power. God thereby chooses not to retain all creative and other forms of power. God is a power-sharing, not a power-hoarding, God. As noted, this sharing continues in a post-sin world (Psalm 8). That the command to "subdue" is needed at all means that "good" [5] does not mean "perfect." This text is to be linked to 2:5 (cf. 2:15), where the presence of a human being to till (ʿbd) the ground is considered indispensable for the development of the creation. Human beings are given responsibility for intra-creational development, bringing the world along toward its fullest possible potential. Creative capacities have been given to the created. God creates a "paradise," but the resultant world is not static; a highly dynamic situation is present in which creaturely activity is crucial for the becoming of the creation.

(7) This theme is explicitly developed in 2:18–25. God here evaluates the creational situation and announces (probably to the divine council) that it is "not (yet?) good." This link back to 1:26 correlates God's "let us" to the divine council and God's relationship with ʾādām. In the divine actions that follow God implicitly speaks a "let us" to the human, inviting ʾādām to participate in the creative process. God places various creative possibilities before the human and ʾādām responds. The initially negative human response to God's presentation of the animals—the human does not simply acquiesce to what God offers!—sends God back to the drawing boards. Human decisions are honored by God and taken into account in moving into new stages of creaturely development.

In the process of finding "a helper as his partner," the ʾādām names the animals and the woman (*God* had named other creatures in 1:5–10). In so doing, the human participates in the creative ordering of the world, discerning the nature of intracreaturely relationships (hierarchical understandings seem not to be present). Phyllis Trible says it well; God is present "not as the authoritarian controller of events but as the generous delegator of power who even forfeits the right to reverse human decisions."[10] *Whatever* the human being called each animal, that was its name (2:19). Evaluative words (!) regarding the woman (2:23) on the part of the *human being,* parallel to God's evaluations in chapter 1, recognize that the creation has moved from "not good" to "good." Human decisions have shaped the

---

10. Phyllis Trible, *God and the Rhetoric of Sexuality* (OBT; Philadelphia: Fortress, 1978), 93.

future in a decisive way. These texts suggest a relational model of creation. Both God and creatures (especially the human) have a key role in the creative process. A deep dependence of the creatures upon the Creator for their existence and continuing life is evident in Genesis 1, which stresses the divine initiative, imagination, transcendence, and power in a way that Genesis 2 by itself does not. Yet, there is already a leaning toward Genesis 2 in Genesis 1. In these texts together, the issue of dependence does not travel one way (human dependence on God). The texts suggest certain levels of interdependence, in which God gives over power and responsibility to the human and in such a way that results in divine dependence. This seems to be more than dependence in the sense of entrusting the human with responsibilities (though it is that). Amid the order and the freedom of the creation, a degree of openness and unpredictability is present wherein God leaves room for genuine human decisions in the pursuance of the divine purposes for the creation. Even more, God gives humans power and responsibility in a way that commits God to a certain constraint and restraint in the exercise of power in the creation. This is a risky move for God, for it entails the possibility that the creatures will misuse the power they have been given, which is in fact what occurs. A reclamation of creation will be needed, but the human, even in sin, is given an important role in that task. [6]

2. The Kind of Human Being with Whom God Works in the World

Several texts emphasize the continuing role given to the human. These texts show that God has chosen to be dependent upon human beings in varying ways in the divine working in the world. It may be that the biblical materials do not speak with one voice about these matters, but the following texts represent a significant cross-section of biblical thought.

Human Beings Help God. I consider here an apparently straightforward text, Judg 5:23: "Curse Meroz, says the angel of the Lord, curse bitterly its inhabitants, because they did not come to the help (*'zr*) of the Lord, to the help of the Lord against the mighty." Certainly the biblical texts speak primarily of human beings as needing help from God (e.g., Ps 121:2), but here the situation is reversed. Some Israelites not only did not come to God's help, at the command of God's own messenger they are to be cursed for not doing so.

How one is to develop such a verse theologically is not altogether obvious, but its concern reaches across many OT traditions (e.g., Ps 132:1–5; see the discussion of 1 Kings 1–2 below). One could claim from this verse that, at the least, God demands help or desires help. Yet, the verse seems to push us even further, namely, God *needs* help, or at least has chosen to be dependent upon that which is not God to get certain objectives accomplished. It seems clear here (and in texts such as Judges 1) that not everything God desired in the settlement of the land was accomplished because of the failure of those who did not properly use the power they had been given (e.g., to eliminate the source of Canaanite religious influence). Does not human sin and failure inhibit God's objectives in this situation of conflict? In other words, does not God's freely made decision to work in and through that which is other than God negatively affect what God wants to get done? God's will proves to be resistible. Even more, given God's way of relating to the Israelites, God does not overpower them in getting them to do what God wants done.

A Human Role in Judgment and Salvation. Many scholars would maintain that certain texts, if not the biblical witness as a whole, are opposed to talk about divine dependence upon the human. I consider one example briefly: Claus Westermann on Isa 45:7, a text which speaks of God forming/making/creating light and darkness, weal [šālôm] and woe [raʿ]. It is "hard to see why this verse does not disturb commentators more than it seems to do," for "each and every thing created, each and every event that happens, light and darkness, weal and woe, are attributable to *him, and to him alone*" (emphasis mine).[11] In such a "divine pancausality" reading, King Cyrus, though called a "messiah" (45:1), is only a divine puppet, whose will and power count for nothing. One is given to wonder why God even bothers with him. An important exilic text that also uses šālôm and raʿ together is Jer 29:11–14 [NRSV: "welfare" and "harm"]. This text brings together divine "plans" and human prayer in an interdependent way; in Jer 18:11–12, a pre-exilic text, divine and human "plans" had come into conflict with dire consequences for Israel.

The language of darkness and woe (raʿ) in Isa 45:7 is not cosmic in orientation, but language typical in the prophets for *specific* (historical) divine judgments, whether against non-Israelites (perhaps especially in this context, see 47:5, 11) [7] or Israel itself (commonly; e.g., Jer 32:42; see Isa 42:7). Israel's God is often the subject of verbs of judgment; "there is no other" god who is responsible. Yet, God's "creating" here is not *ex nihilo*, but action which gives specific shape to a situation of historical judgment (for other historical uses of brʾ in Isaiah 40–55, see Isa 41:20; 43:1, 7; 45:8; 48:7; 54:16). The common language of "punishment" for divine judgment is problematic: most NRSV uses of "punishment" translate words for "sin," especially ʿāwôn; NRSV "punish" usually translates pqd, "visit." For Israel,

---

11. Claus Westermann, *Second Isaiah* (Philadelphia: Westminster 1966), 161–62. Comparably, the note on Isa 45:7 in the Oxford Annotated Bible (NRSV) states, "Cyrus is unaware of his charge from God, who *alone* determines history's course" (emphasis mine; note the move from knowledge to power). My approach is dependent on the thoroughgoing analysis of the so-called "divine pancausality" texts in the OT by Fredrik Lindström, *God and the Origin of Evil: A Textual Analysis of Alleged Monistic Evidence in the Old Testament* (ConBOT 21; Lund: Gleerup, 1983). Isa 45:7 is considered at length on pp. 178–99. For a survey of recent scholarship on this verse, see Michael DeRoche, "Isaiah XLV 7 and the Creation of Chaos?" *VT* 42 (1992): 11–21.

raʿ grows out of *raʿ;* human wickedness (*raʿ*) issues in divinely mediated disaster (*raʿ*).

The human factor is key in thinking about judgment, whether on the part of those who are its recipients (e.g., Ezek 7:27, "according to their own judgments I will judge them") or those who mediate that judgment within a moral order to which God attends. I would claim that God is in some sense dependent upon Cyrus with respect to both judgment (against the Babylonians) and deliverance (Israel). Though it is not possible to factor out the divine and human powers at work in the situation, Isa 45:7 asserts that God's action is the decisive reality. Yet, no claims are made that God is the all-determinative actor in this (or any other) situation

Perhaps one difficulty with this interpretation of the Cyrus text relates to the fact that Isa 45:7 is associated not simply with matters of judgment but also of salvation (light and *šālôm;* see 42:16; 52:7). A problem in assessing such issues is that Christians often collapse salvation into forgiveness and fail to recognize the wide-ranging meaning of salvation in the biblical texts (including such matters as physical health, deliverance from oppression, peace, security, community stability and well-being). Forgiveness does not exhaust the meaning or experience of salvation. Certainly, God is Savior, whose action is grounded in divine love and faithfulness; Israel cannot save itself. At the same time, God saves by choosing to work through, to be dependent upon nondivine instruments, human and nonhuman (at the Red Sea, the nonhuman is the savior of the human!), within the community of faith and without, including Cyrus. The mind leaps forward to texts such as Rom 10:14: "how will they hear without a preacher?"

A Human Role in Shaping the Future. Another way to speak of divine dependence upon the human relates to future contingencies. God so relates to the world that God waits upon future human activity to shape at least some divine activity. In other words, how God acts is *contingent* upon the nature of the human activity. This understanding is quite wide-ranging in various traditions (the brief comments above on prayer could also be expanded to apply to this discussion).

One such category of texts is prophetic speech wherein God lays out the human future in either/or terms. One example is Jer 22:1–5 (cf. Lev 26:3, 14 for a comparable formulation in the law). Two possible futures are given to Israel, depending upon whether they ". . . act with justice and righteousness, and deliver from the hand of the oppressor anyone who has been robbed. And do no wrong or violence to the alien, the orphan, and the widow, or shed innocent blood in this place" (22:3). The way in which Israel treats the poor and the needy will shape their future. If they do obey this word, they will experience one kind of future; if they do not, they will experience another kind of future. The actions of the people not only affect their own future, however, they affect *God's* future as well. What [8] God will do in the future is said to depend at least in part upon what the people do.

Even more, for both of these options to have integrity, they must be genuine possibilities, for *both* God and people.

Another category of pertinent texts is also prophetic, but it is embedded within a narrative wherein the prophetic (or other divine) word can be seen to function in relation to ongoing events. Here I work with several texts from Kings.[12] Several issues come to the fore wherein human activity needs to be considered in relation to issues of both divine power and divine knowledge of contingent futures.

In working with Kings, I am struck by the number and kind of statements made by commentators about divine control, similar to those noted above regarding Isa 45:7. Note this quotation from Richard Nelson's commentary: "In all that follows [in Kings], Yahweh will be in complete control of events."[13] The meaning of the word "control" is elusive (e.g., total control, ultimate control, crowd control), but a *complete* divine control would seem to include even "mind control." Would not this mean that Solomon's sin and Jeroboam's, of which Kings never tires of speaking, are in *reality God's* problem?

Some comments regarding the intrigue associated with the accession of Solomon (1 Kings 1–2) lay further groundwork for our consideration of divine oracles. How the divine purpose in the accession is to be related to this human intrigue is an important issue. Initially, David, though in failing health, sees through the human maneuvers and manipulations and recognizes that God's will has been done here (1 Kgs 1:28–30, 47–48). God has worked in, with, and under human intrigue to accomplish the divine purposes. God's action has been key to Solomon's becoming king.

It would not be true to say, however, that *only* God has brought this event about, as if the human actions involved were finally of no account. What the supporters of Solomon did, not least the cleverness and heightened rhetoric of Nathan and Bathsheba, truly counts for something in bringing about the desired result. Moreover the wisdom of Solomon is specifically associated (by David, 2:6, 9) with his elimination of threats to his power. In pursuing the divine purposes, God does not act alone, but works with what is available, with human beings as they are, with all their foibles and flaws, as well as their wisdom. God does not perfect people before working in and through them; God can work even through human evil toward the divine purposes (see Gen 50:20).

This divine action does not necessarily confer a positive value on the specific human means through which God chooses to work. The human means and methods that God uses here (and often elsewhere) are not held up as exemplary behaviors, applicable to any situation. Nelson's claim that

---

12. For further detail on these Kings texts, see my *First and Second Kings* (Louisville: Westminster John Knox, 1999).

13. Richard Nelson, *First and Second Kings* (Interpretation; Atlanta: John Knox, 1988), 23.

"Yahweh's plan and will must be effected, and for God, at least, the ends justify the means"[14] needs several qualifications. God's "plan" must not be reduced to specific details, God's will must not be considered irresistible in every respect, and the ends do not "justify" the means. Nelson's sentence is apt, "Yahweh is an unindicted co-conspirator in this palace intrigue." At the same time, it is not helpful to understand this claim in such a way that God's actions in the event are reduced to these human proportions. To speak unqualifiedly of God being "in charge" or "in complete control of events," as if everything that happens conforms to God's will, is to engage in such [9] a reduction. God is neither limited to human means (as if "God has no hands but our hands") nor all-determining of human action (as if God micromanages the life of the world, including the human mind). But, between those two ditches, it is difficult to factor out the divine and human activity at work in these events. With this perspective in mind, I consider two divine oracles, those regarding Solomon (1 Kgs 9:1–9) and Jeroboam (1 Kgs 11:26–39).

1 Kings 9:1–9. The conditions God lays before Solomon are stated in both positive and negative terms. That is, God holds out the possibility of both a positive (v. 5) and a negative future (vv. 7–9). It is clear from the entirety of Kings that the negative future comes to pass, first for the Northern Kingdom (2 Kgs 17) and then for the Southern (2 Kgs 24–25).

The "if . . . if not" perspective of this text makes it clear that the negative future has not been established in advance (remembering, of course, that the narrator lived in a time after the negative future had occurred). This way of putting the matter says something important about both God and Solomon/Israel with respect to the future. The way in which these human beings respond to God and God's ways makes a difference with respect to the shape the future takes for both God and Israel. What the king (and his descendants) do and say actually counts in shaping what will happen. As in Jer 22:1–5, the future of people and God is said to be dependent upon human action in at least some respects.

Moreover such a text has implications for divine knowledge and divine integrity within relationship. Both of these futures must be considered genuine possibilities for God as well. For God to hold out the possibility of a positive human future, when it was not in fact a possibility, would be an act of deception (and there is no warrant in the text for such an interpretation, unlike, say, 1 Kgs 22:19–23). If *both* futures are possible for God, then God has not established which future shall come to be, and God also does not *finally know* for certain which one shall occur. God knows these futures as genuine *possibilities,* though God may be said to know which future is more probable (perhaps shown in the detail given to the negative possibility). But God's knowledge of future *human* responses is not absolute. At the

---

14. Ibid., 22.

same time, God gives some specification regarding *what God* will do in view of the possible human responses.[15]

The modern reader can recognize that the exile is in view in this text (especially 9:8–9), but too much can be made of that, as if that future were a certainty at this point in the text (and in the story behind the text). These words of God, in which Solomon's and Israel's faithfulness are said to be decisive for shaping the future, show that what people do makes a difference, not only for them but for God. Finally, this word should be recognized as a gracious word, for God speaks of the future in a way that clearly lays out the real possibilities of blessing or judgment.

Consideration should also be given to the apparent conditioning of the Davidic covenant in 9:5 (cf. 2:4) and its relationship to the unconditional formulation of 2 Sam 7:14–16 (cf. 2 Kgs 8:19). Various efforts to resolve this tension have issued in no real consensus, though it is common to claim that there were different Israelite perspectives on the matter. My sense is that, for Kings at least, the unconditionality of the basic Davidic covenant remains intact; the reference to "Israel" in 9:5 refers to *all* Israel (and hence the positive future goes by the boards in 1 Kgs 11:11). [10] Kings *never* states—despite many opportunities (e.g., 2 Kgs: 23:26–27)—that the Davidic covenant as such has been set aside (though some scholars claim that Kings implies this or is at least ambiguous about it, cf. 2 Kgs 25:27–30). In other words, I would claim that for these texts the essence of the Davidic promise is not made dependent upon future human obedience. Individuals and communities can remove themselves from the sphere of promise and its fulfillment, but the promise remains in place regardless.

This raises a related issue. It is evident elsewhere in Kings that prophetic words of *judgment* with respect to the future do not set that future in stone (e.g., 1 Kgs 21:27–29; 2 Kgs 20:1–7). One cannot argue from the perspective of fulfillment that a judgmental word of God about the future would *inevitably* have occurred in just that way. That some prophetic announcements of judgment do not necessarily or fully or precisely come to fulfillment in Kings means that all such words must be understood as having that *potential* when they are spoken. God does not leave such a word to function on its own; God goes with that word and, in interaction with human beings and the community's ever-changing history, may make adjustments in that

---

15. Texts such as these do not call divine omniscience into question, only an understanding of divine foreknowledge as absolute. God knows all there is to know (omniscience), but there is a future which is not yet available for knowing, even for God. Moreover the philosophical issue of whether absolute foreknowledge does or does not entail predetermination (an issue that seems to me to be undecideable, at least at present), does not come into play. The issue here is not absolute foreknowledge in some abstract sense, but specific texts wherein specific divine words about the future of individuals or other entities is expressed in terms of possibilities. On this issue, and the divine use of words such as "perhaps" and "if," see Fretheim, *The Suffering of God,* 45–59.

word.[16] Such cases, it seems to me, witness to a divine freedom *within re-lationship* (which makes for certain divine constraints) that qualifies any thoroughgoing notion of divine dependence.

1 Kings 11:26–39. God held out high hopes for Jeroboam and his reign. Indeed, God's will spoken through the prophetic word is clearly on record; God wants Jeroboam to be king, and God anticipates a Jeroboam dynasty like unto that of David, though with conditions (11:37–38). God's desire for his kingship is real, and the conditions stated are actual conditions. God no doubt sees the potential in Jeroboam, that he has the strength to resist the oppressive forces at work under Solomon and Rehoboam. God raises him up as, in effect, a savior figure (see 2 Kgs 13:4–5; 14:27).

The reference to Jeroboam's rebellion against Solomon (11:27) is not inconsequential; causation in this situation is not ascribed only to God and God's word. Though the rebellion itself is delayed until chapter 12 and God's powerful word through the prophet fills this scene, the word "rebel" stands at the beginning of this narrative and has important content. This point finds a parallel in 11:14–25; Hadad and Rezon are rebellious figures *before* God raises them up. To recognize this is important for how one thinks about the prophetic word and what follows.

For one thing, God works in and through what people do and say. What Jeroboam has done and will now do counts in charting a future course, not simply what God does or what God's prophet says. Both Jeroboam and God/God's word are effective agents. Jeroboam's faithfulness ("if you will listen," v. 38) is seen to be crucial for the course that that future takes (note that the possible negative future is only implied in this text).

Moreover, the positive future possibility that God's word gives to Jeroboam in v. 38 is real; it has not been "closed off by prophetic foreknowledge."[17] The text gives us no reason to believe that God is being deceptive here or is playing a game, as if God knows for sure that this future will not come to pass, but lays it out anyway. God's "if" is a real if. In fact, God uses important theological language for this word to Jeroboam; God will "take" him and he shall reign and be king; and "I will be with you" and "build" you an "enduring house," i.e., an enduring [11] dynasty. God sees a potential in Jeroboam's rule comparable to David's, as was the case with Solomon. In fact, 1 Kgs 12:15, 24 indicate that God has been at work to fulfill the prophet's word.[18] All this loaded theological language shows that

---

16. An important discussion of the power of words, and more particularly the word of God, is that by Anthony C. Thiselton, "Supposed Power of Words in the Biblical Writings," *JTS* (1974): 283–99. This article stands as a corrective of many discussions of "word" by biblical scholars, including that of Gerhard von Rad.

17. *Contra* Nelson, *First and Second Kings,* 73.

18. 1 Kgs 12:15 is an assessment by the narrator as to why Rehoboam heeded the advice of his younger advisors and did not listen (*šemaʿ*) to the people's request for relief from oppression. He did not listen "because it was a turn of affairs brought about by the Lord that he might fulfill his word" (NRSV; literally: "for it was a turning [*sibbāh*] by [*mēʿim*

God is not being deceptive here. This word to Jeroboam is a *genuine possibility* for the future for *both* Jeroboam and God. God treats Jeroboam *with integrity* in the outline of possible futures. What God does in that future will depend at least in part on what Jeroboam does.

But God's will for Jeroboam is not realized, not because God has failed, but because Jeroboam has. Jeroboam's sins are of such a magnitude that they successfully resist the will of God for him and his dynasty. The only other interpretive option for understanding Jeroboam, it seems to me, is to view the litany of his sins in 12:28–32 as the will of God. Yet, whatever historical judgments one might make about the calves (whether originally apostate or not), the narrative in chapters 12–14 is critical of his actions in uncompromising terms. Given what Jeroboam has done, the will of God is *now* evident in the *condemnation* of his actions.

Such an interpretation is also supported by the divine anger against Jeroboam (14:9,15). This twice-noted provoking of God to anger is important for what it reveals about God's original word to Jeroboam; it demonstrates again that God's word to Jeroboam about establishing his throne was not a sham. If God absolutely knew in advance that these things would happen to Jeroboam, it makes no sense for God to be provoked to anger at this point; God should, indeed would (given God's moral integrity), have been angry at the point of the divine knowledge of it. God certainly knew that these developments were possible, but the extent of the divine disillusionment (and the divine feeling language in these texts is strong, e.g., 14:9–10) suggests that they were not viewed as probable at the time of the original prophecy. More generally, it is important that God not be imaged as a wrathful God (here or elsewhere), as if anger were a divine attribute. God is *provoked* to anger. Anger is a divine response to a specific human situation. If there were no sin, there would be no divine anger.[19]

The book of Kings will pass a theological judgment on subsequent Israelite kings in terms of how they relate to Jeroboam's apostasy (over twenty times; first in 1 Kgs 15:26; finally in 2 Kgs 17:22–23). The assumption is that not only Jeroboam, but (at least some of) Jeroboam's successors could have reversed this state of affairs. But none of them did (2 Chr 28:9–15 and 30:6–11 cite exceptions), and it no doubt became more difficult (and eventually impossible) to do so as time passed. Jeroboam, who started out

---

away from?] the Lord that he might fulfill his word"). Again, Rehoboam is the subject of the verb *šmʿ*; that he did not listen is something that he himself chose. It is not clear what the "turning" means or even who the subject is. (This word occurs only here.) At the same time, the claim is clear that Rehoboam did not act alone. God was at work in this situation on behalf of the future outlined by Ahijah, even through the bumbling efforts of Rehoboam's listening and not listening, and that work of God was effective in this instance toward that end. But, God's will as articulated through the word of the prophet Ahijah is clearly resistible, as evident in the actions of Jeroboam.

19. I find the most helpful treatment of divine anger to be that of Heschel, *The Prophets*, 279–98.

as a savior ends up as such a sinner that the last state of affairs for Israel is worse than the first. God's hopes for him are dashed and God's saving will for Israel is frustrated, if not finally abrogated.

In a variety of texts and traditions, we have seen that God's way into the future is dependent at least in part upon what human beings do and say. Perhaps one reason (apart from more general understandings of God and the human) that such an interpretation of these texts has not been common is that it brings human responsibility to the forefront of the conversation. Many of us would just as soon leave everything up to God, and God (and/or the devil) can then be blamed when things go wrong, tragically or otherwise. God has freely chosen to enter into the kind of relationship with human beings that treats the human party with integrity and honor and entrusts them (even as sinful creatures) with significant and future-shaping [12] responsibilities. A way between pessimism in the face of the difficulties, on the one hand, and a Messiah complex on the other will not always be easy to locate. But God calls human beings to take up these God-given tasks with insight and energy—for the sake of God's world and ours. Some comfort can be found in the assurance that in this effort we do not act alone and that God will remain faithful to promises made.

The Repentance of God: A Key to Evaluating Old Testament God-Talk

Divine repentance is one of the most neglected themes in biblical scholarship. To my knowledge only one monograph has ever been devoted to such a study, and that quite recent.[1] Scholarly articles have been few and far between.[2] Old Testament theologies have treated the subject in passing, if at all.[3] Even commentaries on those books which contain the nearly 40 explicit references to divine repentance (*nicham*) tend to skip past this theme with little or no comment.[4]

This is not a recent development. As early as the Septuagint and the Targums there is evidence that translators had difficulty coming to terms with this anthropopathic language.[5] A survey of Jewish and Christian

---

This essay was originally published in *Horizons in Biblical Theology* 10 (1988): 47–70.

1. Jörg Jeremias, *Die Reue Gottes, Aspekte der alttestamentlichen Gottesvorstellung* (BibS[N] 65; Neukirchen: Neukirchener Verlag, 1975). Cf. H. van Dyke Parunak, "A Semantic Survey of *nhm*," *Bib* 56 (1975): 512–32; H. J. Stoebe, "*nhm*," in *THAT*, 2:59–66.

2. Among the few are those of Lester Kuyper, "The Repentance of God," *RR* 18 (1965): 3–8; "The Suffering and Repentance of God," *SJT* 22 (1969): 257–77. Cf. also Johannes Hempel, "Gottes Selbstbeherrschung als Problem des Monotheismus und der Eschatologie," in *Gottes Wort und Gottes Land: Hans-Wilhelm Hertzberg zum 70. Geburtstag am 16. Januar 1965 dargebracht von Kollegen, Freunden und Schülern* (Göttingen: Vandenhoeck & Ruprecht, 1965), 56–61.

3. Cf. H. H. Rowley, *The Faith of Israel* (London: SCM, 1956), 67; Edmond Jacob, *Theology of the Old Testament* (New York: Harper & Row, 1958), 291. Gerhard von Rad, *Old Testament Theology* (2 vols.; New York: Harper, 1962–65), 2:198–99, deals with the matter only parenthetically when, in commenting on Jeremiah 18, he wonders about the "oddly theoretical" sense of the passage, which almost makes "Jahweh's power dependent upon law rather than freedom." Walther Eichrodt, *Theology of the Old Testament* (2 vols.; Philadelphia: Westminster, 1967), 1:217, notes the matter only in passing, though he quotes (from Schultz) an important statement: "The repentance of God ... grows from the assured conviction that human development is not for him an empty, indifferent spectacle, that it is just this immutability of his being, which excludes that dull, dead unchangeableness which remains outwardly the same, however much the circumstances may change." Cf. T. C. Vriezen, *An Outline of Old Testament Theology* (Oxford: Blackwell, 1958), 77, 168, 240. A book such as Robert C. Dentan, *The Knowledge of God in Ancient Israel* (New York: Seabury Press, 1968), does not even mention the subject, except to affirm that God is one who does not repent (p. 151).

4. Some exception to this is found in discussions of Hos 11:8–9.

5. Cf. Raphael Loewe, "Jerome's Treatment of an Anthropomorphism," *VT* 2 (1952): 261–72. Yet, no thoroughgoing anti-anthropomorphic perspective seems to have been attempted.

biblical interpretation through the centuries reveals a variety of attempts to escape from interpretations which would place in question prevailing understandings of God.[6] Commonly, however, alternatives were not even raised or considered, so entrenched, presumably, were prevailing theistic perspectives.

Similar factors may account at least in part for the contemporary neglect of this theme. The nature of the discipline today, however, is such that it tends to inhibit theological conversation, so it is difficult to be sure. Perhaps it is due to theological disinterest, or not knowing what to make of the theme, or not having the theological sophistication to deal with it confidently. I have sought to make the case elsewhere that "OT scholarship is strongly informed implicitly or explicitly by a move toward theological convergence with traditional Christian or Jewish theological formulations."[7] At the least, when compared to other aspects of the discipline, it seems to be clear that OT scholarship is moving in new directions theologically at a rather slow pace.

Robert Oden Jr. in his recent book, *Bible without Theology,* states that "the theological tradition carries with it clear limitations [48] that have threatened and still threaten to restrict the range of questions considered appropriate to raise of texts and themes in the Bible," and often resorts to "explanation by reference to the inexplicable."[8] It may well be that the study of divine repentance heretofore could be noted as a case in point. But certainly another, probably more important factor could be cited: the neglect of a rigorous interdisciplinary approach to theological matters in the biblical texts.

That is to say, it is not likely that a greater commitment to historical or literary or comparative scholarship in isolation will enable new theological directions. It is only when comparable commitments and energies are devoted to the *biblical-theological task per se* that theological issues will be opened up. Without this, the tendency will be to interpret texts within inherited, usually quite traditional theistic categories and perspectives; all too often this means that the God of the text is assumed to be in absolute control of the situation, sees everything in advance, and is responsive only to God's own will in the situation. As an example of the difficulties this can generate, consider the image of God recently thought to be pervasive in the Saul cycle.[9] The God of the text is thought to be "savage," manipulative, merciless, and predisposed to reject Saul from the beginning. It appears

---

6. Cf. Loewe, ibid., but especially Kuyper, "The Suffering and Repentance of God." Cf. also H. M. Kuitert, *Gott in Menschengestalt: Eine dogmatisch-hermeneutische Studie über die Anthropomorphismen der Bibel* (Munich: Chr. Kaiser, 1967), 192ff.

7. Terence Fretheim, *The Suffering of God: An Old Testament Perspective* (Philadelphia: Fortress, 1984), 20.

8. Robert Oden, Jr., *Bible without Theology* (San Francisco: Harper, 1987), vii–viii.

9. Cf. T. Fretheim, "Divine Foreknowledge, Divine Constancy, and the Rejection of Saul's Kingship," *CBQ* (1985): 595–602.

that this view has emerged because its proponents are operating essentially with a traditional theistic perspective regarding the God of the text and find it problematic. But, if the God of the text is not correspondent with this traditional perspective, then this entire interpretation becomes itself problematic.

It is striking that, while interdisciplinary efforts abound in, e.g., literary, sociological, and anthropological aspects of OT study, and are often accepted as methodologically legitimate (and evaluated largely in terms of their payoff in interpretation), comparable efforts in the study of the theology in[10] the texts are in their infancy and often suspect methodologically (perhaps largely because the study of theology is thought to be a more subjective matter than other disciplines). I would contend *(pace* Oden) that it is in fact my study of the theology in the text, undertaken within the context of a study of contemporary constructive (as well as more traditional) theologies, [49] rather than special attention to other aspects of OT study, that are most decisive in pushing me into new theological directions in the study of the text. It is this which has given me (and others) different sets of questions to ask of the text, which is also the primary effect of interdisciplinary approaches in other areas of OT study. The consideration of the divine repentance theme will benefit from some of these questions (our purpose here).

It is important to make a distinction between the regnant theologies of the church and synagogue and more recent constructive efforts, the result of which have only begun to filter down and affect traditional formulations (and, as always, in an uneven way). This divergence is very evident regarding the theological issues raised by the divine repentance theme. Ronald Goetz makes this clear in the following remarks:

> Theologically ours has been the century of the suffering of God—the Theophaschite Century. The rejection of the ancient doctrine of divine impassibility and immutability among contemporary theologians has become epidemic. Apart from certain conservative defenders of older theological traditions, the vast majority of constructive theologians, silently or noisily, as the case may be, have throughout the century been abandoning the traditional view. Just as significant perhaps is the fact that, even among those theologians who . . . have not embraced modern Theopaschism, there has failed to develop a creative, modern restatement of the older dogma.[11]

While Goetz might speak of an "epidemic" among systematic theologians (often informed by a more open reading of the biblical materials), this is

---

10. I speak of the "theology in the text" rather than the theology of the text in order to stress the theological particularities within a given text as over against an attempt to state the theology of a text as a unit.

11. Ronald Goetz, "Karl Barth, Juergen Moltmann and the Theopaschite Revolution," in *Festschrift: A Tribute to Dr. William Hordern* (ed. W. Freitag; Saskatoon: Univ. of Saskatchewan Press, 1985), 17.

certainly not the case in synagogue and church, nor among biblical scholars, if one can judge from exegetical results. It is not common to see an exegesis forthrightly informed by what Karl Barth, in connection with his consideration of the divine repentance texts, calls "the holy mutability of God."[12] More generally, given the fact that God is the subject of thousands of verbs in the OT, it is not as commonly recognized as it ought to be that one's theistic perspective will often profoundly affect how those verbs [50] and sentences will be interpreted. It is the interdisciplinary theological conversation more than anything else which will make us aware of the interpretive options.

Repentance as Metaphor

Repentance is a metaphor whose roots are to be found in the dynamics of interpersonal human relationships. Generally, the use of the word "repentance" presupposes that one has said or done something to another and, finding that to be hurtful or inadequate or dissatisfactory in some way, seeks to reverse the effects through contrition, sorrow, regret, or some other form of "turning." It is a word which assumes real change on the part of the one who repents; something formerly said or done is no longer held to be right or appropriate. It is also a word for which temporal sequence is integral; it is change with respect to some past statement or action. It is commonplace to observe human beings engaging in words and acts of repentance in order to move toward some change in a relationship with other human beings or with God, with the most common usage captured in the phrase, "repentance of sin." Given this usage for human activity, what might the metaphor mean when used of God, as is common in the OT?

The problem is rooted in the fact that the word "repent" is a translation of two Hebrew terms, *nicham* and *shuv*. The former is the word normally used for divine repentance, the latter for human repentance of sin (and also sometimes for divine repentance). While *nicham* may occasionally be used for human repentance, it is doubtful that it ever refers to repentance of sin.[13] Moreover, God is never said to have committed any sin of which God needs to repent; all of God's actions are considered appropriate and justifiable. Divine repentance thus has reference to an activity for which the word is not commonly used in contemporary English. The older English versions (e.g., KJV; Coverdale) translated both Hebrew words with "repent," for at that time the word had a somewhat broader general reference in everyday usage than what it has today. With the narrowing of

---

12. Karl Barth, *Church Dogmatics* (New York: Scribners, 1957), 2/1:496.
13. Of the passages where this has been suggested, Job 42:6 best carries the sense of "foreswear" (cf. J. Gerald Janzen, *Job* [Interpretation; Atlanta: John Knox, 1985]). Exod 13:17 has the sense of "relent." Jer 8:6 is the only instance where *ra'ah* is an object of the verb used with human beings; yet, the "What have I done?" may indicate that the reference is more to the effects of the sinful behavior (cf. NEB).

the meaning of "repent" in more recent English parlance, contemporary translations have sought to find other words to translate *nicham* (though RSV usually retains it). The most common translations are: regret, be sorry, grieve, have [51] compassion, retract, change one's mind (cf. TEV!), think better of, go back on one's word, and most commonly, relent. Normally, a translation will use a number of these words, depending upon the nuance called for in a given context. Yet, there seems to be a general sense to which one can point: the reversal of a direction taken or decision made. Wolff's suggestion captures the sense even more fully: "a change of mind prompted by the emotions, a turning away from an earlier decision on the part of someone deeply moved."[14] Thus, the word appears to include not only the sense of reversal, but a reversal prompted by one's being moved by the situation in view.

Given this sense of the word, how ought it be related to an understanding of metaphor? While this is not the place to discuss metaphor more generally, suffice it to be said here that I understand such language to be "reality depicting."[15] The metaphors used to speak of God are realistic, having cognitive value. The metaphors do reveal an essential continuity with the reality which is God; they do in fact contain information about God. At the same time, they disclose that which is discontinuous with the divine reality. Each metaphor speaks both a "yes" and a "no" (an "is" and "is not") with respect to God. In the history of interpretation the temptation has been to fall off this horse on one side or the other, either interpreting the metaphors literally in every respect or (more commonly today) denying any essential relationship between the metaphor and God.

How does one then move from metaphor to essential definition? By interpreting "along the metaphorical grain" and not contrary to it, by "following the thrust of the analogy."[16] If one moves against the natural implication of the metaphor, one is misinterpreting it. At the same time, one must always be attentive to that in the metaphor which is discontinuous with the reality which is God, a God who cannot finally be captured within any metaphor(s).

---

14. Hans Walter Wolff, *Joel and Amos* (Hermeneia; Philadelphia: Fortress, 1977), 298. Jeremias thinks that the verb loses its emotional content in later usage. Parunak ("A Semantic Survey of *nhm*," 525–26) thinks the basic meaning of the verb is "be comforted," and relates every usage of the word to that basic sense; but this seems unlikely in many contexts. Efforts to discover the meaning of the word through etymology have not been successful. See H. van Dyke Parunak, "A Semantic Survey of *nhm*," 513–15; Stoebe, "*nhm*," 59; James Barr, *The Semantics of Biblical Language* (Oxford: Oxford University Press, 1961), 116–17. Moreover, because the reversal could be favorable or unfavorable for the affected party, the word in itself cannot mean either "forgiveness" or "condemnation."

15. See the discussion with bibliography in *The Suffering of God*, 512. On metaphors, models, concepts, etc., and their relationship, see Sallie McFague, *Metaphorical Theology* (Philadelphia: Fortress, 1982), especially pp. 14–29.

16. J. Gerald Janzen, "Metaphor and Reality in Hosea 11," *Semeia* 24 (1982): 19, 26.

Hence, to speak of God as a repenting one, the basic "grain" of the metaphor having to do with reversal and change with respect to some past statement or action must be followed. It is at this point where the "yes" of the metaphor is to be found. At the same time, there is no one-to-one correspondence between the way human beings and God repent. Thus, for example, there are certain matters [52] concerning which God never needs to repent (e.g., sin). The OT expresses one aspect of the "no" of the metaphor in the phrase, "God does not repent" (cf. Num 23:19; 1 Sam 15:29). In these passages it is explicitly stated that God does not repent because "God is not a human being." Yet, even when God *does* repent (e.g., Hos 11:8–9) it is said that God does so because "God is not a human being." Thus, in both God's repenting and not repenting, there is a "no" in the use of the metaphor. It remains to be determined what the content of the "no" is, but suffice it to be said at this point that it is focused on a divine faithfulness and steadfastness which finds no parallel among human beings.

Repentance as Controlling Metaphor

Not all metaphors have the same value when used to speak of God.[17] In other words, one might speak of metaphors in terms of degrees of revelatory capacity. God as dry rot (Hos 5:12) would have a low capacity compared to God as lover (Hos 11:1). The high capacity metaphors have a certain controlling function, i.e., they delimit metaphorical possibilities (Why is criminal not an appropriate metaphor for the God of any OT tradition?); they serve to qualify other metaphors (God is not simply father; God is a loving father); and they are especially helpful in bringing coherence to a wide range of biblical language about God (a metaphorical canon within the canon). The evidence suggests that divine repentance is a controlling metaphor of some consequence (and hence a model in McFague's sense, p. 23). On what grounds are these judgments made? Two bases might be cited: (1) the fullness of correspondence that can be discerned between the tenor and vehicle of the metaphor as related to life experience, and (2) the internal witness of the Old Testament, which reflects the first basis.

The first factor noted is a general literary observation pertinent to the assessment of the value of metaphors in any context. Certain metaphors have a greater richness of association in human experience; such metaphors ring true to life in special ways, revealing a breadth and depth of fitness with respect to that experience. They have a high level of capacity to capture, illuminate, organize, and communicate our experience and understanding of God (or anything else), to focus our thinking, feeling, and acting with respect to [53] our life experience. Generally, with respect to God language, it would appear that metaphors drawn from interpersonal relationships have the greatest such capacity.

---

17. See Fretheim, *Suffering of God*, 10–12.

Second, the internal witness of the Old Testament. Generally, the following factors might be considered: (a) the pervasiveness of the metaphor, (b) the traditions with which the metaphor is associated; (c) the genres within which the metaphor is used.

a. Pervasiveness

The frequency of metaphors does say something about the value they must have had for Israel. It is without question that the most frequent metaphors for God in the Old Testament are drawn from the sphere of the human. While the repentance metaphor is not as common as some others, it is more pervasive than is commonly thought. An outline of the usage of *nicham* will help to demonstrate this:

1. Rejection of an already accomplished act: Gen 6:6–7; 1 Sam 15:11, 35 (distinguished by a following *ki* rather than *al* or *el).*
2. God does not repent:
   a. With respect to certain matters: 1 Sam 15:29; Num 23:19; Ps 110:4. Always related to certain promises by which God will stand forever. They are centered in the Davidic traditions, with Num 23:19 tying God's commitment to David and Israel together. Some other verbs are the semantic equivalent of this sense of *nicham (shuv; sb; sur).*[18]
   b. With respect to certain occasions: Jer 4:18; 15:6; 20:16; Ezek 24:14; Hos 13:14 (noun); Zech 8:14. Always related to specific occasions of judgment and applicable only to that occasion.
3. Reversal of what God said he would do or has already started doing:
   a. General affirmation: Joel 2:13; Jonah 4:2.
   b. In (potential) response to prayers/repentance: Ps 90:13; 106:44–45; Isa 57:6 (?); Jer 18:7–10; 26:3, 13, 19; Joel 2:14; Jonah 3:9–10. [54]
   c. In response to an intercessor: Exod 32:12–14; Amos 7:3–6. The seriousness which God gives to human considerations in shaping the future is especially striking here.[19]
   d. For God's sake, with no apparent human mediation: Deut 32:36; 2 Sam 24:16; 1 Chr 21:15; Jer 42:10; Judg 2:18; Ps 135:14?; Hos 11:8 (noun). Each of these passages has to do with a divine reversal with respect to a judgment that is already in the process of execution; the judgment is stopped to prevent total destruction.

Divine repentance appears in other formulations in various traditions. For example, God's actions with respect to Ahab (1 Kgs 21:27–29), Hezekiah (Isa 38:1–6; 2 Kgs 20:1–11), and Rehoboam (2 Chr 12:1–12; note that the parallel in 1 Kings 14 does not contain this theme) are in fact instances of divine repentance without the specific language. God's turning (*shuv*) from his wrath is also a comparable theme (cf. Deut 13:17; Josh 7:26; 2 Kgs

---

18. See the discussion in idem, "Divine Foreknowledge."
19. For some of the theological implications of this, see idem, *The Suffering of God*, 49–53.

23:26; Isa 5:25; Jer 4:8; cf. its use in the Hiphil in Ps 78:38; Ezek 20:22; cf. also the role of the mediator in Num 25:11; Ps 106:23; Jer 18:20). It is precisely this sort of history with its God that prompts later Israel to interpret its earlier history in terms of divine repentance.

b. Tradition

Generally, the broader the representation of a metaphor in OT traditions, the more revealing of God and God's activity it must have been for various Israelite authors/groups in different historical periods. While the importance of a metaphor for Israel cannot be measured simply by counting traditions represented, its frequency would have some bearing on determining its perceived value for theological reflection on the part of Israel's theologians. Divine repentance is in fact found within a variety of traditions, northern and southern, early and late: Jahwist/Elohist; David-Zion; Deuteronomic History; eighth- and seventh-century prophets; exilic and post-exilic prophecy; psalmody. It is thus not the property or perspective of a small number of circles within Israel.

In addition, one should consider the overall perspective or *Tendenz* of a tradition in seeing how a given metaphor functions [55] within it. One example would be the formulation, "God does not repent" (2a above), though its infrequency should occasion caution in drawing conclusions. It would appear that this particular formulation and its semantic equivalents have a special place within the David-Zion traditions (though the tradition represented in Num 23:19 is not altogether clear) and are used to emphasize the steadfastness of the divine promise to Davidic Israel (note that this usage is prominently featured in the NT).[20] Or, consider the formulation that God will not repent of judgment (2b above). This usage is confined to prophetic oracles delivered on the eve of a specific judgment. But, the fact that one of these prophets (Jeremiah) in a number of other passages (3b) holds out the possibility of divine repentance is both a redactional and a theological problem. While these passages may well have historical roots related to earlier and later stages in Jeremiah's preaching (in the absence of repentance, history's passing inexorably narrows Israel's possibilities for the future), having now been intermixed redactionally, they serve theologically to show that what became inevitable was not always so and the change in the range of divine options for response must be placed squarely at the door of Israel's non-response to the divine call for repentance. The

---

20. See Rom 9:6; 11:29; Titus 1:2; Heb 6:17–18; 7:21. These references do not refer to the unchangeableness of God in a general way but to two specific unchangeable matters: God's loyalty and purpose, and his justifiable judgment. It is in this latter sense that Mal 3:6 is to be understood. The more general reference in Jas 1:17 refers to God's total reliability not to tempt God's children with evil, to bestow good and perfect gifts. The correspondent NT passages to God's repenting are those which refer to the divine forebearance, patience, and self-restraint in judgment (see Luke 11:5–8; 13:6–9; 18:7–8; Mark 13:30; Matt 24:22; Rom 2:4; 3:25; 9:22; 1 Pet 3:20–21; 2 Pet 3:9, 15).

particular nuance given to divine repentance is thus related to the interests
central to a given tradition, but certainly in a way that is not entirely removed from historical realities out of which the tradition arose.

Whether one can track the history of this metaphor through the various
traditions in which it is used and discern historical shifts in its meaning is
uncertain. In the only monograph on this subject, J. Jeremias seeks to show
some development in its meaning through the years. He considers it to be
the product largely of later theological reflection, having been built back
into older traditions in some cases.[21] This is problematic not least because
the dating of a number of the traditions is so difficult (e.g., Exod 32:11–14).
Even then, he thinks he can demonstrate that relatively earlier instances
of *nicham* evidence an emotional content, while in the later stages it has
become a regularized divine response to certain human actions. But, rather
than an evolution of meaning, the evidence is more suggestive of shifts in
nuance due to functional factors within [56] a given tradition. It is important to observe, however, that the metaphor appears primarily in later traditions; its broader usage is the product of years of reflection on the nature
of God's activity.

Divine repentance became one of the important vehicles by which Israel
interpreted the significance of older traditions and the divine activity reported therein. For example, in one of the few instances where a prophetic
voice from the past is quoted (Mic 3:12 in Jer 26:18), divine repentance
constitutes the key to the interpretation of a prophetic word. A prophet's
announcement regarding the future did not come to pass because God repented. Or, God's *not* repenting of judgment in the past is used to ground
God's not repenting of good in the future (Zech 8:14–15). Also, its function
in Israel's confession regarding God (e.g., Joel 2:13) mirrors no little reflection on the nature of God's activity in Israel's history over the years.

Whatever decisions one makes regarding the historical development
of this metaphor, its role in the present canonical shape of the OT must
be carefully considered. At the same time, the historical factors and the
canonical factors cannot be dissociated from one another. That is to say,
if divine repentance is a metaphor which commonly functions for later
Israel as a key to interpreting the nature of God's activity over the years,
then there is an inner OT warrant for its important role canonically, reading the whole from the perspective of the "end" of the history (not unlike one would use the Christ-event to interpret the OT). One important
observation in this regard is that the metaphor appears at some of the key
junctures in the canon: the flood story; the Sinai revelation; the institu-
tion of the monarchy; the fall of the northern and southern kingdoms;
throughout the prophets; psalmody. Thus, whether the "early" passages
are in fact so or have been built back in from the perspective of later Israel,

21. Jeremias, *Die Reue Gottes*, 14.

divine repentance is understood to be an important interpretive vehicle for understanding the divine activity throughout the canon. Canonically speaking, therefore, its role is very significant. This conclusion will be supported by a consideration of genre.

What then of the relationship between the function and nuance of the metaphor in an individual tradition and its role within the [57] canon as a whole? Or, how is the God who repents in Jeremiah related to the God who repents in Samuel, for example? The preceding and following considerations suggest that, while the use of the theme in each tradition must be carefully explicated on its own terms, this is not finally enough. They *also* constitute the raw materials for an integrative theological task, seeking to integrate the particular nuances of the metaphor in a given tradition/genre into an overarching canonical sense of divine repentance without losing the edges provided by the traditions. The understanding of divine repentance in the various traditions when integrated with one another result in a many-faceted perspective on divine change.[22]

c. Genre[23]

Genre determination will commonly have much to do with how one understands and explicates a text, including its theology. For example, having God as the subject of verbs in historical narrative enables one to say some things about the kind of God such a God is, e.g., God is a participant in human history. At the same time, it would take a much closer analysis of the text to determine just how this God is related to history. Or, seeing God depicted as the addressee in the lament psalms will say something very important about that God; God is one who is easily and forthrightly addressed, and has entered into an open and dialogical relationship with those who pray such prayers. At the same time, one would have to consider whether the severities of the suffering situation prompted a speaking of God that is theologically imprecise, albeit very important. Literary form and theological understandings are closely interrelated, but one must move beyond genre designation to get at the details or nuances of the theology in the text itself.

Genre determination is of no little help in discerning the place and understanding of the divine repentance metaphor. It appears in narratives of various sorts, indicating that the metaphor is closely related to the divine interaction with the world so characteristic of those materials. In prophetic

---

22. Cf. John Goldingay, *Theological Diversity and the Authority of the Old Testament* (Grand Rapids, MI: Eerdmans, 1987), 183–84. "OT theology is thus a constructive, not merely a reconstructive task. . . . The new whole is more than the parts it began from, not less than them. . . . Working with these materials, we seek to construct a whole which does not correspond to anything that any individual OT writer knew, but does justice to what he knew."

23. See the paper by John J. Collins, "Is a Critical Biblical Theology Possible?" 13–17, presented to the SBL at its Atlanta convention.

oracles it is often found in direct divine speech (e.g., Jer 26:3). It is not unimportant that God himself is understood to use such language; it is not simply used in human reflection on God's activity but is understood to convey God's own understandings. There is thus portrayed a fundamental continuity between God's own reflections (God in himself) and God's specific [58] activity in the world. Or, the fact that this theme occurs in an "oddly theoretical" (von Rad), perhaps even "dogmatic" (Carroll) statement, in Jer 18:7–10 betrays the fact that it has been the subject of very close theological scrutiny. And this text is ascribed to God himself!

Of special interest is the appearance of the theme in psalmody and creedal statements; these are leaner forms of literature in which Israel's faith was expressed. These genres are explicitly confessional in character. When the community of faith incorporates this theme into its hymnic literature (e.g., Ps 106:45) and praises God for God's repentant ways, it has achieved an important place in Israel's confession regarding God. This is demonstrated in even more striking ways by the fact that the theme is incorporated into Israel's most basic creedal statement regarding God:

> Thou art a gracious God and merciful, slow to anger,
> abounding in steadfast love, and repentest of evil.
>   Joel 2:13; Jonah 4:2

The final phrase of this creedal statement is missing in earlier formulations (e.g., Exod 34:6–7). This suggests some development in the importance given to the idea in Israel *generally* (whatever its importance to individual authors). Divine repentance here stands alongside some of the most fundamental statements Israel ever makes about its God (each clause, of course, being as anthropopathic as the next); it is believed to be just as characteristic of God as grace and mercy. This is a confession that is abstracted from the particularities of Israel's history, and (along with other factors) becomes the basis for saying that God is like this wherever and whenever God is being God (witness its use for non-Israelites in Jonah 4:2 and Jer 18:7–10). I have discussed these creedal statements elsewhere;[24] let the following quote suffice:

> Just as the historical recitals determined those events in Israel's history which were constitutive of its present existence, and thus separable from all other events as crucial for faith, so also these generalizations about God provided the appropriate interpretive clue for the determination of the meaning of that history.

[59] In other words, the late inclusion of divine repentance to a position alongside steadfast love, etc., in Israel's most basic statement about the kind of God in which it believed, provides additional evidence for speaking of an inner OT warrant for evaluating all OT God-talk in such terms. It

---

24. Fretheim, *The Suffering of God*, 25–29, especially p. 28.

becomes one of those deep, underlying assumptions about God which now suffuses all of Israel's efforts to speak of its God. Divine repentance thus becomes one of the controlling metaphors for understanding the God of Israel, providing a hermeneutical key for interpreting OT texts which speak of God. It must be a prominent theme at the center of all efforts to bring coherence to a wide range of OT reflection about God.

Divine Repentance Theologically Considered

Fundamental to any consideration of divine repentance in the OT is a prior question. To be able to speak of God as one who repents assumes a basic understanding of God such that God is the kind of God who could so act. It should be clear that divine repentance is not something unusual in the OT understanding of God. The language of repentance is part and parcel of a much broader range of language used to speak of God. More basically, it has to do with divine affectability by the creation. The God who repents is also a God who is provoked to anger, who rejoices over the creation, who responds to prayer. This is a God who has chosen to enter into a relationship with the world such that it is a genuine relationship.

Whence such change language for God? Fundamental to this is the theophany, in which God appears in human form in order to reveal himself to people. For God to assume such a form means that God freely undergoes change, experiencing that which God has not experienced heretofore. Even if one were to say that God foreknew that God would assume such a form, one would still have to reckon with the fact that the actual experience of being "clothed" in the form of the human is different from merely foreknowing such. It is different to know something as actuality rather than only as possibility. In other words, the most basic form in which God reveals himself to Israel, namely the theophany,[25] provides the most fundamental basis for considering a God who in freedom changes for the sake of personal encounter with the creation. [60]

Important here is the recognition that the God who appears in human form is not a divine creature, with the real God remaining in heaven. Nor have we to do here with only a part of God or something less than God. Though clothed in human form, and hence more than God, it is *God* who appears.[26] So, it is actually *God* who undergoes change in assuming human form, revealing himself as one who is not immutable in some absolute sense, and inviting those who see and hear to relate to God who will enter into genuine (and hence change-filled) relationships with the creation. By the way, it could be argued that one of the reasons for Israel's aniconic perspective is that idols do not change (cf. Ps 115:5–7; Jer 10:4–5). I have

---

25. Idem, "The Color of God: Israel's God-Talk and Life-Experience," *WW* 6 (1986): 259–63.

26. On the human form of God, see idem, *The Suffering of God*, 101–6.

sought to show elsewhere that the most basic reason for the prohibition of images is a concern to protect God's relatedness rather than God's transcendence.[27] Also, according to the OT, one of the characteristics of the gods of the nations is that they cannot be moved or affected (cf. 1 Kgs 18:27–29).

We now look at some representative repentance texts, first the general affirmations (Joel 2:13; Jonah 4:2). What does the addition of the phrase regarding divine repentance add to this list of divine characteristics? It would be redundant if repentance were nothing more than another way of speaking of God's love or mercy. Love is that in which the divine repentance is grounded (Ps 106:45), and the application of repentance is certainly a gracious act. But something new must have been intended. It must have been added because it was believed to reflect another dimension to Israel's understanding of its own experience with this God. To confess that God is a God who repents says something about a God who is ready to reverse himself, who stands ready to back away from judgments announced (so Jonah) or judgments already in process (so Joel). It says that God's own history (what has been said and done in the past) may not be fully adequate for dealing with a changed present. Given God's faithfulness and the constancy of God's loving purposes, it may be that God will have to forsake God's own past in order to be true to those purposes, indeed for the sake of God's own name (the latter is the prevailing theme in the passages listed in 3d above). Simply to speak of God's love, mercy, and graciousness would not necessarily carry such freight. Given the implicit reference [61] to God's past activity in Israel's life in this confession, repentance must have been recognized as an important interpretive key to the nature of this God and God's involvement in Israel and the world.

It is thus clear that this confession stands in sharpest contrast to any arbitrariness of divine action. Rather, it reflects the extent to which this loving and gracious God will go in order to execute God's uncompromising salvific intentions. The confession as a whole announces the priority of grace in all of God's dealings with the world. God's constant availability for repentance stands in the service of this unchanginng divine intention, not simply for Israel (so Joel) but also for the world (so Jonah). To speak in other terms, it would appear that it is essential to speak of both immutability and mutability as essential divine attributes, each in its own sphere.

Secondly, some specifics regarding Israel's experience of divine repentance. God may repent in response to an intercessor (3c above) or for God's own sake (3d above), but I concentrate here on passages where God's repentance is related to human repentance (3b above). It is clear that God in fact has repented in view of human repentance in the face of the announcement of judgment (e.g., Jer 26:18–19) or in the midst of a judgment (e.g., Jer 42:10). In other passages divine repentance is promised if human

---

27. See idem, "The Color of God," 265.

repentance is forthcoming (e.g., Jer 26:3). The fundamental motivation for divine repentance is clear. God's desire is for life, not death. In fact, it may be said that God hopes that the announcements of judgment will not have to be fulfilled, so that God's salvific will can be realized. God's will is done, it would seem, when prophecies of judgment fail or, if deemed finally necessary, are stopped short of proceeding to their destructive end. In other words, God hopes to be able to reverse himself; God is open to change precisely in order that the people may experience salvation rather than judgment or final judgment.

The passage in Joel is especially interesting for a number of reasons. One, it provides for God-given vehicles for a repentant response on the part of the community, even down to liturgical details (2:12–17). And yet, for all the repentant activity, the divine repentance is not automatically conceived, as if human repentance were not only the necessary, but also the sufficient, cause for the divine [62] response. Joel 2:14 states, "Who knows whether God will turn and repent and leave a blessing behind him?" (cf. the "perhaps" of Jonah 3:9; Zeph 2:3). This is a way of saying that the human return is the necessary precondition, but not the ground, of God's repentant activity. God's repentance rests finally in God's love, so that grace remains truly grace. Thus, the focus of concern is not on God's freedom[28] but on the safeguarding of the divine grace. It prevents any simple *quid pro quo* understanding of the relationship between human and divine repentance.

Secondly, the divine repentance is not to be related to forgiveness but to the alleviation of the judgment being suffered. The prayer in 2:17 relates to the "sparing" of the people, and the action of God reported in 2:18–20 has no reference to forgiveness. It is God's repenting of *evil*, that is, executed judgment or, in other words, the effects resultant from a build-up of sin in the community (cf. the use of "Who Knows?" in 2 Sam 12:22). The key issue here is not whether the people will be forgiven their sin (it is not mentioned here as it is in 2 Sam 12:13, but may be assumed). Moreover, it is clear that God's will is to save his people (v. 13); that is never in doubt. The uncertainty relates to deliverance from the effects of sinfulness, that is, evil; whether a blessing will be "left."

Thus, there is an element of uncertainty in all of this not only for the people but also for God, that is, whether the accumulated effects of sinfulness can be countered by this human-divine repentance in time for it to affect the present community. It may be possible for God to repent, but for a blessing not to be left, not because God does not will it to be so, but because the effects of sinfulness may even be beyond the possibilities of being affected by the divine reversal. In other words, it is not at all certain that the divine repentance will in fact be effective in a given situation.

---

28. Contra Wolff, *Joel and Amos*, 48.

Some final theological observations are in order.

While there are not many abstract statements about God in the OT, the fact that there are some, including a number concerned with divine repentance, indicates that it is likely that the God of other OT sentences has a meaning in some way related to those abstractions. In other words, any attempt to speak canonically about [63] God must incorporate such abstractions and relate them to all OT speech about God. Or, we are invited by the OT itself to engage in some general reflections about these matters.

In considering this matter, one must avoid two extremes, either that God is immutable in any absolute sense, or that God is mercurial, or capricious, or unstable. In other terms, one must avoid both the idea that God engages in relationships outside of his own heart and the idea that God is not constant in will or purpose or in the loving execution thereof. To be affected and to interact genuinely does not mean some imperfection in God. In fact, it should be said that not to be able genuinely to respond or interact, not to be open and vulnerable, or refusing to change are in fact signs of imperfection. In all of this, it is important to say that God changes as *God,* not as the creatures.[29]

These directions for reflection may be especially fruitful:

1. *Divine self-limitation.* The formulation, "God does not repent," affirms this theme. The promise associated with David (1 Sam 15:28–29) indicates that God will go with David come what may. God thereby limits his options for activity in the world. And this means that God will go with human beings in all of their weakness as the means in and through which God will act in the world.

2. *The primary attributes of God.* Divine repentance enables one to keep the primary attributes of God more in focus, namely, his steadfast love and mercy. With this attention given to God's openness to change, just what it is about God that is unchangeable is brought more sharply into focus. God is revealed not as someone who is unbending or unyielding, as a focus on immutability suggests. God is shown to be other than one who does what

---

29. It is interesting to see how Barth (*CD,* 2/1:497, 502, 506–7) expresses some of these matters: "It would be most unwise, then, to try to understand what the Bible says about God's repentance as if it were merely figurative. . . . It would be just as foolish to try to see in the alteration which is certainly contained in the idea of repentance only alteration in his relation to God, but not an alteration in God in His relation to man. . . . [It would] not be a glorifying, but a blaspheming and finally a denial of God, to conceive of the being and essence of this self-consistent God as one which is, so to speak, self-limited to an inflexible immobility, thus depriving God of the capacity to alter His actions and attitudes. God is Himself in all His attitudes and actions (Ps 102:26f.). . . . He neither loses Himself nor becomes untrue to Himself. . . . Yet . . . He is not prevented from advancing and retreating, rejoicing and mourning, laughing and complaining, being well pleased and causing his wrath to kindle, hiding or revealing himself. . . . God has a real history in and with the world created by Him. . . . His being and action as Creator and therefore His divine being as such acquires contours which are inconsistent with a general concept of immutability. . . . God surpasses Himself in this new work."

God says regardless—a take it or leave it, like it or lump it, perspective. God will move from decisions made; God will change course in midstream in view of the interaction with the world. God's steadfastness has to do with God's love; God's faithfulness has to do with God's promises of salvation; God's will has to do with desiring that people be saved and come to the knowledge of the truth. While we do not want to lose sight of the truth in a word like immutability (better, constancy), divine repentance enables us to place it in its proper perspective and limit its sphere of applicability. [64]

3. *A personal God.* Divine repentance indicates that the world is not in the hands of an iron fate or an impersonal power. God is revealed as one who is not ensconced in some exalted detachment from the life of the world but enters into genuine interaction with its creatures. Among other matters, this will shed light on the meaning of God's holiness (cf. particularly Hos 11:1–9). The "Holy One in your midst" is revealed in God's repentant activity! Holiness or transcendence thus has to do with the *way in which* God personally relates to the world and not in the way in which God is removed from its life. It might also be noted here that this makes inadequate any simplistic distinction between God in himself and God as relating to the world. The God who is revealed is in all essentials continuous with the personal God God actually is.[30] The biblical materials sense no incompatibility between God's honor and dignity and God's vulnerability and openness to change. The essential blessedness of God is affirmed rather than denied by a forthright acceptance of such biblical material much more than by a clever exegesis which would seek to protect God from contamination by too close a brush with the world.

4. *A relationship of integrity.* Divine repentance enables us to see that the relationship between God and world has an essential integrity. The relationship is in fact a relationship, with the wide range of meanings most such metaphors for God imply (e.g., marriage). God takes the response of the other part to the relationship with seriousness; God does not act *upon* the world. God is affected by what is done by and happens to the people, and adjusts modes and directions (though not ultimate goals) in the light

---

30. Abraham Joshua Heschel (*The Prophets* [New York: Harper & Row, 1962], 224–25) has a fund of materials which help to express the importance of this biblical material, though he does not focus on the issue of divine repentance. God is "moved and affected by what happens in the world, and reacts accordingly. . . . Quite obviously in the biblical view, man's deeds may move him, affect him, grieve him, or, on the other hand, gladden and please him." But Heschel (p. 226) also says that creatures affect not only their own life "but also the life of God *insofar as* it is directed to man" (emphasis mine). The emphasized phrase is problematic in Heschel's formulation. One must say that God entirely corresponds to himself in his revelation and activity. There is not evidence in the OT that there is a God in himself who is invulnerable to this interaction with the world. There is no duality between God in himself and God in his relation to the world; whoever says God, says the God who reveals and acts. There is no other God behind the God who participates in the history of the world.

of their response within the relationship. This theme sharpens the meaning of the responsiveness of God. At the same time, this responsiveness is not narrowly related to Israel's disobedience or obedience, as if it were conceived in mechanical or external or formal terms. Divine repentance is understood within the context of a living, dynamic relationship; hence, it cannot be programmed in advance. At the same time, the creation can know that from God's side it will be marked by an essential integrity and that God's will for the people will remain the same in everything. Among other things, divine repentance will enable one to cut across any controlled retributionary [65] theory. Again and again, Israel does not receive the deserved judgment.

5. *An open future.*[31] Divine repentance means that the future is genuinely open. The future is not blocked out in advance. What happens within the relationship has a *direct* bearing on the shape of Israel's life in the world, and indeed the life of all, for God's repentance is available to the entire world. Moreover, it has a direct bearing on the future of God himself, how God will respond within the relationship and the extent to which God's activity is marked by success or failure. God does not have an unchangeable will with regard to every matter the prophets ever discussed concerning the future. In much prophetic interpretation, it is as if there is nothing God or people could do about the future; it is only a matter of those words making their way across history until they find their "home." One should really use the language of fate for such interpretations, for the future is all locked up in prophecies spoken in earlier times.

An appropriate emphasis on divine repentance, however, means that there must always be a reckoning with the effects of the continuing divine-human conversation when thinking about the future. God is ever about the business of making new decisions for new times and places in the light of that ongoing dialogue, which decisions are always in consonance with God's most basic purposes to bring salvation to all. God has not strait-jacketed himself for the future, simply pulling strings to make things happen in accordance with ancient prophecies. In order to accomplish God's

---

31. One will need to consider the extent to which foreknowledge and omniscience are related to this issue. Can one speak of genuine change if the future is fully known? It would seem that one can do so only if future contingencies are known only in terms of possibilities, so that change is experienced in the move from possibility to actuality. In this connection, it would appear that Goldingay's remarks will not work (*Theological Diversity*, 17): "Whereas human beings make their decisions unaware of all their consequences, so that those consequences catch them out, God (so the OT assumes) can foresee not only the consequences of his own actions but also the nature of the response they will meet with . . . so that he can in turn formulate his response to these in advance. So the interaction between divine and human decision-making is real (there are genuine human acts to foresee), yet God is not caught out by the latter, and in this sense he does not change his mind." It is not clear in this formulation in what sense God would change his mind with regard to any matter.

unchangeable salvific will, God can cut off a prophetic word altogether. What happens to the relationship between people and God in history will have a great deal to say regarding the question of fulfillment.

And so, to conclude. The OT is not at all embarrassed about saying that God is open to change. As groups and individuals change, as nature and history develop, God is responsive to what is happening and incorporates all that God experiences in interaction with the world into the shaping of the future. And yet always in view will be God's steadfast love, God's faithfulness to God's promise, and God's ultimate salvific will for all. At this point, one can talk about divine constancy and unchangeability; God will always act in ways that are consonant with this goal. But it is precisely in the light [66] of that unchanging and unchangeable will for the world that God will change God's ways in order to accomplish God's purposes. And so we can join the Psalmist in praising the repentance of God:

> He regarded the distress of his people, when he heard their cry. He remembered for their sake his promise, and repented according to the abundance of his steadfast love. . . . Blessed be the Lord, the God of Israel, from everlasting to everlasting. And let all the people say, "Amen! Praise the Lord!"
>
> Ps 106:44–45

The God Who Acts:
An Old Testament Perspective

"The God who acts." "Revelation in history." Those who cut their biblical-theological eye teeth in the third quarter of [the twentieth] century learned to sing this song in the confidence that it captured the essence of biblical theology. G. Ernest Wright's *God Who Acts* and Gerhard von Rad's *Old Testament Theology* provided the basic lyrics and the melody, and the song was taken up with gusto by preachers and teachers.[1] Its reverberations deeply affected formulations in every theological discipline. The tune proved to be so catchy that the song lingered long after theologians began to question its centrality, accuracy, uniqueness, and value. One still hears its echoes, even in sophisticated theological formulations. Once a tune gets into your head, it is difficult to shake. Most of the notes still do capture the biblical perspective, but we must somehow change the tune.

History and Divine Agency

The word "history" in the phrase "revelation in history" usually refers to certain key events in the course of Israel's actual history in which God's action is dramatic and decisive, such as the exodus and accompanying events. By the way in which God acts, Israel is able to *infer* (a key word) certain things about God and God's ways with the world, for example, that God is one who intervenes on behalf of the oppressed. This sentence in *God Who Acts* captures the perspective well: "Biblical theology is *the* [7] *confessional recital of the redemptive acts of God* in a particular history, because history is the chief medium of revelation."[2] In saying further that "the Bible relates a certain history in a confessional manner," Wright desires to keep both actual history and the emergent confession together. This understanding was a reaction against both conservative and liberal perspectives on revelation, as either the conveyance of propositional truth or the generation and development of human insight.

This essay was originally published in *Theology Today* 54 (1997): 6–18.

1. G. Ernest Wright, *God Who Acts: Biblical Theology as Recital* (London: SCM, 1952); Gerhard von Rad, *Old Testament Theology* (2 vols.; New York: Harper & Row, 1962). In the latter, von Rad works from the foundations provided in his "The Form-Critical Problem of the Hexateuch," in *The Problem of the Hexateuch and Other Essays* (London: Oliver & Boyd, 1966), 1–78.

2. Wright, *God Who Acts*, 13. Wright explicitly cites von Rad in the development of his thesis (ibid., 70).

That such a perspective has continuing value is evident. The Old Testament itself indisputably witnesses to a God who acts in the world. At the same time, many problems have emerged in the way in which this testimony is theologically developed. Over the last half century, these issues have been raised especially from the perspective of systematic and philosophical theology, and less so from biblical scholars.[3]

The following inadequacies of this approach have been noted: the neglect of nonhistorical material (for example, wisdom); the emphasis upon historical event to the diminishment of God's activity in verbal event, natural event, and liturgical event; the stress placed on dramatic events to the neglect of the more unobtrusive forms of divine activity in everyday experience; the emphasis on early historical events and depreciation of later ones; the use of virile language (for example, intrusion, intervention) in the descriptions of God's activity; the emphasis upon drawing inferences about God from external events; the impersonal character of events over against personal divine encounters; the emphasis upon Israelite distinctiveness in this matter and the refusal to acknowledge that Israel's theological claims were positively informed by its encounter with other ancient Near Eastern religions. More theoretical considerations of such matters as divine agency, revelation, history, and "act of God" have also complicated this discussion. Especially important is the recognition that the language of divine act, whether of doing or speaking, is not literal but analogical. Yet, sorting out the continuities and discontinuities in this language with the reality that is God is no simple matter (for example, can God speak with an audible voice?). Several of these matters will be considered more fully in the following constructive statement. [8]

A Constructive Statement

With the above-noted criticisms of the traditional God-who-acts paradigm in mind, I make the following constructive statements regarding the Old Testament understanding of divine action. While these perspectives may not be characteristic of every Old Testament tradition, they are significantly represented across various genres and traditions. In what

---

3. The basic studies include the following. From the biblical side, James Barr, "Revelation through History in the Old Testament and in Modern Theology," *Int* 17 (1963): 193–205; Paul Hanson, *Dynamic Transcendence* (Philadelphia: Fortress, 1978); Werner Lemke, "Revelation through History in Recent Biblical Theology," *Int* 36 (1982): 34–46; Leo G. Perdue, *The Collapse of History: Reconstructing Old Testament Theology* (Minneapolis: Fortress, 1994); David Penchansky, *The Politics of Biblical Theology: A Postmodern Reading* (Macon, GA: Mercer University Press, 1995). From the systematics side, Langdon Gilkey, "Cosmology, Ontology, and the Travail of Biblical Language," *JR* 41 (1961): 194–205 has been particularly influential; other works include Owen Thomas, ed., *God's Activity in the World: The Contemporary Problem* (Chico, CA: Scholars Press, 1983); Thomas F. Tracy, *God, Action and Embodiment* (Grand Rapids, MI: Eerdmans, 1984); idem, ed., *The God Who Acts: Philosophical and Theological Exploration* (University Park: Pennsylvania State University Press, 1994).

follows, I do not pretend to be making a descriptive statement about what Israel believed; that is no longer possible to do. Every discerned meaning is the product of the interaction of the text and the reader; so what follows is a constructive statement shaped in decisive ways by my reading of these texts as a person who believes in the God portrayed therein.

(1) God is *present and active* in all the world. God "fills heaven and earth" (Jer 23:24; see Psalm 139). God is part of the map of reality and is relational to all that is not God. The earth is also "full of the steadfast love of God" (Ps 33:5; 36:5). God is not simply "here and there"; God is always *lovingly* present, in every divine act, whether of judgment or salvation. Hence, God's presence is not a static or passive presence but a presence *in relationship,* profoundly grounded in and informed by steadfast love and working for the good of all, even in the midst of judgment.

The numerous active verbs of which God is the subject demonstrate that Israel's God is an acting God; indeed, God is active in every event. Such activity includes speaking; no wedge should be driven between a speaking God and an acting God. One might be able to construct an intelligible account of such events for a variety of purposes without reference to God (for example, historical research), but no *full* account of any event of which the text speaks is possible without factoring God into the process.

According to Ps 104:1–3, God has made the time and space of this world God's very own dwelling place. The result, to use the language of Isa 66:1, is that heaven is God's throne and the earth is God's footstool. Hence, any movement of God from heaven to earth is simply a movement from one part of the created order to another. God—who is other than world—works from within the world, not on the world from without.

(2) God acts in the *world.* The focus on history and on decisive events in that history narrowed the range of God's activity. The Old Testament witnesses to a much more comprehensive divine working. God's acting is focused in Israel, and God's speaking is especially articulate there, but the divine activity is not limited either to Israel or to historical events.

Genesis 1–11, for example, in introducing the canon, provides a universal frame of reference for all that follows; these chapters portray a God whose *universal* activity includes creating, grieving, judging, saving, electing, promising, blessing, covenant making, and law giving. And the text has not yet spoken of Abraham or Israel! God's actions in and for Israel thus occur *within* God's more comprehensive ways of acting in the larger world and are shaped by God's overarching purposes for that world. Other texts (for example, Amos 9:7; Gen 20:3–7) reinforce the understanding [9] that even God's salvific actions, as well as a knowledge of God, are not confined to Israel or effected only through Israel's mediation.

From another perspective, one might speak of wisdom's interest in discerning the activity of God not in remembered historical events but in everyday human experience. It might be noted in this connection that, contrary to earlier understandings, the idea that the divine is active in history is not unique to Israel, though it may be more predominant there. Even more, Israel drew on such understandings for its own formulations (see the common themes in a text such as Exodus 15).

(3) God's actions occur from within *relationships established with the world.* These relationships with the world are grounded in the very nature of God. This grounding is evident in those texts that speak of God acting within the *divine* realm (for example, Gen 1:26–27; Ps 103:20–21; Jer 23:18–22). These texts testify that God is a social being, functioning within a divine community in a relationship of mutuality. The creation of human beings, for example, is understood to be the result of an inner-divine dialogue ("let us"); God chooses to share the creative process with that which is not God. In other words, relationship is integral to the divine realm, independent of God's relationship to the world.

This relational God freely enters into relationships with that which has been created. That this is the case can be seen generally in the language used to speak of divine action. Such language is drawn primarily from the sphere of interpersonal relationships (parental and marital metaphors are especially prominent). Even where the language is not personal, it is relational: "Be thou a strong rock of refuge for me, a strong fortress to save me" (Ps 31:2). This relational focus is evident also in the strong emphasis on God as one who not only communicates but is desirous of the creatures' voice in return (Isa 65:1–2). Moreover, God gives the divine name(s) to Israel, thereby identifying the divine self as a distinctive member of the community of those who have names.

The relationships into which God enters are committed relationships. This can be seen already in the creation account, where God speaks to the newly created human beings, choosing to share power and responsibility in relating to that which is nonhuman (Gen 1:28). As such, God commits God's self to a certain kind of relationship, which entails a divine constraint and restraint in the exercise of power in the world (so also Gen 8:21–22). Even beyond human sin, God keeps the commitment to share power with human beings (Gen 3:23; Psalm 8).

Moreover, the covenants into which God enters, from Noah to Abraham to Israel to David, are relational by their very nature. God therein makes commitments that God will honor come what may, even placing God's own life on the line (Gen 15:7–21). In texts such as Exod 2:24 and 6:4–5, that prior divine act of covenanting is remembered *by God* in the context of new forms of divine activity. Continuity is thereby seen not only in God's activity for Israel but also in Israel's confession regarding God's prior commitments.

So, in the spheres of both creation and redemption, God's actions occur from within committed relationships that God will honor come what may—because of who God is. [10]

(4) God's actions are *an activation of the divine will.* God's actions are intentional, not idle or accidental. Every divine act is an act of will. God's acts always serve God's purposes in the world. God's speaking, for example, represents a decision by God to accomplish God's will in a given situation. God's word does not simply add something to a situation but renders a divine decision concerning it. The word does not make God present but seeks to clarify and direct God's will within an already pervasive presence. The word makes available to the world what would not otherwise be available, namely, a living experience (including knowledge) of the will of God. Every divine action is informed by God's ultimate salvific will for the world, by God's faithfulness to promises, and by God's steadfast love for all. As such, that will is made available to all those who have eyes to see, both within Israel and without.[4]

(5) This God usually *takes the initiative* in acting in the world. An obvious example would be the creation of the world. At the same time, once relationships with the world and Israel are established, God also *acts in response* to creaturely initiative. For example, God hears the cries of the Israelites in Egypt and "remembers" the covenant (Exod 2:23–25). In the call of Moses, God interacts with him in an extended dialogue wherein Moses' responses are taken seriously by God. Moses' responses lead to new divine speech (Exodus 3–6). Moses' recognition of God's holiness (Exod 3:6) does not lead to passivity in the divine presence. God does not demand a self-effacing Moses. Indeed, Moses' questions find an openness and willingness in God and lead to fuller knowledge of God and God's ways. Moses' persistence in pressing the issues with God increases the revelatory possibilities. God's way into the future is thus not dictated solely by the divine word and will; God's word interacts with the human word and together (though not in a way that can be factored out) their words and actions shape the future.

(6) God's acting in the world is always *situationally appropriate,* fitting for specific times and places. God's actions are always related to particular situations in the world and are designed to make a difference in those situations in service of the will of God. God's seeing often precedes the divine acting (Exod 3:7–10; compare 2:24–25). God is a master at discernment, seeing what is needed and acting in a way that fits the needs of that moment. At the same time, within those focused actions, God has the more comprehensive divine purposes in view: "that my name may be declared in all the earth" (Exod 9:16).

In the very structure of Exodus 1–15, God's acts are related to the specifics of Israel's situation. The acts of God are not isolated from human experience; indeed, they are shaped by that experience. Hence, God does [11] not respond to human oppression of a sociopolitical sort by ignoring

---

4. For detail, see Terence E. Fretheim, "Will of God in the OT" and "Word of God" in *ABD* 6:914–20, 961–68.

those realities in the shape that God's salvation takes. God here acts to save Israel from the effects of other people's sins; God does not act to save Israel from its own sins. God's saving actions in connection with the return from exile, however, have different needs of Israel in view; Israel is forgiven its sin and saved from the effects of its own sinfulness (see Isa 43:25; 40:1–11).

(7) God's activity is *effective* in the world, from the creation of the world to the deliverance of Israel from Egypt to the judgment on Israel by various foreign armies. God does get things done in the world, though God's work is not always successful.

Among the various types of effects, two more comprehensive outcomes might be noted. For one, God's acts issue in *new knowledge*. Promises are stated that were not known before, responsibilities are delineated, and matters are clarified and judged. The effect is new knowledge of God and of God's purposes in the world. Given the experiential character of knowing for Israel, this divine action affects not simply "head knowledge" but the entire relationship between the knower and the known.

The importance of verbal events for such new knowledge should be highlighted more than has commonly been the case. Key historical events, such as the sea crossing, do not stand in isolation from the larger pentateuchal context, including the divine speaking to Abraham (Genesis 15; 17) and Moses (Exodus 3). The significance of later historical events is revealed to Moses in a verbal encounter (Exodus 3–6); meaning is not simply "inferred" from the event itself. This verbal encounter gives Moses the capacity to see the "something more" in the events, and the events' occurrence confirms and fills out that knowledge. A similar understanding is characteristic of the various words of the prophets.

God's acts also issue in *a becoming*. God's actions have not simply to do with revelation (as the juxtaposition of the phrases "the God who acts" and "revelation in history" may suggest). God's actions effect a new relationship with God and a changed status for human beings and communities, for example, freedom from oppression.

God's action in liturgical event has often been neglected in this discussion. Israel understood that God acted in and through various forms of its worship life. The dramatized festivals (Passover, Weeks, Tabernacles) are considered vehicles for God's ongoing salvific activity among the people of God; God's saving activity in historical event is made newly available to Israel in liturgical event. Moreover, Israel's sacrificial system has a sacramental structure in and through which God acts to forgive the penitent worshiper. Israel's worship thus constitutes an important matrix for God's [12] saving activity as well as the reception of new knowledge of the God who acts therein.

God's actions may also issue in new knowledge and becoming for God. Human responses to God's actions may lead to a new level of divine knowing (see Gen 22:12; Deut 8:2), which can lead to new directions in divine action. Or, the laments of the Psalter call for God to receive the human situation into the divine self and to know it first-hand (see also Exod 3:7). New divine commitments made and new relationships established make for a changed situation for God. In some sense, one must speak of a newness in God as well.

(8) God's activity in the world is *not inevitably successful*. This is the case for all divine actions, both words and deeds. Regarding God's speaking, for example, God continues to work beyond the speaking on behalf of a word. But the word once given is now not only in God's hands; it is also in the hands of those who can misuse it. God's will may not always get done. Both finitude and sin may lead to misunderstanding and disloyalty. However powerful God's word may be (like fire and a hammer crushing rocks [Jer 23:29]), it may be resisted (Ezek 2:7), questioned (Jer 1:6–7), rejected (Zech 7:11–12), ridiculed (Gen 18:12–13), scorned (Jer 6:10), despised (Jer 23:17), doubted (Judg 6:13–17), or disbelieved (Ps 106:24). The word of God is therefore not only powerful, it is vulnerable. No good reason exists to deny that God's activity in nonverbal ways would be any less resistible.

At the same time, God will keep promises made, though it is not possible to factor out just how such promises were or will be fulfilled. One might speak generally of an open future, within which human response participates in shaping life in the world, but God works purposefully within the complex of worldly events in such a way that a new heaven and a new earth will certainly be brought into being.

(9) God *works through human language and various human and nonhuman agents* to get things done in the world. God acts directly, but always through means. And the variety of means is impressive. God works through that which is already created to bring about new creations (Gen 1:2, 11, 20, 24); God works through human language to call Abraham as well as through the dynamics of his interrupted journey to Canaan (Gen 11:31–12:3); God works through nonhuman agents in the plagues, at Passover, and at the Red Sea (the nonhuman is the savior of the human!); God works in and through the sacrificial rituals to bring about forgiveness of sin and reconciliation with God; God works through nonchosen, non-Israelite kings and armies to send Israel into exile and to bring the nation home again; God works through prophets to speak God's word of judgment and grace. [13]

God's use of means does not mean that God works *in*directly. God does not, for example, give the word to Isaiah to speak and then leave, but God goes with that word, working in ways to make it effective. It is God, who has an ongoing relationship with the word, who brings about the fulfillment of a word, not the word in itself in some autonomous fashion (see Isa 44:26; 48:3). The fulfillment of a divine word is fundamentally a testimony to God's work, not to a word's mysterious power.

In such divine activity, creaturely agency is not reduced to impotence; God's activity is not all-determining. There is neither a "letting go" of the creation on God's part nor a divine retention of all power. God has chosen to be dependent upon creatures in the carrying out of God's actions in the world. Both God and creatures are active and effective agents. Because the instruments are not perfect, God's actions through them will always have mixed results. As an example, force and violence are associated with God's acts in the world at least in part because they are characteristic of those in and through whom the work is being carried out.

Generally, this divine work in the world must not be understood in either *deistic or deterministic* ways. God neither remains ensconced in heaven watching the world go by nor micromanages the world to control (a much abused word) its every move so that creaturely agency counts for nothing. But between these two ditches, the biblical texts do not always provide clear direction (hence the variety of theological formulations).

(10) While all of God's acts are related to worldly situations in a meaningful way, some divine actions *are more significant than others.* That Israel understood this to be the case is shown both by the vocabulary used (not all acts are called "mighty acts"; see Ps 145:4,12; 150:2) and by the genres employed, that is, the gathering of certain divine acts (for example, the exodus) but not others into creedal formulations (see Deut 26:5–9; Josh 24:2–13).

This greater level of significance is most fundamentally related to the kinds of *effects produced* at the levels of both knowing and becoming. Regarding becoming, certain events are constitutive of the community, without which Israel would not be what it is. Regarding knowing, these events are more translucent with respect to God's purposes, bringing sharper coherence and clarity to the larger range of divine purpose and activity.

(11) These greater levels of significance may be, but are not necessarily, related to the events' being *"extraordinary"* or *"miraculous."* Where these elements do occur in the texts they are not easily sorted out. The following matters may be noted:

(a) The extraordinariness is not understood in terms of divine intervention or intrusion, as if God were normally not present and then intervenes at certain moments to make things happen. As I have noted, God is present and active in every event, and that reality is not usually considered extraordinary or miraculous. God is likely understood to act in and through the means provided by the causal continuum, and sufficient "play" exists in that continuum to allow for God to work and the unusual event to occur. [14] For example, Job 38–41 seems to speak of the looseness of the causal weave with its interest in ambiguity and unexpectedness in the creation; and Eccl 9:11 and 1 Sam 6:9 recognize the role of chance.

(b) Issues of *genre and rhetoric* are important. The language used for the exodus events includes extraordinary features, from the plagues to the passover epidemic to the sea crossing. On the other hand, the fall of Jerusalem and the return of the exiles are described in more mundane terms as the effects of Babylonian army movements and Persian royal policies. Isaiah 40–55 uses extraordinary images to speak of a future return (including profound changes in nature) and links this extraordinariness to God's new work. But the texts descriptive of the return itself do not use such rhetoric. This separation of the event itself and the rhetoric of extraordinariness regarding the divine action is different from the exodus account, where they are integrated. This difference raises questions about the genre of the exodus material and the extent to which the extraordinary elements are intended to be reflective of actual happenings or constitute more of a rhetorical strategy in line with that used by Deutero-Isaiah.

The passover text, for example, is clearly overlaid with elements of later liturgical practice. This elevates the dramatic character of the retelling. In the plague narratives, a hyperbolic way of speaking is typical (the word *kôl*, "all," occurs over fifty times!). A liturgical setting for the entire exodus complex may inform and heighten the dramatic character of the telling. We have here to do with an act of God, but the text's extraordinary features may have to do more with rhetorical strategy than with literal description.

The much-discussed question of the relationship between Israel's actual history and its confessed history might be raised in this connection. The extraordinariness in Deutero-Isaiah's testimony regarding the return from exile need not be literally descriptive of Israel's actual history in order to speak the truth about God's acts and be theologically and religiously significant. Yet, if no links exist between the confession and Israel's actual life, at least in its broad strokes, then the confession does become problematic. The "happenedness" of those events that Israel has confessionally interpreted as *constitutive* of its identity is indispensable for faith, even if they cannot finally be verified; these events have been drawn into Israel's basic credal statements. But divine activity should be linked not only to the events themselves but also to the confessional activity that interprets them; the texts refuse to separate these realities. They belong together in any statement about the God who acts; only God's act in the gift of faith enables the confession that God has acted in Israel's external world (see Exod 14:31 and what follows).

(c) God is not the only agent associated with certain of the extraordinary elements. Both human and nonhuman agents are engaged. In the plagues, for example, divine agency is explicitly associated with only six plagues (1, 4, 5, 7, 8, 10); Aaron and/or Moses are involved in three of these in a dual role (1, 7, 8), and a nonhuman agent is cited in the eighth plague. In four cases, only human agency is cited (2, 3, 6, 9). In the four cases where a [15] plague is removed (2, 4, 7, 8), a dual role is again evident as God "did according to the word of Moses" (8:13). In the summary to the account, only the agency of Moses and Aaron is acknowledged (11:10), while only God's agency is cited in the introduction (7:3). Both God and Israel recognize this dual agency (3:8–10; 14:31), but the texts do not seek to factor out just how this duality works.

(d) Efforts have been made to "explain" the extraordinary elements in "natural" terms. For example, in the plagues, the frogs leave bloody water, and flies are drawn to dead frogs. The gifts of manna, quail, and water have also been so "explained." Sometimes, such reflections are thought to "explain away" the divine factor. But not necessarily, if God is kept in the picture (as has not always been the case). Any consideration of divine providence ought not to be divorced from a recognition of nature's God-given potentialities. To cite one example, in Exod 17:1–7, God is not creating water out of thin air, nor is nature disrupted. Water does course through rock formations; the actions of both God and Moses enable their hidden potential to surface. God works in and through the natural (and the human) to provide water for the people, as God does throughout the exodus complex of events.[5]

(e) The texts give us good reason to suppose that God acts differently in some events than in others. How to articulate this difference is difficult, but I would speak of variations in the *intensification* of divine action.[6] For example, compare God's presence in the story of Joseph and God's indwelling the tabernacle (Exod 40:34–38; compare 24:9–11). In the former, God's presence is more unobtrusive; God never appears to Joseph or his brothers yet is an effective agent (Gen 50:20). In the latter, God's presence is more intense, even having visible elements. In developing a typology of divine presence, one might speak of variations in intensification in comparing God's general (or creational) presence, God's accompanying presence, God's tabernacling presence, and God's theophanic presence.

These distinctions no doubt relate to the needs of the situation and God's purposes related thereto. One might also speak about God's concern for human life and freedom in the face of too-sustained a divine intensity ("you cannot see God and live"). But such differences also involve the dynamics of the God-world relationship and God's commitments related thereto. For example, God's promise at the end of the flood never to act in that way again (Gen 8:21–22; 9:11) limits the divine options with respect to any related matter. One could say something comparable with respect to all of God's promises. Or, the intensity of the divine presence may be affected by the depths of human sinfulness. So, for example, God is *driven* [16] from the temple by Israel's abominations (Ezek 8:6), and its iniquities "make a

---

5. For this and similar ways of dealing with the various wilderness stories, see Terence E. Fretheim, *Exodus* (Interpretation; Louisville: John Knox, 1991), 177–78, 182, 190–91.

6. For a fuller analysis of varying divine intensifications in Old Testament reflections on divine presence, see idem, *The Suffering of God: An Old Testament Perspective* (Philadelphia: Fortress, 1984), 60–78. A case is therein made that Israel does not speak of God's absence.

separation between you and your God, and your sins have hid his face from you so that he does not listen" (Isa 59:2). Such negative human responses can push God back along the continuum of presence so that it becomes less intense, and hence less felt and less positively effective. Positively, human need and powerlessness may call forth intensity in God's presence (see Deut 32:36). God's possibilities are closely related to the nature of the situation. So, for a variety of reasons, God does act differently in various events, but one cannot finally sort out the factors at work within these differences.

To summarize: The present and active God acts in the world within committed relationships in accordance with the divine will. God's actions are always situationally appropriate and effect new knowledge and becoming, though that divine action in both word and deed is resistible and hence may not always be successful. God acts directly through various means, both human and nonhuman, so that not only is the world dependent upon God, but God has also chosen to be dependent on the world. God's actions may be of varying intensities, and some acts are more significant than others, but their import is not necessarily related to the extraordinariness of events.

The Issue of Genre

Objection might be raised to this systematizing approach to the theological issues at stake here, though my outline of material follows no systematic presentation known to me and I attend often to narrative portrayals of God. A brief consideration of genre and the theological task may be helpful in filling out this proposal.

Much attention has recently been given to the *biblical narrative* as that which makes the characters (such as God) come most alive and reveals their identity most clearly.[7] God's identity is narrated, not reduced to attributes or abstractions. Narratives do indeed provide depth to God's character without bringing closure to the depiction of God; they do present God as a living reality with all of the attendant ambiguity and complexity. At the same time, the biblical texts refuse to be content with narratives in their portrayal of God. Interwoven with the narratives are more generalized statements about God. These nonnarrative genres, which gather claims about God, are more important for this discussion than commonly recognized.[8] [17]

---

7. For a brief discussion of the God-who-acts debate from this perspective, see William Placher, "The Acts of God: What Do We Mean by Revelation?" *ChrCent* 113 (1996): 337–42. For an analysis and critical evaluation of narrative theology, see Perdue, *The Collapse of History*, 231–62. More generally, see Walter Brueggemann, "A Shape for Old Testament Theology, I: Structure Legitimation," *CBQ* 47 (1985): 28–46; idem, "A Shape for Old Testament Theology, II: Embrace of Pain," *CBQ* 47 (1985): 395–415.

8. For an earlier attempt to discern the theological import of this genre distinction, see Fretheim, *The Suffering of God*, 24–29.

Two types of gathering genres might be noted here, both of which may be designated as "credal." One type of credal statement gathers claims about God that focus on divine acts (for example, Deut 26:5–9; Josh 24:2–13); these confessions have been emphasized particularly in the work of von Rad. While von Rad's approach has come under criticism, the identification of this genre and its function within the larger narrative is still an important issue.

Another type of credal statement articulates those claims about God in more abstract ways: God is compassionate (Exod 22:27); gracious, merciful, slow to anger, and abounding in steadfast love (Exod 34:6–7; Num 14:18);[9] holy (Lev 19:2); great, mighty, awesome, is not partial and takes no bribe, executes justice for the orphan and the widow and loves the stranger (Deut 10:17–18).

The integration of these types of credal statements within narrative suggests that they represent some kind of centering amid the Bible's theological pluralism. The regular appeal of the book of Psalms—which presents the faith in its leaner form—to these generalizations is noteworthy in this regard. In general, just as the historical recitals determined those events in Israel's history that were constitutive of its present existence and thus separable from all other events as crucial for faith, so also the generalizations about God provided an interpretive clue for the kind of God whom Israel believed to be active in those events.

These generalizing genres make *truth claims* about God and God's relationship to the world. These statements cannot be reduced to story form, though they were no doubt generated by narratives, and the latter carry truth claims in their own way, often displaying concretely and in recognizable patterns the claims of the credal genres. As such, the generalizing genres provide *inner-biblical* direction for interpreting the God references that occur in the narratives. That is, the God who is the subject of sentences in narrative is to be related specifically to these generalizing truth claims.

In this interaction, space is provided for developments in the credal formulations in view of ongoing experience. That is, these credal materials were not finally fixed but remained open to new knowledge of God. While the core of the creeds remained essentially intact, they were supplemented with new formulations in view of the community's experience of God (for example, the divine repentance in Jonah 4:2; Joel 2:13; the creation in Neh 9:6). More generally, these credal materials do not insist on an absolute coherence or univocal way of speaking about God in the Old Testament. Theological "pluralism has been canonized."[10] Some narrative portrayals of God may not "fit" the predominant confession. As such, they witness

---

9. It is noteworthy that the initial canonical statement in Exod 34:6–7, while spoken by God, is in the third person, suggesting an original function as a confession of faith by the community.
10. My formulation in *The Suffering of God*, 19.

to a kind of theology in process, raising up reflections and challenges [18] regarding God that the creeds must take into account in the ongoing discussion in Israel regarding the divine identity.

It must be admitted that this text-internal direction is only a relative positioning. Subjective factors are at work in claiming such a role for the biblical credal statements. But the identification of generalizing genres does give a somewhat objective basis upon which to stand in making such a claim; the absence of a consideration of genre in much of the discussion about the God of the Old Testament is not a minor matter.

The importance of the text-internal direction provided by these credal statements is especially evident in view of God's "character traits" as discerned by some recent readers of the narratives.[11] A list of traits from such readings includes the following: God is mean-spirited, unreliable, unstable, deceptive, irascible, irrational, savage, sulky, and capricious. A simple narrative approach to these matters will tend to pit one reading against another. The end result of a consideration of such differences in narrative readings will probably most often mean simply staying with traditional readings and classical formulations regarding God. But with the generalized truth claims about God present within the narrative and elsewhere, the reader has inner-biblical direction for assessing the value for Israel of the "character traits" of the God who acts that readers of narrative claim to see. On the other hand, such readings continue to challenge the confession, probing its continuing adequacy and resisting an easy settled-ness.

In the constructive analysis above, I have sought to order the material systematically, while appealing to narrative portrayals. If we are to work theologically with these texts, we must do both: attend to genres that tell the story and to those that gather the material into more generalized forms.

---

11. Many examples could be cited. One important reading is that of Danna Nolan Fewell and David M. Gunn, *Gender, Power, and Promise: The Subject of the Bible's First Story* (Nashville: Abingdon, 1993). See also Walter Brueggemann, *Theology of the Old Testament: Testimony, Dispute, Advocacy* (Minneapolis: Fortress, 1992).

Some Reflections
on Brueggemann's God

I am delighted to contribute to this volume honoring Walter Brueggemann. He has been a colleague, mentor, and friend. He has informed my
work by his tenacious attention to specific texts, his relentless pursuit of
theological issues, his fresh use of language, his voracious reading, and his
concern to link biblical thought and contemporary life.

My intent here is to reflect on some (!) aspects of his understanding
of the God of the Old Testament. I trust it will be evident that his pro-
posals have considerable evocative and provocative power. Getting a firm
grasp of his theology is not an easy task, not least because his publications
never quit and, despite much consistency, his understandings are always
on the move. For purposes of this essay I will center on two programmatic
pieces and draw on his magisterial *Theology of the Old Testament,* which I
have studied in manuscript form.[1] First of all, I offer some more general
observations.

For Brueggemann "the primal subject of an Old Testament theology is of
course God" (*TOT,* 117), evident not least in the sheer volume of his treatment of God in his *TOT.* But to speak of Israel's God is for him not simply a
matter of describing an ancient faith. "Everything depends on our confession of God. . . . Let none among us imagine that the right discernment of
God does not matter. . . . there will be no community on earth until there
is a fresh articulation of who God is. What the church can be depends on
that. There will be no new community on earth so long as we rally round
old God-claims of self-sufficiency and omnipotence."[2] The passion [25]
and urgency evident in this statement suffuse his work. I enter into this
conversation because I share these commitments and concerns.

This essay was originally published in *God in the Fray: A Tribute to Walter Brueggemann* (ed.
Tod Linafelt and Timothy K. Beal; Minneapolis: Fortress, 1998), 24–37.

    1. Quotations from Brueggemann's *Theology of the Old Testament: Testimony, Dispute,
Advocacy* (Minneapolis: Fortress, 1997) will be cited as *TOT* within the text. The two other
essays are "A Shape for Old Testament Theology, I: Structure Legitimation," *CBQ* 47 (1985):
28–46; and "A Shape for Old Testament Theology, II: Embrace of Pain," *CBQ* 47 (1985):
395–415. These articles now appear with related essays in his *Old Testament Theology: Essays on Structure, Theme, and Text* (ed. Patrick D. Miller; Minneapolis: Fortress, 1992), 1–21,
22–44, respectively.

    2. "Covenant as a Subversive Paradigm," in *A Social Reading of the Old Testament:
Prophetic Approaches to Israel's Communal Life* (ed. Patrick D. Miller; Minneapolis: Fortress,
1994), 43, 46–47. Published originally in *ChrCent* 97 (1980): 1094–99.

Brueggemann's understanding of Israel's God does not fit neatly into any systematic categories, not least because he allows himself to be pushed and pulled around by specific texts, and the texts will not sit still any more than he will. The lack of univocity in the biblical witness to God is a virtual refrain in his work; but this pluralism is not simply a matter of information, it is *theologically* important in itself. "Biblical faith, of course, is not static. It is not a set of statements that are always and everywhere true; therefore, contemporary biblical theology must not be reductionist in order to make all of the Old Testament fit together."[3] Israel does not offer a finished portrayal of God. For Brueggemann, theological pluralism has been canonized. Thus, any approach or flat thematization that diminishes this pluralism in the interests of congruence with, say, a systematic theology is suspect. He warns against the Western and churchly propensity to universalize at the expense of the particular, to smooth out the rough edges of the testimony. He admits that the Bible itself moves toward certain generalizations about God, but he views them as provisional and they may be challenged by countertestimonies.

At the same time, the biblical theologian must be conversant with systematic and philosophical efforts, and Brueggemann often calls upon such scholars to elucidate the text and to shape his own work (e.g., Paul Ricoeur, Karl Barth, the Yale school). His own identification with the Christian tradition in its Reformed expression plays an important role in his reflection. The Reformed centering in the sovereignty of God is always near at hand, and in it he seems to rest when his theological back is up against the wall. Though he breaks out of traditional understandings of sovereignty in many ways (e.g., attributes such as impassibility and immutability), his not uncommon appeal to such matters as divine intervention, control, irresistibility, and "unlimited" sovereignty shows that this tradition is still important for him (e.g., *TOT*, 66–67). One is given to wonder whether he has sufficiently followed through on his own emphases. Even more, I think that, at the end of the day, his emphasis upon an unsettled and an unsettling God is a *postmodern restatement of sovereignty* (see below).

For Brueggemann, Israel's God is dependent on speech, on Israel's "testimony" and the utterance of the texts produced. "The God of Old Testament theology . . . lives in, with, and under the rhetorical enterprise of this text, and nowhere else and in no other way" (*TOT*, 66). Even more, there [26] is a rhetorical "restlessness and openness" in Israel's God-talk that has to do not simply with the task of theological formulation but with God's own self. God himself has chosen to be caught up in this dialogue and has been affected thereby so that God's very self is "in process."

Within this testimony Brueggemann makes a distinction between "core testimony" and "countertestimony," and has major treatments of each. The

---

3. "Embrace of Pain," 23.

core testimony is Israel's "characteristic" and "habituated" speech about God (*TOT*, 122). The countertestimony consists of themes and texts (e.g., divine hiddenness, the lament) that challenge or protest the more "normative" speech. Yet this testimony does not have a second-class status, but makes the core testimony "fuller and richer" and shows forth the "dialectical, resilient, disputatious quality that is definitional for this faith" (p. 400). The net effect, however, is that the line between these testimonies becomes blurred. For example, violence "belongs to the very fabric of this faith" (p. 381) and "savageness . . . belongs to the core claims of Yahweh" (p. 276).

Brueggemann focuses on narrative, especially verbal sentences, which feature Yahweh as "actor and agent"; these "were Israel's first and foremost strategy for making available the character of Yahweh." (It is not clear to me why and how nominal sentences become secondary [see *TOT*, 123–24 n. 17], but it may be related to his theological commitments; as with his neglect of the psalms of orientation, they reveal a less unsettled God.) The density of this narrative, irreducible to simple or coherent formulations, reveals "the density of its God who refuses every exhaustible domestication." This narrative is a "theo-drama," mediating a God who cannot be controlled or made safe, who "deabsolutizes and destabilizes" what the world regards as given; this God is complex, elusive, and even "odd" (*TOT*, 69–71).

Brueggemann may be too easily settled in a narrative theology (under the influence of the Yale school). Though he is not uncritical, such a theology finally stands somewhat at odds with the God he himself finds in the Scriptures. I pursue one point here (on genre issues, see below). He acknowledges that textual "exposition is always conducted in the presence of two audiences," the believing community and the larger public. But this larger public seems only to be "listening"; Israel's rhetoric is only a speaking "*to*" this public (*TOT*, 87–88). But more must be said here. The God of the Bible, according to its own witness, is actively engaged in the world outside Israel; this work has good effects and shapes Israel's own testimony. God's continuing activity in that extrabiblical story is of such a character as to bring a potentially critical word to bear on the Bible and its testimony regarding God (one thinks of patriarchy) and to enable its readers to hear more clearly where *the Bible itself* is being self-critical, where the [27] Bible would say no to one or another element in its own testimony. Difficult issues of discernment and criteria are quickly at hand, but we cannot in the face of those difficulties retreat into the narrative world of the Bible, so that the text is thought to absorb every human story into its own. God, and certainly the God of Brueggemann's analysis, could never simply be "at home" in such a narrative retreat.

I now take a closer look at the two programmatic articles revealing of Brueggemann's approach to and understanding of the biblical God. These articles are basic for his *TOT.* I begin by noting his conclusion:

The God portrayed here is an *ambiguous* one, *always in the process of deciding*. For Israel, the issue is whether to be "like the nations" or to be a "holy people." Israel dared to say that its God, Yahweh, *lived* in the same *ambiguity: whether to be* "like the other gods" or to be a holy God, "the Holy One in our midst," who had *learned* from Abraham fresh subversive notions of ṣĕdāqâ and mišpāṭ.[4]

I have emphasized the word *ambiguity*. The word refers not to God's external acts and Israel's understanding thereof, but to the divine "interiority,"[5] to God's own unresolved interior life and decision making. This ambiguity refers not to one moment of decision, nor is it just that God "noted, responded to, and embodied the pain that Israel was also to embody."[6] God *"lived"* in ambiguity, was *"always"* in the process of deciding," "whether to be" a certain kind of God.

Brueggemann frames this divine decision-making process by positing a dialectical interaction of "structure legitimation" and the "embrace of pain." Another pair of phrases he uses: God is "above the fray" and "in the fray." This distinction seems to correspond to the traditional distinction between transcendence and immanence.[7] These formulations are problematic. The biblical God is transcendent *within* relationship (never "above" it); the God active "in the fray" and "embracing pain" is so engaged as the immanent *and* transcendent one. The godness of God is revealed precisely in *that* God wills—once and for all (see below)—to enter into the fray and by *the way in which* God embraces the pain: steadfast in love, faithful to promises, and unwaveringly willing the salvation of Israel and world. This God is so committed to full participation in a genuine relationship with Israel and the world that God no longer has the option of finally pulling back [28] from it. But we cannot factor out what it takes for God to be this kind of God; God will make surprising, unsettling, and sharply judgmental moves, particularly in the encounter with creaturely resistance. But all such divine moves occur *from within* this resolve.[8]

For Brueggemann a "common theology" of the Near East has taken root in Israel, evident in creational and covenantal understandings that issue in "structure legitimation" and "contractual theology." This "tight system of deeds and consequences" allows "no slippage, no graciousness, no room for failure."[9] Such a perspective is reality for both Israel and God. But be-

---

4. "Embrace of Pain," 43–44 (emphasis added).

5. "Structure Legitimation," 35; cf. 44; "Embrace of Pain," 408.

6. "Embrace of Pain," 415.

7. This is also Leo Perdue's interpretation of this point in Brueggemann's work in *The Collapse of History: Reconstructing Old Testament Theology* (OBT; Minneapolis: Fortress, 1934), 287. In his *TOT*, "mutuality" may speak "against" transcendence or is associated with fidelity but not sovereignty, both problematic formulations.

8. For a more complete statement, see Terence E. Fretheim, *The Suffering of God: An Old Testament Perspective* (OBT; Philadelphia: Fortress, 1984), esp. pp. 70–71.

9. "Embrace of Pain," 405; "Structure Legitimation," 42.

cause "it lacks a human face," it needs to be submitted to sharp critique.[10] I believe that this "system" is much looser than he supposes; it does not function mechanically, even in Deuteronomic theology (e.g., Deut 4:31; Judg 2:1; 1 Sam 12:2; 2 Samuel 7). The language of "contractual theology" will simply not do for the God-Israel relationship in any Old Testament tradition, though it had its adherents in popular understanding, then as now (e.g., the friends of Job). We should not forget that "covenant" is used metaphorically, carrying both a yes and a no with respect to the socio-political analogue.

For Brueggemann, this contract is one to which Israel's God is committed. Yet Israel's life experience intrudes upon this settled structure and issues in various forms of protest—the laments of the psalmists, the "alternative consciousness" of the prophets, and Job. Changes in this structure are generated not from God's side but from the human side; indeed, the human experience of pain "forces" change on God's part.[11] Israel's prayers "evoke from God a new posture of relationship."[12] This experience (and the extent to which Brueggemann understands experience to figure in Israel's changing theological formulations is notable) occasions an "in-house struggle," between the "common theology" and "mutations which seek to transform" it.[13] But, and this is a key point, these "mutations" are not simply expressed by Israel's theologians; rather they are "going on in the very person of God," disclosing "God's own life, which is troubled, problematic, and unresolved."[14]

Another way in which Brueggemann speaks of the God who is "lodged in a 'common theology'" with Israel is that "two moves are underway at [29] the same time, and in opposite directions." One move is "an *intensification of Yahweh's anger and impatience*"[15] at Israel's waywardness that finally issues in the destruction of Jerusalem. In this common theology, "the outcome of judgment for Jerusalem is tightly tied to disobedience." A second and *concurrent* move within God is "an enormous patience, a holding to promises, even in the face of disobedience, a resistance to the theological categories which conventionally give God self-definition."[16] This movement within God (apart from Israel's response) occasions a divine "reluctance" about simply being an "enforcer" of the contract; indeed God *"wills"* to be other than this. This occasions an "unbearable incongruity" in God. God is "committed to a structure of sanctions, and yet with a *yearning* for a [renewed?]

---

10. "Structure Legitimation," 42.
11. "Embrace of Pain," 402, 404.
12. Ibid., 404.
13. "Structure Legitimation," 34, 43.
14. Ibid., 35, 44.
15. "Embrace of Pain," 397.
16. Ibid., 397.

relationship with this disobedient partner." Again and again, God must decide "how much he must implement its [the contract's] claims, and how much he can resist."[17]

This second movement, however, seems to me to be not an integral aspect of the common theology, but already stands over against it. The point is an important one: Israel discerned such "resistance" and "reluctance" in God *apart from* Israel's prayers or appeals to God. Israel understood that its God was not a simple upholder of the contract come what may. Israel could appeal to God precisely because God was discerned to be already open to, "yearning for," such a direction. In any case, why this situation should be described as an "unbearable incongruity"[18] for God is not clear to me. Brueggemann suggests where God's "will" is in all of this, namely, in being other than simply an enforcer of the contract; this use of "will" language would seem to make clear that this is for God more than simple "reluctance." Is it not a positive willing, which assumes a relationship with Israel that has its best interests at heart ("an enormous patience, a holding to promises")? Yet Brueggemann also states that Israel had only a *"hunch* that this God does not want to be an unchallenged structure . . . and tests the hunch."[19] On what grounds is this only a "hunch"? When Moses, for example, makes his plea to God, he appeals to God's promise to Abraham (Exod 32:13). God's being "committed to a structure of sanctions" does not ever fully comprehend the divine will for Israel. Generally, the *will* of God is a neglected theme in Brueggemann's theology.[20] [30]

Brueggemann's statement about the "will" of God stands in no little tension with his comments that "God *may wish* to be 'above the fray,'" or that "Israel's laments *force* God to recharacterization," indeed "a new identity."[21] Brueggemann even speaks of God's response to such prayers as a "galling" experience; at one point he speaks of "the transformative power of Yahweh, of which Yahweh is indisputably capable, *depends upon* the triggering power of the human agent" (*TOT,* 472–73, emphasis added). Indeed, "Israel's vigorous protest has moved Yahweh *back to fidelity"* (*TOT,* 440, emphasis added). Brueggemann claims that Israel's laments and acts of protest to God stand "in deep tension with the reality of God's sovereign freedom to be who God *chooses* to be."[22] But if God's choosing to be, which must include God's willing, already moves beyond a commitment to structure before any lament is heard, then it seems incongruous to speak of incongruity. In other words, there is within God a leaning toward Israel and

---

17. Ibid., 398.
18. Ibid., 397.
19. Ibid., 401 (emphasis added).
20. For my own reflections on this theme, see "Will of God in the OT," *ABD* 6:914–20.
21. For the first quotation see "Embrace of Pain," 403; cf. "above the fray" on p. 406. For the others see ibid., 402, 404, 407 (emphasis added).
22. Ibid., 402 (emphasis added).

being *for* Israel by virtue of the divine purpose and promises (see below). God's decision-making and actions toward Israel and the world will always be informed by that loving purpose and those promises.

This is true even in judgment, the exercise of God's "ferocious sovereignty." Brueggemann's exposition of the theme of divine anger and judgment suggests otherwise, however. His treatment of Exod 34:6–7, with its combination of divine love and graciousness and yet taking violators seriously, is taken as an example of such "incongruity," though there is no signal in the text of its being so (both come into play again in Numbers 14).[23] Why should love be inconsistent with "just judgment"? Why is divine judgment an act of unfaithfulness? Why cannot judgment be in the service of graciousness? Why is a word or act "against Israel" by Yahweh incongruous with God's will "for Israel"? I would claim that divine judgment is *always* in the service of God's loving and saving purposes, and their juxtaposition in Exod 34:6–7 says precisely this.

I offer some reflections regarding judgment along these lines. God's anger is an exercise of the *circumstantial* will of God, which always stands in the service of God's *absolute* will for life and blessing.[24] Or, from another angle, wrath (unlike love) is never for Israel considered to be an attribute of God; if there were no sin, there would be no wrath and no judgment. Wrath issuing in judgment is a contingent response to a specific situation. Wrath/judgment is never God's final word for Israel or the world (though [31] Israel may wonder about that, especially when untrusting of the promises). But, precisely in order to be faithful, God *must* judge. Fidelity calls for a harsh sovereignty in some situations.

Israel may not *know* how God is working out the divine will in such circumstances, and deeply question God, but that does not mean that God has a divided will with regard to the divine purpose. Several times in his *TOT* Brueggemann will say something like this: Yahweh's exercise of power is linked to Yahweh's fidelity "but not always" (p. 276). Or, Yahweh may act in any circumstance in gracious fidelity "and often does" (p. 271). The "not always" and "often" would mean that Yahweh's faithfulness or saving purposes have been bracketed out in certain divine activities. At times Brueggemann places such an emphasis on "sovereign freedom" that Yahweh can even "cancel the commitment" to Israel (*TOT*, 410). Sovereignty clearly takes priority over fidelity in such formulations. This direction of thought opens up the possibility that the interpreter can decide where and when God is acting faithfully to the divine purpose and promises. Moreover, if God is not always faithful, then *all* God's words and deeds are in question, and one has to do with a "however" theology. "God is faithful, however. . . ." "God is loving, but. . . ." This is not love or faithfulness in any genuine sense. I

---

23. Ibid., 414; pursued with much detail in his *TOT,* e.g., pp. 215–24.
24. On this distinction within the will of God, see Fretheim, "Will of God," 915.

would appreciate a closer study of the relationship of divine love, saving will, and grace to wrath and judgment.[25]

To return to a level of Brueggemann's thought noted above, these texts make available an unsettled God, who is uncertain, indecisive, ambiguous, and conflicted. His thesis as stated in his *TOT*:

> Yahweh is a Character and Agent who is evidenced in the life of Israel as an Actor marked by unlimited [!] sovereignty and risky solidarity, in whom this sovereignty and solidarity often converge, but for whom, on occasion, sovereignty and solidarity are shown to be in an unsettled tension or in an acute imbalance. *The substance of Israel's testimony concerning Yahweh, I propose, yields a Character who has a profound disjunction at the core of the Subject's life.* (p. 268)

He even claims this unsettledness within Yahweh to be "the central datum of the character of Yahweh" (p. 282), belonging "definitionally to the character of Yahweh" (303). This unsettledness is grounded in Yahweh's "excessive self-regard," or "singular preoccupation with self," which is "massive, savage, and seemingly insatiable" (272–79, 293, 556). These comments constitute a *rationale* for Yahweh's unsettling actions, an "explanation" for the fact that "Yahweh has not yet got it right" (331). Again, [32] any concern that Yahweh may have for the relationship with Israel and the world is given a secondary place, as is the will of God. This unresolved tension is finally to claim that the sovereignty of God (see his "definitionally") is the centering metaphor for an Old Testament theology. Though, at one point in his *TOT* (312) Brueggemann will say: "in the end, from the perspective of the final form of the text, fidelity dominates the vision of Israel."

I do not say that God never has any decisions to make in view of the interaction with Israel's laments and protests, or that God cannot agonize regarding such decisions. Brueggemann is right in so forthrightly lifting up these themes. Yet the texts make distinctions among divine decisions. For example, God does make once-for-all decisions, *within which* other decisions are made. Not every divine deciding constitutes a return to ground zero.

Three such divine decisions are especially momentous—once-for-all decisions that shape God's relating to the future of both the world and Israel. First, in Gen 8:21–22 (and 9:8–17) God decides never again to visit the earth in floodlike ways; God will go with the world come what may. This promise grounds certain prophetic texts having to do with *Israel* amid the experience of exile (Jer 31:35–37; 33:19–26; Isa 54:4–10). Lam 3:22–33 puts this divine resolve and Israel's experience together in its claim that, while God has "rejected" God's people, God's steadfast love for Israel persists through exile.[26] Second, in Gen 15:7–21, God passes through the fire

---

25. Abraham Heschel's *The Prophets* (New York: Harper & Row, 1962), 279–306, has influenced my thinking in this area.

26. Brueggemann considers several of these texts (though not Lam 3:22–33) in "A Shattered Transcendence? Exile and Restoration," in *Old Testament Theology*, 183–202. The is-

in committing the divine self to the promises to Abraham (reaffirmed in the covenant with David); God places God's own life on the line on behalf of those promises. Third, in a text parallel to Genesis 8–9, God makes a comparable decision regarding the future of Israel (Exod 34:10), grounded in the Abrahamic covenant (32:13) and in the very nature of God (34:6–7).

To reiterate, these decisions that God makes *for* the world and Israel are once-for-all decisions; God will never go back on the promises to Noah and to Abraham-Israel, even in the midst of the fires of judgment. At the same time, people can reject God and remove themselves from the sphere of the promise, a move that God will honor if not finally be settled with. The texts that speak of God before and during the making of these once-for-all decisions cannot necessarily be used to characterize the God who acts after [33] them. Moreover, those once-for-all decisions are grounded in an ultimate or fundamental divine will *for* Israel and the world. Hence it seems clear that each decision-making moment does not entail God's deciding "what kind of God to be,"[27] as if God had an option not to be a God of, say, steadfast love and faithfulness. In summary, we might speak of three levels of divine decision making: God's ultimate will; three (at least) once-for-all decisions that implement that will; and various circumstantial decisions. God's *ongoing* "ambivalence" is related only to the last.

From another angle, this interpretation is not "incongruous" with our understanding of relationships more generally (Brueggemann's discussion of God in relationship comes late in his *TOT* and does not decisively shape his discussion). In parental and marital relationships (two primary metaphors used for the God-Israel relationship), a commitment to structure *and* an openness to change are integral to genuine relationship. To be true to such relationships one must be committed concurrently to both constancy and change. This is not "incongruity," but revealing of the heart of what it means to be in a relationship of consequence. God is one who enters into such relationships with integrity. On the one hand, God will be steadfast in love, constant in saving will for the world, and faithful to promises made. On the other hand, God will move with the world, interacting in view of developments in the relationship and changing times and places, disciplining and judging, responding to prayers of lament, and (not) repenting of *specific* directions taken in view of that interaction. In traditional language, God is both mutable and immutable; which term one uses depends on the topic under discussion. God's transcendence is revealed in both such moves.

---

sue of the relationship between divine love/will/purpose and judgment/rejection emerges also in this article. When Brueggemann states that *"the transcendence of God is placed in deep jeopardy* by the exile" (p. 199), it is not clear to me what the word *transcendence* entails. Taken at its face value, this would mean that God could cease to be God.

27. "Embrace of Pain," 410.

We return to Brueggemann's concern to address entrenched theologies of various sorts. For him, the texts of God's heavy-handedness and destructive judgments are problematic for "normative theology." In the steady reference throughout his *TOT* to Israel's testimony to Yahweh as both unsettled and unsettling, the range of descriptors used for God is remarkable: savage, odd, abusive, mean-spirited, wild, self-indulgent, unreliable, unstable, capricious, irascible, irrational, sulky, and more (none of them biblical words any more than much churchly language for God has been). Again, this language suggests that, whatever is said about divine fidelity, sovereignty admits of no qualification by the relationships with Israel and the world into which God has entered. Brueggemann does speak of partial qualifications of divine sovereignty by the divine fidelity in some texts, but these seem not to be hermeneutically significant for the larger biblical picture. Countertestimony finally has just as much standing as core testimony. [34] But does every text and every metaphor carry equal weight in considering Israel's understanding of God (see below)?

Brueggemann may insufficiently recognize that there are some theologians (whether evangelical or orthodox) who appeal precisely to these unsettling judgment themes to keep the troops in line with an image of a scary God! Brueggemann's relentless attention to unsettling images for God speaks against settled establishment types who champion a "settled 'establishment' Yahweh," the better to maintain control over life and thought. Not in his purview (from a personal conversation) is a significant theological establishment for whom an unsettling God is precisely the trump card to keep matters settled. Such a portrayal of God "on the loose" is designed to keep people on edge, always looking over their shoulders wondering what God is going to do next if they do not toe the mark. This is another form of sovereignty, and of a hardened sort, for it often has none of the restraints and constraints that genuine relationship entails. In other words, Brueggemann's God may be used in ways that are just as controlling as any other, and I know several folks who will be delighted to be able to appeal to him to substantiate their version of orthodoxy. What guards Brueggemann's work from being so understood and used? The "antidote" can in fact intensify the problem that Brueggemann is rightfully concerned to address.

A further issue may be raised in this connection. What counts as being "unsettling" with respect to God? Does this include the portrayal of God in terms of patriarchy—integral even to Israel's core testimony? For moderns, this is indeed an unsettling aspect of the testimony to Yahweh. But is it an appropriate unsettling? I understand that Brueggemann does not treat patriarchy as an appropriate dimension of the Bible's portrayal of God, though he uses the word *reliable* for the biblical testimony. Brueggemann does, however, in several publications (including his *TOT*), consider violence an appropriate unsettling matter in Israel's God-talk; in fact, he speaks of violence as belonging to the "very fabric" of Israel's faith, as "situated in God's own will and purpose" (pp. 381, 497). Again, no distinctions are made within the divine will; it is as if love and violence belong eternally together in God (an eternal dualism is close at hand).

Violent images (e.g., God as warrior) do disrupt traditional attempts to domesticate God. But on what grounds is God's exercise of violence (and other testimonies to "irascible" and "irrational" divine behavior) understood to be appropriately unsettling, but not patriarchy? Moreover, does this include every violent image? One thinks of the common prophetic witness to a God who lifts up Israel's skirts and exposes her genitalia (e.g., Isa 3:16–17). Another unsettling image! But appropriately so? Criteria must [35] be developed to sort out these testimonies, to make distinctions regarding appropriateness among images of God. Without this, *all* talk about Israel's unsettling testimony regarding God is called into question.

The Bible itself recognizes this issue. One might speak of a biblical capacity to be self-critical regarding its imaging of God. Some studies have shown that certain texts have a subversive role to play regarding patriarchy; the same could be said about violence.[28] Other (implicitly) critical voices regarding various matters are to be found (e.g., Gen 18:25). These testimonies to an internal critique regarding unsettling divine activity need to be more explicitly developed. Such a study will have implications for contemporary usage, not least giving readers permission to ask into the continuing appropriateness of its unsettling testimony without being charged with escapism. We have an inner-biblical warrant to be comparably critical (though we do not finally stand on neutral ground in making this observation). Bible readers should deal with and be confronted by every text, allowing them to be "in our face," but this does not necessarily affirm that every image of God is appropriately unsettling. Some unsettling images for God ought not put the fear of God in anyone![29]

Another way into this discriminating enterprise in view of inner-biblical warrants is through an analysis of genre and other narratological features. In conclusion, I raise questions in three areas, but focus especially on the issue of genre.

1. Point of view. In drawing upon Israel's testimonies to God, Brueggemann explicitly makes no important distinction between Israel's speech *about* God and the word spoken *by* God to Israel; this is surprising given his emphasis on the word and its rhetorical shaping. This decision diminishes

---

28. For example, Phyllis Trible, *God and the Rhetoric of Sexuality* (OBT; Philadelphia: Fortress, 1978); on violence, see Erich Zenger, "The God of Exodus in the Message of the Prophets as Seen in Isaiah," in *Exodus—A Lasting Paradigm* (ed. B. van Iersel and A. Weiler; Edinburgh: T. & T. Clark, 1987), 22–33.

29. For a study of the appropriateness and reliability of God images in the Old Testament, see my *The Bible as Word of God in a Postmodern Age* (Minneapolis: Fortress, 1998), with Karlfried Froehlich.

a rhetorical feature such as "point of view" in assessing the text's testimony regarding God and makes possible a claim that words placed in the mouth of God have no special standing in Israel's God-talk.

2. Character. It has become commonplace to consider God a character just like other characters in the narrative, and Brueggemann generally speaks as if this were the case. But are there no differences to be taken into account? Might the differences between Yahweh and other gods (e.g., theogony) be compromised by a collapse of character differences? What difference does it make that all language for God is analogical? In thinking [36] about such matters as divine anger or divine speech, one must take into account both a yes and a no with respect to the human analogue. With respect to every divine "character trait," indeed every divine action, one must seek to discern where the yes and the no lie. Is not the distinction between the textual God and the actual God somewhat different from the textual-actual distinction with other characters? Does not the narrative itself present God as one who transcends the narrative in ways distinct from other characters? God does enter deeply "into the fray," but not in such a way that God ceases to be God. These are questions that, to my knowledge, have not been adequately addressed in recent literature about God. I would eagerly appreciate an effort by Brueggemann to do just this; he is one of the few biblical theologians who could handle the issue in a theologically sophisticated way.

3. Genre. To my knowledge, Brueggemann does not address the issue of genre with respect to God-talk in any sustained way.[30] What effect does the identification of genre have on the readerly move to theological construction? Take the laments and protests. How does one "translate" the language of these genres into theological formulations? People (then and now) say all kinds of things about God when they are in dire straits, but would never so speak in a carefully formulated theological statement. One thinks of bargaining or the use of hyperbolic language or the use of metaphors designed to get attention. How does one assess the theological value of such outbursts? When the psalmist complains, "Why do you sleep, O Lord? . . . Why do you forget?" (Ps 44:23–24, NRSV) is one to conclude that he thought that God was actually sleeping or forgetting? Is he speaking hyperbolically? Even more, that these expressions occur in *poetry* is important for theological reflection. One must sort out the rhetorical function of this language and its metaphorical character before discerning how to use it in theological formulation.

Another case in point: What does it mean that Israel gathered claims about God into creedal formulations? They are present in two primary

---

30. For fuller discussion, esp of creedal genres, see my "God Who Acts: An Old Testament Perspective," *ThTo* 54 (1997): 6–18. For an earlier effort regarding the import of generalizing genres for theological formulation, see my *Suffering of God,* 24–29.

forms, historical recital (Deut 26:5–9) and more abstract confessions (Exod 34:6–7; Deut 10:17–18). Echoes of these credos are found in numerous texts, especially hymnic literature (which gathers the "leaner" forms of Israel's faith), and they are woven into narratives. They would seem to say: This is the kind of God with whom Israel has to do in every circumstance. Just *how* God will be this kind of God in any moment cannot be predicted in advance, nor how Israel will appropriate this material, or even contest it [37] (Jonah 4:2). But such generalizing genres would seem to provide an inner-biblical basis for interpreting the God who appears in narrative.[31] They represent some kind of centering amid the Bible's theological pluralism, so that "core testimony" does have a distinctive theological value.

Brueggemann does seem aware of this genre issue at various points in his discussion. For example: "Israel does not always stay within the rhetoric of specificity. . . . Israel transforms its testimony about Yahweh from specificity to a larger, more general claim" (*TOT*, 213). The question then becomes: What rhetorical function does this move from specifics to generalizations have within the larger narrative? And what import do the generalizing genres have for the theological interpretation of the specifics of the narrative? Brueggemann does say they are "provisional," and we can observe additions to both the historical recitals (e.g., creation in Nehemiah 9) and the more abstract confessions (e.g., divine repentance in Jonah 4:2; Joel 2:13), though their core claims remain essentially intact. But are they any more provisional than, say, the Apostle's Creed is for Christians? He cites Psalm 136 as a prime example of this generalizing move: "the concrete verbal action of Yahweh cited [in the first half of each verse] permits the larger sweeping affirmation" (*TOT*, 214). Yet the connecting *kî*, "for" (which he neglects), suggests that the move is actually more complex: God acted in this way *because* God's "steadfast love endures forever." God will be steadfast in love wherever God is speaking or acting in any such specific situation. While God's specific actions may well have given rise to such generalizations, and continue to be important to support them, the latter now become a general testimony that can be confessed apart from an immediate experience of such action (as does, say, Lam 3:22–33).

Narrative readings will continue to challenge the core confessions, probing their continuing adequacy in a "theology in process" and resisting an easy settledness. Brueggemann has attended to this challenge in particular in a way that leaves us all profoundly indebted to his work.

---

31. I lay out three criteria for discerning the "confessional" status of certain claims about God (pervasiveness, genre, and tradition) in "The Repentance of God: A Key to Evaluating Old Testament God-Talk," *HBT* 10 (1988): 47–70.

Part 3

God and Suffering

What Kind of God?

It is not enough to say that one believes in God. What is important finally is the *kind* of God in whom one believes.[1] Or, to use different language: metaphors matter. The images used to speak of God not only decisively determine the way one thinks about God, they have a powerful impact on the shape of the life of the believer. They may, in fact, tend to shape a life toward unbelief.

In his autobiography, the American journalist and critic Thomas Matthews, a preacher's kid, writes:

> Try as I may, I cannot altogether shake off my habitual awe of the church nor completely dissociate it from the far more fearful God to whom the church makes its ritual obeisance. I still think of God—no, not think, but apprehend, as I was trained as a child to envision him—as a watchful, vengeful, enormous, omniscient policeman, instantly aware of the slightest tinge of irreverence in my innermost thought, always ready to pounce if I curse, if I mention him in anger, fun or mere habit (though with ominous patience he might hold his hand for a time). . . . But how can that kind of fear of that kind of God be the beginning of wisdom?[2]

All too often the sole focus of the ministry of the church has been on *whether* one believes in God. Insufficient attention has been given to the kind of God in whom one believes, often with disastrous results. Witness any number of atrocities, from the Inquisition to Jonestown, committed in the name of God by those who believe in God. Moreover, to define God solely or primarily in terms of activity can get one into comparable difficulties. The God of Jonestown was a creator and redeemer God who had a clear plan and purpose, moving [2] the people toward a specific goal. The question of the kind of God in whom one believes is not only important, it is crucial. It is a question of images. Metaphors matter.

The OT tells us that the people of God were often guilty of worshiping idols, of making up their own god, of creating gods, or even Yahweh, in a certain image. We oversimplify this matter if we think of such images solely in terms of wood or stone; the plastic image conveyed a particular way of understanding these gods or Yahweh. And, we have learned over the years that idolatries do not need the plastic form to qualify as such.

This essay was originally published as the "Introduction" in Terence E. Fretheim, *The Suffering of God: An Old Testament Perspective* (OBT; Philadelphia: Fortress, 1984), 1–12.

1. I use the phrase "kind of God" in the same sense as in such common phrases as "What kind of person is Sarah?"

2. Thomas Matthews, *Under the Influence* (New York: Macmillan, 1977), 343.

One can move directly to mental images which construct a false image of God and have the power of wreaking havoc in people's faith and life. Metaphors matter.

This issue can be approached from a different perspective. The preaching and teaching of the church have commonly been so focused on a certain portrait of Jesus that many of the biblical images for God have been neglected, and stereotypical images have been allowed to stand unchallenged. It is almost as if faith in Jesus were thought to take care of the picture of God automatically; thus, one need pay no special heed to it. But this assumption has commonly created inner tensions for the faithful, perhaps even intolerable tensions; for the picture of Jesus presented often stands at odds with the commonly accepted picture of God. Attributes such as love, compassion, and mercy, accompanied by acts of healing, forgiving, and redeeming, tend to become narrowly associated with Jesus, while the less palatable attributes and actions of holiness, wrath, power, and justice are ascribed only to God. What tends to fill the mind is God as Giver of the Law and Judge of all the earth. If God is not the cause of all the ills in the world, God is still seen as the one who is to blame for not really doing anything about them. It is the goodness of God that is ignored, not the goodness of Jesus. One can almost hear someone say: "If only Jesus were here, he would do something about all our troubles!" People often seem to have a view which suggests that Jesus is friend and God is enemy. An understanding of the atonement gets twisted so that Jesus is seen as the one who came to save us from God.

One wonders whether the creeds of the church have not in some ways contributed to such perspectives. God the Father gets one line of the Apostle's Creed, and (unlike the Nicene Creed) the fatherhood of [3] God is not separated from almightiness; the emergent image is one of an authoritarian Father—an impression somewhat at odds with the biblical metaphor. Moreover, the saving and blessing activity of God is not directly suggested. Repeated Sunday after Sunday, one wonders about the Creed's effect on the understanding of God. When this influence is combined with a common tendency to ignore the reading of OT lessons, and an absence of regular preaching on OT texts, people tend to continue with their stereotypical images of God, which become even more deep-seated in the process.

Such perspectives regarding God and the relationship between God and Jesus, even if exemplified in nothing more than a tendency in language and thought, have probably commonly led to a kind of "Jesusology," in both naive and more sophisticated forms.[3] God remains at a distance as someone to be feared, while Jesus lives tenderly in one's heart. Or, when combined with an idea that God is really unknowable, one is led to a no-

---

3. Cf. the discussion of "Christomonism" in G. E. Wright, *The Old Testament and Theology* (New York: Harper & Row, 1969), 13–18.

tion that Jesus is finally all we have, and commonly only in a very human form: Jesus, not Jesus Christ. A very close correlation can be seen between the idea of a God who is "wholly other," totally removed from the world, and "God is dead" proclamations, whether the last phrase be understood literally or figuratively. This tendency is reinforced by secularistic trends which have made the activity of God in the world problematic, while Jesus continues to be seen as an actual historical figure; hence one can talk about his spirit living on in the hearts of the faithful with less difficulty.

From another perspective, the mission of the church can be seriously hindered by misconceptions, particularly among those whose difficulty with the church is due to a certain image of or questions about God. The message of the church may be so narrowly focused that it simply does not address the question of God's nature for such individuals, and the proclamation of divine love may indeed pass them by. Anyone seriously concerned with mission or evangelism must be concerned about people's questions, including their questions about God. They often have to be answered before the gospel of Jesus Christ can receive a hearing. Thus, a much more concerted effort to deal with the God of the OT needs to be engaged in by the church at all levels, if it is to reach out to those who have intellectual difficulties with this matter. [4]

Considerations about the relationship between God and Jesus, according to the NT, should assist us in our deliberations, the Gospel of John in particular:

I and the Father are one. (10:30)

The word which you hear is not mine but the Father's who sent me. (14:24))

All that the Father has is mine. (16:15)

He who has seen me has seen the Father. (14:9)

It would appear that, whatever one might say about classical doctrinal formulations, Christian preaching and piety fail to take such statements with sufficient seriousness. It would be unfair to say that there is no talk about the love, grace, and mercy of the Father in the event of Jesus, but the fatherhood of God more generally seems to be seen narrowly in terms of authority and even domination. Such NT statements, however, insist that in Jesus Christ we are in the fullest possible sense looking at the heart of God the Father, the God of the OT. The coming of God in Jesus Christ is indeed the coming of God in a quite concrete way in the entire life of a human being. That is the special force of the NT message: God, unsurpassably enfleshed in the human being, Jesus of Nazareth. The claim would seem to be clear: The point of fulfillment is not alien to the promise, nor to the presence and activity, of the God of Israel. There is a decisive continuity in the history of the God of the OT and the God and Father of our

Lord Jesus Christ. Those central touchstones in the life of Jesus—Incarnation, Ministry, and Cross—are neither foreign to, nor a departure from, the portrait of God revealed to us in the pages of the OT. I intend to show how I believe this to be so.

The relationship between the two testaments is more than simply verbal, with words of promise or prophecy finding their fulfillment in the life, death, and resurrection of Jesus Christ. It is more than typological, with patterns of speech and action having points of continuity across the testaments. It is more than historical and theological, with all the family resemblance that can be discerned by [5] probing into roots and ideas. There is also a decisive continuity in the history of God, who is the same yesterday, today, and forever. An important way to discover that continuity is through an analysis of key metaphors for God. The metaphorical continuity between the Testaments has a considerable capacity to reveal what kind of God it is who is involved in this history. It leads not to information about God, in a narrow sense, but to a knowledge of God in a more holistic sense, a kind of participation in what the journey has meant for God. It gives some sense of identification with what the story of God has been like. And for one who "experiences" the metaphors across the Testaments, the history of God is seen to be coherent, consistent, and marked by certain constants that are finally unsurpassably exemplified in the life and death of Jesus Christ. "He who has seen me has seen the Father" can, in at least one significant sense, be turned around to say: "He who has seen the Father has seen the Christ."

Anthropomorphic Metaphor

Having noted the central importance of metaphor in any study of the God of the OT, a sketch of the meaning and use of metaphor which informs this discussion needs some attention.[4] A basic definition of metaphor is in

---

4. There are many helpful studies of metaphor, too numerous to cite here. From the perspective of OT studies, see James Barr, "Theophany and Anthropomorphism in the Old Testament," *Congress Volume: Oxford, 1959* (VTSup 7; Leiden: Brill, 1959), 31–38; David J. A. Clines, "Yahweh and the God of Christian Theology," *Theology* 83 (1980): 323–30; Johannes Hempel, "Die Grenzen des Anthropomorphisnaus Jahwes im AT," *ZAW* 57 (1939): 75–85; idem, "Jahwehgleichnisse der israelitischen Propheten," in idem, *Apoxysmata: Vorarbeiten zu einer Religionsgeschichte und Theologie des Alten Testaments* (BZAW 81; Berlin: de Gruyter, 1961), 1–29; H. M. Kuitert, *Gott im Menschengestalt* (Munich: Chr. Kaiser Verlag, 1967); Phyllis Trible, *God and the Rhetoric of Sexuality* (OBT 2; Philadelphia: Fortress, 1978); Wilhelm Vischer, "Words and the Word: The Anthropomorphisms of the Biblical Revelation," *Int* 3 (1949): 3–18; cf. also the summary of Ulrich Mauser's work in "Image of God and Incarnation," *Int* 24 (1970): 336–56; Walter Wifall, "Models of God in the Old Testament," *BTB* 9 (1979): 179–86; Bruce Vawter, "The God of the Hebrew Scriptures," *BTB* 12 (1982): 3–7. From other perspectives, see Sallie McFague, *Metaphorical Theology: Models of God in Religious Language* (Philadelphia: Fortress, 1982); Ian Thomas Ramsey, *Models and Mystery* (New York: Oxford Univ. Press, 1964); Max Black, *Models and Metaphors*

order, first of all. Black's formulation is helpful:[5] "A memorable metaphor has the power to bring two separate domains into cognitive and emotional relation by using language directly appropriate to the one as a lens for seeing the other." In other words, a conventional understanding of a matter (e.g., a body, a parent) becomes a window through which we can gain insight into another matter, usually less well known (e.g., the church, God). A metaphor always has a duality of association: the surface associations, drawn from life as experienced, and the analogical association. But insight into the latter can be attained and, indeed, retained only by reflecting on the former in relationship to it. Such insight comes, not only through observing what is similar between the two terms, but also through that which is different. Crucial to a proper understanding of a metaphor is the recognition of both similarity and difference.

It has been rightly stated that virtually all of the language used in the Bible to refer to God is metaphorical; the word "God" would be an exception.[6] Occasionally such language is drawn from the natural world, both animate (God is an eagle, Deut 32:11) and inanimate [6] (God is a rock, Ps 31:2–3). The vast majority of the metaphors for God in the OT, however, are drawn from the sphere of the human: (a) form, with its function (mouth, speaking, Num 12:8); (b) emotional, volitional and mental states (rejoicing, Zeph 3:17); (c) roles and activities, within the family (parent, Hos 11:1) or the larger society (shepherd, Ps 23:1). The natural metaphors are important, particularly as they demonstrate an integral relationship, between God and the nonhuman created order, with continuities seen between God and that world. My primary concern here, however, is with the anthropomorphic metaphor,[7] speaking of God in language drawn from the human sphere.

Anthropomorphic metaphors have tended to be depreciated, even denigrated, in the history of Judeo-Christian thought and OT scholarship in particular.[8] This attitude can be traced from Philo of the first century (for the benefit of those whose "natural wit is dense and dull, whose childhood

---

(Ithaca, NY: Cornell Univ. Press, 1962); David Tracy, *The Analogical Imagination* (New York: Crossroad, 1981); Mark Johnson, ed., *Philosophical Perspectives on Metaphor* (Minneapolis: Univ. of Minnesota Press, 1981); Andrew Ortony, ed., *Metaphor and Thought* (New York: Cambridge Univ. Press, 1979); especially helpful is J. Martin, "The Use of Metaphor as a Conceptual Vehicle in Religious Language" (Ph.D. diss., Oxford, 1982).

5. M. Black, *Models and Metaphors: Studies in Language and Philosophy* (Ithaca, NY: Cornell University Press), 237. Contrast the discussion of Martin at some of these points ("Use of Metaphor," 75ff., 133ff., 212ff.). She makes a strong case that the metaphor does not have a double meaning, literal and metaphorical, but a single meaning which results from the "interanimation" of two "networks of associations" (the tenor and the vehicle).

6. G. B. Caird, *The Language and Imagery of the Bible* (Philadelphia: Westminster, 1980), 17ff.

7. This more accurately states the kind of language with which we are dealing than anthropomorphism does. See the reservations regarding the latter term in Abraham Joshua Heschel, *The Prophets* (New York: Harper & Row, 1962), 268ff.

8. See especially Mauser, "Image of God"; Kuitert, *Gott im Menschengestalt*; Clines, "Yahweh." See n. 4 above.

training has been mismanaged")[9] to contemporaries such as H. H. Rowley ("mere accommodations to human speech, or vivid pictures used for their psychological effect rather than theological in significance").[10] Yet, there have always been those who have sensed a deeper importance in this material, for instance, E. Jacob: "A line not always straight, but nonetheless continuous, leads from the anthropomorphisms of the earliest pages of the Bible, to the incarnation of God in Jesus Christ."[11]

It is ironic that OT interpretation should have problems with these concrete ways of depicting God. To understand this language in a purely figurative sense would mean that it is thought finally to stand over against the concreteness and realism commonly said to be characteristic of OT thought. A figurative interpretation buys abstraction at the expense of concreteness. A further irony can be noted in the fact that anthropomorphic metaphors predominate in Israelite talk about the deity in a way that is not the case elsewhere in the ancient Near East (cf. the use of animal-human hybrids).[12] This preponderant tendency is thus a point of distinctiveness in the OT understanding of God, which many would try to explain away.

It is also ironic that Christians should have trouble with this language.[13] In the incarnation, God has acted anthropomorphically in the most supreme way. The NT, far from being the culmination of a progressive spiritualization in the understanding of God, speaks of [7] God unsurpassably enfleshed in the human. Apart from the Christ-event, the NT continues to speak of God in terms of such metaphors. This continuity is consonant with developments within the OT itself, where one is struck by the constant use of such language. There are no anti-anthropomorphic tendencies to be discerned; even in dreams or visions or glimpses into heaven God is spoken of in such ways.[14] Such later passages as Isa 42:14; 63:1–6; and Dan 7:9 contain some of the more daring anthropomorphic metaphors in the OT.

One of the most basic issues relating to the understanding of metaphor is the relationship between metaphor and essential definition. We need to steer between Scylla and Charybdis in dealing with this matter.

On the one hand, there is the danger of positing no real or essential relationship between the metaphor and God as God really relates to the world. Thus, people speak of "mere" metaphor, or consider it to be only illustrative or decorative of thought, to be dispensed with as one moves on to more abstract definitions. But, as with all metaphors, while there is no one-to-one correspondence, the metaphor does say some things about God that correspond to the reality which is God, while saying other things as

---

9. Cited in Clines, "Yahweh," 324.
10. H. H. Rowley, *The Faith of Israel* (London: SCM, 1956), 75.
11. Edmond Jacob, *The Theology of the Old Testament* (New York: Harper & Row, 1958), 32.
12. See especially Hempel, "Die Grenzen."
13. This is emphasized in Mauser, "Image of God," and Kuitert, *Gott im Menschengestalt.*
14. See Barr, "Theophany," 33; see chap. 6 [not reprinted here] for further discussion.

well. To use the language of Jerald Janzen: "For all their manifold richness and overtone and allusion, metaphors at their center do imply one thing and not another; and the most natural procedure is to take the metaphor as adumbrating an essential character which is analogous to the metaphoric vehicle, and not contrary to it."[15] The metaphor does in fact describe God, though it is not fully descriptive. The metaphor does contain information about God. The metaphor does not stand over against the literal. Though the *use* of the metaphor is not literal, there is literalness intended in the relationship to which the metaphor has reference. God is actually good or loving; God is the supreme exemplification of goodness and love. One must say that such metaphors reveal that God is literally related to the world, unless one is prepared to say that God is literally not in relationship to the world.[16] The metaphors do reveal an essential continuity with the reality which is God; to use J. Martin's apt phrase, the metaphors are "reality depicting."[17]

On the other hand, there is a danger of suggesting that a literal correspondence exists between metaphor and reality in every respect. In popular theology this will often entail a portrayal of God in terms, [8] say, of an old man with white hair (cf. Dan 7:9). While the tendency in the first danger is to make God so wholly other as to make relationship, let alone knowledge, impossible, the danger here is to reduce God to human frailty; both directions lead to idolatry. On this point, the discontinuities inherent in the metaphor need to be lifted up. Anthropomorphic metaphors ought not be conceived in terms of pictures, replicas, scale models, copies, or the like. The variety of biblical metaphors should prevent us from such literalism: for example, to combine the husband-wife and the parent-child metaphors in literal fashion will create problems! There is always that in the metaphor which is discontinuous with the reality which is God. God outdistances all our images; God cannot finally be captured by any of them.

Steering between these two poles, how does one move from metaphor to essential definition? By interpreting "along the metaphorical grain" and not contrary to it, by "following the thrust of the analogy."[18] If one moves against the natural implication of the metaphor, one is misinterpreting it. At the same time, while the metaphor primarily generates insight into the divine reality at the basic thrust of the analogy, it also does so more indirectly at those points where it is discontinuous with the reality which is God.

---

15. Jerald Janzen, "Metaphor and Reality in Hosea 11," *Semeia* 24 (1982): 26.
16. See Schubert Miles Ogden, *The Reality of God and Other Essays* (New York: Harper & Row, 1966), 171ff., 149ff.
17. Martin, "Use of Metaphor," 208ff.; cf. 111ff.
18. So Janzen, "Metaphor and Reality in Hosea 11," 19, 26.

Let me illustrate this last point with some of the metaphors central to this study. To speak of God as one who repents, with the basic ideas of reversal and change, does have some basic points of continuity with the way God actually relates to the world. Yet, there is no one-to-one correspondence between the way people and God repent. Or, to speak of God as one who suffers is to take with utmost seriousness the continuity inherent in certain metaphors (e.g., God as mourner). At the same time, God does not suffer in exactly the same way as humans do, and to try to get at that is important. Or, to use temporal categories for God is to interpret along the grain of certain metaphors (e.g., God as planner); yet, the dissimilarities are also important, that is, God is not subject to the ravages of time.

We now need to inquire into the importance of the great number and variety of the anthropomorphic metaphors for God in the OT, and issues of their relative value. One of the dangers for the people of God in any age is that they will be content with a rather limited fund of metaphors. Thus, for example, the court of law metaphor has [9] become predominant in the thinking of some people regarding God, with other metaphors being subordinated to this or blocked out altogether. The particular danger is that the power such metaphors have in the shaping of thought and life is not always recognized. Metaphors work not simply at cognitive levels, but at the levels of emotion and will as well. To understand this phenomenon is to focus on the very issue we have been raising. The metaphors with which one lives shape one's life. The predominance of the law court in our operative fund of metaphors may effectively cut us off from a side of our experience of God, shaping our religious attitudes and sensitivities adversely. It is not a matter of exchanging one metaphor for another, but of evaluating our operative metaphors and working to extend that list. This is one of my basic concerns: to lift up certain neglected metaphors so that our operative fund of them will be more congruent with the biblical witness and our experience of God in the world. While even a multitude of metaphors will not in itself guarantee this objective, their availability can provide greater balance in our understanding of God as they shed light on, and even correct, one another.

The tendency in OT scholarship has been to forfeit many such metaphors, primarily by collecting a large number of them and drawing a few general conclusions (e.g., God is personal, living),[19] rather than examining each in turn for the insight it might generate. Thus, for example, one needs to ask what speaking of God's eyes and ears (2 Kgs 19:16) adds to the understanding of the relationship of God to world that living, seeing,

---

19. E.g., Walther Eichrodt, *Theology of the Old Testament* (Philadelphia: Westminster, 1961–67), 1:210ff. Eichrodt's suggestion that Israel understood the anthropomorphisms "in a quite literal way" goes beyond the evidence.

and hearing do not.[20] Such language makes the idea that God receives the world into himself vivid and concrete. God's experience of the world is not superficial; God takes it in, in as real a way as people do who use their eyes and ears. At the same time, in ways that people do not, God takes it *all* in (Jer 32:19), and not with fleshly eyes (Job 10:4).

Nevertheless, while examining each metaphor in its specificity is important, the general conclusions drawn continue to be significant. In addition to revealing God as living and personal, they testify to the intimate relationship between God and world. The continuities between God and world are at the heart of every such metaphor. Images drawn from personal life—home, fields, and shops—are those used to speak of God. This frame of reference serves to anchor the experience [10] of God in human experience, especially the public arena. As a result, talk about God is strikingly "secular," inextricably interrelated to an amazing array of those things which characterize the world, yet without collapsing God and world into one another. The metaphor is continuous with both God's presence in the world and God's self-revelation.

While discerning the variety of metaphors in both their specificity and generality is important, not all have the same value. This is true at two related levels. First, we need to recognize what might be called the "varying degrees of correspondence"[21] between the two terms of the metaphor. One might speak of degrees of revelatory capacity. There are those with a low capacity (God as dry rot, Hos 5:12; God as lion, Hos 5:14; God as whistler, Isa 7:18), with a moderate capacity (God as rock, Ps 31:2–3; God's arm, Isa 53:1), and with a high capacity (God as parent, Hos 11:1).[22]

Those of low correspondence are not communal property and tend to be used for their surprise or shock value, especially in Hosea. Those with high correspondence are communal, having found a staying power in the life of the community of faith over a longer period of time. Most common among these are the interpersonal metaphors, though those drawn from the human relationship to the nonhuman (e.g., farmer) are also often rich, largely because the God/human relationship is primarily in view (Isa 5:1–7).

Why are these metaphors so central?[23] They have a richness of association in human experience; they are true to life, revealing a certain fitness

---

20. There is, of course, only a relative distinction between the psychical and physical anthropomorphic metaphors. There are times when scholars seem to argue that certain metaphors are truly revealing of God (e.g., love), while denying an essential continuity to others, perhaps especially when traditional understandings of God, such as immutability, are threatened by a metaphor such as divine repentance. All metaphors need to be probed for their insights, though not all are of equal value, as we shall see.

21. Caird, *Language and Imagery*, 153. See Barr, "Theophany," 31, who distinguishes between anthropomorphisms and theophany; only the latter is a serious attempt to come to terms with the form of God.

22. Cf. Caird, *Language and Imagery*, 154ff.

23. Ibid., 176ff.

with respect to that experience. They have a capacity to capture, organize, and communicate our experience and understanding of God; to focus our thinking, feeling, and living. They can often be extended to capture many facets of an experience (e.g., family interrelationships). They lend themselves to "a two-way traffic in ideas."[24] For example, the father metaphor moves not only from human fatherhood to God, but doubles back and helps shape the human father into the likeness of God. But, the understanding of the human as created in the image of God (Gen 1:26) is of central importance here. These metaphors are especially important because Israel believed that "the pattern on which man was fashioned is to be sought outside the sphere of the created."[25] Rather than accommodating God to the level of the human or raising human characteristics to [11] the nth degree, the human is seen to be fashioned in the likeness of God. Hence, the human is seen in theomorphic terms, rather than God in anthropomorphic terms.[26] Thereby, the essential metaphorical process is revealed to us. The "image of God" gives us permission to reverse the process and, by looking at the human, learn what God is like.

This brings us to our second point on the relative value of such metaphors: the idea of a controlling metaphor. One of the more important issues here is how to determine whether a given metaphor is appropriate, is being misused, or has been exhausted. It is clear from a survey of the OT metaphors for God that some elements of the human experience are not considered appropriate, even in part:[27] death, sexuality, embitterment, lack of wisdom, and capriciousness, as well as certain roles (e.g., criminal), to name a few. These and others can be eliminated because certain metaphors function to delimit metaphorical possibilities. The bulk of these controlling metaphors are probably to be found in passages like Exod 34:6–7. Through the years they have gained a special place in the community. (See chap. 2 [not reprinted in this volume].)

Such controlling metaphors also function in other ways. They not only serve a limiting purpose, but as metaphors among metaphors, not unlike a "canon" within the canon, they are able to bring coherence to a range of biblical thinking about God; they provide a hermeneutical key for interpreting the whole. The sovereignty of God and the grace of God are two obvious examples in the history of biblical interpretation.

Finally, we note the qualifying function such controlling metaphors have. For example, the metaphor "father" in and of itself is not capable of constant meaning or value to those who hear it or use it. The use and

---

24. Ibid., 17ff.

25. Gerhard von Rad, *Old Testament Theology* (New York: Harper & Row, 1962–65), 1:146.

26. Both Mauser ("Image of God") and Heschel (*Prophets*) also speak in these terms. See my discussion in chap. 6 [not reprinted in this volume].

27. See especially Hempel, "Die Grenzen."

meaning of metaphors is heavily dependent upon historical-cultural factors, especially those of our individual experience. The meaning of a metaphor varies from culture to culture, and even from individual to individual within a single culture. A child, for instance, with a brutal or incestuous father will hear the word "father" for God with far different ears than I will. Certain common metaphors for God may, in fact, be closely related to the worst experiences in the lives of people. While this argues for the importance of using a variety of metaphors in our talk about God, it also [12] means that every metaphor finally needs to be qualified by the controlling metaphors of the community of faith. Thus, God is not simply father; God is a certain kind of father. God is a loving father, always (Hos 11:1). And God is not simply mother; God is a certain kind of mother. God is a mother who will not forget her children, ever (Isa 49:15).

To Say Something—About God, Evil, and Suffering

Faced with the realities of suffering and evil, Christians can say something, but they cannot say everything or even as much as they might like to say.[1] They cannot "explain" suffering or "resolve" the problem of evil or provide "answers" to these issues or develop an airtight "theodicy." Such words are sometimes used to characterize or caricature efforts to say something, often as a distraction from pursuing the questions or as a way of shutting down the conversation. In response, the Bible does give its readers some room to speak between silence and "explanation," though it does not propose a single place to stand in that room, as if pastoral discernment were not needed.

The Bible, not least the Old Testament, knows of the experience of suffering and evil at both individual and communal levels, and speaks about those realities in forthright terms (e.g., the laments). The Bible also dares to connect God with both suffering and evil and invites its readers into a conversation about the nature of that connection (e.g., divine judgment). Generally, biblical texts bring various angles of vision to bear on the complexity of the realities of suffering and evil and God's relationship thereto.

At the least, biblical perspectives can rule out several overarching "explanations." To know of these can be pastorally and theologically helpful, though this [346] knowledge does not eliminate the responsibility of discernment. For example, the Bible does not claim that *all* suffering is the will of God or that *no* suffering is the will of God. Or, that *all* suffering is due to sin or that *no* suffering is due to sin. Or, that *all* suffering is bad and to be avoided at all costs or that *no* suffering is bad. More generally, deism (the absence of God from involvement in the life of the world) seems not to be represented in the biblical writings. At the other extreme, a monism or a divine micromanagement of the life of the world seems rarely to be claimed, if at all.[2]

This essay was originally published in *Word and World* 19 (1999): 339–50.

1. Paul Sponheim and I have taught an interdisciplinary course on this topic for several years, and the articles collected in *Word and World* 19 (1999) reflect some of the concerns addressed in that course. Professor Sponheim wrote his article first, and I am much indebted to the range and rigor of his work. I responded by attending to comparable themes from a biblical perspective.

2. Among the "divine pancausality" texts sometimes cited are Job 1:21; 2:10; Amos 3:6; and Isa 45:7. On these types of texts, see Fredrik Lindstrom, *God and the Origin of Evil: A Contextual Analysis of Alleged Monistic Evidence in the Old Testament* (Lund: CWK Gleerup, 1983). On the basis of close exegetical work, Lindstrom claims that no monistic texts are

I. A God of Relationships

Fundamental to thinking about suffering and evil from a biblical perspective is the belief in a God who is in genuine relationship to the world. That this relationship is asymmetrical is evident in such biblical themes as God's holiness, eternality, and the inability to plumb the depths of God. At the same time, God wills to be known, has revealed God's self in manifold ways (Heb 1:1–2), and denies any interest in keeping the chosen people ignorant of the divine ways (Gen 18:17–19; Jer 33:3; Amos 3:7; see John 16:12–15). Indeed, human engagement with God will elicit knowledge of God and God's ways in a manner that passivity or self-effacement will not (witness the interaction between God and Moses in the call narrative in Exodus 3–6).[3] The important testimony that God's thoughts are not our thoughts or God's ways our ways (Isa 55:8), which contextually refers to God's surprising plans for a dispirited Israel's deliverance, is spoken amid amazingly forthright and clear oracles regarding the divine salvific intentions for the exiles in the midst of their suffering (see Isa 48:6).

God's will for a genuine relationship with all creatures is grounded in the relational life of God, evidenced initially in the dialogical way in which God creates humankind (Gen 1:26) and henceforth in God's way of relating to the world (e.g., Jer 23:18–22). Relationality is fundamental to God's way of being and doing, and hence relational categories are key to interpreting such realities as suffering and evil and God's relationship thereto. Generally, God's relationship with the world is such that God is present on every occasion and active in every event, no matter how heroic or Hitlerian, and in every such moment God is at work on behalf of the best possible future for all creation, whether in judgment or salvation. That God is always and everywhere present, however, raises sharp issues regarding the nature and dynamics of the relationship. In the remarkably modern words of Gideon: "But sir, if the Lord is with us, why then has all this happened to us?" (Judg 6:12–13).

Though the nature of the relationship between God and world cannot be factored out in any precise way, the biblical material witnesses to several directions of thought. For example, God has freely entered into relationships in such a way that God is not the only one who has something important to say. Prayer, for example, is God's gift to human beings precisely for the sake of communication within relationship. Again and again, God honors such prayerful responses within relationship (e.g., Exod 32:11–14; 2 Kgs 20:1–7). Such human words bring new ingredients—will, energy,

---

to be found in the Old Testament. See also the helpful article that touches on some of these themes by Frederick J. Gaiser, "'To Whom Then Will You Compare Me?' Agency in Second Isaiah," *WW* 19/2 (1999): 141–52.

3. On the theological implications of this call narrative, see my *Exodus* (Louisville: John Knox, 1991), 52–53.

insight—into a situation in which God is at work; they constitute a genuine contribution to the shape of the future that is at stake. Generally, prayer is a God-given vehicle that can make a difference both to God and to the situation being addressed, though its inner workings cannot be plumbed.[4]

For another example, God has freely entered into relationships in such a way that God is not the only one who has something to do and the power with which to do it. The first words that God speaks to the newly created human beings (Gen 1:28), in developing what "image of God" means, involve commands that entail the possession and use of creaturely power: be fruitful, multiply, fill the earth, subdue, have dominion. God thereby freely chooses, for the sake of a genuine relationship, not to be the only one with power in the world, entrusting creatures in the use of their God-given powers. God moves over, as it were, and makes room for others to be what they were created to be. In honoring this basic character of the Creator-creature relationship, God chooses to exercise constraint and restraint in the exercise of power in the life of the world. This is a risky move for God, as becomes shortly evident in Genesis 3 and beyond; yet, even in the face of human sinfulness and its disastrous effects, God continues to entrust human beings with creaturely responsibilities and the power to carry them out (see Gen 3:23; Psalm 8). This honoring of relationship is also risky in that it opens God up to the charge of neglect; God may well look bad in the eyes of those who think that God should not exercise such constraint and should simply take charge of every detail in our lives. From another angle, it opens God up to the charge of violence, for God chooses to act in and through instruments who often use violent means (e.g., the Babylonian armies). God's efficacy in and through such less-than-perfect instruments will always have mixed results, and be less in accord with God's good will than what would have happened if God had chosen to use power alone.

This divine exercise of constraint is intensified in the story of the flood, wherein God promises never to visit the earth in flood-like ways again, sealed by the rainbow (Gen 8:21–22; 9:8–17). God thereby limits the divine options in responding to the world's sin and evil. Judgment will certainly occur so that sin and [348] evil do not go unchecked in the life of the world, but it will be limited in scope and intensity. Even more, the flood story witnesses to a new divine strategy in dealing with human wickedness and its ill effects. The God who so puts constraints upon the divine activity is the God whose response to human wickedness "grieved him to his heart" (Gen 6:5–6). Deciding to go with a wicked world come what may, with all of the suffering and evil that that will mean for individuals and communities, means for God a continuing grieving of the heart (see Ps 78:40; Eph

---

4. For a thorough study of biblical prayer in terms of divine-human relationality, see Samuel Balentine, *Prayer in the Hebrew Bible: The Drama of the Divine-Human Dialogue* (Minneapolis: Fortress, 1993); see also Patrick D. Miller, "Prayer as Persuasion," *WW* 13/9 (1993), especially pp. 361–62.

4:30). For the sake of the continued life of the world, indeed for the sake of its salvation, God bears that grief and suffering within the divine self (see Isa 43:23–25; Hos 11:8–9). The reader of the New Testament knows that this divine way of being with and for the world is supremely embodied in Jesus the Christ.

II. The Whence and Whither of Suffering

The biblical material, too, asks the questions "Whence?" and "Whither?" and almost precisely in those terms. Indeed, these kinds of questions are not simply addressed in more general ways; they are brought directly into the presence of God. God engages those questions and is moved to respond.

The biblical laments are filled with questions of "Why?" and "How?" regarding both individual and communal suffering situations (e.g., Psalms 13; 44). Even Jesus voices that kind of question from the cross (Mark 15:34).[5] Key figures such as Abraham, Moses, and Jeremiah sharply question God regarding such issues (e.g., Gen 18:25; Exod 32:11–14; Jer 12:1–4), and in each case God responds and in varying ways. Job also confronts God with questions and challenges regarding his suffering situation (e.g., Job 23:1–7), and God evaluates Job's speaking as "right" (Job 42:7).[6] Challenging questions addressed to God regarding issues of suffering and evil are deeply set within the biblical tradition in which we stand. Even more, books such as Job and Ecclesiastes, and segments of several others (e.g, Psalms 49; 73), move beyond the voicing of laments and questions in the midst of suffering to struggle in more intellectual ways with the theological issues involved. These biblical traditions invite their readers to engage in reflections on these matters with equal rigor, sharp probing, and intellectual integrity.

Regarding the "whence" of suffering, the biblical material permits us to make several distinctions,[7] though without suggesting that every suffering experience can somehow be named or gathered in these terms. At the same time, a possible discernment of the specific "whence" can importantly shape the nature of the pastoral or theological or ethical response to the question of "whither." [349]

1. Human beings are created with limits—of intelligence, agility, and strength. When we stretch those limits (in, say, education or sports), we

---

5. On the importance of biblical lament, see Walter Brueggemann, "The Costly Loss of Lament," *JSOT* 36 (1986): 57–71; Daniel Simundson, *Faith under Fire* (Minneapolis: Augsburg, 1980).

6. On issues of God and suffering in Job, see my "God in the Book of Job," *Currents in Theology and Mission* 26 (1999): 86–93.

7. For an earlier formulation, see my *About the Bible: Short Answers to Big Questions* (Minneapolis: Augsburg, 1999), 82–85. I am indebted to Douglas John Hall, *God and Human Suffering: An Exercise in the Theology of the Cross* (Minneapolis: Augsburg, 1986), 53–67, for prompting this type of reflection.

may suffer for the sake of gain. If such suffering serves life, it can be called good, and part of God's intention for the creation. Or, when we test those limits (in, say, climbing), we may suffer (in, say, a fall), not because we sin but because we make mistakes, or someone else does. Accidents happen. God has not created a risk-free world (for example, the law of gravity is both gift and danger). Importantly, as noted, God has assumed risks as well. Sin, however, can intensify the risk (for example, we may fall because we are inebriated).

2. God has created a dynamic world; earthquakes, volcanoes, glaciers, storms, bacteria, and viruses have their role to play in this becoming of the world. This is an orderly process in many ways, but randomness also plays a role; in the words of Eccl 9:11, "time and chance happen to them all." Because we are part of this interconnected world, we may get in the way of these processes and get hurt by them. One thinks of the randomness of the gene pool or tragic encounters with certain storms or viruses. Sin, however, can intensify the encounter and the associated suffering (for example, improper use of alcohol by a mother-to-be can damage the fetus).

3. Individual sins can cause suffering to those who commit them because God made a world in which our actions have consequences for both individuals and communities, though not in some mechanistic fashion. The Bible names these effects as divine judgment, as God, usually in non-forensic ways, sees to the workings of the created moral order and mediates "the fruit of their schemes" (e.g., through the Babylonian armies [Jer 6:19; 21:14] or authorities more generally [Rom 13:4]).[8]

4. We often experience suffering, not because of something we have done, but because of what others have done to us. The Israelites in Egypt suffered because of the harsh policies of others. Importantly, as one thinks of directions for response in other oppressive situations, God did not advise the Israelites to endure their suffering, but moved to get them out of that abusive situation, the results of which are called "salvation" (Exod 15:3). Some of the sharpest indictments of human sinfulness and announcements of divine judgment are directed at those who abuse the less fortunate neighbor (e.g., Exod 22:21–28).[9]

5. We also suffer because we belong to communities that have had a long history of sinfulness with the result that its effects, which can be named "evil," are integrated into the very structures of our life together. Manifested in such realities as ageism, racism, and sexism, everyone will make

---

8. On the contingent character of divine wrath and judgment, see the excellent discussion by Abraham Heschel, *The Prophets* (San Francisco: Harper & Row, 1962), 279–98.

9. On issues of moral order, see Klaus Koch, "Is There a Doctrine of Retribution in the Old Testament?" in *Theodicy in the Old Testament* (ed. James Crenshaw; Philadelphia: Fortress, 1983); Patrick Miller, *Sin and Judgment in the Prophets* (Chico, CA: Scholars Press, 1983).

their own contribution to these [350] systemic evils to be experienced by coming generations![10] In thinking about these forms of evil taking on a life of their own, we move toward biblical thinking about the demonic. In the latest Old Testament texts and into the New Testament there emerges something approaching a limited cosmic dualism (Satan). This reality is represented as a metaphysical power that stands temporally (not eternally) between God and world, opposing and subverting God's work. In terms of the development of such thinking, one may speak of anti-God forces, initially embodied in historical figures (e.g., pharaoh), which in theological reflection over time are thrown onto a cosmic screen, taking on metaphysical proportions (see Isa 30:7; Ezek 29:3–5; 32:2–8). Or, in more objective terms, a build-up of historical evil over time becomes systemic, affecting even cosmic spheres.

6. Suffering may be the effect of a vocation to which we have been called by God (see 1 Pet 2:21; Mark 8:34). Such vocational suffering, which is explicitly taken up for the sake of the neighbor and could be avoided, may be called the will of God (see Isa 53:10). The God who calls others to a vocation that may entail suffering is no stranger to that kind of vocation and to that suffering. The God who "knows" the sufferings of Israel (Exod 3:7) has entered deeply into our suffering world in Jesus Christ and made it his own so that neither suffering nor evil constitutes a final word for the creation.

God is linked to each of these types of suffering in varying ways, and how that linkage is made with respect to specific situations will shape pastoral directions to be taken. God creates a world with risks and challenges wherein suffering is part of life apart from sin,[11] but also a world wherein sin is possible and can intensify that suffering experience and bring still further suffering in its train. God sustains a world wherein sin and its effects are carried along and are built more deeply into the structures of existence over time. God judges the world in and through the created moral order, acting within the interplay of human actions and their consequences, so that sin and evil do not go unchecked in the life of the creation. God saves the world by taking its suffering into the very heart of the divine life, bearing it there, and then wearing it in the form of a cross.

---

10. For varying ways in which the Old Testament speaks of the perseverance and power of evil, see Jon Levenson, *Creation and the Persistence of Evil: The Jewish Drama of Divine Omnipotence* (San Francisco: Harper & Row, 1988).

11. The discussion of Hall, *God and Human Suffering*, 53–67, is most helpful in drawing out the biblical themes that support this assertion.

Suffering God and Sovereign God in Exodus: A Collision of Images

A survey of Exodus studies from the perspective of their God-talk reveals a predominant use of sovereignty metaphors.[1] It is a sovereignty commonly defined in a certain way. God is not only king, lord, and judge, but also one who stands outside of the world and speaks and acts on the creation with absolute authority. Or, God is presented not only as one who takes the initiative, articulates a purpose and sets the agenda, but also as one who is in total control of nature and history, who brooks no opposition and bends every power in heaven and earth to fulfill the divine word and will.[2] I would contend that sovereignty cannot be so defined and still be true to the texts; it needs some correction in view of other metaphors for God in Exodus. Moreover, it is not common for such studies to be mindful of the range of suffering images for God to be found in Exodus, that is, those metaphors that reflect a divine entry into the sphere of the created such that God and God's ways with the world are genuinely affected thereby.[3]

This essay was originally published in *Horizons in Biblical Theology* 11 (1989): 31–56.

1. These reflections emerge from the writing of a commentary on Exodus, in the Interpretation series (Louisville: John Knox, 1991), as well as a critique of my book *The Suffering of God* (Philadelphia: Fortress, 1984), namely, that I gave insufficient attention to how the suffering and monarchical images of God were to be related. This paper begins to address that issue.

2. As examples, see M. Sternberg, *The Poetics of Biblical Narrative* (Bloomington: Indiana University Press, 1985), 101: The Bible "not only assumes or deploys but also inculcates a model of reality where God exercises absolute sway on the universe (nature, culture, history) in conspicuous isolation and transcendence"; yet, strangely, he can also speak of God as one who "at times yields to despair" (p. 109). T. W. Mann, *The Book of the Torah: The Narrative Integrity of the Pentateuch* (Atlanta: John Knox, 1988), 84–85: "Perhaps the most important way [of exalting Yahweh] is to show that Yahweh is in control of events in the narrative from the outset." Even in the opening two chapters of Exodus, where God is rarely noted, it is not uncommon for such language to be used. See, for example, the statement in Cheryl Exum's fine study regarding Moses' mother entrusting him to the boat on the river: "Matters are now in the hands of the deity." But the narrative states only that Moses is in the hands of women, especially Pharaoh's daughter ("'You Shall Let Every Daughter Live': A Study of Exodus 1:8–2:10," *Semeia* 28 [1983]: 77).

3. I use the word *suffering* in a broad sense, encompassing such matters as receptivity, affectivity, vulnerability, pathos, passion, empathy, genuine interaction with the world, dependence on the created orders of being, and even self-limitation, if carefully defined. The word *suffering* makes clear that this is a matter of actuality for God, not just potentiality. Moreover, as will be made clear, suffering is an active, not a passive word. For recent

A few scholars have lifted up the role of Moses, and Jon Levenson has worked in helpful ways with divine and human interrelationships in the Sinai texts.[4] But, a sustained look at the God of the book of Exodus, especially taking into account the suffering metaphors, remains to be undertaken.[5]

Out of an interest in content issues, I will be all too brief in outlining my approach. My look at some pertinent Exodus texts proceeds on the basis of the final form of the text. The interpreter is therein faced with a composite text addressed to an unknown historical setting. At the least, however, this redaction is not socially or theologically disinterested; something is at stake for the redactor, but what is at stake is uncertain at the present level of inquiry. This theological study may help get at that; an initial probe suggests an exilic provenance, in which captive Israel finds itself in straits similar to its forebears in Egypt and in the aftermath of the golden calf apostasy. Israel in exile stands in need of *both* deliverance and forgiveness. [32]

While this layered text shows linguistic and rhetorical signs of attempts to unify the material, it has not been at the expense of flattening it out into a narrative that is theologically tension-free. One is faced with some jarring theological juxtapositions—often recognized by source critics. For example, the pyrotechnic theophany of chap. 19 in which God is unapproachable, even dangerous, is set alongside the quiet theophany of chap. 24, in which God is quite approachable and no special precautions need be taken.

The relationship between theology and narrative continues to be a problem of some consequence.[6] We learn from a number of Old Testament texts that story and generalization do not stand opposed to one another; in fact, they may be integrated (e.g., Exod 34:6–7). While not many statements about God move within a more abstract sphere, the fact that they exist at all indicates that the God who is the subject of sentences in the narrative has a significance in some way related to those abstractions. In other words, we have an *inner–Old Testament warrant* to engage in more general reflections about the God who is rendered in the story. That there is a certain deliberateness regarding the God who is so rendered can be seen, for

discussions of divine suffering, see Paul Fiddes, *The Creative Suffering of God* (Oxford: Clarendon, 1988); Warren McWilliams, *The Passion of God: Divine Suffering in Contemporary Protestant Theology* (Macon: Mercer University Press, 1985).

4. See George Coats, *Moses: Heroic Man, Man of God* (Sheffield: JSOT Press, 1988); Jon Levenson, *Creation and the Persistence of Evil* (San Francisco: Harper & Row, 1988).

5. One example of a helpful, if isolated reflection is that of Moshe Greenberg: "Those who are brought close to God retain their integrity even in moments of closest contact. They are not merely passive recipients, but active, even opposing respondents. There is true address and response, genuine give and take. The human partner has a say in shaping the direction and outcome of the events" (*Understanding Exodus* [New York: Behrman, 1969]), 94.

6. See my initial suggestions in "The Repentance of God: A Key to Evaluating Old Testament God-Talk," *HBT* 10 (1988): 47–70; *The Suffering of God: An Old Testament Perspective* (Philadelphia: Fortress, 1984), 24–29.

example, in the virtual absence of God-talk in some Exodus narratives (e.g., 1:1–2:22; 5:4–21).

One way to look at such theological matters is to probe the God-talk in the various narrative units in terms of the metaphoric semantic fields represented and then explore possible interrelationships. I here single out suffering and sovereignty.[7] I believe this probe will show how *common understandings* of sovereignty in Exodus (and elsewhere) are subverted by suffering metaphors, and an understanding of sovereignty more congruent with the text can emerge.

I have come away from my study of Exodus with two primary theological convictions: (I) A theology of creation shapes the book of Exodus in a fundamental way; (II) The God of Exodus is both sovereign and suffering. We will take a brief look at the first in order to set the stage for the second. The way in which God is perceived to be related to the world will shape what is impossible in terms of talk of God's sovereignty and suffering. [33]

I. A Theology of Creation

Exodus presents the redemption from Egypt within a context informed and undergirded by a God who acts as Lord of heaven and earth. It is the Creator God who redeems Israel from Egypt. Until recently, the interpretation of Exodus has been overwhelmed by attention to the theme of redemption. So much so, that standard introductions to the Old Testament often start at this point. The theme of creation is often ignored or noticed only in bits and pieces of text, with no overarching importance for the interpretation of the book as a whole. Certainly von Rad's important article from the 1930's has had an inordinate influence at just this point, with its claim regarding the secondary role of creation in Israel's theological formulations.[8] Recent discussions, however, have commonly shown the inadequacy of this claim.[9]

Generally, God's work in *creation provides the basic categories and interpretive clues* for what happens in redemption. God's work in creation has been shown to be life-giving, life-preserving, and life-blessing (e.g. 1:7, 12, 20). What God does in redemption is in the service of these endangered divine goals in and for the creation. The hymnic celebration of that redemptive act in Exodus 15 is permeated with creation-talk, in terms of vocabulary, structure, and theme. Not only is an *experience* of God's work as creator necessary for participation in the exodus—otherwise there would be no people

---

7. This presupposes my discussion of anthropomorphic metaphors in *The Suffering of God*, 5–12.

8. Gerhard von Rad, "The Theological Problem of the Old Testament Doctrine of Creation," in *Creation in the Old Testament* (ed. B. W. Anderson; Philadelphia: Fortress, 1984), 53–64.

9. E.g., these two articles in *Creation*: H. H. Schmid, "Creation, Righteousness, and Salvation: 'Creation Theology' as the Broad Horizon of Biblical Theology," 102–17; Claus Westermann, "Biblical Reflections on Creator-Creation," 90–101.

to redeem, an *understanding* of God's work as creator is indispensable for the proper interpretation of what happens—there would be no exodus as *we know it* without it having been informed by that understanding.

The basic creation themes in Exodus are:

(a) A creation theology provides the *cosmic purpose* behind God's redemptive activity on Israel's behalf. While the liberation of Israel is the focus of God's activity, it is not the ultimate purpose. The deliverance of Israel is ultimately for the sake of all creation. As 9:16 states: "I have let you live so that my name may be declared throughout all the earth." The issue for God finally is not that God's name be made known to Israel, but that it be declared to the entire earth. God's purpose in these events is creation-wide. What is at stake is God's [34] mission to the world, for as 9:29 and 19:5 (cf. 8:22; 9:14) put it, "all the earth is God's." Hence, the *public* character of these events is a very important theme throughout the book. It is crucial that all the world be able to observe what God is doing for Israel, for they are the ultimate object of that activity (see 15:14–16; 18:1, 8–12).

(b) God's redemptive activity is set in terms of a *creational need*. The fulfillment of God's creational purposes in the growth and multiplication of Israel is endangered by Pharaoh's attempted subversion thereof. If Pharaoh persists in his anti-life policies at precisely that point at which God has begun to actualize the promise of creation (1:7) — cutting off Israel's fruitfulness (1:8–14), then God's very purposes in creation are being subverted, and God's creational mission will not be able to be realized. God's work in and through Moses, climaxing in Israel's crossing of the sea on "dry land," constitutes God's efforts of re-creation, returning creation to a point where God's mission can once again be taken up.

(c) God's redemptive activity is *cosmic in its effects*. Generally speaking, the Lord of heaven and earth is active throughout Exodus, from acts of blessing to the use of aspects of nature in the plagues, the sea crossing, and the wilderness wanderings. More specifically, Exodus 15 confesses that God's victory at the sea is not simply a local or a historical phenomenon, but a cosmic one. God's defeat of the powers of chaos results, not simply in Israel's liberation, but in the reign of God over the entire cosmos (15:18).[10]

(d) God's calling of Israel is given *creation-wide scope*. The theme of "all the earth is God's" is picked up again in 19:4–6, a divine invitation to Israel to be a kingdom of priests and a holy nation.[11] Israel is called out from among other nations and is commissioned to a task on behalf of God's

---

10. In some ways, Exodus 15 is to the Old Testament what Colossians is to the New Testament. Exodus 15 is also one of the texts appointed for Easter Sunday. Such expressions of triumph must not take away from the reality of the pain and suffering experienced on the way to that point in the journey. This is particularly important for those readers, such as the exiles, for whom the triumph can only be hoped for.

11. My understanding of covenant in Exodus 19–24 is in terms of a vocational covenant within the context of the Abrahamic covenant. See my commentary, *Exodus*, for details.

earth. Israel is to function among those nations as a priest functions in a religious community. Israel's witness to God's redemptive activity (18:8–12) and the obedience of the law is finally for the sake of a universal mission.[12]

(e) Finally, God's own relationship to the creation is seen in terms of an *immanental involvement*. As we shall note below, God has not chosen the way of *radical* transcendence. God has entered into the very life of the world and is fully engaged there on behalf of the [35] divine purposes. The primary "form" in which God has chosen to be so engaged is in the human form of the theophany— from the call of Moses (3:1–6) to the sea crossing (14:19) to Sinai (24:9–11). This action bespeaks God's: (i) identity with human beings, a sharing in the human condition; (ii) willingness to undergo change, taking on a non-divine form and directly experiencing what that entails; (iii) vulnerability, risking a response in the human encounter that is other than faith or obedience. But God does not thereby give up sovereignty; indeed, it is a sign of strength for God to do just this. God's sovereignty is made manifest in assuming a vulnerable form in the midst of the world.[13] This leads to the next section.

II. God Both Sovereign and Suffering

Generally, Exodus presents God as highly engaged in the events of which it speaks, though a more unobtrusive, behind-the-scenes activity is evident in chaps. 1–2, 5, and 18. Images of divine sovereignty are certainly prominent. For example, God's lordship is evident in the proclamation of the law and the call to obedience; God's judging is experienced by the Egyptians. God's kingship, however, is explicitly confirmed only once (15:18), somewhat surprising given the sovereignty issues in the narrative. At the same time, there seems to be a difference in the effectiveness of God's activity, indeed the very nature of the divine sovereignty, depending upon whether God is working in history or nature. We look at each in turn.

(a) *God's sovereignty over nature.* God's relationship to nature is apparently conceived in terms of sovereign control. God seems to be able to work in and through the natural order at will, wherever and whenever God wills to accomplish the divine purpose. Witness the plagues, the use of wind and sea, the provision of food and water in the wilderness, the natural pyrotechnics at Mount Sinai. The natural order is not resistant to the divine will; it "fulfills his command" (Ps 148:8).

At the same time, the narrative introduces at least four qualifications to this divine sovereignty in nature. [36]

(i) The divine working in nature is usually in coordination with human activity. Hence, the use of the rod by Moses/Aaron in the plagues or at the

---

12. The discussion of E. W. Nicholson, *God and His People: Covenant and Theology in the Old Testament* (Oxford: Clarendon, 1986), 172–75, is helpful here.

13. For further discussion of these aspects of theophany, see my *Suffering of God*, 79–106.

sea crossing or in the wilderness is an integral element in what happens in the natural order. Human agency is especially clear in the sweetening of the bitter waters and the provision of water from the rock (15:22–27; 17:1–7). Or, in the four cases where a plague is removed, God acts "according to the word of Moses" (8:13). There is a complex understanding of agency in connection with each of the plagues. Moses and Aaron would not be effective without God's power working in and through them, and God is dependent on Moses and Aaron, working in the world of nature in and through that which is not divine.

(ii) The divine use of nature is not "supernatural" or "unnatural," but congruent with what is possible for nature to become if properly used or improperly exploited. For example, the provision of food and water in the wilderness is, in each instance, a divine use of normal creational processes (e.g., manna and quail). Or, the strong east wind pushes the sea back. Or, the plagues (including the final plague) are instances of divine judgment in which the natural orders are caught up in a sin/consequence vortex, either as cause or victim. Pharaoh's anti-life measures against God's creation have unleashed chaotic powers that threaten the very creation God intended.

Without going into detail, those elements of the natural order that are on the *victimizing* side are all out of kilter with their created way of being (much beyond any "pain" built into the creation). They all appear in distorted form. Water is no longer water; light and darkness are no longer separated; diseases of people and animals run amok; insects and amphibians swarm out of control. While everything is unnatural in the sense of being beyond the bounds of life as created, "hypernatural" (that is, nature in excess) may better capture that sense of the natural breaking through its created limits, not functioning as God intended. This is a picture of creation gone berserk, reverting to a state of chaos. The theological grounding for this is an understanding of the symbiotic relationship between moral order and cosmic order, where the divine judgments grow out of, are intrinsically related to the (evil) deed. In effect, God gives Pharaoh up to reap the "natural" consequences of his anti-creation deeds. Moderns who look in the face of the consequences of an abuse of the environment, e.g., the depletion of the ozone layer or the misuse of atomic energy, know something of what this is about. A kind of hypernaturalness is often the result.

(iii) The divine use of nature is, therefore, not arbitrary, but responds to specific situations in the created order. The plagues are not some capricious divine move, but congruent with the anti-creational sins of Pharaoh. Or, the use of the wind and the waves in the sea crossing is congruent with the cosmic nature of the struggle. The battle was not simply against "flesh and blood," but against the cosmic forces of evil, embodied in the Pharaoh. (At the same time, Pharaoh is an historical figure who is individually responsible.)

(iv) The factors of timing, placement and range for both plague execution and removal no doubt give testimony to the divine control of nature, but these factors are also to be related to the stylized form of the narrative. The formally controlled character of the narrative and the hyperbolic use of language (cf. the pervasive use of *kol,* all/every) suggests a special literary purpose, even the possibility of a dramatic setting for this material. While this does not finally take away the witness to divine control, it introduces an element of qualification.

The upshot of this is that the language of divine sovereignty is certainly appropriate, though not in an unqualified way. God does not act in nature in ways totally independent of the created order of being. We cannot factor out the complexities of the divine, human and cosmic interaction, but God's use of nature certainly exhibits a strong element of rule and control.

(b) *God's sovereignty over the human order.* This order of divine rule seems to be differently conceived, in terms other than absolute rule or control. Unlike nature, human beings have sufficient freedom and power to be resistant to the word and will of God. This becomes a point where the metaphors of divine suffering become prominent in the narrative, subverting a common understanding of sovereignty in Exodus, while enabling a more appropriate view to emerge. The hardening of Pharaoh's heart has tended to crowd out consideration of God's relationship to other human beings in Exodus. [38] Placing Pharaoh in this larger relational context may help shed some light on this perennial discussion. Among the many examples one might cite, let me take up four types:

(i) *The divine decision* (3:7–10; cf. 2:25). This divine word to Moses, part of the first word from God in Exodus, is *programmatic;* the narrator's report in 2:24–25 helps establish this. *The God who acts in the narrative is understood to be the kind of God portrayed here.* This divine word is in the first person, coming directly from God's own heart and will. Characteristic of this word is an interweaving of metaphors of sovereignty and suffering, signaling a way in which subsequent God-talk is to be interpreted.

God's sovereignty is evident in the divine initiative, the setting of the agenda, the will to deliver Israel, and the announced ability to accomplish this. Alongside this, however, is a sphere of God-talk uncommonly related to sovereignty.[14] God sees Israel's afflictions and "knows" their sufferings. For God to "know" the people's sufferings testifies to God's *experience* of this suffering, indeed God's *intimate* experience. God has so entered into their sufferings as to have experienced what they are having to endure. God does not remain safe and secure in some heavenly abode, untouched

---

14. The kingship ideal in Israel (and the ancient Near East) includes such themes as the care and protection of the poor and needy (cf. Psalm 72). At the same time, it would be over-extending the metaphor, and even reductionistic, to suggest that every instance of the divine pathos is interpretive of sovereignty metaphors. Moreover, the way in which such metaphors function (for any people) is decisively informed by the experience of imperfectly realized forms of human sovereignty. Other metaphors are needed in order to realize what shape the divine sovereignty truly entails.

by the sorrows of the world. God is not portrayed here as a typical monarch dealing with the issue through subordinates or at some distance. God does not look at the suffering from the outside as through a window; God knows it from the inside. God is internally related to the suffering, entering fully into the oppressive situation and making it God's own. For God to *know* suffering is, to follow the metaphorical grain, to allow suffering to enter deeply into the divine being.

Yet, while God suffers with the people, God is not powerless in the face of it. However much God's work may be complicated by it, the actual situation does not finally define what is possible for God. This evidences the divine sovereignty. Even more, the divine suffering is in itself a powerful force, focusing the divine energies on the situation. But, for God to deal with such a situation by entering into it, and working on it from the inside rather than from the outside, charts certain directions for the nature of the divine involvement and [39] delimits the divine possibilities. Or, as will be made clear below, sovereignty and suffering qualify one another.

It is also to be noted in this text that God does not act alone in bringing Israel out of Egypt; both God and Moses are the subject of the exodus (3:8, 10; cf. 6:13, 26–27; 32:7). The divine sovereignty is seen in that God takes the initiative, invites Moses, sets the purpose, and is engaged in the task. But God does not act alone and depends on Moses in carrying out the tasks involved. This means that God gives up total control of the ensuing events. Responsibility has been placed in Moses' hands to do with as he will. God will now have to work in and through Moses' frailties as well as strengths. This will mean something less than what would have been possible had God acted alone. Israel recognizes the importance of this non-divine involvement in its post-exodus confession (14:31): "they believed in the Lord and in his servant Moses."

(ii) *Divine engagement with individuals. The five women in chaps. 1–2.* The virtual absence of God as subject in these chapters (though enough is said to place God on the scene) introduces one way in which God is active in the Exodus narrative. Ironies abound in these chapters, including the decision of Pharaoh to let daughters live, with the effect that their activity thwarts his plans. This also becomes a point of *divine irony.* God uses the weak, what is low and despised in that world, to shame the strong (see Jer 9:23; 1 Cor 1:26–29). Rather than using power as it is usually exercised in the world to carry out the divine purpose, God works in and through persons who have no obvious power; indeed, the women chosen are unlikely candidates for the exercise of power. The high role given Pharaoh's daughter (a non-Israelite at that!) is seen in the direct verbal and thematic parallels between her activity and that of God in chaps. 3–18: she "comes down," "sees" the child, "hears" its cry, takes pity on him, draws him out of the water, and provides for his daily needs.

In such moves, God opens himself up to risk and vulnerability, for these persons could fail and God would have to begin again. God, whose plan for Israel's future rests squarely on the shoulders of a baby in a fragile basket, places the preservation of that future in the hands [40] of five lowly women. Yet, they prove to be highly effective against ruthless forms of systemic power, and God is not the subject of a single verb in their various undertakings. God works throughout this section of Exodus in unobtrusive, unlikely and vulnerable ways.

This sets the stage for what follows. While God will fill the scene more evidently in the ensuing narrative, these opening chapters provide a hermeneutical base from which one is to interpret the fundamental character of that divine activity.

Moses.   The dialogical interchange between God and Moses in chaps. 3–6 consists of eight objections raised by Moses to the divine commission, with various divine responses. Moses is anything but deferential; disagreement, argument, and even challenge play an important role. This response on Moses' part is due to the kind of God who has confronted him. God's word to Moses has been of such a character that it draws the other into a genuine conversation. The divine holiness (3:6) is of such a nature that it invites rather than repels human response. God does not demand a self-effacing Moses, but draws him out and works with him, "warts and all." The oft-noted speech disability of Moses adds an ironic twist to this point. It is not only a human being that challenges God; it is an inarticulate one who does so and holds his own!

Moreover, God treats the dialogue with Moses with integrity and honors his insights as important ingredients for the shaping of the task. God is clearly the authority, but God's approach is non-authoritarian in nature. God will move with Moses, even adapting original divine plans (e.g., the role of Aaron) in view of Moses' considerations. God's way into the future is thus not dictated solely by the divine word and will. God has now placed that word and will in the hands of another to do with what he will.[15] That is for God a risky venture, fraught with negative possibilities. At the same time, this enhances rather than compromises the kind of sovereignty which Exodus wishes to claim for God.

Even more, it is Moses' persistence that occasions a greater fullness in the divine revelation. Human questions find an openness in God and lead to fuller knowledge. God thus reveals himself, not simply at the divine initiative, but in interaction with a questioning human [41] party. Simple deference or passivity in the presence of God would close down the revelatory possibilities. It is important to note that God is not thereby de-mystified

---

15. See the comparable statement of von Rad, *Old Testament Theology* (New York: Harper & Row, 1965), 2:73: "What makes it [prophecy] such a tremendous responsibility is the fact that the prophet is thus the one who puts the will of Jahweh into effect: Jahweh thereafter commits himself to stand by the decision of his ambassador."

through further understanding. In fact, the more one understands God, the more the divine inexhaustibility becomes apparent.[16]

From another perspective, this text witnesses to God's initial lack of success in persuading Moses to take up his calling. All of God's persuasive powers are brought to bear on Moses and he remains unconvinced for some time. God's best efforts do not meet with instant success. Whatever power God uses in this encounter, it does not overpower Moses. Hence, in 4:10–17, in the face of Moses' resistance, God must resort to Plan B, calling Aaron to be Moses' voice. Obviously, God is not delighted with this option; in fact, God is angry. But God goes with what is possible; using Aaron is now the best option available to God. God always aims for the best in every situation, but God must often work with options that are less than the best (witness Aaron's later failure as a leader in chap. 32). God often has to accept what people do with the powers they have been given, even to resist God's efforts to persuade.

This dialogue is picked up again in chaps. 32–34. Once more Moses enters into debate with God, this time regarding the initial divine response to Israel's apostasy. In view of Moses' argumentation, God reverses himself with respect to the announced judgement (32:14).[17] What Moses has to contribute counts with this God. *God has so entered into relationship with him that God is not the only one who has something important to say.* In fact, the ongoing conversation in chaps. 32–34 issues in a number of shifts in the divine response to what has happened, climaxing in the decision to accompany Israel on its journeyings and to renew the covenant.

In this context, God proclaims to Moses the most basic characteristics of the divine nature (34:6–7): merciful and gracious, slow to anger, abounding in steadfast love and faithfulness, keeping steadfast love, forgiving iniquity and transgression and sin, but not neglecting just judgment. It is noteworthy that this common confession, in which *God* defines the most basic divine character, is filled with metaphoric language that does not bespeak kingship, judgeship or lordship, at least [42] in terms of the basic grain of those images. The final phrases do speak of judging, and that is not unimportant, but this is not presented as a constant divine attribute and the other images fill the scene. And, yet, the very way in which God chooses to exercise those attributes bespeaks sovereignty (see 33:19).

This discussion should also be related to the text's clear indication that God's knowledge of the future is limited (4:8–9). In the midst of their continuing dialogue, God acknowledges to Moses the uncertainty of the people's response by repeatedly using conditional language. *If* they do not

---

16. See Eberhard Jüngel, *God as the Mystery of the World* (Grand Rapids: Eerdmans, 1983), 330: "The more one understands God the more mysterious God becomes. And the deeper one penetrates this mystery the more interesting it becomes."

17. On the divine repentance theme, see my "The Repentance of God."

believe the first sign, they may believe the second. *If* they do not believe these two signs or listen to Moses' voice, a third sign will be given. This suggests that God is certainly aware of the possibilities of their response; one might even say that God, given a thoroughgoing knowledge of Israel, knows what the response is likely to be. There will be no surprises for God in the sense of not anticipating what might happen. Yet, in God's own words, God does not finally know. It is possible that a spontaneous response on the part of the people will issue in a result different from what God now sees as probable.[18]

Pharaoh. The long history of interpretation associated with the hardening of Pharaoh's heart makes this issue more complex than it is. In this context, we can only give some basic directions.[19] The character of the above-noted divine-human interaction suggests that God is no more controlling of Pharaoh's will than of Moses' will. In fact, a certain parallel is evident between Moses' numerous objections and those of Pharaoh; in both cases God struggles at length with the will of a human leader. Overall, the issue of the hardening of Pharaoh's heart is best explained via Jeremiah, where the theme of hardening is related to the people of Israel (e.g., 7:26).

Both God and Pharaoh are subjects of the hardening verbs, and in the plague sequence, God first becomes the subject only after the sixth plague. Even then, God's hardening does not control the situation (note that God has to harden repeatedly), as Pharaoh's repentance of sin makes clear (9:27; 10:16; note the *narrator's* acknowledgment of "sin" in 9:34). Finally, however, it may be said that God's hardening activity gathers momentum and drives the judgmental events [43] to their disastrous end (as in the fall of Jerusalem). God's activity hardens Pharaoh's own obduracy to the point of no return. Ps 81:11–12 captures this sense: "But my people did not listen to my voice; Israel would have none of me. So I gave them over to their stubborn hearts, to follow their own counsels." Thus, there is a limited amount of deterministic language that one can use at the end of the narrative (if you come too close to the falls in your canoe, the trip over the edge becomes inevitable). But Pharaoh's own decisions have been important in moving the course of events to this point.

Generally, the struggle with Pharaoh would not redound much to the glory of God if it were only a matter of God's outwitting a windup toy. For God's victory to mean something, the opposition cannot be a pushover. If Pharaoh is a puppet in the hands of God, then God's renown is not particularly enhanced, one of the divine objectives of the narrative. As elsewhere in the Old Testament, God does not rid the world of evil with a snap of the divine finger.

18. For further Old Testament examples, see my *The Suffering of God*, 45–49.
19. See my commentary on *Exodus* for discussion.

Certainly one basic concern of chaps. 1–15 is who will finally be recognized as the sovereign one, Pharaoh or Yahweh. But a parallel issue is: *what is the appropriate nature of sovereignty?* Pharaoh's and Yahweh's ways of being sovereign are often contrasted. To anticipate the discussion below: Yahweh's sovereignty is qualified by suffering, Pharaoh's is not. It is Pharaoh who is the unmoved mover.

More briefly, let me cite two spheres of divine activity that reveal a sovereignty that is less than absolute:

(iii) *The people of Israel* (13:17–21). More generally, one might cite the oft-noted movement of Israel from lament to praise in chaps. 1–15. The very shape of the narrative is such that God enters into an interresponding relationship with human beings.[20]

In this transitional passage, the narrator highlights the divine leading. God is concerned that Israel not take the most traveled route from Egypt to Canaan. The divine concern is that the people might change their mind if forced into battle. This shows that God must take into account prevailing socio-political forces as well as people's emotional make-up in charting a way into the future. One might expect that God, with all the power at the divine disposal, would not back off from leading the people into any situation. God would just mow the enemies [44] down! No, the human situation makes a difference regarding the divine possibilities, and hence affects the divine decisions. The exercise of the divine sovereignty in providential activity is thus shown to be of such a nature that it could not ignore or override whatever obstacles might come along. In fact, this divine concern suggests the possibility of failure; the people could decide to return to Egypt. Divine providence is thus shown not to stand over against careful divine planning in view of human circumstances.

(iv) *The world* (2:23–25). In this transitional passage, which moves quickly from earthly palace to heavenly throne, the narrator shows that happenings on the world scene make a difference with respect to the divine possibilities. When kings die, it makes a difference to God. The death of the king of Egypt provides for new possibilities or opportunities for God. Changes in world situations provide the occasion for change in God's way of relating to that world. The long period of waiting in Egypt, then, has been due not to some divine quietism, but to God's waiting for the right configuration of human and natural events to put a new level of activity together on Israel's behalf.

---

20. See Claus Westermann, *Elements of Old Testament Theology* (Atlanta: John Knox, 1982). See also the unpublished 1984 Heidelberg dissertation of Frederick Gaiser, "Songs in the Story." He states helpfully regarding this pattern: God's "guidance of history is pastoral, interested not so much in simply making things happen, but in bringing his people more closely into a trusting relationship with him and securing their ongoing existence."

Some general observations.   The net effect of the discussion to this point is that we have side by side in various Exodus narratives some strong uses of both sovereign language and suffering language. A theological consideration must ask how these metaphoric fields might be related to one another.

One of the issues with respect to images of God has to do with what may be called a metaphorical canon within the canon. Certain images of God are more central than are others; these then function to determine whether a given metaphor is appropriate, is being misused, has been exhausted, or is of low referential value, and how it is to be qualified. For example, one can claim that Hosea's metaphor of "dry rot" (5:12) for God has a low revelatory capacity by measuring it over against such "controlling" metaphors. The task is to sort through the images used in the Old Testament, seeking *by inner-biblical warrant* to determine those that are central. I have sought to show elsewhere[21] that such inner-biblical criteria would include: pervasiveness, distribution, and the nature of the genres and the traditions in which the metaphor is used. Extra-biblically, one might speak of these criteria: [45] how true they are to life; the richness of association in common human experience; their capacity to capture, organize, focus and communicate the experience of God. Clearly, metaphors from both the sovereignty and suffering metaphoric fields would belong among the "controlling" category of metaphors.

The neglect of the suffering metaphors in the history of God-talk shows, however, not only how difficult it has been to hold these metaphoric fields together in the same mind, but also that the metaphors of sovereignty have more often than not been *the* controlling sphere of images (see below). One effect of this has been that the sovereignty metaphors have commonly been left largely unqualified, with a consequent univocal reading of them. And one way to define *idolatry* is: a univocal reading of metaphors for God.[22] A recovery of the "controlling" status of the suffering metaphors will have a decisive effect on common understandings of sovereignty.

As we have shown, both of these spheres of language are interwoven in the book of Exodus. When one lets these metaphors engage one another, even struggle with one another, what sort of theological coherence becomes available? This is possible only if, in this engagement, these two metaphoric fields significantly qualify one another, with sovereignty qualifying suffering and suffering qualifying sovereignty. The end result is that suffering and sovereignty stand alongside one another in a metaphorical dialectic. *Suffering and sovereignty are internally related to one another in God, such that the sovereign God is always suffering and the suffering God is always sovereign.* Contextual factors, however, the needs of a given time and place,

---

21. "The Repentance of God," 52–59.

22. One might suggest that the theologies of the death of God in the 1960's were concerned precisely with this point.

may call for one metaphoric field to achieve some ascendancy over the other. Hence, given the present common understanding of sovereignty, suffering will have a more decisive effect on sovereignty than the other way round. Our study to this point has shown how the suffering images in Exodus subvert such a common understanding of sovereignty, correct our reading of the text, and help to lift up proper understandings.

In the first instance, the qualification of divine suffering that occurs in view of divine sovereignty particularizes the "is not" side of the metaphor drawn from human suffering. For example, God is not [46] overwhelmed by the experience; indeed, God is energized by it. God does not become incapacitated or stymied in the face of suffering; God is able to use suffering to find ways of moving into the future when all hope seems to have faded away. God suffers *as God;* hence, God's Godness is not adversely affected thereby. God's saving will does not waver. God's purposes for the creation remain constant. God's love continues steadfast. God's faithfulness perdures in the face of human disloyalty.

In the second instance, suffering qualifies sovereignty. Having decided to relate to the world in such a way as to be genuinely affected thereby, God becomes vulnerable. The "is not" side of metaphors such as king, judge or lord thereby comes into view. God will work in the world in and through that which is not God with all the potential for disappointment, frustration and failure that that entails. Even more, God will not pull back into a sovereignty without suffering, even temporarily, for that would break the divine resolve to be so related to the creation.[23] This means that common understandings of divine sovereignty must be transformed in view of a God who resolves to suffer so.

Let me work briefly with three recent studies as a way of illustrating how this perspective might be used in an evaluative way as well as help us move this discussion along.

(1) E. W. Nicholson.[24] This book, helpfully concerned with the development of covenant as a theological idea in Israel, has a major concern with texts in Exodus 19–24. I am most interested in sparring with Nicholson in his chapter on the "distinctiveness of Israel's faith," particularly on the understanding of God which emerges. A few representative theological statements (emphases mine):

> "In the Old Testament Yahweh is creator but *radically* transcends his creation. The *distance between him and the human world is polarized"* (p. 200). He speaks of "a *radical* differentiation between the divine and the human world, between God and his creation" (p. 207). "Such 'disenchantment of the world' [elsewhere 'desacralization'] is represented by . . . the decisive

---

23. Sternberg (*Poetics of Biblical Narrative*) seems at times to exercise this option. For example, God retains "the privilege of intervening at any moment" or can engage in a "suspension of omnipotence" (p. 110).

24. *God and His People*, 191–217.

break with the typical creation-theology of the ancient Near East: God is not continuous with his [47] creation, *does not permeate it,* is not to be identified with, or represented by, anything within it, but stands *outside* his creation confronting it with his righteous will" (pp. 207–8). "The making of the covenant was not only upon Yahweh's initiative; more than that, he himself was a partner to it . . . life for Israel was understood as *fellowship* with Yahweh who had entered a covenant with this people" (p. 215). He also wants to speak of Israel's *"free* decision to be obedient and faithful to him" (p. 216).

The predominant images for Nicholson are certainly those of sovereignty, but it is sovereignty informed by a view of the relationship between God and world such that they are "radically" distinct. But, how is it theologically possible to use words like "partner" or "fellowship" for God if God stands "outside" the creation? How can a "radically transcendent" God be a "partner" in any genuine sense? That's having your cake and eating it, too! In these formulations God and creation are so disjunctive that any contact between the two could only be seen in terms of lightning bolt or laser beam. The only way in which "partner" and "fellowship" could fit with this is if they have an esoteric meaning quite removed from their normal senses. In other words, if language such as "partner" is going to be used, and Nicholson is quite correct in doing so, it will qualify sovereignty in a fundamental way, and the radically disjunctive language will have to be set aside. Nicholson is to be commended for joining the crowd in breaking away from treaty or agreement or contractual language for covenant, but he also needs to break with the kind of divine sovereignty language often so much a part of that view of covenant.

Moreover, the strong element on human choice and free decision in his discussion has a sharp ironic sense. The only way in which one can have such a strong view of human freedom in the face of such a sovereign God is with a heavy dose of deism—a move that Nicholson does not want to make. It is also time to rid the world of "desacralization" language; as Jer 23:24 puts it, "the world is full of God."

(2) Patrick Miller.[25] I'm appreciative of this article for the important place divine sovereignty is shown to have in the Old Testament (including Exodus) and the clarity with which it raises a number of these [48] issues. Finally, however, I do not think Miller has sufficiently considered the qualifying role of the suffering images. He claims that King, Judge and Warrior are "controlling images" for God in the Old Testament (pp. 129, 141). I assume that this means that they exercise a qualifying impact on all other metaphors. Hence, whatever other metaphors might mean, they have to be congruent with the basic meaning of these controlling metaphors.

---

25. "The Sovereignty of God," in *The Hermeneutical Quest* (ed. D. G. Miller; Allison Park, PA: Pickwick, 1986), 129–44.

At one point in his article, Miller shows how this might be done. He speaks of an "opening up" of the definition of kingly power so that shepherd can become incorporated among these images, yet "the meaning and force of this [kingly] theme remains the same throughout the Bible" (pp. 130–31). Among those meanings is God's *"control* of nature and history," a recurring theme (pp. 130, 133–34, 141; his italics, though it is not entirely clear how strong he considers "control" to be). It seems clear that here the king metaphor norms the shepherd metaphor; shepherd only enhances the "protection and care" elements in the controlling king image. Whatever the shepherd metaphor might entail, it is subordinate to the king metaphor. Any aspect of the shepherd metaphor that is not congruent with the king's "control of nature and history" belongs to the "is not" of the shepherd metaphor.

At the same time, there are three places in the article where the consistency of this perspective seems to falter. In a one sentence comment on the royal theme in the New Testament (p. 131), Miller speaks of "a suffering love that is willing to take all their [the enemies] attacks." It is not typical of (even ideal) kings, however, that they simply suffer all attacks from their enemies. Hence, clearly, the king metaphor is being qualified by a metaphor of another sort. I would suggest that the field of suffering metaphors has entered into the discussion unacknowledged.

Or, in connection with the judge image, he speaks of God being "not dispassionate, but passionate and compassionate" (p. 131). Yet, dispassionateness" is certainly one thing a true judge is all about. Once again, the judge metaphor is being qualified by a metaphor of another sort. Moreover, his citation of Gen 18:25, "Will not the Judge of all the earth do right?" in this connection might also be noted. Here [49] Abraham calls God judge, but at the same time calls the judge to account in terms of an inherent righteousness in the created order of things. God certainly created such a moral order in freedom, but once having created it, God's sovereignty is thereby qualified. God is subject to the very moral order God put into place, in the sense of having to respond to injustice in some way. God cannot not respond to injustice.[26] This also qualifies the king metaphor, in the sense of one who is in control of things and who cannot be called to account.

Finally, in connection with the warrior image, Miller says that "the struggle [against the principalities and powers] goes on" (p. 134). If God

---

26. Contra Levenson, *Creation and the Persistence of Evil,* 149–50, who wishes to speak instead of God's "unlimited freedom, a freedom unlimited even by his own principles of justice and generosity." Yes, the decision will be God's, but not finally in independence of God's own righteous order. What remains open in the text is what it will take for God to be righteous. Levenson's work is a powerful testimony to the witness of some Old Testament traditions to the vulnerable sovereignty of God as Creator. He does not, however, consider how this vulnerability might be related to the work of God in the exodus, though his discussion of covenant suggests a direction in which he might go.

is King and Warrior who "controls nature and history," is it meaningful to speak of a "struggle" in any real sense? Another metaphor has entered the picture, such that some basic meanings of God as Warrior (and King) have been subverted. If the struggle in which God is engaged against the powers of evil is a genuine struggle, then the metaphors of King and Warrior have been transmuted by another set of metaphors.

It appears that there is, finally, a recognition that the metaphors of King, Judge and Warrior are basic, but that they need to be qualified by another metaphoric field. Whatever place these three metaphors may have in the Old Testament's understanding of God, metaphors from the suffering field qualify them in important ways.

(3) Erich Zenger.[27] For Zenger, Israel's situation in exile is seen to parallel that of the exodus; they are "afflicted, wretched, and poor." God's response to this situation, while often cast in terms comparable to, and grounded in, God's earlier action on behalf of Israel is a new reality. The exodus has revealed the kind of God God is, but the *means by which God will act this time* differs from the exodus in substantial ways. "The first exodus involved the annihilation of Israel's enemies, but this destructive aspect has now faded away" (p. 26). In this new exodus, "God will end Israel's suffering without the use of war and destruction." It will be a "peaceful miracle."

In Isa 51:9–10, Israel calls on God to do things in accord with the ways of the first exodus. In 51:12–16, "God takes up this appeal to unlimited power but gives it a new direction intended to wean Israel away from all ideas of a strong God who destroys the others; he wants [50] Israel to discover that he is a loving God who wants to bestow new life, firstly and foremostly to Israel" (p. 27). God is still the transcendent Lord, but without recourse to the mythology of the struggle of the gods. In fact, the theology of war has had a baneful effect on Israel. "Those for whom victory or defeat are the only alternatives are easily led by historical realities to declare God a loser" (p. 28).[28] Rather, God "turns to Zion like a loving mother in a personal relationship." The servant Israel "cries for vengeance, but in reply God puts forward the picture of the Suffering Servant who, by renouncing power and accepting suffering, becomes a witness to the power of reconciliation and love that can change the world" (p. 28). The vision of Isa 2:4 captures this sense of the effects of God's new way of being the Exodus God. The other nations of the world are *drawn* into this sphere of peace and well-being.

Zenger's language is not entirely consistent in seeking to describe what has happened to the images for God. He speaks of the metaphors of war and power as *"transmuted* into that of the caring shepherd of his people"

---

27. "The God of Exodus in the Message of the Prophets as Seen in Isaiah," in *Exodus: A Lasting Paradigm* (ed. B. van Iersel and A. Weiler; Edinburgh: T. & T. Clark, 1987), 22–33.

28. One might also ask whether "loser" language is only appropriate for warrior metaphors, indeed, whether it would be entirely inappropriate to use failure language for God in some texts (e.g., Hos 11:1–9).

(Isa 40:9–11). Moreover, in Isa 52:7–10, the theme of the arm of the Lord "is taken over from the tradition of the struggle of the gods and the Exodus battle and *transformed* into a 'pacifist' sense" (p. 29; emphases mine). The new Exodus will be a peaceful, solemn procession (52:11–12). But, then, he changes the verb and says that Yahweh the Shepherd "once again *replaces*" Yahweh the Warrior described in the first Exodus.

To transmute or transform is not to replace, however. It must be insisted that the Isaianic hermeneutic consists, not in jettisoning the old imagery of God as Warrior, but of transforming it, now to function as God's powerful ways of love and suffering. Sovereignty language for God must be given a more prominent place than Zenger seems to suggest. For example, he shortchanges the theme of divine wrath in the later Isaianic corpus (e.g., 47:14–15). At the same time, Zenger's work shows that it is a sovereignty that is not correspondent with the usual ways of thinking about such an image. God's rule is of a different order. To use other words, the images of the suffering [51] God have served a qualifying function. Sovereignty has taken suffering into account, while itself retaining an important qualifying role for suffering.

As a way of concluding, let me raise two questions that Zenger does not address: To what degree is the Isaianic interpretation new? Our study has uncovered a hermeneutic within Exodus itself that anticipates the Isaianic perspective. Isaiah is not a radical reinterpretation of Exodus, but extends a direction of thought already present there. A suffering God is clearly in evidence in Exodus, and it remains for later witnesses such as Isaiah and the New Testament to work this out at greater depth. In other words, the transmutation of sovereignty metaphors in view of suffering ones is characteristic of both traditions.

If this is true of two such significant Old Testament traditions, any contemporary formulation of divine sovereignty and divine suffering must give this perspective a significant place. The upshot of this is that the divine suffering metaphors have a place of prominence not commonly given them. In New Testament terms, this means that the cross must be a primary qualifying metaphor for any doctrine of God. So often the Christological formulations of the church have been accompanied by an amazingly imperious notion of God. These reflections suggest that those contemporary theological formulations of the doctrine of God that give as prominent a place to suffering metaphors as sovereignty metaphors are truest to at least one central strand of Old Testament thought. In other words, the sovereignty of God must finally be defined in terms of how it looks when nailed to a cross. The oft-used phrase, "crown of thorns," captures this dialectic well. 1 Cor 1:27–28 would seem to be dependent upon these Old Testament themes (cf. also Jer 9:23–24): "God chose what is foolish in the world to shame the wise, God chose what is weak in the world to shame the strong, God chose what is low and despised in the world, even things that are not, to bring to nothing things that are."

A second question: To what degree can the Exodus texts serve as a paradigm for contemporary Christian reflection and action?[29] The answer to this question is by no means obvious, not least given certain reservations about this paradigm expressed among even liberation theologians.[30] Do we now read Exodus *only* through the eyes [52] of Isaiah, so that Isaiah's fuller transmutation of the warrior metaphor is the definitive one? From the perspective of the canon as a whole, one could say that Exodus can no longer be read in isolation from Isaiah. But, does Exodus still offer some important insights into God's ways with the world independent of this reading? Zenger seems to recognize only these matters: the Exodus remains foundational in showing that God enters into the struggle on behalf of the poor and afflicted. It serves to demonstrate where God's priorities are, defining who God is and what this God is about in the world. The new work of God emerges out of that experience, in continuity with that old work, but now in view of new times and places.

But, further questions need to be raised. Is the Isaianic development a matter of *Israel's* progress in understanding? Or, does Isaiah witness to an evolution in the *divine* way with the world, a change of means and methods by which to achieve the same divine goals in view of *God's* experience? Have all of God's ways with the world been transmuted into "Love your enemies," heaping coals on their heads? Or, is it a contextual matter? For the circumstances inherent in the Egyptian situation, God's warrior ways, as qualified by the suffering images of Exodus, were the only possible mode in order to accomplish Israel's liberation. For Isaiah's time, God's warrior mode is more completely transmuted. Yet, there may be other times and places for God to act as warrior in a less qualified way.

In other terms, does God deal with the Hitlers of this world only in terms of suffering love and patience, or is there room for God to take the way of Exodus again in view of the circumstances? If the latter, any execution of judgment of a coercive sort on God's enemies must be congruent with the images of divine suffering. How this can be made coherent is beyond the scope of this paper, but two directions for thought might be noted.

---

29. See the collection of essays in Bas van Iersel and A. Weiler, eds., *Exodus: A Lasting Paradigm* (Edinburgh: T. & T. Clark, 1987).

30. In liberation theology the images of the exodus God can be sharply rejected or function paradigmatically. Hence, J. S. Croatto (*Exodus: A Hermeneutics of Freedom* [Maryknoll, NY: Orbis, 1981], 29), who rejects the metaphor, 'lord,' because "that is to project onto God the 'shadow' of the oppressor whom we know and who plays with the lives of others," can in the next sentence speak of "God acting violently because the situation of the Hebrews admitted of no other path. . . . Justice is a radical good that demands of *love* (paradoxical as it may seem) a *violent* action." On the other hand, Carol Christ (*Laughter of Aphrodite* [San Francisco: Harper & Row, 1987], 73–81) rejects the warrior God of exodus as a liberating image for feminist theology: "This God of war stands for too much that I stand against." See also the use only of non-violent exodus themes in the writings of Martin Luther King, Jr.

One, the wrath of God—which participates in both suffering and sovereign metaphoric fields[31]—would seem to function only in a non-interventionist fashion in the life of the world; it is a divine seeing to the moral order of things. Two, whether human beings are ever to serve as instruments of the wrath of God, either to exact punishment or to take up arms in the name of God, would seem to be even more difficult to justify.

31. See the discussion of the wrath of God in terms of the divine pathos in A. Heschel, *The Prophets* (New York: Harper & Row, 1962), 279–306.

"Evil" after 9/11:
A Consequence of Human Freedom

I'll always remember that 9/11 was a Tuesday. So also will some sixty students and my colleague Paul Sponheim as we met at 10:40 A.M. that day for our "God, Evil, and Suffering" class. One week into the course, and we had a test case on our hands. Lecture notes were set aside and questions filled the air. As the titles of numerous books, documentaries, and sermons would also show, the primary question was some version of: "Where in the world was God?" Or, truer to the lament form: "Where in the world were you, God, when all that hell broke loose?" In the face of such questions the Christian is not reduced to silence, not least because the Bible forthrightly speaks about evil and God's relationship to it. While neither Bible nor tradition provides an "explanation" of these realities, many helpful things can be said and done, and many unhelpful things left unsaid and undone.

For one thing, we can bring perspective. In the long history of evil and its ill effects, many events have occurred that we could name "evil." As Peter Steinfels put it in the *New York Times* (August 31, 2002): "Where was God, after all, on Sept. 10—when tens of thousands of parents, as on every day, watched their malnourished infants expire, . . . when in Africa, as on every day, more people died of AIDS than were killed in the twin towers, and when traitorous arteries and rebellious brain cells, as on every day, stifled vibrant personalities into silence and stupor?" Moral evil and natural evil are certainly different (and we focus here on the former), but both are descriptive of life in a world full of creatures (human and nonhuman) given freedom by God to be themselves, wherein interrelated individual choices and random events often have devastating consequences. One might fault God for creating creatures with such possibilities, but a world of divine puppetry would deny a genuine relationship between creature and God.

And so we can speak of relationships. We live in an increasingly interconnected world, one effect of which is that any evil act will more immediately and intensively reverberate and affect everyone physically and psychically (witness our increased anxiety). That nineteen men can so deeply continue to affect the life of us all is testimony to just such a world. Among other things, interrelatedness teaches [207] us that 9/11 cannot simply be laid at the feet of those hijackers. Their characters had been formed by their education and life experience, and words and deeds having their roots in American life helped shape the individuals they had become. In such an

This essay was originally published in *Word and World* 24 (2004): 205–7.

interrelated world, we have increasingly good reason to speak of multiple causes for such events, and each of us in our own way will have made contributions to this reality. At the least, this means that, in such events, we are not simply victims, and we ought not speak and act as individuals or communities in ways that would nurture a sense of victimhood.

Because God will honor commitments made to the creation, this faithfulness will entail constraint and restraint in any related divine action. This divine self-limitation, necessary for the genuine freedom of creatures within the relationship, is a key factor in understanding evil. The world's long story of resistance to the will of God has had deeply evil effects on every aspect of life, and the resultant reality complicates God's working possibilities in the world. Because of God's committed relationship to the world, no resolution will be simple, no "quick fix" available, even for God. One might wish that God would force compliance and stop evil in its tracks, but for the sake of a genuine relationship God has chosen not to micromanage life. Rather, God chooses to immerse the divine life into evil's very heart, supremely in Jesus Christ, and overcome it from within rather than overpower it from without.

We can also help sort out the complex and elusive notion of evil. As in English, the word "evil" in Hebrew (*ra'ah*) can refer to both the wicked deed and its ill effects, which may be named the judgment of God, mediating the effects intrinsic to the deed (*ra'ah* leads to *ra'ah*). Such evil effects may be due to one's own sin or to the reverberating sins of others in an interrelated world (witness Israel in Egypt). In addition, we must speak of evil as more than individual acts and their effects: evil has become systemic, built up over time into the infrastructure of life, whether we personalize it or not (as, e.g., Satan). Yet, we are not so permeated with evil that we cannot name it or act against it. The temptation of an overly dualistic perspective is that we will be reduced to passivity in the wake of a cosmic battle or claim that "the devil made me do it." We have responsibilities to speak and act against evil in individual and community life, and we confess that God has entered deeply into our lives to enable that work to be and to bring good.

Part 4
God and Wrath

God and Violence in the Old Testament

The Old Testament has a reputation: it is a book filled with violence, including the violence of God. The New Testament commonly avoids such a charge; but it, too, is filled with violent words and deeds, and Jesus and the God of the New Testament are complicit in this violence.[1] Yes, the Bible does often promote *nonviolence*; indeed, the basic eschatological reflections of the Old Testament are marked by visions of peace and nonviolence, extending even to the animal world (e.g., Isa 2:2–4; 65:17–25)—these texts constitute a fundamental witness that violence is an unwanted intruder in God's world. At the same time, the Bible also—and often—defends the use of violence, including capital punishment, war, and self-defense. The New Testament especially, with its talk about hell, even envisions an eternal violence, in which God is very much involved (e.g., Matt 13:36–50; Rev 14:9–11).[2] [19] My task is to reflect on some theological directions for considering the violence in Old Testament texts, especially divine violence.

The recent proliferation of literature regarding the Bible's violence and, more generally, the linkage between religion and violence is remarkable, sparked not least by the end of the millennium, 9/11, and other terrorist activities in the name of religion.[3] At the same time, Stephen Stein rightly

This essay was originally published in *Word and World* 24 (2004): 18–28.

1. On the much neglected theme of violence in the New Testament, see, e.g., Michel Desjardins, *Peace, Violence, and the New Testament* (Sheffield: Sheffield Academic Press, 1997); George Aichele, "Jesus' Violence," in *Violence, Utopia, and the Kingdom of God: Fantasy and Ideology in the Bible* (ed. George Aichele and Tina Pippin; New York: Routledge, 1998), 72–91. Jesus' violent language and predictions in, e.g., Luke 19:41–44 and Matt 13:23 are illustrative. The violence of God is evident in texts such as Acts 5:1–11 and Revelation 14. On the "anti-Judaism" of the New Testament, certainly a form of violence with long-term and recent violent effects, see Gerd Lüdemann, *The Unholy in Holy Scripture: The Dark Side of the Bible* (trans. J. Bowden; Louisville: Westminster John Knox, 1997), 76–127. That this issue of *Word and World* has no article on violence in the New Testament might reflect a common opinion.

2. Remarkably, eternal violence is rare and late in the Old Testament (e.g., Dan 12:2).

3. For a recent treatment, see John J. Collins, "The Zeal of Phinehas: The Bible and the Legitimation of Violence," *JBL* 122 (2003): 3–21, and the literature cited therein. More generally, see Stephen J. Stein, "The Web of Religion and Violence," *Religious Studies Review* 28 (2002): 103–8, for a review of seven recent books on the topic. Much attention has been given to the work of René Girard on violence; see, e.g., *Violence and the Sacred* (trans. Patrick Gregory; Baltimore: Johns Hopkins University Press, 1977). For a recent review of his work, including essays from a biblical perspective: *Violence Renounced: René Girard, Biblical Studies, and Peacemaking* (ed. Willard M. Swartley; Telford, PA: Pandora, 2000).

claims that "the systematic study of the relationship between religion and violence is not very far advanced." Stein's indictment of the church and other religious communities for this inattention is appropriate; he speaks of "the relative absence of self-reflection by the religious traditions on their role in generating, sponsoring, promoting, supporting, and maintaining such violence."[4] That would include the role that the Bible has played in the perpetration of violence across the globe over the centuries.

In thinking through the violence in the Bible, the need for a closer definition of violence quickly comes into view; it must be a definition that can encompass both divine and human violence. For many people, especially in these post-9/11 days, only physical violence truly qualifies as violence. But, certainly, violence is more than killing people, unless one includes all those words and actions that kill people slowly. The effect of limitation to a "killing fields" perspective is the widespread neglect of many other forms of violence. We must insist that violence also refers to that which is psychologically destructive, that which demeans, damages, or depersonalizes others.[5]

In view of these considerations, violence may be defined as follows: any action, verbal or nonverbal, oral or written, physical or psychical, active or passive, public or private, individual or institutional/societal, human or divine, in whatever degree of intensity, that abuses, violates, injures, or kills. Some of the most pervasive and most dangerous forms of violence are those that are often hidden from view (against women and children, especially); just beneath the surface in many of our homes, churches, and communities is abuse enough to freeze the blood. Moreover, many forms of systemic violence often slip past our attention because they are so much a part of the infrastructure of life (e.g., racism, sexism, ageism).[6] [20] If the Bible had described the course of the twentieth century, it would be a much more violent book than it is[7]—not least because there are so many more people around to be violent!

4. Stein, "Web," 108.

5. Robert McAfee Brown (*Religion and Violence* [2nd ed.; Philadelphia: Westminster, 1987]) is correct in claiming a broad definition: anything that "violates the personhood" of another (p. 7). Unfortunately, it does not take into account violence against the non-human. See also Leo D. Lefebure, *Revelation, the Religions, and Violence* (Maryknoll, NY: Orbis, 2000), 13–14. The issue of spiritual violence—the use of theological and churchly matters to browbeat or threaten others—also needs attention; it has not commonly been addressed in the life of the church.

6. People will differ on what constitutes violence, to some extent, especially moving across time and from one culture or church to another (e.g., refusals to ordain women or gays/lesbians could be considered policies of violence, but some would disagree).

7. See Rudolf Rummel, *Death by Government* (New Brunswick, NJ: Transactions, 1994). He counts 170 million *civilians* who fall into the title's category.

Human Violence

The Old Testament certainly knows of human violence that fits our definition. This is the case, most basically, because the world of which it speaks is filled with violence, including institutionalized violence, and the Old Testament does not shrink from telling it like it is. Readers should be grateful that the Bible does not try to paper over what life is really like for individuals, families, and communities.

Violence—from robbery to rape to homicide to war—appears near the beginning of the Bible and does not let up along the way. Gen 6:11–13, reporting the violence of "all flesh" that led to the violence of the flood, tells the story of our own—and every—time: "Now the earth was corrupt in God's sight and the earth was filled with violence." We should be thankful that God has promised never to visit the earth in flood-like ways again (Gen 8:21)!

Besides the physical violence to which the Bible witnesses, especially to be noted is the exercise of violence through the use of words, e.g., slander, false charges, character assassination, and gossip. Such language has the capacity to promote distrust, disrespect, and enmity, which often lead to physical violence (e.g., Ps 140:3, 11; Prov 10:6, 11; 16:27–30; Jer 9:2–8; note the link between "peace" and violent speech in Ps 34:13–14). Perhaps especially uncomfortable is the extent to which violence is associated with economic issues, not least the pursuit of wealth; as Mic 6:12 puts it without qualification: "Your wealthy people are full of violence."

The most common Hebrew word for "violence" (חָמָס) is used almost exclusively for human violence and is almost always condemned, implicitly or explicitly.[8] God sharply rejects violent people: "The Lord . . . hates the lover of violence" (Ps 11:5), commands that Israel "do no wrong or violence to the alien, the orphan, and the widow" (Jer 22:3), demands that violators of the command "put away violence and oppression" (Ezek 45:9), and condemns those who do "violence to the earth" (Hab 2:8, 17; see Zeph 1:9). The divinely appointed Davidic king's "job description," [21] mirroring that of God, is to redeem people "from oppression and violence" (Ps 72:14). Knowing that God has these commitments, and expecting God to be on their side, the psalmists cry out to God for deliverance from those who are violent, from "the dark places of the land [that] are full of the haunts of violence" (Ps 74:20; see also Ps 25:19; 140:1, 4, 11). The righteous think they have a just case to bring before God and they seek to motivate

---

8. The verb and noun are used only 68 times in the Old Testament (and synonyms such as "oppression" are not common either); this relatively infrequent usage in view of the amount of violence reported assumes that the reader will be able to name the reality for what it is from concrete cases. Dictionary articles on violence can be misleading if they focus only on certain words. But, it is not unimportant that חָמָס only rarely has God as a subject (Job's accusation, Job 19:7; Jeremiah's lament, Jer 20:8; cf. Lam 2:6).

God to act on their behalf by claiming that they have "avoided the ways of the violent" (Ps 17:4). And then, when they have been delivered from violent people, they sing songs of thanksgiving (2 Sam 22:3, 49; Ps 18:48). The righteous are confident that God will see to a future when "violence shall no more be heard in your land" (Isa 60:18). Such a resolute divine *opposition* to human violence is important to remember in reflecting upon divine violence. In sum: if there were no human violence, there would be no divine violence.

To this interhuman violence, we must add the violence of the human against the nonhuman. It is recognized as early as Gen 9:2 that, in the wake of human sin, animals live in fear and dread of human beings. More indirectly, *interhuman* violence has a devastating effect on the environment. For example, Hos 4:1–3 establishes a clear link: human swearing, lying, murder, stealing, adultery, and bloodshed have highly adverse effects upon the land, animals, birds, and fish. On the other hand, the violence of nonhuman creatures against human beings is no small matter (e.g., Gen 9:5; Exod 21:28).

Divine Violence

If human violence were the only story about violence in the Bible, this could be a briefer, if bloody, discussion. But that is not the case. The most basic theological problem with the Bible's violence is that it is often associated with the activity of God; with remarkable frequency, God is the subject of violent verbs:[9] From the flood, to Sodom and Gomorrah, to the command to sacrifice Isaac, to the plagues, to all the children killed on Passover night—and we are not yet through the book of Exodus![10] What will we make of this divine violence?

Questions raised about God's violence in the Bible are not simply of recent vintage. The concern goes back at least as far as the second-century gnostic Marcion, who set aside the Old Testament (and much of the New Testament). He made this move at least in part because of the violence of God portrayed therein, [22] and he has had many followers through the centuries.[11] The church rightly rejected the approach of Marcion, but the

---

9. Cheryl Kirk-Duggan (*Eerdman's Dictionary of the Bible* [Grand Rapids, MI: Eerdmans, 2000], 1358) notes that God is the subject of violence (some 1,000 times) much more than human beings (some 600 texts).

10. For a treatment of God and violence in the prophets, see my "'I Was Only a Little Angry': Divine Violence in the Prophets," *Int* 58 (2004): 365–75.

11. One thinks of Schleiermacher, Ritschl, and Harnack. Marcion promotes "a better god, who is neither offended, nor does he get angry, nor does he take vengeance" (so Tertullian, *Adversus Marcionem* 1.27). For a recent statement along this line, see Kari Latvus, *God, Anger, and Ideology: The Anger of God in Joshua and Judges* (Sheffield: Sheffield Academic Press, 1998): "The God that deuteronomistic theologians created in their own image was the God of strict dogmatism, intolerance and fundamentalism—and, of course, the God

disquiet about the Bible's divine violence has been intensifying in recent biblical work.[12] Some studies even want to set aside the references to divine violence, at least in terms of serious theological consideration, if not actually to remove them from the biblical text.[13] At the same time, and in possible reaction to such views, the church and its spokespersons have often gone to the other extreme and sought to defend the Bible's portrayal of the violence of God, of whatever kind, at all costs.[14]

I seek to steer between these two extremes. On the one hand, I want to claim that the Bible's talk about divine violence must be taken seriously into account in any accurate portrayal of the biblical God. Even more, divine anger and judgment, which may entail violence, are absolutely crucial to our continued reflection about God and God's ways in the world. On the other hand, some of the ways in which God's violence is depicted in the Bible should not stand unchallenged. I take a closer look at these two perspectives, though much work remains to be done.

---

of anger. . . . the God of the crucified and powerless Jesus cannot be the same as the deuteronomistic God of anger" (p. 91). Such a perspective is common among clergy and laity, evident not least in the highly selective use of Old Testament texts in preaching and teaching, prompted in significant part by lectionaries that tend to avoid judgment texts. The issue of divine impassibility is prominent in the history of reflection on this theme, but this is not a common reason for the difficulty regarding divine anger/violence today.

12. Among more recent scholarly efforts that raise serious questions regarding the Bible's violence and God's common association with it, refusing to excuse it or to interpret it away, see Collins, "The Zeal of Phinehas"; Lüdemann, *The Unholy;* David Penchansky, *What Rough Beast? Images of God in the Hebrew Bible* (Louisville: Westminster John Knox, 1999); several essays in David Penchansky and Paul L. Redditt, eds., *Shall Not the Judge of All the Earth Do What Is Right? Studies on the Nature of God in Tribute to James L. Crenshaw* (Winona Lake, IN: Eisenbrauns, 2000). Female scholars and others have been particularly pointed in their critique of those texts wherein God's violence is associated with female imagery. See, e.g., Renita J. Weems, *Battered Love: Marriage, Sex, and Violence in the Hebrew Prophets* (Minneapolis: Fortress, 1995); among many articles one might cite, that of Diane Jacobson offers a clear and well-balanced approach ("Hosea 2: A Case Study on Biblical Authority," *Currents in Theology and Mission* 23 [1996]: 165–72). I have sought to work with this issue in several publications, especially "Is the Biblical Portrayal of God Always Trustworthy?" in Terence E. Fretheim and Karlfried Froehlich, *The Bible as Word of God in a Postmodern Age* (Minneapolis: Fortress, 1998), 97–111 (reprinted: Eugene, OR: Wipf & Stock, 2002).

13. For example, the introduction to the Hebrew prophets by Carol J. Dempsey (*The Prophets: A Liberation-Critical Reading* [Minneapolis: Fortress, 2000]) often calls into question (rejects?) the prophetic portrayal of God in terms of violence. In speaking of Amos 2:1–3, for example, she says: "Again, God's response to violence is violence! And again, we ask, 'Is this the way of God?'" (p. 14).

14. Indeed, an openness to critique the Bible's theological perspectives of any sort, including its depiction of God, has traditionally been considered out of bounds. See, e.g., the response of Froehlich to Fretheim in *Bible as Word of God,* 127–32.

The Theological/Ethical Importance
of Divine Wrath and Judgment

God's *uses* of violence—and that phrasing is important[15]—are associated with [23] two basic purposes: judgment and salvation. Sometimes the same event may have both effects; for example, Persia under Cyrus mediates salvation for the exiles in Babylon and, at the same time, passes judgment on Babylon. Such divine activity often entails God's use of agents that are capable of violence, both human (e.g., Israelites, Nebuchadnezzar, Cyrus) and nonhuman (e.g., clouds, darkness, waves, etc. at the Red Sea).[16] Much of the divine violence in the Old Testament is associated with these contexts, but there are important exceptions, not least the book of Psalms, which is filled with violence.[17]

Judgment. Divine violence seems always to be related to human sin.[18] Generally speaking, if there were no human violence, there would be no divine wrath or judgment, which may take the form of violence, depending upon the agent used. Abraham Heschel has stated well what is at stake in this matter: "[Our] sense of injustice is a poor analogy to God's sense of injustice. The exploitation of the poor is to us a misdemeanor; to God, it is a disaster. Our reaction is disapproval; God's reaction is something no language can convey. Is it a sign of cruelty that God's anger is aroused when the rights of the poor are violated, when widows and orphans are oppressed?"[19]

Violent human actions lead to violent consequences. *That* there are such consequences to human violence is named divine judgment. Just how God relates to the movement from sin to consequence, however, is not easy to sort out.[20] Generally [24] speaking, the relationship between sin

---

15. Wrath and violence are not divine attributes, but responses to creaturely sin, indeed the sins of violence. For discussion, see Terence E. Fretheim, "Theological Reflections on the Wrath of God in the Old Testament," *HBT* 24 (2002): 14–17.

16. For a discussion of God's use of agents, see Terence E. Fretheim, *Jeremiah* (Macon, GA: Smyth and Helwys, 2002), 35–39; idem, "The Character of God in Jeremiah," in *Character and Scripture: Moral Formation, Community and Biblical Interpretation* (ed. W. P. Brown; Grand Rapids, MI: Eerdmans, 2002), 211–30.

17. There are over 100 references to enemies in Psalms. The lament psalms, especially the imprecatory laments, are difficult to interpret in view of the way that the psalmists call upon God to visit their detractors with violence. For an excellent study of these psalms, see Erich Zenger, *A God of Vengeance? Understanding the Psalms of Divine Wrath* (trans. Linda Maloney; Louisville: Westminster John Knox, 1996).

18. God's command to Abraham to sacrifice Isaac seems not to be an exception, given the "test" in view of Abraham's prior sinful behaviors (e.g., Genesis 20).

19. Abraham J. Heschel, *The Prophets* (New York: Harper & Row, 1962), 284–85. This volume remains one of the most cogent treatments of divine wrath.

20. For discussion, see Fretheim, "Wrath of God," 19–24. Helpful resources include Gerhard von Rad, *Old Testament Theology* (trans. David Stalker; vol. 1; New York: Harper & Row, 1962), who speaks of a "synthetic view of life" (p. 265) in which "the retribution is not a new action which comes upon the person concerned from somewhere else; it is

and the judgment of violence is conceived in intrinsic rather than forensic terms; consequences grow out of the deed itself. That is, God mediates the consequences of sin that are already present in the situation,[21] rather than through the imposition of a penalty from without. Ezek 22:31 well illustrates the point. God declares, "I have consumed them with the fire of my wrath," and immediately states what that entails: "I have returned [נָתַתִּי] *their* conduct upon their heads."[22] Israel's sin generates certain snowballing effects. At the same time, God is active in the interplay of human sinful actions and their effects, and God uses "third parties" as agents for that judgment (e.g., the Assyrians). Both divine and creaturely factors are interwoven to produce the judgmental result, which may include violence. Such consequences do not take place in some inevitable or mechanical way; the causal weave is complex and loose so that, for example, the wicked may prosper (see Jer 12:1–4) and room is left for chance ("time and chance happen to them all," Eccl 9:11).[23]

Remarkable correspondences exist between God's actions and those of Nebuchadnezzar.[24] God will not "pity, spare, or have compassion" (Jer 13:14), because that is what the Babylonians, the instruments of divine judgment, will not do (Jer 21:7; see 27:8). The violent words/deeds appear to be used for God because they are used for the actions of those in and through whom God mediates judgment; the latter will certainly act as kings and armies in that world are known to act. *The portrayals of God's wrath and*

---

rather the last ripple of the act itself which attaches to its agent almost as something material. Hebrew in fact does not even have a word for punishment" (p. 385); Patrick D. Miller, *Sin and Judgment in the Prophets: A Stylistic and Theological Analysis* (Chico, CA: Scholars Press, 1982); Klaus Koch, "Is There a Doctrine of Retribution in the Old Testament?" in *Theodicy in the Old Testament* (ed. James Crenshaw; Philadelphia: Fortress, 1983), 57–87; and more recently, Gene Tucker, "Sin and 'Judgment' in the Prophets," in *Problems in Biblical Theology: Essays in Honor of Rolf Knierim* (ed. Henry Sun et al.; Grand Rapids, MI: Eerdmans, 1997), 373–88. How these judgment texts are to be related is best seen in the work of H. H. Schmid, who places them under the umbrella of creation theology: "Creation, Righteousness, and Salvation: 'Creation Theology' as the Broad Horizon of Biblical Theology," in *Creation in the Old Testament* (ed. Bernard W. Anderson; Philadelphia: Fortress, 1984), 102–17.

21. Interpreters have used several different formulations: God midwifes, facilitates, sees to, puts in force, or completes the connection between sin and consequence. Sometimes God as subject stands in a prominent position (e.g., Jer 19:7–9); elsewhere, God's stance is passive (e.g., Hos 4:1–3) or withdrawing (Isa 64:6–7), but deism is ruled out of court.

22. There are over fifty texts in the Old Testament that link divine wrath and violence with such formulations (e.g., Ps 7:12–16; Isa 59:17–18; 64:5–9; Jer 6:11, 19; 7:18–20; 14:16; 17:10; 21:12–14; 44:7–8; 50:24–25; Lam 3:64–66).

23. On the import of divine grief accompanying divine wrath, see Fretheim, "Wrath of God," 7–8.

24. For a partial list, see Fretheim, *Jeremiah*, 36.

violent action are conformed to the means that God uses. God thereby accepts
any fallout that may accrue to the divine reputation.[25]

The ethical implications of such an understanding of divine anger are
considerable. I have stated it this way: "Human anger at injustice will
carry less weight and seriousness if divine anger at injustice in the service
of life is not given its proper place. If our God is not angry, why should
we be?"[26]

Salvation. Violence becomes the means by which God's people are delivered from violence. So, for example, violence *against* the Egyptians leads
to Israel's salvation from Egypt's violence (e.g., Exod 15:1–3). Or, God uses
the violence of the Persians under King Cyrus against the enslaving Babylonians as a means to bring [25] salvation to the exiles (e.g., Isa 45:1–8). In the
first case, God uses violence to save Israel from the effects of *other people's
sins.* In the second, God uses violence in order to save God's people from the
effects of *their own sins,* which got them into exile in the first place. Salvation
is thus comprehensively conceived.[27]

These two ways of speaking of God's use of violence may be reduced
to one. That is, God's use of violence, inevitable in a violent world, is intended to subvert human violence in order to bring the creation along to
a point where violence is no more. Walter Brueggemann says it well: "It is
likely that the violence assigned to Yahweh is to be understood as coun-   ·
terviolence, which functions primarily as a critical principle in order to
undermine and destabilize other violence." And so, God's violence is "not
blind or unbridled violence," but purposeful in the service of a nonviolent
end.[28] In other words, God's violence, whether in judgment or salvation, is
never an end in itself, but is always exercised in the service of God's more
comprehensive *salvific* purposes for creation: the deliverance of slaves from
oppression (Exod 15:7; Ps 78:49–50), the righteous from their antagonists
(Ps 7:6–11), the poor and needy from their abusers (Exod 22:21–24; Isa
1:23–24; Jer 21:12), and Israel from its enemies (Isa 30:27–33; 34:2; Hab
3:12–13). "This is one of the meanings of the anger of God: the end of
indifference" with respect to those who have suffered human cruelty.[29] In
so stating the matter, the divine exercise of wrath, which may include violence, is finally a word of good news (for those oppressed) and bad news
(for oppressors).

---

25. That God is not the only effective agent in these events is made clear by the divine
judgment on *Babylon* (Jer 25:12–14; 50–51; Isa 47:6–7; Zech 1:15). God takes a risk that
God's name will become associated with the violence, indeed the excessive violence, of
the Babylonians. See John Sanders, *The God Who Risks: A Theology of Divine Providence*
(Downers Grove, IL: InterVarsity, 1998).

26. Fretheim, "Wrath of God," 3.

27. For detail, see Terence E. Fretheim, "Salvation in the Bible vs. Salvation in the
Church," *WW* 13/4 (1993): 363–72.

28. Walter Brueggemann, *Theology of the Old Testament: Testimony, Dispute, Advocacy*
(Minneapolis: Fortress, 1997), 244.

29. Heschel, *Prophets,* 284.

Calling Into Question Certain Ways
of Depicting Divine Violence

As I have noted, the Bible understands that some forms of violence, both human and divine, are legitimate. Here I consider several forms of violence whose theological legitimacy has been called into question.[30] The above considerations should make it clear that I do not hereby intend to make the God of the Bible more palatable to contemporary taste. We are always in danger of doing this, of course, especially regarding matters of judgment; we must certainly learn to read the Bible over against ourselves, allowing the text to interrogate us, to be "in our face." But is everything in the Bible that offends us appropriately offensive (e.g., the Bible's patriarchy)? [26] Is it not also dangerous simply to repeat uncritically those texts that denigrate the place of women and portray God as one who orders the wholesale slaughter of cities?[31] And, if we are not critical of those texts wherein the God of the Bible engages in such violent acts and violent speech, does not that, however subtly, commend a way of life for those who follow this God?

It is important to note that an inner-biblical warrant exists for the people of God to raise questions and challenges regarding God's (anticipated) actions. Examples include the biblical laments (e.g., Ps 44); Abraham's challenge in Gen 18:25, "Shall not the Judge of all the earth do what is just?" and that of Moses in Exod 32:7–14. Do not such texts show the way for the important work we have to do regarding this interpretive issue? Moreover, we will be helped if we talk about a biblical center in terms of which all other texts are to be interpreted, evident most clearly in the creedal formulations of both Old Testament and New (e.g., Exod 34:6–7).[32] That center provides a kind of canon within the canon that means that not everything in the Bible is to be placed on the same level of importance and may provide a place on which we can stand to bring a critical word to bear regarding some portrayals of God.

At the least, we must be honest in recognizing the problems the Bible raises regarding divine violence.[33] As I have stated elsewhere: "The

---

30. See the literature cited in n. 12 for further examples.

31. For further reflections about these matters, see Fretheim, "Biblical Portrayal of God," 100–111, where I develop several criteria for determining the kinds of violence that should be rendered problematic. See also n. 32 below.

32. For the crucial issue of genre in determining such a center, see Terence Fretheim, "The God Who Acts: An Old Testament Perspective," *Theology Today* 54 (1997): 16–18; idem, "Some Reflections on Brueggemann's God," in *God in the Fray: A Tribute to Walter Brueggemann* (ed. Tod Linafelt and Timothy Beal; Minneapolis: Fortress, 1998), 36–37. [Both essays are reprinted in the present volume, pp. 58–70 and 71–83.]

33. This is stressed by Collins, "The Zeal of Phinehas," 20. Collins concludes his article with a helpful claim that links a defense of the Bible's violence to certitude, citing Hannah Arendt's phrase regarding a "God-like certainty that stops all discussion": "The Bible has contributed to violence in the world precisely because it has been taken to confer a degree of certitude that transcends human discussion and argumentation. Perhaps the

patriarchal bias *is* pervasive, God *is* represented as an abuser and a killer of children, God *is* said to command the rape of women and wholesale destruction of cities, including children and animals. To shrink from making such statements is dishonest." Even more, the church must recognize the long history of negative effects that many biblical texts about God have had on our life together. "With all the emphasis these days on what a text *does* to a reader, we should be absolutely clear: among the things that the Bible has *done* is to contribute to the oppression of women, the abuse of children, the rape of the environment, and the glorification of war."[34]

Attempts are often made to explain away the force of these texts or to soften their impact.[35] Take the violence of the conquest as an example; Deut 20:16–17 [27] puts the issue squarely before us. God commands, "But in the cities of these peoples [Canaanites] that the Lord your God gives you for an inheritance, you shall save alive nothing that breathes, but you shall utterly destroy them" (see 1 Sam 15:3). Israel carried out this command in various battles recorded in Joshua 6–11.[36] These divine and human activities have often been spiritualized ("put on the whole armor of God"), historically adjusted (turn the conquest into a land settlement or a primitive view that Israel outgrew), idealized (taking a utopian stand against idolatry), viewed as a metaphor for the religious life, or reduced to God's mysterious ways.[37]

No satisfactory "explanation" of this Israelite practice is possible, or, for that matter, of the other uses of divine violence noted above. Yet, certain considerations may help us understand such violence, if not to excuse in

---

most constructive thing a biblical critic can do toward lessening the contribution of the Bible to violence in the world, is to show that that certitude is an illusion" (pp. 20–21). I have also expressed concern that "a myth of certainty about the Bible" is at the heart of this discussion ("Biblical Portrayal of God," 99).

34. Ibid., 99–100.

35. Such a move is driven by several points of view. An approach from the perspective of the "peace churches" seeks to lift up the role of Yahweh as warrior as the decisive factor, diminishing the human role in warfare (see, e.g., Millard C. Lind, *Yahweh Is a Warrior: The Theology of Warfare in Ancient Israel* [Scottdale, PA: Herald, 1980], 169–74). The effect of such an approach is ironic in that the violence is then assigned largely to God. See a critique of several theological approaches in Lori Rowlett, *Joshua and the Rhetoric of Violence: A New Historicist Analysis* (Sheffield: Sheffield Academic Press, 1996), 65–70.

36. Israel's rationale for its ethnic cleansing of the Canaanites is expressed in two ways: one, so they would not be led astray by their seductive religious practices (Deut 7:1–5, 16; 20:18); two, they were instruments of divine judgment against Canaanite wickedness (Deut 9:4–5; see Gen 15:16).

37. Appeal to mystery is too often used to stop the conversation, even though the texts themselves have a remarkably "plain sense." For a fuller survey of these efforts, see Collins, "Zeal of Phinehas," 4–14; Lawson G. Stone, "Ethical and Apologetic Tendencies in the Redaction of the Book of Joshua," *CBQ* 53 (1991): 25–36. See also the studies of Susan Niditch, *War in the Hebrew Bible: A Study in the Ethics of Violence* (New York: Oxford University Press, 1996); L. Daniel Hawk, *Every Promise Fulfilled: Contesting Plots in Joshua* (Louisville: Westminster John Knox, 1991). For an earlier formulation, see my *Deuteronomic History* (Nashville: Abingdon, 1983), 61–75.

every respect the God who is portrayed here (nor those who carried out the divine commands).

(1) God works in and through human beings, with their foibles and flaws, in the achievement of God's purposes, and God does not perfect them before deciding to work with them. God works with what is available, including such institutions in that ancient context involved in the waging of war and other governmental trappings. Violence will be associated with God's work in the world because, to a greater or lesser degree, violence is characteristic of the persons and institutions through whom that work is done. Thus, such work will always have mixed results and will be less than what would have happened had God chosen to act alone. Moreover, God does not necessarily confer a positive value on those means in and through which God works (e.g., Isaiah 47).

(2) Human beings will never have a perfect perception of how they are to serve as God's instruments in the world. Israel's perceptions were often expressed in terms of the direct speech of God. Inasmuch as this is a phenomenon rare in the [28] New Testament, should we understand that Israel may have put into direct divine speech understandings they had gained through study and reflection rather than through an actual hearing of God's words? And they may not have fully or properly understood.

(3) That God would stoop to become involved in such human cruelties as violence is, finally, not a matter for despair, but of hope. God does not simply give people up to experience violence. God chooses to become involved in violence so that evil will not have the last word. In everything, including violence, God seeks to accomplish loving purposes. Thereby God may prevent an even greater evil. By so participating in our messy stories, God takes the road of suffering and death (e.g., Exod 3:7). Through such involvement, God absorbs the effects of sinful human efforts and thus suffers violence (not least because a divine promise of land for Israel lies behind the whole affair).

There remains a certain ambiguity of the Bible toward violence. God does not intend the violence that disrupts the life of the world, rooted as it is in the sinfulness of humankind. Again and again, God takes the side of those afflicted by violence. God so engages the divine self on behalf of those entrapped in violence and its effects that God enters deeply into the life of the world, most supremely in Jesus Christ, and shows thereby the most basic stance of divine nonviolence in the face of violence. But, in order to accomplish God's work in the world, God may respond in violent ways in and through various agents so that sin and evil do not go unchecked in the life of the world.

Theological Reflections on the Wrath of God in the Old Testament

Hope has two beautiful
daughters, anger and courage;
anger at the ways things are,
and courage to work to make
things other than they are.
—Augustine[1]

The "wrath of God" has considerable currency in everyday parlance. The Google search engine reveals over 83,000 entries. The media have found the phrase useful to refer to a remarkable range of phenomena. The History Channel has a feature entitled, "The Wrath of God: Hurricanes, Blizzards, Tsunamis, and Firestorms," and touts its "wrath of God video series." *Time* magazine ran an interview with Osama bin Laden simply entitled, "Wrath of God."[2] Two recent articles on computer viruses and other tech problems had "The Wrath of God" in their titles.[3] The wrath of God does not have to be explained to a general audience: that which is unpredictable, irrational, and capable of striking unexpectedly, with ruinous consequences in spite of the best human preparations.

In exploring various facets of the wrath of God, especially in the prophets, I seek to keep together those dimensions of the theme that are often driven apart: personal and natural; personal and political; wrath and grief; emotion and reason; covenant and creation; historical and eschatological. [2]

That biblical studies have not often considered the wrath of God in detail may indicate scholarly discomfort with the theme, if not outright rejection.[4] Such a conviction can be traced back to Aristeas and Philo, and

---

This essay was originally published in *Horizons in Biblical Theology* 24 (2002): 1–26.

1. Quoted by Robert McAfee Brown, *Religion and Violence* (2nd ed.; Philadelphia: Westminster, 1987), xxii, without citation.
2. January 11, 1999.
3. *USA Today,* January 17, 2001; *Slate,* May 5, 2000.
4. See Rudolf Otto, *The Idea of the Holy* (London: Oxford University Press, 1923): "from many passages of the OT this 'wrath' has no concern whatever with moral qualities . . . is nothing but the *tremendum* itself, apprehended and expressed by the aid of a naïve analogy from . . . the ordinary passional life of men" (p. 18). See Abraham Heschel, *The Prophets* (New York: Harper & Row, 1962), 306, for a response. Wrath is not commonly associated with the specific language of holiness (Ps 78:41); indeed, in Hos 11:9 they are set against one another.

especially to Marcion ("a better god, who is neither offended, nor does he get angry, nor does he take vengeance"—for Marcion, God must be impassible).[5] The issue of divine impassibility is prominent in the history of reflection on this theme, but seems not to be a common reason for the reticence/rejection of divine anger today. Marcion has had many heirs, for example, Schleiermacher and Ritschl,[6] who considered divine wrath to be an unworthy element of Christian theology; this is true even in more recent scholarship.[7] Among important exceptions to this recurrent effort, the Reformers are to be noted.[8]

More generally, this implicit or explicit rejection of the God of anger of the OT may reflect a concern to stress a God of love and peace, not wrath and violence.[9] Witness this concern in the common lectionary, where promissory prophetic texts are decisively favored over those that [3] feature wrath and judgment (hymnody is another example, and *lex orandi lex credendi* considerations are immediately at hand). When such texts are used, God's anger is often directed against the "outsider," whether unbelievers or individuals who do not conform to certain moral imperatives. In such an understanding, divine wrath often amounts to little more than a cover for human hatred (witness some responses to the Sept. 11th tragedy). The prophets, of course, directed much of their rhetoric of judgment against "insiders," with special attention to communal rather than individual behaviors.

The role of the church in violent activities over the years could be added to the list of concerns. Has not the church learned its violence from the Bible, especially the OT? The question often follows: should not the church pass a sharp judgment on the violence in its own tradition? Many recognize the importance of such a critique on the post-biblical churchly tradition. But such a valuation of the Bible itself is less common.[10] The

---

5. So Tertullian, *Marc.* 1.27. See the brief survey of anger in the history of Christian thought in Heschel, *The Prophets,* 299–306.

6. For Schleiermacher, see Stephen D. Paulson, "The Wrath of God," *Dialog* 33 (1994): 245–51. For Ritschl, see Paul Jersild, "The Judgment of God in Albrecht Ritschl and Karl Barth," *LQ* 14 (1962): 328–46.

7. See Heschel, *Prophets,* 305; for a more recent perspective, see Kari Latvus, *God, Anger and Ideology: The Anger of God in Joshua and Judges in Relation to Deuteronomy and the Priestly Writings* (JSOTSup 279; Sheffield: Sheffield Academic Press, 1998), 91. Christoff Schroeder ("'Standing in the Breach': Turning Away the *Wrath of God*," *Int* 52 [1998]: 16–23) shows how the work of René Girard on violence is fundamentally Marcionite in its pitting of the OT God, wherein human aggression is projected into the sphere of transcendence, against the NT God.

8. For Luther, see Paulson, "The Wrath of God"; Egil Grislis, "Luther's Understanding of the Wrath of God," *JR* 41(1961): 277–92.

9. Fifty years ago, R. V. G. Tasker put the issue in comparable terms (*The Biblical Doctrine of the Wrath of* God [London: Tyndale, 1951], v).

10. See Terence Fretheim & Karlfried Froehlich, *The Bible as Word of God in a Postmodern Era* (Eugene, OR: Wipf & Stock, 2002).

images of wrath in some texts, if not the idea, do need to be examined for their appropriateness, both then and now (e.g., Jer 13:20–27; 19:3–9; Ezekiel 16; 23).

The wrath of God is not only an important biblical theme, but also continues to be valuable in our reflection about God. Erich Zenger rightfully claims that to eliminate wrath from our reflection on God's involvement in creation "would reduce God to a spectator uninterested in the world, to a *deus otiosus,* and thus to an *idea* of God that, moreover, would be lacking in every kind of social-critical potential."[11] To speak of the wrath of God is to say something important "about the violent and wretched state of society and the world," which is neither God-created nor God-given. As Zenger suggests, the ethical implications of neglecting this theme are considerable. Human anger at injustice will carry less weight and seriousness if divine anger at injustice in the service of life is not given its proper place. If our God is not angry, why should we be? [4]

The Vocabulary of Wrath and Its Canonical Distribution

Among the few monographs devoted to the wrath of God are those of Bruce Baloian[12] and A. T. Hanson.[13] There are several helpful briefer studies.[14]

Some ten Hebrew terms denote the idea of "wrath" or "anger." These words are translated in various ways (anger, wrath, ire, rage, fury, indignation, aggravation), but differing nuances that may exist do not seem to make any appreciable theological difference, used as they often are in parallel constructions and in clusters (e.g., Jer 21:5). No sharp separation of anger as an inward expression and anger as an outward expression seems present. The purpose of this paper is not to engage in a lexical analysis of these words; that task has been amply treated in several studies, with very similar results.[15] Our purpose is to draw on this lexical work, take into ac-

---

11. E. Zenger, *A God of Vengeance? Understanding the Psalms of Divine Wrath* (trans. L. Maloney; Louisville: Westminster John Knox, 1996), 73 (emphasis his).

12. B. Baloian, *Anger in the Old Testament* (New York: Peter Lang, 1992).

13. A. T. Hanson, *The Wrath of the Lamb* (London: SPCK, 1957). Hanson's formulation, however, is ultimately tinged with a Marcionite perspective. Such is the judgment of Baloian (*Anger,* 82). See his discussion of scholarly work on the issue (ibid., 2–4; also 132 n. 50 for a brief discussion of older historical work).

14. For example, Gary A. Herion, "Wrath of God," *ABD* 6:989–96.

15. For a basic study of these words, see Elsie Johnson (with J. Bergman), "אָנַף, אַף," *TDOT* 1:348–62. See also Hermann Kleinknecht, Johannes Fichtner, and Gustav Stählin, *Wrath* (Bible Key Words; trans. from *TWNT;* London: Black, 1964). See also Baloian, *Anger,* 5–7; Herion, "Wrath," 990–91. These works offer a basic treatment of wrath in ancient Near Eastern literature, the results of which seem to offer no special insight into the biblical theme (see n. 48 below).

count the contexts in which the words are used, and consider the wrath of God from a theological perspective.

Issues of distribution of this theme across the various traditions should be noted. Most words for wrath/anger are used of both God and human beings, though references to divine anger outnumber references to human anger by almost three to one. These words refer to divine anger over 500 times in over 380 contexts in virtually every book in the Hebrew Bible,[16] nearly half of them in the prophets (especially [5] Jeremiah and Ezekiel) and the Psalms (over seventy instances). The first canonical instance of the exercise of divine anger is embedded in the call narrative of Moses (Exod 4:14), where, interestingly, God's anger leads to a change in *God's* plan for Moses' call.

The metaphors used to portray the divine wrath (and its effects) are remarkable in their range, many of them drawn from the sphere of the nonhuman. They include: fire (smoke/oven/melt), water (flood/rain/hail), and storm/clouds (e.g., Isa 30:27–30). These images in turn lead to the use of certain verbs, such as "consume" (Exod 32:10), "pour out" (Hos 5:10), "come down" (Jer 7:20), and "drinking" from the cup (Jer 10:25). That such images are so often used to depict wrath and its effects suggests that wrath is commonly understood in natural terms (see below).

Innerbiblical Development?

Whether any traditio-historical development in the OT understanding of divine wrath can be discerned is disputed. Hanson offers a diachronic presentation of wrath in the OT in broad terms.[17] Israel's understanding of wrath moves from irrational/mysterious understandings (e.g., 2 Sam 6:7–8), named such because there is no evident motivation, to the "moralizing" understandings of the prophets and the Deuteronomistic History (a personal, emotional divine response to sin; God is angry), to an impersonal sense of sin working itself out in history, especially prominent in the post-exilic period. Hanson's impersonal sense is important background for his analysis of the NT understanding of wrath. Remarkably, the NT never directly states that God is angry. The fact that the direct speech of God is rare in the NT may help explain its reticence. [6]

For Baloian, "there appears to be no traditio-historical development of the theological understanding of anger."[18] He considers all OT references to divine wrath to fall into Hanson's second category; God's anger is always personal, though that is stressed more in some texts. The "irrational" texts

---

16. See the charts in Baloian, *Anger*, 189–210.

17. For a summary, see Hanson, *Wrath*, 36–40.

18. Baloian, *Anger*, 174. For a comparable judgment regarding divine vengeance, see H. G. L. Peels, *The Vengeance of God: The Meaning of the Root NQM and the Function of the NQM-Texts in the Context of Divine Revelation in the Old Testament* (OtSt 31; Leiden: Brill, 1995), 295–97.

can be explained in other terms (see below) and, in any case, such texts are too rare to constitute a separable view. Baloian's assessment seems closer to the mark as far as supposed developments in the OT understanding of wrath. At the same time, the absolute use of "wrath" and the replacement of the "wrath of Yahweh" in 2 Sam 24:1 with the divine agent Satan in 1 Chr 21:1 may indicate some finer distinctions were being made in the later OT period.

Human Anger and Divine Anger

That the same terms are used for both human and divine anger shows that God's anger is considered analogous to that of human beings.[19] In any assessment of such an "anthropomorphic metaphor" for God, it is important to claim both a "yes" and a "no" with respect to the human analogue.[20] This task is not easy to pursue, not least because of the difficulty of discerning appropriate human anger. Human beings can "be angry and sin not" (Ps 4:4); anger is to be controlled, not eliminated altogether. "Righteous indignation" has a place, though most expressions of human anger are "infected" with sin. It may be suggested that wherever human anger serves life in God's [7] creation (e.g., regarding injustice[21]), it is appropriate. Analogously, God's anger is exercised in the service of life, but (recalling the "no" in the analogy) it is *always* so exercised.

Generally speaking, the category of relatedness is basic. For God or humans, anger is always relational, exercised with respect to others. Even more, as with human anger, the divine anger is a sign that the relationship is taken seriously (apathy is not productive of anger). God is deeply engaged in this relationship and is passionate about what happens to it. As such, anger is always *provoked* from within such relationships, testifying to the affectivity of both human beings and God (e.g., 2 Kgs 21:6, 15).

Divine Wrath and Divine Grief

Another matter that features the human analogue is that of grief accompanying anger. Commentators increasingly assign many lament-filled texts in the prophets to divine speech.[22] For some readers it is incongruous that expressions of profound grief accompany wrath. But such statements

---

19. Baloian (*Anger*) is especially concerned to understand divine anger in terms of the human analogue.

20. On the interpretation of such metaphors, see Fretheim, *Suffering*, 5–12. The distinction between human and divine wrath is blurred in Jeremiah ("I am full of the wrath of the Lord," 6:11); the wrath of the Lord comes to reside in the very person of Jeremiah (who eats the word of the Lord, 1:9; also Ezek 3:1–3).

21. Baloian places considerable emphasis on the link between anger and justice (*Anger*, e.g., p. 154).

22. For example, Mark E. Biddle, *Polyphony and Symphony in Prophetic Literature: Rereading Jeremiah 7–20* (Macon: Mercer University Press, 1996).

seem to be purposively interwoven, especially in Jeremiah (e.g., see 8:19c in context; 9:10 with 9:11; 9:17–19 with 9:22).[23] Tears and anger are held together in God, as they commonly are in people who have suffered the brokenness of intimate relationships. The dominance of marital metaphors in Jeremiah (and elsewhere) suggests that such relationships inform its portrayal of God's character. God mediates judgment so that sin and evil do not go unchecked in the world, but God does so at great cost to the divine life. [8]

Without the intermittent references to divine tears, the judgment texts would be even harsher and God much more removed and unmoved. Anger accompanied by weeping, while still anger, is different—in motivation and in the understanding of the relationship at stake. God's judgment is not matched by an inner harshness. Words of wrath are proclaimed reluctantly and with great anguish. In putting both wrath and grief on public display, the prophetic strategy is to portray the kind of God with whom their readers have to do, namely, a God for whom anger/judgment is neither the first word nor the last. A word about such a God can be productive of hope.

We have noted that, if there is no *divine* anger at sin and evil, then human anger toward that which is oppressive and abusive does not carry the same weight and seriousness. At the same time, if there is no sorrow associated with divine anger, then human anger is given a freer range regarding harshness.

Personal Emotion and "Political Emotion"

Yet another issue arises in seeking the (dis)continuities that may exist between human and divine anger: anger as an expression of the personality or character and anger as an expression of the "office" held.[24] It seems difficult to make this distinction absolute, for certainly the anger expressed by human officeholders in the exercise of their authority is not without an emotional component. Yet, such "official" anger is related especially to the preservation of the good order of community and creation so that it is not a strictly personal matter. Erich Zenger speaks of anger as "a personal aspect of God's responsibility for the world" and anger as "a political-juristic category," but insists that these two dimensions of anger must be linked in our theological considerations [9].[25] God is "personally touched" in matters of judgment; "God is not only to exercise the office of judge, but in doing so to communicate *God's own self*" (his emphasis).

---

23. For an analysis of the divine suffering texts, see Fretheim, *Suffering*, 107–26. For the texts in Jeremiah, see Terence Fretheim, *Jeremiah* (Macon: Smyth & Helwys, 2002).

24. On this distinction, with ANE parallels, see Herion, "Wrath of God," 991–95. George Mendenhall, *The Tenth Generation: The Origins of the Biblical Tradition* (Baltimore: Johns Hopkins Univ. Press, 1973), 69–104, similarly understands "vengeance," i.e., the exercise of the *imperium*.

25. Zenger, *Vengeance*, 72.

Texts that associate wrath with a role may be especially noted when they include metaphors for God such as King (Jer 10:10), Warrior (Jer 21:5), and especially Judge (Ps 7:11). At the same time, caution is urged. Zenger shows that, in thinking about God as judge, "the public system of justice remains only an analogue for what is at stake in talk about God." God is not at all "a neutral representative of an independent court of justice." Human judges, when they are doing their job well, seek to be objective and dispassionate (imagine courtrooms where judges displayed their anger and anguish!).

God, however, is not cool and detached. God has a binding relationship with those at whom the divine anger is directed, is openly anguished over present and future possibilities (e.g., Hos 6:4), and is personally caught up in the situation. Such features of the character of God constitute a decisive "no" in the metaphor of God as judge (or any "official" role). The personal dimension of wrath qualifies juridical understandings, while the juridical/political sense qualifies the personal. The personal and political senses of wrath must remain linked, but not collapsed. Thinking of God as judge, remember that the judge behind the bench is the spouse of the accused one in the dock.

Wrath, Covenant, and Creation

The discussion of God's wrath is often related to covenant.[26] This linkage is explicit in some texts (e.g., Lev 26:25), but is inadequate as a primary reference point for understanding wrath, not least because about half of the references to divine anger are in the prophets, who rarely reference the covenant. A word such as "relationship" would be [10] truer to the texts: a violation of Israel's relationship with God is a key factor in the exercise of wrath. In any related discussion, it would be important that covenant not be reduced to political or contractual understandings.[27] Covenant has a certain amount of "play" in its basic sense, one that allows for divine patience and change of mind; the result is that God's responses to human sin can never simply be collapsed into "justice."[28]

The divine anger is often directed against foreign nations; the motivation given often has to do with issues of human justice (e.g., Jer 51:45, 49). This exercise of divine wrath is obviously not associated with covenant

---

26. See, e.g., Walter Eichrodt, *Theology of the Old Testament* (2 vols.; Philadelphia: Westminster, 1961), 1:259–60.

27. As does Assmann in Zenger, *Vengeance,* 72. Notably, Eichrodt, *Theology,* 1:52, 68, warns against this legal sense of covenant.

28. Moreover, covenant does not have a univocal meaning in the OT; for example, Moses, in his intercession for Israel in the face of divine wrath, can appeal to the Abrahamic covenant just at the point where the Sinai covenant has been sharply violated (Exod 32:13). Note that Paul (in Romans 4 and Galatians 3) stakes out a claim for the priority of the Abrahamic covenant as well. Paul has learned this from Moses.

(e.g., Obadiah; Nahum).[29] Rather, these texts are rooted in a creation theology, wherein knowledge regarding matters such as social justice is believed to be available to those outside Israel, in terms of which they can be held accountable.[30] This point leads back to Israel's understanding that roots its own law in a creation theology.[31] And so Israel's violation of matters relating to social justice, and God's wrath related thereto, cannot be reduced to matters of covenant. *God's creation is at stake in Israel's behaviors, not simply their more specific relationship with God.* This is made concretely evident in the fact that Israel's sins have a devastating effect on the environment, to which God's wrath is often specifically related (e.g., Jer 4:23–26). Readers [11] might be prompted to ask whether God does not make things worse for the environment, but such texts witness to the deeply interconnected world in which we live.

Wrath and Judgment

The theme of divine wrath is closely correlated with the more comprehensive theme of divine judgment and cannot be considered apart from it (on God as Judge, see above). *That* sins have consequences *is* judgment and that can be named an experience of the wrath of God. Most basically, the wrath of God is a divine response that signals God's opposition to sin and evil in the creaturely sphere. Divine wrath precedes divine judgment and accompanies that judgment, so much so that "wrath" may *metonymically* specify the judgment itself (e.g., Hos 11:9; Jer 49:37, where "fierce anger" and "disaster" are in apposition).[32] In such terms, wrath is in effect viewed as a divine agent. Occasionally, the anger of God is mentioned without noting the specific effects (1 Kgs 16:26, 33) or the effects are only anticipated (Exod 32:9). But these effects are often specified in detail (e.g., Jer 19:3–9) and are amazingly wide-ranging, including individual and community, human and nonhuman, physical and psychical, religious and socio-political, chosen (Amos 3:2) and non-chosen.[33] That is, judgment is the working out of God's wrath in the world and is of such a nature that creatures [12] are

---

29. Notably, God's anger is never directed against the Canaanites in holy war texts in Joshua or Judges.

30. See, e.g., John Barton, *Ethics and the Old Testament* (London: SCM, 1998).

31. For details on this point, see Terence Fretheim, "The Reclamation of Creation: Redemption and Law in Exodus," *Int* 45 (1991): 354–65; idem, "Law in the Service of Life: the Dynamic Sense of Law in Deuteronomy," in *A God so Near: Essays on Old Testament Theology* (ed. B. A. Strawn and N. R. Bowen; Winona Lake, IN: Eisenbrauns, 2003), 183–200.

32. The concern of Heschel, *Prophets,* 280, not to reduce wrath to being *simply* a metonym or a synonym for punishment is important.

33. Baloian lists the following effects (*Anger,* 99): "military defeat (136 times), death (89 times), plague or sickness (26 times), famine (29 times), destruction of the agricultural capacity and actual cities of the land (25 times), captivity (33 times), scattering of the population without captivity (9 times), earthquakes (3 times), desecration of the cult (7 times), loss of leaders or positions of power (11 times) and finally, not being to enter the promised

comprehensively and adversely affected. God's wrath does not always lead to judgment (e.g., Exod 4:14), but it usually does.[34]

Historical Wrath and Eschatological Wrath

Many in Israel thought they were immune to judgment and need never fear the wrath of God (see Amos 5:18–20). Whatever may be said about *eschatological* wrath (cf. 1 Thess 1:10), faithfulness may not protect from *historical* wrath (witness those faithful Israelites caught up in the fall of Jerusalem). While God's advance warning may enable some to hide (Isa 26:20), no guarantees are given. Everyone may be caught up in the experience of wrath, not least because the wrath of God, mediated as it is by non-divine agents such as the Babylonians, does not cut clean. As a contemporary example, should the ecosystem be damaged by moral evil to the point where all creatures are adversely affected—that would be an experience of the wrath of God, to use biblical categories (whether we can speak in these terms today is another question). Should faithful ones get caught up in such a *communal* experience (as they have and will), they will be fearful, but they should not be afraid of God; they can claim the promise of Jer 31:3: "I have loved you with an everlasting love; therefore I have continued my faithfulness to you."

Wrath and Divine Temporality[35]

For many commentators, divine anger is synonymous with action, or, more precisely, for God to be angry is to put its effects immediately into motion ("wrath signifies the actual implementation of the [13] judgment").[36] But this way of formulating the issue is problematic, not least because of the metonymic use of wrath. Moreover, such an understanding implies that every divine thought is actualized, as if there were no such thing as a divine plan that took time to develop and gave temporal space for response before execution (see, e.g., Isa 48:3; Jer 18:11; 50:45). But God's anger, which threatens judgment, can be turned aside by human repentance (Joel 2:13) or intercession (Exod 32:9–14) or by God's own independent decision (Exod 4:14; Hos 11:8–9).

Other formulations regarding anger suggest this idea. For example, Josiah understands that "great is the wrath that is kindled against us" (2 Kgs 22:13), but covenant renewal may forestall its taking effect in judgment.

---

land (Moses, 4 times)." Also, emotional and mental effects, including "sorrow (11 times), terror (12 times), perception of God's abandonment (16 times) and shame (28 times)."

34. For a fuller exposition, see Terence Fretheim, "Divine Judgment and the Warming of the World: An Old Testament Perspective," in *God, Evil, and Suffering* (ed. T. Fretheim and C. Thompson; Word and World Supplement 4; St. Paul: Word and World, 2000), 21–32.

35. On this issue, see Fretheim, *The Suffering of God*, 39–44.

36. Baloian, *Anger*, 102.

This sense of things suggests a temporal distinction between wrath being kindled and wrath being executed. This text also notes that wrath can be "great," which assumes that that is not true in all cases, and also implies that such intensified wrath may be more difficult to turn away.

Generally speaking, God is open to redirection in view of human response or further divine reflection. This point stresses the genuine character of the God/Israel relationship. God is open to taking new directions in view of the dynamics of ongoing experience. At the same time, such openness may no longer be available, *even for God;* the ineffectiveness of intercession in some cases (e.g., Jer 11:14; 14:11) witnesses to the inexorable flow of certain historical events. Other OT texts introduce an even more specific temporal element. A key phrase that characterizes Israel's God is "slow to anger," that is, patient (e.g., Exod 34:6–7). Or, God is angry only momentarily or at least anger is temporally limited (e.g., Ps 30:5; Isa 54:7–8). Elsewhere, God is said (not) to restrain anger (e.g., Ps 78:38; Isa 48:9) and to hold his peace (e.g., Isa 57:11; Ezek 16:42, "I will be calm [= at peace] and will be no more angry"). [14]

These references to divine wrath are coherent only if placed along a time line, so that one can speak of delay, a time of provocation, a time of execution, and an end. God's anger is *historical* anger; it has its time and a time when it is not, with effects on both God and world. More generally, that God is "provoked to anger" by specific historical acts or situations (e.g., Jer 8:19) is temporally important. The texts never suggest that God was provoked from all eternity by any sin that would ever be committed (an absolute foreknowledge position) and that each such "historical" provocation is an actualization of that prior provocation. *Wrath is a contextualized reality.*

Wrath as Contingent: Motivations for Wrath

Virtually all references to divine anger are linked to a motivation, either directly or in the larger context.[37] Two commonly cited exceptions are 2 Sam 6:6–7 and 2 Sam 24:1 (divine anger becomes Satan in 1 Chr 21:1, an agent of divine wrath). Yet, the absence of motivation in these texts may only be apparent; the text could be ambiguous, overly subtle, textually problematic (as with 2 Samuel 6), or the issue may not be within the purview of the narrator.[38] Indeed, given the remarkably common presence of motivations, readers in that culture would probably have sought to supply them (even if they did not agree [15] with them, witness Job). Yet, one

---

37. Baloian (ibid., 72) claims that wrath is motivated by wickedness toward other human beings in about 50% of the texts, while about 75% are marked by infidelity to God, such as idolatry. The percentage total (125%) indicates the presence of both motivations in many contexts (about one-third of the cases).

38. For a survey of possible interpretations of these difficult texts, see ibid., 81–92.

should not go to great lengths to make every text fit; the OT is too sprawling a text to be absolutely consistent.[39]

The Prophets.   The prophets never introduce motivations designed to protect God or God's holiness or moral perfection. The prophetic concern in stating motivations is to make sure that people know the grounds for the judgment that occurs. Note, for example, the remarkable range of concern in Jeremiah that the "Why?" questions of the exiles be addressed (e.g., Jer 5:18–19).[40] These question-answer formulas make clear that God's anger and the adverse effects being experienced are rooted in human sin and not God.

Job and Psalms.   Some texts contest the appropriateness of God's wrath, especially in Job (e.g., 9:13–15). Readers know that Job is not suffering because of divine wrath, but Job understands it so. Hence, in essence, Job agrees with the friends' linkage of suffering and wrath because of sin (4:8–9), though Job claims the divine anger functions inconsistently (21:17, 30). So Job assumes that God must have a motivation for what he has had to endure, but the motivation is not what he thinks it is.

Given these references in Job, readers must be prepared to find comparably inappropriate claims regarding divine wrath elsewhere (e.g., lament psalms), though, unlike Job, they may not protest the anger (e.g., Pss 88:7, 16; 102:10; cf. 27:9; 89:38, 46). The penitential laments, however, understand that the experience of divine wrath has been appropriate, perhaps evident in being convicted of sin (e.g., Ps 6:1). Other laments, especially communal laments, raise questions about the length and breadth of divine anger, while understanding that it was not inappropriate (e.g., Pss 60:1; 90:7–11). [16]

Still other psalmists assume that they have a proper case to make against their enemies before God, and call upon God to act in wrath against them (e.g., Ps 7:6). If they have not provided a motivation for God to act, then the divine wrath would not be forthcoming. This point regarding motivations is the other side of the prophetic word regarding why God is angry with *Israel.* As God regularly gave motivations in the prophetic oracles of judgment, so the psalmists believed that, in their calling upon God to act on their behalf, they were being consistent in providing God with such motivations.

---

39. Walter Brueggemann speaks of the "profound irrationality" of Yahweh, a "Yahweh who is out of control with the violent, sexual rage of a husband who assaults his own beloved" (*Theology of the Old Testament* [Minneapolis: Fortress, 1997], 383). He appeals to Ezekiel 16 and 23 as examples. These are deeply problematic texts, but God's wrath is clearly motivated by infidelity, so the word "irrational" is not appropriate. For this marital metaphor, and it is metaphor, see Renita Weems, *Battered Love: Marriage, Sex, and Violence in the Hebrew Prophets* (Minneapolis: Fortress, 1995).

40. See Terence Fretheim, *Jeremiah* (Macon, GA: Smyth and Helwys, 2002), 4–11.

Baloian refers to these motivations as evidence for a divine wrath that is in accord with just legal procedures, that is, giving good reasons for the judgment.[41] Certainly there is some truth to this point, but to understand the divine justice simply in legal terms is insufficiently relational, and does not adequately take into account either the divine patience or the divine repentance (see discussion on God as Judge). It is remarkable that divine anger has such a prominent place in Israel's prayers, whether that anger is directed against the pray-er, the psalmist makes a case for wrath against the enemy, or the pray-er raises objections because of the severity of the wrath. Given these prayer contexts, God's anger must be understood in relational, indeed personal terms. An angry God is understood to be approachable in prayer; human beings can stand in the face of consuming divine anger and have their say (e.g., Exod 32:7–14).

Cultic Matters. In several texts the wrath of God is associated with breaches in the cultic sphere, including the tabernacle, its furnishings and leadership (e.g., Lev 10:1–6), and other sacral matters as well (e.g., Neh 13:18). Several scholars speak of a close link between wrath and holiness; wrath is "a manifestation of God's holiness."[42] While not eliminating this idea, a broader approach seems preferable, not least because holiness is seldom associated with wrath in the OT.[43] The strict measures regarding worship places and practices in this tradition seem [17] not to be concerned to protect God from the people or the people from God (though violation could mean violence, Num 1:53), but rather, given the people's propensity to apostasy, to preserve the proper, but asymmetrical *relationship* between God and people. The use of comparable language with reference to idolatry (2 Chr 24:18) also suggests such an understanding.

I conclude this segment with three more abstract points. (1) Because wrath is always "provoked," wrath is not a divine attribute,[44] and hence different from, say, love; "if there were no sin, there would be no wrath."[45] In Eichrodt's terms, wrath is never "a permanent state of affairs for God in relation to humanity."[46] See also Peels's language: "Wrath is not a permanent 'attribute' of God, but neither is it 'uncharacteristic' of God."[47] To claim wrath as an attribute would entail an eternal dualism and a compromise of Israel's monotheism. (2) Anger cannot be construed simply in terms of emotion, for God gives reasons. God's wrath is not "irrational"; from the general understanding of God in the OT, one may infer that God's actions

---

41. Baloian, *Anger,* 77–98.
42. For example, ibid., 80–81.
43. See n. 4 above. Note that holiness does not mean unapproachableness (witness Moses, priesthood).
44. On this point, see esp. Heschel, *Prophets,* 279–306. This study remains one of the most cogent contributions to the topic.
45. So Stephen H. Travis, "Wrath (NT)," *ABD* 6:997.
46. Eichrodt, *Theology,* 1:262, 266.
47. Peels, *Vengeance,* 289.

always serve God's purposes even though hidden with respect to specific motivation ("there can never be any question of despotic caprice striking out in blind rage").[48] Emotion and reason come together in God's anger. God's wrath is "voluntary and purposeful, motivated by a concern for right and wrong."[49] (3) God is angry because God's will is not being done; hence, God's will is resistible. If this were not the case, then God's anger would, finally, only be directed to God's own self. If God's will is irresistible, God's anger is meaningless. [18]

Turning Wrath Away

Wrath's contingency is also evident in the divine openness to avert wrath, through human prayer (e.g., 1 Kgs 8:46–53) or action (e.g., 2 Chr 29:10), or God's own (re)assessment of the situation. Several texts portray key leaders as "standing in the breach" between God and Israel.[50] Moses intercedes for an idolatrous people and turns away God's wrath, saving them from destruction (Ps 106:23). That God responds to prayer is a sign that God values the human contribution, revealing the personal character of wrath. For all of wrath's "intensity, it may be averted by prayer."[51]

Jer 15:1 also recalls Moses' intercessory activity and adds Samuel (1 Sam 12:17–18), but specifies that intercessory activity would be fruitless at this point in Israel's life. In other words, there has been a buildup of the effects of human sin to such a degree that wrath (understood as the functioning of the moral order) could not be held back (there is not even enough "room" for God to reverse the situation; see 2 Kgs 23:26). Such an understanding can also be seen in those texts where wrath became "(so) great" that there could be no remedy (see 2 Kgs 22:13). Ezek 22:30–31 has a somewhat different story; God looked for someone to stand in the breach and none was found; therefore, God poured out his wrath. This individual would not have been a scapegoat, taking God's wrath upon himself, but may have prevented the wrath of God from having its judgmental effects in the first place. The use of this image in Isa 58:9–12 suggests that the necessary action to be taken in the face of judgment may be caring for the needy.

In addition to human beings standing in the breach, God can (in effect) stand in the breach. God can decide for the sake of God's own purposes to withhold wrath (e.g., Ezek 20:21b-22) or turn wrath away (Isa 12:1). The parade example of this divine move is Hosea 11:9; God chooses not to "execute his wrath" for God's own reasons. Wrath has [19] been provoked in Yahweh by human infidelity, but God chooses not to let it go forward

48. So Eichrodt, *Theology*, 1:265. So also Heschel, *Prophets*. This claim is one of the points wherein a contrast is often drawn between Yahweh and the gods of the ancient Near East, where the anger of the gods is often malicious and grounded in envy.
49. Heschel, *Prophets*, 282.
50. See esp. Schroeder, "Standing in the Breach."
51. Heschel, *Prophets*, 286.

to work (complete?) the deed of judgment. This text suggests that God can interrupt God's own wrath, at least up to a certain point (as also with the divine "repentance," e.g., Jer 26:3, 13, 19). The Godness of God is such that God chooses to take the wrath into the divine self and suffer it there rather than letting it go forth to destruction. This (potential) change in God is another reason why the law court metaphor is finally not adequate.[52] Moreover, the change in God in Hos 11:8–9 comes after some adverse effects have been experienced (vv. 5–7). So, averting wrath may come before it begins to be executed or it may come after it is already in progress; while anger has a course to run (Isa 5:25), it may be able to be interrupted (Isa 10:25). Ezekiel especially speaks of anger as "rested, spent" or "completed," that is, having run, or not run, its course (e.g., Ezek 5:13).

Wrath as Personal and Natural

Wrath as personal and wrath as natural should not be split apart, but seen as integral dimensions of a single reality; we are not forced to make a decision for one or the other. Indeed, keeping the personal and the natural together will, among other things, enable us to steer clear of both deism and determinism in considering this matter. I suggest this formulation: God's personal anger works in and through the natural order.

Wrath as personal divine response has been evident in several ways. We have shown that the personal and the official must be kept together and considered matters such as divine repentance, restraint, and temporality. Such a view is also supported by the fact that God's anger is often associated with divine *speech* (e.g., Jer 11:17). Or, to say that Jeremiah is "full of the wrath of the Lord" and "weary of holding it in" (6:11), as God is "weary" (15:6), suggests that "wrath" is both the *word of judgment* that Jeremiah is called to speak and is personally [20] embodied in the prophet. To embody a word of wrath and to speak that word is part of the process of judgment itself. It is difficult to imagine these divine activities if we are dealing simply with an impersonal principle.

At the same time, we have noted that several scholars focus on wrath as an "impersonal" phenomenon (especially A. T. Hanson[53]). Several texts would seem to support this claim. For example, in Jeremiah wrath "goes forth" because of the people's evil (Jer 4:4), is like "a whirling tempest," (23:20), "bursts upon" (23:19) or "is poured out upon" the people (6:11), and is like a fire that burns (4:4). The absolute use of the word "wrath" in several texts should also be noted (particularly קֶצֶף and זַעַם). While wrath "goes forth" (or other verbal formulations) and may be said to come from

---

52. Contrary to Baloian, *Anger*, 97.

53. Hanson states that Paul "transformed the wrath from an attribute of God into the name for a process which sinners bring upon themselves" (*Wrath*, 69). The word "attribute" skews the discussion.

Yahweh (Num 16:46), it is often used without explicit reference to Yahweh (e.g., Num 1:53).[54]

Certainly many of these texts could be understood in terms of the use of natural metaphors for wrath or the created moral order, but to consider them impersonal goes beyond the evidence. Psalm 78, for example, with its many uses of anger language (vv. 21–62) juxtaposes both personal and natural understandings (see also Num 16:22 with 16:46; Josh 22:18 with 22:20; 2 Chr 28:9 with 28:13; Ps 79:5–6; Ezek 7:3, 8, 12, 14). These juxtapositions are too frequent to be considered anomalous; the personal and the natural are not considered incongruous. Generally speaking, if certain texts explicitly state that wrath comes from Yahweh, readers would likely have understood that Yahweh was its source even when it is used absolutely (e.g., 2 Chr 28:11 with 28:13; 2 Chr 32:25 with 32:26; Ezek 7:12 with 7:14; Ezra 7:23 with 9:14). Moreover, if an explicit reference to *God's* anger is absent, such texts should also be linked to the metonymic use of wrath. Yes, wrath is "in play" in that sin works itself out in the course [21] of history in terms of a moral order of things, but that does not necessarily entail a deistic move that God is removed from personally "seeing to" the move from sin to consequence.

This moral order, grounded in God's creative work, does not function in a precise or mechanistic way; the causal weave is complex and loose so that, for example, the wicked may prosper (see Jer 12:1–4) and room is left for chance (Eccl 9:11). God is to some degree subject to this just order (see Abraham's question in Gen 18:25), though this cannot be factored out except to say that the looseness of the causal weave allows God to be at work in the "system" without violating or (temporarily) suspending it and, in these terms, God is certainly an agent. Just how God so functions is difficult to sort out, not least because the OT does not approach the matter of agency from a single perspective.

Many texts demonstrate that God as an agent functions within the moral order in various ways. God's giving people up (Rom 1:24–28) is paralleled in many OT texts (e.g., Ps 81:11–16). This giving up is not an arbitrary divine act, but a giving the people up to the consequences of their own choices. Ezek 22:31 is a striking text in this respect. God declares: "I have consumed them with the fire of my wrath." What that entails is immediately stated: "I have returned their conduct upon their heads" (similarly, see Ezek 16:42–43a; 7:3–4, 8–9; 7:14, 27; 9:8–10; 24:13–14). This language is witness to an intrinsic relationship between sinful deed and consequence. God introduces nothing new into the situation (such as a penalty), but sees to the functioning of the moral order.[55]

---

54. For a survey of wrath in the intertestamental period, see ibid., 41–67. This sense of wrath is continued in the deuterocanonical books (e.g., Sir 7:16).

55. Over fifty texts link wrath with such formulations (e.g., Ps 7:12–16; Isa 59:17–18; 64:5–9; Jer 6:11, 19; 7:18–20; 21:12–14; 44:7–8; 50:24–25; Lam 3:64–66).

Several matters of translation and interpretation come together in thinking through this issue. For example, the noun רָעָה occurs eighty-five times
in Jeremiah (related forms over fifty times). Sometimes this word refers
to human wickedness, sometimes to its effects, commonly [22] translated
"disaster" (the word עָוֹן "iniquity," is also used in both senses in the OT,
see Gen 19:15).[56] This verbal linkage shows that the judgment experienced
flows out of Israel's own wickedness.

This understanding of רָעָה issuing in רָעָה may be observed in several
formulations. God's wrath is to be poured out (Jer 6:11) and that brings
disaster (רָעָה), which is "the fruit of *their* schemes" (Jer 6:19; see Hos 8:7;
10:13). Or, "I will pour out *their* wickedness upon them" (14:16). Note that
wrath and "their wickedness" are parallel; the pouring out of divine wrath
is the pouring out of the people's wickedness. Or, God gives to all "according to their ways, according to the fruit of their doings" (Jer 17:10). Like
fruit, the consequence grows out of (or is intrinsic to) the deed itself. This
leads to a certain amount of correspondence thinking in the prophets—
like produces like (e.g., Jer 50:29); the people will stew in the juices they
themselves have prepared.[57] This type of thinking may have its roots in a
concern for fairness; in terms of any human canons of accountability, the
judgment fits the crime.

This dynamic understanding of sin and its effects can also be observed
in the use of the verb פָּקַד, "visit." Its translation as "punish" in NRSV is
problematic, as in 21:14: "I will punish you according to the fruit of your
doings." A more literal translation is clearer: "I will visit upon you the fruit
of your doings" (see 5:9; 14:10). It needs to be considered whether the word
"punish" is ever an appropriate translation [23] of the verb פָּקַד (see also the
related noun פְּקֻדָּה, often translated "punishment," e.g., Jer 46:21).[58]

These various formulations show that God mediates the consequences
of that which is already present in the wicked situation. The people's sin
has had a significant level of "negative fallout," given the interrelatedness

---

56. In view of these two senses of רָעָה its translation varies somewhat in the versions.
The RSV (following the KJV) tends to translate "evil" for both senses of the word (e.g., Jer
18:8). The NRSV, however, commonly changes the translation to "disaster" when it refers
to the effects of human evil (e.g., Jer 18:8), though, strangely, not consistently (e.g., Jer
18:11; cf. 11:11, 23 with 11:17). Among other translations, the NIV translates "disaster"
consistently (e.g., Jer 18:11). The NEB is nearly as consistent and in the two texts where it
translates "evil" (Jer 18:8, 11), its successor (the REB) changes both to "disaster."

57. This understanding can be ascribed to the root נקם, commonly (and unhelpfully)
translated "vengeance" and linked with wrath (Mic 5:15; Isa 59:17; Ezek 25:14, 17). The
root נקם also occurs within "what goes around, comes around" contexts, for example, Jer
50:15 (cf. Isa 59:17–18; Jer 50:28–29; 51:6).

58. Gerhard von Rad speaks of a "synthetic view of life" in which "the retribution
is not a new action which comes upon the person concerned from somewhere else; it is
rather the last ripple of the act itself which attaches to its agent almost as something material. Hebrew in fact does not even have a word for punishment" (*Old Testament Theology*
[2 vols.; New York: Harper & Row, 1962], 1:265, 385).

of all creatures; God brings those consequences to completion. Though the agency issues cannot be factored out with precision, some helpful claims are made in various texts (e.g., Hos 8:7; 10:13–15; 13:7–9, 16). Israel's sin generates certain snowballing effects. At the same time, God is active in the interplay of human sin and its effects, and God uses "third parties" as agents for that judgment. Both divine and creaturely factors are interwoven to produce the judgmental result.[59] Humans and not God are fundamentally responsible for wrath and its effects, bringing people's deeds back upon their own heads. But God is ultimately the source of wrath in that God created the world in which the moral order plays a role, but in that order God works in and through creaturely agents rather than with a divine immediacy.

The nature of the link between the execution of divine wrath and the fruit-producing deed is difficult to articulate.[60] Several images have been [24] suggested for God's involvement in the move from sin to consequence: God mediates, midwifes, facilitates, sees to, carries the mail, puts in force, or completes the connection (שָׁלֵם) between sin and consequence. God's personal anger may be said to be a "seeing to" this movement from deed to consequence that is the moral order. In some texts God takes an active role, at other times a more passive, withdrawing role (e.g., Isa 64:6–7). While this idea could be expressed in language such as "you reap what you sow" (Prov 22:8), God is not removed from the link between sin and consequence (deism is not an OT perspective). This conception gives full stature and respect to both human and divine action.

God's Agents of Wrath

God chooses to work through human (and nonhuman) agents in the exercise of wrath. Numerous texts illustrate the point (e.g., Jer 50:25, "the weapons of his wrath"; Isa 10:5, "Assyria, the rod of my anger"). Indeed, the divine anger is a mirror of the anger of the agent (Ezek 23:25, "I will direct my indignation against you, in order that *they* might deal with you

---

59. See Fretheim, *Suffering of God,* 77.

60. Helpful resources are Patrick D. Miller Jr., *Sin and Judgment in the Prophets: A Stylistic and Theological Analysis* (Chico, CA: Scholars Press, 1982); Klaus Koch, "Is There a Doctrine of Retribution in the Old Testament?" in *Theodicy in the Old Testament* (ed. J. Crenshaw; Philadelphia: Fortress, 1983). More recently, Gene Tucker, "Sin and 'Judgment' in the Prophets," in *Problems in Biblical Theology* (ed. H. Sun et al.; Grand Rapids: Eerdmans, 1997), 373–88. Tucker delineates several formulations, texts that are "dynamistic" and have no explicit reference to God (e.g., Isa 3:9–11; Hos 10:13–15), those in which God makes the connection between sin and consequence (e.g., Jer 6:19; 21:14) and, least common, those that have a juridical element (e.g., Amos 4:1–3). How these "judgment" texts are to be related is best seen in the work of H. H. Schmid, who places them under the comprehensive umbrella of creation theology: "Creation, Righteousness, and Salvation: 'Creation Theology' as the Broad Horizon of Biblical Theology," in *Creation in the Old Testament* (ed. B. Anderson; Philadelphia: Fortress, 1984), 102–17.

in fury"). Ezek 21:31 reinforces the point: God will "deliver you into the hands of brutal men." Wrath is linked to deliverance into the hands of those who execute the wrath. Nonhuman agents are also common (e.g., Ps 104:4, including sickness and famine [e.g., Num 11:33; Deut 28:20–24]). More could be said here about the issue of agency; but I refer to other writings in which this issue has been more fully developed.[61]

That God is not the only effective agency in these events is made clear by the divine judgment on *Babylon* (Jer 25:12–14; Isa 47:6–7; Zech 1:15). Babylon exceeded its mandate, going beyond its proper judgmental activities, and committed iniquity itself. It is assumed (cf. the [25] oracles against the nations) that standards are known by the nations and to which they are held accountable. The exercise of divine wrath against Babylonian excessiveness shows that God did not micromanage their activities; they retained the power to execute policies that flew in the face of the will of God. Hence, the will of God active in these events is not "irresistible."[62] God risks what the Babylonians will do with the mandate they have been given. One element of that risk is that God's name will become associated with violence, indeed the excessive violence of the agents.[63]

This perspective is witness to a fundamentally *relational* understanding of the way in which God acts in the world. Creation has an ordered freedom, a degree of openness and unpredictability, wherein God leaves room for human decisions as they exercise their God-given power. Even more, God confers responsibilities in such a way that *commits* God to a certain kind of relationship with them. This entails a divine constraint and restraint in the use of power in relation to these agents. They overdid it!

Wrath within God's Saving Purpose

God's anger is never an end in itself, but is always exercised in the service of God's more comprehensive *salvific* purposes for creation (see also above on turning wrath away). Generally speaking, wrath may be considered God's circumstantial will that stands in the service of God's ultimate will for life and salvation.[64]

At one level, "Divine sympathy for the victims of human cruelty is the motive of anger."[65] God's wrath means the deliverance of slaves [26] from oppression (Exod 15:7), the righteous from their enemies (Ps 7:6–11), the poor and needy from their abusers (Exod 22:21–24), and Israel from its

---

61. See Terence Fretheim, "The Character of God in Jeremiah," in *Character and Scripture: Moral Formation, Community, and Biblical Interpretation* (ed. W. P. Brown; Grand Rapids: Eerdmans, 2002), 211–30; idem, *Jeremiah*, 35–39.

62. Contrary to Brueggemann, *Jeremiah*, 222.

63. See John Sanders, *The God Who Risks: A Theology of Providence* (Downers Grove: InterVarsity, 1998).

64. For this distinction, see Terence Fretheim, "Will of God in the OT," *ABD* 6:914–20.

65. Heschel, *Prophets*, 288.

enemies (Isa 30:27–33). "This is one of the meanings of the anger of God: the end of indifference" with respect to the victims of human cruelty.[66] In so stating the matter, God's exercise of wrath is, finally, a word of good news (for those oppressed) and bad news (for oppressors). Such wrath gives hope that evil will not have the last word; it makes a more positive future possible for those who have no other hope.

At another level, the warning of divine wrath is intended to lead to repentance (Jonah 3:8–9) and, if judgment is forthcoming, its purpose is to refine and cleanse the people for life on the far side of disaster (e.g., Isa 48:9–11). God's salvific motivation is made clear in Ezekiel's refrain, that "they may know that I am the Lord" (e.g., Ezek 7:27). This objective is more than didactic; it has in view a restored relationship between people and God, a restoration that will bring honor to God's name (Ezek 36:22–23).

God's comfort for the people lies on the far side of anger (Isa 12:1). God would prefer to avoid wrath altogether (Isa 27:1–5), evident not least in the divine patience (Exod 34:6), "the restraint of justifiable anger,"[67] and the divine change of mind, a theme usually associated with judgment (Exod 32:7–14).[68] God has no pleasure in judgment (Lam 3:33) or "in the death of anyone," even the wicked (Ezek 18:23, 32). Isa 54:7–8 sharpens the point: overflowing divine wrath is but for a moment (though it may have felt as if it would last forever, Lam 5:22), but God's love is everlasting (so also Jer 31:3; Mic 7:18). God's anger is finally in the service of this kind of loving relationship; "its purpose and consummation is its own disappearance. . . . This is the dream of God: . . . to say of Himself: 'I have no wrath'" (Isa 27:2–3).[69]

---

66. Ibid., 284.
67. Ibid., 285.
68. See Terence Fretheim, "The Repentance of God: A Key to Evaluating OT God-Talk," *HBT* 10 (1988): 47–70.
69. Heschel, *Prophets*, 286, 294.

The Self-Limiting God of the Old Testament and Issues of Violence

The God of the Old Testament is associated with a remarkable range of problematic words and actions, especially regarding violence. A lively concern about this sort of language is nothing new in the academy or religious communities.[1] Already in the second century, Marcion had great difficulties with the Old Testament image of God, not least the divine anger and violence; he emerged with a truncated New Testament emptied of any remnants of problematic Old Testament God talk. Marcion has had many heirs. In the academy, this concern may be manifested in minimalist theological attention given to difficult God texts and/or sharp criticism of patriarchal and violent images, perhaps even an outright rejection of them.[2] In the church, there has never been a time when the Bible did not create problems in and through what it did or did not say about God. These matters have been raised to new intensities in recent decades, not least because of changing cultural sensitivities and an increasingly diverse readership. At least one effect of these changing times is that both church and academy have begun to give new attention to difficult images of God.[3]

One might ask whether at least some of these difficulties with the God of the Bible are related, not to the textual images as such, but to the impact of traditional understandings of God on Bible readers. These traditional understandings include divine characteristics such as these: omnipotent, omniscient, [180] immutable, impassible, and atemporal. Though the Bible

This essay was originally published in *Raising up a Faithful Exegete: Essays in Honor of Richard D. Nelson* (ed. K. L. Noll and Brooks Schramm; Winona Lake, IN: Eisenbrauns, 2010), 179–91.

1. I speak from the perspective of the church; other religious communities might be included. I would like to thank my student assistant Michael Chan for his comments on an earlier draft of this paper.

2. See, for example, Kari Latvus, *God, Anger and Ideology: The Anger of God in Joshua and Judges in Relation to Deuteronomy and the Priestly Writings* (JSOTSup 279; Sheffield: Sheffield Academic Press, 1998), 91: "The God that deuteronomistic theologians created in their own image was thus the God of strict dogmatism, intolerance and fundamentalism. . . . The God of the crucified and powerless Jesus cannot be the same as the deuteronomistic God of anger."

3. For example, Eric Seibert, *Disturbing Divine Behavior: Troubling Old Testament Images of God* (Minneapolis: Fortress, 2009). For my own work, see "God and Violence in the Old Testament," *WW* 24 (2004): 18–28; idem, "'I Was Only a Little Angry': Divine Violence in the Prophets," *Int* 58 (2004): 365–75.

uses none of these words,[4] their associated ideas have had an immense influence, consciously or unconsciously, on the way in which we interpret the word *God* whenever we encounter it in the text. The result is that many of the actual biblical images for God have been neglected or harmonized to fit with these divine attributes. The discussion of issues such as violence with respect to the God of the Old Testament often assumes textual commitments regarding divine omnipotence, or at least unlimited omnipotence (as it is usually considered), and related claims.[5] The extent to which these traditional assumptions affect the conversation needs forthright attention before problematic issues such as divine violence can be fully considered.

One of the ways in which this conversation can be furthered is by drawing out certain characteristics of the God of the text that seem to stand over against the God of classical theism. To this end, I would like to explore this matter through a close examination of the images of God that are present in the creation story (Genesis 1–2) and the story of the flood (Genesis 6–9), especially the image of divine self-limitation.[6] These Genesis texts often challenge traditional descriptors of God (though this is not often made apparent in the various expositions). In addition, I suggest that the placement of these narratives at the beginning of the Bible invites readers to study all texts that follow through the theological lens they provide. How one reads the God that is presented in succeeding texts, not least the more problematic images, is to be shaped by these opening accounts. At the same time, it should be made clear that not everything that is said about God in the Old Testament/Bible can be fully harmonized.[7] [181]

---

4. Occasionally an equivalent is claimed (see, for example, Jer 32:17, 27), but it seems doubtful that phrases of this sort correspond to the traditional language (see my "Is Anything Too Hard for God? [Jeremiah 32:27]," *CBQ* 66 [2004]: 231–36). Later in this essay, I will work with the possibility of divine omnipotence for the sake of argument.

5. I have deeply appreciated Richard Nelson's work over the years, not least his willingness to engage in theological issues presented by texts. This article is prompted in part by my response to several of his theological reflections. In his treatment of 1 Kings 1, for example, Nelson claims that "Yahweh's plan and will must be effected, and for God, at least, the ends justify the means. . . . The good news is . . . that God is in charge even of the dark side. . . . In all that follows, Yahweh will be in *complete* control of events" (*First and Second Kings* [Atlanta: John Knox, 1988], 22–23 [italics mine]). Elsewhere, Nelson speaks of "God's control of international affairs" and "the future of Jeroboam's dynasty has already been closed off by prophetic foreknowledge" (p. 73).

6. The language of "self" limitation does have some inadequacies, perhaps suggesting to some readers that it contemplates a diminishment of the divine self. I use this language to reference the idea that God is the subject of the limitation, not that which is other than God. It is God alone who limits the divine self.

7. To return to the traditional claims about God of which we have spoken (for example, immutable, impassible), it is remarkable that these theological claims seem at best to be tangentially correspondent with the centering witness about God present in many texts (for example, creedal statements about God such as Exod 34:6–7). The God in these creedal statements is a deeply relational God—a key point—a perspective that seems not to be central to at least some of the more traditional language regarding God.

Divine Self-Limitation in Genesis 1–2

How we think about the God of Genesis, indeed of the Bible as a whole, will be sharply affected by how we portray the God of the creation accounts. It is common among commentators to say that God created the world alone, with overwhelming power and absolute control, working independently and unilaterally. But, if this understanding of God in creation is correct, then the beings created in God's image could *properly* understand their role regarding the rest of creation in comparable terms—that is, in terms of power over, absolute control, and independence. By definition, the natural world thus becomes available for human manipulation and exploitation. In other words, how one understands the God of the creation accounts will have a significant impact on one's view of the world, environmental sensitivities, and the urgency of one's practices.[8]

What if the God of the creation accounts is imaged more as one who, in creating, chooses to share power in relationship, with a consequent self-limitation in the use of divine power and freedom? Then the way in which the human as image of God exercises dominion is to be shaped by this model. Even more, if the God of the creation accounts is imaged as one who involves creatures (human and nonhuman) in still further creations, as we will see, then this should inform our understanding of the value that they have been given by God. I see three types of textual evidence that can assist us in reflecting on this angle of vision.[9]

1. God creates in and through the use of existing matter. Male and female, for example, are not created "out of nothing" but out of already existent creatures, both human and nonhuman (Gen 2:7, 22). The Creator is not external to the creative process but "gets down in the dirt" (see God in human form in Gen 3:8) and creates in direct contact with the stuff used to create; God creates from within creation, not from without. This is an act of self-limitation.

2. God speaks *with* already existing creatures and involves them in creative activity: "Let the earth bring forth," and "the earth brought forth" (Gen 1:11–13); "let us make humankind" (Gen 1:26). This is mediated rather than [182] immediate creation. God's creating is not accomplished alone; God seeks assistance from the creatures in creating. This is an act of self-limitation.

3. Gen 1:28, "Be fruitful and multiply, and fill the earth and subdue it, and have dominion." This first divine word to the newly created human

---

8. For an earlier reflection on this theological issue, see my *God and World in the Old Testament: A Relational Theology of Creation* (Nashville: Abingdon, 2005), 48–53.

9. For detail, see my *Creation Untamed: The Bible, God, and Natural Disasters* (Grand Rapids, MI: Baker Academic, 2010). I assume literary and historical reflections on these texts. For a basic and thorough discussion, see Claus Westermann, *Genesis 1–11*: A Commentary (trans. J. J. Scullion; Minneapolis: Augsburg, 1984). See also J. Richard Middleton, *The Liberating Image: The Imago Dei in Genesis 1* (Grand Rapids, MI: Brazos, 2005).

being constitutes a sharing of power, which would be characteristic of any relationship of integrity. In other words, God gives up a monopoly on power for the sake of a genuine relationship with the world.[10] From the beginning, God chooses not to be the only one who has creative power and the capacity to exercise it, indeed the obligation to do so. Human beings are invited, indeed commanded by God to play an important role in the becoming of their world in and through the exercise of power. God certainly is the one who invites their participation in the use of power. But, having done so, God is committed to this way of relating to them. Given this commitment, forfeiting or suspending this status of the human being for shorter or longer periods of time is not a divine option. God will be faithful to this way of relating to the human beings created in the divine image.

As an example, God lets the *human being* determine whether the animals are adequate to move the evaluation of the creation from "not good" to "good" (Gen 2:18–21). The human being, not God, deems what is fit for him. God places the creative possibilities before the human being, but it is the creature that is given the freedom to decide. God, in turn, accepts the human decision and "goes back to the drawing board." One might also cite Eve's testimony to both human and divine involvement in the birthing of the first human being (Gen 4:1). These are acts of divine self-limitation.

In sum, God takes the ongoing creational process into account in shaping new directions for the world, one dimension of which is engaging creatures in creative acts. Divine decisions interact with both human decisions and nonhuman activity in the becoming of the world. Creation is process as well as punctiliar act; creation is creaturely as well as divine. While creatures are deeply dependent on God for their creation and life, God has chosen to establish an *interdependent* relationship with them regarding both originating and continuing creation. God's approach to creation is thus communal and relational; in the wake of God's initiating activity, God works from within the world rather than on the world from without. God's word in creation is often a communicating word with others, rather than, say, a top-down word.[11] The actions of humans [183] and other creatures make a difference with respect to the future of the creation, indeed *God's* future with creation.

These texts from the creation accounts are a witness to divine self-limitation in creation. God lets the world be involved in its continuing creation, indeed to create itself. In terms of the text, God keeps the Sabbath

---

10. This would mean that any direct or indirect use of metaphors for God such as *king* cannot be construed to suggest that only the superior has genuine power.

11. While the biblical testimony, finally, witnesses to creation out of nothing (Rom 4:17, Heb 11:3), there is strong consensus that this idea only exists on the edges of Genesis 1–2 (and, in any case, would apply to several details rather than creation as a whole—for example, Gen 1:6–7, 14–19).

day (Gen 2:1–3). God rests, without managing the creaturely activity and lets the creatures be and become what they were created to be. God limits both the divine power and the divine freedom because God is committed to the sharing of power and freedom with the creatures.

Foundational to these understandings of the God of the creation accounts is that God has entered into a genuine relationship with the world.[12] God does not remain aloof and, like some divine mechanic, seek to work on the world from the outside. God personally involves the divine self in its life and chooses to work from within. This dimension of the text is revealing of a major Old Testament conviction—namely, the centrality of relationality at three levels of consideration: within God (see Gen 1:26), between God and world, and among the creatures. For the Old Testament, relationships are constitutive of life itself; all things are woven together in and through relationships. To live in a relational world of this sort means at least this: all creatures will be affected by every other creature. We are bound up with one another in such a way that each of us is involved in the plight of all of us. And God has chosen to be caught up in this spiderweb of relationships in a self-limiting way. God will move with the creatures into a future that is to some extent unsettled, dependent in part on what they do with the powers they have been given.

Divine Self-Limitation in the Story of the Flood

A basic list of what God as subject does in the flood story[13] is remarkable in its range: God expresses sorrow and regret (but not anger); God judges but does not want to; God goes beyond justice and decides to save some creatures; God pulls back from an initial decision to "blot out" the world (Gen 6:7), deciding to deliver both human beings and animals; God changes but people do not (Gen 6:5, 8:21); God is receptive to doing things in new ways in view [184] of new divine experience with the world; and God commits to the future of a less than perfect world. God's promising never to act in such a destructive way again, twice stated and formalized in covenantal terms (Gen 8:21–22, 9:8–17), entails an eternal, divine self-limitation in the exercise of power in response to evil in the world.[14]

---

12. For detail, see my *God and World*, 13–22.

13. I assume basic historical and literary perspectives regarding this text and move immediately to theological considerations. Some literary observations: the flood story contains little direct speech and no dialogue; Noah never speaks a word. There is also minimal description of the disaster itself and no reaction from any individual. There is virtually no textual attention to the plight of the victims or to their fearful response or to scenes of death and destruction—in contrast to the many horrific artistic renditions of the flood and modern media portrayal of disasters. Why is the text so reticent regarding the suffering of the victims, not least in view of the fact that the text claims it is their guilt that has occasioned the disaster?

14. The reference to "seedtime and harvest" in Gen 8:22 suggests that the divine promise is more extensive than a simple reference to "no more floods."

From the perspective of many a Bible reader, including many theologians, these are problematic images for God indeed—and commentators often move past them quickly. I suggest once again that these understandings of God have a strategic canonical placement and, as with the opening pages in any good book are intended to provide an important theological lens through which to read subsequent biblical descriptions of God, especially as related to violence.[15] Moreover, the fact that the flood story takes up so much textual space—longer than the creation stories—has long bedeviled scholars. Might the very length of the story suggest the theological importance it was believed to have in the biblical witness about God? When all is said and done, this conversation about the flood story's language for God will leave us with questions, but this in itself is an invitation to consult other texts and to engage in further reflection.

The following points overlap with one another, but they deserve separate consideration; at the same time, they are not of equal import, nor do they stand or fall together. From several perspectives, they are further witness to divine self-limitation.

1. I begin with a more general point: this text is testimony to the affectability of God. God is deeply and personally moved by what has happened to the relationship with humankind. "And the Lord was sorry that he had made humankind on the earth, and it grieved him to his heart" (Gen 6:6). God is revealed as one who is affected by creatures both human and non-human (not just humans and not just Israel); God is not removed and detached from this world but is genuinely engaged with it and affected by this engagement. Several of the following points particularize this.

2. God repeatedly "regrets, is sorry"[16] that God created humankind in the first place (Gen 6:6–7). God knows what might have been and profoundly desires [185] that things had not come to this! Here the past of God, what might have been, seems to stand in disjunction with the present of God, what actually is, and the collision of past and present in God occasions a deep divine regret and accompanying suffering for God. I might add that this point is also testimony to the temporality of God, who has so deeply entered into the life of the world that past, present, and future are real for God. This witness regarding divine temporality is also evident in God's resting on the Sabbath for a specific period of time (Gen 2:1–3).

---

15. Even more, the story witnesses to a God who acts in saving ways beyond the walls of the chosen community. Indeed, in the larger creational context in which the flood story is embedded, God is the subject of a remarkable string of activities that are all too commonly reserved for the chosen community (by the chosen community!): God elects, reveals, saves from danger and death, and makes promises. And this is long before Abraham! And the story suggests: long after Abraham.

16. These are the usual translations of the verb נחם (Niphal; see NIV, "grieve"). On these "anthropomorphic metaphors," see my *Suffering of God* (Philadelphia: Fortress, 1984), 5–12; and, for a study of נחם in its various contexts, idem, "The Repentance of God: A Key to Evaluating Old Testament God-Talk," *HBT* 10 (1988): 47–70.

3. God's regret seems to assume that God did not certainly know that creatures would take this turn (as also in Gen 22:12, Deut 8:2). This does not mean that God is not omniscient, though some definitions of omniscience might be threatened by this understanding.[17] The claim is still available that God knows all there is to know, including all possibilities, but there is a future that is not yet available for knowing, even for God.[18] "Regret" language of this sort would challenge any position that God predetermined that the creation would take this course. What has happened to the creation is due most basically to creaturely activity, not divine. At the same time, God bears some responsibility for these developments by setting up the creation in a way that it could go wrong and could have such devastating effects. God created the world good, not perfect.

4. God's response of regret assumes that human beings have successfully resisted God's will for the creation. Thus, this text is a witness to divine vulnerability in the unfolding creation. This God is a God who takes risks, who makes the divine self vulnerable to the twists and turns of creational life, including human resistance. The resistibility of the will of God is a key to understanding many a biblical text that follows, not least the many passages that speak of divine anger. Should one resist this understanding of God, it might be asked (though not a feature of this text): if God's will were never successfully resisted, why would God get angry?

5. God's initial decision to "blot out" human beings and other creatures seemed to allow for no exceptions (Gen 6:7), but God's pain and sorrow seem to lead God to a decision regarding Noah that changes this judgmental direction, with positive effects for "all flesh."[19] The idea that God changes the divine [186] mind (נחם) is a relatively common biblical theme. At the same time, importantly, this change is not a change in the character of God or the being of God but a change in divine strategy in view of new experience with the world. Only the language of change seems capable of describing the God at the beginning of the flood story and the God of the end of the story, who promises never to do this again. It is God who has changed, not human beings (although there are fewer of them around!), as the text makes clear (Gen 8:21). Yet, as always, God's action stands in the service of the divine immutability regarding being faithful and always acting in the best interests of the creation.

---

17. Ps 139:16 is sometimes cited to support divine omniscience (for example, NRSV, NIV), but see the quite different translations of this verse in the KJV, NJPS, and NEB.

18. Regarding God's power, it is often said to be illogical to ask: can God make a rock so big that God cannot lift it? Comparably regarding God's knowledge, it is illogical to ask: can God know a future that is not yet there to know? At the least, the divine knowledge is not based on the experience of that future.

19. Nothing that Noah has done is said to prompt Noah's finding favor with God. Yet, Noah's faithfulness is not just a blip on the cosmic screen, somehow irrelevant to God. Noah's walking with God counts with God; but it is understood to be a (not inevitable) consequence of God's prior action.

6. The image of God in the flood story is perhaps best described as a grieving and pained parent, distressed over what has happened to the human race (see Gen 6:5–7; compare with Ps 78:40–41, Isa 63:7–10).[20] The NIV says it well: God's "heart was filled with pain"; the same word is used for the pain of the man and the woman in Gen 3:16–17, and God is now said to share this pain. The basic character of the human heart in Gen 6:5, "every inclination of their hearts was only evil continually," is set alongside the disappointed and sorrow-filled response of the divine heart (Gen 6:6). The wickedness of humankind and the associated judgment about to fall have touched God deeply.

While the external and more objective picture in this story is one of disastrous judgment, the internal, subjective image is of divine grief. The judgment talk in the prophets is comparable; grief is what the Godward side of judgment and wrath often looks like.[21] For example, Jer 9:10 (NIV): "I will take up weeping and wailing for the mountains and a lamentation for the pastures of the wilderness, because they are laid waste, so that no one passes through, and the lowing of the cattle is not heard; both the birds of the air and the animals have fled and are gone." This image of God weeping over the judgment that has deeply affected humans and animals alike is paralleled in the flood story (see also Jer 9:17–21, 13:17, 14:17). The fact that divine judgment and divine tears go together has considerable theological import. Without the references to tears, God would be much more removed and unmoved. Judgment accompanied by weeping, although it is still judgment, is different—in motivation and in the understanding of the relationship at stake. God's harsh words of judgment are not matched by an inner harshness.[22] [187]

The narrative strategy in Genesis 6–9 is to portray the kind of God with whom the entire world has to do, not only Israel. This is a God for whom judgment is neither the first word nor the last and hence is a God of hope. While God may give the people up to the effects of their sinfulness, God does not finally give up on them. In other terms, the circumstantial will of God in judgment is always in the service of the ultimate will of God to save. To this end, God can use judgmental *effects* for a variety of positive purposes, such as refining, purification, insight, and discipline.

7. Inasmuch as human beings are said to be just as sinful after the flood as before it (compare Gen 6:5 with 8:21), pain will be an ongoing reality for

---

20. Despite sometime claims to the contrary, the text makes no mention of the anger of God. Is this omission deliberate?

21. For detail, see my "Theological Reflections on the Wrath of God in the Old Testament," *HBT* 24 (2002): 1–26.

22. The ethical implications of this understanding of God are considerable. If there were no *divine* judgment on sin/evil, then *human* judgment toward what is oppressive and abusive would not carry the same weight. At the same time, if there were no sorrow associated with divine judgment, then human judgment would be given a freer range regarding harshness.

God. That is, the flood did not end the reason for the divine suffering; it may have been designed initially to do this, but God's change of the original decision to "blot out" all living creatures had long-term suffering effects for God. While not resigned to sin and evil, God decides to continue to live with these resisting creatures (not the response of your typical CEO!). This divine decision to allow a wicked world to exist, come what may, means for God a *continuing* grieving of the heart. Indeed, the everlasting, unconditional promise to Noah and all flesh that follows *necessitates* divine suffering; a pain-free future is now impossible for God. In other terms, the future of the creation that now becomes possible is rooted in this divine willingness to bear ongoing pain and sorrow. God determines to take the sin and resultant suffering of all creatures into God's own being and bear it there for the sake of the future of the world. In some sense, the world's future becomes dependent on this divine suffering. God's suffering proves over time to be very powerful; indeed it might be said that, finally, suffering is God's chief way of being powerful in the world (see 2 Cor 12:9–10).

8. This divine move leads finally to God's promises. Gen 8:21 addresses two related matters: (a) God "will never again curse the ground because of humankind";[23] (b) "nor will I ever again destroy every living creature," continuing the basic elements of the created order (formalized with a covenant in Gen 9:8–17). The first has reference to the created moral order; God places limits on God's possible actions relating to the move from sin to consequence within the natural order. That is, the move to "blot out" (Gen 6:7) that God makes in the wake of the human condition announced by God in Gen 6:5 will no longer be available to God in view of God's own edict. The second has [188] reference to the effect of this new boundary for God; it is first stated negatively (no destruction of "every living creature") and then positively ("seedtime and harvest, cold and heat, summer and winter, day and night shall not cease," Gen 8:22).[24]

This multifaceted divine promise means that the route of world annihilation has been set aside by God as a divine possibility. God's promise is not a promise to eliminate, say, all natural disasters. Divine judgment there will be (for example, Genesis 18–19), but it will be limited in scope. Sin and evil and their now-limited effects will be allowed to have their day,

---

23. This phrase has been thought to refer to (a) no more floods; (b) no additional curses on the ground (see Gen 3:17); (c) the abandonment of the existing curse; or (d) the end of the reign of curse. It seems best to regard the phrase as some combination thereof; that is, God's newly stated word provides for a constant natural order within which life can develop without any concern about human sin "triggering" another disaster of the magnitude of the flood. That is, God places an eternal limit on the functioning of the moral order. See discussion in Westermann, *Genesis 1–11*, 454–56.

24. Comparable divine promises are also found in Jer 31:35–37, 33:19–26. See the examination of related texts in Katherine J. Dell, "Covenant and Creation in Relationship," in *Covenant as Context: Essays in Honour of E. W. Nicholson* (ed. A. D. H. Mayes and R. B. Salters; Oxford: Oxford University Press, 2003), 111–33.

and God will work from *within* this sort of world to redeem it but will not overpower it from without. God remains committed to the freedom of the creatures, even though the effects may be horrendous. Indeed, their exercise of freedom may result in, *not* the end of the world, but the end of *their* world.[25] Regardless of what people do, however, God will remain faithful to the promises regarding creation, sealed by the rainbow.

What do these promises mean for God? For God to promise not to do something ever again entails an eternal divine self-limitation regarding the exercise of *both* freedom *and* power with respect to any related matters.[26] God thereby limits the divine options in dealing with evil in the life of the world.[27] And, given the fact that God will be faithful and keep promises, does this not mean that divine self-limitation yields real limitation for God? God may be said to be *capable* of doing anything, but the certainty of God's faithfulness means that God *cannot* break a divine promise. Consider, say, the marital relationship (an oft-used metaphor for God and Israel): the individuals involved *are capable of*, say, "playing around," but they *cannot* do so and still be faithful.

These several characteristics of God seem to be fundamentally in tune with the biblical center about a God who is gracious and merciful, slow to anger, and abounding in steadfast love (Exod 34:6–7 and its many parallels). It is this *kind* of God with whom Israelite readers have to do, and it is primarily the word of divine commitment to promises made that they most need to hear.[28]

Implications and Conclusions

Initially, how is this divine self-limitation regarding the flood and its aftermath related to the divine self-limitation we have seen to be present in the creation accounts? Generally speaking, in the wake of the flood God addresses a situation in the ongoing life of the created order that calls for a new divine response. That situation is depicted in Gen 8:21 and speaks of a continuing human reality that is deeply problematic: "The Lord said in his heart . . . the inclination of the human heart is [still!] evil from youth." What God does in the face of a *continuing* human situation of wickedness is of special import. That is, inasmuch as the wicked situation of Gen 6:5

---

25. For this language and a helpful commentary on divine judgment in Ezekiel 6–7, see Joseph Blenkinsopp, *Ezekiel* (Louisville: John Knox, 1990), 44–51 (esp. p. 50).

26. For a discussion of divine self-limitation regarding the exercise of power and freedom in Jeremiah, see my "Character of God in Jeremiah," *in Character and Scripture: Moral Formation, Community, and Biblical Interpretation* (ed. William P. Brown; Grand Rapids, MI: Eerdmans, 2002), 217–19.

27. Except perhaps as a means to bring the world to an end?

28. Some kind of devastating situation in Israel's history is probably in mind, though it could have a multigenerational applicability. The destruction of Jerusalem and the exile would be an especially appropriate context for a promise of this sort.

led to the flood, and this same situation of wickedness continues in a post-flood world (described in Gen 8:21), the threat of repeated floods (or other natural catastrophes) remains—if *the basic cause-and-effect structures of the world were to continue unchanged.*

Thus, a significant shift in the very structures of the world is necessary if the world is not to experience ongoing convulsions. We have seen that God's way with the created order has been shaped from the beginning in terms of divine self-limitation. Faced now with potentially recurrent flood-like devastations in the world's experience because of continuing human sin, God does not pull back from this basic self-limiting direction in relating to the world. Instead, God intensifies this divine way with the world, entering even more deeply into self-limiting ways.[29]

As noted, the claim made in Gen 8:21 may give us a clue regarding this new direction for God: "I will never again curse the ground [or, regard the ground as cursed] because of humankind."[30] This announcement, which introduces the statement about human sin ("for"), means that God thereby explicitly places a limit on the actions of the divine self relative to this continuing sin ("never again"). This divine self-limitation entails a fundamental shift or adjustment in the way in which the created order functions. This change needed to be put into place by God so that the promise could be kept.

Claus Westermann correctly notes (contrary to several scholars) that Gen 8:21 is not a note regarding a transition from curse to blessing; the effects of the curse continue in significant ways.[31] At the same time, Westermann does not go far enough when he claims that the "never again" only means that God "decides to put up with this state of evil. . . . He can simply let things be, [190] putting up patiently with people just as they are with their inclination to evil."[32] At the least, his comments do not take into account the continuing divine suffering that we have noted. He is closer to the mark when he speaks of the world's "stabilization."[33] But more seems to be at stake.

God's "never again" regarding the curse seems to signal a substantial change in the created moral order, or what might be called the causal weave. In effect, God puts into place a new boundary for the functioning of the created order. In other terms, God determines that the divine self-limitation that has been in place since the creation needs to be made

---

29. Michael Chan pointed out to me that Gen 6:3, "My spirit shall not abide in mortals forever, for they are flesh; their days shall be one hundred twenty years," is another act of limitation by God that entails self-limitation (regarding the divine spirit). See also God's self-limiting action "for the sake of his servant David" (2 Kgs 8:19).
30. See the discussion of scholarly views in Westermann, *Genesis 1–11*, 454–58.
31. Ibid., 454.
32. Ibid., 456.
33. Ibid., 457.

deeper and more precise in view of humanity's unchanging wickedness. The world (which acquired a life of its own already in God's rest in Gen 2:1–3) is given divinely established boundaries within which it now functions in ways that will not allow for another flood-like response.

In sum, what God does in the flood story *recharacterizes* the divine relation to the world. God qualifies the workings of divine judgment, placing constraints on the effects of sin and God's own actions relating thereto, and proceeds to promise an orderly cosmos for the continuation of life. Human beings have not been changed by the flood but, in view of God's experience with this world, God charts new directions in relating to this world. In canonical perspective, it is this *kind* of God who provides a basic lens through which readers are invited to interpret the God who is presented in all the biblical texts that follow.

If a change of this sort in God's relationship with the world in this early story of the Old Testament can be so characterized, might this help readers come to terms with later biblical texts that speak of violence, indeed divine violence?[34] Associations of God with violence will pervade the texts that follow in the Old Testament, from natural disasters to invasions of foreign armies to destructions of cities and civilizations. What difference might it make in the interpretation of these texts if they are read in and through the images provided by the flood story, wherein *God places a limit on what God can do about violence?* Indeed, is it not the case that the recharacterized divine way with the world may issue in even more violence? That is to say, by promising "never again" to bring a violent world to an end, does not God thereby open up this world to unending violence, whether generated by human beings or natural forces, even if not catastrophic? From another angle, by loosening the divine control of the world (which the divine "never again" entails), God becomes even more closely associated with its potential for violence and its actual violence [191]. In light of this reality, how might the divine association with violence in the post-flood world be articulated in more detailed ways?

One potential direction for reflection resides in the divine decision to use human agents in carrying out acts of judgment. It may be said that much, if not all of the violence associated with God in the Bible is due to God's decision to use agents that are capable of violence, though not of the world-ending sort (and God does not remove the divine self from continuing levels of involvement, which will entail suffering for God).[35] Obviously, God does not perfect agents before deciding to work in and through

---

34. While "later" refers to a canonical reading of this text, the basic perspectives present in Gen 8:21–22 are usually assigned to the Yahwist, probably an early form of the narrative.

35. See above discussion. See also this earlier language from my *Suffering of God,* 76: "force and violence are associated with God's work in the world, because, to a greater or lesser degree, they are characteristic of the means of those in and through whom the work

them; this will also mean that God does not necessarily evaluate the work of the agents in positive terms. God's agents may exceed the divine mandate, going beyond anything that God intended (for example, Zech 1:15). Notably, God will assume a share of the responsibility associated with this violence and will take on a certain degree of blame for using these agents (Jer 42:10).[36]

Most fundamentally, however, God engages in a new way with the world in and through the articulation of a self-limiting promise, the first formally stated promise in the Bible. In the language of Claus Westermann, "God promises that he will never again allow humanity to be destroyed. . . . There is no power that can shake this promise."[37]

---

is carried out. In order to achieve God's purposes, God will in effect 'get his hands dirty.'" For details regarding divine judgment, see my *God and World*, 157–65.

36. For details on these texts, see idem, "I Was Only a Little Angry" [reprinted in this volume, pp. 172–184].

37. Westermann, *Genesis 1–11*, 456. Compare the statement of William P. Brown, *The Ethos of the Cosmos: The Genesis of Moral Imagination in the Bible* (Grand Rapids, MI: Eerdmans, 1999), 57: "God's unconditional commitment to remain true to creation's formfulness and integrity without destructive intervention."

"I Was Only a Little Angry": Divine Violence in the Prophets

A biblical understanding of God's relationship with Israel and the world helps us interpret passages in the prophetic literature that link God and violence. With tears, lament, and regret, God takes into the divine self the violent effects of sinful human activities and thereby makes possible a non-violent future for God's people.

"I was only a little angry; they made the disaster worse." This seemingly minor quotation from Zech 1:15, which witnesses to the excessive actions of divine agents, may provide a helpful angle on the interpretation of violence in the prophets. After some introductory comments, I consider these basic claims: God's relationship with Israel is genuine; God acts in Israel and in the world in and through agents; God's agents of judgment commonly exceed their mandate; God's response to the consequent disasters includes tears, lament, and regret.

Prophetic literature is filled with violent speech and action, both human and divine. But let it be said immediately: if there were no human violence, there would be no divine violence.[1] Gen 6:11–13 announces a pattern regarding divine and human violence that will persist throughout the canon: "I have determined to make an end of all flesh, for the earth is filled with violence because of them." A more specific form of human violence, namely war—including its anticipation, execution, and aftermath—provides the context within which most of the prophetic literature was written. Another particular form of violence—the oppression of the poor and needy—will often be associated by the prophets [366] with the outbreak of war (e.g., Isa 10:1–5; Mic 2:1–3; Ezek 22:29–31). Violence brings violence in its wake. Inasmuch as the prophets are not deists, the God of whom they speak will be involved in the violence associated with oppression and war. Trying to sort out the nature of that divine involvement is our most basic task.

Divine violence has often been troubling to biblical commentators—and for good reason. One need only note the devastating effect of God's judgment on children, women, and the environment (e.g., Lam 2:19–21; 4:4, 10; 5:11). Such texts have led to various attempts to "shelve" the topic of divine violence: spiritualizing it ("put on the whole armor of God"),

---

This essay was originally published in *Interpretation* 58 (2004): 365–75.

1. For a survey of the issue of violence in the Old Testament, see T. E. Fretheim, "God and Violence in the Old Testament," *WW* 24 (2004): 18–28.

reducing it to the mysterious ways of God (though the texts have a re-markably "plain sense"), "projections" of human behaviors, or even cut-ting these texts out of the Bible, whether practically (as in lectionaries) or actually.

This concern about divine violence in the Old Testament has intensified in recent years.[2] Reasons for this development include the following: the cumulative violence over the course of the 20th century with increasingly lethal weapons, more recent experiences (9/11, terrorist activities), and the spread of interreligious conflict—all of it available in the media on a daily basis.[3] Also to be noted is the increasing realization that the Bible's violence has played a part in the spread of the world's violence. Altogether too often the actions of the God of the Bible have been claimed as justification for the violence, from the crusades to slavery to the denigration of women.[4] One may claim that the Bible has not been properly used when this oc-curs, but at the least readers must admit that the Bible has not provided safeguards for preventing such interpretations and should also consider whether some of its violence is "out of bounds."[5]

Some interpreters may think that voicing such probing questions about the violence of God is inappropriate. Such questioning, however, has long been integral to the Judeo-Christian tradition, and has roots deep within the biblical texts. One need only note questions raised by Abraham (Gen 18:25) and Moses (Exod 32:1–14) regarding divine violence. Habakkuk is a prophetic example. In Hab 1:2–4, the prophet complains to God about the violence Israel has had to endure, to which God responds with an oracle of judgment (vv. 5–11). [367] God is "rousing" the Babylonians, who will "come for violence." Habakkuk's second complaint (vv. 12–17)

---

2. Among more recent scholarly efforts that raise serious questions regarding the Bible's violence and God's common association with it, see J. J. Collins, "The Zeal of Phine-has: The Bible and the Legitimation of Violence," *JBL* 122 (2003): 3–21, and the literature cited therein. Others have been particularly pointed in their critique of those texts wherein God's violence is associated with female imagery. See, e.g., R. J. Weems, *Battered Love: Mar-riage, Sex, and Violence in the Hebrew Prophets* (Minneapolis: Fortress, 1995); among many articles one might cite, that of Diane Jacobson offers a well-balanced approach ("Hosea 2: A Case Study on Biblical Authority," *CTM* 23 [1996]: 165–72). I have worked with this issue in several publications, especially "Is the Biblical Portrayal of God Always Trustworthy?" in T. Fretheim and K. Froehlich, *The Bible as Word of God in a Postmodern Age* (Minneapolis: Fortress, 1998), 97–111 (reprinted: Eugene, OR: Wipf and Stock, 2002).

3. For a review of seven recent books on the topic, see S. J. Stein, "The Web of Reli-gion and Violence," *RSR* 28 (2002): 103–8.

4. E. Zenger, *A God of Vengeance? Understanding the Psalms of Divine Wrath* (trans. L. Maloney; Louisville: Westminster John Knox, 1996), 84: "[T]he history of the impact and reception of an individual text in the annals of Judaism and Christianity must also be taken into consideration when we reflect on its revelatory character . . . [some texts] can have been received in such a destructive way that the very knowledge of this negative his-tory of reception becomes a constitutive part of the revelatory dimension of these texts."

5. See Fretheim, "God and Violence," for efforts to make some distinctions regarding the appropriateness of the Bible's ascription of violence to God.

"attacks God's announced solution to injustice as being more unjust than the original problem."[6] Given Babylon's violent ways and means, how can God use such a people as divine agents to overcome the wicked? God is too pure and holy to use such agents for divine purposes! We return to this issue below.

Let it be clearly said that the prophets and their God often promote non-violence. The eschatological reflections of the prophets are marked by visions of peace and non-violence, extending even to the animal world (e.g., Isa 2:2–4; 65:17–25); such texts demonstrate that Israel considered violence to be an intruder in God's world. Moreover, some texts witness that God makes every effort to stop the violence, *but is not successful in doing so;* people can make choices that successfully resist the will of God. For example, in the face of the post-597 B.C.E. Babylonian threat, God calls Jeremiah to bring a word that is intended to reduce the violence: Israel is to submit to Babylon's hegemony (Jer 38:17–18). Demonstrating a political realism, God announces that if Israel would not rebel, its future would take a less violent course. Israel's own use of violence would lead to its experience of even greater violence. God, too, has a stake in Israel's decision: a positive response would lessen God's association with violence.

Violence and Relationship

A key factor that must inform considerations of biblical violence is the centrality of relationship for Israelite theological reflection.[7] For the Old Testament, relationships are constitutive of life itself; through relationships all things are woven together like a spider web. Interrelatedness is a basic characteristic not only of the God-Israel (and God-world) relationship but also of the very nature of the created order. Human sin ripples out and affects the entire creation (see the linkage between human violence and the nonhuman in Hos 4:1–3). To live in a relational world inevitably means that every creature will be affected by every other; each individual is involved in the plight of all. Violence perpetrated anywhere reverberates everywhere through this relational structure of life, leading to even further violence. Because Israel understood that God is related to, and indeed deeply engaged in the affairs of this world, even the Creator will be affected by and caught up in every act of violence. Though there may be

---

6. J. J. M. Roberts, *Nahum, Habakkuk, and Zephaniah* (Louisville: Westminster John Knox, 1991), 81.

7. For a sophisticated effort to speak of relationship as key to understanding violence and its effects, see M. Suchocki, *Fall to Violence: Original Sin in Relational Theology* (New York: Continuum, 1994). For a fuller explication of the category of relationship, see T. E. Fretheim, "Divine Dependence on the Human: An Old Testament Perspective," *ExAud* 13 (1997): 1–13; "Old Testament Foundations for an Environmental Theology," in *Currents in Biblical and Theological Dialogue* (ed. J. K. Stafford; Winnipeg: St. John's College, 2002), 58–68.

non-violent breakthroughs, an avoidance of interrelational violence is simply not possible for either Israel or God.[8] The Bible tells it like it is.

This understanding of relationship places a key question on the table: What does it [368] mean for God to be a faithful member of this relationship with Israel (and the world) in the midst of all its violence? I make a claim at this point and return to it below. God so enters into these relationships that God is not the only one with something important to do and the power with which to do it. Creatures in relationship with this kind of God have been given genuine power (e.g., Gen 1:28), and God so honors this relationship—indeed is unchangeably faithful to it—that God will be self-limiting in the exercise of divine power within such relationships.[9] This divine self-limitation, necessary for the genuine freedom of creatures within the relationship, is a key factor in understanding violence. Israel's (and the world's) long story of successful resistance to God's will for non-violence has had deep effects on every aspect of life and the resultant violent reality complicates God's working possibilities in the world. Because of God's committed relationship to the world, no resolution will be simple, no "quick fix" available, even for God. The enemies of God cannot be overcome with a flick of the wrist. One might wish that God would force compliance and stop the violence, but, because of the genuine relationship, God's efforts to that end will entail constraint and restraint in the use of power. And so, with continued resistance to the will of God for non-violence, laments will continue and suffering will go on for both the world and God.

God's Use of Agents

God works through various human and nonhuman agents to get things done in the world. God acts directly, but always through means. The variety of means that God uses is impressive. God works through already existing creatures to bring about new creations (Gen 1:11), through human language to call the prophets (Isa 6:8–13), through nonhuman agents at the Red Sea (the nonhuman is the savior of the human!), through sacrificial rituals to mediate forgiveness of sin, through non-Israelite kings and armies to effect both judgment and salvation, and through the created moral order. The latter two are interrelated and particularly pertinent for this discussion.

1. *God's Use of Human Agents.* God's use of human agents is amply demonstrated in texts such as Jer 50:25 ("the weapons of his wrath"),

---

8. The violent events of Sept. 11 are a superb demonstration of this reality; every human being has been deeply affected by the violence of a few, not least through intensified forms of anxiety. No matter how personally we may be in control of our own violent tendencies, we are personally often invaded by a horrendous amount of violence, and that will have deep effects individually and communally.

9. See, e.g., T. E. Fretheim, *The Suffering of God: An Old Testament Perspective* (Philadelphia: Fortress, 1984), 71–78, for a more extensive treatment.

Isa 10:5 ("Assyria, the rod of my anger"), and Isa 45:1 (God's "anointed," Cyrus of Persia). God's word regarding the fall of Jerusalem to Babylon in Jer 27:8 puts the matter in a nutshell, "I have completed its destruction by his hand." Remarkably, God refers to Nebuchadrezzar as "my servant" in Jeremiah (25:9; 27:6; 43:10). Others whom God designates "my servant" in Jeremiah are David, the prophets, and Israel![10] As with these other agents, in some sense God has chosen [369] to be *dependent* on Nebuchadrezzar and his armies in carrying out that judgment.[11] The latter will certainly act as armies in that world are known to act, and God knows of potential problems from experience with conquerors such as these. This portrayal of God constitutes a kind of extreme realism regarding what may happen to the people. Once these armies begin their onslaught, the people will no doubt experience their pillaging, burning, and raping. Exilic readers of these texts will recall that they were real agents indeed.[12]

The frequency with which words of violence have both God and Babylon/Nebuchadrezzar as their subjects is remarkable, especially in Jeremiah. And so, God in judgment will not "pity, spare, or have compassion" (Jer 13:14), because that is what the Babylonians, the agents of divine judgment, will not do (Jer 21:7). God will dash in pieces, destroy, scatter, and strike down (Jer 13:14, 24; 21:6), precisely because that is what Babylon, the chosen divine agent, will do (Jer 48:12; 36:29; 52:8; 21:7).[13] Such harsh words are used with God as subject because they depict the actions of those in and through whom God mediates judgment. *The portrayal of God's violent action is conformed to the means that God uses.*

For these reasons, interpreters must not diminish the distinction between God and God's agents or discount the power of these human armies.[14] Both God and human beings are effective agents; God's activity

---

10. The New Testament also will speak of civil authorities as executors of the divine wrath (Rom 13:4; 1 Pet 2:13–14). In a modern context, one might consider the allied armies as an instrument of divine wrath in the defeat of Hitler; recall also the excessive military activity (e.g., the saturation bombing of Dresden) and the devastating effect of the war on children and other non-combatants.

11. Exod 3:8–10, where both God and Moses (often called "my servant") bring Israel out of Egypt, could function as a paradigm for such considerations. On issues of divine dependence, see Fretheim, "Divine Dependence"; idem, "Creator, Creature, and Co-creation in Genesis 1–2," in *All Things New: Essays in Honor of Roy A. Harrisville* (ed. A. Hultgren et al.; WW Supplement 1; St. Paul: Word & World, 1992), 11–20.

12. Jeremiah also makes this witness when he describes the actual destruction of Jerusalem (Jeremiah 39; 52) in terms that hardly mention God.

13. For a listing of these correspondences, see Fretheim, *Jeremiah* (Macon: Smyth & Helwys, 2002), 36. See also p. 40 for a listing of the use of parallels in the violent speech of God and Jeremiah. For detail on this problematic language, see T. E. Fretheim, "The Character of God in Jeremiah," in *Character and Scripture: Moral Formation, Community, and Biblical Interpretation* (ed. W. P. Brown; Grand Rapids: Eerdmans, 2002), 211–30.

14. A surprisingly common scholarly claim is that God acts in an unmediated way. For example, Walter Brueggemann (*A Commentary on Jeremiah: Exile and Homecoming* [Grand

is not all-determining. God neither "lets go" of the creation nor retains all power. God makes free choices, but those choices are constrained by relationships God has established. One might fault God's choice of agents, but God uses the means available in that time and place to accomplish the divine purposes and, true to the nature of the relationship, does not perfect them before involving them. Hence, God's actions through them will always have mixed results, and God will not necessarily confer a positive value on the violent means in and through which God works (see below). This decision to work through such means is a risky move for God because God thereby becomes associated with the agent's activity. God thereby implicitly accepts any "guilt by association" that may accrue to the divine reputation.

This issue is made more complex by still another reality. One characteristic of *communal* judgment is that no clean distinction can be made between the righteous and the wicked (hence Abraham's questions in Gen 18:25). Because life is so interrelated, the righteous and the innocent (e.g., children) are often caught up in the judgmental effects of other people's sins. In other words, they will undergo the *experience* of judgment in ways that are [370] often devastating to their life and health.[15]

In sum, consideration of God's work through human agents must steer between two ditches. God neither remains ensconced in heaven watching the world go by nor micro-manages the world to control its moves so that creaturely agency counts for nothing. Readers may find more than one place to stand between these two ditches, for the biblical texts do not always provide clear direction, but neither ditch will do. To all external observation, God is not involved in these military and political activities, but the texts *confess* that God's will is somehow at work even in and through violence on behalf of God's salvific purposes.

2. *God Acts in and through the Moral Order.* While interpreters cannot fully account for how God acts in the world, some aspects of the "how" may be evident in terms of the created moral order—a complex, loose causal weave of act and consequence. The basic purpose of the moral order is that sin/evil not go unchecked and that God's good order of creation (= righteousness) can be (re)established.[16] And so, with respect to our topic: *that* sins have consequences, including the sins of violence, is a working out of the moral order, and can be named the judgment of God.[17] God is

---

Rapids: Eerdmans, 1998]) often makes such claims: "The army may be Babylonian, but the real agent is Yahweh" (pp. 54, 70, 176, etc.).

15. It remains a lively question whether it is helpful to continue to speak of "judgment" when its effects are so all encompassing, but the biblical texts do so.

16. See H. H. Schmid, "Creation, Righteousness, and Salvation: 'Creation Theology' as the Broad Horizon of Biblical Theology," in *Creation in the Old Testament* (ed. B. W. Anderson; Philadelphia: Fortress, 1984), 102–17.

17. Though the language of judgment is commonly associated with the court of law, juristic categories do not fully comprehend the workings of divine judgment.

to some degree subject to this just order (so Abraham's question in Gen 18:25 assumes, "Shall not the Judge of all the earth do what is just?"); God has built this self-limitation into the very structures of creation for the sake of a genuine relationship with it. At the same time, the looseness of the causal weave allows God to be at work in the "system" without violating or (temporarily) suspending it. One possible example of such divine work is Jer 51:11: God "stirred up the spirit of the kings of the Medes."[18]

Just how God relates to the movement from sin to consequence is not easy to sort out.[19] But, generally speaking, the relationship between sin and consequence is conceived in intrinsic rather than forensic terms; that is, consequences grow out of the deed itself.[20] At the same time, Israel insists that God mediates the consequences of sin.[21] The point is illustrated by Ezek 22:31, wherein God declares: "I have consumed them with the fire of my wrath." What that entails is immediately stated: "I have returned *(nātan)* their conduct [371] upon their heads."[22]

This moral order, however, does not function in any mechanistic, precise, or inevitable way; it is not a tight causal weave. And so it may be that the wicked will prosper (Jer 12:1), at least for a time, and those who are innocent will get caught up in the effects of the sins of others. Eccl 9:11 ("time and chance happen to them all") introduces an element of randomness in relating human deeds to their effects.

Several matters of translation and interpretation come together in thinking through this issue. Sometimes the Hebrew word *rāʿâ* refers to the evil/wickedness of the people, sometimes to the effects of their wickedness, commonly translated "disaster."[23] In other words, the people's *rāʿâ* will issue in their *rāʿâ*.[24] This verbal linkage makes it clear that the judgment

---

18. See also Isa 13:17; 41:25; 45:13; Ezek 23:22; Joel 4:7.
19. For a recent effort, see G. Tucker, "Sin and 'Judgment' in the Prophets," in *Problems in Biblical Theology: Essays in Honor of Rolf Knierim,* (ed. H. Sun et al.; Grand Rapids: Eerdmans, 1997), 373–88.
20. Gerhard von Rad (*Old Testament Theology* [vol. 1; trans. D. M. G. Stalker; New York: Harper & Row, 1964]) speaks of a "synthetic view of life" (p. 265) in which the consequence "is not a new action which comes upon the person concerned from somewhere else; it is rather the last ripple of the act itself which attaches to its agent almost as something material. Hebrew in fact does not even have a word for punishment" (p. 385). The common translation of *pāqad,* "visit," as "punish" is problematic. Notably, God's actions in history are here *grounded* in an understanding of God as *Creator.*
21. Interpreters have used different formulations: God midwifes, facilitates, sees to, puts in force, or completes the connection between sin and consequence. Sometimes God as subject stands in a prominent position (Jer 19:7–9); elsewhere, God's stance is more passive (Hos 4:1–3), even withdrawn (Isa 64:6–7).
22. There are over fifty such texts in the Old Testament that link wrath with such formulations (e.g., Ps 7:12–16; Isa 59:17–18; 64:5–9; Jer 6:11, 19; 7:18–20; 21:12–14; 44:7–8; 50:24–25; Lam 3:64–66).
23. The word *ʿāwōn,* "iniquity," is also used in both senses in the Old Testament.
24. This understanding of *rāʿâ* issuing in *rāʿâ* may be observed in several formulations. For example, God brings disaster *(rāʿâ),* which is "the fruit of *their* schemes" (6:19; see Hos 8:7; 10:13). Or, "I will pour out *their* wickedness upon them" (14:16).

experienced by the Israelites flows out of their own wickedness, rather than from some divinely imposed retribution. While this understanding could be expressed in language such as "you reap what you sow" (cf. Obadiah 15–16), God usually remains explicitly linked to the connection between sin and consequence.

In sum, Israel's sin generates effects in a snowballing, act-consequence pattern. At the same time, God is active in the interplay of sinful actions and their effects and "third parties" are used by God as agents for that judgment. Both divine and creaturely factors are interwoven to produce the judgmental result. In modern terms, our own sin and the sins of our forebears press in upon us, but no less the hand of God. For history is our judgment and God enables history, carrying the world along, not in mechanistic ways, but with a personal attentiveness in view of the relationship. God's salvific will remains intact in everything, and God's gracious concern is always for the best; but in a given situation the best that God may be able to offer is burning the chaff to fertilize the field for a new crop.

3. *Violence in Judgment and Salvation.* The use of violence in the prophets is never an end in itself; it has a twofold purpose: judgment and salvation. So, for example, God uses the violence of the Persians under King Cyrus as *judgment* against the enslaving Babylonians as a means to bring *salvation* to the exiles (e.g., Isa 45:1–8; 47:1–15). In other words, God uses violence both to save Israel from the effects of *other people's sins* (cf. Israel in Egypt; Exod 15:1–3) and to save God's people from the effects of *their own sins*.[25]

These two ways of speaking of God's use of violence may be reduced to one. That is, God's use of violence, inevitable in a violent world, is intended to subvert human violence in order to bring the creation along to a point where violence is no more. Walter Brueggemann says it well: "It is likely that the violence assigned to Yahweh is to be understood as counterviolence, which functions primarily as a critical principle in order to [371] undermine and destabilize other violence." And so God's violence is "not blind or unbridled violence," but purposeful in the service of a non-violent end.[26]

Exceeding the Divine Mandate

A remarkable number of prophetic texts speak of divine judgment on those nations that have been agents of God (Jer 25:12–14; 27:6–7; 50–51; Isa 10:12–19; 47:1–15; Zech 1:15). In effect, Babylon and other agents exceeded their mandate, going beyond their proper judgmental activities in vaunting their own strength at the expense of Israel and in making the land

---

25. Salvation is thus more comprehensive than commonly conceived. For detail, see T. Fretheim, "Salvation in the Bible vs. Salvation in the Church," *WW* 13 (1993): 363–72.

26. W. Brueggemann, *Theology of the Old Testament: Testimony, Dispute, Advocacy* (Minneapolis: Fortress, 1997), 244.

an "everlasting waste" (Jer 25:14).[27] Such texts (cf. the oracles against the nations) assume that moral standards are known by the nations, to which they are held accountable. The exercise of divine wrath against their excessiveness shows that the nations were not puppets in the hand of God. They retained the power to make decisions and execute policies that flew in the face of the will of God; the God active in these events is not "irresistible."[28] God risks what the nations will do with the mandate they have been given. One element of that risk is that God's name will become associated with their excessive violence.[29]

I take a closer look at one of these texts, namely, Zech 1:7–17. The angel of the Lord presses a lament before God: "O Lord of hosts, how long will you withhold mercy from Jerusalem and the cities of Judah, with which you have been angry these seventy years?" (v. 12). The duration of the suffering and the seeming absence of mercy are a dual focus. God's "gracious and comforting" reply is striking: "And I am extremely angry with the nations that are at ease; for while I was only a little angry, they made the disaster worse." This text stands in the tradition of other texts that speak of nations overreaching—an "improper exercise of power toward the object of God's anger, Israel."[30]

Petersen speaks of the angel's "displeasure with the one in control, Yahweh,"[31] but the point of the text is that God is *not* in control of these nations. They exceeded the divine mandate in their violence! God was not *that* angry! And so, the angel's lament (v. 12), "how long will you [God] withhold mercy," has not taken into account a key element: the exercise of power by the nations went beyond God's will for Israel and that misuse of human power [373] complicated God's merciful activity on behalf of Israel. In other words, the "how long?" is not simply up to God, as if God were the only agent at work and could at any time push a button and "fix" matters. The nations have made God's possibilities more complex and hence God's way into the future is not reduced to a simple divine decision to act. Because of God's committed relationship to the world, no resolution will be simple, even for God.

---

27. The relationship of God to Babylon changes in view of Babylon's own conduct as the agent of judgment. When Babylon engages in excessively destructive behaviors, it opens itself up to reaping what it has sown (Jer 50:29; 51:24). God turns against God's own agent on the basis of issues of justice, a divine pattern also evident with respect to Israel (see Exod 22:21–24). If God were not to change in view of changing circumstances, God would be unfaithful to God's own commitments.

28. Contrary to Brueggemann, *Jeremiah*, 222.

29. See J. Sanders, *The God Who Risks: A Theology of Providence* (Downer's Grove, IL: InterVarsity, 1998).

30. D. L. Petersen, *Haggai and Zechariah 1–8* (Philadelphia: Westminster, 1984), 154. While Babylon is no longer the issue at this juncture, it may well continue to be among the nations indicted because of the long-term effects of its policies, leading to "the continued degradation of the Israelite community" (p. 155).

31. Ibid.

This perspective is testimony to a fundamentally *relational* understanding of the ways in which God acts in the world. There is an ordered freedom in the creation wherein God leaves room for genuine human decisions as they exercise their God-given power. Even more, God gives them responsibilities in such a way that *commits* God to a certain kind of relationship with them. God does not micro-manage their activity, intervening to make sure every little thing is done correctly. They overdid it! These texts are testimony to a divine sovereignty that gives power over to the created for the sake of a relationship of integrity. At the same time, this way of relating to people reveals a divine vulnerability, for God opens the divine self up to hurt should things go wrong. And things do go violently wrong, despite God's best efforts.

Divine Anger, Grief, and Regret

What is God's response to this devastating violence visited upon Israel by the overreaching divine agents? Divine anger is kindled toward these agents certainly, but God's response is also one of grief and regret regarding what Israel has had to undergo. Anger, grief, and regret go together for Israel's God and cannot be properly understood apart from each other. I consider each in turn.

God's anger is usually associated with God's judgment.[32] The category of relatedness is basic to the discussion. God is deeply engaged in this relationship and is passionate about what happens to it.[33] God's anger is a sign that the relationship to Israel is being taken seriously, since apathy is not productive of anger. That God's anger is "provoked" (e.g., Jer 7:18; 8:19) reveals that God is moved by what people do and shows that anger is a divine response and not a divine attribute. God's anger is contingent; if there were no sin, there would be no divine anger.

The wrath of God is often imaged in impersonal terms: it goes forth, whirls like a tempest, and bursts upon the head of the wicked (e.g., Jer 23:19). This characterization of wrath is true to the understanding of moral order; human wickedness triggers negative effects in the interrelated social and cosmic orders, which are then linked to God and named as wrath. At the same time, this wrath is named in personal terms: "the anger of the Lord" (Jer 23:20). God's personal anger is a "seeing to" the movement from act to consequence [374] that is the moral order. Abraham Heschel helps capture some of what is at stake in the prophetic witness to the divine anger:

> The wrath of God is a lamentation. . . . [God] is personally affected by what [people do to people]. [God] is a God of pathos. This is one of the

---

32. For details, see T. Fretheim, "Theological Reflections on the Wrath of God in the Old Testament," *HBT* 24 (2002): 1–26.
33. For an excellent treatment of divine anger, see A. Heschel, *The Prophets* (San Francisco: Harper & Row, 1962), 279–306.

meanings of the anger of God: the end of indifference! . . . [Our] sense of injustice is a poor analogy to God's sense of injustice. . . . Is it a sign of cruelty that God's anger is aroused when the rights of the poor are violated, when widows and orphans are oppressed?[34]

Heschel links divine wrath with divine lament, reflecting a deeply relational understanding of God. To speak of tears and anger together is not contradictory (see Jer 8:19c in context; 9:10 with 9:11; 9:17–19 with 9:22). Rather, these emotions are held together in God, as they commonly are in people who have suffered the brokenness of intimate relationships. The internal side of God's external word and deed of wrath is profound grief. And the prophets put both on public display. God's mediation of judgment is viewed basically in terms of a breakdown in a personal relationship with its associated effects—anger, pain, and suffering—on both parties to the relationship. God's judgment is not proclaimed joyously, but reluctantly and with great anguish, not satisfaction. In effect, readers are invited to look back and see that they have been visited not with the strict and icy indifference of a judge, but with the pain and anger of one whose intimacy has been spurned.[35] This interweaving of divine anger and divine sorrow continues into the post-judgment time and Israel's experience of violence (e.g., Jer 4:19–26; 8:18–9:1; 9:10–11, 17–19). Not only are the tears of the people voiced (e.g., Jer 14:19–22), so also are the tears of the prophet and the tears of God. Readers can thereby see that God does not remain unaffected by the violence Israel has lived through.[36]

That divine anger and divine tears go together has considerable theological import. Without the intermittent references to divine tears, God would be much more distant and unmoved. Anger accompanied by weeping, while still anger, is different—in motivation and in the understanding of the relationship at stake. God's harsh words of judgment are not matched by an inner harshness. The prophet's strategy is to portray the kind of God with whom Israel has to do, namely, a God for whom anger/judgment is neither the first word nor the last. A word about such a God can be productive of hope. While God may give the people up to the effects of their sinfulness, God does not finally give up on them. In other terms, the circumstantial will of God in judgment is always in the service of the ultimate will of God to save.[37] To that end, God can use judgmental effects for a variety of positive purposes (refining, cleansing, insight, discipline).

The ethical implications of this understanding are considerable: if there were no divine [375] *anger* at sin/evil, then *human* anger toward that which is oppressive and abusive would not carry the same weight. At the same

---

34. Ibid., 284–85.
35. See T. Fretheim, *The Suffering of God,* 107–26.
36. On the role of emotions in Old Testament God-talk, see J. E. Lapsley, "Feeling Our Way: Love for God in Deuteronomy," *CBQ* 65 (2003): 350–69.
37. See T. Fretheim, "Will of God in the OT,"*ABD* 6:914–20.

time, if there were no sorrow associated with divine anger, then human anger would be given a freer range regarding harshness.

Finally, I look at regret. God's response to Israel's suffering at the hands of overreaching agents is remarkably stated in Jer 42:10, "I am sorry for the disaster that I have brought upon you." For God to say, "I am sorry," regarding God's own actions is a striking admission.[38] How are we to understand this divine lament? The divine response is not prompted by anything that the people have done; this move is made entirely at the divine initiative. The text certainly does not mean that God regrets that the judgment occurred at all; all prophets witness to the appropriateness of God's judgment against Israel. The text could mean that the past stance of God toward Israel has now changed in view of events; God is now open to a future for this people other than judgment.[39] Yet, God has always had a salvific future in mind for this people. The point could be softer, namely, that God is sorry about all the pain that this community has had to experience. This is certainly the case, but the issue seems more complex.

It seems to me that this statement of God carries with it the sense of genuine regret, in the sense that the judgment and its painful effects proved to be more severe than God had intended, or even thought they would be.[40] This direction for interpretation seems especially apt in view of the excessiveness of Babylon noted above. Yet, God does not remove the divine self from responsibility for the choice of means that resulted in an imperfect execution of the mandate. God, who does not foreknow absolutely just what and how the means chosen will speak and act, accepts some responsibility for what has happened.[41] This text reveals something of the inner life of the God who uses agents who cannot be divinely controlled and is deeply pained at the results. God, however, is not bereft of resources to act in the midst of suffering. Indeed, suffering becomes a vehicle for divine action. God does not relate to suffering as a mechanic does to a car, seeking to "fix it" from the outside. God enters deeply into the suffering human situation and works the necessary healing *from within*.[42] For God to so enter into the situation means that mourning will not be the last word (see Jer 31:13–17).

That God would become involved in such human cruelties as war is finally not a matter of despair, but of hope. God does not simply give people

38. The translation of *niham* is difficult (NRSV, "be sorry"; NAB, "regret"; NIV/NAB, "grieve"). Each of these translations carry the sense of a pained divine response to God's own past actions

39. W. McKane, *A Critical and Exegetical Commentary on Jeremiah* (2 vols.; Edinburgh: T. & T. Clark: 1986), 2:1033.

40. For the idea that God thought something would occur, but did not, see Jer 3:7, 19–20.

41. On the issue of less than absolute divine foreknowledge, see Fretheim, *The Suffering of God*, 45–69.

42. See the paradigmatic Exod 3:7, "I know their sufferings," in this connection.

up to violence. God chooses to become involved in violence in order to bring about good purposes; thereby God may prevent an even greater evil. The tears of the people are fully recognized; their desperate situation is named for what it is. But because of the anguish of God, their tears will one day no longer flow. By so participating in their messy stories, God's own self thereby takes the road of suffering and death. Through such involvement, God takes into the divine self the violent effects of sinful human activities and thereby makes possible a non-violent future for God's people.

Part 5

God and the Pentateuch

Preaching Creation: Genesis 1–2

The creation accounts in Genesis 1–2 are referenced five times in the Revised Common Lectionary.[1] These creation texts appear over the course of three years in the seasons of Christmas (St. John Apostle, 1:1–5), Epiphany (Baptism of our Lord, 1:1–5), Lent (First Sunday, 2:15–17; 3:1–7), Trinity Sunday (1:1–2:4a), and Pentecost (Proper 22, 2:18–24). When combined with other creational passages (for example, Gen 9:8–17; Deut 8:7–18; Job 38:1–11; Joel 2:21–27), including new-creation texts (for example, Isa 25:6–9; 35:1–10; Ezek 37:1–14), the lectionary provides regular preaching opportunities with respect to the theme of creation.

But, even with such lectionary provisions, how often does such creation preaching actually take place? Why or why not? And how might the preacher's answer to these questions affect the way in which congregations think and act with respect to matters of the environment and other creational issues?

Creation has been a marginalized theme in the life of the church and its theological reflections for a long time. This has occurred for various reasons, from the influence of a pervasive anthropocentrism to a neglect of Old Testament [76] resources.[2] Only in the last generation or so have significant efforts been made to recover this theme in preaching and teaching. This salutary development is due, in large part, not to the church or to the theological disciplines, but to the emergence of an environmental consciousness in society more generally. It is ironic that the impetus for the church's concern for matters creational has come largely from secular sources. That in itself is a considerable witness to the importance of creation theology: God the Creator is pervasively at work in the larger culture, often independent of the church, and that divine activity has had good effects.

At the same time, it may be said that the last generation or so has seen the advance of significant biblical-theological studies in this area that have enabled creation to assume a more prominent and rightful place in church and academy. Yet, for all the good in this development, the church has not grounded its concern for creation as appropriately as it might. In its

---

This essay was originally published in *Word and World* 29 (2009): 75–83.

1. Seven times, if the annual text for December 27, St. John Apostle, is counted.

2. For a list of eleven factors that have contributed to this neglect, see Terence E. Fretheim, *God and World in the Old Testament: A Relational Theology of Creation* (Nashville: Abingdon, 2005), ix–x. See the footnotes of this volume for an extensive bibliography on this subject.

conversations and formulations about matters environmental, God and Bible seem often to be bystanders in a conversation dominated by other language, for example, that of stewardship (see below for further discussion). I was recently shown the "environmental statement" of a large congregation that mentioned neither God nor the Bible; in many other instances, God and Bible may be mentioned, but the primary grounding for such statements all too often misses a key point: God's special relationship with nonhuman creatures.[3]

I have stated some of the basic claims regarding such a God-creation relationship in these terms: "God is the God of the entire cosmos; God has to do with every creature, and every creature has to do with God, whether they recognize it or not. God's work in the world must be viewed in and through a *universal frame of reference*. That the Bible begins with Genesis, not Exodus, with creation, not redemption, is of immeasurable importance for understanding all that follows."[4] Such a biblical-theological grounding could be stated even more strongly: God has established a special relationship with each and every creature, a relationship to which the Bible witnesses in numerous texts.[5] One thinks of the repeated promise that God makes with "every living creature" following the flood (Gen 9:10, 15–17; see 8:1) or the commitment God has made with respect to the salvation of the animals [77] (for example, Ps 36:6; Isa 11:6–9; 65:25). What does it mean for our environmental considerations that God has made promises to the animals and other creatures?

It is this relationship that God has with every creature that serves as the primary ground for our care for creation. That is to say, if God is so closely related to each creature, we who are created in the image of God must reflect that relationship in all that we do if we are to be and to act appropriately as the image of God in the world. This matter raises at least three key questions regarding the practical and pastoral usage of creation texts:[6] How will we speak of the Creator? How will we speak of the created? How will we speak about the vocation of human and nonhuman creatures alike?

How Will the Preacher Speak of the Creator?

The God of the Genesis creation accounts is not explicitly "defined." Readers are left to infer the identity of this Creator God from various clues

---

3. The word "nonhuman" is unfortunate, defining such creatures by what they are not. But I know of no other term or phrase that designates all such creatures. I seek to be sparing in my usage of the term.

4. Fretheim, *God and World*, xiv.

5. For details, see ibid., especially pp. 249–68.

6. For purposes of this analysis I read the two accounts of creation in Genesis 1–2 as a single whole. In any case, it is likely that the Priestly account of creation (Gen 1:1–2:4a) incorporated the second account (2:4a–25) from the beginning and was never intended to stand alone.

in the text, while drawing on various understandings provided by the larger tradition. In light of such an analysis, readers have often suggested an image of the Creator God that is in absolute control of the developing creation, working independently and unilaterally.[7] In fact, such an understanding has been the dominant image of the Creator God through the centuries in the religious traditions for which these texts are authoritative. But, is this theological understanding fully appropriate to an explication of the creation passages?

A closer look suggests that such a perspective needs to be modified. From a negative perspective, if this understanding of God in creation is correct, then those created in God's image could *properly* understand their role regarding the rest of creation in comparable terms—power over, absolute control, and independence. By definition, if nonhuman creatures are understood to be but passive putty in the hands of God, then the natural world becomes available for comparable handling by those who go by the name "image of God."

From a positive perspective, the creation accounts make available another point of view regarding the Creator God. What if the God of the creation texts is understood to be imaged more as one who, in creating, chooses to share power in relationship? Then the way in which the human as image of God exercises dominion is to be shaped by that model. Evidence for this understanding is more widespread in these accounts than is commonly suggested. One might cite, in particular, the way in which these texts speak of the mode in which God chooses to create. Four models may be suggested:[8] God creates out of already existing materials (for [78] example, the human being out of the dust of the ground, Gen 2:7); God invites already existent nonhuman creatures to participate in further creating activity (for example, the earth and the waters, 1:11–13, 20, 24); God invites the divine assembly to participate in the creation of the human ("let us," 1:26–27); God draws the human being into further creative activity (for example, 4:1, where creating language [קָנָה], used again for God in Gen 14:19–22, is used with Eve as the subject).[9] God's approach to creating in these examples is communal and relational. In the wake of God's initiating activity, the Creator God again and again works from within the world in creating, rather than on the world from without—God employing creatures as genuine agents, rather than working independently. Certainly all creatures, including human beings, are deeply dependent upon God for

---

7. Some formulations of creation by means of "the word" suggest this understanding, as if God's only means of creating is through speaking or speech-events. For ten, perhaps eleven, modes of creation that are described in the creation accounts, see Fretheim, *God and World*, 34–35.

8. These items will be developed further in another article.

9. The woman was created out of man (אִישׁ) in 2:23; in 4:1, man (אִישׁ) is created out of woman.

their creation and continuing life. At the same time, these texts show that God has chosen to establish an *interdependent* relationship with them with respect to both originating and continuing creation.[10]

This interdependent divine way with the world may also be observed in the command to the human: "Be fruitful and multiply, and fill the earth and subdue it, and have dominion." This action on God's part, the first divine words spoken to the newly created human beings, may be considered a power-sharing move. God here chooses not to retain all power, but to share it with human beings: I am giving you specific tasks to accomplish and, by definition, the power with which to carry out those responsibilities. God thereby chooses not to do everything in the world "all by himself."

The thrust of these texts may be developed in more general terms. The words "relationship" and "community" are basic to this conversation about creation. These are "in" words that are current in discussions regarding creational and environmental issues (and in theological work more generally). All creatures of God together constitute a community in relationship. More particularly, human beings are understood, not as isolated creatures of God, but as part of a global community. Human lives touch the "life" of all other creatures, whether for good or for ill. As Denis Edwards puts it: "Any contemporary theology of the human . . . will need to situate the human within the community of life. It will need to be a theology of the human-in-relation-to-other-creatures."[11] Everyone and everything are in relationship; reality is relational. All creatures live in a spider web of a world within which [79] creaturely words and deeds set the web a-shaking, either positively or negatively—especially those perpetrated by human beings. This important relational point has not originated in recent scholarship; it is a strong biblical claim. Indeed, such interrelatedness is so basic to biblical reality that it is understood to be true of God as well as the world of creatures. Both God and world are who they are because of relationships.[12] This manifests itself in the manner in which God engages in creative activity and chooses to relate in an ongoing way to the creatures, both human and nonhuman.

What difference might it make for congregations to hear of God spoken about in such terms? Among other ways of putting the matter, for the preacher to work with this image of the Creator God will have significant implications for further reflection regarding creatures, their interrelationships, and their environmental responsibilities.

---

10. For further discussion of the distinction between originating and continuing creation, and the importance of using creation language for both activities, see Fretheim, *God and World*, 5–9.

11. Denis Edwards, *Ecology at the Heart of Faith* (Maryknoll, NY: Orbis, 2006), 7.

12. For a fuller development of the centrality of relationship in the biblical material, see Fretheim, *God and World*, 13–22.

How Will the Preacher Speak of the Created?

The most basic statement of Genesis 1–2 regarding created beings is that they are "good" and "very good." *Every creature* is evaluated in these terms; the human being is not given a special evaluative word; indeed, human beings are not even given a creation day for themselves as they share the sixth day with the animals. Moreover, this oft repeated evaluation is reported as a direct *divine* evaluation: God saw that it was good; God saw that "everything" was good. This evaluation is not reported as an assessment of the narrator, but as God's own evaluation. What does it mean to be evaluated "good" by God? At the least, it means that God is not done with the creatures once they are brought into being. God experiences what has been created, is affected by what is seen, and passes judgment on the results. This divine way is illumined by the divine evaluation in 2:18, "it is not good that the man should be alone." Such a divine response assumes that the evaluative dimension of creation entails an ongoing process, within which adjustments, even improvements, can be made in view of the divine response and the engagement of the human (as happens in 2:19–22, with v. 23 constituting an evaluation by the human!). Moreover, such an evaluation by God has environmental implications. To use the language of Francis Watson, "Human acts which treat the nonhuman creation simply as the sphere of use-value or market-value, refusing the acknowledgment of its autonomous goodness, are *acts of terrorism* in direct opposition to the intention of the creator."[13]

And what does it mean to be evaluated as "good"? The word "good" carries the sense of being correspondent to the divine intention, including elements of beauty, purposefulness, and praiseworthiness. God observes a decisive continuity [80] between God's intention and the creational result. At the same time, good does not mean static or perfect (in the sense of having no need of improvement or development to be what it truly is). Several clues in the text demonstrate that "perfect" is not the appropriate way to assess the creational situation. Certainly the "not good" of 2:18 pushes in this direction, but the command to "subdue" the earth is the clearest evidence for the claim.[14] This verb, used elsewhere in the Old Testament for coercive human activities against other humans (see Num 32:22, 29), is never applied to relationships with creatures that are not human. Moreover, the verb is here used in a pre-sin context and apparently no enemies are in view. I have suggested that the best sense for the verb is "to bring

---

13. Francis Watson, *Text, Church, World: Biblical Interpretation in Theological Perspective* (Grand Rapids, MI: Eerdmans, 1994), 146–47 (emphasis mine).

14. One might also cite Gen 3:16, which speaks of the "increase" of pain in childbirth, implying that pain would have been experienced in a pre-sin birth. Suffering is thus shown to be not necessarily related to sin, a point also made by the book of Job (see also Jesus' argument in John 9:1–3).

order out of continuing disorder."[15] The command assumes that the earth was not fully developed, that there is not a once-for-all givenness to the creation at the end of the seventh day. God's creation is going somewhere; it is a long-term project, ever in the process of becoming (as the history of nature shows, with the earth-changing activities of such creatures as glaciers, earthquakes, volcanoes, and tsunamis).

This evaluation of "good" is not taken away when sin enters the life of the world. Sin negatively affects the life of human beings, certainly, and through them the life of other creatures. But nowhere do the Scriptures take away the evaluation "good" from any creature. In fact, many texts in the wake of sin will reinforce that evaluation, even in stronger terms. With respect to human beings: "you are precious in my sight, and honored" (Isa 43:4); God continues to regard them as "crowned . . . with glory and honor" (Ps 8:5). While we certainly need to hear that we often think of ourselves more highly than we ought to think, it is also important for us to hear that we often think of ourselves *less* highly than we ought to think. To speak less highly of the human is to diminish the quality of God's own work. And this is the case not least because of God's own continuing evaluation of them as good. The creational commands indicate that God values us, places confidence in us, and honors what we do and say, though not uncritically. Our words and deeds count; they make a difference to the world and to God, not least because God has chosen to use human agents in getting God's work done in the world. We need constantly to be reminded that the Godness of God cannot be bought at the expense of creaturely diminishment. [81]

Another word that can be used to designate the created is "free."[16] One of the ways in which the creation accounts witness to this reality is the seventh day of creation (2:1–3); this day on which *God* rests (not human beings)[17] is testimony to a period of time in which God suspends the divine activity and allows the creatures, each in its own way, to be what they were created to be. God thereby gives to all creatures a certain independence and freedom. With regard to human beings, God leaves room for genuine decisions as they exercise their God-given power (see already Gen 2:19). With regard to nonhuman creatures, God releases them from "tight divine control" and permits them to be themselves as the creatures they are.[18] The latter includes the becoming of creation, from the movement of tectonic plates to volcanic activity, to the spread of viruses, to the procreation of animals. This divine

---

15. See Fretheim, *God and World*, 52–53.

16. One might distinguish between the freedom of humans and that of nonhumans with the terms "free will" and "free process." So John Polkinghorne, *Quarks, Chaos, and Christianity: Questions to Science and Religion* (New York: Crossroad, 1994), 46–47.

17. Later texts will call upon human beings to rest as God rested (Exod 20:8–11; 31:17).

18. So Polkinghorne, ibid., 47. Sin, of course, complicates the understanding of freedom, as does the influence of other creatures on our ways of being and doing.

commitment to the creatures entails an ongoing divine constraint and re-straint in the exercise of power, a divine commitment that we often wish had not been made, especially when suffering and death are in view. But God will remain true to God's commitments, come what may.

What difference might it make for creatures to be described by the preacher in these terms? The high value given to the creatures by God needs careful attention in our preaching and teaching, not least in view of the immense impact of shame on the human psyche in our culture. The high value of the nonhuman creatures is also significant for our reflec-tions on the environment and the urgency of our environmental plans and actions.

How Will the Preacher Speak of the Vocation of Human and Nonhuman Creatures?

It is not uncommon for discussions about the world's creatures to be human-centered. This has not changed significantly over the years, even with the concern for the renewed care of creation as dominant as it pres-ently is. All too often these important considerations entail a movement only from the human to the nonhuman, implying a hierarchy of valuation: God, human, nonhuman. Indeed, in some formulations, the nonhuman is almost a "basket case," as if these creatures did not possess significant capacities both to care for themselves and to be drawn into God's larger purposes for the creation. It must be stressed that the nonhuman crea-tures also have a vocational role to play in God's world and that role often entails a beneficent activity on behalf of the human. Indeed, human be-ings have been saved from much pain and suffering by the participation of nonhuman creatures in their life, though it has often gone unacknowl-edged and insufficiently appreciated.[19] [82] The book of Job, for example, is a remarkable witness to the healing power of the nonhuman world (see especially Job 38–41). We must speak of a mutuality of vocation; the move-ment goes both ways. Both humans and nonhumans are called by God to a vocation on behalf of the other.

What is the best possible language we can use for this mutual vocation? The appeals regarding churchly responsibility for matters environmental seem largely to be couched in terms of stewardship, which Paul Santmire and others have shown to be a deeply problematic way of grounding the conversation and articulating the human vocation.[20] Another problematic

---

19. For a preliminary listing of such activities on the part of nonhuman creatures that benefit the human, see Fretheim, *God and World*, 278–84.

20. For a thorough and careful study of these issues, see the various writings of Paul Santmire. With respect to the problematic issue of stewardship, see his "Partnership with Nature according to the Scriptures: Beyond the Theology of Stewardship," *Christian Schol-ar's Review* 32/4 (2003): 381–412. For an initial assessment, see Fretheim, *God and World*, 273–75.

formulation is that of the 1993 ELCA Social Statement: "[O]ur *primary* motivation is the call to be God's caregivers and to do justice."[21] As fine as this concern is, the word "primary" claims too much. The primary grounding for such considerations is not God's calling to us, but, as we have seen, God's relationship to these creatures.[22] Another formulation, somewhat less problematic, suggests that concerns regarding the environment are grounded in the recognition of the creation as God's gift to human beings. This "gift" formulation is appropriate in some ways in that it suggests that, say, water, earth, and vegetation have a vocation, too. At the same time, the word "gift" can be problematic in that it can be understood simply as that which is given to us for human enjoyment or human life. But, creatures such as water, earth, and vegetation are gifts for *all* creatures, without which life would not be possible for any of them. Indeed, water, earth, and vegetation are more fundamental to life than human beings are. Such a recognition of the foundational role that such creatures play needs always to be remembered when speaking about the special role given to humans in creation. We should state as clearly as possible the nature of God's own relationship to water and vegetation, a relationship that is prior to any creaturely relationship. And so we seek, most basically, to care for [83] such creatures *for God's sake* and not simply for our own sake or for that of other creatures.

It would be good if we gave the language of stewardship a rest for a period of time and used instead other language, for example, that of partnership and/or servanthood. In any case, it is time to be more deliberate about the responsibility of preaching creation, for the sake of both world and God. In view of the presence of creation texts in the lectionary on a regular basis, and the neverending concerns about the environment, almost any season of the year would be an appropriate time to address one or more of these issues.

---

21. From *Caring for Creation: Vision, Hope, and Justice*, ELCA Social Statement, 1993, p. 8 (emphasis mine). Available at www.elca.org/What-We-Believe/Social-Issues/Social-Statements/Environment.aspx (accessed 17 November 2008).

22. The ELCA statement moves close to this way of putting the matter when it states: "Made in the image of God, we are called to care for the earth as God cares for the earth" (p. 2). The divine "care for the earth" may be too narrow an understanding, however; God's care is one dimension of a more comprehensive relationship.

Creator, Creature, and Co-Creation in Genesis 1–2

Interpretations of the creation story in Genesis have been given a new level of urgency in view of the environmental crisis.[1] The role of the human being is especially in need of attention. In the history of the interpretation of Genesis 1–2, the focus has been placed on the sovereign God who has brought such a wonder-filled world into existence. The role of the creature, on the other hand, has been depicted largely in passive and dependent terms. To the extent that interpretation has been attentive to the human role, it has been focused on the dominion passage (1:26–28). Yet, this text has seldom been related to other texts in the creation story with a comparable import. It is the purpose of this article to lift up the creative role of the creature in these chapters and the God/creature relationship therein implied, in view of more recent holistic approaches to pentateuchal texts.

God and World in the Old Testament

As a prelude to this discussion, I would like to gather some basic statements about the God/world relationship in the Old Testament.

(1) God's relationship with the world is such that, in the words of Jer 23:24, the world is full of God. More specifically, the world is full of the steadfast love of God (Ps 33:5) or the glory of God (Isa 6:3). Putting Gen 1:1 together with Isa 61:1 [12] (and Acts 7:48–49) suggests that the cosmos is conceived as the home of God.[2] Where there is world, there God—who is other than world—is lovingly active, working from *within* that world, not on the world from without. From the perspective of Psalm 139, there is

---

This essay was originally published in *All Things New: Essays in Honor of Roy A. Harrisville* (ed. Arland J. Hultgren, Donald H. Juel, and Jack D. Kingsbury; Word and World Supplement Series 1; St. Paul, MN: Luther Northwestern Theological Seminary, 1992), 11–20.

1. This article is an extension of earlier observations regarding the interplay of creator and creature in Genesis 1–2 and elsewhere in the OT in *The Suffering of God* (Philadelphia: Fortress, 1984), 72–75; "The Reclamation of Creation: Redemption and Law in Exodus," *Int* 45 (1991): 54–65; "Nature's Praise of God in the Psalms," *ExAud* 3 (1987): 16–30. See also the issue of *Word and World* devoted to the environment (vol. 11, no. 2, 1991), especially the articles by Jürgen Moltmann, "Reconciliation with Nature" (pp. 117–23), and James Limburg, "The Responsibility of Royalty: Genesis 1–11 and the Care of the Earth" (pp. 124–30). The present article has also been informed in important ways by Michael Welker, "What Is Creation? Rereading Genesis 1 and 2," *ThTo* (1991): 56–71. See also H. Paul Santmire, "The Genesis Creation Narratives Revisited: Themes for a Global Age," *Int* 45 (1991): 366–79.

2. See Fretheim, *Suffering of God,* 37–44; Moltmann, "Reconciliation with Nature," 120.

no time or place in the world, from the macrocosmic to the microcosmic, where one is beyond the presence of God.

(2) God's presence and activity in the world must be conceived in relation to the history of the nonhuman as well as that of the human. In fact, the Old Testament thoroughly integrates these histories in terms of the divine presence and action. Salvation history as usually conceived is much too narrow a category; we have to do with a God who is deeply engaged in every aspect of the life of the world, moving toward the goal of a new heaven and a new earth, and the salvation of both humans and nonhumans is integral to that end. Ps 36:6 is illustrative: "You, O Lord, save (*yāšaʿ*) human beings and animals alike." As in Noah's ark, so in the new heaven and earth, the wolf will dwell with the lamb, and a little child shall lead them.[3]

One of the implications of such a close relationship between God and the nonhuman is that our ecological considerations must be grounded finally, not in a sense of stewardship, but in the relationship that God has established with the nonhuman.

(3) There is an interrelatedness among all creatures within the totality of God's creation. The world for Israel could be imaged as a giant spider web. Every part is in a symbiotic relationship with every other such that any act reverberates out and affects the whole, setting the entire web shaking in varying degrees of intensity. This is to say that the category of relationship is basic to one's understanding of reality from an Old Testament perspective. This may be illustrated in terms of the effect of the moral order upon the cosmic order. Again and again we read that human sin has had an adverse affect upon the entire cosmos (e.g., Hos 4:1–3). If the church had been attending properly to the Old Testament, it would have been in the vanguard regarding ecological issues.

(4) This is not a mechanical model of the universe, however. To be sure, there are the great, consistent rhythms of the world, to which Gen 8:22 bears witness: seedtime and harvest, cold and heat, summer and winter, day and night. But, at the same time, there is recognition of an openness in the created order. God's speeches in Job 38–41, which reveal unpredictability and ambiguity within the created order, are an example of this perspective. That the shape of the future of the creation is strongly informed by such an openness is made clear in texts such as Jer 22:1–5. Here two possible futures are laid before the people, depending on how they respond to issues of social justice. If one were to restate this passage in modern terms of, say, poverty or the environment, it could be brought even closer to home. There is an openness with respect to the future that waits, not only upon God, but upon the decisions creatures make.

---

3. For a consideration of the amazing range of OT texts, see Fretheim, "Nature's Praise of God."

(5) God relates to this interconnected world in such a way that every movement of the web affects God as well. Examples abound in the Old Testament. In Jer 22:1–5 what human beings do will affect the future of God as well as that of the [13] world. God will do different things, depending upon what people do. Generally in the Old Testament, God delights in creaturely responsiveness, is provoked to anger, and weeps with those who weep.[4] God is on the move with the world. At the same time, God's response will always be shaped by the divine salvific will and steadfast love for all and the divine faithfulness to relationships established.

Images of God as Creator

A traditional interpretation of creation in Genesis has tended to favor the lofty formulations and familiar cadences of the first chapter at the expense of the more "naïve" story of chapter two. This tendency has been reinforced by critical decisions. During the heyday of source criticism, Gen 1:1–2:4a was thought to be a Priestly (P) product worked out in independence from the earlier Yahwistic (J) version in Gen 2:4b–25. P and J were believed to have distinctive perspectives on creation. This separation of sources has often been accompanied by a subtle or not-so-subtle conviction that Genesis 1 is a more mature, less primitive theological statement about the Creator and the creation. The result is that the critical perspective has often reinforced the traditional image of God as a radically transcendent Creator, operating in total independence, speaking the world into being.

In more recent studies, however, P is often understood to be the redactor of Genesis 1–2, drawing upon J and other materials and putting them together essentially as we now have them.[5] This means that, while chapter 1 is P's special contribution, it was shaped with a view to what is now present in chapter 2, and was never intended to stand alone. The P perspective on creation is to be found *only* in Genesis 1–2 as a single whole. The oft-noted differences between Genesis 1 and 2 may be understood as internal qualifications. A theologically coherent perspective on creation, which the P writer presumably had, is to be found in these two chapters *in interaction with each other.* This is the only *canonical* perspective on creation Genesis makes available to us.

In view of this, some different theological emphases come into view. The praiseworthy language about a transcendent Creator is now placed in a larger theological context in which other images for God and the God/ creature relationship come more clearly into view. There are some twenty images of God the creator in these two chapters which, when seen in

---

4. A number of OT texts speak of divine suffering in relationship to the nonhuman world (e.g., Jer 9:10, NRSV footnote and most modern translations, which follow the Hebrew text).

5. See F. M. Cross, *Canaanite Myth and Hebrew Epic* (Cambridge: Harvard University Press, 1973), 293–325.

interaction with one another, provide for a more relational model of creation than has been traditionally presented.

We will note briefly the effect that this larger context has on some of the more prominent of these images. This will be followed by a more detailed discussion of chapter two, especially 2:18–25, a text often less than fully examined in this connection.

(1) God as creator/maker.   An apparently more technical term for *God's* creating (*bārā'*, 7×) is qualified already in 1:1–2:4a by the everyday word for human making (*'āśâ*, 10×). This qualification is more sharply in evidence when one includes the verbs of 2:4b–25; e.g., God uses existing materials as a potter and a builder. It is [14] clear that the creative activity of God is not thought to be without analogy in the human sphere.

(2) God as speaker.   This is a more complex divine activity than commonly suggested, namely, God speaks and "poof!" the creation comes into being. For one thing, God's speaking is usually accompanied by God's making (e.g., 1:6–7; 1:14–16). The placement of the phrase, "and it was so," makes it likely that the divine speaking usually announces the divine *intention* to create, and the creative act is not completed until the making language has so informed the reader.[6] Moreover, the divine speaking is often a speaking *with* that which is *already* created: let the earth bring forth (1:11, 24); let the waters bring forth (1:20); be fruitful and subdue the earth (1:28). Here the divine speaking is such that the receptor of the word is important in the shaping of the created order. This is mediate rather than immediate creative activity; it is creation not from outside the created order, but from within. Both human and nonhuman creatures are called to participate in the creative activity initiated by God. This perspective is sharply reinforced in chapter two.

(3) God as consultant of others.   "Let *us* make human beings." This image of God consulting with other divine beings in 1:26 has not been fully appreciated.[7] The creation of humanity is the result of a dialogical act—an inner-divine consultation—rather than a monological one. This has at least two related levels of importance: (a) Those who are not God—other divine beings—are called upon by God to participate in this central act of creation. God chooses not to do everything all by himself, but shares the cre-

---

6. Sometimes "and it was so" occurs as a kind of summary; sometimes it occurs between speaking and acting, hence meaning: And it was so, as God has spoken: (with a colon). Even the creation of light is not complete until it is separated from the darkness (1:4). See J. Rogerson, *Genesis 1–11* (Sheffield: JSOT Press, 1991), 58–60 for detail.

7. This interpretation of the plural is now very common. See P. D. Miller, *Genesis 1–11: Studies in Structure and Theme* (Sheffield: JSOT Press, 1978). An exception is C. Westermann, *Genesis 1–11: A Commentary* (Minneapolis: Augsburg, 1984), 145, whose "plural of deliberation" has not been accepted, largely because it is unable to account for all instances of the use of the plural (1:26; 3:22 and 11:6). The image of God as a consultant is found in a number of OT texts, e.g., Gen 18:17–22. On this, see Fretheim, *Suffering of God*, 49–53.

ative process with others. (b) It is specifically human beings, those created in the divine image, who are the result of such a consultation. Because God is engaged in a relationship of mutuality within the divine realm, does this not signal the nature of the relationship between God and human beings regarding the creative process? The "let us make" within the divine realm is implicitly extended to human beings, who are created in the image of those who first heard that participatory word (though God himself is included in the "us"). Initially, it takes the form of the command, "Be fruitful and multiply."

(4) A number of images depict God as a creator who reacts to that which has already been created: God is evaluator, namer, blesser, bringer.[8] That which is created brings forth varying responses in God. God does not remain removed or uninvolved with the creation once the initial creative acts take place. God's response leads to the further development of the creation and of intra-creaturely relationships.

These texts thus testify to God's *experience* of what has been created before the creating is completed. God sees the created, God is affected by what has been [15] created, and God responds in varying ways to what has been experienced. Hence, once again, God is one whose creative activity is at least in part determined by that which is not God. I take up three texts that further this understanding.

The Creature and the Creative Process

(1) Genesis 1:28.   The very first words God speaks to the newly created human beings assume the gift, affirmation, and exercise of power: have dominion, subdue the earth. God's relationship with the world is such that God from the beginning chooses not to be the only one who has or exercises creative power. God certainly takes the initiative in distributing this power to the creatures and inviting their participation, but once having done so, God is committed to this way of relating to them. God is a power-sharing, not a power-hoarding God.[9] Occasionally a severe reading of Genesis 3 will suggest that, in view of sin, God no longer entrusts the human with such power and responsibility. But the use of this language in the post-fall context of Psalm 8 indicates that this divine sharing of power is not something that is taken away in the wake of human sinfulness (see also the continuing use of image language in 5:3 and 9:6).

The command to "subdue" (1:28), while probably focusing on the cultivation of the ground, generally has to do with creational development, with the becoming of the world (an often harsh reality). This word makes

---

8. This is stressed by Welker, "What Is Creation?" 60–61.

9. The language of dominion has sometimes been thought to justify the exploitation of the earth. But the use of the verb *rādâ*, "have dominion," must be explained in terms of the care-giving sense of Ezek 34:1–4; cf. J. Limburg, "Responsibility of Royalty"; W. Brueggemann, *Genesis* (Atlanta: John Knox, 1982), 32.

it clear that the evaluation "good" does not mean the world is "perfect," either in the sense of needing no further development or capable of being what it was created to be in and of itself, without human attention.

(3) *Genesis 2:5, 15.* Essentially the same point is made in 2:5, where the absence of a human being to till (*'ābad,* "serve") the ground is considered a crucial reality. The earth was in the pre-creation state it was, not only because God had not yet done something, but also because there was as yet no human being active! The divine purpose for the *'ādām* in 2:15, to serve (*'ābad*) and to protect (*šāmar*), specifically connects back to 2:5. This gives responsibility to the human being, not simply for maintenance or preservation, but in intra-creational development, bringing the world along toward its fullest possible potential.

In other words, God intends from the beginning that things not stay just as they were initially created. And this is so not just because God did not exhaust the divine creativity in the first week of the world, but because of the creative capacities built into the very created order of things. God creates a paradise, but that is not a static state of affairs; it is a highly dynamic situation in which the future is open to a number of possibilities and in which creaturely activity is crucial for proper creational developments.

(4) *Genesis 2:18–25.* These themes are developed in a striking way in 2:18–25. This story is probably intended to retell the events of the sixth day of creation, though certainly not in any precise or linear way. In this text God evaluates the creational situation and declares that something *God* has created is not (yet?) good: "It is not good that the *'ādām* should be alone." To whom is God speaking here? It [16] is likely that the reader is once again permitted to overhear the inner-divine reflective process, providing a connection back to the "let us" of 1:26; the *'ādām*'s not being alone is correlated with God's not being alone. Here God identifies a problem within the divine creative work up to this point and moves to find a solution, to make those changes that would enable a different evaluation: it is now good.[10]

Some representative interpretations of these verses will help us focus on one major issue.

(a) This text speaks of a series of divine experiments, a trial and error method of creation. After a series of "false starts," God finally creates what the *'ādām* needs.[11] Unfortunately, this view has often been adjudged to be naive or primitive, and hence to be left behind theologically. From my perspective, this is an experimental divine move within the very process of creation that has deep theological implications. God does indeed learn from experience (see n. 20).

---

10. For a helpful use of this text by a systematic theologian, see Douglas John Hall, *God and Human Suffering* (Minneapolis: Augsburg, 1986), 53–62.

11. Cf. Bruce Vawter, *On Genesis: A New Reading* (Garden City: Doubleday, 1977), 74.

(b) From another perspective,[12] God here "engages in a sharp secularization of the human creature." *God* does not intend to be the helper of the *'ādām*; God is not the solution to the problem of human aloneness. The help that the *'ādām* needs regarding this matter is to be found among creatures, not among the gods.

(c) On the naming of the animals. For Westermann, it is the *'ādām* who "decides what sort of helper corresponds to him." The naming indicates that the *'ādām* "is autonomous within a certain limited area," whereby he "puts them into a place in his world."[13] Von Rad speaks of the naming as an act of ordering, but also in terms of the use of language, "as an intellectual capacity by means of which [the *'ādām*] brings conceptual order to his sphere of life."[14] It is important to stress in this connection that language shapes reality. It is Phyllis Trible who, from a rhetorical angle, has put this point in a most helpful way. She notes that God, who has so dominated the narrative up to this point, now recedes into the background; this indicates that God is now present "not as the authoritarian controller of events but as the generous delegator of power who even forfeits the right to reverse human decisions."[15] Without any qualification, *whatever* the human being called each animal, that was its name (2:19c).

The human being's naming of each creature is meant to be parallel to the divine naming in 1:5, 8, 10. This is not a perfunctory utilitarian move, a labeling of the cages of the world zoo. It is a part of the creative process itself, discerning the very nature of intra-creaturely relationships.

It is noteworthy that the prohibition regarding the tree occurs just prior to this unit, concerning which no debate is invited (2:16–17). (It is striking that there is no counterpart to this command in chapter 1, or any specific concern about faith or trust in God.) The command (there is law within the pre-fall situation!) indicates that, for all the creative power God entrusts to human beings, there is a relationship [17] to God that provides an indispensable matrix for the proper exercise of that power. To obey the command is to recognize that human creativity is derivative, that human beings are not freed from all limitations in its exercise or from the good divine intention for creaturely life. But within these limits, 2:18–23 depicts some remarkable divine moves relative to the role of the human in the development of the created order.

Before proceeding with a closer look at 2:18–23, let me say a word about recent exegetical work relative to an androcentric perspective present in these verses. The perspective is not as pervasive as often thought.

12. Brueggemann, *Genesis*, 47.
13. Westermann, *Genesis*, 228.
14. G. von Rad, *Genesis: A Commentary*, (rev. ed.; Philadelphia: Westminster, 1971), 83.
15. P. Trible, *God and the Rhetoric of Sexuality* (Philadelphia: Fortress, 1978), 93.

(1) For the woman to be created from the rib of the *'ādām* entails no subordination, any more than the *'ādām's* being created from the ground implies his subordination to it.

(2) For the woman to be called helper (*'ēzer*) carries no implications regarding the *status* of the one who helps; indeed, God is more often called the helper of human beings (Psalm 121).

The suggestion that Eve's helping in this text has to do with motherhood is insufficient.[16] Helping for Eve cannot be collapsed into procreation, not least because the immediate outcome specified in vv. 24–25 does not focus on this concern.

(3) For the woman to be named by the *'ādām* does not entail the authority of man over woman, any more than Hagar's naming of God entails such authority in 16:13.[17] Naming has to do with an act of *discernment* regarding the nature of relationships, as in the naming of the animals by *'ādām*. Moreover, if the *'ādām* is already ruler over the woman in chapter 2, then the sentence of 3:16 represents no judgment.[18]

(4) Finally, contrary to some recent opinion, one ought not consider *'ādām* as an "earth creature" without sexual identity before the creation of woman, so that the creation of man and woman is simultaneous.[19] Without an explicit linguistic marker that the meaning of the word *'ādām* changes from "earth creature" to "the man," it will be read the same throughout this section. At the same time, the use of *'ādām* as a generic (see NRSV at 1:26–27; 2:5; 5:1–2) suggests that *'ādām* in these verses can be extended to refer to a *human* role (and hence our use of the phrase "human being" in what follows). In any case, being created first or last has nothing to do with priority or subordination.

We return to the story. How God proceeds to respond to the evaluation of "not good" is impressive; twice, God "brings (*bô'*)" some other creature— first the animals, then the woman—before the human being. Twice, it is *God* who lets the [18] human being determine whether the animals or the woman are adequate to move the evaluation of the creation from

16. See D. J. A. Clines, *What Does Eve Do to Help? and Other Readerly Questions to the Old Testament* (Sheffield: JSOT Press, 1990), 27–37.

17. On the naming act, George Ramsey, "Is Name-Giving an Act of Domination in Genesis 2:23 and Elsewhere?" *CBQ* 50 (1988): 24–35, is especially helpful. Clines, *What Does Eve Do*, 39, may be right that discerning does not necessarily exclude domination, but it does not include it without some contextual marker either.

18. Verses 13–19 have to do with a sin-judgment schema, which God mediates. Of course, such judgments are not intended to be eternal decrees. Hence, in another context, the judged city of Jerusalem can be rebuilt—even at the command of God; or, seeking to overcome patriarchy or relieving the pain in childbirth may be considered the will of God. On 3:16, see especially Carol Meyers, *Discovering Eve* (New York: Oxford University Press, 1988).

19. So Trible, *God and the Rhetoric of Sexuality*, 79–81. For contrary arguments, see Clines, *What Does Eve Do*, 40–41. Note that NRSV does not translate *'ādām* as Adam until 4:25. The NRSV footnotes to 2:20; 3:17, 21 reflect the difficulty of the issue.

"not good" to "good." The human being, not God, deems what is "fit for him." The future in some basic respect lies in human hands.

This portrayal of God, the creator of heaven and earth, leading all the animals one by one, and then the woman, to a face-to-face meeting with the human being is truly remarkable. It suggests the image of God as a servant: God the Creator places himself at the service of the "good" of the human being, indeed at the service of creaturely creativity. God's role is the placing of various creative possibilities before the human being, but it is the creature who is left to decide. God will take into account the human response from within the creative process in shaping the future.[20]

It is remarkable that the human being does not simply acquiesce to what God presents, as if whatever God does must be deemed satisfactory. Indeed, what God initially provides, the human being does not accept! God, in turn, accepts the human decision, and goes back to the drawing boards. God takes the ongoing creational process into account in shaping new directions for the creation. Divine decisions interact with human decisions in the creation of the world. Creation is process as well as punctiliar act; it is creaturely as well as divine.

The future is genuinely open here. It depends on what the human being does with what God presents. Will the human being decide for the animals? The question of not only how, but indeed whether humanity will be perpetuated beyond this first generation is left open-ended, suspended in the mid-air of this creative moment. How the *human being* decides will determine whether there will be a next human generation. The human being at least in part determines how God will be able to move into the future. The human judgment will shape the nature of the divine decision, indeed shape the future of the world.

Is this much different from the contemporary situation, where human ecological sensitivity or the use of nuclear weapons may have a comparable import for the future of the world? Indeed, such decisions could put an end to the human race as decisively as the choice of the animals would have. It is not that human beings have the capacity to stymie God's movement into the future. But God has established a relationship with human beings such that their decisions about the creation truly count.

It is finally recognized by the man that the woman will address the stated need. God recognizes the creational import of the human decision,

---

20. It is likely that the text does not function with a notion of absolute divine foreknowledge. God does not seem finally to know just how the *'ādām* will respond until he in fact does (see Gen 20:12 for another of many such texts). God knows all there is to know, including all the possibilities or probabilities of the future (and hence omniscience is not the issue). I was recently reminded of a statement made by former teacher and colleague, Warren Quanbeck, in an unpublished 1975 lecture: "We have to rethink the omniscience of God. . . . God's omniscience is not the omniscience of everything that's going to happen but a knowledge of all the possibilities." For further detail, see Fretheim, *Suffering of God*, 45–59.

for there is no additional divine word or act. God lets the man's exultation over the woman fill the scene; the *human word* (the first uttered in Genesis) counts for the evaluation that this is now good in lieu of a statement from God. It is left to the narrator to note the rightness of this creative move by drawing the reader into the closeness of the male-female bond, citing the implication of the human decision for the future of [19] the creation. At the same time, this is not reduced to matters of procreation; it includes companionship, intimate and otherwise.

A Relational Model of Creation

These texts contribute to what might be called a relational model of creation. That is, both God and the creatures have an important role in the creative enterprise, and their spheres of activity are interrelated in terms of function and effect. It seems clear that God is not only independent and the creatures only dependent.[21] God has shaped the created order in such a way that there are overlapping spheres of interdependence and creative responsibility shared between Creator and creature. Moreover, the creatures are interdependent among themselves. Both human beings and animals are made dependent on vegetation for their food (1:29–30); the independent role of the animals in 1:22 is not to be violated. Moreover, that which is nonhuman is made dependent upon varying forms of dominion exercised by the human.

Within this relational model, it is important to speak of both distinctions and commonalities among the principals. On the one hand, God is God and freely brings into being that which is not God. There is a deep dependence of the creatures upon the Creator for their existence and continuing life. Chapter 1 stresses this divine initiative, imagination, transcendence and power in a way that chapter 2 does not. The placement of chapter 1 suggests that these divine characteristics should stand at the beginning and in the foreground in any discussion. Yet, no simple or static hierarchy emerges, as there is already a leaning toward chapter 2 in some features of chapter 1.

On the other hand, the realm of the divine and the realm of the creature are not two radically unrelated spheres; there are overlapping powers, roles and responsibilities, to which "image of God" language testifies (1:26–27; 5:3; 9:6).[22] God is not powerful and the creatures powerless; we need constantly to be reminded that the Godness of God cannot be bought at the expense of creaturely diminishment. In the very act of creating, God gives to that which is other than God a certain independence and freedom. God

---

21. On these themes, see especially Welker, "What Is Creation?" 64–68.
22. On the "dyarchy of God and humanity" in connection with this theme, see J. Levenson, *Creation and the Persistence of Evil: The Jewish Drama of Omnipotence* (New York: Harper & Row, 1988), 111–20.

moves over, as it were, and makes room for others. There is an ordered freedom in the creation, a degree of openness and unpredictability wherein God leaves room for genuine decisions on the part of human beings as they exercise their God-given power. But, even more, God gives them powers and responsibilities in a way that *commits God* to a certain kind of relationship with them. This entails a divine constraint and restraint in the exercise of power within the creation. For example, God will not do the procreating of animals or the bearing of fruit seeds in any unmediated way. Human beings have been given the freedom to destroy themselves, though this is not the will of God for them at all.

Another way of moving into this theme would be to say that God does not have a final and solitary will in place from the beginning regarding every aspect of the created order. God makes adjustments in the divine will for the world in view [20] of the ongoing interaction with the world. At the same time, these divine moves will always be in tune with God's absolute will regarding life and salvation for all humankind.

One implication of this is that the divine sovereignty in creation is understood, not in terms of absolute divine control, but as sovereignty that gives power over to the created for the sake of a relationship of integrity. This is a risky move, for it entails the possibility that the creatures will misuse the power they have been given, which is in fact what occurs. A reclamation of creation will be needed.[23]

---

23. For details, see Fretheim, "The Reclamation of Creation."

"God Was with the Boy" (Genesis 21:20): Children in the Book of Genesis

The history of Hebrew children is fraught with turmoil and instability, as they suffered with their elders the effects of centuries of warfare, tumultuous upheavals, and aimless migration. Lamentations of their starvation, slaughter, and enslavement fill the pages of the Old Testament.[1]

The Bible contains many stories where children suffer and simply become dispensable objects in the telling of the story.[2]

Children take center stage in the book of Genesis.[3] This essay attends to those texts in Genesis that are especially important for thinking about the Bible's [4] portrayal of children. The first section focuses on Genesis 1–11; the balance of the article centers on Genesis 12–50 and the place of children among Israel's ancestors. Focused attention will be given to two endangered children: Ishmael and Isaac.

By reexamining Genesis through the lens of "the child," this essay invites readers to discover the critical role that children play in the opening book of the Bible. Children are created in the image of God, promised to barren ones, loved and enjoyed, vulnerable to violence, threatened with death, and engulfed in destructive events. Of special concern is a delinea-

---

This essay was originally published in *The Child in the Bible* (ed. Marcia J. Bunge, Terence E. Fretheim, and Beverly Roberts Gaventa; Grand Rapids: Eerdmans, 2008), 3–23.

1. A. R. Colon, *A History of Children: A Socio-Cultural Survey Across Millennia* (Westport, CT: Greenwood, 2001). Colon cites Nah 3:10; Hos 13:16; and Lam 5:13; many other texts could also be cited. That children lived perilous lives can be observed in studies of several burial sites in Canaan. About one-third of the children buried at these sites had died before age 5, about half of them before age 18. See Carol Meyers, *Discovering Eve: Ancient Israelite Women in Context* (New York: Oxford University Press, 1988), 112.

2. Danna Nolan Fewell, *Children of Israel: Reading the Bible for the Sake of Our Children* (Nashville: Abingdon, 2003), 9. She has stories such as Sodom and Gomorrah in mind (pp. 28–29). The new heaven and new earth are marked by the end of infant mortality (Isa 65:20), indirectly indicating the commonness of the death of young children.

3. It is difficult to know what period(s) of Israel's history are reflected in Genesis. Regarding Genesis 12–50, Walter Moberly (*The Old Testament of the Old Testament: Patriarchal Narratives and Mosaic Yahwism* [Minneapolis: Fortress, 1992]) has shown that some theological dimensions of these chapters seem to reflect a time before the development of much other Old Testament theology. For a careful and thorough sociological study of families in early Israel (which may or may not correspond to familial life depicted in Genesis), see Carol Meyers, "The Family in Early Israel," in *Families in Ancient Israel* (ed. Leo Perdue et al.; Louisville: Westminster John Knox, 1997), 1–47. Her references to Genesis are rare.

tion of the role that Israel's God plays in the lives of these children and in the shaping of their stories.

Genesis 1–11: Children in the Image of God

In the language of Gen 1:26–27, human beings are created in the image of God. We know from the larger context that human beings do not become an "image of God" only when they are adults; the image of God is not something that they "grow up into." This point is made clear in Gen 5:1–3, the beginning of the genealogy of Adam. After noting that male and female were created in the image of God, the genealogical structure of this chapter makes God the "father" of Adam. Gen 5:3 then states: "When Adam had lived 130 years, he became the father of a son in his likeness, according to his image, and named him Seth." Human beings are now the ones who create further images of God. In other words: this first generation of children *is* created in the image of God (even after the fall into sin). This inclusion of both God and Adam in the genealogy suggests that the pro-creation of children is a genuinely creative act (as Eve already recognized in Gen 4:1: "I have created a man with the help of the Lord").

Everything that the image of God is, every child is. These Genesis texts claim that all human beings—regardless of gender, race, social status, or age—are created in the image of God from the beginning of their life. The image of God is democratized to include everyone—a move that kings and other elites probably did not appreciate. And so, every child is created in the image of God and, as such, has special dignity and value to God and for the world—a point made all too uncommonly. [5]

In the divine call to the first human beings in Gen 1:28, as well as to the post-flood families in Gen 9:1–7 ("be fruitful and multiply"), God builds into the very structures of creation the capacity for humans to bring children into being. Unlike the Canaanites, whose *gods* assumed responsibility to generate new life, human beings are here given that responsibility. By being the image of God they were created to be, human beings will naturally perpetuate their own kind. God will not be absent from the gestation and birthing process, as Ps 139:13, among other texts, testifies: "You knit me together in my mother's womb." But human beings will do the procreating, not God!

Libraries are filled with literature about the "image of God," and Sibley Towner's essay in this volume [not reprinted here] reviews various interpretations of the image of God and addresses this theme at length. For the purposes of the present essay and in the context of this discussion of Genesis as a whole, it is important to note that remarkably little scholarly study on the image of God focuses on the word "God."[4] If one understands

---

4. For the most up-to-date study of the image of God, with a thorough analysis of ancient Near Eastern and biblical literature, see J. Richard Middleton, *The Liberating Image:*

the word "God" in terms of its context in Genesis 1, God is one who creates. It would thus follow that human beings created in the image of God are fundamentally creative beings, and this includes children. When we see children play with whatever might be available, we are astonished at their creativity. Their imagination is a grand gift of God, and they demonstrate that they are created in the image of God in every such imaginative moment. Israel did not always honor this high status of children, often treating them as second-class citizens. Yet Israel stakes a claim that children are created in the image of God, and this enhances their stature as creative human beings.

Even more, the God who creates is a deeply relational God, evidenced in the "let us" of Gen 1:26. This reference to the divine council demonstrates that the creation of humanity is the result of a dialogical act—an inner-divine consultation—rather than a monological one. Relationality is thus shown to be basic to the being of God, and hence it is intensely characteristic of all who are created in the divine image. The interrelational capacities of children may, in fact, be said to be a model for all human beings, of whatever age.

With this creativity and relationality in every child, no matter how old, it is no wonder that this world is not a static state of affairs, but a dynamic, relational process of becoming. And the fact that this process is somewhat disorderly, as children will often be, in fact makes excellence possible.[5] With all of [6] these creative children, we have to do with, not automatons and a monotonous cycle of inevitability, but genuine newness at every step. This understanding of children as creative and relational stands as a grand claim about children at the beginning of the Bible. Whenever readers think about children in the Bible, they are called to think about relationality and creativity. The concern for children in the balance of Genesis 1–11 is largely limited to their assumed presence in the several genealogies. Genesis 12–50 will introduce us to children more fully in the context of several stories.

Genesis 12–50

God, Children, and Promises

Children are the focus of God's promises to Abraham, Isaac, and Jacob, for the promise of many descendants obviously depends upon the birth of children.[6] But children are hard to come by in the family of Abraham.

The Imago Dei in Genesis 1 (Grand Rapids: Brazos, 2005). For my own reflections, see Terence E. Fretheim, *God and World in the Old Testament: A Relational Theology of Creation* (Nashville: Abingdon, 2005), pp. 42–43, 48–56.

5. See W. Sibley Towner, *Genesis* (Louisville: Westminster John Knox, 2001), 20–21.

6. It is very difficult to determine the ages of children in the Old Testament. Over a dozen Hebrew words can be translated as infant, child, boy/girl, youth, the young, off-

With all the emphasis upon generating children in the opening chapters of Genesis, it is striking that the chosen family experiences so much barrenness. Sarah, Rebekah, and Rachel all have such difficulties, and this reality regularly complicates the plot, putting pressure on the divine promises (Gen 15:2–4; 18:1–15; 25:21; 30:1–8, 22–24).

Strikingly, such negative developments are not ascribed in any special way to the presence of sin in the world. It is as if these difficulties, not unlike pain in childbirth (see Gen 3:16), were believed to be a normal part of God's world, though, in the wake of sin, they were intensified by moral factors. These recurrent difficulties regarding conception and birth were also exacerbated by the famine, disease, and violence of their world. Child mortality remained high throughout the biblical period. To move all the way through childhood in Israel was a major feat.

These various difficulties were of such intensity that special arrangements were at times made to ensure posterity. Concubines were not uncommon—usually female slaves owned by a household, who bore children to assure the line of the patriarch and to add to the labor pool. For example, Sarah makes arrangements with her slave girl, Hagar, to be a surrogate wife for Abraham. [7] Jacob even made polygamous arrangements, including children born through the slave girls of Leah and Rachel. These sorts of arrangements were made without moral judgment being cast on the persons involved, probably because of the importance of assuring the production of needed children. A related practice was levirate marriage, built into the heart of Israel's laws (Gen 38; Deut 25:5–10); if a husband died, the husband's brother married his widow to raise legal descendants and to transmit the name of the deceased.

Aside from natural difficulties, human behaviors complicated the production of progeny. On three different occasions Sarah and Rebekah are endangered by their husbands (Gen 12:10–20; 20:1–18; 26); related issues of paternity place further pressure on the promises.[7] The competing wives and concubines of both Abraham and Jacob vie for attention in and through their children (Gen 16:1–6; 21:7–21; 29:31–30:24) and make issues of lineage and inheritance highly complex. Those children grow up to make their own contributions to the dysfunctionality of this family, including the continuing endangerment of children such as Joseph.

With these difficult realities of birthing and childhood, it is no wonder that God focuses on children in the ancestral promises. All the promises of God depend upon the birth and continuing life of children (see, e.g., Gen 15:3–5; 22:17; 28:14). Abraham even gives such a high value to a biological heir that an adopted son will not do. The meaning of his life is closely

---

spring, etc. The words are not age-specific and the stages of life not carefully factored out. Some educated guesswork will be necessary.

7. See also Gen 25:1–6 and Abraham's six other children.

bound up with *his* having children, and that is where God's promises center (Gen 15:1–6).

The importance of children can also be seen in the seemingly endless references to blessing. For example, the blessing is spoken to Rebekah before she leaves home to become the wife of Isaac: "May you, our sister, become thousands of myriads" (Gen 24:60). The patriarch is often the one who mediates the divine blessings from generation to generation. For example, Jacob "blesses" his grandsons in Genesis 48 with these words: "The God before whom my ancestors walked, the God who has been my shepherd all my life to this day, the angel who has redeemed me from all harm, bless the boys . . . and let them grow into a multitude on the earth" (48:15–16; Jacob blesses his sons in Genesis 49). So, children are the fulfillment of God's promises to these families, and they in turn carry on those promises of life and blessing into successive generations.

That children play such an important role in these stories can be seen even in the way the narratives are structured. For example, in the middle of the story of Jacob are listed the births of all of Jacob's children except Benjamin (Gen 29:31–30:24). The narrative flows up to this point and then, [8] after the flurry of births, flows away from it. In verse after verse, rhythmic references are made to a child being born and being named, often with reference to God.[8] The reader is being told thereby that these children, the progenitors of the twelve tribes of Israel, are central, not only to the Genesis narrative, but to the entire story of God's people. The births of these children mean that this particular family is flourishing and God is fulfilling God's promises.

Gratitude to God is evident in the responses of these mothers to their newborn children, as elsewhere in the Old Testament. Again and again, children are the source of great joy. Especially to be noted is the response of Sarah to the birth of Isaac (Gen 21:6): "God has brought laughter for me; everyone who hears will laugh with me."[9] Deep appreciation and love for children may also be seen in Jacob's reaction to the apparent death of Joseph (Gen 37:33–35). He cries out for his child with deep intensity, with traditional signs of mourning, lamenting for many days, unable to be comforted by his other children. In another case, if Benjamin does not return with his older brothers, Jacob will be so distressed that he will die, "bringing the gray head of our father down to the grave in sorrow" (44:31). Love and affection for children are often noted in the Old Testament, with both tenderness and discipline evident.

At the same time, children bring great anxiety and, at times, experience remarkably poor parenting. (See examples of poor parenting by Jacob in

---

8. Note the differences in the reference to Jacob's one daughter, Dinah (Gen 30:21).

9. Isaac was a typical Israelite child in remaining under the care of his mother until the time of weaning—about three years old (see Gen 21:8).

Genesis 34; and by David in 2 Samuel 13–19.) That more negative side of the story of children in Genesis will become evident shortly.

One other claim is made about the divine promises. God does not make promises of children only to members of the chosen line. The narrative in Genesis 16–21 is punctuated with references to God's promises to Hagar and Ishmael (I return to them below). Virtually the same language is used for them as in God's promises to Abraham and Sarah (see Gen 16:10; 17:20; 21:13, 18).[10] That God makes promises of children to outsiders as well insiders is significant. Given the fact that God always keeps promises, how might one look for the descendants of Hagar and Ishmael through the centuries?

So God's promises to children and about children fill almost every scene in the book of Genesis. Without these ongoing divine blessings, life for this family and its children would be bleak indeed. [9]

Abraham as Teacher of Children

God specifically commands Abraham to teach his children (Gen 18:19). Abraham is chosen so that "he may charge his children and his household to keep the way of the Lord by doing righteousness and justice; so that the Lord may bring about for Abraham what he has promised him." Notably, the future of God's promise to Abraham is said to involve the teaching of Abraham's children. Abraham is later said to have kept this divine charge to be teacher of his children (Gen 26:5). This divine charge to Abraham is focused on the children's religious education and its implications for their daily walk. The reference to "righteousness and justice" reminds the reader of the depth and breadth of this education. The "way of the Lord" that Abraham is called to teach the children consists, not simply of personal or spiritual issues, but also matters of justice. Abraham is charged to teach his children very public matters, which are understood to be key concerns for God. Or, in other terms, the teaching of children by the community of faith has a very public face that includes the entirety of life in relationship to others.

This Genesis theme is picked up especially in the books of Exodus and Deuteronomy (Exod 12:26–27; 13:8–10, 14–16; Deut 4:9–10; 6:4–9, 20–25; 11:13–21; 31:9–13; cf. Josh 4:6–7, 21–24). Central to several of these texts are the questions of children, which in turn become the occasion for teaching. For example, Deut 6:20–25 reads, "When your children ask you in time to come, 'What is the meaning of the decrees . . . that God has commanded you, then you shall say. . . .'" The focus is not on simple repetition but on an *interpretation* of the tradition in view of the new times and places represented in the book of Deuteronomy.[11]

---

10. The extensive genealogy of another outsider, Esau (Genesis 36), reveals that he is also a richly blessed man.

11. See the essay by Patrick Miller in this volume [not reprinted here].

The Vulnerability and Endangerment of Children

The patterns of the endangerment of children begin in the Genesis texts and become a lens through which the reader can read subsequent texts that imperil children. One thinks of the suffering of children in the flood or in the destruction of Sodom and Gomorrah, for whom Abraham interceded before God, unsuccessfully. Elsewhere in Genesis, one thinks of Ishmael and Isaac, to whom we will return.

Beyond Genesis, the biblical texts often witness to the endangerment of children—chosen and non-chosen. Andreas Michel speaks of "almost 200 [10] texts about violence against children in the Hebrew Old Testament, another fifty from the deutero-canonical writings."[12] The sources of the endangerment of children vary, from war to famine and, as we shall see, even God's action in such situations. Life for children gets so horrific at times that the texts even speak about eating children to survive (Lam 4:10).

God is not removed from such adverse effects upon children. God, using human agents, is a key actor in the judgment of sins that adults have perpetrated (Lam 1:15–16). While God does not directly perpetrate the violence, the children suffer severely in the wake of God's using human agents to exact judgment. The best modern example may be World War II, in which children suffered, not least because of Allied bombs; these allies could be interpreted as the agents of God against the evils of Hitler and his minions. This sin-consequence connection enables many difficult Old Testament texts to be understood, such as Exod 20:5: "God visits the iniquity of the fathers upon the children." This claim is a basic statement about God's created moral order.[13] The moral order functions so that sin and evil do not go unchecked in the life of world. But that moral order does not cut clean, striking only those who are wicked.[14]

God also endangers children through divine choices made and not made. Who will be the son of promise? Ishmael or Isaac? Jacob or Esau? One of Jacob's sons, or all twelve? God chooses some children rather than

---

12. Michel goes on to say that such violence against children occurs primarily "in the context of descriptions or threats of war, usually as brutal and deadly human violence: children become the victims of armed force, cannibalism, imprisonment, slavery and the extermination of dynasties" (p. 51). Andreas Michel, "Sexual Violence against Children in the Bible," in *The Structural Betrayal of Trust* (ed. R. Ammicht-Quinn, H. Haker, and M. Junker-Kenny; Concilium; London: SCM, 2004), 51–71.

13. For a discussion of the created moral order, see Fretheim, *God and World in the Old Testament*, 158–64. See also the essay by Patrick Miller in this volume [not reprinted here].

14. Whole families suffer for the sins of parents—e.g., the rebellion of Korah (Numbers 16); Achan (Joshua 7); sons of Saul (2 Sam 21:1–9). David's child suffers and dies for David's sins, as do many others in the following generations (1 Samuel 12). We know today that the sins of parents often have deeply adverse effects on the children—witness alcoholism.

others and so creates even further conflict within this family.[15] Indeed, God chooses younger children over older children (e.g., Isaac, Jacob), thereby overturning cultural expectations and disrupting family life. The question may legitimately be asked regarding these divine choices: Do they inevitably make life difficult for children? [11] Human beings, including parents, certainly do their share in jeopardizing the life and health of children in Genesis and elsewhere. One thinks of Joseph, whose life is threatened from within his own household (Genesis 37). Joseph's brothers become jealous of their father's favoritism. First they conspire to kill him, then instead they sell him into slavery—a remarkable interruption in his advantaged childhood. Themes in this story include sibling rivalry, parental partiality, and familial violence.[16] The story refuses to shy away from the issue of the child's own culpability in how he is being treated; he is named outright as a tattletale and interprets his dreams in a prideful way.

One also thinks of Benjamin, treated like a pawn in the midst of familial struggles (Genesis 43–44). One thinks of Lot's virgin daughters (Genesis 19); Lot endangers them by offering them to the men of Sodom for sexual pleasure. While their age is not specified, that they are betrothed and yet unmarried suggests that they are youth. Such horrendous actions on the part of a father! No amount of appeal to issues of hospitality will enable Lot to escape from the judgment of the narrator. The daughters he offers are *betrothed* (see the strictures in Deut 22:23–29). Later he has sexual relations with each of them, even if under the influence of alcohol. The narrative judges Lot: just as Lot gave his daughters no voice in the matter of sexual relations, so he is placed in a comparable situation, where his daughters give him no voice. What goes around comes around.

Two Genesis stories regarding the endangerment of children (Isaac and Ishmael) have proved difficult for interpreters, and the story of each deserves special attention.

---

15. This theme is revealing of the fact that conflict in Genesis must *not* be studied simply in sociological or psychological terms. Familial conflict in Genesis has a theological component. Of course, what human beings do with God's choices can make things a lot worse than they normally would be.

16. Danna Nolan Fewell states: "For children who have been the victims and survivors of domestic abuse and who are struggling with issues of forgiveness, the story of Joseph may offer a significant model of psychological and emotional interruption. For although Joseph claims when the brothers are at last reconciled that, though they meant their actions for evil, God used them for good, Joseph is still careful to forgive his brothers only after he is in a position of power, removed from any further abuse at their hands" (*Children of Israel*, 111). The question may be raised as to whether Joseph does not actually refuse to forgive his brothers, for he is "not in the place of God" (Gen 50:19–20).

Two Stories about Children

The Eviction and Rescue of Ishmael

Bible readers should give more time and space to this child of Abraham and Hagar and to the stories associated with him. That so many have been so neglectful [12] of Ishmael's story is sad; we would have been much better prepared for post–September 11 events if we had paid attention to this child.

When it comes to issues relating to children, several verses from the second story of Hagar and Ishmael in Gen 21:14–21 are particularly pertinent. This boy was Abraham's son, but not a member of the chosen line; God makes a covenant with Isaac, not Ishmael. Ishmael and Hagar are outsiders; indeed, they are twice specifically excluded from the chosen family (Genesis 16; 21).

Once again the structure of the Genesis narrative assists us. Prior to Gen 17:15, Sarah has not been named as the potential mother of the children God has promised Abraham. The context shows that having this child via Hagar is Sarah's choice; yet, Abraham voices no objection whatsoever. No judgment is passed on either figure for this means of having children.[17]

After Isaac's birth, Sarah's decision to send Hagar and Ishmael away is contrary to Abraham's wishes, but because God sides with Sarah, they are banished into the wilderness. At this point, when the narrative takes a particularly poignant turn, how striking it is that God becomes so deeply involved in the life of this child, Ishmael. God had come to Hagar's aid earlier in the wilderness, when she had been excluded from the chosen family. At that point God had extended promises to her (Gen 16:10): "I will so greatly multiply your offspring that they cannot be counted for multitude." And a chapter later, when God makes it clear for the first time that Sarah is to be the mother of Isaac, God does not forget Ishmael. Indeed, God reiterates those promises to him in even sharper detail (17:20: "As for Ishmael, I have heard you. I will bless him and make him fruitful and exceedingly numerous; he shall be the father of twelve princes, and I will make him a great nation." Now, in the context of those ringing promises to Hagar and Ishmael, the story of Hagar and Ishmael takes a special turn in Gen 21:14–20.

Notice the specific actions of God and recall the setting—away from the chosen people and out in the wilderness.

1. God hears the voice of the boy; the point is twice spoken. God hears the cries of children; God is not deaf to the seemingly "minor" wailings of the little ones. We are not given Ishmael's words here; there may not even have been words, only cries in the night. In any case, God hears his voice and moves to help him and his mother. Notably, God hears the voice of the boy "where he is" (Gen 21:17). That is, God does not deal with the issue of a desperate child from afar; God goes where the troubled child is. Hagar and

---

17. This also happens later with Jacob (Genesis 30); it is a practice known in other parts of that world.

Ishmael do not [13] have to find God and bring him on the scene. God is already there, quite apart from the ministrations of the chosen family. This theme of divine presence is especially striking in Gen 21:22. Abimelech tells Abraham, "God is with you in all that you do." The same language that was used of Ishmael in 21:20 is here used of God's servant Abraham. The chosen family does not have a corner on the presence of God.

2. God uses human agents to bring the child through the crisis. God makes use of what is available; in this case, it is Ishmael's mother Hagar and a well of water. God tells Hagar: "Come lift up the boy and hold him fast with your hand, for I will make a great nation of him" (Gen 21:18). Lift up this boy; hold this child fast. God opens her eyes, and she spots a well of water and gives him to drink. God does not perform a miracle, manufacturing a well of water out of thin air. Rather, God opens Hagar's eyes to see a well, a resource already available in God's good creation, but unable to be seen in the midst of all the trouble. Hagar, this outsider, becomes God's agent. God provides for the children, even for those who are not from the chosen line. But the importance of the agent should not be diminished; God always acts in and through available creaturely agents. God does not do these caring actions alone.

3. God was with the boy (Gen 21:20). What follows are implications of God's "being with": Ishmael grows up, even in the godforsaken place of the wilderness. He receives an education, becoming an expert in the bow, a key means of food-gathering in that context. His mother continues to be an agent of God in his life; she takes advantage of her Egyptian heritage to acquire a wife for him.

And so here God is involved in the life of an unchosen child. God's will for this child is evident in several ways, but, most basically, the following: that the child live, that the child no longer be deprived, and, more generally, that he thrive in a life of stability. This is a massive testimony to God as one who cares for all children, not just those who are members of the chosen line. Out in the middle of nowhere, God is with this excluded child, a child excluded by good, religious people; God provides for him through means that are available quite apart from a religious community. This text is testimony that God is present and active out and about in neglected parts of the world, providing for the health and welfare of children, both insider and outsider. Wherever the chosen may traverse across the face of the earth, they encounter a God who has long been at work for good in the lives of even the most deprived of people, including children.

This text about Ishmael in Genesis is a lens through which to read the many references to orphans and other underprivileged children in the Old [14] Testament, for he is the first such biblical individual.[18] Stories like those of Ishmael may reflect the development of Israel's special concern about

---

18. An orphan is defined as one who has lost one or both parents. See the essay by Walter Brueggemann in this volume [not reprinted here].

orphans and other such children. The theme of "widows and orphans" becomes a prominent biblical lens for thinking about God's relationship with children (see, e.g., Exod 22:21–24). The mistreatment of children becomes a sign of the unfaithfulness of adults to their God (even among the chosen people!). Images of healthy, thriving children are a divine concern, and sharp penalties are prescribed for those who flaunt it, even if it means that the children of the privileged will in turn be orphaned. God will not tolerate the mistreatment of homeless children.

The Near-Sacrifice of Isaac

Contemporary Questions Raised by the Story

I focus here on the most difficult text regarding children in Genesis 12–50, namely, the near-sacrifice of Isaac. [19]

Genesis 22 is a deeply troubling text, even a hurtful text; it must be used with great care. [20] Religious interpretations, especially since Soren Kierkegaard's *Fear and Trembling*, [21] seem often to intensify the contradictoriness of the story, perhaps in the interests of heightening the mystery of God's ways. While the reader should not discount the unusual, even frightening character [15] of God's command, it must not be exaggerated either, not least because the narrator gives Abraham no explicit emotional reaction.

While this text has long occasioned theological and pastoral problems for interpreters, readerly anxieties have intensified over the course of the last century or so, not least because of the focus given to the abuse of children. Interrelated issues have been raised with respect to each of the three main characters: God, Abraham, and Isaac.

God. What kind of God would command the sacrifice of a child? What does this command say about God's character? Even if God does not intend

---

19. Estimates of the age of Isaac vary. On the one hand, he was old enough to carry wood and ask questions that assume a capacity to analyze a situation and potential problems relating to it (Gen 22:6–7). On the other hand, God refers to him as a "boy" (22:12), and he calls out "Father" to Abraham (22:7). I think of a boy that is 12 to 13 years old. For a more complete study, see Terence E. Fretheim, *Abraham: Trials of Family and Faith* (Columbia: University of South Carolina Press, 2007), 118–39.

20. In the Revised Common Lectionary, the text is appointed for Easter vigil; in the Jewish community, it is annually read on Rosh Hashanah. Repeated efforts have been made to soften the impact of the story; for example, God's test of Abraham was to see whether he would refuse to go forward with the sacrifice of his son. Whatever the interpretation, it must be consistent with God's commendation of Abraham for proceeding with the sacrifice.

21. Søren Kierkegaard, *Fear and Trembling: A Dialectical Lyric* (Princeton: Princeton University Press, 1941). For a critical analysis of Kierkegaard, see Jon Levenson, "Abusing Abraham: Traditions, Religious Histories, and Modern Misinterpretations," *Judaism* 47 (1998): 259–77. For Levenson, the "teleological suspension of the ethical" says too much. Because God's commands in the Bible are not grounded in some universal morality, Abraham is not suspending ethical foundations or "relying on a faith that transcends and diminishes ethical action" (p. 270).

Abraham to follow through and, finally, slaughter his child, what kind of God would test Abraham in such a violent way? This God promises a son, proceeds to fulfill that promise, and then seems to take it back. Can this God be trusted?

Various responses to such questions have been suggested over the years. Sometimes it is thought that, if we consider the text offensive, then the problem is with us and with our relationship with God, and not with the text. A faithful one will follow where God leads, or at least where God is thought to lead, and especially what God commands—come what may. Such a perspective, however, seems to grant to faith in God a blank check; the ethical can be suspended whenever one thinks that that faith is being served. Jonestown and Waco, to name but two examples, seem not too far away.

Abraham. What kind of faith does Abraham have? A blind faith? No questions are asked and no objections are raised. In fact, he shows no emotion whatsoever, though many retellings of the story have portrayed an agonized Abraham. Earlier in the narrative (Genesis 18; cf. 15:2, 8), Abraham could raise sharp questions with God about the fate of the righteous in Sodom and Gomorrah, but he is strangely passive when it comes to his own child. The narrator assures readers that Abraham loves his son (22:2). Yet Abraham apparently thinks nothing of putting him through the trauma that must have been involved. Is this not child abuse? Or is Abraham (and the culture of which he is a part) oblivious to such a reality? If so, does that make the issue of child abuse irrelevant?[22]

A suggestion might be made as to why Abraham raises no objection. It may be that the narrator intends that the *reader,* having learned from Abraham in Genesis 18 how to question God, is the one to ask the questions on this [16] occasion. If so, the narrator has been immensely successful! Initially, one might suggest that Gen 22:8 (and 22:5) is a delayed clue to Abraham's silence on this occasion: Abraham obeyed because he trusted that, given his prior experience, God would provide a way through this moment that would not entail giving up on the promise.

From another perspective, interpreters can get into a kind of quantitative game; does Abraham love God *more than* he loves his son (his love for Isaac is recognized in 22:2)?[23] But this story should not be reduced to a matter of how much love Abraham has for one or the other. To be a genuine sacrifice, it must be an act of faith and love of God, a giving back to God

---

22. See Phyllis Trible, "The Sacrifice of Sarah," in *'Not in Heaven': Coherence and Complexity in Biblical Narrative* (ed. J. Rosenblatt and J. Sitterson; Bloomington: Indiana University Press, 1991).

23. See the argument of Phyllis Trible, ibid., who thinks that the issue is idolatry, becoming more attached to Isaac than to God. On Trible's questionable analysis of "love" in v. 2, see Walter Moberly, *The Bible, Theology, and Faith: A Study of Abraham and Jesus* (Cambridge: Cambridge University Press, 2000), 163–68.

what is truly dear and costly. And so for the sacrifice to be genuine, must not Abraham's love for Isaac and Abraham's love for God be comparably great at the end of the day? Would not, then, issues of the degree of Abraham's love of God compared to his love for his child be beside the point?

Isaac. What kind of son is this who asks only one question and exhibits no struggle? Does this behavior reveal a child who is completely cowed by an authoritarian, if loving father? Or is this a son who trusts his father as his father trusts God?

Is This Child Abuse?

This story has occasioned deep readerly concern about Isaac, especially in this time when the abuse of children has screamed its way into the modern consciousness.[24] A 1990 book by Alice Miller, a Swiss psychoanalyst, has put the question sharply before us.[25] Miller suggests that this text has contributed in subtle ways to an atmosphere in church and society that makes it possible to justify the abuse of children. She grounds her reflections on some thirty artistic representations of this story over the centuries. This includes two of Rembrandt's paintings, in which Abraham is faced toward the heavens rather than toward Isaac, as if in blind obedience to God and oblivious to what he is about to do to Isaac. Abraham has his hands over Isaac's face, seemingly preventing [17] him from seeing or raising a cry. Not only is Isaac silenced; in addition, only his torso is visible, so that his personal features are obscured. Miller says: Isaac "has been turned into an *object*. He has been dehumanized by being made a sacrifice; he no longer has a right to ask questions and will scarcely even be able to articulate them to himself, for there is no room in him for anything besides fear."[26] Even if she is wrong about Isaac asking no questions, does she not raise an important issue?

We have the testimony of a few parents who have in fact killed their children and ascribed the act to obedience to a divine command.[27] It will not do for us simply to dismiss this negative impact of Genesis 22; it would not be the first time that the Bible has been used knowingly or unknowingly in such distorted ways. Hard as it may be to hear, traditional understandings of this text may in fact have contributed to this more recent reading of the

---

24. This story has, of course, long raised troubling issues, but they have largely been focused on the dilemma faced by the parent in the wake of the divine command.

25. Alice Miller, *The Untouched Key: Tracing Childhood Trauma in Creativity and Destructiveness* (New York: Doubleday, 1990). She has been joined by many others.

26. Ibid., 139.

27. See Wayne Oates, *The Bible in Pastoral Care* (Philadelphia: Westminster, 1953), who tells the story about a mother's response to hearing a sermon on this text. On California trials, see Carol Delaney, *Abraham on Trial: The Social Legacy of Biblical Myth* (Princeton: Princeton University Press, 1998). Moberly's claim, "There is no recorded example of Jews or Christians using the text to justify their own abusing or killing of a child," is insufficiently researched (*The Bible, Theology, and Faith,* 129).

text: *the place of the child has been sorely neglected in a centuries-long focus on the trusting response of Abraham to God's testing.*

It seems clear that more recent problems with Genesis 22 have been sparked by the increasing recognition of the lack of societal attention to the issues children face.[28] Such realities of our own context have sharpened our reading experience of Genesis 22. Meanings of texts are always, of course, the product of the interaction of the text and the reader and his or her experience. At the same time, the issue cannot simply be laid at the feet of readers; at the least, the text does not provide safeguards against negative interpretations. Even if child abuse was not in the mind of the narrator or those who heard this text in ancient Israel, what modern readers hear is not totally irrelevant. Indeed, the language of the text itself can contribute to such an understanding, for God asks and then twice commends Abraham for not withholding his son, his only son, "from me" (Gen 22:2, 12, 16). It is as if the child is simply a pawn in the hands of an issue between "adults" (God and Abraham). Of course, [18] modern adults have little room to criticize either God or Abraham, given the extent to which we remain silent about child abuse among us.[29] But some room exists for an evaluative stance on the basis of the Bible's larger perspective regarding children. If the child in the text (Isaac) is carefully and concernedly remembered, can we ignore this direction of reflection regarding abuse?

History and Metaphor

Reading this text in view of the issue of child abuse has not been common among interpreters until quite recently.[30] In response, several scholars have claimed that this approach is a misuse, even gross misuse of the text.[31]

---

28. More broadly, one might cite twentieth-century experiences of poverty, homelessness, and violence that have so often caught up the young. Or one thinks of the sending of young men and women into battle to settle conflicts that adults have failed to resolve; or the saturation bombings of cities that wipe out large numbers of children; or the death camps and gas chambers that snuff out the lives of children; or the virtual ignoring of genocidal activities in far-off lands (e.g., Rwanda, Darfur). Sadly, one could go on.

29. A related theme is present in twentieth-century war literature, e.g., the poem of Wilfrid Owen, who died fighting for England in 1917, "The Parable of the Old Man and the Young." Appended to a posthumous edition was this line: "The willingness of the older generation to sacrifice the younger." See also Danny Siegel's 1969 look at this text in poetic form: "Father Abraham Genesis 22—Slightly Changed."

30. See T. Fretheim, "God, Abraham, and the Abuse of Isaac," *WW* 15 (1995): 49–57. See also the survey in Moberly, *The Bible, Theology, and Faith*.

31. Especially to be noted are Jon Levenson, "Abusing Abraham," in *The Death and Resurrection of the Beloved Son: Child Sacrifice and Its Transformation in Judaism and Christianity* (New Haven: Yale University Press, 1993); Moberly, The *Bible, Theology, and Faith*, 127–31, 162–83, who follows Levenson. Levenson describes this approach in these terms: Abraham's action has been "increasingly and loudly developed into an interpretation of the last trial as an act of unspeakable cruelty, a paradigm not of love, faith, and submission to God, as in Judaism, Christianity, and Islam, in their traditional formulations, but of hatred, mental illness, and even idolatry" (p. 262).

Two directions of response to the "charge" of child abuse might be especially noted: the historical context of the text; and the text as metaphor.
Neither approach, in my opinion, finally succeeds in setting aside the issue
that has been raised.

The Historical Context. Jon Levenson has been particularly concerned
to draw out the religio-historical dimensions of the text. His discussion is
often helpful. Initially, the text speaks of Isaac as a "burnt offering" (Gen
22:2; see Exod 29:38–46; Lev 1:3–17 for details) and a "substitute" sacrifice
is finally given (Gen 22:13). [32] These bookends of the story place the episode
within the context of the sacrificial system. This reality should be placed
alongside the fact (known from other texts) that child sacrifice was an important part of the context within which Genesis 22 was written. [33] More
specifically, "the first-born son was long and widely believed to belong to
God and must be offered to him, either through literal sacrifice (rarely, as
in Genesis 22) or [19] through one or another of the rituals by which a substitution was made" (e.g., Exod 22:28–29; cf. Ezek 20:25–26). The firstborn
son was to be thereby "redeemed" (Exod 13:11–16; 34:20; Num 3:40–51);
in Genesis 22, God does just this in a *narrative equivalent of the ritual*. That
is, God commands that Isaac be sacrificed and then provides an animal "instead of" Isaac. [34] To the father about to make the offering "the prospect was
doubtless painful in the extreme, perhaps too painful for words, but it was
not unconnected to the larger culture and its ethical and theological norms,
nor was it incomprehensible or incommunicable to others in the same cultural universe." An important matter for Levenson is that, "*in the biblical
text, sacrifice is not deemed unethical or irrational,*" and so it requires no more
an act of faith to adhere to such demands than to ethical demands. [35] The
texts generally recognize the difference between murder and sacrifice. [36]

For Levenson, that Abraham's response would not have been offensive
in that era does not in any way imply that a contemporary person of faith
should do likewise; in our culture it would rightly be considered murder.
Between the Akedah and today lies the Torah, with its redemption of the
firstborn, and the prophetic condemnation of child sacrifice (e.g., Jer 9:3–

---

32. On whether it is appropriate to use the language of substitution, see below.

33. It should be noted that we do not know when this chapter was written.

34. Jon Levenson, "Abusing Abraham," 270–71. He cites parallels in the ancient world
in *Death and Resurrection*, 3–24, 43–52. Child sacrifice in general is different and is prohibited in Lev 20:2–5 and denounced by several of the prophets (e.g., Jer 19:3–6).

35. Jon Levenson, "Abusing Abraham," 271 (emphasis his). These comments occur in
a context of a critique brought against Søren Kierkegaard's *Fear and Trembling;* he claims
that Kierkegaard fails to recognize this historical reality and hence "opens a door to those
who judge Abraham to be an unbalanced person."

36. Jon Levenson suggests that this is a difference between Gen 18:16–33, against
which Abraham protests, and Genesis 22; the former is a "forensic" context (where the
death of an innocent person is an outrage, and hence Abraham's intervention), while the
latter is a sacrificial context.

6),[37] and hence one cannot read a validation of child abuse from the text. Levenson goes to great lengths in seeking to demonstrate that Abraham is not a child abuser; in fact, "it is a symptom of acute myopia and mind-numbing parochialism to think that this must also have been the case in a society that practiced sacrifice (even, on occasion and for a while, child-sacrifice) and did not confuse it with murder."[38] [20]

Perhaps so, but I wonder if the factors cited are sufficient to shut down the conversation about abuse. First, three details might be more closely considered. (a) The text bears no explicit mark of being a polemic against child sacrifice (unlike the prophets, e.g., Jer 19:3–6); Abraham, finally, is commanded not to sacrifice his son, but the text does not generalize the point. (b) The text makes no claim to being an etiology of the redemption of the firstborn.[39] Is it because Isaac is not a firstborn son? Is it because the ram is not clearly a "substitute" for Isaac?[40] (c) From another angle, while the factors relating to the emergence of laws prohibiting child sacrifice in Israel are unclear, might it have had to do, at least in part, with observed negative effects on the lives of children and their families?[41]

Second, to speak more generally, to say that the divine command would not have been offensive in Israel's world begs the question as to whether it *should* have been deemed so. Can evaluative judgments not be made of Israelite thought and practice? For example, patriarchy was characteristic of Israel's life, but does this mean that no evaluative words can be directed at those who exercised patriarchal practices?[42] Levenson and others are on target when they criticize those who speak of Abraham being mentally unbalanced or cruel. But if Abraham should not be criticized at those points, given the realities of sacrifice in that world, what of the practice

---

37. It should be noted that child sacrifice was a sometime problem for Israel (cf. Lev 20:2–5; 2 Kgs 3:27; Jer 7:31; 32:35), even if finally abhorrent.

38. Levenson, "Abusing Abraham," 271. Moberly (*The Bible, Theology, and Faith*) is comparably sharp: "To disregard the context which enabled the meaningful preservation of a story about child sacrifice, and then proclaim the story a problem for contemporary readers, is to create a more or less artificial problem. It exemplifies the truism that context is crucial for meaning" (p. 129)

39. The etiological reference in Gen 22:14b is unclear, but it has no known reference to the redemption of the firstborn (see Claus Westermann, *Genesis 12–36*: A Commentary [Minneapolis: Augsburg, 1981], 362–63).

40. See n. 47 below.

41. Jon Levenson ("Abusing Abraham," 277 n. 50), in considering the question of the emergence of the prohibition, considers basically cultic factors, with a mention of Gen 9:6 and not shedding the blood of human beings made in the image of God. Given what we are told about the suffering of children in the fall of Jerusalem (e.g., Lam 4:10) and our knowledge of children more generally, might the suffering of children have been a key factor? The point should at least be considered.

42. Generally on the issue of evaluation of biblical texts, see Terence E. Fretheim with Karlfried Froehlich, *The Bible as Word of God in a Postmodern Age* (Minneapolis: Fortress, 1988). See also Terence E. Fretheim, "Violence in the Old Testament," *WW* 24 (2004): 18–28.

itself? Perhaps even more importantly, the issue should not simply revolve around the issue of the behaviors of the "adults" involved (God and Abraham). Whatever the evaluation of their actions (on either side of the issue), the negative effects on the child (emotional and otherwise) should be placed front and center. Whatever Abraham's (and God's) intent, is it not likely that Isaac was traumatized by the threat of imminent and violent death at the hands of his father?[43] [21]

The Text as Metaphor. Moving beyond simple historical issues, Levenson promotes a metaphorical (he uses the term "symbolic") interpretation of the text. That the sacrificial death "is only symbolic, that the son, *mirabile dictu,* returns alive, is the narrative equivalent of the ritual substitutions that prevent the gory offering from being made."[44] Early in its history, Israel had prohibited child sacrifice as an abomination hateful to God; yet they could see in Abraham's deed "a paradigmatic disclosure of deeper truths." Among the truths he sees in the text: "all we have, even our lives and those of our dearest, belong ultimately to God; His claim must be honored; God's promises are often painfully at odds with empirical reality."[45]

Walter Moberly also speaks of a metaphorical understanding of Genesis 22, joining a long line of interpreters in the life of the church. He admits that the metaphor is a "dangerous" one, open to abuse on the part of the unscrupulous and misguided. But all metaphors are "in some way 'dangerous.'"[46] He summarizes the metaphorical value of this story in these terms:[47] (a) relinquishing to God that which is most precious (Isaac, the beloved son);[48] (b) self-dispossession of that on which one's identity and

---

43. That Isaac did not return with his father, though Abraham had promised that they would both return (Gen 22:5), is sometimes cited as a sign of this, but that remains uncertain.

44. Jon Levenson, *Death and Resurrection,* 59. The force of the word "only" needs discussion.

45. Levenson, "Abusing Abraham," 272–73.

46. Moberly, *The Bible, Theology, and Faith,* 130. I wonder whether this claim slides much too quickly over the vast difference among metaphors regarding their "danger."

47. Moberly, *The Bible, Theology, and Faith,* 182. The extent to which the language of self-sacrifice permeates his discussion deserves closer attention on his part. For example, Abraham is "required to sacrifice to God not only the centre of his affections but that which he has lived for and is the content of his hope and his trust in God" (p. 131). Or, "the whole burnt offering is symbolic of Abraham's self-sacrifice as a person who unreservedly fears God" (p. 118). He seems not to recognize the dangers of this kind of sacrificial language on the shape and character of the life of faith. It should be noted that, after discerning Abraham's faithfulness, God stopped him *before* the ram was spotted (Gen 22:12–13). So the provision of the ram was not necessary to save Isaac. Indeed, Isaac's sacrifice was stopped independent of the role of the ram, so that "instead of" does not have a "substitutionary" sense. Why would the ram, then, be sacrificed? Is it because of the way in which Abraham states the trust in v. 8? Abraham has faith that God will provide an animal for the offering instead of his son, and so that is what God provides.

48. See the common theme of mourning over an only son. The question may be asked: Has Isaac been sacrificed? Certainly in some respects. Perhaps, as Janzen states (*Abraham*

hopes are most deeply based (Isaac as hope for the future); (c) response to God as costly, or even more costly, at the end of one's life than it was earlier on; (d) the outcome of obedience is unknown and cannot be predicted in advance (a real [22] test); (e) the religious community cannot become complacent. In these terms, the story is "a paradigm of life with God." To that end, the "purpose of Yʜᴡʜ's testing is to promote such a way of living."[49] Though the "literal" practice had been set aside, the story as metaphor retained its power as a paradigm of religious life.[50]

In response, it must be said that these points of significance retain a focus on Abraham (the adult) and his faith, moving all too quickly past the child.[51] In any interpretation of the text as metaphor, it is important not to deplete the story of its sheer horror (remembering that metaphor does include a literal dimension). To identify the story as metaphor should not set readers' minds to looking for the "real" meaning of the text and away from the sacrifice of a child.[52] The potential sacrifice of an actual child is certainly intended to come to the mind of the reader, to confront the reader with the difficult nature of the divine command and the complexity of the journey with God. Readers may disagree with the narrator's strategy in doing that, but the point remains: a child has been abused.

Genesis 22 does not finally enable one to sit comfortably with the obvious abuse that Isaac undergoes. Readers have wondered whether this experience is evident in the fact that Isaac does not return with his father in 22:19 (though Abraham had so assured his servants in 22:5).[53] Abraham

and All the Families of the Earth: A Commentary on Genesis 12–50 [Grand Rapids: Eerdmans, 1993]), "Isaac has truly been sacrificed—truly given up and given over to God. The life he will go on to live is now wholly God's, and Abraham no longer has any claim to it" (pp. 80–81).

49. Moberly, *The Bible, Theology, and Faith,* 101. Moberly emphasizes *Abraham's* learning, though Gen 22:12 stresses God's learning.

50. *If* one is to interpret the text as a metaphor for Israel's life with God, it seems to me necessary to understand that Israel is *both* Abraham and Isaac. And so Israel is not simply one who *makes* a sacrifice (Abraham); Israel is also the one who *is* the sacrifice (Isaac). Various issues related to the fall of Jerusalem would come into play at this point, including the Suffering Servant in Isaiah 53.

51. For *Israel* as the firstborn of God, see Exod 4:22, an issue faced by the exiles (Jer 31:9, 20; cf. 2:3). I have spoken of Genesis 22 as metaphor with reference to *Israel* as firstborn (Terence E. Fretheim, "The Book of Genesis," *NIB,* 1:494, 1:499). See also Terence E. Fretheim, "Christology and the Old Testament," in *Who Do You Say That I Am? Essays on Christology in Honor of Jack Kingsbury* (ed. Mark A. Powell and David Bauer; Louisville: Westminster John Knox, 1999), 201–15 [reprinted in this volume, pp. 350–362]. The New Testament connections, which link Jesus with both Abraham and Isaac, should also be cited. For the parallels of Jesus and Abraham, see Ellen Davis, *Getting Involved with God: Rediscovering the Old Testament* (Cambridge: Cowley, 2001), 63.

52. I wonder whether Moberly understands metaphor in such a way that the actual sacrifice of the child is not to come to the mind of the reader.

53. For detail, see the discussion in Hemchand Gossai, *Power and Marginality in the Abrahamic Narrative* (Lanham, MD: University Press, 1995), 158–60. Cf. also M. J. Kohn,

and Isaac [23] never again converse in the narrative that follows, not even in connection with the search for a wife for Isaac (Genesis 24). While Isaac attends Abraham's funeral (25:9), he does not attend Sarah's or even return to her deathbed (Genesis 23). Moreover, why would God, but not Abraham, bless Isaac (25:11)?

Might this distancing between father and son have anything to do with the horrific experience on Mt. Moriah? Might these textual details, even if in subtle ways, recognize that a child has been abused?

What, Then, of the Future of Children for Genesis?

In the wake of such horrendous stories about children in Genesis, two notes of hope for children are lifted up for readers in the last chapter (Genesis 50).

Human Acts of Kindness as God's Agents for Good.   When Joseph and his brothers are reconciled, he gives testimony that God has been at work for good in the midst of evil, "in order to preserve a numerous people" (Gen 50:20). This goodness of God becomes immediately evident in Joseph's own words and actions (50:21): "So have no fear; I myself will provide for you and *your little ones.* In this way he reassured them, speaking kindly to them." Joseph does not retaliate but reaches out to those who have betrayed him and promises to take care of their children.

Ending on a Note of Promise.   Joseph becomes the mediator of God's continuing promises to this people. He says, "God will surely come to you and fulfill the promises that God has extended to your ancestors." God will continue to be present and active in this family, in the midst of the worst the world may throw their way. God will do this on behalf of the divine mission, so often stated in Genesis: through you shall all the families of the earth be blessed, including their children.

Concluding Reflection

So, this essay ends precisely where the book of Genesis ends: on a note of hope for children in the wake of all the violence that they have experienced through the generations. Will that hope be realized?

"The Trauma of Isaac," *JBQ* 20 (1991–92): 96–104. It has also been suggested that this experience may be related to an ineptitude on Isaac's part in Genesis 26–27.

The Plagues as Ecological Signs of Historical Disaster

It has been shown by H. H. Schmid and others that in the ancient Near East, as well as in Israel, the just ordering of society— reflected in its laws— was brought into close relationship with the creation of the world. A breach of those laws was considered a breach of the order of creation. Hence, it had dire consequences on all aspects of the world order, not least the sphere of nature, threatening the world with chaos. There is thus a symbiotic relationship of ethical order and cosmic order. It is the purpose of this article to show how this understanding of the created order undergirds the plague cycle in Exodus. Contemporary understandings of the links between human misuse of the environment and consequent ill effects upon the entire world order may be said to correspond to such ancient views in many ways.

Seen against this background, the following perspective emerges. Pharaoh's oppressive measures against Israel are viewed as fundamentally anti-life and anticreation. They strike right at the point where the creational promise of fruitfulness is being fulfilled in Israel. This link is demonstrated by the use of creational language in Exod 1:7–20 (see Gen 1:28; 9:1, 7). Egypt, Pharaoh in particular, is considered to be an embodiment of the forces of chaos, threatening a return of the entire cosmos to its precreation state. The [386] plagues are the effect of Pharaoh's anticreational *sins,* the functioning of which may be described as divine judgment. At the same time, they are signs pointing beyond themselves to unmitigated historical disaster. The following paragraphs work this out in greater detail.

Some brief comments on introductory matters. Source analysis has discerned three interwoven strata in Exodus 7–11. The J account is usually considered the most extensive, with seven plagues and the basics of the present structure of the text. The degree to which these prior forms of the plague tradition have been preserved in the present text remains uncertain, however, and hence interpretations of their import will always be problematic. The use of the plague tradition in Psalms 78 and 105, with seven plagues presented in ways different from one another and from Exodus, makes the traditio-historical analysis even more complex. Without discounting the importance of this enterprise, this article will work with the final form of the text, the most basic shape of which is probably to be identified with the P redaction.

This essay was originally published in the *Journal of Biblical Literature* 110 (1991): 385–96.

This form of the text is not socially disinterested; it was written with the problems and possibilities of a particular audience in view. An exilic provenance seems likely. Israel in exile finds itself in straits similar to its forebears in Exodus in two major respects: captive to outside forces (chaps. 1–15) and suffering under just judgment because of disloyalty to God (chaps. 32–34), it stands in need of both deliverance and forgiveness. Issues related to law and obedience, divine presence and absence, and appropriate worship places and practices are also central for both Exodus and exilic Israel. At the same time, the material is presented in such a way as to resonate with other comparable situations.

In terms of rhetoric, repetition is noteworthy. For example, the word *kōl* "all," is pervasive, used over fifty times; it may provide an interpretive clue to the narrative. While used in every plague, there is an explosion in its use (as well as *'ereṣ* "earth"—to which we return) as one moves into the seventh plague. This is an extravagance of language, perhaps even a failure of language, in an effort to speak of the increasing intensity in the final plagues: every tree, all the fruit, no one can see, not a single locust, the whole land. Everything is affected or nothing. A hyperbolic way of speaking has taken control of the narrative. These outer limits of language match and convey the content of a creative order breaking out of its normal boundaries. As such, this language serves both a literary and a theological purpose. [387]

This language participates in a dramatic form that has no real biblical parallel. There are significant continuities with certain prophetic traditions, especially Ezekiel. Also to be noted are texts such as Deuteronomy 28 and Leviticus 26, which view Israel itself as the potential object of the plagues (cf. Exod 15:26 with Deut 7:15; 28:27, 60). Regarding social setting, there are links between 10:2 and the retelling notices associated with ritual in 12:26; 13:8; and 13:14. The highly stylized form may reflect the dramatization of some experience that was less comprehensive and intense. A dramatized presentation in a cultic setting is a possibility.

Common parlance refers to these events as plagues (i.e., a blow/stroke), but the text itself primarily uses the language of "sign" (*'ôt*, 4:17; 7:3; 8:17 [Eng. 8:23]; 10:1–2) and "portent" (*môpēt*, 4:21; 7:3, 9; 11:9–10). The sign character of these materials must be taken more seriously than has been the case heretofore. I work with this definition of sign: a specific word or event that prefigures the future by the affinity of its nature (1 Sam 2:34; Jer 44:29; 1 Kgs 13:2; 2 Kgs 19:29; 20:9). As signs/portents the intent of the plagues is not finally to leave observers with mouths open in amazement. Having gotten peoples' attention, they point beyond themselves toward a disastrous future, while carrying a certain force in their own terms. They are both acts of judgment in themselves and point toward a future judgment, either passover or sea crossing or both, and each must be examined in these terms. This present/future correspondence is more broadly evident when viewed in terms of the ways in which these natural phenomena function in divine judgment contexts, especially prophetic. Generally, it may be said that the plagues are ecological signs of historical disaster. They function in a way not unlike certain ecological events in contemporary society, portents of unmitigated historical disaster.

I. The Plagues as Portents of Disaster

The correspondences between the plagues and the Passover/sea crossing are both verbal and imagistic. Each of the plagues is examined in turn. [388]

Exodus 7:8–13: On Swallowing Rods and Egyptians

The swallowing of the magicians' staff by Aaron's does not represent Aaron's superior power to do magical tricks! Only indirectly is it concerned with the power of God. It is a sign of the fate of the Egyptians at the Red Sea. The only other use of the verb *bāla'*, "swallow," occurs in 15:12, where it refers to the swallowing of the Egyptians in the depths of the earth beneath the sea. This results from God's "stretching out his right hand; certainly a reference to God's working in and through Moses' staff (cf. 7:15; 14:16). Moreover, that the word for serpent is different from that used in 4:3 supports this view. *Tannîn* is a more terrifying creature than any snake. Elsewhere, this word refers to the chaotic forces God defeated in the exodus (Ps 74:13; Isa 51:9). Even more, it is used elsewhere as a symbol for the Egyptian Pharaoh (Ezek 29:3–5; 32:2; cf. Jer 51:34). A closer look at the symbolism shows this to be an *ironic reversal*. The staffs of the magicians become *tannîn* and Aaron's *tannîn* swallows theirs. Here God turns the tables, using a dragon to swallow up the chaos monster, as God will use the waters in chap. 15. This is a sign of Pharaoh's fate.

Exodus 7:14–24: Whose Blood in the Water?

The phrase "there was blood (*dām*) throughout all the land of Egypt" (vv. 19, 21) suggests the sign value. The comprehensiveness of the blood in the land is more than hyperbole. While *dām* is not used in chaps. 14–15, the *image* is one of the sea becoming red with Egyptian blood. The language of the oracle against Egypt in Ezek 32:6 is certainly striking in this connection, linking blood in land and water: "I will drench the land even to the mountains with your flowing blood; and the watercourses will be full of you" (cf. 29:4–5; 5:17; 14:19; 38:22; Isa 34:7). Also to be noted is Exod 11:6, where the cry of the Egyptians is as extensive as the blood in this sign. These references show that this sign is more than just a bloody mess, a lot of dead fish, and a headache for waterworks personnel. Blood, which will be a sign of deliverance for Israel (12:13), here becomes a sign of disaster for Egypt. [389]

Exodus 7:25–8:11 [Eng. 7:25–8:15]: The Land Stank

The sign value of this wonder for Pharaoh may be focused at three points. The verb *nāgap*, "smite" (7:27 [Eng. 8:2]), is not used again until chap. 12, where it refers to the smiting of the firstborn (12:23, 27; cf. 12:13; 9:14; Josh 24:5). This is a strong word, often meaning a fatal blow and used in contexts of divine judgment (Isa 19:22; Ps 89:23). It is anomalous that the narrator, out of all the plagues, should raise the specter of fatal blows in connection with frogs! It functions as a sign of something more deadly on the horizon. Further, the reference to the stinking land (8:11 [Eng. 8:14]) is an image of destruction. The death of so many children and animals in the last plague (12:30) would have created a comparable problem for Egypt, and the picture of all the Egyptians piled dead on the seashore (14:30) creates a similar image. Pharaoh's own nose should have told him that something is amiss here! Moreover, the phrase "covered (*kāsâ*) the land of Egypt" (8:2 [Eng. 8:6]) may portend an ominous future, as the waters of the sea "cover" the Egyptians (14:28; 15:5, 10; cf. Ezek 30:18).

Exodus 8:12–15 [Eng. 8:16–19]: From Dust to Dust

This sign functions solely in terms of images. The "dust of the earth" has been turned into gnats. Dust is that from which human beings have come and to which they return upon death (cf. Gen 3:19; Eccl 3:20; Job 4:19; 10:9; Ps 104:29). In fact, it can refer to the grave or the netherworld (Job 17:16; Ps 22:29; Isa 26:19). The image suggests the end of the Egyptians. It is also an image used to speak of the humiliation of those who oppose the God of Israel, including the kings of the earth (Isa 26:5; 41:2; 49:23; Mic 7:17; Job 40:13; Ps 72:9). Generally, the use of "dust" as an image of mortality and humiliation is a sign that Pharaoh ignores at his peril.

Exodus 8:16–28 [Eng. 8:20–32]: The Land Is Ruined

The sole use of sign language within a plague narrative (8:19 [Eng. 8:23]) is in connection with the division between Egypt and Israel. To have flies stopped at the Goshen border, as if by an invisible wall, should have been a sign of some magnitude to Pharaoh (cf. his concern in 9:7). This distinction between Egyptians and Israelites will be disastrously realized in 11:7. Its sign value is enhanced by the reference to "all" the land being "ruined" (*šāḥat*, 8:20 [Eng. 8:24]; note the repetition of *ʾereṣ*, "land"). Such language seems too strong for a fly infestation! This root plays a key role in the Passover story (12:13, 23; cf. its use in Gen 6:11–12 for the preflood state of affairs; Ezek 5:16). The flies are a sign of the destroyer that will pass through the land of Egypt on that fateful night. Moreover, it is to be noted that the flies were removed so that "not one remained" (8:27 [Eng. 8:31]; cf. 10:19). This phrase is [390] repeated in 14:28, where not one Egyptian remained. God's re-creative act is also a sign, a sign of judgment on the oppressors. As it was with the flies, so it will be with the Egyptians. They did comparable damage to the land; they will share a common end. The sign is thus found in both the plague and in its removal.

Exodus 9:1–7: Whose Livestock Die?

This sign takes a significant step beyond nuisance and discomfort. Its sign value lies at two points. The use of *deber* for the plague is an ominous word (note the play on *dābār* in vv. 5–6); it is used exclusively in divine judgment contexts, whether in Israel (Deut 28:21; Ezek 5:12) or among Israel's enemies (and with cosmic effects, Ezek 38:22; Hab 3:5). Moreover, the distinction between Israel's and Egypt's animals (see Ezek 32:13) is again portentous, a distinction also present in the final plague (11:5; 12:29). The use of the word *kōl* for the death of livestock also enhances its sign value.

Exodus 9:8–12: Signs of Mortality

This sign has been prefigured in the sign in 4:6–7; there Moses' hand became leprous and was returned to normalcy. Leprosy is mentioned elsewhere in the OT with the verb used in 9:8–12, *pāraḥ*, "break out," and is specifically connected with boils (Lev 13:18–23). This is an ominous sign of a disease that will be even more devastating for the Egyptians; while the plague that finally falls on them is not identified, it is likely a more intensified form of that which is experienced here. The disease, an obvious sign of mortality and judgment, would serve as an image of more severe possibilities. The power of this plague's significatory value is seen in the later recollection of the "boils of Egypt" as a possible judgment on Israel (Deut 28:27, cf. v. 60; 7:15).

Exodus 9:13–35: A Sign from Heaven

Generally, the plague's intensity and incomparability enable it to function as a sign of the incomparability of the plague of death (11:6). Comparative [391] language now begins to be used (see 9:18, 24; cf. 10:6, 14). As to intensity the extensive use of *kōl* and *'ereṣ* vivify this frightful experience of the weather. Weather-related phenomena often function as images in theophany (Ps 18:12–13; 77:16–20) and divine judgment contexts (Isa 28:2, 17; 30:30–31; Ezek 13:11–13; 38:22–23; Hag 2:17). Hail is a powerful image of God's coming in judgment. Experienced in such an intense form, it should function as a sign for any who would listen.

Exodus 10:1–20: Driven into the Red Sea

The extensive use of *kōl* (eleven times!) and *'ereṣ* again intensifies the absoluteness of the devastation wrought by the locusts. Moreover, the sign values of the plague become more numerous. Given the fact that, like hail, locusts often are a symbol of divine judgment (Deut 28:38, 42; 2 Chr 7:13;

Jer 51:27; Amos 4:9; 7:1; Joel), this is certainly a portentous sign. The use of the image in Joel is particularly similar (1:4, 7, 17–20; 2:9–10, 25). As with the frogs (8:6), they *"cover* the face of the (entire) land" (10:5, 15), a portent of the water covering the Egyptians (14:28; 15:5, 15). A sign may also be present in the phrase "no one can see the land" (10:5); when the destroyer moves through Egypt (12:13, 23), not seeing the blood on the doorposts means tragedy. Once again, the twice-noted incomparability language (10:6, 14) anticipates 11:6. The causal factors at work may also constitute a sign, as the east wind is drawn into the fray (10:13); it will prove to be an agent of destruction at the Red Sea (14:21). Finally, the phrase "not a single locust was left" (10:19; 8:27 [Eng. 8:31]), having been driven into the Red Sea, again prefigures the sea crossing (14:28). As it was with locusts and flies, so will it be with the Egyptians. They will meet a common end. The significatory value of this plague is rich and varied.

Exodus 10:21–29: A Return to the First Day of Creation

The darkness language, anticipated in 10:5, 15, has a high sign value. "Heavy darkness" (*ʾăpēlâ*) is a symbol of divine judgment (Isa 13:10; Joel 2:10), including Ezekiel's oracle against Egypt (Ezek 32:7–8!). The use of darkness with the infrequent language of "feeling, groping" (*māšaš*) is also present in such contexts (Deut 28:29; Job 5:14; 12:25). The narratives that follow are filled with darkness language, both with respect to the tenth plague (11:4; 12:12, 29–31, 42) and the sea crossing (cf. *ḥōšek* in 14:20–21). This plague is the darkness of chaos; it is a reversion to a precreation state of affairs.[1] That is why it is the most serious plague, but one. The sign is [392] beginning to participate in the reality of destruction for Pharaoh. There will be no stopping the disaster at this point.

Such an extensive correspondence of vocabulary and images between the plagues and the Passover/sea crossing is hardly fortuitous.[2] The balance of the article will seek to draw out the implications.

II. The Plagues and the Created Order

The pervasive usage of the word *ʾereṣ*, "earth, land," in every plague story—over fifty times, and intensely from the seventh plague—also provides a clue to this focus: What is happening to God's earth/land? While the center of attention is on the land of Egypt, the word sometimes has a

---

1. So also Z. Zevit, "The Priestly Redaction and Interpretation of the Plague Narrative in Exodus," *JQR* 66 (1975–76): 193–211. Zevit correctly sees the importance of the theme of creation in the plague narratives, but the focus on finding specific links with Genesis 1 is at times strained.

2. The fact that these extensive links are with both Passover and sea crossing may provide further data for the exploration of the relationship of these two traditions. For a discussion of the issues, see G. Coats, "The Sea Tradition in the Wilderness Theme: A Review," *JSOT* 12 (1979): 2–8.

more comprehensive sense. It is commonly recognized that the "knowing" texts are among the most important theologically in the cycle; three of these are concerned with earth/land: God is Lord in the midst of the earth (Exod 8:18 [Eng. 8:22]); there is no God like Yahweh in all the earth (9:14); the earth is the Lord's (9:29; cf. 19:5; Ps 24:1–2). It also appears in the central verse, 9:16: so that my name may be declared throughout all the earth. For the sake of the mission of God, the creationwide proclamation of the divine name, there is a concern for the earth.[3]

Generally for Exodus, God's liberation of Israel is the primary but not the ultimate focus of the divine activity. The deliverance of Israel is ultimately for the sake of the entire creation. The issue for God finally is not that God's name be made known in Israel; the scope of the divine purpose is creationwide, for all the earth is God's. God's purpose is to so lift up the divine name that it will come to the attention of all the peoples of the earth. Hence, the *public character* of these events is very important. To put this in different words: in order to accomplish God's mission in the world, God must have a world teeming with life. If Pharaoh persists in his antilife policies at precisely that point at which God has begun to actualize the promise of creation (clearly laid out in 1:7), then God's very purposes in creation are being subverted and God's mission is threatened. God's work in and through Moses, climaxing in Israel's crossing of the sea on "dry land," constitutes God's efforts [393] of recreation, to return creation to a point where God's mission can once again be taken up.

The plagues need more detailed attention in view of this overarching creational theme. They are fundamentally concerned with the natural order; each plague has to do with various nonhuman phenomena. The collective image presented is that the entire created order is caught up in this struggle, either as cause or victim. Pharaoh's antilife measures against God's creation have unleashed chaotic powers that threaten the very creation that God intended.

First, a word about those elements of the nonhuman order that are on the *victimizing* side; they are all out of kilter with their created way of being. Move down the list—water, frogs, dust and gnats, flies, cattle epidemic, ashes and boils, weather phenomena, locusts, and darkness: none of them appear as they were created by God to be. They all appear in distorted form. Water is no longer simply water; light and darkness are no longer separated; diseases of people and animals run amok; insects and amphibians swarm out of control. What must the numbers have been when every speck of dust in the land became a gnat (8:13 [Eng. 8:17])?! What size must

---

3. For further discussion of this creationwide purpose for Israel, see Fretheim, "Suffering God"; see also M. Greenberg (*Understanding Exodus* [New York: Behrman, 1969], 169–170). The extensive correspondences between Exodus and Genesis 1–11 are detailed in my *Exodus*. The use of ʾereṣ in the patriarchal narratives also needs to be noted (e.g., Gen 18:18; 41:57; cf. 12:3; 28:14).

the hail have been to "shatter every tree" (9:25)?! And the plagues come to a climax in the darkness, which in effect returns the creation to the first day of Genesis 1, to a precreation state of affairs. While everything is unnatural in the sense of being beyond the bounds of the order created by God, the word *hypernatural* (nature in excess) may better capture that sense of the natural breaking through its created limits, not functioning as God intended. The plagues are hypernatural at various levels—timing, scope, and intensity. Some sense for this is also seen in recurrent phrases to the effect that such "had never been seen before, nor ever shall be again" (10:14; cf. 10:6; 9:18, 24; 11:6).

Second, regarding the *victims* of the plagues, scholarly attention has tended to focus on their effects on Pharaoh and other human beings (a typical anthropocentrism). But in every plague there are devastating effects on the nonhuman—water, the land, various plants and animals, even the air—every sphere of the created order is adversely affected. The stress on the word "all" (*kōl*) serves to show that nothing in the entire nonhuman order escapes from these ill effects. Even more, the effects (like the causes) are hypernatural. The hail strikes down *every* plant and shatters *every* tree. There are boils on every beast and every human being. The locust devastation is such that "not a single green thing remains" (10:15) and not a soul can see the land— except, of course, in Goshen, where the hypernatural extends in the other direction, with not a single cow dying from plague, not a single swarm of flies, not a single hailstone falling, and the pitch-black darkness stops dead in the air precisely at the border. The exemption for Israel is but another form of participation in the uncharacteristic, hypernatural behaviors of the natural order. [394]

This means that attempts to see these signs as simply *natural* occurrences are far removed from the point of the text. There is sufficient continuity with the natural to show that it is in fact creation that is adversely affected. Their sequencing does have a certain naturalness to it—frogs leaving bloody water, flies drawn to piles of dead frogs, etc. But these continuities really serve this purpose: to show that the elements of the natural order are *not* what they were created to be and do. Their "behaviors" break the bounds of their createdness. It is a picture of creation gone berserk. The world is reverting to a state of chaos. It is a kind of flood story in one corner of the world, that corner where God's creational purposes were beginning to be realized.

III. The Plagues and the Moral Order

The theological grounding for the plagues is an understanding of the moral order, created by God for the sake of justice and well-being in the world. Pharaoh's moral order is bankrupt, severely disrupting this divine intent, and hence he becomes the object of the judgment inherent in God's order. A key word is *šepeṭ* (6:6; 7:4; 12:12; cf. Gen 15:14; note its predominant use in Ezekiel, including two references to Egypt, 30:14, 19). God sees to the moral order of things, enabling the working out of the effects of Pharaoh's sinfulness. Such judgments are not imposed on the situation from without, but grow out of, have an intrinsic relationship to, the sinful (or good) deed.[4]

Correspondence thinking between deed and consequence is prominent in these texts. It is sharply evident in 4:23: the death of Pharaoh and the Egyptians correlates with that experienced by Israel at his hands. Other verbal and thematic correspondences are: (1) The unjust oppression of the Israelites over an extended period of time and a prolonged oppression of the Egyptians via the plagues. (2) The losses experienced by the Israelites— general well-being, property, land, life—and those experienced by the Egyptians. (3) The bondage of Israel and its ill effects on their personhood and the hardening of the Egyptians' hearts (14:17), an experience of enslavement. The "broken spirit" (6:9) of the Israelites that prevents them from hearing the good news finds a correspondence in the hardening of Pharaoh's heart that inhibits his hearing the word of the Lord. (4) The indiscriminate death experienced by Israelite babies at the hands of a Pharaoh bent on genocide and the death of Egyptian firstborn at all levels of society (11:5; 12:29). (5) The "cry" (*ṣĕ'āqâ*) of the Israelites in bondage (3:7, 9) and the "cry" of the Egyptians on that fateful night (11:6; 12:30). (6) The cosmic sphere in which [395] the plagues function correlates directly with the creational sins of Pharaoh so central in the narrative. Pharaoh has been subverting God's creational work, so the consequences are oppressive, pervasive, public, prolonged, depersonalizing, heart-rending, and cosmic because such has been the effect on Egypt's sins upon Israel—indeed, upon the earth—as the pervasive "land" language suggests.

In those instances where God removes the plague, the appropriate language is that of re-creation. God overcomes the chaos and returns those elements of the natural order to a closer semblance of their created scope and intensity. In some cases the sign of judgment is retained, as we have seen with the phrase "not one remained" (8:27 [Eng. 8:31]; 10:19; 14:28). Here, re-creation entails ridding the world of the perpetrators of evil.

These reversals of the plagues are anticipatory of God's re-creational activity in the narratives that follow. The song at the sea is filled with creational language, and the divine victory over the powers of chaos assumes cosmic proportions. Moreover, these re-creational themes are played out in the gifts of water and food in the wilderness. For example, the result of

---

4. Cf. K. Koch's "fate-producing deeds" in his "Is There a Doctrine of Retribution in the Old Testament?" in *Theodicy in the Old Testament* (ed. J. Crenshaw; Philadelphia: Westminster, 1983), 27–87. See also P. D. Miller, Jr., *Sin and Judgment in the Prophets* (Chico, CA: Scholars Press, 1982).

the first plague was that "they could not drink the water" (7:24). When, in 15:23, "they could not drink the water," the bitter water is made sweet and potable. In fact, the wilderness is filled with springs of water (15:27). This will also be the cosmic effect of a later divine victory (Isa 35:6–7). Or, whereas God "rained" (*mṭr*) hail upon Egypt, destroying the food sources (see 9:18, 23), in 16:4 God "rains" bread from the heavens. Or, as locusts "came up" (*ʿlh*) and "covered" *(ksh)* the land (10:14–15), destroying the food, so in 16:13 the quails "came up" and "covered" the camp, providing food. In the Numbers parallel (11:31), the wind brings quail rather than locusts (Exod 10:13). Or, in 17:5, "the staff with which he [Moses] struck the Nile" brings water for people to drink rather than making all the water in the Nile unfit to drink. At the same time, these signs of the new creation are related to the shape of Israel's life (15:25b–26). The symbiotic relationship between moral order and cosmic order is universal, a matter to which Israel must attend as much as Egypt. The "diseases [= plagues] of Egypt" also stand as a possibility for Israel (see Deut 28:27, 60).

God is certainly portrayed in these texts as active in the interplay of Pharaoh's sin and its consequences (though not without mediation), but in effect God gives Pharaoh up to reap the "natural" consequences of his anti-creation behaviors (hardening of the heart, making the heart something other than it was created to be, is another such instance). God's seeing to this order is not a passive "letting it be," but God does function within the limits provided by that order. The plagues are thus *not an arbitrarily chosen divine response* to Pharaoh's sins, as if the vehicle could just as well have been foreign armies or an internal revolution. The consequences are cosmic because the sins are creational. God thereby acts to reestablish the *rightness* of the created order (ironically confessed by Pharaoh himself in 9:27: "The [396] Lord is in the right" [*ṣaddîq*]). The divine power over all forms of pharaonic power is demonstrated through the moral order for the purpose of re-creating justice and righteousness in the world order.[5]

The sin-consequence schema is not understood in mechanical terms, however, as if all of these results were inevitable and programmed to occur within a certain temporal and causal frame; there is a "loose causal weave" in the moral order. Pharaoh was given opportunity to break into the schema, to turn the situation around. Note also the warning in 9:19–21, where the "fear of the word of Yahweh" provides relief from judgment,

---

5. John Collins has called my attention to the treatment of the plagues in the Wisdom of Solomon. In his *Between Athens and Jerusalem: Jewish Identity in the Hellenistic Diaspora* (New York: Crossroad, 1983), 184, Collins cites 12:27; 15:17; and 16:24 in noting that for wisdom "the events in question are not ascribed to the direct intervention of God but to the constant activity of wisdom in the world. The experience of Israel and its enemies is expressed as an experience of the cosmos rather than a direct encounter with God." He cites A. T S. Goodrick: "Even miracles are regarded by 'wisdom' not as a derangement of the universe but as a rearrangement of the harmony of it."

mitigating the effects and the sense of inevitability (cf. 10:7). God himself enters into the prolongation of the consequences (see 9:16) for the public purpose of mission. But, finally, in the face of continuing and resolute refusal, the only way into the future was for God to drive the consequences to their deepest level.

More generally, such a correspondence at the cosmic level is reflective of the symbiosis between the human and the nonhuman natural orders commonly observed in the OT, from Gen 3:17–18 on (e.g., Hos 4:1–3; Jer 9:10–16, 20–22).[6] The combination of plagues and judgment is also a feature of many prophetic passages, as we have seen. The fall of Jerusalem is in effect a time when Israel also becomes the recipient of plagues (see Deut 28:27–29; Lev 26:14–39; Exod 15:26; Jer 4:23–28).[7]

The complexities of the divine, human, and cosmic interaction in the narrative cannot all be factored out, but the divine purpose for Israel in and through this entire experience is clear: to get Israel through the waters of chaos and to enable them to walk on the "dry ground" of creation. Hence, the creation themes will become prominent once again in Exodus as God works his re-creative deed (15:1–21).

In this ecological age we have often seen the adverse cosmic effects of human sin. Examples of hypernaturalness can be cited, not least in the mutations occasioned by ecological disasters and the use of atomic energy. The "nuclear winter" presaged by many is often depicted in plaguelike terms. The whole creation groaning in travail waiting for the redemption of people needs little commentary today (Rom 8:22).[8]

---

6. On this symbiotic relationship and God's relationship to the nonhuman in the Psalms and the prophets, see T. Fretheim, "Nature's Praise of God in the Psalms," *ExAud* 3 (1987): 16–30.

7. Cf. also the extensive use of the plague tradition in the book of Revelation.

8. This material is a reworking of the section on the plagues in Exodus. An earlier form of this paper was read at the SBL Annual Meeting in Anaheim in November 1989.

The Reclamation of Creation:
Redemption and Law in Exodus

Whereas in modern times Genesis has been read in the light of Exodus, and creation has been understood in the light of redemption and the giving of the law at Mount Sinai, it now seems clear that one must reverse the order. Exodus is to be understood in the light of Genesis and redemption and law in the light of creation.

Genesis does come before Exodus, but this canonical ordering has seldom been important, let alone decisive, for the way in which the Old Testament has been interpreted in modern times.[1] The usual attempt to begin reading the Old Testament from the perspective of Exodus rather than Genesis seems to be grounded primarily in the centrality of the category of revelation in modern theology.[2] This has received paradigmatic expression in statements such as this: Israel came to know God as Creator only in the light of its experience of God as Redeemer. Ironically, given the usual theocentrism of this perspective, *Israel's knowledge* of God as Creator has [355] thereby often assumed theological priority over God's creative activity itself. The net effect has been that the order of knowing has eclipsed the order of being, and creation has received much less than its just place in theological treatments of the Old Testament.[3]

In recent years, this situation has begun to be rectified. The work of H. H. Schmid in relating ancient Near Eastern and Old Testament material and that of Westermann on creation and blessing might be cited, as well as

---

This essay was originally published in *Interpretation* 45 (1991): 354–65.

1. This article extends the argument in my commentary on Exodus in the Interpretation series (Louisville: Westminster John Knox, 1991). My views have been informed by the work of the Swedish theologian Gustaf Wingren, see *Flight from Creation* (Minneapolis: Augsburg, 1971), *Creation and Law* (Philadelphia Muhlenberg, 1961). Wingren is a student of Irenaeus, see his *Man and the Incarnation: A Study in the Biblical Theology of Irenaeus* (Edinburgh: T. & T. Clark, 1959).

2. This perspective has also been influenced by socio-cultural factors, such as the use of creation theology in National Socialism or the giving of the topic over to the field of modern science, as well as by a focus on a theology of history. It is doubtful, however, that these factors would have been decisive without the fit with contemporary theological perspectives.

3. Cf. Gerhard von Rad, "The Theological Problem of the Old Testament Doctrine of Creation," in *The Problem of the Hexateuch and Other Essays* (Edinburgh: Oliver & Boyd, 1966), 131–43. That von Rad, in his *Old Testament Theology* (2 vols.; New York: Harper, 1962), 1:136–65, did consider creation before redemption had little theological impact on his discussion of either.

a number of other articles.[4] Yet, much work remains before creation is truly reclaimed for Old Testament theology.

The Importance of Genesis as the First Book of the Bible

As one contributing factor to this renewed enterprise, it is imperative to begin reading Exodus, indeed the entire Old Testament, with Genesis as the point of departure. The implications of this canonical placement are more far-reaching than is commonly realized.[5]

This canonical ordering was *theologically* significant for Israel. Those who put the canon together in its present form were certainly reflecting existing community perspectives rather than promoting an innovative theological strategy. This is evident from the fact that two traditions (J and P) preface specifically Israelite texts with creation materials. If the Yahwist is given its usual tenth-century dating, such a perspective would have been in place throughout much of Israel's history and would have informed its most basic theological developments, implicitly or explicitly. The theological factors reflected in this canonical ordering include the following:

(1) The actual sequence of divine activity in the world. God's creative activity not only brought the world into being in the first place but also was effectively engaged in the lives of individuals and peoples long before Israel came into being. Both Genesis 1–11 and 12–50 (e.g., Gen 12:10–20) witness to this universal activity of God, a crucial reality for understanding [356] the place of Israel within the divine economy (see below). God was at work in the world, even in and through the earliest glimmerings of what later became Israel, on behalf of the divine creational purposes. This was the case before Israel understood or articulated what this divine activity was all about.

(2) Priority of place is given to God's actions in the world, rather than to human knowledge of what God has done. While one ought not discount the importance of Israel's knowledge of creation and associated issues of revelation, this amounts to Israel's "catching up" with what God has long been about. The canonical ordering constitutes a demonstration that the

---

4. See H. H. Schmid, "Creation, Righteousness and Salvation: 'Creation Theology' as the Broad Horizon of Biblical Theology," in *Creation in the Old Testament* (ed. B. W. Anderson; Philadelphia: Fortress, 1984), 102–17. In the same volume, cf. George Landes, "Creation and Liberation," 135–51. For Westermann, see *Blessing in the Bible and the Life of the Church* (Philadelphia: Fortress, 1978) and *Creation* (Philadelphia: Fortress, 1974). See also Rolf Knierim, "Cosmos and History in Israel's Theology," *HBT* 3 (1981): 59–123; O. H. Steck, *World and Environment* (Nashville: Abingdon, 1980).

5. Cf. B. S. Childs, *Introduction to the Old Testament as Scripture* (Philadelphia: Fortress, 1979): "The canonical role of Gen 1–11 testifies to the priority of creation. The divine relation to the world stems from God's initial creative purpose for the universe, not for Israel alone" (p. 155). This helpful observation, however, is not carried beyond a concern for the present shape of Genesis.

history of theological developments in Israel, such as the emergence of a creation theology,[6] is a level of consideration secondary to God's actual engagement with the world.

(3) The sequence of the human experience of God's activity. Human beings in all times and places, including ancient Israel, have experienced (even if they have not known) God's creative acts (e.g., conception and birthing) prior to and alongside of God's redemptive acts. Human beings receive their life from the Creator quite apart from their knowledge of its source. This is a given by virtue of being a part of the created order; it is not the product of a human decision.[7] The redemptive work of God takes place within a world, indeed within individual lives, that have been brought into being and sustained by God's creative activity. God's redemptive work does not occur in a vacuum but within a context decisively shaped by the life-giving, creative work of God both within Israel and without (e.g., Egypt).

Within Genesis–Exodus this point is made very clear in a number of texts, especially those that see in the fruitfulness of Israel *in Egypt* a fulfill-ment of the creational word of God (cf. Exod 1:7 with Gen 1:28; 9:1, 7; 17:6). God's creative work of growth and blessing experienced by the people of Israel does not simply happen to be a reality prior to God's redemptive work; it is necessarily so in order for there to be a people to redeem.

(4) The intentions of God's redemptive work. The placement of Genesis shows that God's purpose in redemption is not finally centered on Israel. God as Creator has a purpose that spans the world, and since divine deeds are rooted in the divine will, God's redemptive activity on Israel's behalf must be understood to serve this universal intention. A proper understand-ing of Israel's place in the purposes of God is clear only from within a creation-wide perspective. Hence, even in the midst of a situation focused on the people [357] of Israel, it is God's universal will for the creation that remains in focus: "that my name may be declared throughout all the earth" (Exod 9:16).[8]

Redemption and the Reclamation of Creation

It has long been recognized that Exod 15:1–18 employs the language, style, and literary structure of the creation myths of the ancient Near East. What is not agreed upon, however, is the extent to which this pattern has

---

6. This probably occurred much earlier than is often suggested. If older texts such as Exodus 15, replete with creation theology, are any indication, it may have been a theo-logical given for those who first articulated a theology of Israel's redemption. See Schmid, "Creation, Righteousness and Salvation."

7. Though one could claim that no experience of God's activity occurs independently of already existing creational structures. Every divine act is immediately contextual or rela-tional, the experience of God is always mediated, and hence never a "naked" experience.

8. On the "will of God" in the Old Testament, see my forthcoming article in the new *Anchor Bible Dictionary*.

influenced the theology of this chapter. For example, B. W. Anderson claims that whatever may have been the case in other Old Testament literature, in Exodus 15 "there is no suggestion here of creation in a cosmic sense"; rather, the language is entirely in the service of historical concerns, namely, the coming to be of a people.[9]

This formulation is problematic, for several reasons. (1) It suggests that the admittedly mythological material can somehow remain selectively relevant, carrying only a historical point. (2) It seems to set myth and history against one another, as if the text could affirm only one or the other. (3) It fails to account for the profound role of the cosmic in the text, on both sides of the conflict. (4) Issues of intertextuality seem not to be taken with sufficient seriousness, that is, that other Old Testament texts interpret the Exodus in both historical *and* cosmic terms (e.g., Ps 74:12–14; Isa 51:9–10).

For our purposes, it is only necessary to note the extent to which cosmic issues play a role in the conflict between God and Pharaoh. Exodus 1 sets up the issue as a creational one. Pharaoh seeks to subvert the divine creational work among the Israelites (1:7). The cosmic effects of this conflict are especially evident in the plague cycle.[10] A number of Old Testament texts identify the chaos monster with Pharaoh/Egypt (cf. Ezek 29:3–5; 32:2–8; Ps 87:4; Isa 30:7; Jer 46:7–8); this may be recognized in Exodus at those points where the conflict at one level is within the realm of the divine (e.g., 12:12; 15:11; 18:11). Egypt is considered a historical embodiment of the forces of chaos, threatening to undo God's creation.

Given the anticreational forces incarnate in Egypt and the Pharaoh, no simple local or historical victory will do; God's victory must be and is cosmic in scope. God, therefore, fights with "weapons" appropriate to the enemy; it is God's activity in *creation*—the use of nonhuman rather than human forces—that conquers chaos. God's redemption is an overcoming of anticreational forces at every level, including the cosmic.

It is precisely because what happens here is cosmic that it has universal [358] effects. Hence, all of Israel's future enemies between the sea and the promised land tremble and "melt away" (Exod 15:13–16). After the divine victory such conflicts are already settled, and the enthronement of God in the promised land is a reality *already at the sea* (Exod 15:17–18). A kind of "realized eschatology" is in place here.

When God delivers Israel from bondage to Pharaoh, the people of Israel are reclaimed for the human situation intended in God's creation. In redemption, God achieves those fundamental purposes for life and well-being inherent in the creation of the world. When the anti-creational forces embodied in Pharaoh have been destroyed, life begins to grow and

---

9. See "Mythopoeic and Theological Dimensions of Biblical Creation Faith," *Creation in the Old Testament* (ed. B. W. Anderson; Philadelphia: Fortress, 1984), 5.

10. See my forthcoming article, "The Plagues as Ecological Signs of Historical Disaster," *JBL* 110 (1991) [reprinted in this volume, pp. 225–235].

develop once again in tune with God's creational designs. It is important to note that this is not a "back to Eden" scenario, as if the effect of God's redemptive work were a repristination of the original creation. The image to be considered here is spiral, not cyclical. This consideration has to do with two major factors: the nature of the original creation and the effects of redemption.

(1) In the first instance, the original creation was not static and immobile, perfectly developed, complete in every respect. The command to "subdue the earth" (Gen 1:28 [as well as "be fruitful and multiply"]) clearly indicates that the meaning of "good" does not entail complete development or perfection. These divine commands built into the very created order of things indicate that there is to be development in the world. Envisaged is a becoming of the world in such a way that the creation will in time look other than it did on the seventh day. And that, too, will be very good. God's creation is a living, moving, dynamic reality. For the creation to stay just exactly as God originally created it would be a failure of the divine design.

There are certainly continuities with the original creation to which one must attend in this discussion (cf. Gen 8:22), but development and change are central to what God intends in creation.[11] Exod 1:7 already witnesses to a new creational reality, far beyond Eden. The rest of the Old Testament testifies in a massive way to God's continuing work in creation, bringing into being that which is new and different. There is no aspect of daily life that does not testify to this ongoing creative work of God (see Pss 104:27–30; 139:13; Isa 43:7; Jer 1:5; Job 10:8–12; 12:10; 34:14–15). God did not exhaust the divine creativity in the first week of the world!

(2) Secondly, God's redemption, being the historical act that it is, enters into a point in history where some of that becoming of the world has already begun to take place. Because God's continuing creative work is not neutral [359] or negative, redemption does not do away with these proper creational developments. God's redemptive acts reclaim all that makes for life, including that which is truly human. Redemption is in the service of creation, a creation that God purposes for all. Because God is a God of life and blessing, God will do redemptive work, should those gifts be endangered. *The objective of God's work in redemption is to free people to be what they were created to be.* It is a deliverance, not from the world, but to true life in the world.

---

11. A narrow definition of creation may complicate this discussion, either in terms of the beginning of things or in terms of result. God is engaged in creative activity in every moment. H.-J. Hermisson's statement about wisdom applies generally to the Old Testament: "Creation did not only happen at the beginning of the world, but takes place continuously; *therefore,* the orders have not become rigid, but necessarily remain flexible" (emphasis mine). "Observations on the Creation Theology in Wisdom," in *Creation in the Old Testament* (ed. B. W. Anderson; Philadelphia: Fortress, 1984), 122.

Negatively, this entails freeing Israel from all that oppresses or victimizes, from inner spirit (cf. Exod 6:9) to socio-political sphere to cosmic realm. Positively, God's redemptive act reclaims Israel as God's own and reconstitutes them as a living, growing people. Even more, this act restores the life-giving potential of all aspects of the created order, to which the wilderness texts testify (see below).

What happens in redemption is not something extracreational or extrahuman, something different from what God gives in creation. Redemption makes ordinary human life possible once again. Yet creation and redemption, though integrally related, are not to be equated with one another. Redemption as well as distinguishable continuing creative acts (e.g., in the wilderness) are the means; creation is the end.[12] Redemption is the divine act in and through which the forces that threaten life and creation are overcome. Redemption is in the service of a creational end, ultimately a new heaven and a new earth (Isa 65:17; cf. 2 Cor 5:17), preliminarily realized in the rest in the promised land (cf. Exod 3:8). The effect that God intends in the act of redemption is a new creation—in the dynamic sense.

For all the potency of God's redemptive victory, however, this reclamation is not a matter of a divine flick of the wrist, as if everything now is immediately restored to its full creational life. The people of Israel are indeed liberated, entirely by God's doing; but they move from the Red Sea into a godforsaken wilderness, where the reclamation only *begins* to take effect in the gifts of food and water and in the overcoming of still existing oppressive forces such as the Amalekites (Exodus 15–17). The redemptive victory of God frees the creation *to become* what God intended. Redemption, for all its decisiveness, does not cancel out the becoming character of creation, a becoming in which God continues to be active as the creator of the world. The gifts of God in the wilderness, by which God enables new life and growth for Israel *and* the nonhuman order, are the initial stages of the history of God's *continuing creative giving* to the community on its way.

The law given at Sinai (see below) is part and parcel of these new [360] possibilities for human life and growth within the social sphere. As in the original creation, a divine command is given to human beings, catching them up in the pursuit of this new potential for life in God's creation. This helps explain the noteworthy attention given in Deuteronomy to issues of life and growth, "that you may be strong, . . . that you may live long" (Deut 11:8–9; cf. 4:40; 16:20; 22:7). This emphasis picks up on the fruitfulness theme of the creational divine purposes, made possible once again by God's redemptive action.

---

12. The word "salvation" refers to the *effects* of God's redemptive *and* God's creative activity (both deliverance and, say, healing). The word "soteriological," though linguistically related to salvation, should be reserved for specific acts of redemption (or forgiveness). Note that the language of salvation, in both Testaments, is rarely used with sin as the object (cf. Matt. 1:21); in such contexts sin is best understood as referring to the *effects* of sin.

Creation, Abrahamic Covenant, and Sinaitic Covenant

It has long been recognized that Gen 12:1–3 is a fulcrum text that ties the chapters that precede to what follows. The divine election of Abraham is immediately related to "all the families of the earth," the subject of Genesis 1–11. The covenantal relationship with Abraham is thus claimed to have a universal import, explicitly connected to God's larger creational purposes.[13] The unconditional promise to Abraham is not simply for the sake of his posterity but for the sake of the world. Those who are drawn into the orbit of this family will experience the same blessings. The covenant with Abraham will have a positive *creational* effect on others.

A long-standing question in Old Testament scholarship is how the Abrahamic and Sinaitic covenants are to be related. It is commonplace to claim that they belong to different covenantal traditions and to conclude that, among other things, the Abrahamic covenant is unconditional while the Sinaitic is conditional.[14] Whatever the truth in this point of view from the perspective of the history of traditions, the present canonical arrangement compels us to recognize that the "two" covenants are integrally related, with the Abrahamic covenant providing the framework within which the Sinaitic covenant is developed.

A key text to consider in this regard is Exod 32:13 (cf. 33:1):

> "Remember Abraham, Isaac, and Israel, thy servants, to whom thou didst swear by thine own self, and didst say to them, 'I will multiply your descendants as the stars of heaven, and all this land that I have promised I will give to your descendants, and they shall inherit it for ever.'"

This text presupposes earlier references to the Abrahamic covenant in Exodus (2:24; 6:4–5, 8; cf. 3:6, 15–17; 12:25; 13:5, 11), which provide the theological grounding for God's redemptive action. In the wake of the golden calf apostasy, and God's preliminary decision to destroy the people, Moses intercedes on Israel's behalf. Among the reasons Moses gives for God [361] to repent of this decision is the covenant with Abraham.[15] God has sworn, *by God's own self,* regarding the promises of descendants and land. In effect, Moses claims that God's own life has been put on the line with respect to these promises.[16] At least from Moses' perspective, these unconditional promises remain *even with the Sinaitic covenant in place.* Hence, whatever

---

13. H. W. Wolff, "The Kerygma of the Yahwist," *Int* 20 (1966): 147–58, shows how this theme permeates the subsequent narrative.

14. That this has become standard fare in Old Testament studies can be seen in their separate treatments in *IDBSup,* 188–97.

15. On divine repentance, see my "The Repentance of God: A Key to Evaluating Old Testament God-Talk," *HBT 10* (1988): 47–70.

16. Note that Moses' prayer overstates the point, for these promises could still be fulfilled even if God had to start over again with Moses.

one might say regarding the "conditions" of the Sinaitic covenant, the promises of God to Abraham, Isaac, and Israel still stand. The Sinaitic covenant does not make these particular promises conditional.[17]

It may be asked, however, that if the Abrahamic covenant remains in place as the fundamental grounding for God's relationship with Israel, of what basic significance is the Sinaitic covenant within this framework? I would suggest (and the details are developed in my Exodus commentary) that the Sinaitic covenant, far from establishing the relationship between God and Israel as is commonly thought, is a *vocational covenant* with those who are already God's people.[18] Israel's status as the people of God is explicitly in place throughout the early chapters of Exodus (e.g., 3:7, 10; 5:1; 7:4; cf. 4:22–23; 15:16). Sinai may be said to provide *a closer specification* of what is entailed in that relationship in view of what Israel has become *within* its status as a people of God, that is, a people redeemed. The Sinai covenant is a matter, not of the people's status, but of their vocation. It is a formal act of promising only in this sense. One could also note that 19:5–6 suggests that there is something new at stake in this for God as well.[19]

The Sinaitic covenant, then, may be said to specify more closely the responsibilities of the descendants of Abraham for the sake of all the families of the earth (cf. Exod 19:5, "for all the earth is mine"; Deut 4:6). The function of the law is to set out Israel's vocation in the world, to bring the created order—human and nonhuman—into closer conformity with the creation as God intended it, characterized in particular by righteousness, mercy, and the fear of God. This conformity between social order and cosmic [362] order can be observed particularly in the Psalms (e.g., 97:2, 6; 33:5; 85:10–13).

Law and the Reclamation of Creation

As B. D. Napier stated long ago: "Hebrew Law, in its present total impression, has its clearest roots in [Israel's] creation-faith."[20] Even more,

---

17. Other texts within the Pentateuch affirm this perspective as the only proper canonical one, e.g., Lev 26:44–45; Deut 4:31; 9:27; cf. Judg 2:1; 1 Sam 12:22.

18. See, e.g., Dale Patrick, *Old Testament Law* (Atlanta: John Knox, 1985), 225; the covenant "formally established a relationship in which Yahweh was Israel's God and Israel was Yahweh's people." E. W. Nicholson (*God and His People: Covenant and Theology in the Old Testament* [Oxford: Clarendon, 1986], 210) speaks of the Sinai covenant as both "Israel's constitution as the people of Yahweh" and as "Israel's vocation to be the people of Yahweh." Nicholson makes an important case for the latter, but not the former.

19. It has been common over the last generation to claim that the Sinai covenant was based on analogy with international political treaties of the suzerainty type. But the application of this analogy, especially to the texts in Exodus, has been seriously challenged, and it plays little role in many recent discussions (see Nicholson, *God and His People*).

20. "Community under Law: On Hebrew Law and Its Theological Presuppositions," *Int* 7 (1953): 413. Cf. Jon Levenson, "The Theologies of Commandment in Biblical Israel," *HTR* 73 (1980): 28–33.

one could say that the law actually belongs to the sphere of creational thought. Basic to this view is the symbiotic relationship between cosmic and social orders. H. H. Schmid, in his study of creation in Israel and the ancient Near East, notes this parallel: "Legal order belongs to the order of creation." Negatively, "an offense in the legal realm obviously has effects in the realm of nature (drought, famine) or in the political sphere (threat of the enemy)."[21] Positively, the law is a means by which the divine ordering of chaos at the cosmic level is actualized in the social sphere, brought into closer conformity with the creation God intended. Thereby God's will is done on earth as it is in heaven, and the cosmic and social orders are harmoniously integrated. For Israel, obedience of the law means doing justice to, conforming oneself to, that creational order that God has by the divine redemptive activity put right. The object of Israel's ethic is not asceticism or removal from the sphere of creation but immersion within the very sphere that has been reclaimed by God's redemptive work. Israel now joins God in seeking to keep right what God has put right, and to extend that rightness into every sphere of daily life.

God's redemptive activity does not cancel or negate that which is human or natural. Rather, it has the effect of reclaiming and enabling true human life, freedom, *and responsibility* within the created order of things. As a newly redeemed community by and under God, Israel is in effect addressed as humanity was on the sixth day of creation. In the gift of the law, Israel is thereby given specific tasks in the tradition of Gen 1:26–28. Israel now stands before God and hears anew the command of God to have dominion over the earth, to till and keep the land, and to be its brother's keeper (the narratives subsequent to Genesis 3 are also revealing of creational commands). Israel, by attending to its relationship with Yahweh and to the commands given at Sinai, grows toward God's intention for the human, indeed the entire world, laid out in the creation. [363]

The original creation was not without law (Gen 1:26–28; 2:14–16; cf. 9:1–6; 18:19, 25; and 26:5, the pre-Exodus, pre-Sinai placement of which must be taken with full seriousness!). Creation entails demand for at least two reasons: (1) The life established by God in creation is not free from all threats; it will not be maintained in the fullest sense regardless of what human beings do with the gifts they have been given. Hence, law is given within the very creation for the sake of the preservation of God's creative work. This will entail the recognition that every human being as creature

---

21. Schmid, "Creation, Righteousness and Salvation," 104–5. He notes, for example, that Hammurabi's giving of the law comes in a creation context, and "so does every ancient Near Eastern legal code with the same structure" (p. 105). Cf. Douglas Knight, "Cosmogony and Order in the Hebrew Tradition," in *Cosmogony and Ethical Order: New Studies in Comparative Ethics* (ed. R. Lovin and F. Reynolds; Chicago: University of Chicago Press, 1985), 133–57.

is related to the law by virtue of being creature. Human beings are not free of the creational demand just because they do not belong to the chosen people.[22]

(2) Even more, this preservation, as we have noted, is not understood in a static sense. Creational law joins other creational activity in being given in the service of creation's proper development, for there is not a once-and-for-all givenness about all aspects of the creative order. This dynamic sense of the law is canonized in the redactional incorporation of the shifts and changes in pentateuchal law over the centuries. This is in recognition of the fact that the law must constantly be on the move if it is to connect with the actual realities of creation which are constantly changing. Understanding the creation as mobile and flexible helps keep the law from becoming a static reality (and vice versa). In other words, a proper creation theology should be in constant challenge of the status quo rather than in support of it. This dynamic sense of creation is what animates all the talk about newness in the theology of Deutero-Isaiah.

The law given at Sinai, then, is not a new reality but a fuller particularization of how the community can take on its God-given *creational* responsibilities in view of new times and places. Sinai is a drawing together of previously known law, and some natural extensions thereof; it intensifies their import for this newly shaped community. In most respects, Sinai is simply *a regiving of the law implicitly or explicitly commanded in creation.* Sinai reiterates for those redeemed the demands of creation.

The Exodus does not bring a new ethic into being, as if all that follows in the law were new expectations for Israel or the world. To suggest that law is grounded fundamentally in the Exodus experience is to deny the central role of law in the creation before Sinai.[23] God's redemptive work in the Exodus does give Israel some new *motivations* for keeping the law (Exod 22:21; 23:9), indeed empowers Israel to that end. The Exodus also sheds new [364] light on the creational expectations of the redeemed in view of their own experience. At Sinai, the divine demand now becomes known in a more explicit way to Israel in no little detail. Non-Israelites may in fact conform their lives to one or more aspects of these laws (e.g., Pharaoh's daughter), but without knowing that these behaviors are in fact the divine intention for the creation. At Sinai, Israel comes to know that it is the Creator God who issues these commands, and hence Israel is *expected*

---

22. John Barton, "Natural Law and Poetic Justice in the Old Testament," *JTS* 30 (1979): 1–14. Note that later Judaism sometimes viewed the law of Moses as preexistent, serving as the pattern God used in making the world. The identification of Wisdom and Torah could also be profitably related to this discussion.

23. Note that if the law at Sinai only grows out of the redemptive act, there is no grounding for the law for persons other than Israelites.

to obey them for the sake of the creation. But the Exodus is not an event that *creates* the law.[24]

Those commands that may be said to be peculiar to Israel's life with God do not stand over against this perspective. To the extent that there are laws intended specifically for the redeemed community (e.g., pertaining to worship), they are *both* grounded in, and in the service of, divine creational purposes. At one level, commands regarding worship as a creational reality are implicit in the story of Cain and Abel and the appropriateness of their offerings (cf. also Gen 2:1–3; 4:26; 8:20–21). But even more, Israelite worship is a means by which the world is created and re-created in every new ritual activity.

A recent study of the Priestly legislation by Frank Gorman, building on the anthropological work of Mary Douglas and others, demonstrates this integration of worship and the creation:[25] "The Priestly ritual system is best understood as the meaningful enactment of world in the context of Priestly creation theology." This is defined as "the bringing into being and the continuation of the order of creation . . . that reflects the original good order of God." Certain rituals are necessary for the continuation of the world order; others are needed to effect a restoration upon disruption. In view of Genesis 1, "human beings are called to become participants in the continual renewal and maintenance of the created order." The ritual legislation becomes one means by which human beings act out this role in creation. Thus, even though these laws are intended specifically for Israel, the concerns and the effects of such *local* ritual activity are *cosmic*. Obedience is not conceived simply in individual or even social terms but as actions that affect and encompass the entire created order.[26] [365]

The parallels to many Israelite laws in the cultures surrounding Israel must be placed within this theological context. Few of the social laws are in fact uniquely Israelite, and there are many parallels to various ritual activities (e.g., sacrifices); what is unique is the particular configuration of material collected here and its being related in specific ways to Yahweh. But

---

24. Jon Levenson says it well: "In this theology, the commandments appear not as the yield of a historical event, or at least not exclusively so, but as the extension into human society of cosmic order, divinely ordained and sustained" ("Theologies of Commandment," 28). He also cites Psalms 19, 119, noting that the latter makes no allusion to Israel's history. Though he speaks of this as one of a number of theologies of commandment, the discreteness of the "theologies" he isolates is open to debate. See above on "motivation."

25. *The Ideology of Ritual Space, Time and Status in the Priestly Theology* (Sheffield: JSOT Press, 1990), 9, 18, 230–34. Cf also Walter Brueggemann, *Israel's Praise: Doxology against Idolatry and Ideology* (Philadelphia: Fortress, 1988), 1–28.

26. Gorman's conclusion (p. 230) that the incompleteness of the created order in Genesis 1 is understood by the Priestly writers to be *"fully* finished" (emphasis mine) in the ordering of *Israelite* society around the tabernacle is problematic. His discussion moves from Israel to the generally human (pp. 230–32) without sufficient consideration of the relationship between Israel and the larger creation.

the existence of much of this legal material in the surrounding cultures is testimony to God's work as creator among these peoples. One result of this divine activity is the development of law for the ordering and preservation of human life, and this is prior to and independent of God's redemptive work. God uses such laws for the benefit of life, quite apart from both redemptive activity and the world's *knowledge* of the origins of the laws. This is further evidence for the fact that the law does not grow out of redemption but is brought into the light of day for Israel as the law of God for the sake of creation. It is now made clear to the redeemed people what their responsibilities are in God's reclaimed world. The law is given to be of service in the ongoing divine task of the reclamation of creation. In the obedience of the law, Israel in effect becomes a *created co-reclaimer* of God's intentions for the creation.

The first commandment becomes pivotal in this understanding, recognized not least by the way in which its various formulations regularly punctuate the legal corpus.[27] Only as the community remains in a right relationship with God (see Deut 6:5) is obedience of the law truly possible. It is as a redeemed people trusting in God alone that the reclamatory work of God can be extended out into the larger world in and through them.

---

27. Even the first commandment can be said to be at least implicit in the creation materials. Genesis 3 and the subsequent narratives are hardly comprehensible without some such understanding.

Law in the Service of Life:
A Dynamic Understanding of
Law in Deuteronomy

I. Introduction

Christians commonly do not know what to do with the law texts in the Pentateuch. One practical effect of this uncertainty is that these texts are virtually ignored in the common lectionary. Besides the Decalogue, the exceptions are Deut 6:4–9 and Lev 19:11–18—probably because Jesus quotes from these texts and claims that no laws are "greater" than these and commends the scribe for saying that they are "more important" (Mark 12:28–34). There are many reasons Christians tend to ignore the law texts: their ancient cultural context; their claimed obsolescence; their hard-nosed, albeit selective, use by some believers; confusion over the polysemic word "law"; and their remarkable capacity to make readers feel uncomfortable (e.g., Exod 22:21–28; Deut 15:7–11). A less visible, but perhaps more basic reason for this neglect is the sense that Old Testament laws are to be understood in static terms, given by God and never to be changed; hence, readers will either agree or disagree and treat them accordingly. In this essay I will argue that *the legal texts themselves* understand the law in dynamic terms. I focus on the book of Deuteronomy, but draw other law texts into the conversation.

At stake in these reflections is not simply an understanding regarding whether and how individual laws pertain to Christian faith and life, but a [184] continuing positive view of the basic concerns that undergird and inform these laws. Specifically, many laws articulate Israel's deep concern for justice for the less advantaged; by neglecting these law texts we lose so much grist for our consideration of these issues. More generally, these laws, both individually and in their entirety, are a gracious gift of God for the sake of the life, health, and well-being of individuals in community. This is made especially clear in the book of Deuteronomy. As Deut 5:33 puts it: these laws are given to God's people "that you may live, and that it may go well with you, and that you may live long on the land that you are to possess." God gives the law in the service of life. If for no other reason than that, they deserve our close attention.

This essay was originally published in *A God So Near: Essays in Old Testament Theology in Honor of Patrick D. Miller* (ed. Brent A. Strawn and Nancy R. Bowen; Winona Lake, IN: Eisenbrauns, 2003), 183–200.

Scholars have long been at work tracking the development of Israel's legal tradition. While the canonical presentation of the emergence of Israelite law covers a span of some forty years (from Mt. Sinai to the plains of Moab), interpreters usually understand that these laws developed over many centuries, from pre-monarchical times to the postexilic period. Various repetitions and inconsistencies in the laws have been especially important in drawing this conclusion. Broadly speaking, it is now commonplace to distinguish the Book of the Covenant (Exod 20:22–23:33), Deuteronomy 12–26, and the Priestly tradition (Leviticus); and that is the usual chronological ordering. At the same time, these complexes of law are themselves composite and it is usually thought that they underwent a complex development over many centuries in view of ongoing changes in community life before being drawn into their present canonical orbit.[1]

Yet, while there has been a long-standing awareness that Israel's laws developed over time and were not understood in a static sense, this has been more an historical judgment than a canonical one.[2] Does the *canonical* presentation of law, set as it is in the wilderness period, reveal a comparable perspective regarding law? In my judgment the answer is affirmative: despite the ascription of all law to the Mosaic era, there are several different signs that the law as canonically presented is not understood to be timeless and immutable.

I make several claims as a way of beginning. The laws that God gives Israel are understood basically in terms of creation and vocation. For example, for Deuteronomy to speak so basically and persistently of the law as [185] being in the service of life and well-being means that its understanding of law is dynamic and is fundamentally creational in its orientation. To speak so of Deuteronomy also carries the claim that its understanding of law is seen basically in vocational terms. God gives the law not only for the sake of the life of those who receive it but also for the sake of the life of the neighbor, indeed all of creation, whom they are called to serve.

II. Creation and Law

Links between Deuteronomy and the creation story in Genesis have often been noted,[3] but here I speak of the relationship between law and creation in the Pentateuch more generally, a perspective in which Deuteronomy

---

1. For a helpful analysis of the development of the Book of the Covenant, showing that it is not "an immutable, timeless law," see Paul D. Hanson, "The Theological Significance of Contradiction within the Book of the Covenant," in *Canon and Authority* (ed. George W. Coats and Burke O. Long; Philadelphia: Fortress, 1977), 110–31.

2. A recent, important book, focusing on this issue relative to the book of Deuteronomy that informs my discussion is Bernard M. Levinson's *Deuteronomy and the Hermeneutics of Legal Innovation* (New York: Oxford University Press, 1997).

3. For a brief summary, see Terence E. Fretheim, *The Pentateuch* (IBT; Nashville: Abingdon, 1996), 56–58.

participates. The sequence of redemption followed by law in the book of
Exodus can be misleading; it may prompt a view that God's act of salvation obligates obedience to the law.[4] But such an understanding cannot be
maintained. Rather, Israel's laws are grounded in God's work in creation. As
B. D. Napier stated long ago, "Hebrew Law, in its present total impression,
has its clearest roots in [Israel's] creation-faith."[5] Generally speaking, that
many Pentateuchal laws have their predecessors and parallels in other ancient Near Eastern cultures demonstrates their roots in creation rather than
redemption (which Israel itself recognized, see below on Deut 4:8). More
specifically, in his study of creation in Israel and the ancient Near East,
H. H. Schmid claims unambiguously, "Legal order belongs to the order of
creation." In his view, there is a symbiotic relationship between cosmic
and social orders. Negatively, "an offense in the legal realm obviously has
effects in the realm of nature (drought, famine) or in the political sphere
(threat of the enemy)." Positively, the law is a means by which the divine
ordering of chaos at the cosmic level is actualized in the social [186] sphere,
which is thereby brought into closer conformity with the creation that God
intended.[6] The law is given because God is concerned about *the best possible
life* for *all* of God's creatures.

    The book of Genesis supports this understanding of creational law. Law
is integral to God's creative work and is formulated both as prohibition
(Gen 2:16–17) and as positive command (Gen 1:26–28). Law is thereby
recognized as a pre-sin reality, part and parcel of God's good creation, given
for the sake of a good life for all its creatures. This creational law is reiter-
ated and extended after sin enters the life of the world (Gen 9:1–7) and
these early narratives reveal something of this creational law (e.g., the story

---

    4. An example of the difficulties such an understanding can generate may be seen
in a statement by James W. Watts, *Reading Law: The Rhetorical Shaping of the Pentateuch*
(Biblical Seminar 59; Sheffield: Sheffield Academic Press, 1999), 95: "Because YHWH has
done and will do these things for Israel, Israel *owes* YHWH obedience" (emphasis mine; cf.
similarly, p. 125: "the exodus has obligated Israel to YHWH"). The word "owes" draws on
imagery from the world of finance and suggests that Israel is in debt to God and hence
is obligated to repay God for what God has done. But if God is truly gracious, as Israel's
central confession states (Exod 34:6–7), the language that Israel has an obligation to pay
God back for services rendered compromises the claim regarding grace.
    5. B. D. Napier, "Community under Law: On Hebrew Law and Its Theological Pre-
suppositions," *Int* 7 (1953): 413. Cf. Jon Levenson, "The Theologies of Commandment
in Biblical Israel," *HTR* 73 (1980): 28–33. Important for these considerations generally is
the work of Gustaf Wingren, especially his *Creation and Law* (Philadelphia: Muhlenberg,
1961).
    6. See H. H. Schmid, "Creation, Righteousness and Salvation: 'Creation Theology'
as the Broad Horizon of Biblical Theology," in *Creation in the Old Testament* (ed. Bernhard
W. Anderson; IRT 6; Philadelphia: Fortress, 594), 104–5. He notes, for example, that Hammurabi's giving of the law occurs in a creation context, and "so does every Near Eastern
legal code with the same structure" (p. 105). See also Klaus Koch, "Is There a Doctrine of
Retribution in the Old Testament?" in *Theodicy in the Old Testament* (ed. J. Crenshaw; IRT
3; Philadephia: Fortress, 1983), 57–87.

of Cain and Abel assumes that Cain should have known that murder is wrong, Gen 4:10–13).

The ancestral narratives also witness to pre-Sinai law; especially to be noted is Gen 26:5 (cf. 18:19, 25): "Abraham obeyed my voice and kept my charge, my commandments, my statutes, and my laws." This text is no simple anachronistic reference to the law given at Sinai; it witnesses to the narrator's understanding of the place of law in the pre-Sinai period.[7] This text stands in basic continuity with earlier articulations of God's will in the creation. Abraham's conformation to the will of God shows that his life is in tune with God's creational purposes and models for later Israel the right response to law. These ancestral texts also demonstrate that law cannot be collapsed into the law given at Sinai. At the same time, they show that Sinai law basically conforms to already existing law; that is, the law given at Sinai stands in fundamental continuity with the law obeyed by Abraham.

The place of law in Exodus 15–18 makes the same point (e.g., 15:25b–26; 16:4, 26; 18:13–27). Exod 18:13–27 may carry a special force, situated as it is just before the revelation at Sinai (and somewhat disjunctively so). Jethro identifies his wisdom regarding the right ordering of the community with what God has *commanded* (18:23), even though he had not received a revelation from God. This understanding is important for at least two reasons. [187] First, it makes possible a more open understanding of the ascription of the Sinai laws to God's specific revelation. If Jethro can attach a "God commands you" to his own discernment, then readers are put on the alert that the phrase "the Lᴏʀᴅ spoke to Moses" (or the like) does not necessarily exclude human insight and reflection in the development of these laws (though no explicit credit is so given). This understanding may be parallel to the description of mediated divine *action* in Exod 3:7–10 where both God and Moses are agents of the exodus, though God is often the only subject of the verbs (e.g., Exod 14:13, 31). This point may be supported by the textual recognition of the distinction between God speaking the Decalogue directly (see Deut 5:22–27) but mediating other laws through Moses. Even more, the additional distinction between law spoken by God to Moses (Sinai) and law spoken by Moses (Deuteronomy) makes the latter one step further removed from the mouth of God. In the latter, God's laws pass through a human mind (narratively) and that inevitably involves interpretation and reflection (see Acts 15:28, also in a law-giving context). God's revelation is therefore the decisive, but not the only factor in the giving of the law.

---

7. See James Bruckner, "The Creational Context of Law before Sinai: Law and Liberty in Pre-Sinai Narratives and Romans 7," *ExAud 11* (1995): 91–110. See also his Luther Seminary dissertation, "A Literary and Theological Analysis of Implied Law in the Abrahamic Narrative: Implied Oughts as a Case Study," forthcoming from Sheffield Academic Press.

Second, "The *specific revelation of God at Sinai,* now to be presented, is thus seen to stand in *fundamental continuity* with the discernment of the will of God in and through *common human experience.*"[8] To cast this point in general terms, human constructs for the ordering of community may be revealing of the divine intention quite apart from the reception of a specific divine directive to that effect. This observation, in turn, links back to the development of law in ancient Near Eastern societies and, I might add, in every society since that time.

This understanding may be supported further by Deut 4:6–8. As noted above, we know that many of Israel's laws find their parallel in ancient Near Eastern law codes. That Israel also knew this to be the case is clear from this text. Other peoples do have "statutes and ordinances," but they are not as "just" as Israel's (4:8); theologically, this recognizes the work of God the Creator among such peoples in the development of law. Note also that the difference in the "just" character of the laws involved pertains to the "entire law"; this may recognize that the *individual ordinances* of other peoples could not always be so described. Even more, the knowledge of the law by other peoples entails a quality of discernment on their part; they recognize the wisdom of Israel's laws (4:6; cf. their discernment in Deut 29:24–28; Jer 22:8–9). This text understands that ultimately there were human agents, both within and without Israel, involved in the ongoing evaluation and development of Israel's laws. [188]

The law is given in creation for two fundamental reasons, both of which are basically concerned about life:

1. to preserve God's creative work in the face of threats that may arise to creation's well-being. For example, creation will not remain "good" and engendering of life regardless of what human beings do with the gifts they have been given. The created order is not so fixed that it is immune to significant damage; human sin can negatively affect the created order so that it ceases to serve life in the way that God intended (see Deut 11:13–17; Hos 4:1–3). The law is given in creation so as to keep cosmic order and social order integrated in a harmonious way. This creational context for law also means human beings are not free of creational demands just because they do not belong to the chosen people. It is just such an understanding that informs many biblical texts relating to non-Israelites (e.g., Deut 4:6–8; or the oracles against the nations, e.g., Amos 1–2).[9] Nations are held accountable to creational law quite apart from their knowledge of the God who gave it.

---

8. Terence E. Fretheim, *Exodus* (Interpretation; Louisville: John Knox, 1990), 200.

9. See John Barton, "Natural Law and Poetic Justice in the Old Testament," *JTS* 30 (1979): 1–14. Note that one perspective within later Judaism was that the law of Moses was preexistent, serving as the pattern God used in making the world.

2. to serve the proper development of God's good but not perfect creation. The command to "subdue the earth" (1:28) indicates that the creation was not fully developed at the beginning. God does not establish the created order as a fixed, polished entity; it was not intended to remain forever just as it existed at the end of the first week of its life (as the history of nature well demonstrates). This openness to the future exists not only because God did not exhaust the divine creativity in the first week of the world (see Ps 104:30), but also because of the creative capacities built into the order of things and the charges given its creatures (see Gen 1:11–12, 20, 24, 28; 2:18–23).[10] To be sure, there are the great rhythmic givens of creation that perdure: seedtime and harvest, cold and heat, summer and winter, day and night (Gen 8:22; Jer 31:35–36), but God's creation is also understood to be a work in progress. God creates a paradise, but the effect is not a static state of affairs; the creation is a highly dynamic reality in which the future is open to a number of possible developments. [189]

If the law was given in creation in the service of developing God's creation toward its fullest possible life-giving potential, then for the creation to stay just as God originally created it would be a failure of the divine design. Development and change are what God intends for the creation and human beings are charged with responsibilities for intra-creational development. A fundamental implication of this kind of reflection is that "natural law" is not understood to be a fixed reality; it, too, is open to development in view of a changing world. In other words, a proper creational understanding of law entails something other than the maintenance of the status quo; existing understandings of "natural law" are in need of ongoing scrutiny in view of what creation is becoming (and this is borne out by experience). For example, the command to "fill the earth" (Gen 1:28), understandable in view of its ancient setting, may need to be reexamined in view of changing population patterns. New situations will teach new duties in view of the developing created order, including natural law.

III. Law and Vocation

The covenant at Sinai with its accompanying laws is concerned most fundamentally with Israel's vocation in the world in the service of life. The Sinai covenant does not establish God's relationship with Israel; the Israelites are "my people" early in the book of Exodus (e.g., Exod 3:7–10). These people are the inheritors of the promises given to their ancestors (Exod 3:15–17; 6:4, 8), a covenant that God remembers (Exod 2:24; 6:4–5)

---

10. On the interpretation of these texts as witnessing to a creation in process, see Terence E. Fretheim, "The Book of Genesis," *NIB*, 1:343–46, 352, 357. For an important statement of this perspective, see Michael Welker, "What Is Creation?: Rereading Genesis 1 and 2," *ThTo* 45 (1991): 56–71.

as given to the ancestors and to their "descendants" (Gen 17:7). It is this ancestral covenant that grounds Moses' appeal to God when the people break the Sinaitic covenant (Exod 32:13), indicating that the Abrahamic covenant is more foundational for the God-Israel relationship. The Sinai covenant is a matter of Israel's vocation not its status. It is a formalization of Israel's role in the world—to be a holy nation and a kingdom of priests (Exod 19:5–6). The giving of the law to an already redeemed people is in the service of this vocation, to which the people agree to be obedient (Exod 19:8; 24:3, 7).

In being given the law at Sinai, Israel, like the first human beings, is caught up by God in avocation that involves the becoming of the creation. Sinai law is not a new reality but a fuller particularization of how the community can take on its God-given *creational* responsibilities for the sake of life in view of new times and places. Sinai draws together previously known law and develops new law for this redeemed and called community. In most respects, Sinai is simply a regiving of the law implicitly or explicitly commanded in creation or made evident in common life experience (within Israel and without). The exodus gives Israel some new motivations for keeping the law, indeed empowers Israel to that end, but, as I have already [190] noted above, the law is grounded in Israel's creation-faith, not God's redemptive activity.[11] To obey the law is to live in harmony with God's intentions for the creation. As Deuteronomy never tires of telling readers, the law is given for the sake of the best life possible; the law stands in the service of a stable, flourishing, and life-enhancing *community* (the community language is important). Sinai law sketches a vocation to which Israel is called for the sake of the neighbor and the creation. Because of the way in which Deuteronomy often identifies the neighbor in relationship to specific life situations (e.g., 24:10–22), it reveals a dynamic sense of law.

I return to the salvation wrought by God at Passover and sea crossing. When the Israelites sing the song of Exodus 15, "the LORD has become my salvation," it is important to note what salvation means in this context. Salvation means that the Israelites are delivered from the effects, not of their own sin, but of the sins of other people (the Egyptians). When God delivers Israel from this abusive situation, the people are reclaimed for the life and well-being that God intended for the creation. As such, God's salvation stands, finally, in the service of creation, freeing people to be what they were created to be and having a re-creative effect on the nonhuman world as well, as life in the desert begins to flourish once again.[12] And the central concern of the law for the poor and other disadvantaged people is,

---

11. For an earlier formulation of these understandings of law, see Terence E. Fretheim, "The Reclamation of Creation: Redemption and Law in Exodus," *Int* 45 (1991): 354–65.

12. For details, see idem, "The Plagues as Ecological Signs of Historical Disaster," *JBL* 110 (1991): 385–96 [reprinted in this volume, pp. 225–235].

for Deuteronomy, for the sake of life, or, in other terms, to make sure that God's *salvation* extends deeply into the life of the community. God's work of salvation has the effect of reclaiming and enabling not only true human life and freedom, but also *responsibility* for the sake of life for all. As a newly redeemed community, Israel stands before God and is in effect addressed as human beings were on the sixth day of creation, called to take up this vocation.

IV. A Dynamic Understanding of Law

I now consider various matters that more fully indicate that the law is understood to be a dynamic rather than a static or fixed reality.

Law and Context

It is of no little import that the wilderness is the context for all Pentateuchal law. This is true of the major blocks of law given at Sinai and [191] Moab, but especially to be noted are the wilderness narratives (Exod 15:22–18:27; Num 10:11–36:13), where laws emerge periodically as new situations develop for the journeying community (e.g., Exod 15:25b–26; Numbers 15; 18–19; 27–36). The book of Deuteronomy, whether viewed canonically (forty years after Sinai) or historically (most basically, the seventh century B.C.E.), is a major exemplar of law emerging in view of changing circumstances (see further below). The forty years between Sinai and Deuteronomy should not be downplayed, especially in view of its recollection of Israel's most recent history and its anticipation of a new context in the promised land. This span of time is sufficient to demonstrate that the text recognizes that Israel's life situation has now changed and new formulations of law are needed. Deuteronomy would have to be interpreted quite differently if its laws had been given at Sinai.

In tracking the way in which the law is literarily presented in Exodus through Deuteronomy it is immediately apparent that law and narrative are interwoven.[13] In other words, the law is not presented as a code but is integrated with the ongoing story of the people of God, unlike the law codes of the ancient Near East (or of contemporary societies). Law for Israel is always intersecting with life as it is lived—filled with contingency and change, complexity and ambiguity.

That Israel's laws emerge in connection with the wilderness experience is significant; it indicates that the wilderness is an image for the basic character of law. On the one hand, the law provides something of a compass for wandering in the wilderness. On the other hand, the contingencies of wilderness wandering keep the law from becoming absolutized in a once-for-all form and content. Law in and of itself tends to promote a myth of certainty regarding the shape of life; actual life, however, especially when

---

13. For the theological significance of this literary reality, see idem, *Exodus*, 201–7.

seen from the perspective of the wilderness narratives, is filled with contingencies, in which nothing on the ship of life seems to be tied down. This means that new laws will be needed and older laws will need to be revised or perhaps put on a back burner. So, for example, in Deuteronomy there are laws regarding kingship and prophecy in anticipation of the coming settlement in the land.

The image of wilderness lifts up that which is basic to the development of law (and all relationships for that matter): constancy and change. Law takes ongoing experience into account while remaining constant in its objective: the life, health, and stability of the community. Both constancy and change are basic to law because they are basic to life, indeed the life that God intends for all creatures. They are also basic for God, a matter to which I now turn. [192]

Law and God

That all Pentateuchal law is ultimately attributed to God has created something of a problem in thinking about the God of these texts, especially in view of their inconsistencies. Is God inconsistent or represented as inconsistent or is some other explanation possible? Various harmonistic efforts, both Rabbinic and Christian, have been attempted to make sure that a consistent God emerges, but at the expense of a straightforward reading of the text. At the same time, critical scholars sometimes make claims about God that may intensify the God issue unnecessarily. But some implications of the interweaving of law and narrative noted above deserve further consideration.

1. The law is a gracious gift of God. The law is more clearly seen to be a gracious gift because it is episodically integrated with the story of God's other gracious activities. God's actions in the narrative show that the law is not arbitrarily laid upon the people, but is given "for our good always, that God might preserve us alive" (Deut 6:24). The gracious purposes of God for Israel evident in the narrative demonstrate that the law is fundamentally gift, not burden.

2. The law given by God has a fundamentally personal and interrelational character. God introduces the law with highly personal statements regarding what God has done on behalf of the people (Exod 19:4; 20:2). Obedience to law is thus seen to be a response within a relationship, not a response to the law as law. Moreover, in the narrative, readers are confronted with a God who personally interacts with Israel through every stage of their journey. God's giving of the law does not stand at odds with this kind of interactive God-people relationship. And so God does not give the law in a once-for-all form but takes the ongoing relationship into account in giving shape to the law.

3. God's gracious gift of law meets a creational *need*. God's ongoing work of providence and salvation in Pentateuchal narrative is always related to

the needs of the people, for example, delivering them from Egyptian abuse and providing food and drink in the wilderness. That God's narrative actions are so correlated with the people's needs argues for a comparable understanding of law. God's law takes into account what the people need for the best possible life. This means that the laws are not arbitrary; they are given in view of specific human needs, and this at several levels. For example, God gives the sacrificial laws in Leviticus 5 because of the people's need for atonement. At the same time, it is made clear that the wealth of the worshiper is taken into account in determining the type of offering. Individual situations of need affect how the law is to be applied.

4. The basic shape for a life lived in obedience to law is drawn most basically from Israel's narrative experience with God, rather than from [193] abstract ethical argument or even divine imperative. God "loves the strangers, providing them food and clothing. You shall also love the stranger, for you were strangers in the land of Egypt" (Deut 10:18–19). "Be merciful, just as your Father is merciful" (Luke 6:36). God's will for Israel does not remain at the level of general principle; it moves into life in all of its particulars, for that is where the law often makes the most difference for people's well-being (e.g., Deut 24:19–22).

That the law is developed as an exegesis of divine action means that believers are always being called to go beyond the law. The range of God's actions is not *legally* circumscribed (e.g., Jer 3:1–5, 11–12). God is always doing new things, and so this will mean imagining ever-new ways in which the law and the consequent shape of people's lives can reflect God's actions in the world. Such an understanding also prevents the believer from equating obedience to the law with doing what is right. Law may not have caught up with the community's confession regarding God or its understanding of life and well-being (and so it may be that the legal act is not necessarily a moral act).[14]

5. God does not simply give the law to the people by divine fiat; God accompanies the law with motivations to obey the law.[15] These motivations are revealing of the kind of God that stands behind the law; God does not just lay down the law, but gives Israel good reasons to obey. For Deuteronomy (e.g., 5:33; 22:6–7!), it is in Israel's self-interest and in the best interests of the human and nonhuman community; especially the vulnerable and marginalized, to obey—"that it may go well with you and that you may live long." This, of course, is not the language of reward; rather, such benefits are intrinsically related to the deed; they grow out of the deed itself. To obey is a reasonable thing to do (Deut 4:6); right obedience is always an intelligent obedience.[16] The concern of the law is not to bind Israel to some

---

14. Hanson, "Theological Significance," is particularly forceful on this point.
15. For a brief, helpful survey of these motive clauses, see Watts, *Reading Law*, 65–67.
16. See Miller, *Deuteronomy*, 55.

arbitrary set of laws but to enable them to experience the fullness of life in relationship.

The most basic motivation given Israel for obeying the law is drawn from its narrative experience with God as deliverer: "Remember that you were a slave in the land of Egypt" (e.g., Deut 24:18, 22). Because of God's stance towards the disadvantaged Israel must also shape its life toward the disadvantaged in ways both compassionate and just. God's saving deeds call forth this grateful response from Israel. For what is Israel to be grateful? Most basically, it is the gift of life, and obedience to law extends that gift out into all the highways and byways of the community. [194]

6. God's giving of the law, understood in vocational terms, means that God has chosen to use human agents in carrying out the divine purposes in the world. God moves over, as it were, and gives to the human an important role to play in taking initiative and assuming responsibility for the world of which it is a part, including furthering the cause of justice and good order in Israel and the larger creation. God is the kind of God who has chosen not to do everything "all by himself."

7. Given these comments about the law, let me interact briefly with statements about God made by two scholars who have been very helpful in developing our thinking about the law.

James W. Watts, in his excellent book, *Reading Law: The Rhetorical Shaping of the Pentateuch,* makes certain claims regarding the God of the law that are sometimes problematic.[17] He states: "Because Yʜᴡʜ rules in Israel, fidelity and obedience is demanded and enforced."[18] But this kind of formulation implies an unacceptable purpose for God's giving laws to Israel. It is as if God reasoned, "I'm king and you're my subjects, and hence you are obligated to obey me." God's purpose in giving the law looks quite different if understood in more creational and relational terms. That is, God gives the law and commands obedience for the sake of the life and well-being of the creatures, not out of a self-serving notion that the people *must* obey because God is, after all, their ruler.[19]

Bernard Levinson, in his article, "The Human Voice in Divine Revelation: The Problem of Authority in Biblical Law," asks some rhetorical questions about the God of the law that are also problematic: "Once a

---

17. Watts, *Reading Law,* 91–109, claims that the primary metaphor for the God who gives the law is "just king." He draws this conclusion primarily on the basis of certain parallels with ancient Near Eastern law texts. He recognizes that kingship language for God in the Pentateuch is rare, but that recognition should have proved decisive in rejecting such a primary metaphor. If Israel did borrow legal ideas, conventions, genres, etc., it is remarkable that they did *not* bring the royal language along with it. The most likely reason is that Israel did not find royal images particularly helpful in thinking about their relationship with God. This is borne out by the uncommon use of this imagery in the rest of the Old Testament, where it is used primarily in contexts relating to other nations.

18. Ibid., 108.

19. See also the comments in n. 4 above.

law is attributed to God, how can it be superseded, which is to say, annulled, without the prestige or authority of the divine law being thereby impaired? . . . Could one imagine, for that matter, that the divine himself should suddenly deem inadequate one of his own rules?"[20] These questions assume that the will of God (and God?) is immutable, at least as revealed in the law. [195] But on what grounds is such a claim made? Why would a divine change in God's own law be considered problematic for either the law or God?[21] Would it not be much more problematic for both God and the law if God were not able to revise God's own law or to choose to set one or more laws aside in view of new needs in the people's lives? God's (and the law's) "prestige" and "authority" are more tied up with the divine ability to know what is best for people's lives, not the ability to put laws in place that never need changing. It might be noted that the *historical* recognition on the part of most scholars that the canon reveals an ongoing revision of God's own law has probably enhanced the divine reputation, not damaged it.

Law and Spirit

One of the more striking characteristics of the book of Deuteronomy is the passion and energy with which the law is set forth. The parenetic form of presentation ("preached law") addresses the reader directly. This spirit in which the law is presented reveals a dynamic understanding of law that often entails a degree of open-endedness. For example, Deut 15:7–11 speaks of the treatment of the poor in the language of spirit rather than letter: "do not be hard-hearted and tight-fisted toward your needy neighbor; you should rather open your hand, willingly lending enough to meet the need"; "give liberally and be ungrudging when you do so"; "open your hand to the poor and needy neighbor in your land."

This hortatory language is not related in a literal way to the actual law regarding remission of debts (15:1–3). Rather, the language urges readers to *interpret* the law and even go *beyond the law* (e.g., "give liberally"; "enough to meet the need"). Once this rhetoric is introduced into the text, then what it takes for individuals (or the community) to obey the law becomes a somewhat open-ended matter, subject to interpretation (for example, "liberally" is not defined and discerning what is "enough" to meet the need is left open). The laws regarding the less advantaged are often generally stated (e.g., Exod 22:21–24); what it means to care for them entails the use of

---

20. Bernard Levinson, "The Human Voice in Divine Revelation: The Problem of Authority in Biblical Law," in *Innovation in Religious Traditions* (ed. M. Williams et al.; Berlin: de Gruyter, 1992), 45.

21. It might be noted that there are many texts in the Old Testament where the divine will changes in view of changing human circumstances, especially regarding announcements of judgment (e.g., Exod 32:14; 2 Kgs 20:1–7; Jer 26:18–19).

the imagination (Exod 22:25–28 may provide an illustration of the general principle articulated in the prior verses).

Revision of Law within the Pentateuch

The literary history of Pentateuchal law is ostensibly denied by the attribution of all law to God in the wilderness setting. Levinson in his penetrating study of Deuteronomy seeks to uncover the human voice that lies [196] beneath the surface of the text. While some aspects of Levinson's proposal are problematic, his work opens up new avenues for conversation.[22] He speaks of a "rhetoric of concealment" in Deuteronomy whereby, through various literary devices, changes in the law are deliberately camouflaged through a variety of literary means, not least casting the whole in terms of its ancient Mosaic setting. They employed "the garb of dependence [on the Covenant Code] to purchase profound hermeneutical independence."[23] While the text of Deuteronomy presents the law in terms of the divine voice, Levinson's proposal reveals the concealed human voice in the material. His proposal joins other analyses of the text that give evidence for ongoing human involvement in the development of law.

I would like to pick up on a somewhat isolated statement by Levinson regarding the juncture between his historical work and the canonical shape of the law; he calls the inclusion of both the Covenant Code and Deuteronomy within the Pentateuch "a major irony of literary history."[24] In other words, the canonical process has given a status to the Book of the Covenant that the Deuteronomic authors would not have shared. Whatever one may think of Levinson's historical proposal, that Deuteronomy has been placed on a canonical continuum that includes older law, that very fact indicates that Deuteronomic law is considered a revision of prior law and has in turn been opened up for further revision.

---

22. See Levinson, *Deuteronomy*. For Levinson, the Deuteronomic authors assert their freedom to revise the canonical law, but sense that they must do so "under the table," so to speak. They assume that their program would not be acceptable in Israel if presented in a straightforward way. Is it clear that they could not have done this more openly? Or, from another angle, who is fooling whom? In addition, if the Deuteronomists sensed that they could do this only in a subversive way, as Levinson claims, where from within Israel came the understanding that this would be an appropriate thing to do? If God had spoken in a prior generation, and this was generally recognized in Israel, whence their theological moxie that they felt that they could *completely* abrogate that earlier divine word? Levinson skirts the danger of making the Deuteronomists into religious charlatans; they camouflage their innovations "by feigning a cunning piety with respect to the very authoritative texts that they had subverted" (p. 48). The Deuteronomists are "subversives," religiously intolerant and "tendentious" folk, who sought to "silence," indeed "eliminate" the opposition, defining their new vision as normative while regarding the existing legal traditions as "odious" and "deviant" (p. 144–50). Such judgments on the prior tradition seem unlikely and, in any case, the final form of the canon declares otherwise.

23. Ibid., 149.

24. Ibid., 153 (cf. p. 94).

Notably, the inconsistencies in the laws are not ironed out in the canonical form. What if one worked with the assumption that these inconsistencies are a plus and are revealing of a complex understanding of the development of law *within* the canonical shape of things? This dynamic understanding of the law may be demonstrated by a comparison of law texts [197] to one another. A long-recognized example are the changes that Deuteronomy makes with respect to the laws in the Book of the Covenant in view of new times and places (changes in Leviticus and Numbers could also be noted).[25] These changes are not explicitly acknowledged in Deuteronomy (hence Levinson's proposal), but readers of the final form of the Pentateuch would recognize them as such.

To illustrate this situation, two texts may be cited. The Ten Commandments, redactionally placed at a crucial position in both Exodus and Deuteronomy, introduce the two major bodies of law in the Pentateuch. Given their standing, it is striking that the Deuteronomic version varies from that in Exodus; the changes are minor, but that they exist at all is important. The coveting commandment(s) is notable, with the interchange of "house" and "wife" (Exod 20:17; Deut 5:21); this change may reflect a change in the status of women in Israelite society (and any contemporary revision would make sure that the "neighbor" is no longer only the male!). This change may be related to a more significant revision in the slavery laws where, for example, Deuteronomy does not distinguish between treatment of male and female slaves in their manumission whereas Exodus does (cf. Deut 15:1–18, esp. v. 17, with Exod 21:2–11, esp. vv. 2, 9).

This recognition of inner-biblical development in the law is of considerable import, not only for understanding biblical law but also for postbiblical developments. The tensions and inconsistencies in the law texts are testimony to the ongoing, unresting divine effort to link the law to life in ever new times and places. Watts says it well, "Contradiction in Pentateuchal law . . . authorizes legal change as a natural part of Torah."[26] Because God is the author of all these laws, Israel's legal traditions "cast God as the principal instigator of change within law."[27] If these law texts were (are) all smoothed over, then they would be testimony to an immutable law for which new times and places were irrelevant. The very roughness of the material is an ongoing witness to the changing character of life and the changing character of the will of God as it relates to that life. And so *development in the law* is just as canonical as individual laws or the various collections of law. God's will for Israel is understood to be a living will. God moves with this people on their life's journey and God's will for them changes because they are changing. For God's will to be linked to life in

---

25. Dale Patrick, *Old Testament Law* (Atlanta: John Knox, 1985), 97, lists twenty-two instances.
26. Watts, *Reading Law*, 119.
27. Ibid., 104.

such a central way makes the law an even more gracious gift than it would be if understood as immutable. [198]

Even more, the Pentateuch's *preservation of older law alongside newer law is* an important matter to consider. Leaving the Book of the Covenant stand in the canon in its given form along with Deuteronomy is not considered a threat to the law's integrity; rather, old law and new law remain side by side as a canonical witness to the process of unfolding law. At the same time, all laws remain God's laws—older laws from God and newer laws from God—and hence cannot be declared devoid of value. As such, the Book of the Covenant maintains its value for ongoing legal reflection and innovation. This means that in moving toward any new formulation of law, every word from God was thought to need careful consideration. In revising the law it was deemed necessary to go back over all the laws from God; it was precisely in the imaginative interaction of older laws and current laws that new laws were generated for changing times and places. As such, Pentateuchal law unfolds in a way comparable to the ways in which new law is developed in our own time, where older laws that are no longer "on the books" continue to be a resource for legal reflection.

And so, instead of an immutable, timeless law in the Pentateuch, we have preserved for us a developing process in which experience in every sphere of life over time is drawn into the orbit of the law and preserved for the consideration of successive generations. For the sake of the best life possible!

The New Testament Witness to This Pattern

The New Testament texts pick up on this Old Testament witness to a dynamic, unfolding law. The New Testament community doesn't simply accept every Old Testament law as binding law; it works through the laws in a variety of ways in view of the new situations in which it finds itself (e.g., Acts 15:1–35; note especially vv. 28–29). As such, it follows a trajectory already set by the Old Testament community.[28] The New Testament thereby provides a broad pattern for interpretation and sets an agenda for both church and society in its ongoing consideration of Old Testament laws.

For example, the laws regarding clean and unclean food are rethought (e.g., Mark 7:1–23; Acts 10:1–16) and the result is that older laws regarding these matters now have a different standing in the canon for Christians. At the same time, the food laws have not been cut out of the canon or declared of no value. They remain the laws of God for an ancient time and place, but they have an ongoing import precisely because of that. They served life at [199] one time and it remains to be asked; how might the most basic concerns that inform the food laws continue to be of value for contemporary life? One may well look to contemporary food laws designed

---

28. Patrick Miller's reflections on this "trajectory" in both of the works cited in the note on p. 183 have been important for my thinking about relationships between Old Testament and New on matters of law.

to preserve life and health as descendants of that ancient biblical concern (e.g., the Food and Drug Administration). I would argue that every law of God continues to have value for contemporary communities *at some level.*

V. A Point of Contemporary Significance

Over the course of the last two centuries much blood has been spilled over the question of the continuing applicability of particular Old Testament laws. In the nineteenth century, disagreement over texts regarding slavery spawned conflict and split communities, churches, and families. In more recent times, disagreement over law texts regarding homosexual behavior threatens to do the same. In my estimation, these conflicts have not been accompanied by much sophistication in understanding how to work with these and other laws. However well-intentioned, such argumentation is all too often a cut-and-paste enterprise.

The post-biblical formulation of new laws by human beings should be seen as being in tune with the divine intention regarding creational life and well-being evident in biblical law. Because these ever-emerging laws, however, are usually associated with legislatures, courts, arid church assemblies, and developed by human beings, we tend not to think of them as God's laws; but of course they are (see, e.g., Rom 13:1–7). It may well be that some of these newer laws will stand over against their biblical predecessors, but this would be not unlike their biblical predecessors in, say, Deuteronomy.

The above discussion of inner-biblical development in the law—as much a canonical reality as the laws themselves—may provide a canonical warrant for thinking through post-biblical developments in the law in a new way. Interpreters should not make a blanket statement about all biblical laws, as if they were all equally applicable or obsolete; we are called to study each and every law seeking to discern whether it continues to serve the life and health of the community and see what might come of that conversation. While the New Testament has done some of that work for us regarding Old Testament laws, we are called to do a careful and thorough consideration of *all* biblical law, to think through God's purpose in giving it and to read back through it for insights it may continue to provide in moving toward new formulations. It is precisely in the interaction of older words from God and newer words from God, words that may stand in tension with one another, that revisions or abrogations of law are determined and new laws are developed. [200]

If it is granted that the biblical law texts witness to a dynamic process of revising law in view of new times and places, then that testimony provides an important canonical basis for considering every biblical law as open to revision, but without treating any one of them with disdain. This way of thinking about biblical law may change attitudes toward the law and, I might add, toward the God who has so graciously given us such a dynamic law for the sake of life.

Part 6

God and the Prophets

Divine Foreknowledge, Divine Constancy, and the Rejection of Saul's Kingship

Much scholarly ink has been spilled trying to make sense of the divine-repentance theme in 1 Samuel 15.[1] There are two primary issues. From one perspective, it is often thought that the picture of God in these verses is less than laudable, to say the least. What kind of God is it who would choose Saul to be king and then, for seemingly little reason, change that choice? One way of moving through this issue, hitherto unexplored to my knowledge, is to focus on the matter of divine foreknowledge. What if God did not know with certitude what would happen with the kingship in Saul's hands? I have tried to show elsewhere that this limited divine knowledge of the future is a basic substratum of much, if not all, OT thought.[2]

From another perspective, it is often thought that the chapter is incoherent. It moves from the repentance of God (vv. 10–11) to an affirmation [596] that God does not repent (vv. 28–29), and then it returns to repentance in v. 35.[3] It is almost as if God cannot make up his mind to change his mind. This has occasioned not a few attempts on the part of scholars to bring their own sense of order into the text.[4] But, whatever development

---

This essay was originally published in *Catholic Biblical Quarterly* 44 (1985): 595–602.

1. There has been much recent discussion of the Saul cycle, much of which can be considered a development of the insights of G. von Rad, *Old Testament Theology* (New York: Harper & Row, 1962), 1:324–27. Especially important is the work of D. Gunn, *The Fate of King Saul* (JSOTSup 14; Sheffield: JSOT Press, 1980). See also B. Birch, *The Rise of the Israelite Monarchy: The Growth and Development of I Samuel 7–15* (SBLDS 27; Missoula, MT: Scholars Press, 1976); R. Knierim, "The Messianic Concept in the First Book of Samuel," in *Jesus and the Historian* (ed. T. Trotter; Philadelphia: Westminster, 1968), 20–52; D. Jobling, *The Sense of Biblical Narrative* (JSOTSup 7; Sheffield: JSOT Press, 1978). One might also cite three articles on the Saul cycle by W. Lee Humphreys: "The Tragedy of King Saul," *JSOT* 6 (1978): 18–27; "The Rise and Fall of King Saul," *JSOT* 18 (1980): 74–90; "From Tragic Hero to Villain," *JSOT* 22 (1982): 95–117.

2. See T. Fretheim, *The Suffering of God: An Old Testament Perspective* (Philadelphia: Fortress, 1984), 45–59.

3. The only monograph-length treatment of this theme is Jörg Jeremias, *Die Reue Gottes: Aspekte der alttestamentliche Gottesvorstellung* (BibS[N] 65; Neukirchen-Vluyn; Neukirchener Verlag, 1975). See also H. van Dyke Parunak, "A Semantic Survey of *nhm*," *Bib* 56 (1975): 512–32; H. J. Stoebe, "*nhm*," *THAT* 2:59–66; L. Kuyper, "The Suffering and Repentance of God," *SJT* 22 (1969): 257–77; J. Hempel, "Gottes Selbstbeherrschung als Problem des Monotheismus und der Eschatologie," in *Gottes Wort und Gottes Land* (FS H.-W. Hertzberg; ed. H. G. Reventlow; Göttingen: Vandenhoeck & Ruprecht, 1965), 56–61. The various OT theologies give only passing treatment to the repentance of God, if at all.

4. See, e.g., P. K. McCarter, Jr, *I Samuel* (AB 8; Garden City, NY: Doubleday, 1980), 268; A. Weiser ("1 Samuel 15," *ZAW* 54 [1936]: 4–5) considers vv. 25–30a secondary. R. Klein

267

these materials may have undergone, I believe that clear and straightforward sense can be made of them in their present context. The key is to be found in the nature of divine constancy.

As G. von Rad has noted,[5] it is important to keep in mind that the stories about Saul are written with an eye cocked for the one who is to come—David. Put simply, these stories are written from a later perspective.[6] Certain basic questions seem to inform the thought of those responsible for putting these traditions into their present form. There were, of course, such realities as the fact that kings were traced from David, not from Saul, and that God's rejection of Saul's kingship was therefore final and unconditional. 2 Sam 7:15 seems to point the way to the heart of the concerns nurtured by a writer of a later generation: ". . . but I will not take my steadfast love from him, as I took it from Saul, whom I put away from before you."[7] The unconditionality of the promise to David is set specifically over against the situation prevailing in Saul's case. [597]

While one might trace this material back to circles concerned for the legitimacy of the Davidic dynasty,[8] the emphasis in 2 Sam 7:15 is not on legitimacy, but on what might be the effect of the Davidic king's sinfulness, given what happened to Saul. The divine rejection of the kingship of Saul (note, not a rejection of the person of Saul), though not without motivation, must have been considered somewhat extraordinary for it to have been mentioned in just this way. It seems to have occasioned questions such as the following. Could the divine freedom evident in God's rejection of Saul's kingship also become operative with respect to the Davidic kingship? Given the fact that members of the Davidic dynasty had, like Saul, "rejected the word of the Lord" (vv. 23, 24, 26), was it not possible that God would reject the Davidides as he had rejected Saul as king? Given the fact that prayer and repentance were not effective in turning back the divine decision with respect to Saul (vv. 11, 24–25, 30), was it not possible that such means would be equally ineffective with respect to the members of

---

(*1 Samuel* [WBC 10; Waco, TX: Word, 1983], 155–56) treats the chapter as a unity, but chooses to leave the tension unresolved.

5. Von Rad, *Old Testament Theology*, 1:325.

6. Various theories regarding date have been suggested. See Birch, *Rise of Israelite Monarchy*, 152–53; Humphreys, "From Tragic Hero to Villain," 107–9. Pro- and antimonarchical perspectives seem not to be in order in any consideration of this chapter. At the very least, the chapter is not informed by an anti-Saul perspective, see Birch, *Rise of Israelite Monarchy*, 106. The surrounding of the passage with a very powerful note of grief, the full opportunity given Saul to explain his behavior, and the clear distinction made between Saul's failure as king and his continuing faith in God—all cast the passage in a sympathetic hue, rather than in black and white. Such sympathy may explain in part why some interpreters are able to detect some imbalance between Saul's disobedience and his rejection as king.

7. The fact that the parallel in 1 Chr 17:13 does not mention Saul specifically suggests that this issue is no longer of the same magnitude in the community.

8. So Jeremias, *Die Reue Gottes*, 32–33.

the Davidic dynasty? Something very much like the situation of Psalm 89 needs to be envisaged as the context for this chapter in its present form. That this approach to the text is justified seems borne out by parallels other than 2 Sam 7:15. But we must first take a closer look at 1 Sam 15:29: "And also the Glory of Israel will not lie[9] or repent, for he is not a man, that he should repent." Although it is sometimes claimed that this verse intends to make clear to the insistent Saul that God will not change his mind regarding his rejection as king,[10] it almost certainly has reference to David.[11]

Verse 28 states that God has taken the kingdom from Saul and given it to David; v. 29 then proceeds to speak to this particular action of God: With regard to the giving of the kingdom to David, this is a matter concerning which God will not repent, come what may. Then, as if to give a reason to those who might wonder about such a decision in the light of what has happened to Saul, Samuel says, in effect: Unlike the fickleness so characteristic of human action, God has made a decision with respect to David, and with respect to that decision God will not repent. This statement, therefore, does not have general reference to God as one who never repents with regard to anything. Rather, it has reference to God's decision to give the kingdom to [598] David. That decision is irrevocable. God has chosen to limit his options in this regard. The point is not that God's repentance is a divine action which is not to be repeated ever again in any situation;[12] the point is that God's repentance regarding the promise to David is foreclosed. There may well be other persons and actions concerning which God will repent of a promised good (cf. Jer 18:9–10).

The other two passages that have reference to God not repenting of a certain matter also pertain almost certainly to the Davidic kingship.[13] Ps 110:4, "The Lord has sworn and will not repent, 'You are a priest forever after the order of Melchizedek,'" while perhaps speaking to a special

---

9. See Ps 89:35 (English verse enumeration; 89:36 in MT), which indicates that this word was used in Davidic covenant contexts.

10. So McCarter, *I Samuel*, 268.

11. See Jeremias, *Die Reue Gottes*, 32–34. The repentance-parallels to be noted below are centered around promise and David; see also 1 Kgs 11:11–13. If this statement referred to Saul, it would be a general reference regarding divine repentance and would thus stand in contradiction to vv. 11 and 35. If, however, it has specific reference to God's decision to give the kingdom to David, it can have a future reference with respect to this particular matter.

12. So ibid., 35–36. Generally, the idea of divine repentance is not as extreme an idea as Jeremias would have us believe (see p. 37) This conclusion results in a very negative judgment of Jeremiah 18 by Jeremias (see pp. 38–39).

13. A distinction needs to be made between God's not repenting of certain matters and God's not repenting on certain occasions. The latter set of passages almost all have reference to God's not relenting with respect to the judgment of 587 B.C. (see Jer 4:28) and are thus applicable only to that situation, with no binding of God to a commitment beyond that. In the commitment not to repent regarding a certain matter, God binds himself to stand by it for all time.

aspect of the kingship, in effect affirms the eternal nature of the dynasty.[14] Num 23:19, "God is not a man, that he should lie, or a son of man, that he should repent," is also generally recognized as having Davidic connections.[15] Given the certain concern for the Davidic dynasty in the larger context of the Balaam speeches (Num 24:7, 17–19; cf. 23:21), this passage may well be intended as a word which roots the irrevocable promise to Davidic Israel in the constitutive era of Israel's life.

The use of *šûb*, *šbʿ*, and *sûr* in similar contexts suggests that we have to do with a semantic field related to the Davidic covenant of which "God does not repent" is an integral part. Thus, Ps 132:11, "The Lord swore to David a sure oath, from which he will not turn back [*šûb*]," assures that one of David's sons will succeed him on the throne.[16] The use of *šbʿ* in Pss 110:4 and 132:11 also suggests that the phrasing is a semantic equivalent for "will not repent" (see also especially 2 Sam 3:9–10; Ps 89:3, 35, 49).[17] Finally, it might [599] be noted that *sûr* is used in these same contexts, so that "will not turn (depart)" is the semantic equivalent of "do not repent" as well (see 2 Sam 7:15; 1 Chr 17:13; 1 Sam 16:14; 18:12; 28:15–17).[18]

1 Samuel 15 is thus shaped by those who would deny that one can draw any conclusions regarding the Davidic dynasty on the basis of extrapolations made from God's relationship to Saul's kingship. The situation has changed. Indeed, God made an unconditional commitment to David, which means that God has given up the kind of freedom displayed in the rejection of Saul's kingship. The relinquishment of freedom in a given sphere is, of course, entailed in any statement of promise. While the kingship of Saul was explicitly conditioned by the obedience of both king and people (1 Sam 12:14–15, 25),[19] the kingship of David was not. God placed the kingship on an entirely new footing compared to that of Saul.

---

14. Space does not permit a discussion of the relationship of this passage to Gen 14:18 and the pre-Davidic priest-kingship of Jerusalem within which David is here said to stand.

15. See Jeremias, *Die Reue Gottes*, 33–34.

16. Ps 132:12 conditions accession beyond that to at least some extent. It is likely that this unusual condition is to be interpreted in the light of 1 Kgs 11:11–13, 31–39, especially v. 35. That is to say, the stress in Ps 132:12 may well be on "your throne" (that is, the entire kingdom), which, in the light of 1 Kings 11, is divided. Thus the "sons" rule over only a portion of the Davidic kingdom as a result of Solomonic disobedience. See T. Fretheim, *Deuteronomic History* (Nashville, TN: Abingdon, 1983), 112. See also R. Nelson, *The Double Redaction of the Deuteronomistic History* (JSOTSup 18; Sheffield: JSOT Press, 1981), 99–118.

17. On *šbʿ*, see also Deut 4:31; Judg 2:1; Isa 14:24; Mic 7:20.

18. On *sûr*, see Isa 54:10; Ps 66:20, where it is applied to an individual; see also Isa 31:2, which is a specific, contextual statement and not a general affirmation.

19. It should be observed more often that the "burden" of obedience does not fall only upon Saul. The future of his kingship is made conditional upon the obedience of the people as well; see 1 Sam 12:14–15. While the focus is rightly on Saul as the anointed one, so that his disobedience provides the center of attention, first in the rejection of his dynasty (13:13–14) and then in the rejection of himself as king (15:28), the sinful role of the people (and Saul's acquiescence thereto, 15:24) is also seen to play a part in these developments (see 13:6–8, 11; 14:33; 15:21, 24).

Why? Because God learned something from the experience (and experiment) with Saul.

It is striking how much recent literature has raised the issue of divine fair play in this regard.[20] Was not God unduly harsh with Saul, even petty? Why should David be favored with such an unconditional promise and not Saul?[21] Such an objection seems to presuppose an understanding of God not compatible with these narratives. That is, it is assumed that God could [600] clearly see what the outcome of Saul's kingship would be. God, however, could only see the possibilities. If the alternatives offered in 1 Sam 12:14–15 are indeed genuine possibilities, then the future is open. If the negative possibility is known in advance, then to hold out the positive possibility is a deception of Saul and the people. For each of these options to have integrity, they must both be understood to be possibilities, and only possibilities.

The conditioning of Saul's kingship, along with strictures related thereto, was related to the special circumstances surrounding the rise of the kingship and the concern that Israelite kingship would go the way of all the nations. If this occurred, it would entail the compromise or outright rejection of the divine kingship (see 1 Sam 8:7–9, 19–20; 10:25; 12:14–15, 24–25). Safeguards were called for in the light of the situation, and the ground rules established were clear to all, including Saul.[22] In a quite remarkable

---

20. Gunn and Humphreys, in particular, have emphasized this. Humphreys ("From Tragic Hero to Villain," 100, 106) even speaks of a "savage God" who is revealed in at least one level of this passage; see also n. 23 below. One is given to wonder, however, whether that is actually an aspect of the God revealed in the text, or whether scholars have more personal theological problems with the way in which the God of the text speaks and acts. There seems to be an inordinate amount of interest in these studies in portraying the "tragic" character of the story, in lifting up Saul as an unwitting victim of circumstances beyond his control; see n. 22 below. It seems to me that the story is here being pushed into a literary mold that simply is not there.

21. One item commonly mentioned is the apparent lack of positive divine response to Saul's twice-affirmed repentance (15:24, 30). But it is important not to cast this matter in inappropriate terms. The OT always makes a clean distinction between forgiveness and salvation (see Isa 40:1; 2 Sam 12:13–14), between forgiveness and the effects forgiveness may have upon the life of the forgiven. The effects of forgiveness depend upon the depths of the situation of evil in which the forgiven find themselves. While the text does not explicitly say whether Saul is pardoned or not, such forgiveness, if it did occur, would not necessarily have entailed the socio-political effect of the return of the kingship to Saul; see n. 6 above.

22. Knierim ("Messianic Concept," passim) especially points out that the issue at stake here does not relate to Saul as human being, but to Saul as the anointed one of God (note that 15:1, 17 set the parameters for this chapter, cf. 9:16; 10:1). Thus, certain expectations are set for him, of which he is aware, that are not expected of, e.g., Jonathan (see 14:45). 1 Sam 15:22–23 focuses precisely on the point of the rejection of the Word of the Lord. The text is very clear on this point (cf. 15:11). Given the level of Saul's awareness of the expectations, Gunn's attempt (*Fate,* 124) to show that his rejection is "radically out of balance with the nature of his 'crimes'" is not commensurate with the assumptions of the text, cf. Moses' not being allowed entry into the land. To suggest that Saul is somehow "fated" to this end has no basis in the text either. It is Saul's failure, he *could* have succeeded. He

consent to the desires and argumentation of the people, God himself ends up initiating the monarchy (see 1 Sam 9:16–17; 10:1; 12:13; cf. 8:7, 22) as the best way to proceed in Saul's time and place.

This picture of divine acquiescence and initiation reveals a God who is anything but legalistic, or unwilling to compromise, or insistent upon his own way.[23] God moves with the people; God is willing to try new directions; God takes the people's point of view into consideration in determining the shape of the future. It is clear from a remarkable variety of OT passages that God takes into account human thought and action in moving into the future (see Exod 32:11–14; Num 14:11–20).[24] It is this view of God which is the decisive one for the entire Saul narrative; for without it, Saul's kingship [601] would not have existed, at least from the point of view of the narrator. This is also the way to understand Samuel's response to God in 1 Sam 15:11. He was seeking to persuade God to take another course with Saul. God had given Samuel an opportunity to respond before the decision became irrevocable. The extensive narrative which follows may be seen as Samuel's attempt to discern the appropriateness of the divine decision and to make matters clear to Saul.

Given what has happened to the conditionally established kingship of Saul, God determines that only a new tack will have a chance of succeeding, viz., an unconditional commitment to the Davidic king. Now there will be only unconditioned promises. It is of great importance to recognize that God's primary concern in all of this is for the future of *Israel* (cf. 1 Sam 9:16; 10:1; 12:22). Saul's disobedience and other unkingly behavior may not seem to our minds to be sufficient justification for the divine rejection. But chaps. 13–15 (cf. 1 Sam 28:18) would seem to be concerned to chart a trend or direction in the nature of Saul's kingship (chap. 14 has a number of references to Saul's ineptitude as king). It is possible that the whole people would be swept away (12:14–15, 25) if this pattern in the kingship were allowed to continue. It thus becomes necessary to intervene in the situation before it gets out of hand, i.e., before the pattern of Saul's disobedience gets to such a point that *not even God* could retrieve the situation and start again with this people.[25] God has made a commitment to the

---

is no "innocent victim" (Gunn, *Fate,* 123). Knierim ("Messianic Concept," 38) speaks of a "radically defined messianology" at work here. Yet, while this may have been true with Saul, God proceeds in a new direction with David, with more limited expectations.

23. It might also be noted here that Samuel is often judged in similar terms. But the sustained grief of Samuel for Saul (see especially 16:1), his efforts to dissuade God (v. 11), and his full exploration of the circumstances before the matter is finalized, belies any view of Samuel which considers him to be harsh and sharply anti-Saul in his orientation (contra Gunn and Humphreys). Verse 31 is also sympathetic, following as it does upon a confession of Saul which does not place significant blame upon the people (in contrast to vv. 24–25).

24. See Fretheim, *Suffering,* 49–53.

25. See n. 21 above.

people in which God himself has a stake (cf. 1 Sam 12:22, "for the sake of his name"). It may therefore be said that Saul suffers for the sake of this overriding concern, and thus his kingship could be said to have a positive value. In some sense he is a "scapegoat" for *Israel's* insistence on trying this new way. The kingship of Saul must go if the people are to survive.

This narrative, then, is a vivid testimony to the *historical* character of God's activity in the world, both in what God does to initiate the kingship in the first place and in the changes God makes in view of new circumstances. God works with what is available at any moment, with human beings as they are, with all their foibles and flaws, and within existing societal structures and possibilities, however inadequate. But God does not only "make do" with what is there to work with; at the same time God places a high level of confidence in the human instruments chosen—in this case Saul, as well as the people. God's activity is thus conditioned and limited by such structures, which in turn are always changing, and with which God needs to move as well, given the way in which he has chosen to relate to the world. We would [602] thus have to speak of divine self-limitations with respect to his exercise of power in the world.[26]

This divine way of working is also a testimony to how God subjects himself to extreme vulnerability. God goes along with the people in their desire for the kingship, and by so doing opens himself up to criticism, even failure. For if the kingship does not work because of human or structural failure (and God knows that this *may* happen), then God too is made to "look bad" (this is the truthful element in D. Gunn's approach to the text) and will have to start all over again with the possibilities inherent in the new situation. The factors that determine God's decisions and actions are not always fathomable, but they are always motivated by the best interests of those involved. The shift from Saul to David, from the conditional to the unconditional promise, shows not only what God has learned, and how God adjusts in view of such learning,[27] but also how those who are heirs to the Davidic promise have reaped the benefits of this divine readjustment.

---

26. See Fretheim, *Suffering*, 71–78.

27. Gunn (*Fate*, 123) speaks of God's "transition in attitude," an appropriate direction of thought if properly defined ("attitude" is an inexact term, to say the least). Such a change, however, is not capricious, but is dictated by the circumstances. To speak of Saul as "kingship's scapegoat," as a means by which God demonstrates the weakness of human kingship and vindicates his initial hostility to the kingship, flies in the face of God's stated objectives with respect to the kingship of Saul (9:16 10:1). The text must certainly be taking God's moves here as properly motivated (contra Gunn [ibid., 124] God is not "predisposed to reject him as king") and in Israel's best interests. One may well agree with Gunn that the "dark side" of God is revealed here, but to suggest that this is a "merciless manipulation" of Saul with "less than honorable motives" goes far beyond the text. "Dark side" talk needs to be balanced by the clarity with which the text as a whole speaks of God's faithfulness in pursuing goals which are in the best interests of Israel and its future (see 9:16; 10:1; 12:22, and the deuteronomic history as a whole).

The Prophets and Social Justice: A Conservative *Agenda*

The prophetic word about social justice is often associated with liberal causes. Indeed, the prophets are sometimes depicted as if they were free-floating radicals from the '60s! This may in part explain the not uncommon negative reaction to discussions of social justice and related sociopolitical considerations in the church—especially in the sermon! In the face of such opinions, it must be emphasized: the prophets were fundamentally conservative (and public!) in their approach to these issues. The prophets discerned that social justice was a long-established value, richly embedded in the traditions they inherited, though often neglected. Generally speaking, the prophets were deeply indebted to their ethical and theological past, one key dimension of which had to do with social justice.[1]

This point is made convincingly in a somewhat neglected article by James Barr:

> Certainly it is true that the prophets insisted on social justice, and they were not afraid in its name to challenge the established authorities of their time. But the prophets for the most part were not reformers, and they had no new insights into [160] the working of society to offer. Theirs was not a novel analysis, on the ground of which new perceptions of social need might arise, from which in turn demands for righteousness and mercy in new dimensions might be heard. On the contrary, in this respect *the social perspectives and perceptions of the prophets were essentially conservative. . . .* Their message was not a new morality. . . . In other words, the traditional liberal and reformist perception that the system is wrong and that the system has to be changed if justice is to be possible is lacking from the prophetic perspective. Practically never do we find the prophets putting forward any sort of practical suggestions for change in the structure of society.[2]

This essay was originally published in *Word and World* 28 (2008): 159–68.

1. It should be made clear that the prophets seldom accuse Israel of breaking specific laws; rather, they "appeal to known norms of humane conduct, of 'justice and righteousness,' norms which are exemplified in the 'apodictic law,' but cannot be limited by it." So Walter J. Houston, *Contending for Justice: Ideologies and Theologies of Social Justice in the Old Testament* (London: T. & T. Clark, 2006), 70–71.

2. James Barr, "The Bible as a Political Document," *Bulletin of the John Rylands Library* 62 (1980): 278–279 (emphasis added). Without reference to Barr, J. David Pleins, *The Social Visions of the Hebrew Bible: A Theological Introduction* (Louisville: Westminster John Knox, 2001), makes a related statement: "Indeed, the major drawback to adopting a so-called prophetic critique, as is so popular in some circles today, is that the prophetic literature

It is not that the prophets had nothing new to say about social justice, but their radicality consisted more in their rhetorical strategy than their ideas, in their forceful and intense way of speaking older understandings into a new time and place, and by the remarkable way in which they got "in your face" with respect to long-standing communal commitments. Listen to these texts:

> And the LORD said to me. . . . "Hear this, you that trample on the needy and bring to ruin the poor of the land!" (Amos 7:15; 8:4)

> "What do you mean by crushing my people, by grinding the face of the poor?" says the Lord GOD of hosts. (Isa 3:15)

> "Should you not know justice?—you who hate the good and love the evil, who tear the skin off my people, and the flesh off their bones; who eat the flesh of my people, flay their skin off them, break their bones in pieces, and chop them up like meat in a kettle, like flesh in a caldron." (Mic 3:1–3)

> "For scoundrels are found among my people; they take over the goods of others. Like fowlers they set a trap; they catch human beings. . . . They know no limits in deeds of wickedness; they do not judge with justice the cause of the orphan, to make it prosper, and they do not defend the rights of the needy. Shall I not punish them for these things?" says the LORD. (Jer 5:26–29)[3]

Nothing fundamentally new is presented in these texts (see, e.g., Exod 22:21–24). But the remarkably uncompromising and "get under your skin" images of the writing prophets and the fervor and candor with which they address specific issues give them a new force. From another angle, unless these social justice concerns of the prophets were reasonably well known by their audiences (from whatever source), their message would have been obscure, even unintelligible, and they could be faulted for seeking to hold people responsible to unknown or little-known standards.

More generally, the prophets believed that issues of social justice were public [161] matters and they voiced these concerns in the public square to their "congregations"; these issues were not simply a matter of private morality. This approach was much disputed by the prophets' audiences, who complained (in remarkably familiar language!): "'Do not preach'—thus they preach—'one should not preach of such things'"! (Mic 2:6).

The public character of their preaching is one of the distinguishing marks of the writing prophets (beginning with Amos) as over against their forebears (e.g., Nathan or Elijah): they addressed themselves publicly to

---

often fails to advocate the kind of concrete mechanisms that would be necessary for the alleviation of poverty in society" (p. 78).

3. When I have read these texts out loud to students and others, the silence in the room is often palpable.

the entire community, not just to individuals (usually kings). Moreover, these prophets believed that the future of their communities was at stake; *communal* judgment was commonly envisaged by them as a possibility or even a certainty.[4] Issues of social justice were understood to be very public matters in which the *community* must become deeply involved in seeking to resolve the issues raised or it would face a disastrous future (and, in fact, that often happened). To be true to the tradition they had inherited, they *must* preach it!

If we were to seek to articulate this point in today's terms, we could say something like the following: the concern for matters of social justice is deeply rooted in the biblical tradition (over six hundred texts could be cited).[5] Anyone who is committed to that tradition will be truly concerned about social justice and, in every age, will seek to address these issues anew with *communities* of faith in very public ways.[6] To be concerned about social justice in this way is then, basically, a conservative agenda. It could be said that anyone who does not attend carefully and explicitly and publicly to issues of social justice in our life together betrays the cause of conservatism. [162]

God, Social Justice, and Salvation

What are the sources of this pervasive and wide-ranging prophetic concern for social justice?[7] First and foremost, we must make reference to who

4. For an emphasis on community in considering these matters, see Bruce C. Birch, *Let Justice Roll Down: The Old Testament, Ethics, and Christian Life* (Louisville: Westminster John Knox, 1991).

5. For a recent, thorough study of poverty in the Bible, see William Robert Domeris, *Touching the Heart of God: The Social Construction of Poverty among Biblical Peasants* (New York: T. & T. Clark, 2007). A summary statement regarding the prophets: "The underlying message of the prophets is one not just of poverty, but of the oppression of the poor. The peasants of Israel are facing more than the simple struggle of peasants worldwide. They are facing a collapse of social structures with endemic oppression, violence and injustice" (p. 22). See also David Pleins, *Social Visions*; Hemchand Gossai, *Justice, Righteousness, and the Social Critique of the Eighth-Century Prophets* (New York: Peter Lang, 1993).

6. Birch, *Let Justice Roll Down,* makes a clear and helpful statement of the "dialectic" between the old and the new: "Calls for radical change apart from rootedness in the faith tradition are likely to express only our own desires and not the divine will. Preaching of our historic moral traditions as an end in itself robs us of participation in what God is doing anew in our time, and suggests that we do not believe in the power of God's word to affect the course of history anew" (p. 257). See also C. J. H. Wright, *Walking in the Ways of the Lord: The Ethical Authority of the Old Testament* (Leicester: Apollos, 1995).

7. I cite texts from the Pentateuch and from a wide swath of Israel's history. Many of these texts originated in a time when the prophets had already been at work. At the same time, these passages are deeply rooted in *pre*-Israelite concerns for the poor and the needy (see below), are *canonically* presented as pre-prophetic (a point not often explored, but here assumed), and their basic orientation in terms of the exodus (and related) events suggests a concern to ground these understandings in Israel's early life, even if the particular formulations are much later. See also David Pleins, *Social Visions,* 75–81.

God is and what *God* has done for Israel and continues to do.[8] The prime example of divine justice in the Old Testament is God's deliverance of Israel when they were enslaved in Egypt: "Israel knew well what social injustice was because it had been born in that condition" (see Exod 1:11–14).[9] The point is often repeated in the Old Testament: the Israelites were the helpless victims of abuse and exploitation at the hands of the most powerful nation of that age, and God, who identified *himself* as compassionate (Exod 22:27), delivered them.

The book of Exodus roots this divine deliverance deeply in the tradition, namely, "the covenant with Abraham, Isaac, and Jacob" (Exod 2:24); "covenant" in this context is to be equated with promise, an obligation that God takes upon himself.[10] The Israelites "groaned under their slavery, and cried out. Out of the slavery their cry for help rose up to God" (Exod 2:23; cf. Judg 2:18). And God "heard" and "remembered his covenant" and "looked upon" them and "knew" what they were going through (Exod 2:24–25; see the similar string of verbs with God as subject in the divine word to Moses in Exod 3:7–8). A key point emerges here (and in Exod 6:4–8) with the use of the language of "covenant," which God "remembers" and to which God will be faithful: "I am the Lᴏʀᴅ, and I will free you from the burdens of the Egyptians and deliver you from slavery to them. I will redeem you" (Exod 6:6). God liberated the Israelites from sociopolitical bondage because God had *promised* to do so (see the divine promises to do so throughout Genesis, e.g., 15:12–16; 46:3–4; 28:15; 17:6–8; see also Deut 7:8).

This explicit link between divine promise and social justice should not be lost on modern readers. What God will do on behalf of an abused and oppressed people is made a matter of divine promise. And God's deliverance of the people of God from abuse and oppression in Egypt is believed to be the fulfillment of such a promise. That this divine action is called "salvation" in Exod 15:2 should expand our understanding of what salvation is all about; in a given context, salvation may include a sociopolitical dimension. What might it mean theologically that the language of salvation is associated with the divine practice of social justice?[11] Might the

---

8. See Birch, *Let Justice Roll Down*, 37–41. John Rogerson (*Theory and Practice in Old Testament Ethics* [London: T. & T. Clark, 2004]) claims that the purpose of the law was "to make a theological statement about the character of God" (p. 26).

9. Bruce V. Malchow, *Social Justice in the Hebrew Bible: What Is New and What Is Old* (Collegeville, MN: Liturgical Press, 1996), 5. Malchow obscures this point by neglecting the fact that covenant with its associated promises *precedes* salvation in the canonical ordering.

10. Unfortunately, much discussion seeking to relate the Pentateuch to the prophets considers only the Sinai covenant. To speak about divine liberation without promise is theologically shortsighted.

11. For detail, see Terence Fretheim, "Salvation in the Bible vs. Salvation in the Church," *WW* 13/4 (1993): 363–72.

ongoing practice of social justice be salvific in some basic sense? God's concern about matters of social justice was believed to be so strong and so pervasive that it was built into the very heart of the covenantal promises. And God was and will be faithful to such promises.

At a later time in Israel's history, when the sociopolitical context was exile, promise and social justice are brought together in a similar way: Israel's Lord is "a God of justice" (Isa 30:18), who "loves justice" (Isa 61:8) and "delights" in it (Jer 9:24). To the exiles comes this repeated word: God has chosen a suffering servant as a divine agent and has put God's "spirit upon him; he will bring forth justice to the nations . . . he will faithfully bring forth justice. He will not grow faint or be crushed until he has established justice in the earth" (Isa 42:1–4; see 32:16–17; 51:4; 9:7). And God was faithful to promises made as Israel is brought home from the oppression of exile. Notably, this justice is spelled out in very specific ways and is given to the servant as a vocation to be pursued: "to open the eyes that are blind, to bring out the prisoners from the dungeon, from the prison those who sit in darkness" (42:7; see Isa 11:1–5; 49:6; 61:1–11).

In both exodus and return from exile (see the justice connection in Jer 23:5–8 to both old and new) social justice is linked to divine promise; this linkage lies at the center of Israel's faith tradition from the beginnings of their existence as a community and moves into ever new moments. This divine action against social injustice on behalf of God's people in fulfillment of divine promise *twice* proves to be a constitutive and salvific event: without it, they would not be who they are. Return from exile, God's "new thing" (Isa 43:19), in some sense "replaces" the exodus in Israel's confession of faith in Jer 16:14–16; 23:7–8, but the continuity with the "old" is remarkably strong. In some basic sense, both of these events were to Israel what the cross and resurrection of Jesus Christ are to Christians.

God, Social Justice, and Law

The significance of these salvific traditions (especially the exodus) for issues of social justice is made evident in numerous texts. For example, observe the way in which texts such as Deut 10:17–19 move from God's action to Israel's action: "For the Lord your God is God of gods and Lord of lords . . . who executes justice for the orphan and the widow, and who loves the strangers, providing them with food and clothing. You shall also love the stranger, for you were strangers in the land of Egypt." One might also note that the Ten Commandments are introduced by this [164] theme (Exod 20:2; Deut 5:6). The action of God in Israel's past history is to ground and shape Israel's own continuing action on behalf of those comparably abused and marginalized (it is a matter of continuing debate whether one can speak here and elsewhere of the "imitation of God"[12]).

---

12. See the brief discussion in John Barton, *Understanding Old Testament Ethics: Approaches and Explorations* (Louisville: Westminster John Knox, 2003), 50–54. See also John

This line of argument often appears in the tradition. I cite but four such texts here. In Exod 22:21 (see 23:9): "You shall not wrong or oppress a resident alien, for you were aliens in the land of Egypt." Indeed, "you shall love the alien as yourself, for you were aliens in the land of Egypt" (Lev 19:34). "If any of your kin fall into difficulty and become dependent on you, you shall support them. . . . I am the Lᴏʀᴅ your God, who brought you out of the land of Egypt" (Lev 25:35–38). "And when you send a male slave out from you a free person, you shall not send him out empty-handed. Provide liberally out of your flock, your threshing floor, and your wine press, thus giving him some of the bounty with which God has blessed you. Remember you were a slave in the land of Egypt, and the Lᴏʀᴅ your God redeemed you; for this reason I lay this command upon you today" (Deut 15:13–15).

Texts such as these must be linked to the ancestral promises noted above; together they show that Israel's concern for the less fortunate is deeply grounded in God's concern to be faithful to promises made, which included social justice. That concern was not based on wise social planning, family values, or even existing laws. Such matters may be important, but they do not provide sufficient explanation for Israel's pervasive commitment to care for the disadvantaged. For Israel's tradition, caring for these needy ones was a *religious* matter grounded in a *theological* claim about God. The authority behind the concern for the less fortunate has to do with Israel's relationship with a God who makes promises, keeps them, and acts justly to that end again and again. The prophets were inheritors of this tradition regarding divine justice and divine promise, and such theological claims shaped their basic understandings of and commitments to human justice.

Whatever the prophets' specific dependence on such ancient traditions, from within Israel or from without, such concerns and understandings are evident from an early time in Israel when the basic structure of Israel's society was the family and the clan. Over the course of Israel's history this situation began to deteriorate, for several reasons: the effects of ongoing war, which yielded many widows, orphans, and refugees (hence the refrain, "alien, orphan, and widow," especially in Deuteronomy, e.g., 24:19–22); royal policies that ignored tradition; the growth of cities that broke down traditional family ties to the land, shifting the economic point of gravity, with wealth becoming more and more concentrated in the hands of a few (an ongoing story!). Old Testament literature reflects these socioeconomic changes, with considerable attention given to the less fortunate in text after text. Prophets from various historical settings become involved in these issues. [165]

While the prophets do not often become involved in matters of social justice in the historical books, there are some notable exceptions, focused on individual cases. As an example, take the story of Naboth's vineyard in

---

Rogerson, *Theory and Practice,* 18–19, who speaks about a "morality of grace" and an "imperative which derives from God's salvation" (pp. 19, 25–28).

1 Kings 21. In the face of demands by King Ahab to acquire his vineyard, Naboth responds: "The LORD forbid that I should give you my ancestral inheritance" (1 Kgs 21:3–4). Ahab honors this customary law of the ancestors, albeit sadly, for he knows that Naboth is legally right; such ancestral property must remain in the family in perpetuity (for a later formulation, see Lev 25:1–34). It is only when Jezebel becomes involved that this law is set aside and Naboth is killed, providing opportunity for Ahab's acquisition of the property. At this point the prophet Elijah becomes involved and passes judgment on the king, not on the basis of some new prophetic insight, but on the grounds of already existing custom and legislation. Elijah is a conservative![13]

Or, take the story of the ewe lamb, told by Nathan the prophet to David the king in the wake of his sins against Uriah (2 Samuel 12). John Barton's language helps make our point: "David is properly furious at the case presented to him because it involves not simply theft but the exploitation of the poor man by his rich neighbor. The parable will work only if Nathan can take it for granted that the king . . . will be outraged by a man who has all he needs and yet exploits the poor."[14] Again, the assumption is that Nathan brings no new prophetic insight into this situation (nor does he cite a specific law); he works with existing understandings of human moral responsibility that he believed David would recognize and even honor, and he presses them home. In making charges of abuse against David, Nathan is dependent upon a long-standing tradition. The prophet is a conservative.

God, Social Justice, and Creation

Casting the net more broadly, one can say that the lively concern for the underprivileged in the Old Testament has roots in Israel's larger world. One may speak both more generally of "natural law" and more explicitly of ways in which such ethical concerns found their way into ancient Near Eastern literature![15] [166]

Regarding the latter, one can discern an advocacy for matters of social justice in literature of the ancient world before there was an Israel (e.g., the

---

13. See the comments by Waldemar Janzen on this text (*Old Testament Ethics: A Paradigmatic Approach* [Louisville: Westminster John Knox, 1994]): "Thus a prophet acts properly as a prophet when he brings God's word to bear on the actions of persons (or groups) so as to judge (positively or negatively) such actions in terms of their own proper ethical paradigms, rather than according to a distinctive prophetic paradigm" (p. 19). More generally he says that "the prophets did not promote an ethic of their own" (p. 161) or "a new ethic for a new time" (p. 169). He holds up a "familial paradigm," which highlights the key dimensions of life, land, and hospitality, as basic to the prophetic way of thinking (pp. 26–54).

14. Barton, *Understanding Old Testament Ethics*, 5.

15. Barton, ibid., 32–44, 48–50, speaks of the importance of "natural law" for Israel, not least in the prophets (he speaks especially of Amos and Isaiah, pp. 77–153).

Code of Hammurabi).[16] As Bruce Malchow puts it: "justice for the weak was a common concern throughout the Near East long before Israel existed," even if it was not as heavily accented as in Israel.[17] He makes the point more explicitly: "Israel accepted its neighbors' belief that justice was the responsibility of all of its citizens and especially of the ruler. It agreed that the special objects of social concern were the poor, widows, fatherless children, and sojourners." It simply "adopted Near Eastern injunctions on just judgment of the weak, lack of partiality in lawsuits, refraining from bribery, just weights, not moving landmarks, and charity to the poor."[18] In many other matters, Israel adapted such ideas in view of its particular faith convictions, but it is notable the extent to which Israel adopted such matters unchanged.

Regarding natural law, one might speak of the prophets' appeal, not least in their oracles against the nations (e.g., Amos 1:3–2:5), to "a kind of conventional or customary law about international conduct."[19] For example, John Barton speaks of the prophet Isaiah in these terms: "By far the greater part of Isaiah's references to the people's sin deals with matters which either were not in fact the subject of law (e.g., drunkenness) or could not be in the nature of the case" (e.g., excessive luxury).[20] Among Barton's conclusions regarding Amos's oracles against the nation is this: "no interpretation of the prophet can be correct which regards him as an innovator" with respect to foreign nations being subject to certain moral obligations.[21] Barton goes on to speak of "conventional morality" as a key factor among those leading to the prophetic indictment against abuse and oppression.[22]

---

16. For a convenient survey of these ancient Near Eastern roots, see Malchow, *Social Justice in the Hebrew Bible*, 1–4, 76–78. For an extensive treatment, see also Domeris, *Touching the Heart of God;* Moshe Weinfeld, *Social Justice in Ancient Israel and in the Ancient Near East* (Minneapolis: Fortress, 1995). See also Barton, *Understanding Old Testament Ethics,* 120–26.

17. Malchow, *Social Justice,* 4. This has its modern counterpart, wherein the care of many a non-Christian for the less fortunate outshines that of Christians, sometimes far outshines them. God the Creator has long been at work far beyond the boundaries of Israel (or the church), and that creative work of God in the lives of people has had many salutary effects.

18. Malchow, ibid. 76. He also includes Israelite adaptations of ancient Near Eastern practice.

19. Barton, *Understanding Old Testament Ethics,* 78.

20. Ibid., 36. Barton also importantly states: "Natural law and positive law, in classical theory, are two ways by which ethics flows from God: they are not to be opposed as respectively human and divine" (p. 51). Nor are they to be opposed as scriptural and nonscriptural; natural law has a significant presence in the Scriptures themselves. See also James Barr, *Biblical Faith and Natural Theology* (Oxford: Clarendon, 1993).

21. Barton, *Understanding Old Testament Ethics,* 80.

22. Rogerson, *Theory and Practice,* uses the phrase "natural morality" in this context and distinguishes it from "natural law" to refer to "a moral consensus common to sensitive and thoughtful people, religious and nonreligious alike" (p. 16). This is a phrase that Barton could accept (*Understanding Old Testament Ethics,* 179 n. 16).

In any case, these kinds of prophetic appeals do not constitute new directions with respect to matters of social justice; rather, they are reiterations of existing understandings of "natural law" in Israel and the larger cultural context. Again, this prophetic move, dependent as it is on existing standards, should be considered basically [167] conservative, while articulating these concerns with a new intensity and fervor in view of their particular time and place. If one were to speak of the prophets' novelty, Barton suggests that it would consist in their "maintaining, against popular opinion, that social morality (understood as impartiality in justice and care for the rights of the helpless) is not a mere piece of arbitrary divine legislation, nor merely a human convention, but almost part of the order of nature—self-evident to any right-thinking person."[23] He adds: "Since the rightness of the obligations laid on Israel [by God] ought to be as obvious as if they were agreed on by everyone in the world, how much worse their guilt is when they also have the advantage of a special personal contact with God to endorse them!" (see Amos 3:2).

In his discussion of Amos and Isaiah, John Barton allows that "natural law" appeals do not cover all of the prophets' references to the people's sin ("by far the greater part"). This suggests that one should be on the lookout for the occasional reference to Israelite law in the prophets, though, in the cases that follow, Israel is in turn dependent upon already existing Near Eastern law. At the same time, it seems to be the case that the prophets' sources are more comprehensive than the Torah's sources; as a result of this exposure, they "bring to light injustices left unaddressed in the Bible's legal traditions."[24]

Two examples may be illustrative. In Isa 3:13–15, God "argues his case" and "enters into judgment with the elders and princes of his people: It is you who have devoured the vineyard; the spoil of the poor is in your houses. What do you mean by crushing my people, by grinding the face of the poor?" Isaiah almost certainly has reference to existing laws regarding the harvesting of crops, namely, that some of the crop must be left behind "for the alien, the orphan, and the widow" (so Deut 24:19–22; Lev 19:9–10; 23:22; cf. Exod 23:10–11 for a different formulation of the same concern).[25] This practice, which allows the poor to eat without having to beg for food, is well illustrated in the story of Ruth (2:1–10). But, Isaiah charges, the leaders of Israel have not done this; they have "devoured" the vineyard, that is, they have taken every last olive, sheaf, and grape out of their fields

---

23. Ibid., 118.

24. Pleins, *Social Visions*, 81.

25. I recognize that there are issues of dating here; Isaiah 3 precedes Deuteronomy in its present form. At the same time, we do not know how old the roots of the deuteronomic formulations are, though they are likely pre-Isaianic, not least because such laws are present elsewhere in the ancient Near East (e.g., *Instruction of Amenemope*). See the discussion in Pleins, *Social Visions*, 75–81.

for themselves. They have left nothing for the poor, but instead have proceeded to fill their own pantries. Given the prevalence of this reference in both law and narrative, it is likely that [168] Isaiah is here not voicing a new concern, but is dependent upon existing tradition and law.[26]

Another example is Amos 8:4–7 (see also the parallels in Hos 12:7; Mic 6:10–11; Ezek 45:10–12), where God calls the people to account in these terms: "Hear this, you that . . . say, 'When will the new moon be over that we may sell grain; and the Sabbath, so that we may offer wheat for sale? We will make the ephah small and the shekel great, and practice deceit with false balances.'" This concern for proper weights and balances, scales that have been rigged in the merchant's favor, does not originate with the prophets, but is dependent upon already existing tradition and law (see Deut 25:13–16; Lev 19:35–36, noting the reference to the exodus events).[27] Such concerns were widespread in the traditions inherited by the prophets and so their appeal to these matters is markedly conservative, but the intensity and frequency of their rhetoric sharpens the concern.

Among the implications of this discussion for a "prophetic ministry" today, let the words of Walter Brueggemann, who speaks of the "alternative community of Moses" and whose personal commitment to social justice is deep and broad, express a key point:

> The church will not have power to act or believe until it recovers its tradition of faith and permits that tradition to be the primary way out of enculturation. That is not a cry for traditionalism but rather a judgment that the church has no business more pressing than the reappropriation of its memory in its full power and authenticity. . . . The prophet is called to be a child of the tradition . . . who is so at home in that memory that the points of contact and incongruity with the situation of the church in culture can be discerned and articulated with proper urgency.[28]

---

26. For other points of dependence on the law, see, e.g., Isa 1:17, 21–23; 5:23; 10:1–2 (murder; theft; bribery; lack of justice in the courts; lack of care for the widow and the orphan). For a convenient outline of sins in Isaiah, see Barton, *Understanding Old Testament Ethics*, 134–35.

27. See also the references in wisdom literature (e.g., Prov 11:1; 16:11; 20:10, 23).

28. Walter Brueggemann, *The Prophetic Imagination* (2nd ed.; Minneapolis: Fortress, 2001), 2.

Caught in the Middle:
Jeremiah's Vocational Crisis

Jer 20:7–18 is the most intense of the prophet's many laments.[1] Some scholars think it bespeaks a crisis of Jeremiah's very faith in God.[2] This deep anguish, however, is best interpreted in terms of a *vocational crisis*, the prophet's distress at being stuck between an insistent God and a resistant people. As such, this lament of Jeremiah (with others) may prove especially helpful to pastoral leaders who face a comparable crisis. Such laments are revealing of an important dimension of a faithful, interactive relationship with God.

Scholars have sometimes claimed that Jer 20:7–18 is so filled with agony because the prophet sympathizes with the people in their certain death and destruction.[3] But, in fact, because Jeremiah's antagonists can be identified with these very [352] people, he expresses no sympathy for them at all.

This essay was originally published in *Word and World* 22 (2002): 351–60.

1. This article is based on my commentary, *Jeremiah* (Macon, GA: Smyth & Helwys, 2002) especially pp. 289–301. Readers should know that I have made several different interpretive moves here from those presented in the commentary.

2. For studies of Jeremiah's laments, see Kathleen O'Connor, *The Confessions of Jeremiah: Their Interpretation and Role in Chapters 1–25* (Atlanta: Scholars Press, 1988); A. R. Diamond, *The Confessions of Jeremiah in Context: Scenes of a Prophetic Drama* (Sheffield: Sheffield Academic, 1987); see the summary discussion of Walter Brueggemann, *A Commentary on Jeremiah: Exile and Homecoming* (Grand Rapids: Eerdmans, 1998), 114–15; S. Balentine, *Prayer in the Hebrew Bible: The Drama of the Divine-Human Dialogue* (Minneapolis: Fortress, 1993), 150–68. See my *The Suffering of God: An Old Testament Perspective* (Minneapolis: Fortress, 1984), 156–59.

3. This textual segment is commonly thought to consist of two laments of Jeremiah (vv. 7–12 [13], 14–18). The common lectionary (which includes only vv. 7–13) assumes this understanding. Verse 13, a call to praise, is often considered interruptive. Yet, praise language and the certainty of a hearing are often found in laments, both within the psalm (see Pss 35:9–10; 144:9) and as concluding words (see Pss 13:6; 59:16–17; 109:30–31). See, e.g., O'Connor, *Confessions;* D. J. A. Clines and David Gunn, "Form, Occasion, and Redaction in Jeremiah 20," *ZAW* 88 (1976): 390–409. The call to praise in Ps 22:23 (in the middle of the psalm) and Ps 31:24 (cf. 27:14) at the end are important parallels. It is sometimes suggested (as here) that vv. 7–13 and vv. 14–18 belong together (see, e.g., J. G. Janzen, "Jeremiah 20:7–18," *Int* 37 [1983]: 179–83). Concluding sharp laments and questions after a strong confession of faith are attested elsewhere (e.g., Lam 5:20–22 after 5:19 and 3:22–33; cf. Psalm 89). It seems best to understand vv. 7–18 as a single lament that includes elements of complaint, confession of trust, petition, certainty of being heard, and thanksgiving, concluding on a sharp note of questioning. This lament brings together several themes previously lifted up by Jeremiah, including complaints of hardships in carrying out his commission (cf. v. 7 with 15:15–18), and calls for judgment against his persecutors (cf. vv. 10–12 with 17:14–18; 18:19–23).

Rather, he fervently prays that God's judgment be quickly forthcoming on the whole lot (20:12)! Jeremiah's crisis is better interpreted in specifically vocational terms.

This text also functions at another level, this time with implications for those who listen to the word of God. In reading Jeremiah a distinction must be made between the audience for the *preaching* of the prophet and the audience for the *book* (though these audiences overlap).[4] The opening lines (1:1–3) make clear that the present form of the book is addressed to an audience on the far side of the destruction of Jerusalem; the earlier preaching of Jeremiah has been appropriated as a resource to speak a new word into a new context (probably the exile). A key question for modern readers is this: How would *exiles* have read this lament? It is unlikely they could identify their anguish with Jeremiah's anguish; the prophet's lament could not become their lament.[5] After all, they had been (and perhaps still were) the problem to which Jeremiah speaks. At best, reading this text might engender remorse and/or repentance among them, as they observe the agony through which they put both prophet and God. Look at what it took—such personal cost—for the prophet to speak the word of God to them. In short, the text in its present form functions not as prophetic (auto)biography, but as *proclamation;* the word of God is conveyed in and through a suffering prophet who is *textually embodied.* As such, this text speaks not only to leaders in vocational crisis, but also to those people of God who are resistant to the word that the leader proclaims.

God "Dupes" and "Prevails"

This lament is remarkable for the strength of its images; given the sharp address to God, it has even been called blasphemous. I begin with the verbs in v. 7, the translation of which will deeply affect the interpretation of the text.

The initial verb (פתה) is difficult and translations vary widely. It can have the sense of seduce (so JB; see Exod 22:16), allure/entice (so NRSV; see Hos 2:14), persuade (Prov 25:15), dupe/make a fool of (so NEB/REB, NAB; see Job 5:2), and deceive (so NIV; see 1 Kgs 22:20–22). The verb is used twice in v. 7 and again in v. 10 [353] with Jeremiah's persecutors as subject (see below). The translation "take advantage of"[6] could make the point, but "deceive" or "dupe" carries the basic sense well. This is, of course, Jeremiah's interpretation of what God has done.

The sense of the next verb (חזק) is also difficult. It can mean "overpower" in, say, a military or physical sense (1 Kgs 20:25; 2 Sam 13:14; so NRSV, NIV, JB) or, somewhat softer, "be strong" (cf. NAB; NRSV in 1 Kgs 20:23–25). NEB/

4. For detail, Fretheim, *Jeremiah,* 4–11.
5. Contrary to Ronald Clements, *Jeremiah* (Atlanta: John Knox, 1988), 123.
6. So Brueggemann, *Jeremiah,* 181.

REB translates "outwit," hence, *mental* strength; such a translation would fit well with "dupe." Perhaps especially important, it can refer to the effect of *words spoken* (e.g., 2 Sam 24:4).

Whatever the nature of the divine action, Jeremiah acknowledges that God has "prevailed" (יכל), the third verb in v. 7. Inasmuch as Jeremiah uses the same verb in v. 9 (I "can[not]" hold the word in; NRSV), that usage may inform its sense in v. 7, that is, God's *word* has prevailed in Jeremiah's life. The issue is not a question of God's power in a general way,[7] as if it were a test of sheer strength. The power with which Jeremiah has to do is the power of the word of God that he hears or that wells up within him. The issue for God is to overcome Jeremiah's strong resistance (v. 9) to speak the word he has been called to speak and in fact has already often spoken, and God is successful in doing so. Even so: Does God prevail because God dupes? Jeremiah apparently believes so.

We return to the issue of God's deception/duping of Jeremiah or at least Jeremiah's sense of having been deceived. Some scholars relate this to God's failure to deliver on the word that Jeremiah proclaimed (to this point). Yet, while Jeremiah may be impatient for the word to be fulfilled (18:19–23), the timing issue is not raised in this context and Jeremiah is confident that fulfillment will come (v. 11). Other scholars think the deception relates to the lack of a positive response from the people.[8] Yet, his unrelenting announcement of the coming judgment, and the stubbornness of the people evident in both his indictment (e.g., 16:12) and their own admission (18:12), suggests that he was not naïve in this regard. The sense of personal failure seems to be on the edge of this lament, at best.

Another direction for thinking about the deception is preferable, namely, his sense of *entrapment* between a compelling word from an insistent God and a stubborn and derisive people. As has been pointed out, Jeremiah interweaves attention to God (vv. 7a, 8a, 9) and to his persecutors (vv. 7b, 8b, 10).[9] Recall especially v. 7 in light of v. 10, where פתה and יכל are also used for the actions of his persecutors. Jeremiah has been deceived by God (v. 7), and the people are trying to do the same thing to him (v. 10). These repeated verbs frame the vocational issue for Jeremiah: he is beset by the word of God on the one hand and beleaguered by antagonists on the other.

Whether or not God intended to dupe him, Jeremiah feels that he has been drawn into a vocation that is much more intense and difficult than God had led him to believe. Though God had clearly warned him of difficulties, God had also promised to deliver him from his antagonists (Jer 1:8, 19), a promise remaining to be fulfilled. Jeremiah did not fully realize what

---

7. Ibid., 181; William Holladay, *Jeremiah I* (Philadelphia: Fortress, 1986), 553, speaks of God's use of "brute force."

8. Clements, *Jeremiah*, 122.

9. So Clines and Gunn, "Jeremiah 20," 390–409.

he was "getting into," and he laments regarding the two parties responsible for his personal quandary.

At the same time, Jeremiah's approach to God and the persecutors is different. Though God is sharply addressed, it is doubtful that the language is accusatory (as it is usually designated). Jeremiah's complaint does not stay focused on God; it immediately (and often) moves to the response that God's word has engendered. God's call has placed Jeremiah directly in the line of fire and he finds that oppressive, but he recognizes that this is due, finally, to his antagonists' failure to acknowledge the truth of the word he speaks. His sharpest complaints are about his persecutors, and his *only* petition relates to them (v. 12). Yes, God did dupe him, but he recognizes that action for what it was and he has done what he was called to do, however much he has struggled with the call. *Deception recognized* changes the equation. Jeremiah's complaint is accompanied by the acknowledgment that the divine action was in the service of a compelling truth; he never intimates that God's word was a false word. Jeremiah believes not that God's *word* is deceitful (see v. 11), but that God has called him into a vocation wherein he feels trapped, caught in the middle, squeezed between these two parties that have quite different "agendas." Jeremiah expresses confidence that God will deliver him (vv. 11–13),[10] recalling God's early assurances that his persecutors will not "prevail" (1:19). But that does not lessen the deeply troubling dimensions of his vocation, especially when deliverance seems nowhere in sight.

How Is God's Word Compelling?

An associated dimension of the accusation of deception immediately follows (vv. 8–9). Jeremiah bemoans his inability to stop speaking the word of God—so [355] compelling is it. He "must" speak it, even the language about violence and destruction. The latter has a double reference: the violence perpetrated by the people, which in turn flows into its violent consequence, that is, the judgment of God (v. 8). Because of this word of God that Jeremiah speaks he has become a reproach and is derided "all day long." In other words, *because he embodies the word of God regarding violence he suffers what that word suffers at the hand of others.*

When he resolves not to speak God's word because of all the "guff" he receives, he is not able to maintain that stance.[11] The word so burns within him that he "cannot" (יכל, as in God's "prevailing" in v. 7) but speak it. He suffers if he speaks the word of God and he suffers if he doesn't, and the God who called him from the womb is ultimately responsible for *both*

---

10. This expressed confidence is a move beyond Jeremiah's accusation of divine deception in 15:18 and picks up the assuring language of God's response to that lament in 15:20–21.

11. Following REB, v. 9a is a reference to "it," the word of God, rather than "him," God (NRSV).

realities. *Therein lies the essence of the deception.* Trying to hold back the judgment word of God produces a profound weariness (as in 6:11). Notably, God also experiences such weariness (see 15:6). God is weary from holding back the judgment on an unrepentant people. So Jeremiah, in being unable to hold back the word, is conformed to the very word of God he embodies. His weariness and God's are of one and the same piece; as it is with God, so it is with Jeremiah.

This being the case, Jeremiah's inability finally to resist should not be interpreted as a clinical compulsion, but as a theological and vocational one. He finally speaks because he comes to the point where he believes that this is what he must do. The continuing divine pressure on him to speak words of judgment is real, and Jeremiah recognizes that he cannot be true to himself or to his calling by being silent. Jeremiah finally does not speak *against* his own will, as if he were forced to do so; what he says is really what *he* says and not the word of God in some unmediated way (cf. 23:9; Amos 3:8; 1 Cor 9:16). He remains a genuine human mediator of the word.

William McKane says it well: the inner conflict of the prophet over whether to speak "is not to be interpreted as rebellion and guilt or reduced to human frailty."[12] Jeremiah's lament is an honorable one within a genuine relationship. Even more, if Jeremiah

> speaks against his will, his freedom is overwhelmed by a force which he cannot resist, and his utterance is no more his than that of a man whose integrity has been destroyed by violence or torture or drugs. . . . The most that can be made of 'compulsion' is that what we are loath to utter and can only utter after overcoming inner resistance is not so subject to the dangers of willfulness, self-assertiveness or self-deception as those utterances which we have a natural inclination to make. The thoughts which are congenial to us and which we are inclined to embrace, or the attitudes which are agreeable with our desire for security are more liable to error than those which force themselves on us because [356] they have a truth which we cannot ultimately evade and to which we must give expression, even if we fear or shrink from the consequences of so speaking.[13]

The most basic personal effect of this divine commission is that Jeremiah has been made to look the fool, a laughingstock to "everyone" (v. 7). People ridicule him and subject him to rebuke and censure. From their perspective, Jeremiah is a disgrace (v. 8, see v. 18). Moreover, they engage in a "whispering campaign," and Jeremiah quotes them twice in v. 10. They sarcastically repeat his message that "terror is all around" (see v. 3; Ps 31:13), for to all external appearances that is not the case. They conspire among themselves to "get him." Even his close friends and neighbors are

---

12. William McKane, *A Critical and Exegetical Commentary on Jeremiah*, vol. 1, *Introduction and Commentary on Jeremiah I–XXV* (2 vols.; ICC; Edinburgh: T. & T. Clark, 1986), 1:474.
13. Ibid.

on the watch (see 11:21); they look for missteps so they can obtain a firmer basis on which to silence him. Indeed, they hope to trick him into making a blunder (see Luke 20:20); then they can get rid of him and his accusing words, making him suffer the very end he has been predicting for them ("revenge"; see v. 12).

For all of Jeremiah's lamenting about the situation into which God has called him, he expresses great confidence that God will provide a "way out" for him (v. 11). His God is a "great warrior" and will turn the tables on his behalf. God would prevail against them rather than they against him. They, not he, will be a "disgrace" (NRSV, "dishonor") as they so judged the word of God and the prophet in v. 8 (NRSV, "reproach"). For God to visit them with "vengeance"[14] refers to the "revenge" planned by them against Jeremiah ("what goes around comes around").

Verse 12 virtually repeats the words of 11:20; it is often thought to provide an inclusio for Jeremiah's laments. He commits his cause to God, trusting that God will see that his persecutors are judged appropriately. This language is not a personal vendetta, but reveals that his stance toward these unfaithful people now conforms to that of God. Jeremiah's wrath mirrors the wrath of God.[15]

The language of testing (v. 12a; see 17:16) is a personal reflection on Jeremiah's own situation with respect to God. In effect, he moves to the point of responding to his own initial complaint. Testing is inherent to all relationships of consequence: Will those involved remain faithful to the relationship in the face of every circumstance? Jeremiah understands his negative situation to have constituted such a test, but he also proceeds to call upon *God* to be true to the relationship by delivering him from his persecutors.

Then, in v. 13 Jeremiah urges praise to God, inviting exilic *readers* to do the same. He is certain that God will hear his lament and deliver him from his enemies (see Psalm 70), returning to God's assurance in his call (1:8, 18). But this response proves not to be Jeremiah's settled disposition on the matter. [357]

Jeremiah's Cry of the Heart

Jeremiah's cry in vv. 14–18 has occasioned much discussion and has often been interpreted as a sign of Jeremiah's deep despair. The search for language to describe the prophet has ranged widely, including self-hatred and self-curse. Links with Job 3:3–26; 10:18–19 have suggested the latter. From this perspective, these verses are not a prayer addressed to God; they are self-directed. In fact, however, Jeremiah does not direct the curses toward *himself*, but to the day of his birth and to the messenger who announced

14. So NIV and most translations; NRSV, "retribution," is too forensic a notion.
15. See Fretheim, *Suffering of God*, 156–59.

it. A key question for readers: Is the word "cursed" a call for his birthday (and the messenger) to be cursed, or is it a declaration that they are in fact cursed? The latter interpretation is much more likely![16]

To curse something/someone is to call down death or destruction on them; it is the opposite of blessing, which is directed toward life, fertility, and well-being. But the day and the messenger lie in the past, irretrievable except to memory; Jeremiah cannot get at them with a retroactive curse. But as a *personal* declaration that these realities *are in fact cursed*, it states what Jeremiah believes their (*ongoing*) status to have been.[17] As such, these realities associated with his birth signify to him that, in view of God's choosing him in the womb (about which he could do nothing), he has personally embodied death and destruction from that point on (see 1:5). This is who he is and it's not pretty!

While vv. 14–18 are not specifically addressed to God (nor is 15:10–11), and no petition is stated, the cry to God is probably implicit. A sharp cry in the night ending in a sharp question is one way of thinking about the lament. As noted above, laments could end with deep questioning even after statements of trust and confidence (notably, there is no curse of God in this lament).

The wish that he would have been killed in the womb (see 15:10 for related motifs) refers to his becoming a dead fetus in the womb ("my grave"), which his mother would have carried to her grave. Inasmuch as he was called from the womb (1:5, a possible inclusio with this chapter), this strongly expressed language is, in effect, a fervent wish that he had not been called to this kind of vocation.

Even more, Jeremiah *declares as cursed* the man who delivered the joyful news about his birth (vv. 15–17).[18] But why would this messenger be singled out for such a fate? The role of the messenger has been linked to other reports of bad news (e.g., 6:22–26) [358], to which Jeremiah or others respond in anguish. The messenger who brought the news about Jeremiah's birth announced it as good news, but he should have brought *bad* news, for

---

16. Holladay, *Jeremiah*, 560–61.

17. The verbs beginning the two halves of v. 16 are often translated as jussives ("let . . ."), following the LXX rather than the Hebrew. They are probably better translated as simple future (NEB), present, or even past (see Holladay, *Jeremiah*, 560). As for the last line in v. 14, it can be translated, "it could never be blessed," or similarly. These translations would support the understanding that Jeremiah's use of the word "cursed" (in vv. 14–15) is a declaration, not a petition or desire.

18. Most commentators consider the phrase "like the cities that the LORD overthrew" to be a reference to Sodom and Gomorrah (see Gen 19:25). Yet, these cities are *named* elsewhere in Jeremiah (23:14; 49:18; 50:40) and the phrase "without pity" is not used of those cities. Exilic readers (at least) would probably see in this a reference to the cities of *Judah* that God overthrew without pity (v. 16a; for the pitiless theme, see 4:28; 16:7; 13:14; 21:14). They would have recalled that during that disastrous time they had voiced the "outcry" and heard the "alarm" (see 4:19; 11:11; 18:22).

he *himself* will be caught up in the devastation that Jeremiah announces. If he had instead killed Jeremiah in the womb he may have saved not only himself but also an entire people from death and destruction. Alternatively, the subject of the first line of v. 17 may be not the messenger ("he"), but indefinite and translate something like REB, "since death did not claim me before birth."[19]

Jeremiah's final question encapsulates the basic point of the prior verses (cf. the "why?" questions of Gen 25:22; 27:45; Lam 5:20–22). Why did he come forth from the womb to be a prophet and suffer so? From the womb he has been the embodiment of God's word, a word decisively shaped by the message of sword, famine, and death. As a consequence he has had to live a life of great hardship and anguish (cf. Baruch in 45:3), having to spend every day dishonored by his compatriots and friends (see 17:18). Why?!

The apparent lack of a divine response to Jeremiah is often noted. But is God silent? As for the *textual* Jeremiah (we don't have access to the *actual* Jeremiah), God does *not* respond with silence. Jeremiah speaks his words of complaint and curse, and God is right there with another word to speak (21:1). It is not a word of commiseration or assurance, as many readers might like, but it is, in effect, a word to continue doing what he has been called to do (not unlike 12:5–6; 15:19–20). As if to provide an immediate illustration of Jeremiah's point in 20:8–9, God insists that he keep speaking no matter how he feels. At least from the text's perspective, God does not allow Jeremiah to linger in his despair; God keeps the pressure on. Such is the life of a prophet.

A Crisis of Faith or Vocation?

Keeping vv. 14–18 together with what precedes, and adopting the above sense of curse, probably makes Jeremiah somewhat less despairing than is commonly thought and makes the issue less a psychological problem. Words like self-pity and self-hatred do not capture the point. If this cry is *vocationally* oriented, then the issue is less that his life has no value than that his life as prophet is so caught between God and people that it has not been worth the trouble. This is *not* a crisis of faith in the sense that if he had a stronger faith in God he wouldn't go through such times. To say that Jeremiah accuses God "of having broken the relation which he had initiated" is unacceptable.[20] Or, to claim that Jeremiah had a "love-hate relation" with [359] God is much too psychological an assessment.[21] People with genuine faith can use accusatory language—if that's what this is—in prayer to God (e.g., Ps 44:22–23) and raise sharp questions with God (e.g., Gen 18:25). This is the type of honest interaction that God encourages in

19. See McKane, *Jeremiah,* 488.
20. Holladay, *Jeremiah,* 522.
21. Ibid., 559.

relationships, and the many biblical laments are witness to that. Persons of sharp insight and rich faith in God often have such moments, as a survey of the lives of faithful people through the centuries will show. God is part of the problem, but that is, finally, occasion for hope, not despair.

This is a crisis of vocation for Jeremiah. For him, it is an issue of having to *be* (!) a certain kind of person. Jeremiah has expressed certainty that God would deliver him from his persecutors, but he still feels squeezed between an insistent God with a compelling word and a resistant people with a derisive word. He has had to voice violence and destruction, and he has had to deal with a people who have done violence to him for doing just that. He is caught in the middle—the story of many a prophet and preacher.

Daniel Berrigan's recasting of Jeremiah's last lament (20:7–18) is remarkable in the way in which it gathers new images to make the lament sing once again.[22] But note that he has changed the order of the verses; v. 13 is placed at the end. This move, of course, changes the rhetorical character of the poem, and it now stands more like many a lament in the Psalter. At least the book of Jeremiah does not want to leave it like this for the reader.

> Yahweh, you trickster,
> with a flick of your finger
> you whirl me about—
> this way, that, a weather—
> vane in your wild weathers,
> whim, tornado, mood.
>
> Never shall I countenance
> this mad charade of yours!
>
> You wound me, spur my flanks—
> I must
> under your whip
> a cowering beast
> neigh, whinny, roar—
> "Root up, Tear down!"
> On every side
> ridicule greets me,
> disdain, scorn.
>
> In corners they gather,
> like whispering spiders [359]
> weaving rumors—
> "Malcontent, he sees
> through a glass, darkness only."
>
> Friends grown sly,
> weave their spells—

22. Daniel Berrigan, *Jeremiah: The World, The Wound of God* (Minneapolis: Fortress, 1999), 86–88.

"Only wait,
await his downfall!"

My soul beleaguered
whispers;
   Peace, poor soul, peace—
let pass this awful
behest of His
in sweet forgetting!

Then
I swear it
your word erupts—
a fire shut in my bones
smolders there, consuming—
I cannot contain, endure it!

Cursed, thrice cursed
be the ill-starred
night of my birth,
a mother's womb my tomb!
Cursed the gladdening word—
"A child is born, a son!"

Good news?
No. A plague—
sorrow, disgrace my lot.

Nevertheless,
   You
cloud of unknowing,
of undoing—
I cling to You, fiery pillar cling to You, burn of you
and I sing, I raise
a song against the night;
my Scandal
my Love—
stand with me in the breach!

The Character of God
in Jeremiah

How is God's character depicted in the present (MT) form of the book of Jeremiah?[1] Of what import is this portrayal for the shaping of human character? With these two questions in mind, I will treat various aspects of the character of God in Jeremiah, especially God's violent action and speech.

Point of View in Jeremiah

Various points of view on the character of God are presented in Jeremiah, and they are often difficult to assess. For example, the people's point of view is presented in various quotations.[2] To cite one instance: "My Father, you are the end of my youth" (3:4). God is both father and friend, two metaphors juxtaposed—the subject for an intriguing exercise in metaphorical theology. Although the people's understanding of God is sometimes presented as distorted (e.g., 2:35), the theology in their laments does not seem to be so (14:7–9, 19–22). Which is the case in 3:4? The view of the false prophets (e.g., 23:16–17) is declared to be false, and the theology of many individuals (e.g., Zedekiah in 21:2) is regarded with suspicion. These and other voices present the reader with a theological cacophony. To discern the portrayal of God that the editors of the [212] book commend to readers in the face of falsehood becomes an important, if complicated, exercise.

Two points of view that the book presents are especially important, those of Jeremiah and God. Words placed in the mouth of God apparently have a standing in the book that Jeremiah's words do not have (see God's rebuke of Jeremiah in 15:18–19; cf. 12:5–6). Yet, certainly, when the prophet is expressly speaking the word of God, he is presented as the embodiment of God's own word.

This observation relates to another difficulty in a surprisingly large number of texts: identifying whether the speaker is God or the prophet. Their

This essay was originally published in *Character and Scripture: Moral Formation, Community, and Biblical Interpretation* (ed. William P. Brown; Grand Rapids, MI: Eerdmans, 2002), 211–30.

1. It would be an important exercise to lay out the portrayal of God in the LXX and see the similarities and differences from that presented in the MT. More speculative would be an effort to discern differences in the portrayal of God in the various levels of redaction in the book (e.g., Deuteronomistic).

2. See T. Trapp, "Jeremiah: The Other Sides of the Story," in *Was ist der Mensch? Beiträge zur Anthropologie des AT* (ed. F. Crüsemann et al.; Munich: Chr. Kaiser, 1992), 228–42.

voices often "bleed" together, and scholars frequently disagree regarding the identity of the speaker. Such disagreement may be due to the personal theological perspectives of interpreters, especially when assigning speakers to texts of weeping and lamenting (e.g., 8:18–9:1 [MT 8:18–23]; 13:17; 14:17). Traditional understandings of the immutability and impassibility of God may be at work, though they are usually not explicit. One example from the NRSV is 9:10 [MT 9:9]. Is it because of the theological difficulty of having God say "I will take up weeping and wailing for the mountains and a lamentation for the pastures of the wilderness" that the translators have decided to go to the versions ("Take up weeping and wailing. . .") rather than to stay with the Hebrew?[3]

In describing the character of God in Jeremiah, it makes a difference if one usually or always assigns the texts that describe weeping to the prophet. Doing so makes the texts describing judgment even harsher and God much more removed and unmoved. Anger accompanied by weeping, while still anger, is different—in motivation, in the understanding of God, and in the relationship at stake. If these texts are, at least, sometimes assigned to God, the harsh words of judgment are not matched by an inner harshness, an important matter for exilic readers to see. Words of judgment are proclaimed reluctantly and with great anguish. The internal side of God's external word and deed of wrath is profound grief.[4] [213]

For some readers, it is incongruous that expressions of profound grief accompany anger and the announcement of judgment (e.g., 9:10–11 [MT 9:9–10]; see below). Yet such statements seem to be purposively interwoven. God mediates judgment so that sin and evil do not go unchecked in the life of the world, but God does so at great cost to the divine life. In terms of ethical implications, if there is no *divine* anger at sin and evil, then *human* anger toward that which is oppressive and abusive does not carry

---

3. One might ask whether this translation is testimony to an anti-anthropomorphic tendency.

4. Note that the anger of God is "provoked." This language for divine anger is common in Jeremiah (7:18; 8:19;11:17; 25:6–7; 32:29–32; 44:3, 8) and reveals several things about God. For one, God is moved by what the people do. For another, it reveals that anger is not an attribute of God, as if anger were no different from, say, love. Rather, God's anger is contingent. If there were no sin, there would be no divine anger. To say that God is always angry, that anger, like love, is integral to the divine identity is to fall back into a kind of dualism.

References to God's wrath being "poured out" (7:20; also 6:11; 10:25; 42:18; 44:6) provide another insight into the divine anger. While there is a personal dimension to God's anger, wrath is also impersonally conceived in Jeremiah (cf. Num 1:53; 16:46). Wrath is not only "poured out" but "goes forth" because of the people's wickedness (*rōaʿ*, 4:4 = 21:12) like "a whirling tempest" (23:19), "is not turned away" (4:8; 23;20), "bursts upon" the head of the wicked (23:19), and is like fire that burns (4:4; 7:20; 15:14; 17:4; 21:12; 44:6). In this way of thinking, wrath is an effect that grows out of a violation of the moral order of God's creation (cf. Deut 28:15, 22, 45). God's personal anger may be said to be God's "seeing to" this movement from deed to consequence that is the moral order.

the same weight and seriousness as it would if that divine anger were present. If there is no sorrow associated with divine anger, then human anger is given a freer range regarding harshness.

Commentators increasingly assign many of these lament-filled texts to divine speech.[5] Yet this more recent willingness to speak of God as one who weeps and laments raises new theological issues that play a role in interpreting the character of God in Jeremiah. For one thing, how one speaks about the suffering of God is important.[6] For another, and more important for our purposes, it is not common for interpreters to work out the *implications* of having a God who suffers—who laments, weeps, and anguishes over decisions. Not uncommonly, alongside the acceptance of such language of suffering for God is the continued affirmation of "classical"— but now deeply problematic—understandings such as: God is immutable, "irresistible,"[7] the only "real agent," [214] radically free, and unqualifiedly sovereign, even in "absolute control."[8] Generally, I would characterize this mixed theological situation as follows.[9]

So-Called Contradictions in Jeremiah and Theological Coherence

The claim of theological incoherence in Jeremiah is often due to the theology of interpreters; something does not make sense from within their own theological framework, which is laid over the various perspectives of God in the book. For example, Kathleen O'Connor's helpful work on the character of God claims that the book presents images for God that "contradict each other." And so, "divine tears put aside punishment . . . and

5. K. O'Connor, "The Tears of God and Divine Character in Jeremiah 2–9," in *God in the Fray* (ed. T. Linafelt and T. Beal; Minneapolis: Fortress, 1998), 172–85; M. Biddle, *Polyphony and Symphony in Prophetic Literature: Rereading Jeremiah 7–20* (Macon, GA: Mercer University Press, 1996); T. Fretheim, *The Suffering of God: An Old Testament Perspective* (OBT; Philadelphia: Fortress, 1984).

6. There are important differences among those who have worked with the theme of the suffering of God, a matter that needs exploration. At least three different perspectives might be examined: those of A. Heschel (*The Prophets* [San Francisco: Harper, 1962], esp. pp. 483–85); W. Brueggemann (e.g., *Theology of the Old Testament: Testimony, Dispute, Advocacy* [Minneapolis: Fortress, 1997], 267–313), and my own work, which differs in several respects from that of Heschel and Brueggemann.

7. W. Brueggemann (*A Commentary on Jeremiah; Exile and Homecoming* [Grand Rapids: Eerdmans,1998], 26, 222, 246) uses this language. Brueggemann's theological work on Jeremiah is unparalleled.

8. So, e.g., L. Stulman, *Order Amid Chaos: Jeremiah as Symbolic Tapestry* (The Biblical Seminar 57; Sheffield: Sheffield Academic Press, 1998), 74, 114; cf. "absolute sovereign rule of YHWH," p. 43. See Brueggemann, *Jeremiah*, 167.

9. The word "contradiction" (or the like) is common in Jeremiah studies and is often linked to theological matters. There may well be some contradictions, but the many claimed "contradictions" immensely exacerbate the theological cacophony in Jeremiah. At the same time, the God of the final form of Jeremiah is an immensely complex character.

characterize God in radically different terms from much of the rest of the book." These tears "provide a glimpse of another kind of deity" from that of "the divine punisher and wrathful judge."[10] To the contrary, anger and tears do go together in Jeremiah (see 8:19c in context; 9:10 with 9:11 [MT 9:9 with 9:10]; 9:17–19 with 9:22 [MT 9:16–18 with 9:21]). These emotions are held together in God, as they commonly are when speaking of people who have suffered the brokenness of intimate relationships. Anger and tears flow together. The use of marital and parental metaphors in Jeremiah suggests that such relationships inform its portrayal of the character of God.

Or, consider William Holladay on issues of agency in Jer 23:1–4; he is puzzled by the change of the subject that "drives away" (*nādaḥ*) the people in 23:2–3. In verse 2, the shepherds do so; in verse 3, *God* drives them into exile (see also v. 8; 8:3; 24:9). Holladay claims that God as the subject of the verb in verse 3 "contradicts the accusation against the shepherds in v. 2."[11] On the contrary, readers are not asked to choose between these statements. Agency is conceived in a complex sense: shepherds, Babylonians, and God are all active agents in the exiling of the people (see 50:17; see below).[12]

Or, for Walter Brueggemann, the judging God and the faithful God are [215] incongruous; "the completed tradition of Jeremiah makes in turn two quite different theological emphases which are impossible to coalesce," namely, judgment and promise.[13] Thus, regarding various texts in chapters 1–25, he makes the following statements: "God has withdrawn fidelity"; God "has ceased to care"; a "complete absence of fidelity on God's part."[14] I have dealt with this dimension of Brueggemann's thought elsewhere.[15] I reiterate: "Why should love be inconsistent with 'just judgment'? Why is divine judgment an act of unfaithfulness? Why cannot judgment be in the service of graciousness? Why is a word or act 'against Israel' by YHWH incongruous with God's will 'for Israel'? I would claim that divine judgment is *always* in the service of God's loving and saving purposes."

Or, for Louis Stulman, in Jeremiah "the jumbled character of God pulsates with tensions and contradictions." By way of illustration, he says that "the reader confronts in the character of God the convergence of power

---

10. So O'Connor, "The Tears of God," 172, 184–85.
11. See W. Holladay, *Jeremiah 1* (Hermeneia; Philadelphia: Fortress, 1986), 615.
12. A similar complexity is evident in the other scattering verb used in these verses, *pûṣ* (cf. 23:1–2 with 9:16 [MT 9:15]; 13:24; 18:17; 30:11).
13. Brueggemann, *Jeremiah,* 270; cf. p. 283. Sometimes this issue is stated in such a way that God's judgment means the end of Israel's election! See, e.g., Stulman, *Order Amid Chaos,* 46–48.
14. Brueggemann, *Jeremiah,* 121, 142, 152, 278.
15. T. Fretheim, "Some Reflections on Brueggemann's God," in *God in the Fray* (ed. T. Linafelt and T. Beal; Minneapolis: Fortress, 1998), 24–37, esp. p. 30.

and vulnerability, love and wrath . . . , hope and disappointment."[16] I can accept "tensions," but the word "contradictions" is not theologically appropriate.

I suspect that the interpreters' own theological perspectives are decisively at work in claiming such incongruities (as they are in my own analysis). This point might be further illustrated with two common themes: divine sovereignty and divine freedom.

The Sovereignty of God

Stulman claims that "Yhwh reigns" is "a root metaphor in the book."[17] He follows efforts to qualify the sovereignty metaphor more generally, such as "dynamic sovereignty."[18] Yet such qualification is insufficient for Jeremiah; the problem is much deeper. A definition of sovereignty must be found that allows [216] for tears and anguish and hesitation. O'Connor broaches the issue when she claims that the tears of God "suggest a deity who vacates sovereignty and hierarchical transcendence, at least temporarily."[19] Yet this direction of reflection is not adequate either, as if God could turn sovereignty or transcendence off and on.

One could say that God's tears *recharacterize* sovereignty, say in the manner of a "crown of thorns" worn by one called "the King of the Jews" (Matt 27:29). If and when we do this, however, we should steer clear of the all too common "classical" descriptions of the God of Jeremiah noted above. Whatever the qualification, the claim that God's ruling is basic to other images for God in the book is itself problematic. Remarkably, the language of ruling is scarcely used for God in Jeremiah.[20]

Stulman's strong language that the God of Jeremiah is "in absolute control"[21] is certainly an ironic claim. He rightly warns against "confident propositional assertions about God's governance,"[22] but to say that God is "in absolute control of history" is just such a statement. If God is in "abso-

---

16. Stulman, *Order Amid Chaos*, 186. Regarding love and wrath, he qualifies himself by saying "or more accurately what Eichrodt called the 'wrath of love.'" One wonders why he retained the original formulation.

17. Stulman, *Order Amid Chaos*, 109.

18. See James L. Mays, *The Lord Reigns* (Louisville: Westminster John Knox, 1994), 6–9.

19. O'Connor, "The Tears of God," 185.

20. None of the verbs to rule or reign (e.g., *mālak, māšal, rādāh*) are used with God as subject (cf. the future rule of the messianic king in 23:5; 30:21; 33:21). Words in this semantic field are also uncommon. For example, *kissē'* ("throne") is used four times, two regarding the future (3:17; 49:38), one by the people (14:21), and one by Jeremiah in hymnic material (17:12). The six references to God as king are in the oracles against the nations (46:18; 48:15; 51:57) or against their idols (10:7, 10) and thus have a focused point of applicability. The other reference is a quotation of the people and is suspect (8:19), Also to be noted is how rarely the word "holy" is used for God ("Holy One of Israel," 50:29; 51:5).

21. So Stulman, *Order Amid Chaos*, 74, 114. The language of divine "control" appears throughout his discussion (e.g., pp. 73, 76, 96, 109–10).

22. Ibid., 161.

lute control," then why is it that God is so often portrayed as one who is in anguish and sorrow? If "ruling" is a primary metaphor for God in Jeremiah, then, given how unruly Israel is, we would have to score God a crashing management failure! The divine responses to Israel in the book must mean their words and deeds stand *against* the will of God; the will of the God of Jeremiah is resistible.

With respect to ethical implications, if God is in (absolute) control, then this becomes a pattern for human activity willy-nilly. Whether God's speaking or acting *should* be a model for human conduct is in many ways besides the point; like it or not, this will happen. In the Old Testament generally, the desired character of persons who follow this God is at least in part to be explicated on the basis of an exegesis of divine action and speech. God "loves the stranger . . . you shall also love the stranger" (Deut 10:18–19). Or, "Be merciful as the Lord your God is merciful" (Luke 6:36). Be in absolute control as God is in absolute [217] control? If monarchical images for God are the dominant ones in the book, then this invites readers to assume such images for their ways of speaking and acting. Perhaps the kings of Israel were especially fond of monarchical images for God![23]

The language of "power" is naturally drawn into any discussion of God being in control, though explicit power language is comparatively infrequent in Jeremiah (primarily with creation, 10:12 = 51:15; 27:5; 32:17). Stulman concludes at one point that "power and powerlessness embrace as divine sovereignty"; but "power," which he has just defined as being in "absolute control," empties the word "powerlessness" of any meaningful content.[24] Tears recharacterize God's power altogether.

It seems wise in the interpretation of Jeremiah to keep the language of sovereignty in reasonable proportion to its usage in the book and qualified by other pervasive images.[25] If one were to pick a "root metaphor" for God in the book of Jeremiah, and probably the Bible, it would be *relatedness*.[26]

---

23. Some statements by J. Moltmann could illustrate this point: "Since the Renaissance, God has always been understood one-sidedly as 'The Almighty.' *Omnipotence* has been valued as the superior characteristic of godliness. God is the Lord and the world is God's property to do with whatever God wills. God is the *absolute subject* and the world is the *passive object* of God's dominion. As God's likeness on earth, humans must understand themselves correspondingly as a subject . . . and the world as their passive object to be conquered. It is only through domination over the earth that humanity can correspond to God, the Lord of the world. Just as God is the Lord and owner of the whole world, so humans must work to become lords and owners of the earth and of themselves. According to this understanding, neither through goodness and truth, nor through patience and love, but through power and domination humans prove their likeness to God" ("Reconciliation with Nature," *WW* 11 [1991]: 118).

24. Stulman, *Order Amid Chaos,* 115.

25. For an earlier effort to qualify the language of divine sovereignty in terms of divine suffering, see T. Fretheim, "Suffering God and Sovereign God in Exodus: A Collision of Images," *HBT* 11 (1989): 31–56.

26. See, e.g., T. Fretheim, "The God Who Acts: An Old Testament Perspective," *ThTo* 54 (1997): 6–18.

Indeed, this metaphor would constitute an essential dimension for every concrete metaphor used for God.

The Freedom of God

Talk about divine freedom is common in Jeremiah studies, but the way in which this matter is formulated is often problematic.

One distinction between true and false prophecy in Jeremiah relates to [218] the preaching of peace and judgment (e.g., 6:14 = 8:11; 23:9–22; 28:1–17). The false prophets brought *only* a word of peace and assurance to an unfaithful people; Jeremiah understood that God would stand in judgment—even of the elect. One way in which this distinction has been articulated theologically is in terms of divine freedom. For example, Brueggemann asserts that "[t]he tradition of Jeremiah asserts God's freedom, even from God's partner. . . . To judge Jeremiah to be true is a theological verdict which allows for something wild, dangerous, unfettered, and free in the character of YHWH."[27] To be sure, it *is* important to affirm that God is free to judge his own people, and to affirm God's freedom more generally. At the same time, God's freedom for Jeremiah cannot be claimed in an unqualified way. For God to enter into judgment is not even fundamentally an exercise in freedom. More basically, God's judgment (or any divine action) is grounded in God's will and purpose for the world; indeed, judgment may be *necessary* if God would be faithful to that purpose. Judgment may be the only way in which God can do justice to relationships established and to a *purpose* to which he is committed (see 9:23–24 [MT 9:22–23]; 29:1–14; 31:1–6).

The immense agony of the God of Jeremiah is a demonstration that God is not truly free of his relationship with Israel. If God had "radical, unquestionable freedom,"[28] then he would not agonize so, either over the breakdown in the relationship or over decisions regarding judgment. If God were truly free, then he could just get up and leave, without hesitation, for he would have no significant commitments to this people. God agonizes over these matters precisely because he is *not* free of these people; God has long been in a committed relationship with a people whom he loves with "an everlasting love" and to whom, even in and through their pervasive infidelity, he has "continued [his] faithfulness" (31:3).

To speak of God's promises (e.g., to Noah, Abraham, David, all alluded to in 3:18; 7:7; 11:5; 30:3, 9; 31:35–37; 33:14–26; cf. 14:21) is to speak of a God who has chosen not to remain unfettered. Indeed, to speak of God's election of Israel and his promise to be their God places limits on any talk about divine freedom (see 30:22; 31:2; 32:38). God has exercised freedom

---

27. Brueggemann, *Jeremiah,* 138.
28. The phrase is that of L. Perdue, *The Collapse of History: Reconstructing Old Testament Theology* (OBT; Minneapolis: Fortress, 1994), 216. Cf. Brueggemann, *Jeremiah,* 138, 168, 215; Stulman, *Order Amid Chaos,* 176.

in making such promises in the first place, but, having freely made them, God's freedom is thereafter truly limited by those promises. God will be faithful to his own promises. Even more, God's history with Israel through the years means that Israel has been caught [219] up into the divine life and has shaped the divine identity. God will *forever* be known as the God of Israel; Israel is now a part of God's identity. It is precisely because of that relationship and related commitments that God grieves. Given the Noachic covenant references, one might also speak more generally of God's relationship with the world, to which God will be true.

To speak of the freedom of God in an unqualified way has ethical implications. If God is radically free, then we who are God's followers will seek to be radically free, wily-nilly; we may even come to believe that we are not bound to our commitments and can get on with our unfettered lives. Certainly one will want to speak of the freedom of the chosen people, but not in isolation from claims regarding commitments.

To summarize, neither the language of sovereignty nor that of freedom can be used for God in an unqualified sense in Jeremiah, for these understandings have ethical implications. This point is supported further by a closer look at the means in and through which God chooses to act in the world.

God Acts through Means:
Divine Dependence in Jeremiah

This section focuses on the portrayal of God in relationship to Nebuchadrezzar and Jeremiah. The general issue pertains to God's use of human beings as instruments in and through which God's purposes are carried out. The issue regarding God and Nebuchadrezzar relates to violent action; the issue regarding God and Jeremiah focuses on violent speech.

The first issue is the surprisingly common claim that the God of Jeremiah is, at least in some texts, imaged as acting in an unmediated way. For example, Robert Carroll, in connection with 13:9, claims that "Yнwн does the destroying rather than Babylon."[29] Several commentators will speak of Babylon as God's "instrument," but then claim that Yнwн is the only "real agent." For example, Brueggemann in a variety of contexts makes claims such as: "[t]here is no mediating agent" and "the army may be Babylonian, but the real agent is Yнwн."[30] He goes on to claim that "the rule of Yнwн is not done 'supernaturally,' but through historical agents."[31] Yet I cannot discern any theological space between God being the only "real agent" and God acting "supernaturally."

---

29. R. Carroll, *Jeremiah: A Commentary* (OTL; Philadelphia: Westminster,1986), 294.

30. E.g., Brueggemnann, *Jeremiah*, 54, 70, 176, 193, 428, 430, 439, 460; Stulman, *Order Amid Chaos*, 123.

31. Brueggemann, *Jeremiah*, 56; Carroll, *Jeremiah*, 763–64, 811.

Such theological statements regarding agency discount the genuine role [220] that the Babylonian armies play; they are no less "real" than YHWH. One must not diminish the distinction between God and his agents or discount the stature and the very real power of that human army. Just how God is involved in this activity cannot be factored out, though 51:11 may contain a clue with its reference to God as having "stirred up (*'ûr*) the spirit of the kings of the Medes" (cf. Zech 1:14; Jer 6:22; 25:32; 50:9, 41; 51:1).

The second issue pertains to the *ethical implications* of God's use of creatures to act in the world in and through *violent action* and *violent speech*. God chooses to be dependent on that which is not God to carry out the divine purposes in the world. This risky move links God with the character and activities of the chosen instruments. God does not perfect people before working through them, which means that one must not necessarily confer a positive value on the results (e.g., Babylon's actions; see below).

God and Nebuchadrezzar

Note the commonality of verbs and metaphors in the chart (see opposite page). Remarkable correspondences exist between God's actions and those of Nebuchadrezzar.[32]

What conclusions might one draw from this common fund of language? Such harsh words appear to be used for God because they are used for the actions of those in and through whom God mediates judgment. God's language in 27:8 puts the matter in a nutshell, "I have completed its destruction by his hand." In view of this mediation, God refers to Nebuchadrezzar as "my servant" (25:9; 27:6; 43:10). Others whom God designates "my servant" in Jeremiah are David, the prophets, and Israel! In some sense God has chosen to be *dependent* on Nebuchadrezzar in carrying out that judgment.[33] Note that Exod 3:8–10, where both God and Moses (often called "my servant") bring Israel out of Egypt, could function as a paradigm for such considerations.

As Nebuchadrezzar is identified as God's servant,[34] so, at the time of the return from exile, another "pagan" king, Cyrus of Persia, is identified as

---

32. Note the virtual absence of God talk in the descriptions of the fall of Jerusalem (39:1–14; 52:3b–30). It is also uncommon in the oracles against Babylon (chs. 50–51). Some violent actions are also ascribed to both Jeremiah and God (cf. 1:10 and 24:6; 25:15–29). For details, see T. Fretheim, *Jeremiah* (Macon, GA: Smyth and Helwys, 2002), 35–41.

33. On issues of divine dependence on the human, see idem, "Divine Dependence on the Human: An Old Testament Perspective," *ExAud* 13 (1997): 1–13. Brueggemann's perspective on this issue is stated in *Jeremiah*, 106 (see also p. 463): God is "not dependent on what is in the world." See also T. Fretheim, "Creator, Creature, and Co-creation in Genesis 1–2," in *All Things New: Essays in Honor of Roy A. Harrisville* (ed. A. Hultgren et al., Word and World Supplement 1; St. Paul: Word and World, 1992): 11–20.

34. Isa 45:4. See T. Overholt, "King Nebuchadnezzar in the Jeremiah Tradition," *CBQ* 30 (1968): 39–48.

God's Actions	Babylon's Actions
13:14—I will dash (*nps*) them I will not pity (*ḥml*), or spare (*ḥûs*),	48:12—they will dash (*nps*) in pieces 21:7—he will not pity (*ḥml*) or spare (*ḥûs*).
or have compassion (*rḥm*), when I destroy (*šḥt*) them (also 13:9).	or have compassion (*rḥm*) 36:29—he will destroy (*šḥt;* also 51:25)
9:16 [MT 9:15]; 13:24; 18:17; 30:11—I will scatter (*pûṣ*)	52:8; 23:1–2—scattered (*pûṣ*) the flock
24:9; 27:10 —1 will drive them away (*ndh*)	50:17; cf. 23:2—Israel driven away (*ndh*)
21:5—I will fight against you (*lḥm*)	21:2—he is making war against us (*lḥm*)
21:6–I will strike down (*nkh*)	21:7—he shall strike them down (*nkh*)
21:14 —I will kindle a fire (*yṣt*)	32:29—they will kindle (*yṣt*) a fire
49:20—God has a plan (*yʿṣ*) and *purpose* (*ḥšb*)	49:30—Nebuchadrezzar has a plan (*yʿṣ*) and purpose (*ḥšb*)
49:38—God will set (*śym*) God's throne	43:10—Nebuchadrezzar will set *(śym)* his throne
19:11(+)—God will break (*šbr*) the people [221]	43:13 Nebuchadrezzar will break (*šbr*) [221]
25:33—those slain (*ḥll*) by the LORD	51:4—Babylon must fall for the slain (*ḥll*) of Israel
27:8—Until I have completed its destruction . . .	. . . by his [the king of Babylon's] hand.
12:12; 47:6—sword of the LORD (also 14:12; 15:9)	20:4—they shall fall by the sword of enemies
25:38; 49:19—God imaged as a lion	4:7; 5:6—foe from the north imaged as a lion
29:4, 7, 14—God sends into exile (*glh*)	29:1(+)—Nebuchadrezzar sends into exile (*glh*)
29:17—God will pursue (*rdp*) them	39:5; 52:8—Chaldeans will pursue (*rdp*) them
30:3—I will bring them back to the land 31:20—I will have mercy	42:12b—he will bring them back to the land 42:12a—he will have mercy

God's "anointed one" (Isa 45:1–7). As with Cyrus,[35] Nebuchadrezzar does not know YHWH. The coalescence of God's actions and those of Nebuchadrezzar are abundantly clear in these texts. God will bring Babylon's armies against Israel and destroy them (and their neighbors); both God and Babylon are agents. God [222] may be the "ultimate" agent in these events, but not in such a way that other agents are less than "real."

Importantly, in this judgmental activity the Babylonians are not puppets in God's hands. That God is not the only effective agent in these

---

35. It is helpful to note that the granting of mercy could take place through the king of Babylon (42:11–12). Both the removal of peace and mercy (see 16:5; 21:7) and its restoration are thus related to his agency.

events is made clear by the divine judgment on Babylon (25:12–14; 50–51; see Isa 47:6–7; Zech 1:15, "while I [God] was only a little angry, they made the disaster worse"; note also the statement of divine regret in Jer 42:10, "I [God!] am sorry for the disaster"). In effect, Babylon exceeded its mandate, going beyond its proper judgmental activities, and committed iniquity itself in making the land an "everlasting waste." It is assumed (as with the oracles against the nations generally) that moral standards are available to which the nations are held accountable. This divine judgment on Babylonian excessiveness shows that God did not micro-manage their activities; they retained the power to make decisions and execute policies that flew in the face of the will of God. Hence, the will and purpose of God, indeed the sovereignty of God, active in these events is not "irresistible."[36] In some sense God risks what the Babylonians will do with the mandate they have been given. One element of that risk is that God's name will become associated with the violence, indeed the excessive violence, of the Babylonians.[37]

Another factor to be considered here are those texts in which God calls Jeremiah to bring a word of nonviolence through Israel's submission to Babylon (see chs. 27–29; 38:17–18). This divine command, which intends to reduce the violence, was announced after Babylon's subjugation of Jerusalem in 597 B.C.E. and before the fall and destruction of 586 B.C.E. With a political realism, God announces that if Israel would not rebel against Babylon, its future would take a less violent course. In other words, Babylon would function as agent of divine judgment in different ways, depending upon how Israel responded to the call for nonviolence. Israel's own resorting to violence would lead to even greater violence and to God's association with such violence, which is in fact what happens.

To recapitulate, God is not the sole agent in this situation; God acts in and through the agency of Babylon. At the same time, the latter will certainly act as kings and armies are known to act. That is predictable, and God (and other observers) knows this from experience with conquerors such as these. So, God in judgment will not "pity, spare, or have compassion" (13:14) because that is what the Babylonians, the instruments of divine judgment, will also not do (21:7). This portrayal of God reflects an extreme realism regarding what is about to [223] happen to the people. When the people do experience the pillaging, burning, and raping by the Babylonian armies, readers can be sure that they were real agents. Jeremiah also makes this witness when describing the actual destruction of Jerusalem (chs. 39, 52) in terms that hardly mention God.

These striking parallels suggest that *the portrayal of God's violent action in Jeremiah is conformed to the means that God uses.* God is portrayed in terms

---

36. Brueggemann, *Jeremiah*, 222.

37. For a comprehensive statement on divine risk taking, see John Sanders, *The God Who Risks: A Theology of Providence* (Downers Grove, IL: InterVarsity, 1998).

of the means available. God thereby accepts any fallout that may accrue to the divine reputation ("guilt by association").

The ethical implications of such a perspective are considerable. If God is the only "real" agent, then the humans through which God works are diminished, and, finally, they do not "count."[38] Such a perspective cheapens their creaturely status and devalues their words and deeds, making them finally inconsequential. For Jeremiah, however, both God and human agents have a crucial role to play, and their spheres of activity are interrelated in terms of function and effect. God is not only independent, and the humans involved are not only dependent. God has so shaped the created order that there are overlapping spheres of interdependence, and creative responsibility is shared with human beings.

This perspective is testimony to a fundamentally *relational* understanding of the way in which God acts in the world. There is an ordered freedom in the creation, a degree of openness and unpredictability, wherein God leaves room for genuine human decisions as they exercise their God-given power. Even more, God gives them powers and responsibilities in such a way that *commits* him to a certain kind of relationship with them. This entails a divine constraint and restraint in the exercise of power in relation to these agents (they overdid it!). These texts in Jeremiah are testimony to a divine sovereignty that gives power over to the created for the sake of a relationship of integrity.

God and Jeremiah

Jeremiah's laments often petition God to visit his enemies with various judgments (11:20; 12:3; 15:15; 17:18; 18:21–23; 20:12; also 6:11; 10:25). A comparison with God's speech shows some twenty parallels in words and phrases (see the chart on the next page).

[224] One question that arises from these comparisons is how the situation with God and Jeremiah relates to that of God and Babylon. Does God use such violent language because that is the language of God's prophet? This would be similar to what happens in any proclamation of the word of God in any age: God becomes associated with the language the preacher uses. This is certainly true at some basic level for God's words in Jeremiah; they are presented in human language. That God criticizes Jeremiah's language (15:18–19) could suggest this approach, though God never criticizes his own violent language. The task of assessing God's violent words would certainly be easier if we could say that God's language has been conformed to Jeremiah's own violent language. Perhaps one could appeal

---

38. Brueggemann uses this language in *Isaiah 40–66* (Westminster Bible Companion; Louisville: Westminster John Knox, 1998), 77. My colleague Frederick Gaiser has addressed the issue of agency in response to such claims in "'To Whom Then Will You Compare Me?' Agency in Second Isaiah," *WW* 19 (1999): 141–52.

God's Speech	Jeremiah's Speech
Wrath (*ḥēmâ*, 4:4; *zʿm*, 10:10)	Filled with *God's* wrath (6:11), indignation (15:17)
—Pour out wrath (*špk*, 6:11; 14:16)	—Pour out wrath (10:25)
Slaughter (*hărēgâ*, 7:32; 19:6)	Set them apart for slaughter (12:3)
Vengeance (*nqm*, 5:9, 29; 9:9 [MT 9:8])	Let me see *your* vengeance upon them (11:20; 15:15; 20:12)
Shame (*bôš*, 2:26), dismay (*ḥtt*, 8:9)	Let my persecutors be shamed, dismayed (17:18; 20:11)
Bring evil/disaster (*rāʿâ*, 4:6; 6:19; 11:23)	Bring upon them evil/disaster (17:18)
Break this people (*šbr*, 19:11) doubly (16:18)	Break them with *double* destruction (17:18)
Give sword, famine (11:22; 14:12; 15:2, 9)	Give them sword, famine (18:21)
"Therefore" (18:13+)	Therefore + announcement of judgment (18:21)
Childless, widowed (6:11b–12; 15:7–9)	Let wives become childless and widowed (18:21)
Young men die by the sword (11:22)	Let young men die by the sword (18:21)
Terror fall[s] suddenly (*pitʾōm*, 15:8)	When you bring the marauder suddenly (18:22)
Crying out (*zʿq*, 11:11–12; 25:34)	May a cry be heard (18:22)
God will not listen after repentance (14:7–11)	Do not forgive their iniquity (18:23)
Trip up, stumble (*kšl*, 6:15, 21; 8:12)	Let them be tripped up (18:23; 20:11)
"Time" of visitation (6:15; 10:15; 11:12–14)	"Time of anger" (18:23; cf. v. 17)
Violence, destruction (6:7)	Must shout, "violence and destruction" (20:8)
Weariness (15:6)	I am weary (6:11; 20:9)
They will not prosper (*lōʾ śkl*, 10:21)	They will not succeed (20:11)

more generally to the interactive character of the God-Jeremiah relationship; identifying who learns from whom is far from clear.[39] [225]

Another interpretation seems more likely, the upshot of which is to distinguish the character of the God-Jeremiah relationship from that of God and Babylon. An examination of Jeremiah's language reveals that he usually uses language that God has used in prior texts. Occasional parallels are found in texts subsequent to Jeremiah's speaking, but most follow the

---

39. It might be suggested that Jeremiah's sharp statement to God in 20:7 constitutes, at least in part, a critique of the word he was called to bring. This seems doubtful. Yes, God duped him with respect to the call, but Jeremiah recognizes that action for what it was, and he has done what he was called to do in the full knowledge of the deception. *Deception recognized* changes the equation, and Jeremiah never intimates that the word he was called to proclaim was a false word.

canonical order (we do not know the historical order, but God's call sets a certain agenda, 1:17–19) . The canonical ordering seems decisive for interpreting the relationship between God's speech and Jeremiah's. One example from the list is Jer 6:11–12. Children (playing in the streets!) are included among those who are *objects* of God's judgment (see 6:21; 9:21 [MT 9:20]; 19:9).[40] The children will not only suffer the effects of the judgment on the community; they are *singled out* for judgment: "Pour it out on the children!" Jeremiah seems to have learned both his rhetoric and its content from God, for a comparable word is heard in his laments (18:21); he calls upon God to give the children of his adversaries over to famine and sword. This prompts the question: why should children be the *specific* object of the wrath of God, made to suffer for what adults have done? Also present in these verses is the ravishing of property, including fields and wives, a fate to which God consigns them (cf. 2 Sam 12:11). This proves to be no rhetorical flourish; the witness to the devastating effect on children, women, and the environment is clear (see Lam 1:5, 16; 2:19–21; 4:4, 10; 5:11; cf. 2 Kgs 6:28–29; Isa 49:26; Ezek 5:10). One might, of course, say that these texts were written in light of actual events; even if this were the case to a greater or lesser degree, the fact that the editors chose to ascribe such language to God remains an issue.

In thinking through these texts, the interpreter should recall that God works judgment in and through the existing moral order.[41] Generally, the Old [226] Testament will not speak of this order in deistic ways.[42] God will

---

40. Some interpreters think that Jeremiah is the speaker of 6:11b (see NEB). Even if this were the case, the other three references noted are sufficient to ground these observations.

41. Helpful resources for this topic include Patrick D. Miller, Jr., *Sin and Judgment in the Prophets: A Stylistic and Theological Analysis* (SBLMS 27; Chico, CA: Scholars Press, 1982); Klaus Koch, "Is There a Doctrine of Retribution in the Old Testament?" in *Theodicy in the Old Testament* (ed. J. Crenshaw; Philadelphia: Fortress, 1983), 57–87. Most recently, see Gene Tucker, "Sin and 'Judgment' in the Prophets," in *Problems in Biblical Theology: Essays in Honor of Rolf Knierim* (ed. H. Sun et al.; Grand Rapids: Eerdmans, 1997), 373–88. See also my article, "Divine Judgment and the Warming of the World: An Old Testament Perspective," in *God, Evil, and Suffering: Essays in Honor of Paul R. Sponheim* (ed. T. Fretheim and C. Thompson; Word and World Supplement 4; St. Paul: Word and World, 2000), 21–32. G. von Rad has provided a helpful (and generally approving) look at these matters (*Old Testament Theology* [trans. D. Stalker; New York: Harper, 1962], 1:264–68, 383–87).

42. Tucker delineates several different formulations: texts that are "dynamistic" and have no explicit reference to God (e.g., Isa 3:9–11; Hos 10:13–15), those in which God makes the connection between sin and consequence (Jer 6:19; 21:14), and, least common, those that have a juridical element (e.g., Amos 4:1–3). How these "judgment" texts are to be related is best seen in the work of H. H. Schmid, who places them under the comprehensive umbrella of creation theology ("Creation, Righteousness, and Salvation: 'Creation Theology' as the Broad Horizon of Biblical Theology," in *Creation in the Old Testament* (ed. B. Anderson; Philadelphia: Fortress, 1984], 102–17). See also W. Brueggemann, "The Uninflected *Therefore* of Hosea 4:1–3," in *Reading from This Place: Social Location and Biblical Interpretation in the United States* (ed. F. Segovia and M. Tolbert; Minneapolis: Fortress, 1995), 231–49.

see to the moral order so that sin and evil do not go unchecked in the life of the world and so that God's good order of creation (= righteousness) can be reestablished. Consistently in Jeremiah, the people's rā‘â (= evil) will issue in their rā‘â (= disaster; e.g., 6:19, "the fruit of their schemes"; 14:16, "I will pour out *their* wickedness upon them"; see also 21:12–14). God does not introduce anything new into the situation; he does not impose sanctions that are distinct from the violations. God's action is usually not described as forensic and external in nature; rather, he mediates the effects of the people's own wickedness, which are intrinsic to the evil deed itself.[43] This divine involvement is not conceived in terms of micro-management, as God's later judgment on the Babylonians for their overkill makes clear (see above).[44]

Readers could also recall that this is a *communal* judgment; once unleashed, Babylon's armies will cut down everything in their path. In war, everyone will suffer (cf. the effects of indiscriminate bombing in World War II). Readers might also recall this kind of rhetoric in the psalms of imprecation (Ps 109:9–10; 137:9).[45] Certainly we do not want to insist that speakers of laments to God be held to careful theological formulations; hurting persons must be allowed to pour out their anger to God regardless of the theological fallout. In this light, perhaps we should allow for such rhetoric in the laments of God as well; God is deeply pained by [227] what has happened, expressing all the sorrow and anger that goes with the breakdown of a relationship of intimacy. But if we do so, then we should seek to tell it like it is for God and not dismiss such words by (easy?) appeals to divine sovereignty or mystery. Yet, however ameliorating such comments may be, standing squarely before us is the command of God to pour out wrath on the children.

This analysis leads to the unsettling idea that, as the canonical editors present the case, Jeremiah has learned to use such violent language against his persecutors from God. In other words, the divine character has shaped Jeremiah's character. His speaking follows a pattern set by God; God's judgment has become his judgment. Jeremiah has become conformed to the wrath of God (see 6:11a; 25:15–17).

---

43. Gerhard von Rad speaks of a "synthetic view of life" (*Old Testament Theology*, 1:265) in which the "retribution is not a new action which comes upon the person concerned from somewhere else; it is rather the last ripple of the act itself which attaches to its agent almost as something material. Hebrew in fact does not even have a word for punishment" (p. 385).

44. See also the statements about divine wrath in n. 4.

45. For a recent helpful study of these psalms, see E. Zenger, *A God of Vengeance? Understanding the Psalms of Divine Wrath* [German, *Feindpsalmen!*] (trans. L. Maloney; Louisville: Westminster John Knox, 1996). These psalms are, of course, words *about* and *to* God, not words *by* God, but they may well assume an understanding of God's own words of judgment such as are found in Jeremiah and other prophets. They can speak this way because they understand God to have spoken in these terms regarding their enemies.

Many interpreters have had difficulty with Jeremiah's outbursts for their harsh and unforgiving nature and sought to explain them (away) in one fashion or another, usually by appealing to Jeremiah's humanity. This is a human being in deep anguish. However, these texts say more than "He's only human." However much Jeremiah's language corresponds to that of the imprecation psalms, it cannot simply be ascribed to outbursts over his suffering at the hands of his enemies. Jeremiah's language has been explicitly shaped by God's language; Jeremiah's character has been shaped by God's character.

Notably, those interpreters who seek to "explain" Jeremiah's language usually do not make a comparable judgment on God's language; God usually gets home scot-free. We would certainly be properly critical of, say, a modern general who gave his soldiers orders to kill children. Why not the God of Jeremiah? Yet on what grounds would we do so? Where does one stand in bringing such a critique? One should be guided at the least by an inner-biblical warrant, seeking to be true to the basic biblical portrayal of God (cf. the common response to patriarchy in biblical texts).[46] Even more, is not this portrayal of God deeply problematic when it comes to thinking about the development of human character? Yet again, on what grounds? One must at least be true to the basic biblical portrayal of the character of those who follow this God.[47]

One way to proceed would be that of Daniel Berrigan, whose reflections on Jeremiah are often helpful, not least on the use of the language of judgment in our own time. Yet listen to his reflections on Jer 18:19–23:[48] [228]

> Who is this God anyway, the God of Jeremiah, what of his moral physiognomy? Do such oracles as are here recorded, with their summons to violent reprisal (a call taken seriously, more, initiated again and again by YHWH), offer sound insight into God, our God as well as Jeremiah's? Insight into God's hope for ourselves? Into crime (ours) and punishment (God's)—an ineluctable hyphenation, a logic of terrifying consequence? Why does the God of Jeremiah never once counsel—forgiveness? For this we are forced to turn in another direction than Jeremiah, to a later time, another seer—maligned as he is, put to scorn, murdered. And amid the infamy, a far different response is offered to his persecutors; a prayer on their behalf, an intercession (Luke 23:34). Jeremiah, we confess in confusion of heart, much resembles ourselves. And Jesus much resembles God. But not the God of Jeremiah, the God of Jesus.

---

46. Criteria and texts would have to be more fully developed. For an initial attempt, see T. Fretheim and K. Froehlich, *The Bible as Word of God in a Postmodern Age* (Minneapolis: Fortress, 1998), 97–126.

47. Again, texts and criteria would need to be fully developed and issues of "canon within the canon" explored.

48. D. Berrigan, *Jeremiah: The World, the Wound of God* (Minneapolis: Fortress, 1999), 84.

But is it so simple? Is this not a return to that old saw about Jesus coming to deliver us from the abusive God of the Old Testament? Does Jesus mean that there is no place anymore for harsh, even unforgiving rhetoric? Yet, if we do not take Berrigan's route, do we simply move over to the other ditch and accept this language without evaluation? It is often argued that God's language is beyond scrutiny, or that biblical usage places an imprimatur on the (indiscriminate) use of such language by those who learn how to speak and act from such a God. However, does not this imaging of God stand for the violence that most of us would stand against?

One might seek a middle way and consider the nature of the situation into which such a word might be spoken. Upon careful discernment of a given situation of, say, the horrific abuse of human beings, one might be called upon to speak such a harsh word (though the words about children seem not to have a conceivable appropriate context). So, this language of God and Jeremiah would be placed in the same rare-use category as the psalms of imprecation and then used only by those whose personal experience calls for such rhetoric, or by those who stand in solidarity with them.

Nevertheless, however important it is to have this language available for such moments, the issue with the God of Jeremiah seems more complex. It is one thing to set a half-dozen psalms on the back burner for potential use; it is another thing to have the unrelenting harsh imagery of a major biblical book drummed into our consciousness on a regular basis. Will we not, as readers and hearers of this word, learn all too well how to speak and act from this portrayal of God?[49] This problem is at least implicitly recognized in the common [229] lectionary, where the only text assigned with such harsh language is Jeremiah's lament in 20:7–13 (11:18–20 is an alternate); God's use of this language is not represented. This may well be an appropriate decision regarding the public use of these Jeremiah texts, but do we leave the texts in this kind of limbo—retaining them in our printed Bibles but making no practical use of them? Several summary considerations regarding the use of these texts seem in order by way of conclusion. We also suggest further work to be done:

1. These texts remind us of the inadequacy of all of our language about God. Every image comes up short; every metaphor has its "no"; every reference to God is in some discontinuity with the reality that is God. Yet, even so, it is important to remember that these images are not "mere metaphors"; they have a great impact on our thinking, feeling, and being. Willy-nilly, they will sink deep into our selves and shape us in ways beyond our knowing. It may be that certain images for God in Jeremiah need to be set aside while retaining the "yes" of which they speak—indictment and judgments.[50]

---

49. For further discussion, see Fretheim and Froehlich, *The Bible as Word of God*.

50. Zenger's comment is helpful in thinking through such issues (*A God of Vengeance*, 84): "[T]he history of the impact and reception of an individual text in the annals of Juda-

2. By recognizing these harsh images for what they are, they can keep us alert to the fact that language about God has powerful effects upon people and world, both positive and negative, and can be used to promote ideas and practices that do not serve life and well-being. We must not be casual or indifferent about the God language we use.

3. Another approach would claim that such language about God is designed to make readers uncomfortable, to show what their sin has wrought, and to reveal the depths of their own violence. To try to escape from the force of texts such as these is a typical sinner's response. But are there no limits to such an approach? It is one thing to be told that our sin has had incredibly negative effects upon the children of the world; it is another thing to say that God directly commands that such violence be visited upon the children. Yet such effects on children are in some sense still related to God's circumstantial will,[51] and we are invited to think further of the kind of God who is often caught up in violent activities that so adversely affect children.

4. To engage texts of this kind could enhance our dialogical relationship with the biblical text more generally. The proper stance of readers in working [230] with the text is not one of passivity or submission or simply listening. As with key figures such as Abraham and Moses, the word of God calls for genuine interaction.

5. By carefully considering this language, and struggling with these texts, our imaginations may be sparked to seek ever more appropriate language for God. Certainly there are inadequacies in our present formulations that need attention, and these texts may not only remind us of this fact but also serve to generate new reflections regarding God.[52]

---

ism and Christianity must also be taken into consideration when we reflect on its revelatory character. . . . [Some texts] can have been received in such a destructive way that the very knowledge of this negative history of reception becomes a constitutive part of the revelatory dimension of these texts."

51. On distinctions within the will of God, see T. Fretheim, "Will of God in the OT," *ABD* 4:914–20.

52. A postscript: I am left wondering whether much of this analysis is not too subtle for the average reader/hearer of Jeremiah. The violence of God's actions and speech in a "naked" form is what people will often take away from an encounter with these texts. They may well understand that such violent actions and language are in some sense a permitted or even mandated human response, to be exercised as they choose. Also, I am grateful to Beverly Stratton and Bruce Birch for their responses to earlier versions of this essay.

Is Anything Too Hard for God? (Jeremiah 32:27)

This study suggests an interpretation of Jeremiah 32 that cuts against the grain of traditional understandings.[1] I wish to argue that Jeremiah understands the purchase of land, not as a sign of *future* restoration but as a sign that God will now bring a halt to the judgment in progress and move directly to restore Israel's fortunes. This interpretation also makes possible a new look at the question of the coherence of the chapter.[2]

My focus for this interpretation is a discernment of the relationship of God's query in Jer 32:27 ("Is anything too hard for me?") to Jeremiah's prior declaration in 32:17 ("Nothing is too hard for you").[3] Commentators generally take [232] God's query as a rhetorical question reaffirming Jeremiah's prior declaration, in effect: that's right, Jeremiah, nothing is too hard for me. Walter Brueggemann even calls it divine "self-praise."[4] The upshot is that Jeremiah's statement and God's are "in essential agreement."[5] At the same time, it has troubled scholars that Jeremiah's statement takes the form of a declaration, while God's response takes the form of a question. Should not Jeremiah voice the question and God declare the theological point?

I think this ordering—declaration followed by question—should be taken seriously, and the effect is that God's question is *not* a way of re-

---

This essay was originally published in *Catholic Biblical Quarterly* 66 (2004): 231–36.

1. This article is a more fully and somewhat differently developed treatment of a point in my commentary, *Jeremiah* (Smyth and Helwys Bible Commentary; Macon, GA: Smyth & Helwys, 2002), 459–68. Detailed studies of Jeremiah 32 are rare; the most recent are those of Walter Brueggemann, "A 'Characteristic' Reflection on What Comes Next (Jeremiah 32:16–44)," in *Prophets and Paradigms* (ed. Stephen B. Reid; Sheffield: Sheffield Academic Press, 1996), 16–32; and Andrew G. Shead, *The Open Book and the Sealed Book: Jeremiah 32 in Its Hebrew and Greek Recensions* (JSOTSup 347; Sheffield: Sheffield Academic Press, 2002).

2. I grant that Jeremiah 32 has had a complex transmission history. Several redactional layers may be discerned, but if this study proves convincing, the number of such possibilities will be reduced. My intent in this article is to work with the final form of the text, and my thesis regarding the interpretation of Jer 32:27 would be supported by a claim that the thought of Jeremiah 32 flows more smoothly as a result.

3. For the purposes of this article, I accept the common translation, "hard," for *pele'*. Shead (*Open Book*, 128) concludes that "G, like Tg and Pesh, took it to mean 'hidden'" because it "avoids the suggestion—even the negative suggestion—that something could be impossible for God."

4. Brueggemann, "'Characteristic' Reflection," 29. Brueggemann elsewhere (*A Commentary on Jeremiah: Exile and Homecoming* [Grand Rapids: Eerdmans, 1998], 307) claims that God's "question corresponds to the assertion of Jer 32:17."

5. William L. Holladay, *Jeremiah* 2 (Hermeneia; Philadelphia: Fortress, 1989), 206.

affirming Jeremiah's claim; it is a more complex reply. The fact that the *kol* in Jer 32:17, 27 is missing from the parallel in Gen 18:14 suggests an emphasis on that word in this context, and that could be used to support either of two understandings of God's question. If God's query is considered a rhetorical question, it should be understood in this way, with emphasis on the first two words: *Is anything* too hard for me? Yes! More likely, God's question is a genuine question to Jeremiah that invites Jeremiah's reflection regarding what he has declared about God: Are there not some things that *are* too hard for God?[6]

A closer look at Jeremiah's prayer (32:16–25) and God's response (32:26–44) provides further support for this reading. It is important to note that Jeremiah's prayer *follows* his purchase of the land. He is not puzzled over whether to obey God's command; he has already done that. His puzzlement (a common sense given to "Ah Lord God," v. 17) is a post-purchase reflection in the form of a prayer. For Brueggemann, this prayer expresses Jeremiah's "trustful incredulity"; this suggestion is helpful so far as it goes.[7] But a further assumption commonly made by interpreters is that Jeremiah in his prayer correctly understands the *timing* of things, namely, that the positive future symbolized by the purchase of land lies *beyond* the disaster. I suggest, rather, that when God commands the purchase of land and interprets the symbolic act in v. 15 ("houses and fields shall again be bought in this land"), Jeremiah understands the purchase not [233] as "nonsensical" in and of itself,[8] but as incongruous because it is applicable in the short term. The issue for Jeremiah is not that he cannot reconcile present disaster and future hope, but that God's word about the purchase of land seems to *override* the announcement of judgment. The issue is not that God opens up a future for Israel,[9] but that God has determined to put that future in place without Israel's having fully to go through the disaster (cf. Isa 31:4–5).

Jeremiah begins his prayer by declaring that nothing is too hard for God and grounds that claim by referring to God as Creator, which in turn

---

6. Brueggemann ("'Characteristic' Reflection," 26) thinks that God's query may be either a rhetorical question (with an implied answer of no) or "a serious probing question which intends to evoke an answer and a commitment from the one who prays." To consider this a "probing question" is helpful, but for different reasons. For if God's point is not different from Jeremiah's declaration in v. 17 it is difficult to see what more God could want from Jeremiah. Holladay (*Jeremiah 2*, 212) calls it an "ironic counter question," which apparently assumes that a question informs Jeremiah's declaration (such as: Do you really believe what you've said?), though, finally for Holladay, the claim being made by both Jeremiah and God is the same.

7. Brueggemann, "'Characteristic' Reflection," 19. This is also affirmed by Patrick D. Miller, "The Book of Jeremiah: Introduction, Commentary, and Reflections," *NIB*, 6:820.

8. See William McKane, *A Critical and Exegetical Commentary on Jeremiah XXVI–LII* (ICC; Edinburgh: T. & T. Clark, 1996), 843; Brueggemann, "'Characteristic' Reflection," 24.

9. See Holladay, *Jeremiah 2*, 206.

elevates God's power (v. 17). Language referring explicitly to the power of God is used in Jeremiah most basically with respect to creation (e.g., 10:12; 27:5; 51:15), but also, as in this prayer, with respect to God's salvific actions on behalf of Israel. Jeremiah proceeds with a creed-like rehearsal of God's "great and mighty" actions in Israel's history, undertaken by God's "great power and outstretched arm." He also includes a statement about the moral order, namely, that God "gives" (*ntn*) to all according to "the fruit of their doings." What is now happening to Jerusalem is the natural outcome of this moral order, and Jeremiah may understand that this fixes the disaster in place. Then Jeremiah moves to the crux of his point: the people have been unfaithful, and the announced disasters being experienced are the just consequence of their deeds. Jeremiah asks God to observe that the word of God he has spoken is in fact coming to pass; the city has been given into the hands of the Babylonians. Yet God has told him to buy this land (NAB captures the sense best)! The address to God is direct: God, nothing is too hard for you, but I don't understand how you can set your own word aside and stop the judgment in its tracks. Jeremiah has some highly pertinent questions, but declares his trust in God's power to bring this strange future about.[10]

God's response in v. 27 picks up on Jeremiah's initial words in v. 17. God's reply, "I am the God of all flesh," grants Jeremiah's point about creation, but then God raises a question regarding Jeremiah's claim that nothing is too hard for God. A frequent way of understanding this query refers it back to the "impossibility"of the future that the purchase of land signifies.[11] In other words, this future may seem to be impossible for God, but for God the impossible becomes possible. I [234] think this interpretation misses the point. At this juncture in their discussion, God is responding to Jeremiah's understanding that the purchase of land is a sign that the judgment has been cut off. God's query invites Jeremiah to consider whether this is indeed possible for God. Might not short-circuiting the judgment be impossible for God?

The movement of thought in the balance of the chapter makes sense as a way of thinking through this impossibility for God; it is expressed in the twofold "therefore" in vv. 28, 36, often puzzling to interpreters. If God's query in v. 27 does have the same sense as Jeremiah's declaration in v. 17,

---

10. This response of Jeremiah may suggest a kind of "desperate hope" that this detour past disaster will prove possible; it may be profitably compared to Jeremiah's initially hopeful response to the prophecy of Hananiah (see Jer 28:6).

11. See, e.g., Patrick Miller ("Jeremiah," 822): "The God who covenants with Israel can break out of all conventions and overcome all seeming constraints, including those of the Lord's own purposive actions [!], to effect a new reality, to turn punishment into redemption, devastation into good, danger and oppression into safety and security." Miller's emphasis upon "all" suggests that God can even bypass judgment on the way to salvation for Israel.

then Holladay is right that God's expressed "words of doom are not germane to the issue."[12] Hence, the scholars who see a basic incoherence to the flow of these verses would be on target.[13] Our understanding of v. 27, however, provides a smoother flow of thought in what follows. The first "therefore" shows that judgment is *necessary* in view of pervasive levels of unfaithfulness. Jeremiah's interpretation of the purchase of land is *not* a possibility for God; "therefore," to make clear why that is the case, God reiterates the indictment and judgment in very sharp terms (vv. 28–35).

The word of salvation that follows is possible only because of the necessary judgment spelled out in vv. 28–35—hence the second "therefore" (v. 36).[14] God thereby demonstrates that it is not possible for God to bypass the destruction on the way to restoration (cf. the similar argument in 33:1–9; note the "second time," as if the point needed to be repeated). That is to say, it is only through judgment that salvation becomes possible. God will be at work within the judgment itself to bring about a new future; the death of the old heart is necessary for the creation of the new heart (v. 42 brings these themes together). At this time and place, there is no other possible way *for God* to move into the future.[15] From God's perspective, what is at stake in this situation are God's promises and Israel's future, and one approach to this dilemma is, in fact, impossible. God is *not able* to take a shortcut into that future and still be faithful to the relationship with Israel.

[235] This discussion has developed an argument that, given the interpretation of Jer 32:27 proposed here, the flow of thought in Jeremiah 32 is much more cogent than is commonly suggested. If so, then that cogency, in turn, becomes an argument for my interpretation of 32:27, at least at the level of the final form of the text.

Several other considerations may be drawn into the argument. The question of divine possibility was certainly raised by exilic readers.[16] Their

12. Holladay, *Jeremiah 2*, 207; comparably, McKane, *Jeremiah*, 847.
13. Robert Carroll (*Jeremiah* [OTL; Philadelphia: Westminster, 1986], 626–27) considers these verses "out of place"; "the spelling out of the claim [in v. 27] does not appear until vv. 37–41." Moreover, for Carroll (p. 631), with the various expansions represented in vv. 27–41, only in vv. 42–44 does the "chapter finally reflect on the significance of Jeremiah's buying family land." McKane (*Jeremiah*, 851) goes farther in stating that v. 42 has "no particular contact with Jeremiah's purchase of a field."
14. Brueggemann (*Jeremiah*, 307) claims that "therefore" is "odd"; such a causal understanding could not "be further from the intended shape of the argument." But, in fact, it is precisely in and through the judgment that "therefore" can be stated. Brueggemann's later (p. 310) reference to a "two-stage" process seen in terms of death and resurrection moves closer to the thought of the passage.
15. The force of God's summary quotation of Jeremiah's message in v. 36 (cf. v. 43), in a quotation of what the people have said, constitutes a reassurance that Jeremiah's word of judgment is still a crucial word in the divine economy, for it is only in and through such judgment that God's salvation becomes possible.
16. For the understanding of an exilic readership for Jeremiah, see Fretheim, *Jeremiah*, esp. pp. 4–11.

"Why?" questions are common in the first half of Jeremiah and elsewhere.[17] It is exactly such a "Why?" question that is voiced by Zedekiah in 32:3–5. His question—unusual in its third-person reference to the speaker—probably reflects a question asked by exilic readers:[18] Why could God not have made possible a future for us short of all the death and destruction? Are not all things possible for God? The upshot of the divine reply to Jeremiah is that their premise regarding the power of God is flawed. This entire narrative, then, may be said to be an effort to challenge the exiles' questions and their premise regarding divine possibilities.

This understanding of Jeremiah 32 might be linked in a helpful way to the Book of Consolation (chaps. 30–31), which, in turn, may further clarify chap. 32. The opening question of 32:3–5, coming as it does following— indeed, interrupting—the repeated promises of restoration in the Book of Consolation, raises a thorny issue regarding divine power (as 32:17 and 27 recognize). If God has this remarkably detailed and seemingly impossible future in store for Israel, why would it not be possible for God to stop the destruction in its tracks and move directly into that future? This direction of thought suggests that the immediately following report of a word from the Lord regarding the purchase of land (32:6–8; already announced in v. 1) might have been interpreted by Jeremiah as God's decision to do just that. In the final form of the text, the Jeremiah of chap. 32 already understands from the content of chaps. 30–31 that God does indeed have a future for Israel.[19] The issue that arises for Jeremiah in connection with the purchase of land is not *that* God has such a positive future but the timing of that future in relation to the judgment already under way.[20] [236]

Finally, I briefly draw into the argument two other features of Jeremiah 32. The frequent first-person reference to divine anger in God's response in vv. 29–37 is noteworthy (eight times!), as is the strong language with respect

---

17. For example, Jer 9:12: "Why is the land ruined and laid waste like a wilderness, so that no one passes through?"(see also Jer 5:19; 13:22; 14:19; 16:10; 22:8; Deut 29:24; 1 Kgs 9:8).

18. If my interpretation of v. 27 is correct, it can be shown that the entire chapter is a response to Zedekiah's question (see Fretheim, *Jeremiah,* 453–68; cf. Gerald L. Keown, Pamela J. Scalise, and Thomas G. Smothers, *Jeremiah 26–52* (WBC 27; Dallas: Word, 1993), 146–47. Verse 26, which refers to Jeremiah in the third person, may suggest otherwise; but see Jer 27:1–2.

19. Patrick Miller speaks of chap. 32 as an extension and confirmation of the Book of Consolation ("Jeremiah," 819); cf. Keown et al., *Jeremiah,* 149. While it is possible that Jeremiah 32 simply repeats the oft-made point of chaps. 30–31, the newly stated question in 32:3–5 and the issues of coherence it raised suggest that another, if related, issue is being addressed.

20. God's command that the scroll be placed in the jar "for a long time" (v. 14) is probably understood by Jeremiah as a reference not to the exile (see Holladay, *Jeremiah 2,* 212) but to the perdurance of what the deed signifies regarding the land. God may have had the exile in mind, yet the pertinence of the deed to Israel's relationship with the land would extend beyond the exile.

to Israel's sin being contrary to the will of God (v. 35; see 7:31; 19:5). This powerfully stated resistance to the express will of God, which intensifies Jeremiah's witness in v. 23, cannot be ignored by God in moving into the future. Indeed, this resistance is understood to be of such a nature that it severely complicates God's working possibilities in this situation (which, in turn, speaks to issues of divine power). God cannot but be angry, of course, for God's will has been so deeply violated.[21] But, even more, the repeated reference to divine anger suggests that the wrath of God is so "aroused" (v. 31) that it cannot simply be stopped in its tracks, even by God (cf. the "spending" of divine anger in Ezekiel, e.g., 5:13). In the words of Jer 4:28, "I have spoken, I have purposed; I have not relented nor will I turn back" (see 15:19; Ezek 24:14). This witness to divine anger and a resistant Israel helps to substantiate God's point that judgment *cannot* be short-circuited. Salvation is possible for both God and Israel only in, through, and beyond judgment.[22]

To conclude on a more general note: issues of divine possibility must be considered from within an understanding of the relationship between God and Israel. Because God honors commitments made with Israel, and given who God is, God is not able to act in ways that would be unfaithful. One way for God to be unfaithful at this juncture in Israel's history would be simply to overlook injustice and to treat infidelity lightly (6:14). Judgment is necessary if God is going to "continue faithfulness" (31:3), do justice to relationships established (9:23–24), and move toward a new world (29:10–11, "only when").[23]

---

21. Generally speaking, if the will of God is irresistible, then God's often-expressed anger is meaningless or directed only at the divine self. If there were no sin, there would be no wrath. For detail, see T. Fretheim, "Theological Reflections on the Wrath of God in the Old Testament,"*HBT* 24 (2002), 1–26.

22. This interpretation is not put in question by the fact that the gift of a new heart is a unilateral, unconditional act of God. In eschatological thinking, God will act in such a way. For example, there will be a new heaven and a new earth come what may.

23. More generally, it might be stated that faithfulness in relationships entails constraint and restraint, even for God. God may theoretically be able to exercise power of any sort, but when presented with cases such as this, God cannot do so and remain faithful.

The Exaggerated God of Jonah

The book of Jonah has generated a wide variety of interpretations; at the same time, a basic scholarly agreement exists regarding the book's presentation of God. My purpose in this article is to suggest an alternative view of Jonah's God.

Scholars have not finally settled the identification of the genre of Jonah. Most understand that the book is not to be interpreted as an (auto) biographical or historical account, even though links can be established with historical realities (e.g., Nineveh; the Jonah of 2 Kgs 14:25). But the next step in genre identification has proved more difficult. Among the suggestions that have been made are: parable, allegory, midrash, parody, satire, didactic story, ironic tale.[1] In any case, the book is imaginative literature. This occasions the question as to whether the *God* of Jonah is also a product of the imagination, at least in part, rather than a traditional or straightforward account.

Exaggeration in Jonah

Most scholars agree that Jonah often uses exaggerated language,[2] especially [126] regarding the city of Nineveh, its size and population (3:3–8; 4:11).[3] The mammoth city, extraordinarily wicked (1:2), experiences a total conversion after one minimalist sermon; even the animals are dressed up

---

This essay was originally published in *Word and World* 27 (2007): 125–34.

1. See James Limburg, *Jonah: A Commentary* (Louisville: Westminster John Knox, 1993): "The book of Jonah may be described as a fictional story developed around a historical figure for didactic purposes" (p. 24). See also Robert B. Salters, *Jonah and Lamentations* (Sheffield: JSOT Press, 1994), 40–50; Daniel J. Simundson, *Hosea, Joel, Amos, Obadiah, Jonah, Micah* (Nashville: Abingdon, 2005), 255–59.

2. Many scholars understand that the book of Jonah is filled with irony; purposeful exaggeration is a way of speaking ironically. For a summary statement, see, e.g., Edwin M. Good, *Irony in the Old Testament* (London: S.P.C.K., 1965), 39–55. For details, see David Marcus, *From Balaam to Jonah: Anti-prophetic Satire in the Hebrew Bible* (Atlanta: Scholars Press, 1995) 93–159. See also the learned essays by Ehud Ben Zvi, *Signs of Jonah: Reading and Rereading in Ancient Yehud* (London: Sheffield Academic Press, 2003). For my own previous work, see *The Message of Jonah: A Theological Commentary* (Minneapolis: Augsburg, 1977), 51–60.

3. Scholars disagree about the size of Nineveh in ancient times. Most common is this assessment from Jonathan Magonet: "Everything about Nineveh is exaggerated, by the author's design" (Jonathan Magonet, *Form and Meaning: Studies in Literary Techniques in the Book of Jonah* [Sheffield: Almond, 1983], 49. For a different view, see Jack M. Sasson, *Jonah* [New York: Doubleday, 1990]). The phrase, "the king of Nineveh" (3:6), is unusual; Nineveh is thereby treated more like a country than a city.

in sackcloth and ashes and cry out to God. One thinks also of the un-precedented idea that a fish swallowed a human being and vomited him up unharmed after three days.[4] Also to be noted are Jonah's composition of a psalm while ensconced in the belly of a fish and the book's unprec-edented concentration of water/Pit images (some twenty-two allusions!). Moreover, a prophet of God becomes very angry at God's positive response to Nineveh's repentance (3:10–4:2); indeed, Jonah had resisted God's call to preach to Nineveh, not wanting to give God opportunity to be true to the divine character (4:2). Ironically, Jonah twice expresses great joy over *his own* deliverance (2:1–10; 4:6)!

Yvonne Sherwood expresses well the book's use of exaggerated language:

> the adjective "big" (*gadol*) is added lavishly to almost every noun (the fish is big, the city is big, the wind is big); "yeast" is added prodigiously (carnival fashion) to reality (*qiqayon* plants grow like triffids, a fish hears and responds to instructions); and verbs are stretched to excess (Yhwh does not send the storm but *hurls* it [1:4], the worm does not nibble at the plant but *smites* it [4:7])—the worm and the plant, like God and Jonah, are engaged in warfare and the reader can almost *see* the words "Pow," "Biff," and "Arghh" writ large over the text.[5]

Sherwood goes on to show that anything can happen "in the strangely counter-intuitive world that is the book of Jonah; a prophet can run away from God; the Assyrians, epitome of wickedness, can be inspired by a five-word oracle and repent in dust and ashes. . . . The plot can go anywhere, do anything, and the accumulation of 'who knowses' and 'perhapses' (1:6; 3:9) acts as wry commentary on the infinite possibility, and 'miraculous' caprice, of its development.'"[6]

I am suggesting that readers of Jonah should bring their understanding of the God of Jonah more into line with the book's exaggerated use of lan-guage and, more generally, its type of literature. If the fish and its capacities, for example, are recognized [127] as high exaggeration, an intensification of incongruities, why not think of the God of the fish in the same terms?[7]

Certainly not all of the God language of Jonah is exaggerated. Several statements stand firmly in the tradition: God is the Creator of the world,

---

4. Historians pay remarkably little attention to the fish and its capacity to accom-modate human beings for three days in undigested form. But, ironically, they do tend to interpret in a straightforward way the God who appoints the fish to swallow and vomit up Jonah.

5. Yvonne Sherwood, *A Biblical Text and Its Afterlives: The Survival of Jonah in West-ern Culture* (Cambridge: Cambridge University Press, 2000), 241. She reviews the range of Jonah interpretations over the centuries, as does Barbara Green, *Jonah's Journeys* (College-ville, MN: Liturgical Press, 2005).

6. Sherwood, *Afterlives*, 241.

7. God's acting in nature is depicted in ways that are almost casual, with no stress on divine power or amazement on the part of the characters.

even if confessed by a runaway believer (1:9).[8] God is gracious and merciful and abounding in steadfast love, even if uttered by an angry and recalcitrant Jonah (4:2). God is a deliverer who rescues the needy (2:2–9). God does relent from judging, not least in view of God's compassion for human and animal alike (4:2, 10–11). God does care about all creatures and, at least indirectly, commends their care to the reader. God's actions in nature do bear some similarity to those cited in texts such as Exodus 14—the wind and the waves. Yet, such divine actions seem to be of a different order than those in Jonah. Nature in Jonah is more like Elijah's ravens (1 Kgs 17:6), Balaam's ass (Numbers 22), and Eden's snake (Gen 3:1–15), all generally interpreted in legendary terms.

Do these more traditional witnesses to God in the book of Jonah make necessary a straightforward interpretation of God as a micromanager of plants, fish, worms, and sultry east winds? This traditional testimony to God in Jonah seems to be combined with the piling up of exaggerated elements. Scholars, however, have generally understood that the God language of the book is to be interpreted in more straightforward ways. Among many examples that could be cited, the following are representative.

For Thomas M. Bolin, the text speaks of "the boundless power, freedom and authority of Yahweh . . . [the] absolute power of Yahweh over all creation coupled with a complete license concerning any act or behavior, beyond human categories of justice or logic."[9] Yvonne Sherwood claims that the God of Jonah is "an irresistible force and a master of strategic planning." The fourfold repetition of God as an "appointer" "emphasizes Yhwh's strategic and effortless manipulation."[10] "Cumulatively, the descriptions [of God] reinforce the image of an omnipotent, omni-controlling [128] divine monarch."[11] Janet Howe Gaines speaks of "[t]he completeness of divine control over natural events."[12] Kenneth Craig claims that the "characterization of the Lord is accomplished by . . . a picture of God the Creator, in complete control of plant, animal, and human life in this story."[13] James Bruckner summarizes, "In the last two centuries, interpreters have tended to

---

8. Jonah's confession of faith may not be so traditional; for Sherwood, it is "a comically apt choice from *select-a-creed" (Afterlives,* 249). Let's see now, how can I flatter God enough to turn this situation around?! At the least, Jonah 1:9 does not speak of divine sovereignty, but of God as Creator. Notably, Jonah confesses this and still resists, as if to suggest that he should have no difficulty fleeing from such a God.

9. Thomas M. Bolin, *Freedom beyond Forgiveness: The Book of Jonah Re-examined* (Sheffield: Sheffield Academic Press, 1997), 147. Without apparent recognition of the issue at stake, he also affirms that the book ends with a debate between God and Jonah, where there is "no clear-cut victor" (p. 149).

10. Sherwood, *Afterlives,* 252, 253 n. 163.

11. Ibid., 253 (cf. p. 283).

12. Janet Howe Gaines, *Forgiveness in a Wounded World: Jonah's Dilemma* (Atlanta: Society of Biblical Literature, 2003), 54.

13. Kenneth M. Craig Jr., *A Poetics of Jonah: Art in the Service of Ideology* (Columbia: University of South Carolina Press, 1993), 146.

see Jonah 1 as a treatise on the sovereignty of God. . . . That God is almighty is a timeless truth of Jonah."[14] Raymond F. Person Jr. is a partial exception to this interpretive trend; he speaks of Jonah's God as "omnipotent, controlling humans and nature."[15] At the same time, Person importantly qualifies this claim in one case: "the Lord is not unlimited for, as is expressed in Jonah's protest (4:2), he is limited by his divine nature of mercy and compassion."[16] Though Person does not consider the relationship between divine omnipotence and a "limited" God, his point pushes in the right direction, as I hope to show.

It is interesting that many biblical interpreters just assume that Jonah was not literally swallowed by a fish and did not actually live in the stomach of a fish for three days. But, as noted, they will often turn around and interpret God's actions in a more literal way. Look how powerful this God is; even the fish and the worms obey him! It is strange, if not inconsistent, to consider many exaggerated materials as evidence of the unhistorical character of the book, but not of the God of the book.

What theological implications might follow if some of the language about God in Jonah is recognized as purposively exaggerated, perhaps even outrageous, to make a point? As such, the exaggerations help shape the message of the book. This ironic cast, this intensification of incongruities, suggests that the author moves beyond direct statements about God to an imaginative effort with theological ramifications. Jonathan Magonet moves toward this point when he states that the "miracles" in Jonah have been referred to as "literary miracles, designed as much to amuse and enchant his readers, as to illustrate their ultimate absurdity in [129] the world in which they lived."[17] This may be the case, but might a more theological point be available for readers?

Divine "Weakness" and Affectability in Jonah

Alongside the deliberately exaggerated themes regarding God in Jonah are claims about God that present a somewhat different point of view. Each of the claims cited below is revealing of a God whose relationship with Jonah, Israel, and other characters challenges the exaggerated themes.

1. Jonah's Resistance to God's Call

Jonah testifies that God is the Creator (1:9), but he still understands that he can resist God's call, and he acts in view of such an understanding. Indeed, his trip to Tarshish, located far from Nineveh and in the opposite

---

14. James K. Bruckner, *Jonah, Nahum, Habakkuk, Zephaniah: The NIV Application Commentary* (Grand Rapids: Zondervan, 2004), 53–54.

15. Raymond F. Person Jr., *In Conversation with Jonah: Conversation Analysis, Literary Criticism, and the Book of Jonah* (Sheffield: Sheffield Academic Press, 1996), 62.

16. Ibid., 88.

17. Magonet, *Form* and *Meaning*, 106.

direction, suggests an element of defiance on his part. Jonah even seems to use the confession to trumpet his resistance before others: God is my Creator and look what I can do! God responds to Jonah by working in and through a natural order that is not resistant to the will of the Creator, which serves to intensify the fact that human beings can be resistant to God's call. Though resisted, God persists, finding ways to interrupt Jonah's recalcitrance. God does succeed in getting Jonah to go to Nineveh, but does not succeed in shaping his graceless message (3:4) or the belligerent anger with which he reacts to Nineveh's repentance and God's response to it (3:10–4:2) or even to God's graciousness toward him (4:6–11). These are not images of a God who is in control.

2. God Is Affected by Prayers

The prayers of the sailors (and their actions with respect to Jonah) result in their deliverance (1:14–15). Jonah's prayer comes to God and is efficacious (2:7). The repentant prayers of the people of Nineveh result in a changed future: "When God saw what they did, how they turned from their evil ways, God changed his mind" (3:10). God is affected by people's prayers, whether they are voiced by the people of God or those who stand outside that community.

3. God and Creatures Act in Concert

Jonah's prayer expresses the belief that *God* has cast him into the sea, though he himself took that initiative with the help of the sailors (1:12–15; 2:3). So Jonah's own decision, the actions of other creaturely agents, and God's own action are related in a complex way; at the least, this complexity indicates that God is not the sole actor in what has happened. This perspective on God is lifted up by the way in which God works through other creatures (the fish, bush, worm, wind). These exaggerated elements serve the point that God chooses not to act alone in the world, but works in and through agents, both human and nonhuman, none of whom are perfect instruments in accomplishing God's purposes. [129]

4. The Words of a Prophet of God Are Not Fulfilled

Jonah's preaching is unconditional; the Ninevites are headed for destruction (3:4).[18] When that word of God does not come to pass, Jonah is very angry (4:1) and continues to hope for Nineveh's destruction (4:5). An Israelite prophet has failed, at least from Jonah's perspective (but see God's perspective in Jer 18:5–10). Is Jonah then a false prophet (cf. Deut 18:22)? Has there ever been in Israel such an incompetent and recalci-

---

18. Some scholars have suggested that the word "overthrown" is ambiguous and could also refer to an inner turning on the part of the Ninevites. Jonah clearly has their destruction in mind. The Ninevites' inner turning could be an ironic reference: Jonah preached one kind of overturning and got another.

trant prophet?[19] God is able to work in and through his inept efforts, but one cannot help but wonder what would have been possible with his full cooperation.

5. God's Willingness to Change the Divine Mind (Jonah 3:10; 4:2; cf. 3:9)

God's way into the future is genuinely affected by what human beings do and say: "When God saw what they did, how they turned from their evil ways, God changed his mind" (3:10).[20] God's future is at least somewhat open. The future is shaped by what happens in that divine-human interaction in view of God's honoring of relationships. The king of Nineveh claims that God's gracious response is not *necessitated* by the human response (3:9, "Who knows?"), yet God's promise in Jer 18:5–10 suggests that God has bound the divine self to so respond, at least in communal situations.[21] As is the case with other divine promises, God's options are thereby genuinely limited.

God's decision in 3:10 to spare Nineveh angers Jonah, and he cites the familiar confession in 4:2 as the reason he did not go to Nineveh. In other words, Jonah specifically relates the divine character in 4:2 to the divine decision in 3:10 to honor Nineveh's repentance. But that element of the divine character that is especially noted is "repenting" (נחם; it is added to Exod 34:6). And so Jonah in 4:2 links divine repentance and divine mercy. They are *both* characteristic of God, and both come into play in this situation. The compassion noted in 4:10–11, working back through the claims about God in 4:2, is viewed as the grounds for the divine decision in 3:10.[22]

It is commonly noted that Nineveh was destroyed in 612 B.C.E.; this state of affairs is probably in place at the time of writing (compare Nah 1:2–3 with Jonah 4:2 [131]). This disastrous development for Nineveh has its parallels in other instances of divine repentance where, over time, it is followed by an act of destruction (Amos 7:1–9).[23] Times change and

---

19. For a more positive assessment of the prophet Jonah, see Green, *Jonah's Journeys*.

20. For a full study of the language involved, see Terence E. Fretheim, "The Repentance of God: A Key to Evaluating Old Testament God-Talk," *HBT* 10 (1988): 47–70; see also idem, *The Message of Jonah*, 112–15.

21. See idem, "Repentance in the Former Prophets," in *Repentance in Christian Theology* (ed. Mark J. Boda and Gordon T. Smith; Collegeville, MN: Liturgical Press, 2006), 25–45.

22. To say that God "repents" with respect to judgment is not equivalent to saying that God forgives the Ninevites (cf. Exodus 32–34 and the Moses-prompted divine moves from initially relenting to finally forgiving, Exod 34:6–7). Cf. Gaines, *Forgiveness in a Wounded World*. A distinction must be made between forgiveness of sin and a reversal of the consequences of sin. The issue of *human* forgiveness might be clearer; God's questions to Jonah about his anger over the divine relenting of judgment on the Ninevites may well reveal Jonah's inability to forgive them for their atrocities against Israel.

23. Compare also Exod 32:14 with 32:35, though the latter is much less severe than God's original word (32:10).

an occasion of divine repentance does not lock a specific future forever
in place. God will take new situations into account in moving into the
future.[24]

It is striking to note that in Exodus 32 God repents regarding Israel quite
apart from any repentance on their part, with only Moses' prayer in view
(Exod 32:14). So, it is possible that God would have changed the divine
mind even apart from Nineveh's repentance, on the grounds of divine
compassion alone (4:11). God's final question in 4:11 includes no suggestion that Nineveh's repentance conditions God's repentance (so also 4:2).
God's compassion prompts God's response to the Ninevite's repentance.
God will spare them because of *who God is* and *who they* are.

6. God Is "Slow to Anger"

God's concern for justice is tempered by the divine slowness to anger
(4:2). The exercise of divine justice in Jonah is shown not to be absolute or
fixed in the way in which it functions in the created order. Indeed, many
people escape from the consequences of their behaviors (see Jer 12:1), not
by virtue of a divine decision, but by a "looseness" in the creational causal
weave that God allows to be what it was created to be (hence, "slow to
anger"). Jonah himself experiences such a "looseness" in his journeys, and
the king of Nineveh understood there to be no fixed link between deed
and consequence (3:9). Both unrepentant Jonah and repentant Ninevites
experience God's slowness of anger and a creational order that does not
function with precision, not least in view of the complexities of the situation (4:11). God's mercy and graciousness, strongly affirmed by Jonah (4:2),
temper the exercise of strict justice.

That God is "slow to anger" is a part of the tradition with which Jonah
disagrees. Not unlike Job's friends, Jonah's justice is strict and precise, almost mechanical. You reap what you sow, period! Jonah knows that God
is merciful and gracious (4:2), but believes that those divine characteristics can obscure God's role as executor of justice on the deserving wicked.
Jonah will now be more just than God is! At the same time, he does not
perceive that, in such a retributive system as he espouses, he himself should
have been the recipient of the wrath of God. [132]

7. God Is Emotionally Compassionate (Jonah 4:10–11)

The ending question of the book (4:10–11) introduces readers to a
deep divine concern. God's final question indicates that God is moved by
Nineveh's weak or morally confused ones (from children to adults) and its
animals (in view of potential disaster). What is happening in Nineveh has
an effect upon God. The verb חוס, "concern for" (NRSV), refers to suffering ac-

---

24. Divine repentance on behalf of non-Israelite peoples is not unique to Jonah; indeed, Jer 18:5–10 universalizes this possibility.

tion, action executed with tears in the eyes.[25] God's concern entails emotional responsiveness.[26] It is suffering action. Here God vulnerably appears to take the evil of Nineveh upon the divine self. God bears the weight of its violence, the pain of a thousand plundered cities, including Israel's. God's tears flow instead of theirs.

8. God Engages in a Conversation with Jonah about His Anger and Seeks to Move Him out of His Resentment over What Has Happened to Nineveh (Jonah 4:8–11)

In this interaction, Jonah is not blown away by divine rhetoric or divine power. God's actions prior to the conversation (4:6–8) contain some of the exaggerated elements in the story. These actions take a "soft" approach to Jonah's dilemma and serve to engage Jonah in a conversation regarding his response to God's mercy and repentance. God thereby hopes to turn Jonah around and engages him in theological conversation to that end.

9. God Does Not Have the Last Word

The book of Jonah ends with a question, with the differences between God and Jonah unresolved. God seeks to convince Jonah of certain understandings regarding God; Jonah continues to resist God's efforts to convince him. No divine success regarding Jonah's perspective is reported. Such divine difficulties do not seem to fit the image of God presented in the exaggerated elements of the book. God is not said to be in control of the response, either of Jonah or of the reader. The future remains genuinely open-ended at the conclusion of this book.

Jonah's problem with God is a theological problem. His disobedience to God's call was theologically motivated. It is not that Jonah disagrees with Israel's basic confession about God (4:2), as we have noted, but he wishes to restrict the range of its applicability. His motivation turned out to be bad theology. God goes to the root of the problem by engaging him in words and actions that are designed to get his theological perspective turned around. If and when Jonah is convinced to make a theological turn, his resistance and despair will take care of themselves. Along the way, the exaggerated actions of God with respect to nature are not life-threatening, but a cleverly designed means of leading Jonah through a conversation designed to move Jonah theologically.

These features relating to the God of the book of Jonah are revealing of a God who is deeply affected by the world, who enters into relationships that honor the [133] creatures and takes their interaction seriously. The effect of

---

25. The link between moved to spare and tears is expressed negatively in Deut 19:13, 21; Isa 13:18; Ezek 5:11; 7:4, 9, where allowing tears to flow would wrongly deter the judgment.

26. The verb חוס is variously translated (NRSV, "concerned about"). For details, see Terence E. Fretheim, "Jonah and Theodicy," *ZAW* 90 (1978): 236–37.

such an understanding is that God has limited God's actions in the world in such a way as to honor God's promises and so that this relationship can flourish, with creatures allowed by God to be what they were created to be.

Preliminary Conclusions

I suggest that the purposeful and multiple exaggerations of God's power and freedom in the book of Jonah constitute a *foil* over against which God's character can be more clearly discerned and God's relationship to God's people—often problematic—can be more sharply delineated. Indeed, might the book of Jonah be saying in and through these exaggerations that, in spite of what readers may think (or hope for!), their God is *not* such a manipulative, all-controlling deity?[27]

Might the purpose of Jonah's exaggerations be to challenge the perspective of those readers who wish, perhaps desperately, that their God was like this, for purposes of rescuing them from disaster or foreign domination or debilitating disease? God should just pop in and fix it! The book is laying claim to the idea that, for all the seeming "miraculous" power of God, Israel's God is not a magician who manipulates creatures, small or large, whenever it serves the divine purposes, however minor or major. God does not actually engage in these exaggerated activities, not least because such divine activity would sharply undercut creaturely responsibility.

This is not to suggest that Israel's God does not have the power to do these things, only that it would be contrary to the divine character to do them. For God to act in this way in the world of nature would be to violate God's own creation, which includes God's giving creatures the "freedom" to be what they were created to be. The gift of such freedom to the creatures means that God is committed to a relationship with human and animal alike, including God's own people, which entails divine restraints and constraints in the exercise of power—for the sake of genuineness in the relationship, the keeping of promises, and the honoring of the creature. Even though such a divine relationship with the world entails risks and engages human beings who can make life difficult indeed for God and for other creatures.

From another angle, the exaggerated language in Jonah relates entirely to God's relationship to the natural order and to non-Israelites—from fish to worms, from sailors to Ninevites. The nonhuman creatures and non-Israelite peoples are imaged as remarkably nonresistant to God's actions in and through them. Indeed, [134] Jonah often benefits from their nonresistant responses. This exaggerated rhetoric serves to intensify the differences with respect to God's relationship to Jonah. From the beginning to the end of the book Jonah is in a resistance mode, from rejecting God's call to his anger

---

27. Such an understanding of an all-controlling God is also common in contemporary religious communities.

at God's gracious response to the Ninevites. In view of these difficulties God has with Jonah, God interrupts their relationship, but not in such a way as to force compliance. And so the book ends with the divine question to Jonah ringing in the air and Jonah's response, indeed every reader's response, waiting in the wings. How will he (and you) respond?

Jonah and Theodicy

The book of Jonah is concerned with the question of theodicy in a fundamental way.[1] It puts the question in a rather unusual manner, however: Are God's *compassionate* actions just? The stumbling block for the faith of Jonah is not so much some ancient counterpart to the Lisbon earthquake, the visitation of evil upon the innocent, but the Nineveh deliverance, the proffering of divine mercy to those who are evil. Jonah's complaint concerns the leniency made available to the guilty. Nineveh had taken up the sword (more than any other known!) and should, if *anyone* should, perish by the sword. But now Nineveh, at whose very hand Jonah's Israel[2] had suffered so mercilessly, was to be offered the chance to escape the guillotine. Israel, God's covenant people, had been destroyed, and now the destroyer was being offered life!

To Jonah this must have been sheer madness. Such a circumvention of all that goes by the name of justice! In the face of such injustice [228] what difference does faith make after all (cf. Mal 3:14–15)? For Jonah, God, if he is to be truly God and if Israel's faith is to be meaningful, must conform to canons of righteousness that relate divine response to human conduct in ways that are consistent, if not predictable.

It is the purpose of this article to re-examine the conclusion of Jonah in the light of this interest in theodicy. First of all, however, it is necessary to consider some preliminary matters.

I

Some scholars[3] speak of Jonah's problem as being related to an incomprehensible God whose actions cannot be schematized. God is one who

---

This essay was originally published in *Zeitschrift für die alttestamentliche Wissenschaft* 90 (1978): 227–37.

1. The author wishes to express his appreciation to Prof. H. W. Wolff, who read the manuscript and offered some helpful suggestions. For suggesting this approach to Jonah, the author is indebted to some sermons on Jonah by Richard Luecke, *Violent Sleep: Notes Toward the Development of Sermons for the Modern City* (Philadelphia: Fortress, 1969), 8–45.

2. The connection between Nineveh and a prophet from the northern kingdom is certainly not fortuitous. Jonah, who had announced the greatness of Israel's future (2 Kgs 14:25), is now called upon to offer a future to the very country that had put an end to Israel.

3. Cf. Alfred Jepsen, "Anmerkungen zum Buche Jona," in *Wort—Gebot—Glaube: Beiträge zur Theologie des Alten Testaments. Walther Eichrodt zum 80. Geburtstag. Zusammen mit Johann Jakob Stamm und Ernest Jenni* (Zurich: Zwingli Verlag, 1971), 300.

cannot be depended upon absolutely, e.g., to fulfil the word spoken by the prophet. Through the introduction of an element of uncertainty in his ways with the world, God makes life miserable for his servants. The issue for Jonah, however, is not so much *that* God repents, but *for whom* God repents. Jonah certainly was aware that Israel's very life depended upon God's repentance. He had no problem with God's changeableness per se. Moreover, the non-fulfilment of his prophecy in and of itself was the least of his problems. He and his compatriots were quite familiar with the contingent element in Hebrew prophecy.

Jonah's problem was the indiscriminate extension of God's repentance. One must be careful not to speak too broadly here, however. It cannot be maintained that Jonah's resistance is related to sharing God's repentance with the heathen per se.[4] The issue for Jonah is not so much the indiscriminate *extension* to the heathen, as the *indiscriminate* extension of God's repentance to those whose cup of evil had filled to overflowing, "whose wickedness has come up before" God (Jonah 1:2).[5] The book presents no *absolute* dichotomy between Israel and the heathen. In fact, Jonah's positive response to the heathen in 1:12, making their deliverance possible ("then the sea will quiet down for you"),[6] makes it clear that Jonah can be discriminating indeed when it comes to the heathen.

The theme of God's repentance must remain tied to that of God's slowness to anger in the face of horrendous evil (as in 4:2). Anger is a [229] central theme in the book, as we shall see. For Jonah, when the cup of wrath is full, it should be poured out. As it was with Israel in 721 B.C. and with Judah in 587 B.C., so it should also be with Nineveh. Such lack of discrimination on God's part is unjust.

This perspective necessitates a re-assessment of a current view[7] which maintains that Jonah belongs to a class of "salvation-prophets," and that the book is to be interpreted as a critique of religio-national pride evident particularly in the eschatological prophecies against the nations.[8] A connection is commonly made at this point between the book and the Jonah of 2 Kgs 14:25. Jonah's prophecies regarding Jeroboam's kingdom were highly optimistic and nationalistic, thus belonging to a type of prophecy

---

4. Contra Jörg Jeremias, *Die Reue Gottes: Aspekte alttestamentlicher Gottesvorstellung* (Neukirchen-Vluyn: Neukirchener Verlag, 1975), 105.

5. Cf. Joel 4:13; Jer 25:29, 31.

6. However one interprets 1:12 (cf. George M. Landes, "The Kerygma of the Book of Jonah: The Contextual Interpretation of the Jonah Psalm," *Int* 21 [1967]: 22–23), the attitude of Jonah toward the heathen is remarkably different in ch. 1 from ch. 4.

7. See Otto Eissfeldt, "Amos und Jona in volkstümlicher Uberlieferung," in *Kleine Schriften IV* (ed. Rudolph Sellheim and Fritz Maass; Tübingen: Mohr, 1968), 137–42; H. W. Wolff, *Studien zum Jonabuch* (BibS[N] 47; Neukirchen-Vluyn: Neukirchener Verlag, 1965), 14f.; Otto Kaiser, "Wirklichkeit, Moglichkeit und Vorurteil: Ein Beitrag zum Verständnis des Buches Jona," *EvT* 88 (1978): 91f.

8. E.g., Joel 4:1–21; Isa 63:1–6; 34:1–17.

condemned by Amos (cf. 6:13–14; 7:1). In using the traditional figure of Jonah, it is thought that the author of Jonah thereby seeks to draw significant parallels at this point between his own time and that of Amos.

This view, however, must now be qualified. We have seen that the issue for the author of Jonah was not shaped in terms of a radical Israel/heathen dichotomy. While Jonah (and those whom he represents) probably would have been sympathetic with the basic outlook of the prophecies against the nations, this only provides background for a more central issue: God's justice.

A brief sketch of the audience to which the author addresses himself (of which Jonah is a type) assists us in illuminating the setting in which this issue is raised. It is common to consider self-confidence, even pride, as characteristic of this audience. A closer look at certain actions and attitudes of Jonah, however, calls for some re-assessment at this point: flight, complaint, frustration, stubbornness, self-pity, anger, repeated and strenuous wish for death. Such characterizations do not suggest self-confidence. In fact, self-pity would seem to preclude self-confidence. Moreover, the stubbornness and dogmatism that we see in Jonah reveal a certain *lack* of self-confidence, a basic inner insecurity. This suggests an audience uncertain about their own future (unlike the contemporaries of Amos), and raising serious questions about their relationship to God's ways with the world. Such a characterization would fit an audience that is experiencing the seeming *failure* of the eschatological prophecies. In such a context the indiscriminate extension of God's pity to those who are evil would have seemed doubly unjust. [230]

It thus seems best to suggest that Jonah was directed to a situation like unto that envisaged in the book of Malachi (cf. 2:17; 3:14–15; 1:2–5).[9] "Everyone who does evil is good in the sight of the Lord, and he delights in them." "Where is the God of justice?"

In this light, the connection of Jonah and 2 Kings 14 deserves another look. The Deuteronomistic interpretation of Jonah's prophecy (virtually canonical for the author of Jonah?) is a highly positive one (2 Kgs 14:26–27). What comparable evidence is there that a negative interpretation of Jonah's prophetic work was available to the author of Jonah? A more satisfactory approach would be to relate the positive perspective to the book of Jonah. The highly compassionate activity of God toward Israel (14:26) and his refusal to blot out Israel's name (14:27) in spite of Israel's persistent sinfulness (14:24) suggests a more than "just" pity for *Israel* on God's part.

---

9. The important place of the question in both books is also to be noted. Every statement directed to Jonah (the author's audience) includes a question. It suggests a situation where dialogue between prophet and people is the common form of discourse. See James Crenshaw, "Popular Questioning of the Justice of God in Ancient Israel," *ZAW* 82 (1970), 380–95.

Thus, if God has been more than just with Israel in the past, Israel should have a broader perspective from which to view the question of God's justice in cases like Nineveh.[10]

We now turn to an examination of the final question of the book in the light of this interest in God's justice. Our arguments here will, in turn, support the above-mentioned considerations.

II

It is common for studies in Jonah to maintain that the final verses (4:10–11) demonstrate that "compassion is supreme in God's way with his creatures; and it is a universal compassion, extending to all [231] of them equally."[11] An argument from creation to compassion seems to be perceived in the text. Nineveh is to God what the plant has become to Jonah. If Jonah pities the plant, which he has neither created nor nourished nor known, then certainly God should pity Nineveh (and, by logical extension, all creatures) because he has in fact created them, provided for them and knows their need. Such a perception assumes the common translation of *ʾaḥûs*, "*Should* (not) I pity . . . ?*" An affirmative answer is considered obvious, which implies an "oughtness" or inevitability to God's pitying action.

There are, however, major difficulties with this interpretation:

1. There is a disjunction between this understanding and the story of Nineveh in ch. 3. It is there made clear that God "repented of the evil which he had said he would do to them," but *only when* "he saw what they

---

10. This may also be the way of relating Jonah and Joel. The close relationship between these two books has often been noted (see Wolff, *Studien zum Jonabuch*, 67ff.). Joel is concerned with a threatened Jerusalem. Upon her repentance of sin God repents regarding the judgment. If the author of Jonah knew Joel, the point made by him may well be stated as follows: God has repented regarding Israel's destruction in a manner quite apart from the question of justice. If one were to ask into Israel's *just* desserts, then God should *not* have had pity. But God's saving action moves beyond the question of justice. Therefore, Israel has no right to raise the question of justice regarding Nineveh. It is probable that Jonah's deliverance from the sea is intended to make the same point. The psalm (reflecting the resolution of a complaint) could then be understood as a paradigm for the appropriate response to *all* of God's more than just saving acts, not only Israel's (within the book the psalm would thus be ironically perceived): "Deliverance belongs to the Lord!" (2:9). For an excellent case for the integrity of the psalm, see especially Landes, "The Kerygma of the Book of Jonah," 22f.

11. Millar Burrows, "The Literary Category of the Book of Jonah," in *Translating and Understanding the Old Testament: Essays in Honor of H. G. May* (ed. Harry Thomas Frank and William J. Reed; New York: Abingdon, 1971), 102. Part of the problem here may be the translation of *ḥûs* as "compassion." "Compassion" should be used only in the sense of a movement from God to people that actually issues in deliverance. Cf. Jeremias, *Die Reue Gottes*, 105. As will be seen below, *ḥûs* does not have reference to a fixed attribute of Yahweh, and hence an abstract statement about his love cannot be understood here. The common rendering "pity" is appropriate, but has no singular sense. Our subsequent discussion will indicate that "pity" in the sense of "moved to spare" seems best in most contexts.

did, how they turned from their evil way" (3:10). Thus God pities (is moved
to spare) Nineveh, not simply because he has created them and knows
their need, but because of their repentant response. The repentance of the
Ninevites provides the necessary (though, as we shall see, not sufficient)
occasion for God's repentance. Thus the argument in ch. 4 cannot move
directly from creation to God's pitying action if it is to be consistent with
ch. 3.

2. There is a disjunction between this interpretation and a key motif in
the book: God's sovereign freedom. While Nineveh's repentance was a necessary condition for God's repentance, it was not in and of itself sufficient.
God's repentance rested finally in his own sovereign decision. The following verses highlight this pervasive theme:

> 1:6—*Perhaps* the god will give a thought to us, that we do not perish.
> 1:14—For thou, O Lord, hast done *as it pleased thee.*
> 3:9—*Who knows*, God *may* yet repent and turn from his fierce anger, so
> that we perish not.

That these statements should be found on the lips of the heathen is, of
course, one of the ironic features of the book.[12] It is the *heathen* [232] who
have such extraordinary insight into the sovereign freedom of God!

Human response is the pre-condition, but not the ground, of God's deliverance. There is no mechanical relationship between human acts of piety or worship and God's saving action. Though God may be motivated
to save because of human prayer and penitence, God remains ultimately
free to decide whether he will have pity. What is true of God's deliverance
is also true of his judgment. The book makes clear that these actions are
parallel as they relate to God's freedom. Just as God's judgment is not an
automatic consequence of sin (God may repent!), so God's pity is not a
necessary consequence of repentance (Perhaps!). Both God's judgment and
his pity are contingent not merely upon human action, but finally upon
the sovereign will of God, who will have mercy upon whom he will have
mercy (Exod 33:19).

Yet it must also be stated that God is not thereby rendered capricious, so
that the community of faith is left in a perpetual state of anxiety regarding
the course of his action. The confession of 4:2 (and elsewhere, e.g., Ezekiel
18) makes it clear that God's will is to save his creatures. His steadfast love
and his wrath are not equally primary attributes. God will always act in
ways that are consonant with his ultimate salvific purposes. But such a con-

---

12. On irony in Jonah, see especially Edwin Marshall Good, *Irony in the Old Testament*
(Philadelphia: Westminster, 1965), 39–55. For a discussion of this "göttliche Vielleicht",
see Jeremias, *Die Reue Gottes*, 74, 78, 87, 97, 107. This idea is found in quite "orthodox"
traditions elsewhere in the Old Testament (cf. Exod 32:30; Amos 5:15; Zeph 2:3; Lam 3:29;
Joel 2:14).

fession of faith is not reducible to a formula whereby it can be determined just how God will act in specific instances. The "divine perhaps" thus safeguards the divine sovereignty and enables grace to remain truly grace.[13]

Thus, if God acts as he sees fit throughout the book, and is not programmed to respond in fixed ways to certain patterns of human behavior, it would be wholly disjunctive for the final verses to be made to speak or imply either an "oughtness" or an inevitability to God's pity which would somehow comproimse his sovereign freedom.

3. The usage of the verb *ḥûs*. God cannot be described as a God who pities, if by that is meant that *ḥûs* is a constant movement of God toward his people. *Ḥûs* does not have reference to a fixed attribute of Yahweh.[14] There is, in fact, frequent reference to God's *refusal* [233] to exercise *ḥûs* (cf. Jer 13:14; 21:7; Ezek 5:11; 7:4, 9). As such, this verb would not be appropriate to an argument which seeks to show from creation that God is a God who has compassion upon all creatures. Such an argument would have to presume that, because God has created, nourished and known the needs of *all* creatures, he would *always* act in a pitying way. The verb *ḥûs* cannot carry that sort of freight.

4. Finally, this interpretation stands in disjunction with ch. 1, God's call to Jonah and Jonah's flight from mission. If God is moved to spare the peoples of this earth quite apart from the preaching of the Word of God, then all human responsibility for the task of mission is emptied of importance, let alone urgency. If such is the case, then Jonah's flight to Tarshish to avoid the preaching task is finally irrelevant. To answer the final question, "Should not I pity Nineveh?" in the affirmative is to place the entire responsibility for the Ninevehs of this world in God's hands. It provides a subtle way for the Jonahs of this world to wash their hands of responsibility for the Ninevehs.

In view of these considerations another approach to the final verses of Jonah must be found. To this end a closer analysis of the larger context in ch. 4 is in order.

---

13. Landes, "The Kerygma of the Book of Jonah," 128; Burrows, "The Literary Category," 100; Jeremias, *Die Reue Gottes*, 92f., 107f. Jeremias (pp. 83ff., 119) reflects a misunderstanding at this point that necessitates his rejection of the theological thrust of Jer 18:9–10. He confuses the unchangeable character of God's salvific purposes for his creation and the particularistic articulation of such purposes to Israel (or any other entity). The former may be absolutely relied upon, but neither Israel nor any other can be *guaranteed* participation in the reality of fulfilment irrespective of their response. God will remain true to his promises, but not in some universalistic sense.

14. *Ḥûs* has reference to concrete actions grounded either in love (Neh 13:22) or anger (Jer 21:5ff.; Ezek 7:3–4, 8–9). Cf. Jeremias (*Die Reue Gottes*, 105), who notes that *ḥûs* has reference less to a subjective "compassion" than to an objective "sparing." It is striking that, with the author's penchant for repetition, a word from 4:2 is not used here.

III

To begin with, it should be noted that ch. 4 has a heavy ironic cast. For example, a prophet of God becomes angry and expresses a wish for death upon a repentant response to his message (4:1, 3), and does not wish to give God opportunity to be true to himself (4:2). Jonah rejoices over a gift of shade when he already had the shade of a hut (4:5, 6), and expresses great joy over his own deliverance, having just expressed great anger over Nineveh's (4:1, 6). The following discussion depends upon the recognition of this literary characteristic.

Besides 4:10–11, the only other direct statements of God in the book are in 4:4, 9. These questions are seldom related to the final verses in any significant way. Moreover, it is common to consider 4:9 as little more than a repetition of 4:4 in God's attempt to move Jonah to repentance. Those two verses are in fact parallel,[15] but their content is quite different: 4:9 concerns destruction, while 4:4 concerns deliverance.

In 4:4 God asks Jonah: Is it right for you to be angry about the deliverance of the city? The essence of this question is: Are you right in passing judgment upon God's sovereign decision *not* to be angry?[16] [234] For Jonah, God was not angry when he should have been angry. Jonah in his anger believes himself to be responding rightly to the situation. This is nothing less than a judgment on God's right to be slow to anger (4:2).[17] According to Jonah's canons of justice, God's non-anger betrays caprice. Jonah by his anger demonstrates the only reaction he believes is truly God-like. He will be just if God will not.

God, by inquiring into the rightness of Jonah's anger, implies that such anger is not right. This explains Jonah's subsequent silence, highlighted by the purposively delayed notice of 4:5.[18] An impasse has occurred, not unlike that which occasioned Jonah's flight in the first place. The placement of 4:5 thus makes clear the unchanged mind-set of Jonah, a perspective firmly set on the destruction of the Ninevites as the only just outcome of their evil deeds.

As in 4:4, 4:9 also concerns the rightness of Jonah's anger. This time, however, it is related not to God's act of deliverance, but to his act of destruction: Is it right for you to be angry about the plant? By his anger Jonah again calls into question the rightness of God's action. He presumes to

---

15. Cf. Carl Keller, "Jonas: Le portrait d'un prophète," *TZ* 21 (1966): 329–340, for chiasmus in ch 4.

16. On the importance of the anger motif, see Wolff, *Studien zum Jonabuch*, 37.

17. That *ḥārâ* is not used in 4:2 is important for showing that the author, though fond of repetition, will not arbitrarily alter inherited linguistic patterns to achieve such. This must be considered in any attempt to argue that the psalm is secondary because of a lack of linguistic connections with the surrounding narrative.

18. On the "catch-up" style of the book, see Wolff, ibid., 40ff.

bring God before the bar of justice and pronounce a verdict of guilty—God's actions are not just.

It is important to note that 4:9 broadens the scope of the issue between God and Jonah in relating the discussion to God's actions of destruction. This demonstrates clearly that the issue between them is not confined simply to the question of the deliverance of Nineveh. The *sphere* of God's activity under discussion is shown here to be limited not merely to Nineveh, but includes Jonah (Israel) as well. Here it is Jonah's experience of destruction at the hands of God that is challenged as to its rightness. What makes Jonah even more angry here and wish even more intensely for death is his perception of the contrasting ways of God's dealings with him (that is, his own people!) and Nineveh. God is not just.

This probably reflects a comparable experience on the part of those Israelites whom Jonah typifies. They had suffered while those who were evil (perhaps rulers to which they were subject) were escaping destruction. But the point now to be made should have been clear to them: the gifts of God were given them in the first place quite apart from the question of justice, hence the loss of such gifts or a comparable gift to others should not raise the question of justice. Thus, the author, rather than providing, say, an eschatological counter-argument (like Malachi), simply shows the inappropriateness of the charge in [235] the first place by an appeal to God's sovereignty. The details of the argument run as follows:

The dilemma set by God for Jonah by his question in 4:9 can be seen more clearly after a consideration of 4:10. Here God indicates to Jonah that the plant has come to him as a pure gift (which, in the final analysis, is true of everything). It was not something which Jonah had coming to him, that he had deserved or earned. It was not something which he had created or even nurtured. Besides, the plant was ephemeral, growing up and perishing in a day. Jonah's ties to the plant were obviously superficial. Moreover, it was only a single plant, and lifeless at that.[19] At every point this stands in contrast to God's relationship to Nineveh.

What is the point made by this sort of recital? It serves to demonstrate that there can be no question of injustice whatsoever in God's taking of the plant from Jonah (we cannot even refer to it as Jonah's plant!). Jonah had no claim on the plant whatsoever. He had no *right* to make any claims regarding it. All of his appeals to justice were simply out of court. Judgments regarding caprice on the grounds of what was due Jonah were not in order. Jonah could not lift himself out of the totality of life in which he was inextricably enmeshed to the point of being able to make claims upon that life in its diverse aspects, of making judgments regarding life and death. He is creature, not Creator.

---

19. The lifelessness of plants (from the perspective of ancient Israel) in contrast to animals and people may be another point of contrast drawn by the author.

The dilemma posed for Jonah by God's question in 4:9 can now be seen more clearly. Is it right for you to be angry about the plant? If Jonah's answer is negative (as it should have been), then, of course, he thereby admits that he cannot make judgments concerning what God has done with Nineveh. On the other hand, if Jonah's answer is affirmative (as it indeed was), then he tacitly recognizes *God's* right to do what he wills regarding Nineveh!

The final verses drive the point home. Jonah actually was in no position to make final demands or judgments about the plant, therefore he certainly was not in any position to make ultimate demands or judgments about Nineveh. But, once having placed himself in such a position through his regret over the plant, he should certainly recognize God's sovereign right to spare Nineveh.

God has the right to do what pleases him regarding Nineveh because he is Creator. Jonah cannot bring God into court on the question of justice or injustice, mercy or condemnation. He is creature. Thus *the argument of the final question of Jonah moves not from creation to redemption, but from creation to sovereignty.* [236]

This interpretation is supported by a closer look at the verb *ḥûs*. It is noteworthy that when used of human beings, *ḥûs* has reference to the actions of a ruler,[20] or a representative thereof in instances of war[21] or administration of justice.[22] Thus there is a sovereign decision or action in view when this verb is used. It characterizes a movement from a superior to those who are subordinate in some way. It relates to superiors who are (or are not) moved to pity toward those who are within their jurisdiction. Clearly implicit throughout the usage of this term is the right of the sovereign (or representative) to have pity or not have pity as he sees fit in specific circumstances of life.

The verb *ḥûs* is thus singularly appropriate for usage in a context concerned with the sovereign right of God. It is also clear from this usage that Jonah had no right to exercise *ḥûs* regarding the plant[23] (and certainly not Nineveh!) for he had no sovereignty relating thereto.[24]

In the light of the objections noted initially and our subsequent discussion a different translation from that commonly given is necessary for *ʾaḥûs* in 4:11. It is probable that "May I not . . ." (i.e., am I not allowed to)

---

20. Cf. 1 Sam 24:11; Ps 72:13; Jer 21:7.

21. Cf. Deut 7:16; Isa 13:18.

22. Cf. Deut 13:9; 19:13, 21; 25:12.

23. Jonah's anger in 4:9 should be considered the ground for the *ḥûs* noted in 4:10 (see n. 14). The only other reference to *ḥûs* in connection with an inanimate object is Gen 45:20. There it has reference to "having no regrets" over personal property left behind. The reference to property is not unrelated to that of rights and the appropriateness of a regretful response.

24. The common exegetical comments to the effect that Jonah *should* have had pity over Nineveh are, of course, quite out of order if this interpretation is correct.

best captures the sense. This would then focus on God's sovereign right to spare Nineveh. Moreover, such a translation does not presume to prejudge God's response to Nineveh, thus safeguarding his freedom. Also, it does not remove the necessity of human repentance or the importance of human responsibility.[25]

If this is the case, then the force of the question at the end of the book has essentially the same thrust as the question at the end of Jesus' parable of the laborers in the vineyard in Matthew 20: "Am I not allowed to do what I choose with what belongs to me? Do you begrudge my generosity?"

One more thing must be said. The use of *ḥûs* in the final question pushes beyond the question of God's rights as sovereign to the *way* in which his rights are exercised. *Ḥûs* is suffering action, action executed with tears in the eyes.[26] God takes upon himself the evil of Nineveh [237] and bears the weight of its violence, the pain of a thousand plundered cities, including Israel's. God chooses to suffer for Nineveh, perhaps even to die.[27]

---

25. If one insists on the common translation "Should I not pity Nineveh . . . ?" then the question must be left without an answer. Such a conclusion, however, would blunt the force of the argument presented in ch. 4, leaving it without a climactic point.

26. See Wolff, *Studien zum Jonabuch*, 36ff.; S. Blank, "'Doest Thou Well to Be Angry?' A Study in Self-Pity," *HUCA* 26 (1955): 29–41.

27. L. Schmidt, *De Deo: Studien zur Literaturkritik und Theologie des Buches Jona* (BZAW 143; Berlin: de Gruyter, 1976), came to my attention after this article was completed. This work, which as a whole is concerned with more theoretical reflections about God in the Old Testament, contains an intricate analysis of Jonah. On the basis of different names for God, he divides Jonah into two major strata (plus a redactor for the psalm and two glossators). While the two strata have somewhat different emphases, both can be characterized as an "erzählte Dogmatik" concerned with a theology of creation within a wisdom-influenced context. The above-noted and disputed argument from creation to compassion in 4:10–11 is strongly affirmed, though its difficulties (not fully perceived) are only partially resolved, and that through a depreciation of the themes of evil and repentance as well as an unlikely division of sources. The book, however, contains a number of provocative suggestions, and his quite correct emphasis on a theology of creation could be made even more meaningful if placed in the context of theodicy detailed in this article.

Part 7

God and the Church's Book

The Old Testament in Christian Proclamation

It is my conviction that the discussion regarding the use of the Old Testament in the church fails to consider adequately what is *experienced* by Christians when they hear Old Testament texts read or preached on. That concern will serve as a motif for the following paragraphs regarding the Old Testament in Christian proclamation.

The Old Testament is the Word of God for the Christian Church. That is, it is a means by which God speaks a word of judgment and grace to the people of God. There are other functions which it may be said to have. It helps to define what the Christian faith was and still properly is, and it assists in delineating a shape for Christian life in the world. But, at the heart of things, the Old Testament serves to bring people face to face with the Father of our Lord Jesus Christ, and in that encounter God speaks. Such a perspective is in decisive continuity with the Old Testament's own "self-understanding" and the New Testament authors' use of the Old Testament (see below).

In Christian circles this understanding of the Old Testament should need no argument, for we have experienced this to be the case again and again. Whose conscience has not been stricken upon hearing, "You shall not take the Name of the Lord your God in vain"? Or, who has not been assured of forgiveness upon hearing these words read or sung: "Comfort, comfort my people, says your God. Speak tenderly to Jerusalem . . . that her iniquity is pardoned"? Or, who among us has not felt the arms of God's providential care upon hearing the 23rd Psalm? Whether it be the Law, the Prophets, or the Psalms, they have served more than a preparatory or propaedeutic function; they have actually spoken an effective Word of God to Christian people: calling, exhorting, warning, judging, redeeming, comforting, and sanctifying.

So what's the problem? Let's just preach on these texts in such a way that the Word of God can be heard, as we would on any New Testament text. After all, whether Old Testament or New Testament, we have to do with the one Bible of the church. Yet, in recent times, the church's preaching has tended to neglect [224] the Old Testament, and that massive reservoir of the Word of God has been held back and not allowed to become the river of life it has the potential of being for the church.

This essay was originally published in *Word and World* 3 (1983): 223–30.

For most of the history of the church this has not been so. Even a cursory look will show that the church through the centuries has experienced the Old Testament as Word of God, and consequently filled its liturgies, its preaching, and its catechetics with a plenitude of Old Testament materials. The whole Bible constituted the *Christian* Scriptures, an *undifferentiated* resource for its primary tasks. As such, the Old Testament has been used largely according to patterns initiated by the New Testament writers. The latter started with the unargued premise that their Scriptures (essentially the same as that of the Jews of the first century) were "sacred writings which are able to instruct you for salvation through faith in Jesus Christ" (2 Tim 3:15). Then, drawing upon virtually every existing interpretive means available to them, Old Testament texts in profusion were used as a vehicle for interpreting *and* proclaiming God's act in Jesus. And so the church has seemed to say for generations: If the New Testament authors did things this way, ought we not follow in their steps?

And so the church did, for centuries. But the rise of an historical approach to the Scriptures changed the picture. The Old Testament was set squarely in pre-Christian times, limited to an historical mode of interpretation, and an immense hiatus between Old Testament and New Testament was created. The struggle to bridge this gap, while remaining true to an historical approach, has occupied the scholars of the church for two centuries and more.[1]

For all the insights of this new approach, it has probably occasioned much of the neglect of the Old Testament in preaching noted above. Of the many factors that could be considered, we shall note five of them. Each of these points will be used as an occasion to reflect on our basic topic.

I. The Question of Methods

The methods used by the New Testament authors in interpreting the Old Testament have been called into question. They paid little attention to the original contexts of Old Testament texts, and hence gave the latter inappropriate meanings, or so it is claimed. Anybody who has tried to link Hos 11:1 and Matt 2:15 or Exod 17:6 and 1 Cor 10:4 knows something of what is involved. Yet, I wonder whether we have not been too hasty here, and that more help is available from the New Testament authors than is commonly claimed.

---

1. For helpful discussions of the issues, see especially J. Barr, *Old and New in Interpretation* (London: SCM, 1966); B. W. Anderson, ed., *The Old Testament and Christian Faith* (New York: Harper, 1963); C. Westermann, ed., *Essays on Old Testament Hermeneutics* (Richmond: John Knox, 1963); A. H. J. Gunneweg, *Understanding the Old Testament* (London: SCM, 1978); H. Gese, *Essays in Biblical Theology* (Minneapolis: Augsburg, 1982); J. Bright, *The Authority of the Old Testament* (Philadelphia: Westminster, 1967). Gunneweg is the most up-to-date full discussion, while Barr remains the most provocative and generative of helpful reflection.

A. Just the fact *that* they understood the Old Testament to be the Word of God and *that* it provided crucial resources for interpreting and proclaiming the Christ-event provides an indispensable starting point for us. There is a givenness here that cannot be put aside; certain claims about the Christ are made on the basis of the Old Testament, and one cannot (logically) have the claims without the basis. The Old Testament is such an authoritative resource, however, not only because the Christ event was interpreted in terms of it, but also because it determined to a considerable degree how Jesus was *experienced* in the first place. Thus, for example, the Old Testament essentially defined the questions that were (or were not) asked (e.g., a Messiah was expected).

So too for modern Christians, the Old Testament should continue to serve that function, helping to determine how the Christ-event is to be interpreted, proclaimed, *and* experienced. The nature of the Christian experience ought not be determined on the basis of the New Testament alone, and we impoverish our people if we seek to do that.[2]

B. In their use of the Old Testament, the New Testament authors employed exegetical methods borrowed largely from contemporary Judaism.[3] Contrary to the Gnostics, the New Testament writers used publicly available canons of interpretation. This gives us permission (obligation?) to make use of whatever public canons may be available today. These canons also provide an important touching-point between the biblical and public worlds; our methods are thus intelligible, an important aspect of mission.

C. The New Testament authors used a variety of interpretive methods.[4] The Old Testament was not used in some monochromatic fashion. This suggests that we ought not seek any single way of appropriating Old Testament material. The richness of the Old Testament demands a variety of angles of vision for proper appreciation and appropriation. This needs to be expanded in a separate point.

D. Generally characteristic of New Testament methodology is this important combination: textual adherence and hermeneutical freedom (with a Christological center). Thus, it is common to appeal to the text over against the meanderings of tradition (see Mark 7:8–13), while at the same time manifesting great freedom in combining texts (Matt 2:6) and interpreting them (Matt 2:15). There is no rigidity of method; there is even an aversion to methodological legalism. Yet there remains a basic faithfulness

---

2. Barr, *Old and New*, 139f., reminds us helpfully that the primary New Testament task was not to explain the Old Testament in terms of Jesus, but Jesus in terms of the Old Testament. He was the one who needed explaining; he still does, and the Old Testament continues to help us do that.

3. There is a continuity in hermeneutics not only with Judaism, but with the Old Testament itself, e.g., in the use of predictive prophecy (see Deut 18:21–22) or typology (see Second Isaiah).

4. Any list would be quite extensive, but the most important seem to be: Midrash, Targum, Pesher, typology, allegory, paraenesis, promise/fulfillment.

to the text as the departure point for interpretation. There is insistence on text-centeredness, but creativity is exemplified in appropriation.

The suggestion here for our use of the Old Testament is to be more centered on the text, while being more imaginative in our hermeneutic. It is, *finally,* the results obtained which are important and not the methods used to get them, and, in any case, the results can, indeed must, be evaluated on grounds [226] other than the methods used.[5] The variety of New Testament methods, then, should be the preacher's invitation to creativity in method, not a limitation to well-traveled ruts.[6]

II. Attention to Sources

The historical approach has given more concentrated attention to sources of biblical books than to their final form. This atomization of the literature has tended to discourage preachers, because of the preparatory time it takes to track down this theory or that, and because it often takes too much explaining before one can get on with the sermon.

Recent literary and "canonical" studies[7] have given renewed importance to the present form of the text. There is now scholarly permission, if you will, to work with the interpretive possibilities of the text as it stands. The literary approach in particular gives promise of being helpful to preachers.

At the same time, one ought not lose sight of the traditioning process that has preceded the final form, not only for its insights into individual texts, but also for the possibilities it bespeaks regarding relationships between texts and Testaments. The Old Testament is seen to be the end product of a long history of many traditions, most of which had a *testimonial* character. That is, for each generation the inherited tradition functioned as an ongoing witness to God's activity, and new shapes of the tradition emerged as these generations added their own witness to that of the old.[8]

---

5. This is important to remember not least because we tend to accept for our own use the conclusions drawn by the New Testament authors regarding the Christ-event, but not all the methods used to arrive at them. On the other side, a flawless use of methods may issue in results incompatible with, say, the theological perspective of a passage.

6. One might suggest that this is, rather, an invitation to anarchy, so that anything goes. However, as long as there are publicly available canons, well-executed, an anarchy of method would not be a bad thing (in fact, not far removed from the present state of affairs!). Even somebody like, say, Hal Lindsay, ought not be condemned for his method *per se* (though it has some esoteric aspects), but on his execution and on the results he achieves. It is true, of course, that certain methods are more productive of insight than are others. Cf. Barr, *Old and New,* 142: "Perhaps modern interpretation, being historical in the way no ancient interpretation was, has its possibilities for creativity enriched *but also narrowed*" (italics mine).

7. From the canonical side, see B. S. Childs, *An Introduction to the Old Testament as Scripture* (Philadelphia: Fortress, 1979). From the literary side, see Robert Polzin, *Moses and the Deuteronomist* (New York: Seabury, 1980).

8. The meaning of a text is thus never exhausted by what the originator of the original form of the text intended it to be (to the extent that that is recoverable). Cf. R. E.

At every stage the tradition functioned as Word of God for Israel. But the old was not superseded in the face of the new, for no Word of God can become antiquated, or lose its value and import. The old remained as living Word of God *and* became part of a new coherent totality so that *together* they witnessed in a new way to God's activities. [227]

Thus, Genesis 2 was not set aside when Genesis 1 was added. The old story retained a distinctive character, but it was no longer simply "old." It became a part of the new to constitute a new story of creation, something more than either was individually. New contexts generate new meanings, opening up the old to new theological functions.[9] The same point could be made regarding Isaiah 1–39 and 40–55, or the various stages of the "law of Moses," or the use of royal texts for messianic expectations, or, in the New Testament, the use of the Markan witness by Luke and Matthew.

In a similar manner one can say that the Old Testament is (often literally) contained within the New Testament; in being so blended into the new, it becomes as new as the new. Together they constitute a new coherent totality, yet without the old losing its character as Word of God. Thus, one might say that the Old Testament constitutes *both* a pre-Christian Word of God, and by virtue of the new totality, a Christian word.[10] This brings us to our next point.

III. Relating Old and New as a Problem

Perhaps most effective in the diminishment of Old Testament usage in preaching is its being anchored so solidly in the pre-Christian era, and the consequent difficulties associated with relating it properly to New Testament realities, without denying its integrity as Word of God for its own times and places.

The issue might be sharpened when questions like these are asked: When the average Christian hears the Word "God" in Old Testament texts, what comes to mind? Is it "God before Jesus"? Do we somehow abstract ourselves from our contemporary situation and live ourselves back into some pre-Jesus time so that we hear these words as ancient Israelites? I suspect that few do. It is, for example, a Trinitarian cast of mind into which these

---

Clements, *Old Testament Theology: A Fresh Approach* (Atlanta: John Knox, 1978), 12: "The very demand of a truly historical criticism requires that we look at the biblical dimension of faith in all of its aspects, and seek to proceed beyond the view that works with simple monochrome meanings for sayings. . . . A single historical context cannot, by itself, determine the meaning of a biblical text."

9. The tradition may be said to be transmitted, not for the sake of preserving the past, but for the sake of providing a point of orientation for present faith and for the embodiment of future hope.

10. The question of unity and diversity pertains not only to the relationship between the Testaments, but within each Testament. One ought to be prepared to discover that there are greater levels of unity between, e.g., Isaiah 40–55 and the Gospel of John than between the latter and, say, James.

texts are placed, whether the preacher makes that explicit or not. That God is our God; there has been no evolution from "one to three" over the years. The words of these pre-Christian texts have become for us Christian words.

But have we not thereby compromised the integrity of these words, giving them a meaning which they did not have in their original contexts? Or have these words *become* something more than they were originally by being placed within the new totality we call the Christian Bible (see previous section)? Indeed, even more, has this context enabled a more accurate assessment of what actually happened in the original situation? Thus, for example, we might say that *we* now realize what *Israel* did not, namely, that the God of whom they spoke *could* (if they had known what is now known) have been described in, say, Trinitarian terms.[11] Thus, while it might be said that we are not being "true to" all aspects [228] of their understanding, we are being *truer* to the kind of God who was actually involved in Israel's life, and are thus more accurate than Israel in speaking of the nature of that involvement.[12] These texts thus have the capacity of being both pre-Christian words, and by virtue of the new context *and* the nature of our experience with the God of the text, Christian words.

But how in preaching do we do justice to both: our *knowledge* of their pre-Christian origins and our *experience* of hearing them as Christian words?

There are no doubt variations in our experience at this point, so that there is no one approach to suggest. Certain texts are more immediate to our experience (say, Psalm 23 over against Psalm 109),[13] hence needing little "translation"; almost any talk about the text rings true. Thus, because of the high degree of commonality of experience, one does justice to both pre-Christian and Christian simultaneously.

Other texts are less immediate to our experience for a variety of reasons (e.g., trans-cultural difference). In such cases more "explaining" is necessary before the horizons of text and hearer meet. This can take many forms, but one way is to talk *about the text,* but in language that enables it to ring true to common Christian experience (hence doing justice to both worlds). There will be no specific point of "application," but a merging of the experience of the people in the text with the experience of the congregation into a single "story." An elision of worlds will have occurred. A variation on this is a one-two step approach, whereby one will first lay out the experience reflected in the text, anticipating in one's description the

---

11. It might be noted that internal to the Old Testament is the development of, say, henotheism to monotheism. But from the perspective of the post-exilic redactions, all texts were read from the perspective of a high monotheism.

12. This would, of course, have implications for matters other than talk about God, e.g., the nature of faith.

13. This is also true of the New Testament, e.g., the Gospel of John and the Book of Revelation. In fact, many Old Testament texts are more immediate to common Christian experience than are many New Testament texts.

commonalities with contemporary experience, and then speak of the contemporary situation in such a way that the commonalities with the biblical generation are transparent, and so that the Word of God which spoke then speaks again.[14]

This approach is especially helpful where the biblical historical context is sharp and clear or where the interpreter is working with a narrative or "story." Thus, e.g., to lay the exilic situation of the people of God (in connection with, say, texts from Isaiah 40–55) alongside contemporary Christian experience makes for some unusually striking commonalities.

One general way to honor the realities of the pre-Christian world is through the careful use of language, avoiding obviously anachronistic language or concepts (e.g., Christology). A preacher need not be explicit with regard to New Testament realities for an elision of worlds to occur. The liturgical setting and the larger Christian tradition "embedded" in the community will play an important role in how a text is heard.[15] [229]

IV. Difficult Passages

The historical approach has prevented many difficult passages from being interpreted in a non-literal way. Thus, holy wars and curse psalms, and other such "crude and primitive" notions have had to be faced head-on. One could no longer "escape" through various forms of an allegorical approach, and the whole Old Testament has tended to suffer from neglect as a result. Yet the Old Testament has taken more than its share of neglect for such a reason, for the New Testament is filled with comparable difficulties, from a demon-filled world, to eternal punishments in gory detail, to prohibiting women a leadership role in churches.[16] One ought not think that all Old Testament texts need somehow to be resurrected for general Christian preaching, and that one has to engage in special pleading or

---

14. The second step need not be an explicit "application" step. It may involve only setting two "stories" side by side (or interweaving them) and letting the congregation draw the analysis as appropriate. They may see more than the preacher.

15. There is, of course, a venerable tradition which has employed explicit Christological language when speaking of Old Testament realities (e.g., Luther, Bonhoeffer); though this practice is rooted in the New Testament (e.g., 1 Cor 10:4), and it is certainly not theologically inappropriate, for the second person of the Trinity was active in Israel's life, it seems best to avoid it so that the pre-Christian context can be seen more sharply, preventing the text from becoming an allegory of our own experience, and maintaining that over-againstness which is so important for insight.

16. This demonstrates that the evaluation of texts for use in contemporary theology and ethics cannot proceed on the basis of the New Testament alone (as many tend to do), for New Testament texts also need to be evaluated. Thus, this can only be done on the basis of a canon within the canon, at the center of which must be the gospel, the proper definition of which is arrived at only on the basis of both Testaments. A determination of what is "Christian," while more directly dependent upon the New Testament, is finally arrived at only with the assistance of the Old Testament. Gunneweg's discussion, *Understanding the Old Testament*, 219ff., suffers at this point.

heavy-handed apologetic to see that they are. Yet, while an historical approach to such texts makes for more work than usual, it is often worth the effort, for they are often "surprise" texts that carry a fresh angle of vision on what the Christian faith is all about.

One example might be cited: the so-called curse psalms of which Psalm 109 is typical. These laments, cries *to God* to be delivered from the hands of oppressors, are rooted in the Exodus tradition and the contest with Pharaoh, and in the legal tradition (see Exod 22:22–24). In essence, they could be said to be prayers that the judgment announced by the prophets on oppressors would be forthcoming (see Jer 5:26–29). One key is to see that these psalms are not model prayers, but occasional ones, used by those who were on their way to an ancient counterpart of Hitler's gas chambers; as such, one dare not stand in judgment over them. We probably have difficulties with these psalms in a way that, say, Namibian Christians would not, for we so seldom (if ever) are the victims of true oppression, and are in fact more often the oppressors. We have not been sufficiently attentive to the ways in which Christians have actually experienced texts like these.

V. Obsolescence

Closely related to these passages are those which speak of practices and institutions (e.g., animal sacrifices) which have been abrogated as a result of the coming of Christ. Because we can no longer allegorize our way through these texts, but must see them as the historical phenomena they in fact are, the effect has been to put many of these texts "on the shelf."

In response, it is to be noted once again that there are comparable realities [230] in the New Testament, e.g., 1 Corinthians 11 or Philemon—passages reflective of early Christian practices that were important for a particular sociohistorical situation, but are no longer significant; in fact, they often *must* be set aside to be true to the gospel. Moreover, within the Old Testament itself there are developments which make earlier practices obsolete (e.g., changes in sanctuaries). In the case of both Testaments, however, such developments do not make these *texts* of no further import.

It might be tempting to suggest that these Old Testament realities are only prefigurations (or types) of New Testament realities yet to come. But that would be effectively to minimize their very important role in the life of a community as real and rich as our own and to see them only as shadows of the real thing. It is difficult to relate to shadows.

Another direction seems preferable. Such materials should be anchored firmly in Israel's history, and seen to be part and parcel of a community of faith with whom God is working to carry out his purposes. Such religious forms provide the matrix for the community's growth in faith and for the maturation of theological perspectives that continue to have considerable significance (e.g., the theology of sacrifice). Such texts are not easy to preach on, but their obvious rootedness in history and in a developing community of faith should enable significant experiential analogies to be drawn for the people of God in any age.

Thus, for example, the laws in the Pentateuch have commonly been put aside without recognizing the ways in which they often touch base with common Christian experience. Certainly Deuteronomy, often referred to as a book of "preached law" (and, one might add, a favorite of Jesus), shows the way here. We see there (and elsewhere) how a key touch point in an old law is used to speak to a new situation. For example, Deut 15:1 picks up on Exod 23:10–11 at the point of concern for the *poor* and gets at the heart of what the law is all about: "You shall open wide your hand to your brother, to the needy and the poor in the land" (Deut 15:11). Again, Lev 25:1–7 picks up on the same law at the point of concern for the *land,* and gets at another key issue: "It shall be a year of solemn rest for the land" (25:4; see what disobedience involves in Hos 4:1–3). Given the widespread concern in the legal materials for matters of justice and ecology (and other "modern" issues), one is given to wonder whether greater attention to these passages by preachers through the years would have made the contemporary church more sensitive.[17]

This leads to a concluding point: The sensitivity of our congregations to such issues will be dependent upon our preaching from Old Testament texts more often than we realize. The authority or value of such texts and their issues in the eyes of people so often depends on preachers having "shown it to be so" only by repeated attention. And one of the best ways to do this is not by treating the text as an object, to be taken out and trumpeted about, but by reflecting on the text as an experience of the people of God, people whose lives are so similar to our own. But, above all, the preacher should show how God pilgrimaged with this people, sharing in their limitations, complexities, and ambiguities, and promising to be with them and for them wherever they went.

---

17. It is said that Marcion was a very wealthy man; no wonder he wanted to get rid of the Old Testament!

Christology and the
Old Testament

Without the Old Testament, there would be no adequate Christology. This claim may state the obvious, but it merits further exploration. The Old Testament has a contribution to make to Christology, not only through the New Testament's use of it but also through the way in which the church (led by the Spirit) reads the Old Testament anew in view of the total canonical witness to God. More continuity between Jesus and the God of the Old Testament is available than is commonly argued, and probably even more than the early Christians realized.[1]

In what follows, I make several introductory comments in relation to this claim and then suggest some ways in which the Old Testament understanding of God is crucial for proper Christological understanding.

Some Introductory Issues

1. The issue in my opening claim is not simply that the followers of Jesus sought to make sense of him by employing terms familiar from their scriptures. The basic issue at stake is not literary or historical. The early Christians make a theological claim on the basis of Old Testament texts; Jesus is the Christ whom God promised. Without the Old Testament and the presuppositions about God that it provides for that claim, Jesus is not the Christ. If the authority of that basis is diminished, as it often is by Christians, the claim that Jesus is the Christ is also diminished. The status given [202] to the Old Testament in the life of the church has significant implications for ongoing theological reflection regarding Jesus Christ.

2. Given the obvious incompleteness in our understanding of Jesus as the Christ, the Old Testament is indispensable for the *continuing* insight it gives regarding his identity. This means that it is insufficient to say Jesus is important for understanding the Old Testament; the interpretive traffic going the other way is even more fundamental. We continue to need the Old Testament in our ongoing efforts to understand Jesus more fully, both historically and theologically.

Just how to read the Old Testament so that it further elucidates the identity of Jesus is not altogether clear. Two factors stand in tension with each

This essay was originally published in *Who Do You Say That I Am? Essays on Christology* (ed. Mark Allan Powell and David R. Bauer; Louisville: Westminster John Knox, 1999), 201–15.

1. I am pleased to be a contributor to this book honoring Jack Dean Kingsbury. We started teaching together at Luther Seminary in 1968, and the helpful conversation begun there on the relationship between the testaments is here continued.

other: the particularity of the Old Testament in its pre-Christian time and place, and the experience of Christians who have for centuries heard the word of God addressed to them through these texts. The one reality that spans these times is God, the God of Israel and of Jesus Christ. In seeking to relate the two testaments, one is called to center one's interpretive strategies on the portrayal of that God.

Seeking out possible New Testament allusions to the kind of God of whom the Old Testament speaks (see below) will remain an important enterprise. But more is at stake. The explicitness of the New Testament references to these God themes may be minimal. Yet, as noted below, the reader still must ask about the effect these themes may have had more generally on the early Christian understanding of God (for example, claims about God in texts such as 2 Cor 5:18–19 or Phil 2:5–11). But even more, modern readers may discern significant connections between the testaments in this regard that early Christians may not have seen. The New Testament does not have the full and final interpretation of the significance of Jesus Christ (witness Chalcedon) or of the links between Jesus and the Old Testament. Postbiblical insights into the God of the Old Testament have the potential of enriching our christological reflections. In such cases, one might speak of the ongoing work of the Spirit, leading the church into all the truth (John 16).

3. The Old Testament has a status for the New Testament claims regarding the identity of Jesus that first-century Judaism does not. I discern some tendency in scholarship to collapse the Old Testament into first-century Judaism, as if to explicate the latter would accurately and adequately mirror Old Testament perspectives. For example, N. T. Wright, in a major recent work, undertakes a lengthy explication of "Israel's" worldview, beliefs, and hope in terms of what "first-century Jews actually believed."[2]

Aside from historical inaccuracies that this collapsing presents, its inadequacy [203] is demonstrated in the fact that the New Testament authors almost always quote the Old Testament in support of their claims, not first-century Jewish sources that were available to them. It is not that early Christians were uninfluenced by contemporary theological and philosophical perspectives or disdained current exegetical methods. But apparently the experience of Jesus (including the tradition of Jesus' own use of scripture) propelled his followers into a new encounter with their scriptures in search for understandings that contemporary Judaism and its interpretation of those same texts was not believed able to provide. They read their scriptures with new eyes in view of their experience with Jesus and the faith in him that experience generated (see Luke 24). One might also speak of

---

2. N. T. Wright, *The New Testament and the People of God* (Minneapolis: Fortress, 1992), 244. Another example of this tendency is the introductory New Testament section in the *NIB*, vol. 8; it contains a "Jewish Context" chapter but none on the use of the Old Testament.

the gift of the Spirit (see John 16:12–15).[3] The effect of Jesus (and the Spirit) on the early Christians leads to a *rediscovery of the Old Testament itself* and to a "sea change" in seeing its interpretive possibilities. (A possible parallel to the depth of this change is the effect of the historical-critical method on modern biblical interpretation.) The early Christians encountered Old Testament and, more specifically, the God of the Old Testament in fresh ways. One effect of these new ways of seeing was that first-century thought may have colored their interpretation of the Old Testament to a lesser degree than might otherwise have been the case.

4. Such a perspective has implications for understanding the nature of early Christian claims regarding God. A common view is that the followers of Jesus engaged in what N. T. Wright calls "a radical redefinition" of their theological heritage.[4] Elsewhere, Wright speaks of a "radically revised Jewish picture of the one true God."[5] One reason for Wright's use of the word *radical* (in a context where he recognizes much continuity) seems to be apparent when he goes on to describe this Jewish God as the "transcendent God who is beyond space and time." But while this phrase may be an accurate portrayal of the God of first-century Judaism, it does not describe the God of the Old Testament. I hope to show that the God of the Old Testament has less "emptying" to do in the incarnation than does a God who is conceived in such "wholly other" terms. One may speak of an early Christian advancing (or filling out) of the Old Testament portrayal of God in speaking of the identity of Jesus, but more continuity is here than the language of radical redefinition or even revision seems able to acknowledge. In what follows, I use the language of *trajectory*.

To use the word *radical* is to stress distance and discontinuity. If one were working with perspectives in first-century Judaism, this theological distance might be claimed with some justification. (A question to be pursued would be how the understanding of God in first-century Judaism, under [204] the impact of Hellenistic philosophy and historical experience, differed from that of the Old Testament.) But the issue of continuity/discontinuity with first-century Judaism should not be collapsed into the issue of continuity/discontinuity with the Old Testament. The religious and theological perspectives of first-century Judaism are an *interpretation* of the Old Testament (informed by other understandings). The question about Jesus' identity hinges most directly on differing interpretations of the *Old Testament*.

3. Several important works on the New Testament use of the Old Testament have recently appeared; for example, Richard Hays, *Echoes of Scripture in the Letters of Paul* (New Haven: Yale University Press, 1989); Robert Brawley, *Text to Text Pours Forth Speech: Voices of Scripture in Luke–Acts* (Bloomington: Indiana University Press, 1995).

4. N. T. Wright, *The Climax of the Covenant: Christ and the Law in Pauline Theology* (Minneapolis: Fortress, 1991), 115–16.

5. Idem, *What Saint Paul Really Said: Was Paul of Tarsus the Real Founder of Christianity?* (Grand Rapids: Eerdmans, 1997), 74.

One could fall into the ditch on the other side of the road and simply flatten out the two testaments theologically or force christological readings of the Old Testament, claiming no newness or advance in theological perspective in view of the Christ event. The interpreter must live with the tensions entailed in staying between the two ditches. The theological tension between the testaments in view of the Christ event will never be overcome, but that tension in itself often generates a fuller understanding of God and God's ways in Jesus.

The early Christians, if asked about the kind of God in whom they believed, would have pointed to various Old Testament portrayals (see below).[6] In view of the fact that the God of the Old Testament is understood to be a certain kind of God, specific claims were made about Jesus' relationship to that God. Placing their experience of Jesus over the template provided by Old Testament understandings of God (and other matters), early Christians discerned a certain fit and the lights went on regarding Jesus' identity.

5. The Gospels have Jesus making some explicit claims about the place of the Old Testament in his self-understanding. Texts such as Luke 24:44–47 (compare 18:31–34; 24:26–27) are startling in this regard. "Then he opened their minds to understand the scriptures, and he said to them, 'Thus it is written, that the Messiah is to suffer and to rise from the dead on the third day, and that repentance and forgiveness of sins is to be proclaimed in his name to all nations, beginning from Jerusalem.'"

Jesus' followers, in turn, "argued . . . from the scriptures . . . and examined the scriptures every day to see whether these things were so" (Acts 17:2–3, 11; see 3:18–26). Paul testified that "Christ died for our sins [and was raised] in accordance with the scriptures" (1 Cor 15:3–4). The reader can be forgiven for wishing that Luke and Paul had cited the specific texts to which they make reference. We would then not expend so much effort in seeking to determine which texts they had in mind and the approach they used in interpreting them.

In this search, textual blocks such as Isaiah 52–53 and various psalms have been brought into play, as well as numerous allusions and "echoes," [205] which join the study of traditional texts, themes, and titles.[7] As important as this exercise has been and continues to be, more seems to be at stake than identifying and explicating specific passages. N. T. Wright's comment in this regard is helpful: "When Paul declared that 'the Messiah died

---

6. For the importance of the issue of "the kind of God," see T. Fretheim, *The Suffering of God: An Old Testament Perspective* (Philadelphia: Fortress, 1984). It is helpful to see that N. T. Wright uses this same language in *The Original Jesus: The Life and Vision of a Revolutionary* (Grand Rapids: Eerdmans, 1996), 79.

7. See, for example, Donald Juel, *Messianic Exegesis: Christological Interpretation of the Old Testament in Early Christianity* (Philadelphia: Fortress, 1988); Nils Dahl, *Jesus the Christ: The Historical Origins of Christological Doctrine* (ed. Donald Juel; Minneapolis: Fortress, 1991).

for our sins according to the Scriptures' [1 Cor 15:3] . . . he does not mean that he can find half a dozen 'proof-texts' from Scripture that he can cunningly twist into predictions of the crucifixion. He means that the entire scriptural story, the great drama of God's dealing with Israel, came together when" Jesus died.[8]

I follow Wright's lead in somewhat different terms: The "great drama" has to do with *two* stories that are woven into a single tapestry, namely, the story of Israel and the story of God.[9]

A fresh encounter with their scriptures in view of their experience with Jesus meant that the early Christians saw with new eyes not only the story of God's people (and their place within it) but also the story of God (and Jesus' place within both). As such, the Christ event is seen to be as much the climax of the story of God as it is the story of Israel. Jesus not only gathers up the people of God in his person and embodies this community. Jesus' story is not simply the story of *human* life and death. Jesus not only mediates the work of God on behalf of this people (as many Israelite "saviors" also did). Jesus is the climactic moment in *God's* own story. So, for example, the suffering of Jesus must be linked not only with the suffering of Israel but also with the suffering of God (see below; Mark 3:5; 14:33–34; compare Eph 4:30). Or, the healing work of Jesus must be linked not only with the prophetic healers but also more directly with the healing work of God (see John 5:17).[10]

Hence, the interpreter who would understand Jesus through an appeal to the Old Testament must tend as much to God's story in the Old Testament as to Israel's story. God's story is more comprehensive, inclusive, and cosmic in scope than that of Israel. For starters, God's story has to do with the world, as does that of Jesus (witness Genesis 1; John 1; Colossians 1). (I wonder whether pursuing the idea of "story of God" has often not been possible because classical theism has for so long assumed that the word *story* does not really apply to God.)

The claims made regarding Jesus are fundamentally grounded in understandings of God and God's story from the Old Testament. For early Christians, the portrayal of God may have proved to be the sharpest point of continuity between their scriptures and their experience of Jesus. Old Testament God-talk provided a substratum of thought for ongoing reflection regarding God's act in Jesus, whether explicitly acknowledged or not.

---

8. Wright, *What Saint Paul Really Said*, 48–49, 50–51.

9. The study of God in the New Testament has been neglected. See Nils Dahl, "The Neglected Factor in New Testament Theology," in *Jesus the Christ*, 153–63. This 1975 essay still pertains for the most part. The extended project of Wright is, in part, to "rectify" this situation (*New Testament and the People of God*, xiv). See also Brawley, *Text to Text*.

10. For a summary account of key New Testament texts regarding the relationship between Jesus and God, see Raymond E. Brown, *An Introduction to New Testament Christology* (New York: Paulist Press, 1994), 171–95.

In [206] other words, certain claims about God that permeate the Old Testament provided a theological matrix within which thinking about Jesus and his identity could develop.

If, for example, as Wright claims, everything Paul "said about Jesus was, for him, a way of talking about God," then it is important to ask *what kind of God* this is.[11] It is often said that the New Testament takes the God of the Old Testament for granted; but at least this key question remains: What kind of God is this God?

The following fundamental convictions about the God of the Old Testament, at the least, should be included in such a list. One may doubt that early christological formulations would, indeed could, have developed as they did without these theological convictions. I list these particular themes in view of my own experience of the witness of both testaments. A next step would be to gather still other New Testament texts in which there are quotations, allusions, or echoes regarding this kind of God.[12] But finally, the theological issue is not simply the use of the Old Testament by the New. The issue is a theological use of the Old Testament that is able to fill out our christological reflections even beyond that of the New Testament, though staying on the same trajectory.

Jesus' Story and God's Story

God in Relationship. First, the Old Testament witnesses to God as one who is *in relationship within the divine realm*. Israel's God is by nature a social being, functioning within a divine community (Gen 1:26; Prov 8:22–31; Jer 23:18–23). These and other passages witness to the richness and complexity of the divine realm. God is not in heaven alone but is engaged in a relationship of mutuality within that realm and chooses to share the creative process, for example, with others. In other words, relationship is integral to the identity of God, independent of God's relationship to the world. A recognition of the sociality of God does not compromise the witness that God is one (Deut 6:4). These Old Testament perspectives on the social nature of God provided understandings that laid the groundwork for later theological developments. Early Christian reflections about God that led to Trinitarian thought were not grounded only in New Testament claims about Jesus and the Spirit.

Second, this relational God freely enters *into relationships with that which has been created*. Biblical metaphors for God, with few if any exceptions, have relatedness at their very core (for example, king–subject, husband–wife, parent–child). Even nonpersonal metaphors are understood [207] in

---

11. Wright, *What Saint Paul Really Said,* 57.
12. Among the key texts that would have to be mined for such linkages are Luke 1–2; John; Acts 17; Romans 8–11; 1 Corinthians 1–2, 8–12, 15; 2 Corinthians 3–5; Galatians 4; Ephesians 1–4; Philippians 2; Colossians 1–2.

relational terms (Deut 32:18; Ps 31:2–3). To characterize these metaphors generally: They are relational, usually personal rather than impersonal, ordinary rather than extraordinary, everyday rather than dramatic, earthly rather than "heavenly," and secular rather than religious. This type of language used for God ties God closely to the world and its everyday affairs. These kinds of images for God were believed to be most revealing of a God who had entered deeply into the life of the world and was present and active in the common life of individuals and communities.

This relatedness is also evident in the fact that God gives the divine name(s) to Israel, thereby identifying the divine Self as a distinctive member of the community of those who have names. Naming entails a certain kind of relationship. Giving the name opens up the possibility for a certain intimacy in relationship and admits a desire for hearing the voice of the other (see Isa 65:1–2). A relationship without a name inevitably means some distance. Naming enables truer and deeper encounter and communication; it entails availability and accessibility. (In the Old Testament period, the divine name was pronounced.) But naming also entails risk, for it opens God up to an experience of the misuse of the name (see the commandment on the divine name).

The pervasive use of anthropomorphic/anthropopathic language is also important in this regard. God is one who thinks, wills, and feels. God has a mouth that speaks, eyes that see, and hands that create. This language stands together with the more concrete metaphors in saying something important about God—one who is living and dynamic, whose ways of relating to the world are best conveyed in the language of human personality and activity. It is ironic that Christians have at times had difficulty with this language, for in Jesus Christ, God has acted anthropomorphically in a most supreme way. (On God and human form, see below.)

The importance of such relational language is also evident in the prohibition of images. The concern of this prohibition is to protect God's relatedness. The idols "have mouths, but they do not speak; they have eyes, but they do not see; they have ears, but they do not hear, and there is no breath in their mouths" (Ps 135:15–17). "They have hands, but do not feel; feet, but do not walk" (Ps 115:5–7; cf. Jer 10:4–5). The implication, of course, is that Israel's God is one who speaks and sees and hears and feels. With the idols there is no deed or word, no genuine presence. This understanding is continuous with that point where the Old Testament speaks of a legitimate concrete image, namely, the human being (Gen 1:26). The human being, with all its capacities for relationships, is believed to be the only appropriate image of God in the life of the world. For the New Testament to [208] use this language for Jesus (Col 1:15) is testimony to him not only as the supreme exemplification of humanity but as one who reveals God most fully and decisively.

Israel's God is transcendent, but transcendent in relationship to the world, not in isolation from it. In the words of Abraham Heschel, "God remains transcendent in his immanence, and related in his transcendence."[13] God has taken the initiative and freely entered into relationships, both in creation and in covenant with Israel. But having done so, God—who is other than world—has decisively and irrevocably committed the divine Self to be in a certain kind of relationship. And so this God chooses to share power and responsibility with that which is other than God (Gen 1:28), to exercise constraint and restraint in the exercise of power in the world (Gen 8:21–22), and to honor promises made, even to the point of placing God's own life on the line (Gen 15:7–21). The incarnation could be said to be on this relational trajectory, being the supreme exemplification of this kind of divine relatedness and its irrevocability.

This God of the Old Testament is not first and foremost the God of Israel but of the world. The opening chapters of Genesis make universal claims for this God. These chapters portray a God whose *universal* activity includes creating, grieving, judging, saving, electing, promising, blessing, covenant making, and lawgiving. God was in relationship to the world before there ever was an Israel, and so God's relationship with Israel must be understood as a subset within this more inclusive and comprehensive relationship. God's acting and speaking is especially focused in Israel, but this divine activity is a strategic, purposive move for the sake of the world (Gen 12:3, "in you all the families [the families in Genesis 10] of the earth shall be blessed").[14]

The God Who Is Present. God's relationship with the world is comprehensive in scope. God is present and active in the *world.* God "fill[s] heaven and earth" (Jer 23:24); indeed, the earth is "full of the steadfast love of the Lord" (Ps 33:5; 36:5). God is a part of the map of reality and is relational, indeed lovingly relational, to all that is not God. Hence, God's presence is not static or passive but *an active presence in relationship,* profoundly grounded in and informed by steadfast love for the good of all.

Even more, the God of the Old Testament, in creating the world, enters into the space and time of this world and makes it God's own. For example, God builds God's own residence into the very structures of the created order (Ps 104:1–3; compare Isa 40:22; Amos 9:6), so that the heavens (or their semantic equivalent) become a shorthand way of referring to the [209] abode of God *within* the world. God's movement from heaven to earth is a movement within the creation. God—who is other than world—works from within the world, and not on the world from without.

A comparable statement can be made with respect to time; God's relationship to the world is *from within* its structures of time. For example, the

---

13. Abraham Heschel, *The Prophets* (New York: Harper & Row, 1962), 486.
14. For the importance of this theme in Luke–Acts, see Brawley, *Text to Text.*

common language for divine planning and execution of plans (Jer 29:11; 51:12) and being provoked to anger or slow to anger (Deut 32:21; Exod 34:6) assumes that temporal sequence is real for God. Timelessness is not descriptive of the God of the Old Testament; God's life is temporally ordered (at least since the creation). God has freely chosen to enter into the time of the world and truly get caught up in its flow. God is the eternal, uncreated member of this world community, but God too will cry out, "How long?" (Hos 8:5).[15] To suggest that God first entered into time and history in the Christ event is to ignore this wide swath of Old Testament material. God's act in Jesus is an *intensification* of this already-existing trajectory of God's way of being present in and relating to the structures of the world.

Understanding divine presence in terms of varying degrees of intensification is already characteristic of Old Testament thought. In human life, differences in energy level, focus, direction, and attention, as well as the competing presence of others, determine our understanding of the intensity of the presence of someone. Regarding the divine presence, something comparable is at work; divine presence is not understood in a univocal way. For example, though Jonah flees "from the presence of the Lord" (1:3), he still professes belief in a Creator God (1:9). The departure of the tabernacling God from the temple (Ezek 10:1–22; 11:22–25) does not mean that God is now absent (see 11:16). The psalmist prays to a God who has forsaken him but is believed to be present to hear (22:1). One might think of a continuum moving from general or creational presence to theophanic presence (see below), with accompanying and tabernacling presence being intermediate points. (Actual absence is not a divine possibility in the Old Testament.) God is believed to be continuously present, yet God will also be especially present at certain times; God is believed to be everywhere present, yet God will also be intensively present in certain places. The language of "glory," often used for an intensified divine presence, is used in connection with both theophanic and tabernacling texts (Exod 24:15–17; 1 Kgs 8:11; Ezek 9:3).

Such texts show that the God of the Old Testament has taken a variety of steps at key times and places to be more intensively present in the life and structures of the world, and of Israel in particular. That this language is used to speak of Jesus Christ (John 1:14; 2 Cor 4:4–6) catches him up [210] in a trajectory of divine movement toward more intensified forms of presence in the life of the world.

God and Human Form.   N. T. Wright states that the biblical God "became human without doing violence to his own inner essential nature."[16] He grounds this statement in an understanding of God as love, who by nature

---

15. For a discussion of the many texts that support this interpretation, see Fretheim, *Suffering of God,* 37–44.

16. Wright, *Original Jesus,* 82.

cannot "remain uninvolved, or detached, or impersonal." He also speaks of several Jewish "symbols" that spoke of their God coming to dwell in their midst (Wisdom; law; temple). But with respect to the human form, another Old Testament tradition is even more important, namely, the *theophany.* Throughout the Old Testament, God takes on human form and appears. God does not become human for the first time in Jesus.

Old Testament texts witness to various types of theophanies, but the most pertinent here are those where God appears in anonymous human form, as a "man" (*'ish*) or "angel/messenger" (*mal'ak;* see Gen 16:7–13; 18:1–19:11; Judg 6:11–24; 13:3–23). These divine appearances are brief, direct, and personal, usually to individuals. Moreover, they are usually not disruptive or extraordinary but occur within the framework of everyday life and experience. God appears, enfleshed in human form. In some theophanies (usually to the community), God appears enveloped in elements of fire, cloud/smoke, or light. These elements probably veil a human form; see the messenger "in" the flame of fire in Exod 3:2 and the appearance of "the likeness as it were of a human form" with the fire round about in Ezek 1:26–28 (see also Exod 24:9–11).[17]

In these theophanies, God appears in the life of the world in a way that is specific, articulate, and tangible; in this form, God speaks, listens, and even eats and touches. The assumption of human form is believed to be integral to the accomplishment of the divine purpose in each case. As such, the human form does not compromise divine transcendence. The finite is capable of the infinite. The empirical world can serve the task of "clothing" God. In these theophanies, God "wears" aspects of the creation in order to be as concretely and intensely present as possible. At the same time, the texts are devoid of speculation; the common partialness of reference (hand, foot, mouth, back) suggests a concern to convey a somewhat impressionistic picture.

In theophany, the personal and relational element is sharpened as the divine address to the whole person is made more apparent. There is greater intensity of presence, with greater potential effectiveness for the word spoken. Appearance makes a difference to words. A God who "appears," and appears in the flesh, says something more about God and the God–people relationship [211] than does a God who only speaks. God's word is embodied; the speaking God is understood to share, if only for brief periods of time, the fleshly form of humankind. Hence, the human response can never be simply to believe or speak; it must also mean to re-embody the word in the world.

---

17. For a discussion of the pertinent texts, see Fretheim, *Suffering of God,* 79–106. A distinction is to be made between these theophanies where God is the bearer of a word and those of God as warrior in times of need, where no word is spoken and no form seen (Psalms 18; 29; 77; Habakkuk 3). On this, see J. Jeremias, "Theophany in the Old Testament," in *IDBSup.*

God's appearance in human form also reveals God's vulnerability. Appearance associated only with storm phenomena would suggest that God remained aloof, only to be feared, in total control of the situation. But for God to enter into the life of the world in human form makes for greater vulnerability; the human response can be derision (Gen 18:12–13) or incredulity (Judg 6:13–17). It is revealing of the ways of God more generally that in such key moments of revelation, God is enfleshed in bodies of weakness within the framework of everyday affairs, and not in overwhelming power. Even in those instances where the vestments of God's appearance are threaded with lineaments of power, they clothe a vulnerable form. (It might also be noted that theophanies witness to divine change, as do other themes, such as divine repentance. Depending on the topic, the Old Testament stakes claims for both divine immutability [better: constancy] and mutability.)[18]

Precritical interpretations of these texts often linked theophanies to the preexistent Logos or the second Person of the Trinity.[19] This is anachronistic language for the God of ancient Israel, of course, but it is significant that this linkage of theophany and Christology has a long tradition. I claim only that these theophanic texts may have provided a perspective on God within which incarnation could be naturally developed. The incarnation would not be a radical move for those steeped in Old Testament texts (see also on anthropomorphisms, above). To use an earlier formulation of mine,

---

18. In the words of Walter Eichrodt, in the theophany "God's connection with the world is most clearly observed"; indeed, Israel's God is one who "can temporarily incarnate himself" (*Theology of the Old Testament* [2 vols.; Philadelphia: Westminster, 1961–67], 2:15, 27). Some scholars downplay the form God assumes in the theophanies. For example, Walter Brueggemann ("Presence of God," *IDBSup*) states that there is "no interest in any form of appearance" (p. 681). Brueggemann's lack of interest in this aspect of theophany is also evident in his *Theology of the Old Testament* (Minneapolis: Fortress, 1997), 567–77. Remarkably, he considers many theophanies to be "unmediated" (even in texts such as Gen 18:1–2). Similarly, Samuel Terrien (*The Elusive Presence* [New York: Harper & Row, 1978]) devaluates references to the "seeing of the eye" in contrast to the "hearing of the ear" (p. 112). Such is the impact of a narrowly conceived theology of the word of God.

In contrast, Edmund Jacob claims that "God always appears in human form," and that theophanies are "approaches to the biblical solution of the divine presence, that of God become man in Jesus Christ" (*Theology of the Old Testament* [New York: Harper & Row, 1958], 74). Gerhard von Rad (*Old Testament Theology* [2 vols.; New York: Harper & Row, 1962]) speaks even more expansively; certain texts claim that, for Israel, "Yahweh has the form of man" (1:145; see also his "divine kenosis" reference on 1:367). That is, God does not simply *assume* the human form for the sake of appearance; there is, for Israel, an essential continuity between that form and the reality of God. Gen 1:26 considers the human to be "theomorphic" rather than God being anthropomorphic (1:146). For further discussion of this issue, see Fretheim, *Suffering of God*, 102–5.

19. Eichrodt's arguments (*Theology of the Old Testament*, 2:28) in setting these Christian interpretations aside from Old Testament perspectives are largely beside the point. The point is not to "Christianize" the Old Testament but to consider the basic theological perspectives that informed Christian theological reflection.

"there is no such thing for Israel as a nonincarnate God."[20] The Old Testament God is a God who is prone to incarnation, and once again, the interpreter can discern a divine trajectory of which *the* incarnation is climactic.

God, Prophet, and the Enfleshed Word. This understanding of God's appearing in human form is extended in the prophetic literature. From a canonical perspective, prophets appear at about the time that the messenger of God ceases to appear. Noteworthy are the significant continuities between them (human form; "man of God" and "messenger" identification; use of first-person singular and similar genres; membership in the divine council). Yet there are new developments (prophets have names and distinctive personalities; their ministries extend over time) so that they are called to function, in effect, as ongoing theophanies.

Thinking of the word of God as embodied in the prophet's person is [212] particularly evident in Jeremiah and Ezekiel. In their call narratives, God does not speak what they are to say; the word of God is placed directly into their mouths (Jer 1:9; 15:16; Ezek 2:10–3:3). The prophet thus ingests the word of God, and "you are what you eat." Gerhard von Rad warns against taking these passages "in too spiritual a way. . . . The entry of the message into their physical life brought about an important change in the self-understanding of these later prophets. (We may ask whether the entry of the word into a prophet's bodily life is not meant to approximate what the writer of the Fourth Gospel says about the word becoming flesh.)" Samuel Terrien speaks of the prophet as a "living incarnator of divinity."[21] The prophets are understood to be vehicles of divine immanence; the word of God is enfleshed in their very selves. In some fundamental sense, the human figure *is* the word of God The story of the prophet is a story of the word of God. The story of God gets caught up in the very life of the prophet.

The Old Testament does not finally come to the conclusion that God was incarnate in a human life in complete unbrokenness or in its entirety. Yet more decisive continuities between this material and the incarnation exist than have been commonly recognized. Those who had been steeped in the theophanic texts of the Old Testament would not have been surprised at incarnation.

God and Suffering. Messiah and suffering seem not to have been linked in pre-Chritian literature; hence, the notion of a crucified Messiah is commonly thought to be a distinctively Christian formulation. At the same time, the Old Testament witness to a suffering God may not have been taken sufficiently into account in this discussion. God did not suffer for the first time in the Christ event; even more, God did not suffer for the sins of the world for the first time on the cross.

---

20. Fretheim, *The Suffering of God*, 106.
21. Von Rad, *Old Testament Theology*, 2:91–92; Terrien, *Elusive Presence*, 241.

The New Testament witness to the finality and universality of Jesus' suffering and death is certainly an advance on Old Testament understandings. But it is an advance on an already-existing trajectory of reflection about a God who suffers. The Christ who suffers and dies on the cross for the sins of the many bears a strong "family resemblance" to the God revealed in the Old Testament, particularly in the Prophets. To see the face of God in a crucified man would not be a radical move for those steeped in Old Testament understandings of God. The *kind of God* whom the early Christians knew from their scriptures was a God who could know the experience of crucifixion.

The Old Testament witness to a suffering God is rich and pervasive.[22] This understanding of God is grounded in a God who has entered deeply [213] into relationship with the world (see above), and with Israel in particular. In opening the divine Self up to the vulnerabilities of a close relationship, God experiences suffering because of what happens to that relationship. God suffers *because* the people have rejected God. In such cases, God speaks in traditional lament language (Isa 1:2–3; Jer 2:5, 29–31; 3:19–20; 8:4–7; 9:7–9); Jesus' words over Jerusalem stand in this divine lament tradition (Matt 23:37). God suffers *with* those who are experiencing suffering (Exod 3:7; Jer 9:17–18; 31:20), to which the Emmanuel theme may be related.

Several texts witness to a divine suffering *for* (Isa 42:14; 43:23–25; Hos 11:7–9). Consider Isa 43:24–25: God here testifies to being "burdened" with the sins of the people (the verb is *'abad,* to which *'ebed,* "servant," is related). This divine carrying of the sins of the people issues immediately in the unilateral announcement of forgiveness "for my own sake" (43:25). To this text should be linked the "bearing sin" passages of Isa 53:4, 11–12 (compare 1 Pet 2:24). The servant of God thus assumes the role that God himself has just played. (See above on the relationship of God and prophet.)

Many of these divine suffering texts make clear that human sin is not without cost for God. For God to continue to bear the brunt of Israel's rejection rather than deal with it on strictly legal terms means continued life for the people. What does such suffering mean for God? In some sense, it means the expending of the divine life for the sake of the relationship with the people and their future life together. In the especially striking Isa 42:14 ("I will cry out like a woman in labor, I will gasp and pant"), God acts on behalf of a barren people, who are unable to bring their own future into being. God engages in such a giving of self that only one of the sharpest pains known can adequately portray what is involved for God in bringing to birth a new creation of Israel beyond exile. For this kind of God, the cross is no stranger.

---

22. For detail, see Fretheim, *Suffering of God,* especially 107–48. The work of Abraham Heschel on the pathos of God in *The Prophets* is indispensable for this discussion.

Salvation in the Bible vs. Salvation in the Church

Have you been saved? This question of street evangelists is often ridiculed, but by and large the church has accepted the spiritualized understanding of salvation implied in the question. In light of such views, Ted Peters recently claimed: "We need to reopen discussion on the nature of salvation."[1] This response explores some Old Testament dimensions of the theme, links them to the New Testament, and draws some implications for ministry.

We live in a salvation-hungry world. Salvation language abounds on bumper stickers (and elsewhere): save the whales; save the planet; save our cities; condoms save lives. Or, note the interest in holistic health and the integration of physical, emotional, and spiritual dimensions of life; the language of salvation, commonly defined as a making-whole, often appears in such discussions. Or, closer to home, some (many?) Christians perceive that the church's idea of salvation is private and disembodied, only indirectly related to life outside of the vertical relationship with God. Can biblical views of salvation connect with these modern concerns? [363]

I. The Meaning and Place of Salvation

At the heart of this matter is the Bible's use of salvation language in association with God's activity in *both* creation and redemption, a range not often recognized in the church. Christians typically relate salvation to forgiveness, which God grants to those who believe in Jesus Christ, crucified and risen (see Rom 5:8–10). The truth and centrality of this is not being challenged here; what is being questioned is any claim that this exhausts the meaning or experience of salvation in the biblical sense, or that the redemption God accomplishes once-for-all in Jesus Christ has only spiritual salvific effects. I provisionally distinguish between the more traditional churchly view (Salvation I) and those more comprehensive dimensions of salvation (Salvation II) and will then make some suggestions as to how they might be related.

This essay was originally published in *Word and World* 13 (1993): 363–72.

1. Ted Peters, "Wholeness in Salvation and Healing," *LQ* 5 (1991): 312. For a survey of the question "What is salvation?" from various perspectives, see *ExAud* 5 (1989).

For Claus Westermann, God's activity in the world can be divided into saving and blessing.[2] Blessing is a "continuous, flowing and unnoticed working of God which cannot be captured in moments or dates," while saving focuses on specific acts of God (e.g, the exodus).[3] This is a useful distinction in many ways, but a problem arises if one translates it directly into a creation/redemption or a law/gospel distinction (Westermann does not make these systematic moves, but he may encourage them by too simply associating saving with history and blessing with creation).[4]

Westermann shows that God's saving work is respondent to specific needs of people, evident in the structure of the saving deed: cry of the needy one; God's saving with respect to that need; response of the saved.[5] In the exodus, e.g, God responds to needs of a sociopolitical sort in shaping the nature of salvation. Mark Powell makes the same point in his study of salvation in Luke–Acts: the content of salvation is "determined in each instance by the needs of the person or persons involved."[6]

Speaking about "salvation" could take in an array of words as used in various genres and traditions. We will focus on *yāšaʿ* and *sōzein* (and related nouns) more generally. In summary, salvation is deliverance from anything inimical to [365] true life, issuing in well-being and a trustworthy world in which there is space to live.[7]

---

2. Claus Westermann, *Elements of Old Testament Theology* (Atlanta: John Knox, 1982); a briefer form of this study is *What Does the Old Testament Say About God?* (Atlanta: John Knox, 1979).

3. See ibid., 44. The "experience of saving belongs to the whole of human [and non-human] existence" (p. 28).

4. For example, God's blessing, from rain to promises realized in history, has to do with *both* creation and redemption (Gen 12:1–3; cf. Deut 28:6–7). For Westermann, God's saving and blessing are "interlocked and combined with each other" (*What Does the Old Testament Say About God?* 52), but he does not think this through very thoroughly. (See T. Fretheim, "The Reclamation of Creation," *Int* 45 [1991]: 357–359).

Creation in the beginning is not a saving act; poetic texts such as Isa 51:9–10 and Ps 74:12–15 use mythological themes for the cosmic effects of *the exodus*. For Westermann, the proclamation of God as Savior is the same in both Testaments (see *What Does the Old Testament Say About God?* 89), but in the New Testament salvation is focused on the right relationship with God through faith in Jesus Christ. One may ask if salvation *was experientially* different for faithful Israelites, however.

5. Conveniently, see ibid., 29–30.

6. Mark Powell, "Salvation in Luke–Acts," *WW* 12 (1992): 5.

7. Salvation language is wide-ranging and occurs across all types of literature from every period. Other words include *nāṣal, pādāh, gāʾal* (deliver, redeem); *ṣedeqāh* (righteousness). U. Mauser (*The Gospel of Peace* [Louisville: Westminster John Knox, 1992]) shows peace/well-being (*šālôm; eirēnē*) has a comparable range of meaning ("the healing of the sick, the feeding of the hungry, the care of the neglected and despised, and the forgiveness of sins are all aspects of the restoration of God's peace. . . . christological and soteriological thought will then be opened up to the material side of human existence," p. 188). That *ṣedeqāh* has a comparably comprehensive meaning is shown by H. H. Schmid, "Creation, Righteousness, and Salvation: 'Creation Theology' as the Broad Horizon of Biblical The-

II. The Use of Salvation Language

I will focus on various overlapping dualisms often implied in the church's use of salvation language.

1. Eschatological and Historical

Salvation may be associated in a narrow way with the next world, as if salvation were only a heavenly experience, but certain texts insist on salvation as a reality in the present world (e.g., many Psalms). With the appearance of the prophets, salvation becomes more focused on the future (e.g., Isa 11:1–9), but without losing its moorings in this life and this world. In the New Testament such a now/not yet dialectic receives varying emphases. In Luke, for example, the present experience of salvation is emphasized (see 4:21; 19:9). For Paul, too, salvation is very much a present reality (1 Cor 5:17; 2 Cor 6:2), yet more oriented toward the future (Rom 8:19–24; 13:11; Phil 3:20). Saving experiences are both real in the present and a sign of the full salvation to come. Such a view opens up the saving work of Jesus to include his earthly ministry, though his death and resurrection remain the focus in any understanding of salvation.

Most Christians know that to be "saved" (Salvation I) does not effect total well-being in all aspects of life, but that salvation in the eschaton is to be so described. Only the latter will reveal the full content of salvation, but the biblical view insists that the continuities between the now and the not yet experiences of salvation are more than spiritual. The objectives of God's work of salvation in the present have not been truncated or trimmed back; they are as "full-bodied" as they will be in the eschaton. The biblical view is not a "salvation *out of* this world but always salvation *of* this world. Salvation in Christ is salvation in the context of human society *en route to* a whole and healed world. The Church's concern for salvation thus has a universal dimension and, with that, a physical and political dimension."[8]

2. Individual and Communal

One may reduce salvation to an individual experience, a personal relationship with God. Without discounting this, the texts insist on a communal experience (e.g., the exodus and the return from exile [cf. Isa 63:8–9]) as well as an [366] individual one (1 Sam 2:1, Hannah; Isa 38:20, Hezekiah; Jer 17:14); the two dimensions are linked in Ps 22:1–5.[9] In the New Testament, salvation does have an individual focus, but also has a communal reference (Matt 8:25; Luke 1:71; Eph 1:14; 2:14–22; images such as kingdom, family, and body).

---

ology," in *Creation in the Old Testament* (ed. B. W. Anderson; Philadelphia: Fortress, 1984), 102–17.

8. D. Bosch, "Salvation: A Missiological Perspective," *ExAud* 5 (1989): 151.

9. Cf. Westermann, *Elements*, 66–68.

In view of this witness, more attention should be given to the communal aspect of God's saving work in the post-biblical world, such as the healing of a dysfunctional family, a divided congregation, a war-torn community, or the ecological structures of reality, but without losing the individual dimension. Indeed, the experience of being (not just becoming) a part of the ongoing life of the community of faith catches individuals up into communal dimensions of God's saving work that enhance personal healing.

3. Religious and Social/Economic/Political

Salvation may be linked solely with the religious sphere. For the Old Testament, however, salvation also catches up the socio-economic-political dimensions of life (e.g, exodus [Exod 15:2], deliverance from exile [Isa 43:2–3], and God's delivering Israel or individuals from enemies [Ps 44:6–7; 59:1–2]). More specifically, the broad concern for the poor and needy is basically an issue of salvation (Ps 72:12–14; 70:4–5; 76:9; 86:1–2). The Israelites are to care for such persons, for they themselves were strangers in the land of Egypt and God delivered them (Exod 23:9; Deut 10:17–22). In effect, this emphasis includes the alienated within the sphere of salvation God wrought on behalf of Israel.

Jesus' ministry is understood in comparable terms in Luke–Acts. The content of God as Savior (Luke 1:47) is spelled out in the reversal of fortunes in Mary's Magnificat (1:48–55), based on Hannah's song (1 Sam 2:1–10) and the tradition of God as "Savior" of the oppressed (Ps 17:7; 2 Kgs 13:5; Neh 9:27; cf. Acts 13:23). In immediately calling Jesus Savior (2:11; cf. 1:69–77), Luke claims this understanding of salvation for Jesus' *ministry* (4:18–21; 7:21–22; cf. 19:10; Matt 11:5). Luke "makes no distinction between what we might describe as physical, spiritual or social aspects of salvation. . . . God is concerned with all aspects of human life and relationships, and, so, salvation may involve the putting right of any aspect of life that is not as it should be." [10]

Also to be noted are instances of deliverance in times of personal danger (e.g., Mark 3:4; 15:30–31; Acts 27:20–34). One might consider these nontheological references, but the reality is more complex, as seen in texts such as Matt 8:25 (cf. 14:30): "Lord, save us! We are perishing!" This saving work of Jesus, wherein life is preserved and the disciples are brought into a safe place, entails a theological content. Paul speaks of his "deliverance" (*sōtēria*) from prison, with the "help of the Spirit of Jesus Christ" (Phil 1:19; cf. Acts 16:16–40; 2 Cor 1:10).

This broader understanding of salvation is common in various forms of [367] liberation theology, which link God's saving activity on behalf of the oppressed in the Bible to similar modern situations. The danger of

---

10. Powell, "Salvation," 7–8; see his chart on pp. 6–7. Cf. D. Tiede, *Luke* (Minneapolis: Augsburg, 1988), 55.

collapsing salvation into a political theology (see below) or neglecting its spiritual dimensions exists, but this ought not detract from the biblically-based point that God's saving activity also has to do with deliverance from oppressive social, economic, and political realities, and that the church somehow needs to relate its life more directly to this divine work.

4. Spiritual and Psychical/Bodily

God's saving work may be reduced to a subjective experience ("salvation of the soul") or equated with forgiveness or focused only on guilt as that from which one needs to be saved. It is true: where there is forgiveness, there is also life and salvation. But forgiveness, for all of its power, does not comprehend all that is entailed in either God's actions of saving or in the human experience of salvation.

Emotional healing is an aspect of divine salvation in the Old Testament. God saves those who are "broken-hearted and crushed in spirit" (Ps 34:18; cf. Exod 6:9), those who "suffer distress and anguish" (Ps 116:3–4) or "shame and dishonor" (69:1–3, 19–20) in the face of rejection or the threat of death. A New Testament counterpart may be the language of salvation associated with the casting out of demons (Mark 1:34; Luke 8:36).

Physical healing, too, is an experience of salvation (Ps 69:29; Isa 38:20–21—note that Hezekiah's healing combines prayer and medicine). Salvation language is used for Jesus' healing the sick and disabled (Mark 5:23; 6:56; Luke 6:9; 17:19; 18:42; John 11:12), raising the dead (Luke 8:50), and a more comprehensive making whole (Luke 9:24; 19:10). Jesus is *born* a Savior (Luke 2:11) and "brings salvation to people throughout his earthly life."[11] Such language is also used for the healing ministry of the disciples and Paul in Acts (4:9; 14:9–10; Jas 5:15). This reaffirms and intensifies Israel's view of salvation, standing in fulfillment of texts such as Isa 35:3–6. Generally, God's becoming physical in Jesus catches the bodily life up into God's saving deeds. In eschatological perspective, salvation includes the resurrection of the body, a psychosomatic experience. Basically, the objective of God's saving work is to enable human beings to be what they were created to be.

Issues of holistic health have recently been given more attention in the church. Carl Braaten gives some specifics in an issue of *dialog* devoted to the body:[12] "My wish is that pastors would include in their teaching the message of the whole person and the whole earth . . . that congregations would develop programs that give people practical concrete life-style alternatives that promote total health, living life to the hilt, optimum well-being." Ted

---

11. So Powell, "Salvation," 8. It will not do to consider this a "secular" usage; *sōzein is* too evocative of a theological frame of reference. Indeed, it is possible that Jesus' *ministry* leads to the confession of him as Savior (note that Luke–Acts does not specifically link "salvation" to Jesus' death).

12. Carl E. Braaten, "The Temple of the Holy Spirit," *Dialog* 27 (1988): 173.

Peters also draws out some practical implications, e.g., that ministry in congregations include a concern for [368] "preventive and wholistic health care."[13] Such suggestions reflect this broader biblical view of God's saving work in the world. It would be possible, of course, to diminish the spiritual dimension in recovering this broader view of salvation, or to become overly optimistic regarding the effects of such forms of ministry.

5. From Sin and from the Effects of Sin

Salvation language may focus on being saved from sin; but, in both Testaments it is rare so to speak (cf. Ps 39:8 [*nāṣal*]; 130:8 [*pādāh*]; Ezek 36:29 [*yāšaʿ*]; Matt 1:21; 2 Cor 7:10). Even in these texts, the primary focus may be salvation from sin's effects (cf. Ps 38:17–22; 78:8–9; Isa 59:9–15). That is, sin brings people into one kind of trouble or another, from which they need deliverance.

One possible approach is to distinguish (though not separate) forgiveness and salvation, as in exilic texts. God unilaterally and unconditionally extends forgiveness to the exiles (40:1–2; cf. 43:25); this is a saving act, but the exiles are not thereby delivered from exile, from all the judgmental effects of their sins. Further divine saving work is needed, namely, to bring them home and establish them in the land, before one can speak of salvation in any full sense (Isa 43:2–3; 46:12–13; 52:7–10).

6. From One's Own Sin and from the Sins of Others

Salvation may be associated only with one's own sin, but salvation in the Bible also refers to deliverance from the (effects of the) sins of others. This is most evident in Israel's liberation from the Egyptians, from the devastating effects of bondage upon life in every respect. For God to have sent Moses only to mediate the forgiveness of Israel's sin would have left Israel in bondage in Egypt.

In a modern case, God's work of salvation in a situation of familial abuse would entail not only forgiveness for the victimizer but healing for the victim. Salvation includes being delivered from the reverberating effects of the sins of others, those whom we know and those whom we do not know. Implications for interpreting the work of Jesus would include confessions such as this: "Jesus Christ died for human hurt as well as human sin."[14]

7. Human and Nonhuman

Salvation may be conceived exclusively in human terms; both Testaments, however, insist on a creation-wide understanding. The eschatolog-

---

13. Peters, "Wholeness," 309.

14. P. Miller, *Interpreting the Psalms* (Minneapolis: Fortress, 1986), 110. "The Gospels make clear that human pain as well as human sin is in view in the redemptive work of God in Christ." For a liturgical use of the laments with this in mind, see Wendell Frerichs, *Take It to the Lord* (Minneapolis: Augsburg, 1982).

ical view is clear: a new heaven and a new earth (where animals and human beings constitute a reconciled community, Isa 11:6–9). The nonhuman, devastated in the experience of God's judgment (Isa 24:1–13; Jer 9:10), will participate in the same salvific event that brings the exiles back home (Isa 35:1–10). That story begins already with Noah, where both humans and animals are saved (see Heb 11:7). Along the way there are startling texts about God's saving the animals (cf. Ps 36:6). The New Testament [369] picks up on this theme in various ways, from Jesus' nature miracles (cf. Matt 8:23–27; 14:28–33; Mark 4:35–41) to Paul's word about the linkage between the redemption of human beings and the entire cosmos (Rom 8:19–24; cf. Col 1:15–20; Eph 1:7–10, 20–23).

In this light, the slogan "save the planet" captures a dimension of the biblical view of salvation. In its reflection about such matters, the church ought not shrink from using salvation language. Certainly most would confess that God is at work on the saving/healing of the cosmic structures of reality, not least through environmentalists both within and without the church (see below). Should moments of such healing take place, we would certainly pray our prayers of gratitude for God's saving work.

8. Event and Process

Many may speak of a moment when one is saved (baptism; adult conversion), which would issue in a state/condition called salvation ("I am saved"). If salvation language is used for specific ways in which God acts in the ongoing life of such a "saved" one, it would focus in forgiveness.

In the Old Testament, to be in a right relationship with God does not mean that one ceases to be in need of God's saving activity (Salvation II). What is stressed is not the state of salvation, but "the *process* of saving," the ongoing saving acts of God, which are "to be expected, to be prayed for, and to be experienced."[15] The "God of our salvation" "*daily* bears us up" (Ps 68:19). The psalmists pray for God to save them from one kind of trouble or another, and the sooner the better. In other words, persons who *are* saved (Salvation I) pray God *to be* saved, and the latter is not to be collapsed into an eschatological not yet. Those who are saved at the Red Sea, as decisive and constitutive as that saving event is, both need and experience further saving acts of God on their journey through the wilderness (Exod 18:8; Num 10:9).

The New Testament also uses salvation language to speak of ongoing saving experiences, from healing to deliverance from danger (see above). Other texts suggest that salvation is more processive, linked with the confession of faith (Rom 10:10) and "grown into" (1 Pet 2:2; cf. Eph 4:15–16) and "worked out" in the ongoingness of life (Phil 2:12–13, explained in 3:12–16?; cf. 1 Cor 1:18; 15:2; 2 Cor 2:15; Acts 2:40, 47), for "God is at work

---

15. Westermann, *What Does the Old Testament Say About God?* 29, 27 (see *Elements*, 45).

in you." Salvation is a present reality, but it is also that which God continues to work in the believer (see 1 Tim 4:16; 2 Tim 3:14–15; the enigmatic 1 Tim 2:15 may also be so understood).

Being "saved" does not effect a state of total well-being, which is the full meaning of salvation. Those ongoing acts of God in life that move toward that "full-bodied" objective are also salvifically described, and ought not be emptied of salvation content.

9. Insider and Outsider

Salvation may be understood as that which divides humanity into the saved [370] and the unsaved. One might agree with this in certain respects (in terms of Salvation I). In terms of Salvation II, however, those who are not a part of the community of faith are also the recipients of God's saving activity (Amos 9:7; Isa 19:19–25; 2 Kings 5). Yet, though they experience God's saving activity, they often do not link God with what has happened. Westermann puts it this way: "no boundaries exist for God's saving action; they occur among the people of God, in the life of the individual, in humanity."[16] This point is important not least because it suggests that God's activity in Salvation II may open up its recipients to God's more wide-ranging saving work.

Faith is commonly, but not always, a way of appropriating God's saving work. Those who call out for God's saving activity are the upright (Ps 7:10; 36:10; 37:39); salvation will come to those who wait in trust for the Lord (Isa 30:15–16). For Paul salvation comes to those who have faith (Rom 10:9–10; cf. Eph 2:8). But for 1 Tim 4:10, God is the Savior "especially" of those who believe! For Luke, Jesus' activity of saving/healing is not always associated with faith (cf. 6:9–10 with 8:48–50). Generally for Luke, Jesus appears as the savior of the outsider: tax collectors, the sick and demon-possessed, the poor, Samaritans, women, and "sinners." The "lost" that Jesus comes to seek out and save (19:10; 3:8; 5:31–32; 7:34) stand outside traditional religious boundaries. These texts link up with the reversal of fortunes in Mary's song (1:46–55).

For the Old Testament, God's invitation of salvation goes out to all (Isa 45:22–23) and will even be exercised on behalf of Israel's enemies (Isa 19:20–25); Israel is to proclaim God's salvation to "all the earth" (Ps 96:1–3), for only God is the hope of the world (Ps 65:5). God intends that Salvation I and II be the experience of all. Such texts ground the broad-based New Testament understanding of the gentile mission (Luke 24:47; Acts 13:47; Rom 15:9–12).

10. God and God's Instruments

God is Savior in both Testaments. God's saving work is grounded in steadfast love (Ps 17:7; 6:4; 31:16; 85:7; 109:26) and faithfulness (Ps 40:10;

---

16. Westermann, *Elements*, 40.

57:3). Israel cannot save itself, by whatever powers it may have at its disposal (Ps 33:16–17; 44:6–7), nor can other gods (Isa 45:20–21). At the same time, God often saves by working through chosen instruments. Moses mediates not only the announcement of saving, but the exodus itself; judges and kings serve as "saviors" (Judg 2:9; Neh 9:27); prophets mediate a saving word. Israel is called to be a light to the nations so that God's salvation, in the broadest sense, may reach to the end of the earth (Isa 42:1–9; 49:6). Cyrus is also such an instrument, though he does not know God (Isa 45:1–8). At the Red Sea, the nonhuman is the savior of the human (Exodus 15; cf. medicines, e.g., the use of figs in 2 Kgs 20:7). In the New Testament, Jesus mediates God's salvation in all aspects of his life and ministry (see the Acts passages mentioned above for other mediators).

That God draws these mediators from within and without the community of faith, and that they are both human and nonhuman, shows that God does not work [371] salvation exclusively through the faithful, though Salvation I is focused there. Regarding Salvation II, modern mediators include the church, as well as social service agencies and hospitals, nurses and counselors, ecologists and medicines developed from yew trees. Modern Cyruses and east winds also can be caught up by God in a ministry of salvation beyond their knowing.

III. Some Concluding Thoughts

Confining God's saving work to Salvation I, centered on the vertical relationship with God, has been a common churchly approach. This attenuated definition of salvation has "inevitably led [the church] to a preoccupation with narrowly defined ecclesiastical activities, which . . . severely complicated the believers' involvement in society since such involvement had nothing to do with salvation except to draw people toward the Church where they might get access to salvation proper." [17]

This narrowing has commonly meant that the range of God's work in Salvation II has been given a second-class status in the life of the church; it is not really "mission" or "outreach" or the proper work of the church. Hence it is often justified among the church's activities in contorted ways (e.g., "auxiliary enterprises"). This contributes to a view that faith is a private matter divorced from the public world. It obscures the nature of the ministry of laity, giving the impression that their vocation is small potatoes compared to that of the clergy; that their activities are only tangentially related to what the church is really about; that their non-verbal or non-explicit christological witness is something about which they ought to feel guilty; that their activity is of value only for this side of eternity, as if the only continuity between God's saving work between now and then is spiritual in nature (as if the need for salvation is less pressing now!).

---

17. Bosch, "Salvation," 143.

Letting Salvation II fill the scene entirely has proved to be attractive as well, and equally problematic. Here salvation may be reduced to a form of social gospel or political theology or holistic health, wherein the improvement of our earthly lot, however laudable a goal, becomes focused on human efforts and programs as means to make this world right again. God is often more facilitator than decisive agent; Jesus is often more teacher or ideal embodiment of the cause than the one in and through whom God has most decisively acted to make the world right. Often, the spiritual dimension of salvation is slighted, commonly with a downplaying of sin and its effects. The often visceral theological reaction to this view, however, has often meant a careening back into the more comfortable churchly view that collapses salvation into the vertical relationship of the individual with God.[18]

Neither Salvation I nor Salvation II comprehends all that the biblical view entails; the church and the world need both. To answer the question, "What are you saved from?" entails a response as comprehensive as the world's needs: guilt [372] and shame; social chaos, war, and other types of violence; abuse in its many forms; mental and physical illness; famine; the rape of the environment. Put positively: it includes forgiveness, mental and physical health, peace, safety in every life setting, harmonious family relationships, community stability and well-being, and a healthy natural order. God is about this full range of saving work in manifold ways in the life of the world through numerous mediators.

How might Salvation I (for which the language of soteriology should be reserved?) and Salvation II be related to one another? Indeed, it may be asked whether this distinction is adequate for the complex reality the Bible shows salvation to be. The distinction might tempt one to think of two separate tracks or a dialectical view. These different dimensions of God's saving work are more interwoven, more circular (in matters like scope and spatial or temporal realities). The direction of the flow is not only from the narrow to the broad, from the vertical relationship out into the horizontal. A more *symbiotic* way of articulating this relationship is needed, not least that God's saving work in the larger creation (not finally separated from the cosmic import of God's work in Christ) has both ontological and epistemological effects. These God-created ways of being and knowing, however provisional and ephemeral, reverberate into the larger world and flow back into the community of faith, shaping its particular word about God's saving work in Jesus and its life in the world. As a consequence, the church may more directly link up with the world's experience of God's broader saving work. God is about saving the world in the widest possible sense, and God is at work on that divine objective for the sake of both present and future worlds in more ways than we can imagine.

The Authority of the Bible and Churchly Debates Regarding Sexuality

Recent churchly discussions regarding homosexuality raise significant questions about biblical authority.[1] My reflections assume that the Bible is the word of God. In saying that, I refer to two roles played by the Bible. Most basically, the Bible has a formational or constitutive role in and through the work of the Spirit. That is, the Bible has a unique capacity to mediate God's word of law and gospel, which can *effect* life and salvation for individuals and communities. Second, the Bible is the fundamental source for shaping and maintaining Christian self-identity. We turn to these books to discern what the Christian faith essentially is and what should be the basic shape for Christian life in the world. This claim grounds these reflections.

As a member of the ELCA Task Force on Sexuality (2002–2005) I interacted with many individuals and congregations regarding issues of biblical authority. [366] I was surprised at how common it was—indeed almost universal—that those who held widely diverse perspectives on the interpretation of biblical texts regarding sexuality were in basic agreement regarding the authority of the Bible.[2] From another angle, a shared high view of the authority of the Bible did not issue in commonality regarding the way in which biblical texts regarding sexuality were (to be) interpreted.[3]

I should not have been surprised. Such a "disparity" has existed through every century of the church's life. Persons with a high view of the Bible's authority have often disagreed over the interpretation of specific biblical texts (from Genesis 1 to Revelation 22) and specific biblical issues (from

---

This essay was originally published in *Word and World* 26 (2006): 365–74.

1. For an analysis of the characteristics of the current context that have problematized issues relating to the authority of the Bible, see Terence E. Fretheim and Karlfried Froehlich, *The Bible as Word of God in a Postmodern Age* (Minneapolis: Fortress, 1998), 81–87. I would emphasize even more strongly today that the Bible's own content creates problems for contemporary readers (e.g., its violence).

2. The initial rhetoric in a conversation did not always bend this way, but upon closer examination this proved to be the case again and again.

3. This experience confirmed several statements by Darrell Jodock (*The Church's Bible: Its Contemporary Authority* [Minneapolis: Fortress, 1989]): "Voices claiming the Bible as their authority advocate widely differing views" on a considerable range of ethical and theological matters (p. ix). And so, for Jodock, "Scriptural authority is not foundational. . . . Disagreements about the Bible are as much the symptoms as they are the causes of disunity" (p. 5).

infant baptism to free will). Indeed, we know instinctively that the ascription of a high level of authority to the Bible does not guarantee the accuracy or truthfulness of our interpretations (witness the Jehovah's Witnesses!), though sometimes we speak as if it does. Again and again, readers with such a view of biblical authority differ widely among themselves on many issues. Indeed, a traditional viewpoint regarding the Bible's authority often issues in various interpretations of the texts relating to sexuality.

Why is this the case? Before responding to this question, I seek to complicate the matter from another perspective.

People with a *low view* of the Bible's authority can have a highly *traditional* view regarding same-sex relationships. Some powerful voices against change regarding this matter see no special value in biblical perspectives, except perhaps as part of a strategy in helping to swell the ranks of those who are comparably committed. Experience with such individuals has sharpened my conviction that issues relating to the authority of the Bible are largely irrelevant in this conversation. Though the heightened rhetoric may suggest otherwise, the importance of biblical authority on this issue does not run deep.

Why is this the case? It appears that there is no single or simple answer to this question, but further reflections are needed before responding.

Some readers claim that interpretations of texts vary as much as they do because of differences in the way the Bible is approached or used.[4] This may be the case in individual instances, but the differences among us regarding the interpretation [367] of sexuality texts cannot be reduced to such a formula. Again and again, those who use the same methods of studying biblical texts (e.g., the latest in historical or literary criticism; a "Lutheran hermeneutic") often come to different conclusions regarding the meaning of texts. This is a truism and characterizes much of the ongoing debate over specific interpretations of this or that element in the biblical texts, not simply the sexuality texts.

Moreover, individuals who have a (highly) traditional perspective on issues of sexuality may have a "contextual" approach to studying the Scriptures, taking into full account the historical evidence available, both within and without the Bible.[5] One thinks of Richard Hays and Robert Gagnon on the more traditional side of this issue and Robin Scroggs and Martti Nissinen on the other side.[6] All of these scholars are quite at home with the

4. See, e.g., Craig L. Nessan, *Many Members, Yet One Body: Committed Same-Gender Relationships and the Mission of the Church* (Minneapolis: Augsburg Fortress, 2004), 23–37.

5. Nessan's claim (ibid.) that "traditional" and "contextual" hermeneutics are "irreconcilable" does not prove to be the case in practice.

6. Richard B. Hays, *The Moral Vision of the New Testament: Community, Cross, New Creation: A Contemporary Introduction to New Testament Ethics* (San Francisco: HarperSanFrancisco, 1996); Robert A. J. Gagnon, *The Bible and Homosexual Practice: Texts and Hermeneutics* (Nashville: Abingdon, 2001); Robin Scroggs, *The New Testament and Homo-*

historical-critical approach to the Scriptures, freely acknowledge this to be the case, and often come out at a different place regarding interpretations of these texts.[7] In other words, individuals who use essentially the same hermeneutic can sharply disagree with respect to the interpretation of the relevant texts regarding sexuality.

Why is this the case? Most basically, the formal use of a specific hermeneutic will be shaped significantly by more "informal" matters, which will make the interpretation of sexuality texts more complex than commonly suggested. I explore two such matters: the "nature" of the interpreter and the nature of the biblical material.

The "Nature" of the Interpreter

Interpreters of the Bible are not blank slates when they read the Bible. As interpreters we are deeply affected by what we have been taught and, more basically, the broad range of our life experiences. Something of "who we are" as interpreters will inevitably be a part of any meaning we claim to see in a text. This point reveals the most basic issue that undergirds churchly differences with respect to the interpretation of sexuality texts. These differences have to do not with biblical authority, but with the often *deep personal convictions*—formed over time—that people have with respect to sexuality and, more specifically, homosexuality.

These personal convictions commonly have their roots in matters such as these: personal experiences with homosexuals, communal and familial influence, assessments of social/psychological and scientific studies (e.g., nature/nurture debates [368]; the "gay gene"),[8] evaluation of the importance of the tradition,[9] convictions regarding matters of "natural law" (e.g., gender complementarity), and one's own personal sexual orientation, practice, and experience.[10] In other words, powerful personal factors are in play—often beyond our knowing—in the varying assessments we make of

---

sexuality: Contractual Background for Contemporary Debate (Minneapolis: Fortress, 1983); Martti Nissinen, *Homoeroticism in the Biblical World: A Historical Perspective* (Minneapolis: Fortress, 1998). For a convenient review of the work of these four scholars on this subject, see Nessan, *Many Members*, 23–37.

7. Though not always. For example, Richard Hays thinks that Genesis 19 is "irrelevant" (*Moral Vision,* 381) to this discussion, while Robert Gagnon considers it of considerable importance (*Bible and Homosexual Practice*, 71–91).

8. Most would agree that such studies were unknown to the biblical authors. If they had had full access to such information, however, we do not know whether they still would have written what they did.

9. The church has long held convictions regarding this matter and, quite apart from personal preferences, some (many?) cannot set that traditional perspective aside—unless the evidence becomes much more decisive than it is at present.

10. On the last-named, the language of Nessan, *Many Members,* seems right: "To speak of human sexuality is to discuss an aspect of human existence that is deeply rooted in what we hold very personal and precious. My beliefs and my emotions are greatly invested

the textual and contextual evidence. The greater the number and intensity of these factors at work in a particular interpreter, the greater will be the impact on the interpretive results. This will be the case regardless of where we stand on the spectrum regarding the issues involved. Such factors are decisive in *undergirding* our current understandings of texts regarding sexuality or in *challenging* interpretations of biblical texts that question our present perspective.

And so it may be said with some confidence that the differences among us regarding the interpretation of texts relating to sexuality are not basically due to a perspective on the authority of the Bible, but to personal convictions about the matter that may be more or less deeply set within ourselves as interpreters.

Bible readers through the centuries have always brought their experience and personal convictions to their reading of the Bible. But the interpretive situation in the present time is quite different in many respects. We now have a much more diverse group of Bible readers than ever before in Christian history—and more numerous (including, e.g., female and third-world biblical scholars). This new reality has complicated these interpretive issues immensely. A much more complex and wide-ranging set of experiences and convictions now characterizes the interpreters of these texts and influences their study of them.

This reality is not simply to be related to texts regarding sexuality, but to numerous texts on various topics. The range of "problem issues" is considerable, including scientific, historical, social, and theological matters. You know them well. Take matters scientific. How is the Bible's talk about creation to be related to more recent scientific research and discovery? How is one to interpret those ancient manuscripts, unearthed in Near Eastern deserts, with numerous biblical parallels? Or, what of matters of human equality and social order across lines of race, gender, and social class? How are we to understand the Bible's apparent acceptance of, say, patriarchy and slavery, and strong rejection of, say, usury and same-sex intimacy? Or, what do we do with the Bible's pervasive violence, wherein both God and God's people are often the subjects of violent verbs (e.g., 1 Sam 15:2–3; Jer 13:14; 19:6–9)? As with issues of sexuality, our experiences and convictions will deeply affect how we read and assess these texts. [369]

All of us are challenged to become as self-aware as possible regarding how these experiences and convictions affect our interpretation of texts. Whether or not we are fully aware of "who we are," we should stand ready to acknowledge that our feelings, thoughts, actions, and associated experiences with regard to any number of issues—including sexuality—are present in *everything* we say about a text.

---

in a certain way of ordering sexual morality. When my own deep convictions confront your own deep convictions, this is a recipe for a clash of views" (p. 23).

Another way of putting the matter is to say that no interpretation of the Bible is value-free. How we interpret texts and the authority we give to the resultant interpretation will reflect (perhaps even promote!) the personal and social values we hold dear. At the same time, because our knowledge and experience are constantly on the move, not least because of the impact of the Bible on our lives, we will read texts with ever new eyes—which may reinforce, challenge, or dismantle our current understandings. Moreover, the culture (family, congregation, community, nation, and world)—always on the move—will continue to affect not only our understandings of biblical texts, but the kinds of questions that we ask of the text in pursuit of those understandings.

The proliferation of (English) Bible translations—and translations are always interpretations—reflects something of this diversity, in the last half century especially. This factor helps to demonstrate the openness of the text itself to different interpretations. And to that reality we turn below.

Authority, Bible, and Interpretation. But first, it should be noted that another reality is commonly at work in the interpretive process we have been describing. Differing personal experiences lead to differences in interpretation of texts and, in turn, lead—recognized or not—to the authority we give to specific interpretations of biblical texts. Over the course of the interpretive process, some *interpretations* of specific biblical texts often take on an authority that approximates the authority of the Bible itself. Not uncommonly, if those interpretations are challenged, then the very authority of the Bible is thought to be called into question. This ascription of authority to *specific interpretations* of texts often goes unrecognized and has, in and of itself, become a major problem in discussions of the sexuality (and other) texts.

At the same time, most readers would say—at least theoretically—that a text's interpretation should not be elevated to a status comparable to the biblical text itself. Given the fact that all interpreters are both finite and sinful, most readers recognize the potential inadequacy of our interpretations and the need to check them over against the interpretations of other individuals and communities. At the same time, interpreters *will* want to make some basic claims about what the Bible says, especially in view of the scriptural center of which the tradition speaks (e.g., [370] christology); but even those claims are not to be given an authority equal to that of the biblical text itself.

Hence, we must make a clean distinction between the text and our own interpretation of the text, for whatever we say *about* a Bible passage is never the same as what the Bible itself says. This includes every Bible translation. Strictly speaking, the only statement that should follow the phrase, "The Bible says," is an actual quotation from the Bible in its original language (and even then our intonation will betray our interpretation!). It is to that biblical text that Bible readers are *finally* held accountable, not to some existing interpretation or tradition, however important these may be as, say, a place to begin and to ground the interpretive process.

To be honest to the interpretive process, we should read the Bible from within an explicit recognition of our own history and social location. These factors are the most basic reason why we remain accountable, first and foremost, to the text itself and not to the tradition of the interpretation of the text. This reality is also one of the most basic reasons why it is important to discuss our interpretations with other persons, including those who come from different traditions and have had different experiences. With regard to every text there will always be more for us to learn, and our openness to the insights of others is a part of what it means to be a faithful Bible reader.

The Nature of the Biblical Material

The Bible itself often makes interpretation difficult and contributes to the problem of its own authority. It has been said that the Bible is its own worst enemy. In addition to matters of content, such as those noted above, is *the way in which the Bible expresses itself.* There are numerous textual uncertainties in the Bible. Such a reality means that the reader will participate more than usual in the making of the meaning of the text. Put more positively, there are points of openness in the text that invite interpreters to use their imagination. Some examples among many that could be cited:

- Grammatical ambiguities, polysemic words, and other uncertainties of translation. For example, there are three perfectly legitimate translations (and at least four interpretations!) of Gen 1:1–3. Which will you choose and why? Could more than one reading be a "right" (authoritative) reading? Your choice will affect how you read the rest of the chapter and beyond.
- Matters of genre and historicity. Is the book of Jonah parable, history, or something else? Is only one decision appropriate? Your decision will deeply affect how you read an entire book.
- Metaphor. Bible readers are invited to unpack metaphors, with the understanding that every metaphor has a "yes" and a "no" (or a "like" and an "unlike"). How will you unpack, say, the various metaphors for God in any given context (e.g., father in Isa 63:16–17 or warrior/mother in Isa 42:13–14)? Will [371] only one interpretation be the right one? Or, is there an openness in the metaphor that allows for several right readings?
- Point of view. The Bible does not always commend the viewpoints it reports. For example, the book of Job gives a negative evaluation of the extensive speeches of Job's friends. Might the author give a comparably negative evaluation of Job's confident words in 1:21 ("the Lord gave, and the Lord has taken away; blessed be the name of the Lord") and the less confident 2:10? Is only one response the authoritative one?
- Silences and gaps. Biblical narratives often do not tell us everything we would like to know. For example, in the story of Cain and Abel (Gen

4:1–17), we are not told why God chose Abel's offering rather than Cain's, where Cain got his wife, for whom he built a city, or why Cain was afraid that someone would kill him. Such gaps in the text invite the use of our imagination in the task of interpretation and occasion much disagreement among scholarly readings. Among the sexuality texts, Lev 18:22 ("You shall not lie with a male as with a woman; it is an abomination") contains several such gaps. Why is only male-male sexual activity referred to? What motivation(s) led to the formulation of this law (for example: threat of disease; creation theology; procreation; idolatrous worship; sexual violence; gender complementarity)? Is this text a command related to sexual activity on the part of *homosexuals* or, inasmuch as the sexual activities in the context of Lev 18:22 always relate to forbidden heterosexual actions, might this text be concerned about *heterosexuals* "behaving badly"?[11]

These and other questions regarding the text have led to detailed scholarly investigations and, often, speculation. Indeed, gaps (openness) in the text invite the use of our imagination in the task of interpretation. The common "gaps" in the text will foster more new insights, give more room for the play of the imagination, encourage deeper conversation, and provide more avenues in and through which the word of God can address people in our ever more diverse communities. This is one basic reason why reading the Bible is always a creative activity.

The net effect of this reality has been that Bible readers commonly emerge from their studies of texts with more than one possible reading. With respect to such efforts regarding almost any text or topic, there will be a common lack of [372] unanimity among interpreters. In this situation, is only one reading the right reading? May more than one reading be appropriate? Readings of texts will always be open-ended to some extent; textual meaning is not as stable as we might think. Think of sermons you've heard on a given text over the years (e.g., the parable of the prodigal son)! Has the interpretation you've developed or discerned always been the same? Is one interpretation more right (authoritative?) than all the other possibilities? The meanings of texts have evolved in some ways in view of the ever-changing experience of both preacher and congregation, new knowledge of the text, and prayerful relationship with the God whose Spirit works in and through our readings.

But these difficulties in the biblical text itself again raise the question of whether the issue of biblical authority is relevant to the interpretation of the details of such texts. The interpreter's view of biblical authority is basically not going to determine how these gaps are bridged. People with

---

11. For this angle of interpretation, see Samuel E. Balentine, *Leviticus* (Louisville: John Knox, 2002), 158–59. Of course, one still has to deal with other texts on the topic, e.g., Rom 1:26–27. But if Richard Hays (*Moral Vision*, 281) is right that Genesis 19 is "irrelevant," then the issue could be said to be primarily a New Testament issue.

widely variant senses of biblical authority may agree (again and again!) on a given interpretation, while those who are like-minded regarding authority may sharply disagree! Personal experience, knowledge, and convictions will once again often come into play.

From another angle, how can we speak of biblical authority when the text itself, again and again, allows for differing interpretations of textual detail? Is only one interpretation of each biblical text authoritative? Is one interpretation more authoritative than another? Or, are all possible interpretations authoritative? What criteria are to be used to decide?

Biblical Reading as Dynamic Process

Reading the Bible should be understood as a dialogical or conversational process in which the Spirit is at work (along with other factors), potentially opening up new possibilities of meaning beyond those with which we are familiar. There is, however, no sure move from the "objective" exegesis of the text to its meaning; contemporary issues are in the room at every stage of the process. The effects of our experience upon our study of the Bible mean that readers do not have direct, unmediated access to meanings the author may have intended or to "naked" meanings of the text itself. Recognizing that we can make no clean distinction between "what the text meant" and "what the text means," the most that we can expect is a *relative* objectivity in reading texts. Yet, for all the uncertainties thereby introduced, that relative openness is a good thing, finally, for *the Holy Spirit works in and through the person you are and the skills you have in* unpacking the text.

The meaning we see in a text is always a product of the *interaction and integration* of the text itself, who we are as individual readers and readers in community, and the Holy Spirit working in and through our hearing and study of the texts. Yet, are there no constraints on meaning possibilities?[12] At least three factors come into play. [372]

1. The text itself is a relatively stable element in the task of interpretation; it influences readings in certain directions and not others. Texts do shape readers; readers do not create meanings out of whole cloth. As such, the text stands reasonably independent of interpretations. At the same time, as we have seen, textual and translation difficulties can present significantly different interpretive options. So, even the texts themselves can be a source of instability in interpretation; the proliferation of differences in Bible translations is witness to this reality. Yet, while texts may mean many things, they cannot mean just anything. Because the texts are what they are, we can eliminate certain interpretations with a reasonable level of probability and we can accept others with a similar probability.

---

12. For detail, see Fretheim and Froehlich, *The Bible as Word of God*, 90–93.

2. Something of the community and tradition of readers will inevitably be a part of the meaning of biblical passages. Texts are not autonomous, independent of long usage in religious communities. This influence, ranging from the reader's inherited/adopted religious traditions (e.g., Lutheran; local congregation) to historical analysis and to the ongoing hearing of the word, will affect meaning possibilities. But, these influences have led communities astray over the centuries, so they are not an absolutely sure guide to biblical interpretation.

3. Prayerful study under the guidance of the Spirit is a key element in the interpretive process. But, even then, not every prayer-filled interpretation is thereby guaranteed to be trustworthy. The language of Acts 15:28 seems appropriate for *every* interpretation of biblical texts: "For it has seemed good to the Holy Spirit *and to us*" (italics mine). On the one hand, what readers bring to the task of interpretation can be aligned with and reinforce the work of the Spirit. On the other hand, we can resist the work of the Spirit in our lives even when our reading of the Scriptures is surrounded by prayer and devotion. Prayer-filled interpretations can often go astray.

We should focus our energies to work with specific biblical passages and interact with one another regarding divergent interpretations. More abstract and technical discussions will be necessary, but the hundreds of congregational studies generated by the ELCA Task Force's *Journey Together Faithfully* showed that *nothing* is more important than getting people together and discussing specific texts and ways of interpreting them.[13] Differences will never go away, but the conversations will lead to greater understanding and open up the Bible for more and more readers. That is good.

These various developments lead me, finally, to ask several questions: Do we need a high view of the authority of the Bible to be effectively about God's purposes [374] in the world? Is the church wasting its time and energy being defensive about the Bible or engaging in debates about its authority, especially when it seems not to affect the basic meanings we see in the text? The word we are to bring to the world is not a word about the Bible and its authority. Any view of the Bible, or any use we make of the Bible, must be of such a nature that it does not detract from the hearing of the word of God. Should we not then just proceed to preach and teach from biblical texts and let whatever esteem the Bible may have grow out of that encounter? This is a "theology of the cross" approach to the Bible; that is, the Bible exemplifies its power in and through weakness. Would not such an approach to the Bible be more consistent with some of our most basic theological instincts?

---

13. *Journey Together Faithfully, Part Two: The Church and Homosexuality* (Chicago: ELCA, 2003).

What Biblical Scholars Wish Pastors Would Start or Stop Doing about Ethical Issues in the Old Testament[1]

How should the Old Testament be approached in matters moral? In addressing this question, pastors often neglect Old Testament scholarship, and understandably so. Much biblical scholarship is narrowly historical-critical and does not seek to draw out the ethical-theological dimensions of the text. Consequently, it takes much time and effort for pastors to wade through the technical details to discern the ethical implications. Old Testament scholars could make their material more "friendly" to readers interested in such questions.

Several other factors are at work in the neglect of the Old Testament by pastors as they seek to address moral issues. I list several of them, which overlap:

1. Our world raises many ethical issues that the Bible does not reference.
2. Scripture works with many perspectives that have little if any pertinence to today's world, from the treatment of women and slaves to severe punishments. [298]
3. The Old Testament especially is thought to be problematic ethically (e.g., its violence; its presentation of God) and hence is less helpful than the New Testament, though New Testament violence finally exceeds that of the Old Testament (especially, *eternal* violence—the gnashing of teeth in the fires of hell for all eternity, e.g., Matt 25:30; see Revelation 14).
4. Questions arise about the authority and consequent use of the Bible. Biblical texts are often cited as authoritative for a given ethical issue— and, all too often, that is the end of the conversation. It should be noted that a distinction between the authority of the Bible and the authority of a particular interpretation of the Bible is often not as crisp as it should be.
5. Ethical differences among Christians are often sharp. The Bible is a significant contributor to this contentiousness, so many stay away from it. It is not enough simply to appeal to the believing

This essay was originally published in *Word and World* 31 (2011): 297–306.

1. The original form of this paper was addressed to Christian ethicists at the Society of Christian Ethics session, Society of Biblical Literature, Atlanta, November 2010.

community, for differences among believing communities are immense. At the same time, such differences on the same topics are also often evident among non-Christians.

In view of these factors, I address six "wishes" for a pastor's use of the Bible as a resource in working with ethical issues. Other "wishes" could certainly be added.

1. I Wish for Greater Concern regarding the Creation-Based Character of Old Testament Law

As B. D. Napier stated long ago: "Hebrew Law, in its present total impression, has its clearest roots in [Israel's] creation-faith."[2] Law is integral to God's work in creation, and it is formulated in the creation accounts both as positive command (Gen 1:28) and as prohibition (Gen 2:16–17). That law is presented in both creation accounts suggests a long-standing linkage of law to creational reflection in Israel (though historical issues are uncertain).[3] At least canonically, law is recognized as a pre-sin reality, part of God's "good, but not perfect" creation.[4] To obey the law is to be in tune with God's creation. And so, before there is any talk about the elect people of God, before there is any reference to God's redemptive work, before there is any appeal to Sinai, sharply drawn ethical considerations are brought forward. Canonically, the law is given a *universal frame of reference.* Other pre-Sinai narratives are also revealing of creational law. For example, no explicit law regarding murder had been given, but human beings like Cain are held accountable (made explicit in Gen 9:1–7). Or, in the story of Sodom and Gomorrah, Abraham appeals to a creational moral standard that holds even God accountable (Gen 18:25).[5] [299]

The law is given in creation because God is concerned about the best possible life for all God's creatures. At least three particular motivations may be given: (a) To keep cosmic order and social order integrated in a harmonious way. For example, human sin can negatively affect the natural order so that it ceases to serve life in the way that God intended (see, e.g., Hos 4:1–3). (b) To make clear that all individuals and communities are accountable to

---

2. B. D. Napier, "Community under Law: On Hebrew Law and Its Theological Presuppositions," *Int* 7 (1953): 413. For my own work in this area, see Terence E. Fretheim, *God and World in the Old Testament: A Relational Theology of Creation* (Nashville: Abingdon, 2005), specifically the chapter on "Creation and Law," 133–56.

3. For a brief discussion of the historical origins of Israel's creation-faith, see ibid., xiv–xvi.

4. For this language, see Terence E. Fretheim, *Creation Untamed: The Bible, God, and Natural Disasters* (Grand Rapids: Baker, 2010), esp. chap. 1.

5. See idem, *God and World,* 135–44. An important, though neglected, study on this matter is James K. Bruckner, *Implied Law in the Abraham Narrative: A Literary and Theological Analysis* (Sheffield: Sheffield Academic Press, 2001).

law; human beings are not free of law just because they do not belong to the chosen people. For example, more than thirty oracles against the nations in prophetic literature hold them accountable (e.g., Amos 1–2). (c) To serve the proper development of God's good but not perfect creation (see Job 38–41). The law is given for the sake of a stable, flourishing, and life-enhancing *creational* community.

Law, then, is not a new reality at Sinai. Rather, Sinai is a fuller particularization of the law given in creation, specifying how the chosen community can take on its God-given creational responsibilities for the sake of life in view of new times and places. Israel, like the first human beings, is caught up by God in a vocation that involves the becoming of the creation. To obey Sinai law is to live in harmony with God's intentions for the creation.

It might be noted that in the common focus on love of neighbor we could become anthropocentric in our ethical concerns. What about the good of the larger creation? Or, note that the Ten Commandments exhibit no special concern for the environment; yet, the Old Testament has many such reflections, grounded in creational law (e.g., Deut 11:10–12). Sometimes, I hear in ethical reflection a remarkable emphasis on motivation centered in God's redemptive work. For example, God has acted redemptively on our behalf; that should motivate comparable action on behalf of the other. But I ask: Can such reflection lead to a "soteriological reductionism" that downplays the work of God in creation, which also provides motivation and energizes ethical reflection? To be sure, what God has done in redemption provides high levels of motivation—but, to engage in what activity?[6] The creational context for law is a crucial foundation for filling out responses to that question.

It is not my purpose in this paper to discuss the significance of law given in creation for reflections on "natural law."[7] But in such discussions, it is important to note that the law is presented in the Bible as an ongoing gift of God in creation and not as a [300] static reality. And that biblical reality needs more careful consideration. God's creation embodies a moral order that is part of the fabric of all existence and is appealed to in many contexts apart from the particular moral traditions of God's revelation to Israel.

---

6. It should be noted that creation theology is a prevailing theme in the book of Exodus in both narrative and law; see Terence E. Fretheim, *Exodus* (Louisville: John Knox, 1991), for references to many texts.

7. See Bruckner, *Implied Law*, and John Barton, *Understanding Old Testament Ethics: Approaches and Explorations* (Louisville: Westminster John Knox, 2003). For a perspective from an ethicist, see Gary Simpson's recent article, "'Written on Their Hearts': Thinking with Luther about Scripture, Natural Law, and the Moral Life," *WW* 30/4 (2010): 419–28.

2. I Wish for More Interest in the Interweaving of Law and Narrative in the Pentateuch and the Implications for Understanding Law[8]

Elucidating Israel's story/narrative has been an important development in thinking about the Old Testament as an ethical resource.[9] In addition, however, it is important to note that narrative is interwoven with law in the Pentateuch. From Exodus 12 on, the rhythm of genres is that of story-law-story-law, etc. (with varying degrees of intensity). God's law is not drawn into a code; it is integrated with the story of God's gracious activity. Law is presented as intersecting with lives filled with contingency and change, with complexity and ambiguity. Hence, Israel's law is not understood to be a static reality, intended to remain the same for all times and places. Indeed, the formulations of Israel's law take ever new experience into account while remaining constant in their objective: the best life for all. This literary reality is a profound witness to the fact that Israel understands *law as process* rather than as a fixed entity.[10] It needs to be emphasized that law and narrative are integrated in the Pentateuch. Neither law nor narrative in itself is sufficient.

3. I Wish for More Attention to the Fact That in Exodus through Deuteronomy the Entire Narrative Context for Law Is Wilderness Wandering or Journey

Wilderness wandering is an image for the basic character of Old Testament law. Law is presented as a dimension of a *journey*, a journey in relationship with God. It turns out to be a journey for both God and Israel.

On the one hand, the law provides something of a compass for wandering in the wilderness. On the other hand, the contingencies of wilderness wandering keep the law from becoming absolutized in a once-for-all content. Law, in and of itself, tends to promote a myth of certainty, suggesting that God's will for every aspect of life is the same in every time and place. Actual life, however, especially when seen from the perspective of a wilderness journey, is filled with changing circumstances, in which nothing on the ship of life seems to be tied down. Such a journey means that new laws will be needed and older laws will need to be revised or put on the back shelf. God will have new words to speak in view of life's ongoing twists and turns. And so, new laws and new formulations thereof emerge periodically as new situations develop for the journeying community (see

---

8. For greater detail, see Fretheim, *Exodus*, 201–7.

9. See, e.g., Stanley Hauerwas, *Peaceable Kingdom: A Primer in Christian Ethics* (Notre Dame, IN: University of Notre Dame Press, 1983), 24–34.

10. For a list of implications of the law/narrative mixture of genres, see Terence E. Fretheim, *The Pentateuch* (Nashville: Abingdon, 1996), 124–25.

Exod 15:25b–26; 16; 18:13–27; Numbers 15; 18–19; 27–36; Deuteronomy 12–28).[11] The community is on the move; the law will not stand still any more than this community will. The laws emerge over a time that is represented [301] as forty years, but that time is actually emblematic of many generations; the whole of Israel's life is imaged in these wilderness wandering texts. "Journey" is both literal and metaphoric. Pentateuchal law thus emerges from within the matrix of life on a journey.

The relationship between laws in Exodus and Deuteronomy regarding the same issues is also revealing of this ongoing development of Israel's law in the wilderness. Some nineteen or more statutes from Exodus 21–23 are recast in Deuteronomy.[12] For example, the laws concerning slaves in Exod 21:1–11 have been revised in Deut 15:12–18. See also the important revision of the Ten Commandments in Deuteronomy 5, compared with Exodus 20 (note, e.g., the switch of "house" and "wife" in the ninth and tenth commandments, where "wife" is no longer on a list of property—a significant shift—and "neighbor" is no longer only male). If the Ten Commandments were written today, they would need to look somewhat different; and such changes would stand in the legal tradition of the Old Testament itself and be informed by Old Testament texts to some degree (e.g., those concerned with environmental matters).

Such texts are a canonical witness to law on the move. Old law and new law remain side by side in the Pentateuch—not unlike a modern lawyer's library—as a canonical witness to the process of unfolding law. The differences are not considered a threat to the law's integrity (or biblical authority). There is no apparent interest in ironing out internal tensions in these laws. Hence, development in the law is just as canonical (or authoritative) as individual laws or the body of law as a whole. Instead of a timeless law, the text witnesses to a developing process in which experience in every sphere of life is drawn into the orbit of law (cf. tax laws today). The ongoing formulation of new or revised laws is in tune with God's intention, though that should happen only after a thorough examination of the old. How to sort out constancy and change is, of course, a big question. But the reality of it in the biblical witness is of great importance.

4. I Wish for More Relational Thinking about the God of the Old Testament and the Impact of Such Thinking on Ethical Considerations

We have begun this conversation, but we must ask more directly about the God who leads Israel in the wilderness. What kind of God is this God?

---

11. Note that Deuteronomy reflects later Israelite institutions, such as prophecy (Deut 13:1; 18:15) and kingship (Deut 17:14).

12. See Gerhard von Rad, *Deuteronomy* (Philadelphia: Westminster, 1966), 13; Dale Patrick, *Old Testament Law* (Atlanta: John Knox, 1984), 97.

What is the nature of the relationship that Israel has with this God? If there is not a uniform [302] imaging of God in the Old Testament, is there a dominant portrayal, one that might even be called "confessional"? How confident can we be in our ability to distill such a view of God from these disparate texts, when they present us with such themes as holy war and violent judgment? One's consideration of biblical-ethical issues will vary depending on the most basic imaging of God that one brings to the conversation.[13]

Much effort has been expended on developing particular themes such as the character of God, the activity of God, the will of God. Less attention has been given to a more basic question: *the kind of God* with which these texts have to do. The classical understanding of God has been commonly assumed to be basic to biblical ethical-theological thought; but might such a perspective be too narrow and insufficiently attentive to biblical understandings? Issues of divine relationality, for one thing, need to be placed more up front in this discussion. How one understands Old Testament law will be sharply affected by the understanding of the God-human relationship that is brought to the table.

I return briefly to the theme of creation. I have sought to make the case that creation is good, not perfect.[14] God decided to create the world relationally or communally, rather than do it all by Godself, with all the uncertainties and messiness that such a decision entails. God determined to catch up the creatures, both human and nonhuman, in the creation of the world. The creation texts are a witness to God's interdependent way of working with the world.

This understanding of God's work in creation is important for one's assessment of law. Though the law is predominantly represented in the text as a word from God, its ongoing link to ever-changing life means that God takes into account the actions of the human (and nonhuman) community in the formulation of ever-new law. Hence, human agency counts in the emergence and shape of ever-new law. Human beings are thereby given important responsibilities in furthering the cause of justice and good order in Israel and the larger creation. Creation is on the move, and hence law also must be on the move, if it would be in tune with God's gracious, relational will for people in ever-new times and places. God is caught up in this story with God's people, because God honors relationships and values human contributions. [303]

---

13. James Gustafson states: "Scripture *alone* is never the final court of appeal for Christian ethics. Its understanding of God and his purposes . . . [and several other matters], however, do[es] provide the basic orientation toward particular judgments"; Gustafson, "The Place of Scripture in Christian Ethics," in *The Use of Scripture in Moral Theology* (ed. C. E. Curran and R. A. McCormick; New York: Paulist Press, 1984), 176.

14. Fretheim, *Creation Untamed*, 9–37.

One implication of this interdependent relationship is that God revises God's own laws (which presumably God has a right to do!). Something like this must be said: God revises God in view of and for the sake of the changing community of God's people. Just because laws are from God does not make them unchangeable; the texts witness to a God who makes changes in the law. If these law texts had been all smoothed over and drawn into a single code, then they could be more easily defended as testimony to an unchanging law for which new times and places were irrelevant. The very textual roughness of the law material is an ongoing witness to the changing character of life and the changing character of the will of God as it relates to that life.

What if the word "relationship" were taken seriously? What might a genuine relationship with God entail?[15] As one example, God is both constant and changing. Ideally, is that not true of the nature of all interhuman relationships: constant in terms of, say, promises made, yet changing as the relationship develops over time? Of course, God will be faithful to promises made in a way that no human being can; God always wills the best; God's love will be there through thick and thin. God's core character will never change. At the same time, to remain true to these relational commitments—indeed, to remain true to God's own character—God must change in view of new times and places in and through which God's people are moving. God must change to remain true to who God is. And so God will, say, change the divine mind with respect to law in view of a variety of human responses.[16]

Some further reflections on the divine will may be helpful at this point. The law is a gracious gift of God. The law is offered—in Genesis as well as Exodus through Deuteronomy—for the sake of the life, health, and well-being of an ever-changing community and each individual therein. In the words of Deut 5:33, God gives the law "so that you may live, and that it may go well with you, and that you may live long in the land that you are to possess." To return to the image of wilderness: this image helps to lift up that which is basic for understanding the will of God for all relationships. God's law is constant in its objective: the best life for all. And that divine constancy will mean ongoing changes in the law in view of life's changes. And so God's will for God's people is not delivered in a once-and-for-all fashion; it is a dynamic reality, intersecting with life and all of its contingencies.[17]

---

15. For amplification of this thought, see idem, *God and World,* 13–22.

16. One might profitably relate this issue to the use of *niham* (change of mind) with God as the subject (almost forty times in the Old Testament, e.g., Exod 32:14; Jonah 3:9–10). See idem, "The Repentance of God: A Key to Evaluating Old Testament God-Talk," *HBT* 10 (1988): 47–70.

17. A remarkable feature of Old Testament law is the admixture of civil, moral, and cultic laws (e.g., laws regarding murder; the honoring of parents; sabbath). For Israel, life

This understanding of the will of God keeps the *personal and relational character* of the law front and center. Experience has shown how easy it is for law to become [304] an impersonal matter, manifested especially in a debilitating legalism. It can become, as it were, a "law unto itself," unrelated to any specific giver, dissociated from the dynamic will of the one who stands behind its formulations, unrelated to life's changes. In the biblical texts, however, one is confronted with the giver of the law as one who is living, personally interacting with people through every step of their journey. Both law and narrative reveal a lively relationship between God and people. Relationship language is crucial here; God is one who gives the law as part of an existing interpersonal relationship, with all that the language of relationship entails.

5. *I Wish for Greater Recognition of the Conservative Nature of Prophetic Perspectives on Social Justice*

The prophetic word about social justice is often associated with liberal causes.[18] Indeed, the prophets are sometimes depicted as if they were free-floating radicals from the '60s! This may in part explain the not uncommon negative reaction to discussions of social justice and related sociopolitical considerations. In the face of such opinions, it must be emphasized that the prophets were fundamentally conservative (and public!) in their approach to these issues. The prophets discerned that social justice was a long-established value, richly embedded in the traditions they inherited, though often neglected. Generally speaking, the prophets were deeply indebted to their ethical and theological past, one key dimension of which had to do with social justice![19] This point is made convincingly in a somewhat neglected article by James Barr:

> Certainly it is true that the prophets insisted on social justice, and they were not afraid in its name to challenge the established authorities of their time. But the prophets for the most part were not reformers, and they had no new insights into the working of society to offer. Theirs was not a novel analysis. . . . On the contrary, in this respect *the social*

---

could not be separated into such categories; the will of God had to do with every sphere of life. So, various types of law from diverse life settings have been integrated into a single fabric. What does this admixture say about the nature of law in these texts and how might that reality affect modern formulations?

18. See the fuller argument in Terence E. Fretheim, "The Prophets and Social Justice: A *Conservative* Agenda," *WW* 28/2 (2008): 159–68; idem, "Interpreting the Prophets and Issues of Social Justice," in *The Bible and the American Future* (ed. Robert L. Jewett; Eugene, OR: Cascade, 2009), 92–107.

19. The prophets seldom accuse Israel of breaking specific laws; rather, they "appeal to known norms of humane conduct, of 'justice and righteousness,' norms which are exemplified in the 'apodictic law,' but cannot be limited by it"; so Walter J. Houston, *Contending for Justice: Ideologies and Theologies of Social Justice in the Old Testament* (London: T. & T. Clark, 2006), 70–71.

perspectives and perceptions of the prophets were essentially conservative. . . .
Their message was not a new morality. . . . In other words, the traditional
liberal and reformist perception that the system is wrong and that the
system has to be changed if justice is to be possible is lacking from the
prophetic perspective. Practically never do we find the prophets putting
forward any sort of practical suggestions for change in the structure of
society.[20]

It is not that the prophets had nothing new to say about social justice, but their radicality consisted more in their rhetorical strategy than
their ideas, in their [305] forceful and intense way of speaking older understandings into a new time and place, and by the remarkable way in
which they got "in your face" with respect to long-standing communal
commitments.

The exodus helps chart a direction for this perspective. This divine deliverance is rooted deeply in the tradition ("the covenant with Abraham,
Isaac, and Jacob," Exod 2:24).[21] When the Israelites "groaned under their
slavery," God "remembered his covenant" (Exod 2:24–25; see 3:7–8). A key
point emerges here with the covenant to which God will be faithful: "I will
free you from the burdens of the Egyptians and deliver you from slavery to
them" (Exod 6:6). God liberated the Israelites from sociopolitical bondage
because God had *promised* to do so.[22]

This explicit link between divine promise and social justice should not
be lost on modern readers. What God will do on behalf of an oppressed
people is made a matter of divine promise. And God's deliverance of them
is believed to be the fulfillment of such a promise. That this divine action is
called "salvation" in Exod 15:2 should expand our understanding of what
salvation is all about; in a given context, salvation may include a socio-
political dimension.[23] What might it mean ethically and theologically that
the language of salvation is associated with the practice of social justice?
Might the *ongoing* practice of social justice be salvific in some basic sense?
God's concern about matters of social justice was believed to be so strong
and so pervasive that it was built into the very heart of the covenantal
promises. And God was faithful to such promises. For the sake of a broader
public acceptance, is there a way in which the prophetic concern for social
justice can be more clearly seen as a conservative cause?

20. James Barr, "The Bible as a Political Document," *Bulletin of the John Rylands Library*
62 (1980): 278–79 (emphasis mine).

21. Covenant in this context is equated with promise, an obligation that God takes
upon the divine self. Unfortunately, much discussion seeking to relate the Pentateuch to
the prophets considers only the Sinai covenant. To speak about divine liberation without
promise is theologically shortsighted.

22. See the divine promises throughout Genesis, e.g., 15:12–16; 46:3–4; 28:15; 17:6–8;
also Deut 7:8.

23. For detail, see Terence E. Fretheim, "Salvation in the Bible vs. Salvation in the
Church," *WW* 13/4 (1993): 363–72.

6. I Wish for a Greater Value Given to the Energetic Rhetoric of Texts Relating to Ethical Issues in Law and Prophecy, Especially regarding the Poor and the Needy

In both the law and the prophets, there is a rhetorical urgency regarding ethical matters, particularly on behalf of the poor and needy. Listen to these texts:

> Should you not know justice?—you who hate the good and love the evil, who tear the skin off my people, and the flesh off their bones; who eat the flesh of my people, flay their skin off them, break their bones in pieces, and chop them up like meat in a kettle, like flesh in a caldron. (Mic 3:1–3)

> You shall not abuse any widow or orphan. If you do abuse them, when they cry out [306] to me, I will surely heed their cry; my wrath will burn, and I will kill you. (Exod 22:22–24)

A rhetorical urgency and resolve permeates these texts, often in direct divine speech; it merits greater attention. Does this rhetorical energy call for imitation? Perhaps the rhetoric is outlandish or insufficiently nuanced, but I wonder. Our language is commonly (much) more cautious; there is a place for caution, but can we find a way to give voice to that divine urgency? Have we overreacted to the shrillness on so many ethical topics in our culture (admittedly, a real problem) that we give up the rhetorical playing field? Or, does such language come too close to home? Or, are we uncomfortable with the God language?

Listen to Abraham Heschel:

> [Our] sense of injustice is a poor analogy to God's sense of injustice. The exploitation of the poor is to us a misdemeanor; to God, it is a disaster. Our reaction is disapproval; God's reaction is something no language can convey. Is it a sign of cruelty that God's anger is aroused when the rights of the poor are violated, when widows and orphans are oppressed?[24]

The hortatory nature of many texts in both law and prophets (including major texts such as Leviticus 17–26 and Deuteronomy) calls for attention—quite apart from specific words they use or ideas they float. The prophets do take sides, without apology; the prophets critique affluence, without qualification; the prophets condemn the life of worship, mercilessly. We might well articulate a concern for social justice, but do we get the rhetoric right? Is our language sufficiently radical on behalf of the less fortunate? Can we capture these key biblical concerns for the disadvantaged with a proper rhetorical energy?

---

24. Abraham J. Heschel, *The Prophets* (New York: Harper & Row, 1962), 284–85.

Publications of Terence Fretheim

Books

Reading Hosea-Micah: A Literary and Theological Commentary. Macon, GA: Smyth & Helwys, 2013.

Creation Untamed: The Bible, God, and Natural Disasters. Grand Rapids, MI: Baker Academic, 2010.

The Child in the Bible. Grand Rapids, MI: Eerdmans, 2008 [co-editor with Marcia Bunge and Beverly Gaventa].

Abraham: Trials of Family and Faith. Columbia: University of South Carolina Press, 2007.

Hope in God in Times of Suffering. Minneapolis: Augsburg Fortress, 2006 [with Faith Fretheim].

God and World in the Old Testament: A Relational Theology of Creation. Nashville: Abingdon, 2005.

Jeremiah: A Commentary. Macon, GA: Smyth & Helwys, 2002.

God, Evil and Suffering: Essays in Honor of Paul Sponheim. St. Paul, MN: Word and World, 2000 [co-editor with Curtis Thompson].

About the Bible: Short Answers to Big Questions. Minneapolis: Augsburg, 1999. Revised 2009.

First and Second Kings. Louisville: Westminster/John Knox, 1999.

In God's Image: A Study of Genesis. Minneapolis: Augsburg Fortress, 1999.

A Theological Introduction to the Old Testament. Nashville: Abingdon, 1999. Revised ed. 2005 [with B. Birch, W. Brueggemann, and D. Petersen].

The Bible as Word of God in a Postmodern Age. Minneapolis: Fortress, 1998 [with Karlfried Froehlich].

Proclamation 6: Interpreting the Lessons of the Church Year. Pentecost 1, Series C. Minneapolis: Fortress, 1997.

The Pentateuch. Nashville: Abingdon, 1996.

"The Book of Genesis." in *The New Interpreter's Bible.* Nashville: Abingdon, 1994.

Exodus. Interpretation. Louisville: John Knox, 1991.

From Eden to Zion. Augsburg Adult Curriculum. Minneapolis: Augsburg Fortress, 1991.

Deuteronomy–II Kings. SEARCH 9 and 10. Minneapolis: Augsburg, 1985.

The Suffering of God: An Old Testament Perspective. Minneapolis: Fortress, 1984.

Deuteronomic History. Nashville: Abingdon, 1983.

The Message of Jonah: A Theological Commentary. Minneapolis: Augsburg, 1977.

Editors' note: The publications in each section of this bibliography are presented in chronological order, beginning with the most recent.

Our Old Testament Heritage. 2 vols. Minneapolis: Augsburg, 1970–71.
Creation, Fall and Flood: Studies in Genesis 1–11. Minneapolis: Augsburg, 1969.

Articles and Essays

"Issues of Agency in Exodus." Pages 591–609 in *The Book of Exodus.* Edited by T. Dozeman, C. Evans, and J. Lohr. Leiden: Brill, 2015.

"What Kind of God is Portrayed in Isaiah 5:1–7?" Pages 53–68 in *New Studies in the Book of Isaiah: Essays in Honor of Hallvard Hagelia.* Edited by Markus Zehnder. Piscataway, NJ: Gorgias, 2014.

"Jacob's Wrestling and Issues of Divine Power (Genesis 32:22–32)." Pages 181–91 in *Where the Wild Ox Roams: Biblical Essays in Honour of Norman C. Habel.* Edited by A. H. Cadwallader. Sheffield: Sheffield Phoenix, 2013.

"Violence and the God of the Old Testament." Pages 108–27 in *Encountering Violence in the Bible.* Edited by H. Hagelia and M. Zehnder. Sheffield: Sheffield Phoenix, 2013.

"Genesis and Ecology." Pages 683–708 in *The Book of Genesis: Composition, Reception, and Interpretation.* Edited by C. Evans, J. Lohr, and D. Petersen. Leiden: Brill, 2012.

"God, Creation, and the Pursuit of Happiness." Pages 33–56 in *The Bible and the Pursuit of Happiness.* Edited by Brent Strawn. Oxford: Oxford University Press, 2012.

"Biblical Theology in Dialogue: Reflections of Terence E. Fretheim, May 2011, with a Response by Walter Brueggemann, July 2011." Pages 151–64 in *Living Countertestimony: Conversations with Walter Brueggemann.* Louisville: Westminster John Knox, 2012 [with Carolyn Sharp].

"The Authority of the Bible, the Flood Story, and Problematic Images of God." Pages 29–47 in *Hermeneutics and the Authority of Scripture.* Edited by A. H. Cadwallader. Adelaide: ATF Theology, 2011.

"The Bible in a Postmodern Age." Pages 123–40 in *The Bible Tells Me So: Reading the Bible as Scripture.* Edited by R. Thompson and T. Oord. Nampa, ID: Sacrasage, 2011.

"Leading from the Wilderness." *International Congregational Journal* 10 (2011): 15–28.

"Some Reflections on Samuel A. Meier's *Themes and Transformations in Old Testament Prophecy.*" *Ashland Theological Journal* 43 (2011): 124–28.

"What Biblical Scholars Wish Pastors Would Start or Stop Doing about Ethical Issues in the Old Testament." *Word and World* 31 (2011): 297–306. [A somewhat fuller version with responses from ethicists Wyndy Corbin Reuschling and Michael Cartwright appeared in *The Covenant Quarterly* (2011): 1–46.]

"Does the God of Genesis 1–11 Cross Cultures?" *The Korean Journal of Old Testament Studies* 16 (2010): 158–76.

Notes on the book of Numbers in *The New Oxford Annotated Bible.* 4th ed., 2010. [Reprinted in *The Pentateuch.* Edited by J. Muddiman and J. Barton. Oxford: Oxford University Press, 2010.]

"Numbers." Pages 153–86 in *The Pentateuch*. Edited by John Muddiman and John Barton. Oxford: Oxford University Press, 2010.

"Old Testament Commentaries: Their Selection and Use." *Theology and Life* 33 (2010): 71–98.

"Response to Reviews of *God and World in the Old Testament: A Relational Theology of Creation*." *Journal of Pentecostal Theology* 19 (2010): 183–218. [Reviews by Robert Stallman, Scott Ellington, and Kenneth Archer. Reply by Fretheim.]

"The Self-Limiting God of the Old Testament and Issues of Violence." Pages 179–91 in *Raising Up a Faithful Exegete: Essays in Honor of Richard D. Nelson*. Edited by K. Noll and B. Schramm. Winona Lake, IN: Eisenbrauns, 2010.

"Interpreting the Prophets and Issues of Social Justice." Pages 92–107 in *The Bible and the American Future*. Edited by R. Jewett et al. Eugene, OR: Cascade, 2009.

"Preaching Creation: Genesis 1–2." *Word and World* 29 (2009): 75–83.

"The God of the Flood Story and Natural Disasters." *Calvin Theological Journal* 43 (2008): 21–34.

"'God Was with the Boy' (Genesis 21:20): Children in the Book of Genesis." Pages 3–23 in *The Child in the Bible*. Edited by Marcia Bunge, Beverly Gaventa, and Terence Fretheim. Grand Rapids, MI: Eerdmans, 2008.

"The Prophets and Social Justice: A Conservative Agenda." *Word and World* 28 (2008): 159–68.

Response to "Draft of ELCA Social Statement on Sexuality." *Journal of Lutheran Ethics* 8 (2008). http://www.elca.org/JLE/Articles/434.

"The Authority of the Bible and the Imaging of God." Pages 45–52 in *Engaging Biblical Authority: Perspectives on the Bible as Scripture*. Edited by William Brown. Louisville: Westminster John Knox, 2007.

"The Binding of Isaac and the Abuse of Children." *Lutheran Theological Journal* 41 (2007): 84–92.

"Creation in Community: Faith and the Environment." *ViewPoint: Theological Investigations in Church and Culture*, 2007. http://www.atthispoint.net/articles/creation-in-community—faith-and-the-environment/177/.

"The Exaggerated God of Jonah." *Word and World* 27 (2007): 125–34.

"The Authority of the Bible and Churchly Debates Regarding Sexuality." *Word and World* (2006): 365–74. [Reprinted in online *Journal of Lutheran Ethics*, 2007.]

"Hope in God in Times of Suffering." *Lutheran Woman Today* (Sept. 2006–May 2007) [9 articles, with Faith Fretheim].

"Repentance in the Former Prophets." Pages 25–46 in *Repentance in Christian Theology*. Edited by Mark Boda and Gordon Smith. Macon, GA: Liturgical Press, 2006.

"Evil after 9/11: A Consequence of Human Freedom." *Word and World* 24 (2004): 205, 207.

"God and Violence in the Old Testament." *Word and World* 24 (2004): 18–28.

"Is Anything Too Hard for God? (Jer 32:27)." *Catholic Biblical Quarterly* 66 (2004): 231–36.

"'I Was Only a Little Angry': Divine Violence in the Prophets." *Interpretation* 58 (2004): 365–75.

"Response to McConville's 'Judgement of God in the Old Testament.'" *Ex Auditu* 20 (2004): 43–46.

"Law in the Service of Life: A Dynamic Understanding of Law in Deuteronomy." Pages 183–200 in *A God So Near: Essays in Old Testament Theology in Honor of Patrick D. Miller.* Edited by Brent A. Strawn and Nancy Bowen. Winona Lake, IN: Eisenbrauns, 2003.

"Caught in the Middle: Jeremiah's Vocational Crisis." *Word and World* 22 (2002): 351–60.

"The Character of God in Jeremiah." Pages 211–30 in *Character and Scripture: Moral Formation, Community and Biblical Interpretation.* Edited by William P. Brown, Grand Rapids, MI: Eerdmans, 2002.

"Conversation or Conversion? Hearing God from the Other." *Word and World* 22 (2002): 304, 306.

"God and the Power of Vulnerability." http://www.catalystresources.org/god-and-the-power-of-vulnerability/. [accessed July 7, 2014]

"Theological Reflections on the Wrath of God in the Old Testament." *Horizons in Biblical Theology* 24 (2002): 1–26.

"The Book of Numbers." Pages 110–54 in *The Oxford Bible Commentary.* Edited by John Barton and John Muddiman. Oxford: Oxford University Press, 2001.

"The Old Testament and Homosexuality: What Is God Doing?" http://www.thelutheran.org/article/article.cfm?article_id=858. [accessed July 7, 2014]

"Old Testament Foundations for an Environmental Theology." Pages 58–68 in *Currents in Biblical and Theological Dialogue.* Edited by John Stafford. Winnipeg: St. John's College Press, 2001.

"Divine Judgment and the Warming of the World." Pages 21–32 in *God, Evil and Suffering: Essays in Honor of Paul R. Sponheim.* Edited by Terence E. Fretheim and Curtis L. Thompson. Word and World Supplement Series. St. Paul, MN: Luther Seminary Press, 2000.

"Does God Really Wrestle?" (Genesis 32:22–32)." *Lutheran Woman Today* 13 (2000): 2–4.

"The Earth Story in Jeremiah 12." Pages 96–110 in *Readings from the Perspective of Earth.* Edited by Norman C. Habel. The Earth Bible 1. Cleveland: Pilgrim Press / Sheffield: Sheffield Academic Press, 2000.

"When the Morning Stars Sang Together (Job 38:7)" *Lutheran Woman Today* 12 (2000): 7–9.

"Which Blessing Does Isaac Give Jacob?" Pages 279–91 in *Jews, Christians and the Theology of the Hebrew Scriptures.* Edited by Alice Ogden Bellis and Joel S. Kaminsky. SBL Symposium Series 8. Atlanta: Society of Biblical Literature, 2000.

"In God's Image: A Study in Genesis." *Lutheran Woman Today* 1999–2000. [series of 9 articles]

"And They Laughed." *Lutheran Woman Today* 12 (1999): 25.

"Christology and the Old Testament." Pages 201–15 in *Who Do You Say That I Am? Essays on Christology*. Edited by Mark Allan Powell and David R. Bauer; Louisville: Westminster John Knox, 1999.

"God and the Meaning of Suffering." *Lutheran Woman Today* 12 (1999): 8–10.

"God in the Book of Job." *Currents in Theology and Mission* 26 (1999): 85–93.

"To Say Something—About God, Evil, and Suffering." *Word and World* 19 (1999): 339, 346–50.

"Some Reflections on Brueggemann's God." Pages 24–37 in *God in the Fray: Essays in Honor of Walter Brueggemann*. Edited by Tod Linafelt and Timothy K. Beal. Minneapolis: Fortress, 1998.

"The Ten Commandments." Pages 204–7 in *The Family Handbook*. Edited by Herbert Anderson et al. Louisville: Westminster John Knox, 1998.

"Divine Dependence upon the Human: An Old Testament Perspective." *Ex Auditu* 13 (1997): 1–13.

"Exodus 3: A Theological Interpretation." Pp. 143–54 in *The Theological Interpretation of Scripture: Classic and Contemporary Readings*. Malden, MA: Blackwell, 1997.

"The God Who Acts: An Old Testament Perspective." *Theology Today* 54 (1997): 6–18.

"About the Bible." *Lutheran Woman Today* 1996–98. [series of 21 articles]

"'Because the Whole Earth Is Mine': Narrative and Theme in Exodus." *Interpretation* 50 (1996): 229–39.

"God, Abraham, and the Abuse of Isaac." *Word and World* 15 (1995): 49–57.

"The Bible Today: God in Exodus." *Creative Transformation* 4 (1994): 1, 3–5.

"Is Genesis 3 a Fall Story?" *Word and World* 14 (1994): 144–53.

"Salvation in the Bible vs. Salvation in the Church." *Word and World* 13 (1993): 363–72.

"Creator, Creature, and Co-Creation in Genesis 1–2." Pages 11–20 in *All Things New: Essays in Honor of Roy A. Harrisville*. Word and World Supplement Series 1. St. Paul, MN: Word and World, 1992.

"Where in the World Is God? Reflections on Divine Presence in the Old Testament." *Lutheran Theological Journal* 26 (1992): 6–13.

"The Plagues as Ecological Signs of Historical Disaster." *Journal of Biblical Literature* 110 (1991): 385–96.

"The Reclamation of Creation: Redemption and Law in Exodus." *Interpretation* 45 (1991): 354–65.

"Suffering God and Sovereign God in Exodus." *Horizons in Biblical Theology* 11 (1989): 31–56.

"The Book of Jonah." *Harper's Bible Commentary*. Edited by James Luther Mays. San Francisco: Harper & Row, 1988.

"A God Who Suffers: An Old Testament Perspective." Pp. 25–37 in *Suffering and Redemption: Exploring Christian Witness within a Buddhist Context.* Chicago: Division for Global Mission, 1988.

"Prayer in the Old Testament: Creating Space for God in the World." Pages 51–62 In *A Primer on Christian Prayer.* Edited by Paul R. Sponheim. Philadelphia: Fortress, 1988.

"The Repentance of God: A Key to Evaluating Old Testament God-Talk." *Horizons in Biblical Theology* 10 (1988): 47–70.

"The Repentance of God: A Study of Jeremiah 18:7–10." *Hebrew Annual Review* 11 (1987): 81–92.

"The Suffering of God and the Power of Jesus." *Entree* 4/5 (1987): 7–9, 19.

"The Color of God: Israel's God-Talk and Life-Experience." *Word and World* 6 (1986): 256–65.

"God and Prophet: An Old Testament Perspective." Pages 31–42 in *God and Jesus: Theological Reflections for Christian-Muslim Dialog.* Minneapolis: Division for World Mission and Inter-Church Cooperation, American Lutheran Church, 1986.

"The Understanding of Mission in the Old Testament." Pages 19–30 in *Bible and Mission.* Edited by Wayne Stumme. Minneapolis: Augsburg, 1986.

"Were the Days of Creation Twenty-Four Hours Long? 'Yes.'" Pp. 12–35 in *The Genesis Debate: Persistent Questions about Creation and the Flood.* Edited by Ronald Youngblood. Nashville: Thomas Nelson, 1986.

"Divine Foreknowledge, Divine Constancy, and the Rejection of Saul's Kingship." *Catholic Biblical Quarterly* 47 (1985): 595–602.

"The Old Testament in Christian Proclamation." *Word and World* 3 (1983): 223–30.

"Old Testament Commentaries: Their Selection and Use." *Interpretation* 36 (1982): 356–71.

"Ten Faces of Ministry: A Conversation." *Word and World* 1 (1981): 382–90.

Augsburg Sermons: Old Testament Lessons A, B and C. Minneapolis: Augsburg, 1979–81. [3 sermons]

"Jonah and Theodicy." *Zeitschrift alttestamentliche Wissenschaft* 90 (1978): 227–37.

"Life in the Wilderness: Numbers 21:4–9." *Dialog* 17 (1978): 266–72.

"The Theology of the Major Traditions in Genesis–Numbers." *Review and Expositor* 74 (1977): 301–20.

"On Being a Servant: Isaiah 50:4–9." *Princeton Seminary Bulletin* 66 (1973): 59–64.

"Jacob, the Church." *Luther Seminary Review* 11/1 (1972): 6–21.

"The Jacob Traditions: Theology and Hermeneutic." *Interpretation* 26 (1972): 419–36.

"The Ark in Deuteronomy." *Catholic Biblical Quarterly* 30 (1968): 1–14.

"The Priestly Document: Anti-Temple?" *Vetus Testamentum* 18 (1968): 313–29.

"Psalm 132: A Form-Critical Study." *Journal of Biblical Literature* 86 (1967): 289–300.

Entries in Encyclopedias and Dictionaries

"Abraham"; "Akedah"; "God, Old Testament View of"; "Image of God." In *The New Interpreter's Dictionary of the Bible*. 5 vols. Nashville: Abingdon, 2006–9.

"Angel"; "Creation"; "God Most High"; "Heaven"; "Jealous"; "Lord of Hosts." In *Westminster Theological Wordbook of the Bible*. Edited by Donald E. Gowan. Louisville: Westminster John Knox, 2003.

"Exodus, Book of." In *Dictionary of the Old Testament: Pentateuch*. Downers Grove, IL: InterVarsity, 2003.

"The Book of Jonah"; "God." In *Eerdmans Dictionary of the Bible*. Grand Rapids, MI: Eerdmans, 2000.

"God"; "Grace, Favor"; "Knowledge, Understanding"; "Pain, Hurt"; "Worship, Serve." In *New International Dictionary of Old Testament Theology and Exegesis*. 5 vols. Grand Rapids, MI: Zondervan, 1997.

"Will of God"; "Word of God." In *Anchor Bible Dictionary*. 6 vols. New York: Doubleday, 1992.

"Elohist"; "Source Criticism." *Interpreter's Dictionary of the Bible: Supplementary Volume*. Edited by K. Crim. Nashville: Abingdon, 1976.

Study Bible Notes

Study Bible notes on the book of Job in the *Common English Bible Study Bible*. Nashville: Common English Bible, 2013.

Contributing editor to *The New Revised Standard Version*. Minneapolis: Augsburg Fortress, 2009.

Study Bible notes on the book of Genesis in *The Westminster Discipleship Study Bible: The New Revised Standard Version*. Louisville: Westminster John Knox, 2008.

Study Bible notes on the book of Numbers in the *New Oxford Annotated Bible: The Revised Standard Version*. 3rd ed. Oxford: Oxford University Press, 2007; and Fully Revised Fourth Edition, 2010.

Reviews in Various Journals

Biblical Interpretation; Catholic Biblical Quarterly; Interpretation; Journal of Biblical Literature; Journal of Religion; Princeton Seminary Bulletin; Theology Today; Word and World

Index of Authors

399

Index of Scripture

Hebrew Bible

New Testament